The Pelagian Controversy

The Pelagian Controversy

An Introduction to the Enemies of Grace
and the Conspiracy of Lost Souls

Stuart Squires

PICKWICK *Publications* • Eugene, Oregon

THE PELAGIAN CONTROVERSY
An Introduction to the Enemies of Grace and the Conspiracy of Lost Souls

Copyright © 2019 Stuart Squires. All rights reserved. Except for brief quotations in critical publications or reviews, no part of this book may be reproduced in any manner without prior written permission from the publisher. Write: Permissions, Wipf and Stock Publishers, 199 W. 8th Ave., Suite 3, Eugene, OR 97401.

Pickwick Publications
An Imprint of Wipf and Stock Publishers
199 W. 8th Ave., Suite 3
Eugene, OR 97401

www.wipfandstock.com

PAPERBACK ISBN: 978-1-5326-3781-0
HARDCOVER ISBN: 978-1-5326-3782-7
EBOOK ISBN: 978-1-5326-3783-4

Cataloguing-in-Publication data:

Names: Squires, Stuart, author.

Title: The Pelagian controversy : an introduction to the enemies of grace and the conspiracy of lost souls / by Stuart Squires.

Description: Eugene, OR : Pickwick Publications, 2019 | Includes bibliographical references and indexes.

Identifiers: ISBN 978-1-5326-3781-0 (paperback) | ISBN 978-1-5326-3782-7 (hardcover) | ISBN 978-1-5326-3783-4 (ebook)

Subjects: LCSH: Pelagius. | Augustine,—of Hippo, Saint,—354–430. | Grace (Theology)—History of doctrines—Early church, ca. 30–600. | Pelagianism.

Classification: BT1450 .S68 2019 (print) | BT1450 .S68 (ebook)

Several sections of this book are based on articles previously published, which I have received permission from the journals to use in this book. These articles are:

- "Augustine's Changing Thought on Sinlessness." *Augustinianum* 54.2 (2014) 447–66.

- "Cassian on Sinlessness." *Cistercian Studies Quarterly* 48, no. 4 (2013) 411–32.

- "Jerome on Sinlessness: A *Via Media* between Augustine and Pelagius." *The Heythrop Journal* 57, no. 4 (2016) 697–709.

Manufactured in the U.S.A.   10/01/19

For Lia, Aspen, and Isaac

Contents

Acknowledgments | ix
Abbreviations | xi
Important Dates of the Pelagian Controversy | xvii
Introduction | xxi

Part I: History

Chapter 1: The Political, Ascetic, and Theological Contexts | 3
Chapter 2: Pelagius: A Man Aflame with Ardent Zeal | 41
Chapter 3: Caelestius: The Commander of the Pelagian Army | 53
Chapter 4: The "Holy Priest" Rufinus | 61
Chapter 5: Augustine: The Doctor of Grace | 68
Chapter 6: Jerome: The Irascible, Morbidly Sensitive Old Curmudgeon | 87
Chapter 7: Orosius: A Useful Vessel in the House of the Lord | 97
Chapter 8: Texts, Councils, Popes, and an Emperor | 102
Chapter 9: Julian of Eclanum: The Architect of Pelagian Doctrine | 144
Chapter 10: John Cassian: Master of the Inner Life | 161

Part II: Theology

Chapter 11: The Theology of Pelagius | 183
Chapter 12: The Theology of Caelestius and the Theology of the Author of the *Liber de Fide* | 194
Chapter 13: The Theology of Augustine (411–418) | 201
Chapter 14: The Theology of Jerome | 220
Chapter 15: The Theology of Orosius | 232

Chapter 16: The Theology of Julian of Eclanum | 238
Chapter 17: The Theology of Augustine (419–430) | 246
Chapter 18: The Theology of Cassian | 262

Conclusion | 278

Bibliography | 295
Text Index | 333
Subject Index | 337
Scripture Index | 343

Acknowledgments

There are many people whom I would like to thank for their support with this project. Sarah Eastlund, Allen Gehring, Jared Ortiz, Marc Rugani, and Andy Staron provided me with their insight and wisdom. The librarians at the Fr. Leonard Alvey Library obtained countless sources for me. My editor, Charlie Collier, carefully shepherded this project through the editorial process. Most importantly, my family buoyed me with their words of encouragement.

Abbreviations

Series

Acta Conciliorum Oecumenicorum	*ACO*
Ancient Christian Writers	*ACW*
Ante-Nicene Fathers	*ANF*
Classics of Western Spirituality	*CWS*
Clavis Patrum Graecorum	*CPG*
Corpus Scriptorum Ecclesiasticorum Latinorum	*CSEL*
Nicene and Post-Nicene Fathers	*NPNF*
Patrologia Graeca	*PG*
Patrologia Latina	*PL*
The Works of Saint Augustine	*WSA*

Multiple Authors

Epistula	*Epist.*
Sermo	*Serm.*

Ambrose of Milan

De officiis	*Off.*

Anastasius I

Ad Ioannem episcopum Hierosolymitanum	*Ad Ioan.*

Athanasius

Vita Antonii	*Vit. Ant.*

Augustine

Acta contra Fortunatum Manicheum	*Fort.*
Ad Cresconium grammaticum partis Donati	*Cresc.*
Ad Orosium contra Priscillianistas et Origenistas	*Priscill.*
Beata vita	*Beat.*
Confessiones	*Conf.*
Contra Academicos	*Acad.*
Contra duas epistulas Pelagianorum	*C. du. ep. Pelag.*
Contra Julianum	*C. Jul.*
Contra Julianum opus imperfectum	*C. Jul. op. imp.*
Contra litteras Petiliani donatistae cirtensis Episcopi	*C. litt. Petil.*
De bono viduitatis	*Vid.*
De civitate Dei	*Civ.*
De correptione et gratia	*Corrept.*
De doctrina Christiana	*Doctr. Chr.*
De dono perseverantiae	*Persev.*
De gestis Pelagii	*Gest. Pelag.*
De gratia Christi, et de peccato originali	*Grat. Chr.*
De gratia et libero arbitrio	*Grat.*
De haeresibus	*Haer.*
De natura et gratia	*Nat. grat.*
De nuptiis et concupiscentia	*Nupt.*
De ordine	*Ord.*
De peccatorum meritis et remissione et de baptismo parvulorum	*Pecc. merit.*
De perfectione justitiae hominis	*Perf.*
De praedestinatione sanctorum	*Praed.*
De spiritu et littera	*Spir. et litt.*
Retractationes	*Retract.*
Soliloquia	*Sol.*

Bede

Historia ecclesiastica gentis Anglorum	*Hist. eccl.*

ABBREVIATIONS

Benedict of Nursia

Regula Sancti Benedicti — *Reg.*

Caelestius

Libellus fidei — *Lib. fid.*

Cassian

Collationes — *Coll.*
De incarnatione Domini contra Nestorium — *De inc.*
De institutis coenobiorum — *Inst.*

Cassiodorus

De divinis lectionibus — *De div.*

Council of Ephesus (431)

Ad Coelestinum Papam — *Ad Coel.*

Eusebius of Caesarea

Historia ecclesiastica — *Hist. eccl.*
Vita Constantini — *Vit. Const.*

Gennadius

De viris inlustribus — *De vir. inlustr.*

Gerontius

Vita Melaniae iunioris — *V. Mel.*

Gregory Thaumaturgus

Oratio panegyrica in Origenem — *Ora. in Orig.*

Jerome

Apologia adversus libros Rufini — *Apol.*

ABBREVIATIONS

Commentaria in Amos	Comm. Am.
Commentaria in epistolam ad Ephesios	Comm. Eph.
Commentarii in Ezechielem	Comm. Ezech.
Contra Ioannem Hierosolymitanum	C. Joan.
Contra Iovinianum	C. Jov.
Contra Vigilantium	C. Vig.
De perpetua virginitate beatae Mariae adversus Helvidium	A. Hel.
De viris illustribus	Vir. ill.
Dialogi contra Pelagianos	Dial.
In Hieremiam prophetam Libri Sex	In Hier.
Interpretatio libri Didymi de Spiritu Sancto	Int. Did.
Praefatio Hieronymi in quatuor evangelia	Praef. in quat. evang.
Vita Hilarionis	Vit. Hil.
Vita Malchi monachi captivi	Vit. Malch.
Vita Pauli	Vit. Pauli

John of Nikiu

Chronicon	Chron.

Lactantius

Liber de mortibus persecutorum	Mort.

Marius Mercator

Commonitorium de Coelestio	Comm.
Subnotationes in verba Iuliani	Sub.

Origen

Commentaria in epistolam Pauli ad Romanos	Comm. Rom.
Contra Celsum	Cels.
Homiliae in Lucam	Hom. Luc.
De Principiis (Peri archon)	Princ.

ABBREVIATIONS

Orosius

Commonitorium de errore Priscillianistarum et Origenistarum	*Prisc. et Orig.*
Historiarum adversum paganos	*C. pag.*
Liber apologeticus contra Pelagianum	*Lib. apol.*

Palladius

Dialogus de vita sancti Joannis Chrysostomi	*Dial.*
Historia Lausiaca	*Hist. Laus.*

Pamphilus of Caesarea

Apologia pro Origene	*Apol. Orig.*

Paulinus of Milan

Vita sancti Ambrosii	*V. Amb.*

Paulinus of Nola

Poemata	*Poe.*

Pelagius

Epistula [ad amicum] de divina lege	*Div. leg.*
Epistula ad Celantiam [matronan]	*Ad Cel.*
Epistula ad Claudiam de virginitate	*Virg.*
Epistula ad sacram Christi virginem Demetriadem	*Ad Dem.*
Expositiones XIII epistularum Pauli	*Expos.*
Libellus fidei	*Lib. fid.*
Liber de vita Christiana (Christianorum)	*Vit. Christ.*

Possidius

Vita Sancti Aurelii Augustini	*V. Aug.*

Priscillian of Avila

Tractates	*Tract.*

ABBREVIATIONS

Prosper of Aquitaine

Chronicum integrum	*Chron.*
Epistula ad Augustinum Hipponensem	*Ep. ad Aug.*
Pro Augustino liber contra collatorem	*C. coll.*

Rufinus (*presbyter*)

Liber de Fide	*Lib. fid.*

Rufinus of Aquileia

De adulteratione librorum Origenis	*Adult. libr. Orig.*
Apologia ad Anastasium	*Anast.*
Apologia contra Hieronymum	*Apol. Hier.*
Prologus in libros peri archon Origenis Presbyteri	*Prol. ad per.*
Prologus in omelias Origenis super Numeros	*Prol. ad num.*

Socrates

Historia ecclesiastica	*Hist. eccl.*

Sozomen

Historia ecclesiastica	*Hist. eccl.*

Sulpicius Severus

Chronicorum libri duo	*Chron.*
Dialogi	*Dial.*
Vita sancti Martini	*V. Mar.*

Tertullian

De praescriptionibus adversus haereticos	*Praescr.*

Theodore of Mopsuestia

Ex libro contra defensores peccati originalis	*C. def.*

Vincent of Lérins

Commonitorium	*Comm.*

Important Dates of the Pelagian Controversy

380–89

384	Approximate year Pelagius went to Rome
384	Jerome wrote his letter (22) to Eustochium
387	Augustine is baptized by Ambrose of Milan

390–99

390–400	Approximate time that Caelestius became Pelagius' disciple
393	Approximate year Jerome wrote *Contra Iovinianum*
393	Origenist controversy begins
394	Paulinus of Nola renounced his immense wealth and career to live as a monk
394	Paulinus of Nola and Augustine began exchanging letters
394	Jerome received letter from Domnio
399–428	Possible years that the *Liber de fide* was written

400–409

400–08	Julian married his wife sometime during this period
404/405	Cassian arrived in Rome
405/406	Approximate years that Pelagius began his Pauline commentaries
406–14	Possible years that Pelagius wrote *De natura*
408	Approximate year Caelestius left Rome for Africa
408	Approximate year Memorius wrote a letter to Augustine requesting a copy of his *De musica* for Julian

IMPORTANT DATES OF THE PELAGIAN CONTROVERSY

408/409	Augustine replied to Memorius' request to send a copy of his *De musica* for Julian
409–15	Approximate years that Orosius left Spain

410–19

410	Rome sacked by Alaric
410	Augustine wrote a letter to Pelagius
410–14	Approximate years Jerome wrote *Commentarii in Ezechielem*
411	Council of Carthage that anathematized Caelestius
411/412	Augustine wrote *De peccatorum meritis et remissione et de baptism parvulorum*
412	Demetrias became a consecrated virgin
412/413	Augustine wrote *De spiritu et littera*
413/414	Augustine wrote a letter to Proba and Juliana
414	Pelagius and Jerome wrote separate letters to Demetrias
414	Jerome wrote letter to Ctesiphon
414	Jerome began writing *In Hieremiam prophetam*
414/415	Orosius wrote *Commonitorium de errore Priscillianistarum et Origenistarum*
414/415	Hilary wrote to Augustine asking for his advice about how to respond to five teachings spread in Syracuse by some unnamed Christians
415/416	Augustine wrote *De natura et gratia*
415	Augustine sends Orosius to Palestine
415	Augustine wrote *De perfectione iustitiae hominis*
415 (Jul.)	*Conventum* in Jerusalem
415	Jerome wrote *Dialogi contra Pelagianos*
415 (Dec.)	Synod of Diospolis
416/417	Julian was ordained a bishop
416/417	Augustine and Alypius wrote to Paulinus of Nola warning him about Pelagius
416–18	Approximate years Orosius wrote *Historiae adversum paganos*
416	Orosius left Palestine
416	Jerome's monastery is attacked

IMPORTANT DATES OF THE PELAGIAN CONTROVERSY

416 (summer)	Latest date that Caelestius was ordained in Ephesus
416 (summer)	68 bishops (including Aurelius) held a council in Carthage
416 (summer)	59 bishops (including Augustine and Alypius) held a council in Milevis in Numidia.
417 (Jan. 27)	Pope Innocent wrote three letters to Africa
417 (Mar. 12)	Pope Innocent died
417 (Mar. 18)	Pope Zosimus elected
417 (Sep. 23)	Augustine preached a sermon declaring the "*causa finita est.*"
417 (Nov. 2)	Letters from Zosimus arrived in Africa
417 (Nov. 8)	Paulinus of Milan and African bishops respond to Zosimus
417	Augustine wrote *De gestis Pelagii*
417/418	Augustine and Alypius wrote a letter to Juliana warning her and her family about Pelagius
418 (Mar.)	Zosimus replied to Paulinus of Milan and African bishops
418 (Apr. 29)	Reply from Zosimus reacting to the response from Paulinus of Milan and African bishops arrives in Africa
418 (Apr. 30)	Emperor Honorius condemned Pelagius and Caelestius
418 (May 1)	200 bishops condemn Pelagius and Caelestius at a Council in Carthage
418 (summer)	Pope Zosimus issued his *Tractoria*
418 (summer)	Augustine wrote *De gratia Christi et de peccato originali*
418	Pelagius died within a few years after his triple condemnation by Honorius, the Council of Carthage, and Zosimus
418 (Dec.)	Pope Zosimus died
418 (Dec. 28)	Boniface was elected Pope, although he was not universally recognized until Easter 419
418/419 (winter)	Augustine wrote Book I of *De nuptiis et concupiscentia*
418–21	Approximate time Julian and other Italian bishops took refuge with Theodore of Mopsuestia in Cilicia
419/420	Jerome died
419 (Jun. 9)	Honorius issues a second rescript banishing Pelagius and Caelestius to the provinces
419 (summer)	Julian wrote *Ad Turbantium*
419–26	Approximate time Cassian wrote *De institutis coenobiroum*

IMPORTANT DATES OF THE PELAGIAN CONTROVERSY

420–29

420–29	Approximate time Cassian wrote *Collationes*
420/421	Approximate time Augustine wrote Book II of *De nuptiis et concupiscentia*
420/421	Augustine wrote *Contra duas epistulas Pelagianorum*
421	Augustine received a copy of Julian's *Ad Turbantium* from an Italian Bishop Claudius
422	Augustine wrote *Contra Iulianum*
423/424	Caelestius' petition to Pope Celestine to return to good standing with the Church was rejected
423	Possible latest year that Orosius died
423–26	Julian wrote *Ad Florum*
425	Theodosius II and Valentinian III demanded that all bishops in Gaul must proclaim their orthodoxy to Bishop Patroclus of Arles against the Pelagians
427	While in Rome, Alypius copied and sent to Augustine the first five books of Julian's *Ad Florum*
428/429	Caelestius returned to Constantinople, but was cast out by Nestorius
428–31	Approximate time Cassian wrote *De incarnatione Domini contra Nestorium*
428	Theodore of Mopsuestia died, causing Julian to move to Constantinople soon afterwards
428	Approximate time Augustine began writing his *Contra Iulianum opus imperfectum*
429	Theodosius II banished Julian from Constantinople

430–55

430 (Aug. 10)	Pope Celestine finally responded to Nestorius' letters inquiring about Julian, causing Nestorius to withdraw his support of Julian
430	Augustine died
431	The Ecumenical Council of Ephesus condemned the Pelagians
431–35	Cassian died
439	Pope Sixtus refused the request of Julian of Eclanum to return to his See
455	Latest year that Julian may have died

Introduction

THE PELAGIAN CONTROVERSY (411–431) was one of the most important theological controversies in the history of Christianity. It was a bitter and messy affair in the evening of the Roman Empire that addressed some of the most important questions that we ask about ourselves: Who are we? What does it mean to be a human being? Are we good, or are we evil? If we are good, why do we do evil? Are we burdened by an uncontrollable impulse to sin? Is it possible to be sinless? What would have happened if Adam and Eve did not eat that fruit? Do we have free will? How should we understand the relationship between God's gracious activity and human freedom? Was sexual desire part of God's plan from the beginning of creation? How should sex and marriage be understood in relation to one another?

This controversy was comprised by a group of men who were some of the greatest thinkers of Late Antiquity. They were deeply immersed in the rich Roman literary and intellectual traditions of that time, and who, along with many other great minds of this period, tried to create equally rich Christian literary and intellectual traditions. Augustine, on one side of the divide, not only produced more literature against the Pelagians than everyone else in this controversy combined, but more of his texts have survived to the present than have survived from any other author from Antiquity; Jerome, an often overlooked player in this fight, translated most of the Bible into Latin, known as the *Vulgate*, which then became the standard translation in the West for centuries; Cassian, who spent years in the Egyptian desert, brought eastern asceticism to the West, and thereby laid the foundation for western monasticism. The Pelagians, on the other side of the divide, also contributed to and influenced the Christian tradition down through the centuries, because some of their texts, such as Pelagius' *Ad Demetriadem*, continued to be read and copied (primarily) under Jerome's name. Pelagius was an innovator who blazed new spiritual and theological paths that would find a better reception in our time than in his; Caelestius modeled how to bring Scripture and logic together; and Julian endlessly defended the goodness of God's creation.

Many of the issues that are disputed today about the human person are echoes of the same underlying questions that were disputed in the fifth century. Certainly, the theology of baptism, the precise definition of grace, and the proper understanding of the story of Adam and Eve (which will be explored in this book) are not hotly contested today in the pages of the *New York Times*, or on cable news. But, there are clear resonances of the aspects of the Pelagian controversy that addressed the proper understanding of freedom, marriage, and sexual desire (which also will be explored in this book) with contemporary fights over the same issues—although the specific grounds on which these battles are fought today, admittedly, are different. The Pelagian controversy, then, which usually is of interest only to historians and theologians of Christianity, should be appreciated by a wider audience, because it was the primary event that shaped the way Christians came to understand the human person for the next sixteen hundred years, and is still relevant today because anthropological questions continue to haunt our public discourse.

This book is intended for readers with a basic grasp of the history of Christianity, students, and scholars in the field. It will introduce this controversy in two movements: the first explores the biographies of the main characters involved, the most important texts that they wrote during the controversy, and the significant events that transpired during it, such as the numerous councils that were convened to address the issues at stake. The second explores the theological ideas both sides espoused. A common caricature describes the Pelagian controversy as nothing more than a tug of war over the single issue between the necessity of grace and the sovereignty of the will, with Augustine championing grace, and Pelagius championing free will. We will see in the second part of this book, however, that not only is the issue of grace and free will much more complicated than how this caricature presents it, but that the Pelagian controversy involved many more issues than just this one.

Before we investigate the Pelagian controversy itself, we first must briefly explore three contexts that set the stage for it. In the first chapter, we will begin by surveying the political landscape of the epoch. We will see that, at the beginning of the fourth century, Christians were a persecuted minority, but, by the end of that century, Christianity had become the official religion of the Roman Empire. Then, we will consider three different forms of the ascetic movement that flourished at roughly the same time that the political situation changed for Christians. Finally, the theological controversy known as the Origenist controversy, which was fought at the end of the fourth century and included several figures who are also important for the Pelagian controversy such as Rufinus of Aquileia and Jerome, will be reviewed.

Part I: **History**

Chapter 1

The Political, Ascetic, and Theological Contexts

The Political Context: The Christianization of the Roman Empire in the Fourth Century

BEGINNING WITH THE EMPEROR Nero (54–68), who blamed Christians[1] for a fire that tore through the city of Rome in 64, Roman authorities sporadically persecuted the followers of Jesus for almost 250 years.[2] One of the most severe of these persecutions, which became known as the "Great Persecution," began during the reign of Diocletian (284–305),[3] who also is known for reorganizing the political leadership of the Empire into the Tetrarchy (Diocletian was the Augustus of the East, Galerius was the Caesar of the East, Maximian was the Augustus of the West, and Constantius, the father of Constantine, was the Caesar of the West) in 293. The Great Persecution began after Diocletian and Galerius partook in an animal sacrifice at Antioch in 299 that failed. The priests had slaughtered an animal, and the soothsayer (*haruspex*) inspected the animal's entrails for divine messages, but found nothing. The priests slaughtered more animals, but these, too, produced nothing. They concluded that the Christians in Diocletian's entourage had made the sign of the cross during the sacrifice, causing it to be inefficacious. Or, as the Christian apologist Lactantius (c. 240–c. 320), who earlier had been hired by Diocletian to be the chair of Latin rhetoric in Nicomedia,[4] would describe it, "the demons were chased away, and the holy rites interrupted."[5] When a final sacrifice was made after the Christian interlopers were expelled, the gods were appeased. Diocletian also sent letters to the military that they, too, must sacrifice, and if any soldiers refused to do so, they must leave the army.[6] In the fall of 302, Diocletian was again in Antioch, and again made a sacrifice to the gods prior

---

1. Scholars generally do not call it "Christianity," but call it the "Jesus Movement," because, at this point in history, it would be misleading to think of it as a separate religion from Judaism. Scholars view it more as a movement within Judaism, and only later did it become its own religion. Harrington, *The Church*, 1–27.
2. Eusebius, *Hist. eccl.* 2.19–26; Chadwick, *Early Church*, 25–26.
3. Barnes, *Constantine and Eusebius*, 19; Leithart, *Defending Constantine*, 19.
4. Drake, *Constantine and Bishops*, 207.
5. Lactantius, *Mort.* 10.
6. Leithart, *Defending Constantine*, 15–18; Barnes, *Constantine and Eusebius*, 18–19.

to conducting official business. A certain deacon named Romanus was scandalized by seeing so many people in the pagan temples there. He interrupted the sacrifice at court in protest, and denounced them all as worshipping demons. Diocletian had him arrested, and Romanus was sentenced to be burned to death. But, Diocletian decided to have his tongue cut out of his mouth instead. Romanus was executed the following year after the persecution of Christians officially began.[7]

Diocletian consulted Galerius about how to handle the Christian population. Galerius strongly pressured Diocletian to begin a formal persecution. Although Diocletian was initially hesitant, he issued the first of four edicts on Terminalia, February 23, 303, the feast of the pagan god Terminus. This first Edict, although severe, did not execute any Christians, as it was clear to the Roman authorities by now that killing them only made the Christian community stronger. Instead, it targeted Christian property and rights. Churches were ordered to be destroyed, as well as homes that contained any church assets, which first were seized for the imperial treasury. Christians could not lawfully assemble, Scripture and liturgical texts were confiscated and burned, Christians who were public officials lost their jobs, and Christian aristocrats lost legal privileges (specifically, they could not be plaintiffs in court cases dealing with theft of property, adultery, or physical injury). Anyone who went to court was required to sacrifice to the gods before they were permitted to speak, which effectively banned all Christians. Christian slaves could not be manumitted, and those former Christian slaves who had been manumitted were required to return to slavery. This Edict, however, did not require Christians to offer a universal animal sacrifice.[8] On the morning of the first day the Edict was issued, the church at Nicomedia, which was visible from the imperial palace, was pillaged, Scripture was burned, and the building was destroyed. The decree was painted onto a wooden board, and placed at the center of the city. A certain Christian named Euethius ripped it down and tore it to pieces. Unsurprisingly, he was arrested, and burned to death that day.[9] In response, Christians of that town set fire to the imperial palace twice within fifteen days, destroying Diocletian's bedroom in the devastation.[10]

A second Edict was issued during the summer of 303. This time, the state took aim at Christian leaders by imprisoning all clergy. The prisons in the East, however, were incapable of holding so many people. A third Edict, therefore, was issued in November that allowed the clergy to go free—if they first were to sacrifice. The final Edict, promulgated a few months later at the beginning of 304, required all citizens,

---

7. Leithart, *Defending Constantine*, 18–20; Barnes, *Constantine and Eusebius*, 20–21.

8. Frend, *Rise of Christianity*, 452–57; Leithart, *Defending Constantine*, 21; Barnes, *Constantine and Eusebius*, 21–22.

9. Lactantius, *Mort.* 12; Williams, *Diocletian*, 175–77; Barnes, *Constantine and Eusebius*, 22.

10. Williams says that the fires were set "within months" of the Edict, while Leithart said that they were set "several days" after the Edict. Williams, *Diocletian*, 177; Leithart, *Defending Constantine*, 20.

THE POLITICAL, ASCETIC, AND THEOLOGICAL CONTEXTS

regardless of age or gender, to sacrifice. Anyone refusing to do so could be imprisoned or executed. This resulted in a general persecution.[11]

A little more than a year later, on May 1, 305, Diocletian, at a parade surrounded by the military in Nicomedia, stunned the Roman world by being the first Emperor to abdicate, and retiring to Split in Dalmatia. He told his troops that he was tired and needed rest, but, more importantly, he had come to the conclusion that emperors should have term limits. He also convinced Maximian to abdicate as well. Constantius replaced Maximian as the Augustus of the West, and Galerius replaced Diocletian as the Augustus of the East. Severus and Maximin Daia were appointed Caesars, while Constantine was passed over to the surprise of many.[12]

Galerius continued the campaign against Christians until he was on his death bed. Lactantius described Galerius's final days with more than a hint of *schadenfreude*. Among other vivid details, he said that

> God struck him [Galerius] with an incurable plague. A malignant ulcer formed itself low down in his secret parts, and spread by degrees. The physicians attempted to eradicate it, and healed up the place affected. But the sore, after having been skinned over, broke out again; a vein burst, and the blood flowed in such quantity as to endanger his life. The blood, however, was stopped, although with difficulty. The physicians had to undertake their operations anew, and at length they cicatrized the wound. In consequence of some slight motion of his body, Galerius received a hurt, and the blood streamed more abundantly than before. He grew emaciated, pallid, and feeble, and the bleeding then stanched. The ulcer began to be insensible to the remedies applied, and a gangrene seized all the neighbouring parts. It diffused itself the wider the more the corrupted flesh was cut away, and everything employed as the means of cure served but to aggravate the disease.[13]

On April 30, 311 (almost six years to the day after Diocletian's abdication), Galerius wrote a letter to the provinces, and had it posted in Nicomedia, that allowed Christians the right to assemble, and freed those in prisons and those who had been sentenced to work in mines, because he finally concluded that Christianity could not be eliminated. He also asked Christians to pray for both him and the Empire. But, he did not take any measures to have the property that had been confiscated from them returned.[14]

The Great Persecution may have come to an end officially, but troubles for the Christians were not over. Almost immediately after Galerius died, Maximin Daia

---

11. Frend, *Rise of Christianity*, 460–61; Williams, *Diocletian*, 178; Barnes, *Constantine and Eusebius*, 22–24.

12. Chadwick, *Early Church*, 122; Frend, *Rise of Christianity*, 462; Leithart, *Defending Constantine*, 46; Barnes, *Constantine and Eusebius*, 26.

13. Lactantius, *Mort.* 33.

14. Chadwick, *Early Church*, 122; Frend, *Rise of Christianity*, 480; Leithart, *Defending Constantine*, 27; Barnes, *Constantine and Eusebius*, 39.

wrote to governors telling them to ignore previous edicts that persecuted Christians, but he did not formally tolerate Christians either. Although he did not issue any new edicts beginning another campaign against Christians, six months later, on November 26, 311, he had Peter, the bishop of Alexandria, arrested and executed, and on January 7, 312 he personally tried a Christian scholar named Lucian, and had him put to death. He forbade Christians from gathering in cemeteries to honor the martyrs, and gave pagan priests the authority to arrest any Christians who refused to sacrifice to the gods. Like Galerius, however, Maximin Daia stopped his informal persecution in late 312, just months before his own death in 313.[15]

The situation for Christians radically changed after Constantine became an Augustus. On his deathbed in York before he died of natural causes on July 25, 306, Constantius declared that Constantine, who was thirty-four or thirty-five years old at the time, would be his successor, a decision that was immediately supported by Constantius's army—but was not immediately embraced by Galerius.[16] A few years later on October 28, 312, Constantine defeated his political rival, Maxentius, at a battle outside of Rome, at which Maxentius drowned in the Tiber near the Milvian bridge.[17]

Prior to the battle, Constantine had some sort of experience that was recounted (with important differences) by two men who knew him: Lactantius[18] (who was a tutor to Constantine's son Crispus),[19] and Eusebius of Caesarea[20] (who claims that he heard the story directly from Constantine).[21] According to Lactantius, Constantine was (anonymously) commanded in a dream (*in quiete*) prior to the battle to place the "heavenly sign of God" (*coeleste signum Dei*) on the shields of his soldiers. He described this sign as "the [Greek] letter X [*Chi*], with a perpendicular line drawn through it and turned round thus at the top, being the cipher of Christ."[22]

Eusebius tells the story differently. He says that Constantine was praying to the Christian God, and asked God to reveal himself to him, and to assist him in the upcoming battle. Around noon, Constantine saw with his eyes a "sign" (*signum, epiphaneia*)—as did his entire army—the "trophy of a cross of light in the heavens, above the sun, and bearing the inscription 'Conquer by This.'"[23] He did not understand what

---

15. Frend, *Rise of Christianity*, 481; Leithart, *Defending Constantine*, 97–98; Barnes, *Constantine and Eusebius*, 40.

16. Eusebius, *V. Con.* 1.21–22; O'Donnell, *Pagans*, 124; Barnes, *Constantine and Eusebius*, 25–28; Leithart, *Defending Constantine*, 57.

17. Eusebius, *V. Con.* 1.37–39; Rousseau, *Early Christian Centuries*, 214; Leithart, *Defending Constantine*, 65–67; Barnes, *Constantine and Eusebius*, 30.

18. Lactantius, *Mort.* 44.

19. Brown, *World of Late Antiquity*, 86; Frend, *Rise of Christianity*, 486.

20. Eusebius, *V. Con.* 1.28–29. It later would be told by Socrates and Sozomen as well. Socrates, *Hist. eccl.* 1.2; Sozomen, *Hist. eccl.* 1.3.

21. Eusebius, *V. Con.* 1.28.

22. Lactantius, *Mort.* 44.

23. Eusebius, *V. Con.* 1.28.

it meant, but that night, while he was sleeping, Jesus appeared to him with the same sign, and told him that he must "make a likeness of that sign which he had seen in the heavens, and to use it as a safeguard in all engagements with his enemies."[24] The next day, he commanded his craftsmen to build the standard that became known as the *labarum*.[25] At the top of the staff, which was covered with gold, was a wreath of gold and precious stones. Inside it were two intersecting Greek letters X (*Chi*) and P (*Rho*), which indicate the first two letters of the word Christ (*Christos*, Χριστός). This symbol—which had not been used previously by Christians, but became widely used through the centuries—later was placed on Constantine's helmet, and it was on his helmet on a coin issued in 315. Beneath the letters on the *labarum* was a portrait of Constantine and his children. Hanging from the cross-bar was a square cloth that also was embroidered with gold and precious stones.[26]

A few months later, in February 313, Constantine and Licinius (now the Augustus of the East) met in Milan during Licinius's wedding celebration. There, they agreed on an imperial policy concerning all religions. On June 15 of the same year, Licinius, now back in Nicomedia, published a letter in Latin signed by both Augusti announcing this policy, and a slightly different Greek version was published in Caesarea shortly afterwards. This policy has become known as the Edict of Milan since the ecclesiastical historian Caesar Baronius (1538–1607) named it so, although it was not an edict, and it was not issued from Milan. This policy is important for several reasons. First, it allowed Christians to practice their religion without molestation by the state (although Licinius later would start his own persecution of Christians in the East before Constantine defeated him in 324 to become the sole ruler of the Empire).[27] Second, it made the Roman Empire the first state in western civilization to permit all of its citizens to worship any deity. The emperors did not grant this out of a proto-Jeffersonian belief in the separation of church and state.[28] Rather, they demanded that everyone pray to their own god or gods for the safety and security of the emperors, and for the good of the empire. Third, any property that was taken from Christians during the recent persecutions must be returned immediately to the Christian communities. Those pagans who owned the property must return it without expecting compensation.[29]

24. Eusebius, *V. Con.* 1.29.

25. Chadwick, *Early Church*, 126; Frend, *Rise of Christianity*, 482; Leithart, *Defending Constantine*, 69–73; Barnes, *Constantine and Eusebius*, 43; O'Donnell, *Pagans*, 139–41; Drake, *Constantine and Bishops*, 203; Merdinger, *Rome and African Church*, 18.

26. Eusebius, *V. Con.* 1.30–31; Sozomen, *Hist. eccl.* 1.4; Leithart, *Defending Constantine*, 69; Drake, *Constantine and Bishops*, 201–3.

27. Eusebius, *Hist. eccl.* 10.5; Eusebius, *V. Con.* 1.51–56, 2.1–16; Sozomen, *Hist. eccl.* 1.7; Barnes, *Constantine and Eusebius*, 70–71.

28. Gaustad, *Sworn*, 51–55, 96–104, 184–200.

29. Eusebius, *Hist. eccl.* 10.5; Christensen, "So-Called Edict," 129; Drake, *Constantine and Bishops*, 194; Meyendorff, *Imperial Unity*, 5; Rahner, *Church and State*, 39; Leithart, *Defending Constantine*, 99–100.

Both of these events, Constantine's experience before defeating Maxentius, and this new religious policy, have led many to claim that Constantine was the first Christian emperor. Although this claim is not entirely incorrect, the reality is much more complicated. Constantine's conversion to Christianity, as many like to call it, is similar to Paul's experience, I would argue. Paul's dramatic encounter with the risen Christ on the road to Damascus, as told by Luke (Acts 9: 1–31), is widely known. Paul's own description of it, however, is often overlooked. He tells us that after God revealed his Son to him, Paul did not immediately consult with anyone about the meaning of his experience, and he did not seek out those who knew Jesus during his ministry. Rather, he went to Arabia, and then returned to Damascus for three years before he went to Jerusalem to meet with Cephas for fifteen days (Gal 1:13–24). Both Paul and Constantine experienced something profound, but they both needed years to process the meaning of their experiences.[30] Constantine's religiosity, then, should not be crammed into twenty-first century assumptions and categories about religious conversion and identity.

There is much evidence to indicate that he did not become a Christian overnight to the exclusion of his pagan background. Only gradually did Christian symbols appear on his coins. Pagan symbols, and images of the Unconquered Sun (*Sol Invictus*), remained on his coins (and official documents) until sometime between 318 and 321. Constantine also received pagan honors from the city of Athens; he took pagan statues from around the East to decorate his new capital; he paid for a pagan priest to travel to Egypt to see the pagan sites there; he remained the *pontifex maximus* of Roman paganism; he allowed pagan temples to remain open; most disturbingly of all, he executed his own wife, Fausta, and his own son, Crispus.[31]

The most important fact that should give us pause before describing Constantine as the first Christian emperor is that he was not baptized until his deathbed in 337. When he finally was baptized, it was at the hands of Eusebius of Nicomedia. Current academic and popular discussions love to debate questions of identity, and, although Avery Dulles has insightfully described the different ways that Christian identity and membership can be conceived,[32] it should be safe to say that the minimum requirement to be a Christian (and therefore to be a Christian emperor) is baptism. Constantine, it must be noted, was not the only person in Late Antiquity to postpone baptism until the end of his life.[33] It was a common practice at that time to delay it.[34] Augustine's mother Monica, for example, arranged to have Augustine baptized as a child when he became ill, but, when he recovered, it was postponed "on the assumption

---

30. Barron, *Catholicism*, 127–34.

31. Sozomen, *Hist. eccl.* 1.5; Brown, *World of Late Antiquity,* 88; Chadwick, *Early Church*, 126; Frend, *Rise of Christianity*, 484–85; Leithart, *Defending Constantine*, 76, 120; Meyendorff, *Imperial Unity*, 6; Merdinger, *Rome and African Church*, 20; Drake, *Constantine and Bishops*, 237.

32. Dulles, "Changing Concepts," 133–52.

33. Eusebius, *V. Con.* 4.62–63; Socrates, *Hist. eccl.* 1.39; Sozomen, *Hist. eccl.* 2.34; Chadwick, *Early Church*, 127; O'Donnell, *Pagans*, 152; Rahner, *Church and State*, 41, 48; Meyendorff, *Imperial Unity*, 6.

34. Ferguson, *Baptism in the Early Church*, 617–33.

that, if I died," Augustine later would write as a bishop, "I would be sure to soil myself; and after that solemn washing the guilt would be greater and more dangerous if I then defiled myself with sins."[35]

Scholars have offered a variety of reasons why Constantine may have chosen to postpone his baptism. Some scholars, like Henry Chadwick, James O'Donnell, and John Meyendorff have assumed that Constantine, like Monica for Augustine, was fearful that his post-baptismal sins might jeopardize his soul—"especially," Chadwick said, "if one's duty as an official included torture and execution of criminals."[36] Hugo Rahner, however, believed that his baptismal deferment was not only out of religious conviction, but for "political expediency,"[37] presumably so that he would not offend and alienate any pagan citizens. Regardless of the reasons why he chose not to be baptized, Constantine spent his entire reign as emperor outside of Christianity, despite the fact that he liked to call himself a "common bishop."[38]

Even though he was not baptized until the end of his life, Constantine supported the church in many ways throughout his reign. He recalled those Christians who had been sent into exile, liberated those who had been imprisoned, and allowed Christians to join the military again.[39] He outlawed crucifixion as a form of punishment.[40] Private divination became illegal, although public divination remained legal. If a *haruspex* were caught divining in a home, he would be buried alive; the person who requested his services would forfeit his property, and be sent into exile to an island.[41] Constantine decreed that no Christians should be in slavery to a Jew, and that the Jew must pay a fine after the slave is manumitted.[42] He gave money to pay for fifty copies of Bible to be made, which he insisted on inspecting when they were completed.[43] Constantine became the first emperor to call an ecclesiastical council when, in August 314, bishops met at Arles in an attempt to resolve the Donatist schism in Africa.[44] In 316, he disallowed facial branding of those who were sent to work in the mines, or who were gladiators, because humans are created in the image and likeness of God (Gen 1:26–7). They only may be tattooed on their ankles or hands.[45] Clergy were exempt

---

35. Augustine, *Conf.* 1.11.17.
36. Chadwick, *Early Church*, 127; O'Donnell, *Pagans*, 152; Meyendorff, *Imperial Unity*, 6.
37. Rahner, *Church and State*, 41.
38. Leithart, *Defending Constantine*, 150.
39. Socrates, *Hist. eccl.* 1.2; Sozomen, *Hist. eccl.* 1.8.
40. Sozomen, *Hist. eccl.* 1.8; Frend, *Rise of Christianity*, 488; Barnes, *Constantine and Eusebius*, 51.
41. Sozomen, *Hist. eccl.* 1.8; Barnes, *Constantine and Eusebius*, 52.
42. Eusebius, *V. Con.* 4.27.
43. Eusebius, *V. Con.* 4.36–37.
44. Eusebius, *V. Con.* 2.66; Merdinger, *Rome and African Church*, 18, 89–90, 201; Leithart, *Defending Constantine*, 157–59.
45. Chadwick, *Early Church*, 127–28; Frend, *Rise of Christianity*, 488; Barnes, *Constantine and Eusebius*, 51.

from all civic duties,[46] and from paying taxes. Bishops received permission to adjudicate civil legal cases in 318.[47] In 320, Constantine reversed inheritance law on the books since the reign of Augustus that penalized those who were unmarried, or who did not have children.[48] Also, any child who had chosen the ascetic life could make a will before the age of puberty.[49] These two laws were enacted to protect those men and women who chose the ascetic life because of their "ardent love of philosophy."[50] In 321 and again in 325, Constantine declared that any manumission of a slave by a clergyman that happened in a church was legally binding.[51] Also starting in 321, he banned the courts from hearing cases on Sundays (except cases manumitting slaves), and he insisted that only work done on farms that day is permitted.[52] He called the Council of Nicaea in 325—which has become known as the first ecumenical council—to address the controversy over the thought of Arius, who claimed that the Father and the Son are not consubstantial.[53] He banned all gladiatorial games,[54] and it is possible that he banned pagan sacrifice, but scholars disagree on this.[55]

Probably the most important way that Constantine (and his mother Helena) showed his favor for Christianity was through the building of churches.[56] His motivation for erecting them, undoubtedly, were manifold. Like almost every other ruler throughout time, he wanted to demonstrate to the world his political and financial might. Building projects are always excellent avenues for self-aggrandizement. But, he also seems to have had genuinely pious reasons for doing so. His most important building projects were erected in Jerusalem and Rome. The first church he constructed, for example, has been called the Basilica Constantiniana, Basilica Salvatoris, and San Giovanni in Laterano. It was built at the top of the Caelian Hill in Rome. Constantine may have conceived of the idea for it shortly after he defeated Maxentius, but it took several years for it to be completed. Unlike St. Peter's basilica, this church, which is the seat of the bishop of Rome, was not built on the site of a Christian shrine, but had been one of Maxentius's military camps. It could accommodate

---

46. Eusebius, *Hist. eccl.* 10.7; Merdinger, *Rome and African Church*, 18.

47. Sozomen, *Hist. eccl.* 1.9; Frend, *Rise of Christianity*, 488; Merdinger, *Rome and African Church*, 86.

48. Sozomen, *Hist. eccl.* 1.9.

49. Eusebius, *V. Con.* 4.26; Sozomen, *Hist. eccl.* 1.9; Frend, *Rise of Christianity*, 488; Leithart, *Defending Constantine*, 204–5; Barnes, *Constantine and Eusebius*, 52.

50. Eusebius, *V. Con.* 4.26.

51. Frend, *Rise of Christianity*, 488.

52. Eusebius, *V. Con.* 4.18; Sozomen, *Hist. eccl.* 1.8; Chadwick, *Early Church*, 128; Frend, *Rise of Christianity*, 488; Leithart, *Defending Constantine*, 201.

53. Eusebius, *V. Con.* 2.61–65, 3.6–21; Socrates, *Hist. eccl.* 1.5–9; Sozomen, *Hist. eccl.* 1.17–25.

54. Eusebius, *V. Con.* 4.27; Socrates, *Hist. eccl.* 1.18; Sozomen, *Hist. eccl.* 1.18.

55. Eusebius, *V. Con.* 4.23–25; Bradbury, "Constantine," 120–21; Rousseau, *Early Christian Centuries*, 219.

56. Eusebius, *V. Con.* 2.46, 3.26–46; Socrates, *Hist. eccl.* 1.3, 1.17; Sozomen, *Hist. eccl.* 1.8–2.3.

approximately three thousand people, and was one of the largest buildings in Rome at the time.[57] The structure as it stands today shows no traces of what it would have looked like in the fourth century.

After Constantine died and was buried in a tomb flanked by cenotaphs of the twelve apostles, power passed to his three sons (Constantine II, Constantius II, and Constans) until his son Constantius,[58] a committed Arian, took sole control in 353.[59] When he died, Julian (361–363), the so-called "Apostate," sent the Christian world into a panic. Julian, Constantine's nephew, had been raised as a Christian. He was baptized, grew up learning the Bible and theology, and became a lector in the church in Nicomedia. He also received a Roman education. After the age of seven, Julian was tutored by a certain Mardonius, who possibly was a eunuch, possibly a Goth, possibly a slave, and possibly a Christian. Mardonius was an important mentor for Julian, and taught him many of the Greek pagan authors, such as Homer and Hesiod.[60]

The circumstances and reasons for Julian's abandonment of Christianity, and his turn towards paganism, are not entirely clear. Although he publicly professed Christianity as shown by his presence at the celebration of the Feast of the Epiphany in Gaul in 360 or 361,[61] Julian had secretly become a pagan in Ephesus around the age of twenty, in 350 or 351, through the influence of a Neoplatonic philosopher named Maximus. He kept his new religious identity private for ten years until shortly before he became the emperor when he wrote two letters while Constantius was still alive—one to Maximus and another to the Athenians—that suggest that Julian already was worshipping the gods publicly, and that he had already reopened pagan temples in Greece after he became a Caesar in 355, which also was the first thing he did when he became the emperor.[62]

For the first five months of 362, Julian issued a variety of laws that would radically change the relationship between the state and Christians, whom he called "Galileans" to emphasize his belief that they were not truly Romans.[63] On January 17, he capped the maximum number of Christians allowed to practice law at Rome to thirty.[64] On

---

57. Curran, *Pagan City,* 93–96; Holloway, *Constantine and Rome,* 57–76.

58. Barnes, *Athanasius and Constantius,* 19–20.

59. Merdinger, *Rome and African Church,* 20.

60. Socrates, *Hist. eccl.* 3.1; Sozomen, *Hist. eccl.* 5.2; Bowersock, *Julian the Apostate,* 24; Tougher, *Julian the Apostate,* 24; Chadwick, *Early Church,* 154; Frend, *Rise of Christianity,* 594–95; O'Donnell, *Pagans,* 166–67.

61. Chadwick claims 360, but Tougher claims 361. Chadwick, *Early Church,* 155; Tougher, *Julian the Apostate,* 55.

62. Bowersock, *Julian the Apostate,* 30, 70; Tougher, *Julian the Apostate,* 22, 29, 55; Chadwick, *Early Church,* 155. The first thing he did after he became the emperor was to reopen pagan temples, many of which were in a dismal state of disrepair, and permitted sacrifice to the gods. Socrates, *Hist. eccl.* 3.1, 3.11, 3.15; Sozomen, *Hist. eccl.* 5.2–3.

63. Socrates, *Hist. eccl.* 3.12.

64. Bowersock, *Julian the Apostate,* 92.

February 9, he recalled all bishops—including Athanasius of Alexandria, Hilary of Poitiers, and a number of Donatist bishops—who had been sent into exile because of intra-Christian fighting.[65] He probably did so because he felt that Christianity could not survive the squabbling of its own leaders.[66] The following month, on March 13, Christian clergy lost all of the privileges they had enjoyed since the time of Constantine.[67] His infamous law, enacted on June 17, 362, prohibited Christian students from attending public schools to learn Greek literature, and to prohibit Christian teachers from teaching grammar, rhetoric, and philosophy. Any teacher, he said, who taught a subject (philosophy) that he did not believe to be true must be morally bankrupt, and should not be allowed to shape the minds of young people. In response, Apollinaris of Laodicea (who later would get himself into trouble for a deficient Christology), and his father, rewrote the Torah in hexameter verse, and the four Gospels and New Testament letters as Socratic dialogues, to ensure that Christian students were exposed to classical literary forms.[68] Julian also prohibited Christians from holding any office at court, from being judges or magistrates, and from being governors of the provinces, because, he said, Christians were not willing to sentence anyone to death due to their aversion to capital punishment.[69] Although Julian instituted these new laws harming Christians, he did not initiate another violent persecution against them, because he knew how powerful martyrs were for the Christian community.[70]

In addition to these new laws, a number of events happened during Julian's reign that impacted Christians. Both Julian and provincial governors exacted immense fines against Christians who refused to sacrifice to the gods.[71] Three Christians, Macedonius, Theodulus, and Tatian, for example, were executed for refusing to sacrifice as punishment for having destroyed the statues of pagan gods in the reopened temple of Merum. Amachius, the Governor of Phrygia who ordered the temple to be reopened, tortured them, and, as the ecclesiastical historian Socrates tells it, Amachius "at last laid them on gridirons under which a fire was placed, and thus slew them. But even in this last extremity they gave the most heroic proofs of fortitude, addressing the ruthless governor thus: 'If you wish to eat broiled flesh, Amachius, turn us on the

---

65. Socrates, *Hist. eccl.* 3.1–10; Sozomen, *Hist. eccl.* 5.5.

66. Frend thinks so, but Bowersock is not convinced. Frend, *Rise of Christianity*, 601; Bowersock, *Julian the Apostate*, 71.

67. Sozomen, *Hist. eccl.* 5.5; Frend, *Rise of Christianity*, 601–2; Bowersock, *Julian the Apostate*, 73–74.

68. Socrates, *Hist. eccl.* 3.12–16; Sozomen, *Hist. eccl.* 5.18; Brown, *World of Late Antiquity*, 93; Chadwick, *Early Church*, 156–57; Frend, *Rise of Christianity*, 604; Bowersock, *Julian the Apostate*, 83–84; Tougher, *Julian the Apostate*, 57.

69. Socrates, *Hist. eccl.* 3.13; Sozomen, *Hist. eccl.* 5.18.

70. Socrates, *Hist. eccl.* 3.12; Sozomen, *Hist. eccl.* 5.17; Bowersock, *Julian the Apostate*, 83–84; Tougher, *Julian the Apostate*, 83.

71. Socrates, *Hist. eccl.* 3.13–17.

other side also, lest we should appear but half cooked to your taste.'"[72] Another important event that revealed Julian's attitude towards Christians was the death of George, the Arian bishop of Alexandria, at the end of December 361. After Christians there paraded some human skulls through the streets that they had found while transforming a pagan temple into a church, pagans killed George and other Christians. Julian responded by castigating the pagans in a letter, but, other than that, took no action against them.[73] He also ordered Bishop Eleusius of Cyzicus to rebuild the Novatian church that his predecessor had destroyed.[74]

The most provocative of all of his efforts to undermine Christianity was his attempt to rebuild the Jewish temple in Jerusalem, which had been destroyed in the year 70. A genuine admiration for Judaism may have prompted him to undertake such a massive building project, because of the importance it historically placed on the cult of sacrifice,[75] as well as a "common hostility"[76] towards Christians that they both shared. It is also likely that he wanted to rebuild it in order to disprove the claim that Jesus had made that not a single stone of the temple would be left on top of another stone (Matt 24:2).[77] Unsurprisingly, the Jews did not entirely embrace the idea—despite the fact that Julian had remitted their taxes to the state—because they expected the temple to be rebuilt with the arrival of the Messiah.[78] Julian, to be sure, was not the Messiah.

Not long after Alypius, the former governor of Britain who had been put in charge of the project, began its construction in March 363, the project came to a halt. Modern scholars usually offer natural explanations for what happened: W.H.C. Frend, for example, said that workers hit hidden gas deposits that exploded,[79] and G.W. Bowersock has claimed that either an earthquake or sabotage caused the work to be abandoned.[80] The ecclesiastical historians Socrates and Sozomen attributed it to supernatural explanations, claiming that first an earthquake scattered the stones of the old foundation of the Temple, then a fire consumed the workmen's tools, and the next night, after a great number of Jews had assembled to witness these miracles, the sign of the cross appeared on the clothing of all of the workmen.[81] Regardless of what exactly happened, the foundation of the temple wasn't even laid before the entire endeavor fell apart.

---

72. Socrates, *Hist. eccl.* 3.15.

73. Socrates, *Hist. eccl.* 3.2–4; Sozomen, *Hist. eccl.* 5.7; Tougher, *Julian the Apostate*, 56.

74. Socrates, *Hist. eccl.* 3.11; Frend, *Rise of Christianity*, 602.

75. Frend, *Rise of Christianity*, 606; Bowersock, *Julian the Apostate*, 89; Tougher, *Julian the Apostate*, 57.

76. Bowersock, *Julian the Apostate*, 89.

77. Sozomen, *Hist. eccl.* 3.22; Tougher, *Julian the Apostate*, 57; Bowersock, *Julian the Apostate*, 89.

78. Bowersock, *Julian the Apostate*, 89.

79. Frend, *Rise of Christianity*, 606.

80. Bowersock, *Julian the Apostate*, 90.

81. Socrates, *Hist. eccl.* 3.20; Sozomen, *Hist. eccl.* 5.22.

PART I: HISTORY

After Julian died in 363 at the beginning of his campaign against the Persians when a spear pierced his abdomen, the army first tried to proclaim the pagan Salutius emperor, but, when he refused, they turned to the Christian Jovian, who accepted.[82] Every emperor after Jovian until the collapse of the Roman Empire was Christian. The most important Christian emperor after Constantine was the Spaniard Theodosius I (379–392 as Emperor of the East, and 392–395 as sole Emperor), whom Hugo Rahner said "brought to term what Constantine had begun."[83] Stephen Williams and Gerard Friell said that Theodosius, along with the Council of Nicaea, "can be considered as the historic founder of the established Catholic church."[84]

In February 380, not long after becoming emperor, Theodosius decreed a new law, *Cunctos populous*, in Thessalonica that required all citizens to become Christians in the tradition that was taught by Peter to the Romans at the beginning of the church, and currently was taught by bishops Damasus of Rome and Peter of Alexandria. This tradition, which is the only one that truly may be called Catholic, professes the Nicene trinitarian formula. Anyone who holds theological opinions contrary to this must be despised, considered heretics, and handed over to the state for punishment. This new law, which has been called a "momentous document that inaugurated a new age,"[85] and "one of the most significant documents in European history,"[86] was not an attack on pagans, but was intended to bring unity to Christianity.[87]

Shortly after this law was put into place, Theodosius became deathly ill. He summoned Bishop Acholius to his bedside in Thessalonica so that he could be baptized. Before he would receive the sacrament from him, Theodosius questioned him about his confessional identity. Once Acholius reassured him that he professed a Nicene theology, Theodosius allowed him to proceed. He recovered his health within a few days, however, and he ascribed his miraculous recovery to the graces he received at baptism. He was the first emperor baptized towards the start of his rule, rather than the end.[88]

That fall, when Theodosius arrived in Constantinople, he began a crackdown on Arian clergy. Demophilus, the Arian bishop of Constantinople, was ousted (as were other Arian bishops throughout the East), and Gregory of Nazianzus was put in his place. Theodosius issued another law directed at the Eunomians, the Photinians, and the Manichaeans for good measure. He also called a council—which met in

---

82. Socrates, *Hist. eccl.* 3.21; Sozomen, *Hist. eccl.* 6.1–3; O'Donnell, *Pagans*, 171; Bowersock, *Julian the Apostate*, 118–19.

83. Rahner, *Church and State*, 68.

84. Williams and Friell, *Theodosius*, 57.

85. Rahner, *Church and State in Early Christianity*, 74.

86. Williams and Friell, *Theodosius*, 28.

87. Sozomen, *Hist. eccl.* 7.4; King, *Emperor Theodosius*, 28.

88. Socrates, *Hist. eccl.* 5.6; Sozomen, *Hist. eccl.* 7.4; Meyendorff, *Imperial Unity*, 7; Williams and Friell, *Theodosius*, 31.

Constantinople in 381 that has become known as the second ecumenical council—that tried to end the Christian infighting that had persisted even after the Council of Nicaea. This council, too, did not end the conflict. Yet another law, in July 381, officially sacked all Arian clergy, and listed specific bishops for major cities (except Antioch) with whom presbyters and deacons must be in communion. The Arians resisted as well as they could, but to little avail. In January 386, for example, Justina—an Arian and the mother of Valentinian II, the young emperor of the West—convinced her son to pass a law giving Arians the right to worship. She also insisted that Ambrose, the bishop of Milan, give the Basilica Portiana to the Arians for their use. Ambrose and his congregation (including Monica)[89] locked themselves inside it to stage a sit-in. Justina, without any options save violence, relented.[90]

Initially, Theodosius's focus on what he considered to be Christian heretics meant that he had little interest in pagans. But, on February 24, 391, he issued the first of four laws that would radically reshape the empire. This law, *Nemo se hostiis polluat*, prohibited sacrifice to the gods, including state sacrifices. It prohibited anyone from entering pagan temples, or worshipping graven images. Anyone with means caught breaking this law would be fined a significant amount of gold. The second law, on June 9 of the same year, prohibited Christians from converting to (or back to) paganism, on the pain of the loss of certain legal rights. The third law, on June 16, echoed the first law against sacrifice, but it specifically targeted Egypt, and the pagan temples in Alexandria. These laws, especially the third law, initiated an outbreak of violence against pagans and their temples, including at Petraea, Areopolis, Canopus, Heliopolis, Gaza, and Gaul. Most significantly, the Serapaeum, the Alexandrian temple dedicated to the god Serapis, was destroyed. After fighting erupted between Christians and pagans in the streets, the pagans took refuge in the Serapaeum, holding several Christians hostage, and then killing them. Theodosius said that, because the Christian dead had been martyred, the pagans should be forgiven. But, there could be no forgiveness for their idolatry. Hearing this, Theophilus, the bishop of Alexandria whom we will discuss in detail later, and the Alexandrian Christians looted and destroyed the temple. The fourth law, not issued until November 8, 392, declared that all sacrifice and divination were punishable by death, and any pagan ritual accoutrements were prohibited.[91]

These four laws completed an almost ninety-year arc that began with Christianity's future in jeopardy because of Diocletian's Great Persecution, and ended with its future fully entwined with state power. This new political reality shaped the way the Pelagian controversy concluded, because the state played a small yet significant

---

89. Augustine, *Conf.* 9.7.15.

90. Socrates, *Hist. eccl.* 5.8; Sozomen, *Hist. eccl.* 7.7–13; Williams and Friell, *Theodosius*, 53–60; King, *Emperor Theodosius*, 32–46.

91. Socrates, *Hist. eccl.* 5.16–17; Sozomen, *Hist. eccl.* 7.15–20; Chadwick, *Early Church*, 168–69; Meyendorff, *Imperial Unity*, 391–92; Williams and Friell, *Theodosius*, 119–24; King, *Emperor Theodosius*, 77–86.

role in its outcome. As will be discussed in detail later, the Emperor Honorius twice intervened against the Pelagians when, in 418, he condemned Pelagius and Caelestius and banished them from the city of Rome—despite the fact that Pelagius was not in the city at that time—and, the following year, banished them from the provinces. Julian of Eclanum, who was sent into exile after he and a number of other Italian bishops refused to sign Pope Zosimus's *Tractoria* condemning the Pelagians in 418, invited the state to get involved when he wrote to a certain Valerius, a military official at the imperial court in Ravenna, asking him to assign impartial judges to adjudicate their case. In 425, furthermore, Theodosius II and Valentinian III insisted that all bishops in Gaul prove their orthodoxy against the Pelagians to Bishop Patroclus of Arles. Theodosius later banished those Pelagians who were in Constantinople in 429. These governmental actions sealed the fate of the Pelagians in a more definitive way than ecclesiastical condemnations alone would have done.

The Ascetic Context: The Rise of Christian Renunciation

Another important part of the landscape of the fourth and fifth centuries that comprised the context of the Pelagian controversy was the Christian ascetic movement. The exact origins of asceticism are unclear, but examples of renunciation can be traced back to the Bible.[92] In the Old Testament, for example, the Nazarites took vows abstaining from all products from grapes, to wear their hair long, and to abstain from contact with a corpse (Num 6:1–8).[93] In the New Testament, John the Baptist wore clothes made of camel's hair, ate locusts and wild honey, and preached in the desert of Judea (Matt 3:1–12).[94] In post-biblical Christianity, evidence shows that ascetics began to appear in the deserts of Egypt and Palestine by the end of the third century,[95] spread to Syria and Cappadocia, and was thriving around the Roman world by 400.[96]

It is not known who these renunciants were. At first, these ascetics were hermits, but organized communities—which has become the standard form until today—quickly began to appear.[97] Most of them were lay Christians,[98] and most did not come from the elite classes of the empire.[99] Scholars disagree about their education level. Henry Chadwick called them "fairly simple folk,"[100] but C. H. Lawrence and Samuel Robinson have argued that many of them maintained letter correspondences, and

92. Robinson, "Christian Asceticism," 50.
93. Chepey, *Nazirites*, 22–40.
94. Saldarini, "Asceticism," 22.
95. Lawrence, *Medieval Monasticism*, 1.
96. King, *Western Monasticism*, 31; Robinson, "Christian Asceticism," 49.
97. Lawrence, *Medieval Monasticism*, 1.
98. Lawrence, *Medieval Monasticism*, 1.
99. Brown, *World of Late Antiquity*, 100.
100. Chadwick, *Early Church*, 177.

many were involved in intellectual pursuits. Origen of Alexandria, for example, was read widely in the Egyptian desert.[101] Scholars also disagree why they abandoned social norms. One possibility is that fugitives had fled to the desert during the Decian persecution (250–251), and decided to remain there after the persecution ended.[102] Another possibility is that, after Constantine began to favor Christianity, the bloody martyrdom of the saints was replaced by a bloodless martyrdom of the ascetics. As R.A. Markus succinctly described this possibility: "the emotional energies previously absorbed by the duty to rise to the demands made on a persecuted Church were largely re-directed towards disciplined ascetic living."[103] In other words, the internal self-persecution of the ascetics took over from the external persecution of the martyrs by the pre-Constantinian state. A third possible reason, also arising from the change in the Christian political reality, was that many Christians desired a more rigorous life in response to a perceived softening of the Christian moral fiber.[104] The most satisfactory reason (while not ignoring the social, psychological, economic, and political factors), however, is that ascetics came to believe that this pursuit of perfection was the necessary precondition to achieve union with God through prayer.[105]

Although asceticism spread all over the Mediterranean world, it was Egyptian asceticism, both in its eremitic and cenobitic manifestations, that captured the imaginations of Christians in the fourth and early fifth centuries,[106] mostly because of the *Vita Antonii*, the hagiography Athanasius of Alexandria wrote about Antony of Egypt. Athanasius (c. 295–373) was ordained the bishop of Alexandria in 328.[107] Because of his battles with the Arians, who refused to accept the Creed of the Council of Nicaea that claimed that the Father and the Son are consubstantial, Athanasius was sent into exile five times.[108] During his third exile (355–362), Athanasius wrote the *Vita Antonii*, which immediately had a transformative effect on the entire Christian world.[109] At the height of his existential crisis in 386, for example, Augustine would recall that, although neither he nor his friend Alypius had heard of Antony at that point, Antony's holiness already had been broadcast widely throughout the East and the West.[110]

Antony (251–356) was born to moderately affluent Christian parents in Egypt. As a child, he hated school, but as an obedient son he dutifully went to school, and also to

---

101. Lawrence, *Medieval Monasticism*, 4; Robinson, "Christian Asceticism," 52–53.

102. King, *Western Monasticism*, 16.

103. Markus, *End of Ancient Christianity*, 70–72.

104. Lawrence, *Medieval Monasticism*, 3.

105. Markus, *End of Ancient Christianity*, 159; Lawrence, *Medieval Monasticism*, 2–3.

106. Brown, "Rise and Function," 82; Lawrence, *Medieval Monasticism*, 3; Robinson, "Christian Asceticism," 49.

107. Kannengiesser, "Athanasius of Alexandria," 479.

108. Gregg, "Introduction," xi.

109. Rousseau, *Ascetics, Authority*, 14–15; Gregg, "Introduction," 2.

110. Augustine, *Conf.* 8.6.14.

church.[111] When he was about eighteen to twenty years old, he became responsible for his sister after their parents died. Less than six months later, he was walking to church and pondering how the apostles had abandoned everything to follow Jesus, and how, in the Acts of the Apostles, many sold all of their possessions for the sake of the community (2:45). Entering the church, he heard the Gospel of Matthew proclaimed that "if you would be perfect, go, sell what you possess and give to the poor, and you will have treasure in heaven" (19:21). Antony understood that God was speaking directly to him through this passage, so he immediately left and gave away his money and possessions (leaving some for his sister).[112] Soon afterwards, he once again heard Matthew proclaimed that he should not be anxious about his life (6:25–34), so he began to imitate the life of an old man he knew who had been a renunciant since he was a child.

From the edge of his village where he now lived, Antony would seek out any wisemen he could find. He began to do manual labor, bought bread to eat with the money that he earned, and donated the rest of his earnings.[113] He often would stay awake all night, would drink only water, would eat only one meal after sundown, would fast for four days at a time, and would sleep on a matt on the floor.[114] This life, however, was not intense enough for him, so he moved farther away from the village, and asked a friend to lock him in a tomb where he could battle the devil in spiritual warfare.[115] In 269 when he was about thirty-five years old,[116] he decided that the tomb still did not satisfy his zeal, so he set off for the wilderness where he discovered an abandoned fortress on a mountain where he sequestered himself. He never left the fortress, nor received anyone who came to see him.[117] Antony lived in seclusion there for twenty years. Only after some friends of his, and others who desired to emulate him, dismantled the door did he finally emerge from his solitude. Rather than appearing emaciated from lack of nutrition, or obese from lack of movement, he looked exactly as he did two decades earlier. Through him, God healed many sufferers of physical disease, purged those possessed by demons, and gave Antony the gift of eloquence despite his earlier dislike of education. His example and eloquence convinced so many to imitate his life that, as Athanasius said, "the desert was made a city by monks."[118]

He was ashamed of the needs of his body, so he would not eat any more than what he needed. When he would eat a meal, he often would leave the other monks because he was fearful that he would blush if others saw him eating. He focused all of his attention on the soul, rather than the body, and offered advice to those who would

---

111. Athanasius, *Vit. Ant.* 1.
112. Athanasius, *Vit. Ant.* 2.
113. Athanasius, *Vit. Ant.* 3.
114. Athanasius, *Vit. Ant.* 7.
115. Athanasius, *Vit. Ant.* 8.
116. Brown, *World of Late Antiquity*, 96.
117. Athanasius, *Vit. Ant.* 11–12.
118. Athanasius, *Vit. Ant.* 14.

listen that they should not allow the soul to be corrupted by the desires of the body. The body should always be in service to the soul, not the other way around.[119] His own attempts to master his body included constant fasting, and wearing clothes inside out with the hair turned towards his skin. He never bathed with water, and refused to wash his feet, nor dip them in water unless it was a necessity. No one ever saw him without clothes on until he died and was buried.[120] Even though he never wrote a *regula*, never took any formal vows, never required anyone else to take any vows, nor established a common form of worship, Antony's way of life became a model for those who came after him.[121]

When Maximin Daia waged his informal persecution, he sent many Christians to the mines and prisons. According to Athanasius, Antony and other desert hermits went to Alexandria in hopes of becoming martyrs, but Antony did not hand himself over to the authorities. Rather, he tended to those who suffered at the hands of the state, and accompanied those who were sent to their deaths by a judge. The judge, seeing Antony's willingness to die, ordered him and all of the other monks out of the city. The others thought it would be best to go into hiding, but the next day Antony defiantly stood at the front of the court, once again inspiring others to a life of renunciation.[122]

When the persecution had ended in late 312, he returned to the desert. But, life there had become too crowded with people, and the temptation of the sin of pride too great, so he intended to retreat even more deeply into the marshes of the upper Thebaid where no one knew him. While waiting on the banks of the Nile for a boat, he heard a voice tell him to go to the "inner mountain" instead, because he would not be able to find the solitude that he sought if he did not. He traveled with some Saracens for three days and three nights, because they knew the way to it. Arriving, he found a hill with clear water at the base, and wild date palms.[123] He lived there for the rest of his life, rarely leaving his seclusion, and dying at the age of 105 years old.[124]

Pachomius (c. 290–347) was the second great figure of fourth-century asceticism, because he was the founder of Egyptian cenobitic monasticism.[125] Our knowledge of him is sketchy, as the sources who wrote about him did not have any personal relationship with him.[126] Palladius described him as "a man of the kind who live rightly," and "exceedingly kind and brotherly,"[127] while Gennadius called him "a man endowed

119. Athanasius, *Vit. Ant.* 45.
120. Athanasius, *Vit. Ant.* 47.
121. Chitty, *Desert a City*, 5.
122. Athanasius, *Vit. Ant.* 46.
123. Athanasius, *Vit. Ant.* 49.
124. Athanasius, *Vit. Ant.* 89.
125. Gennadius, *De vir. Inlustr.* 7.
126. Rousseau, *Pachomius*, xiv.
127. Palladius, *Hist. Laus.* 32.1.

with apostolic grace both in teaching and performing miracles."[128] Philip Rousseau, Pachomius's biographer, described him as "a man of caution and doubt, yet ready to experiment and to adapt to circumstance and personality. He was humble and generous. Above all he was a shrewd judge of character, and able to mold without tyranny those who trusted him."[129]

Pachomius was born to pagan parents in the Thebaid. He was drafted into the army about the age of twenty by Maximin Daia, in 312 or 313, to fight in the civil war with Licinius. One night, he and his fellow soldiers had sheltered in a prison at Luxor. Christians came to the prison with food. Pachomius had never heard of Christians, and did not understand the root of their generosity. When he inquired, he was told that they were followers of the Son of God, and that their charity extended to all people, not just to other Christians. He was shaken to his core when he heard this, and he found a quiet spot in the prison where he prayed, and pledged himself to God for the rest of his life. A few months later, he was out of the army and returned to the village of Chenoboscia in the Thebaid asking to be baptized. Just before his baptism, he had a vision in which dew fell from heaven, dripped into his hand as honey, and spilled onto the earth. A voice told him that this adumbrated his future. For the next three years following his baptism, he lived a simple life in the community, but then began a life of renunciation. He sought out the hermit Palamon to be his mentor, who (like many spiritual masters often did) tried to discourage Pachomius by describing the rigors of his diet, fasts, vigils, and prayer. But, this did not deter him. Like other solitaries in the mode of Antony, Pachomius learned the arduous patterns of the life of the hermits.

A voice spoke to him one day in a vision when he came across the abandoned village of Tabennesis while he was collecting wood. The voice told him to establish a monastery on that spot where many others could come and join him. Palamon helped Pachomius build a cell there, but he died shortly afterwards. Pachomius's older brother, John, soon joined him, but they disagreed on how big the monastery should be, John favoring a smaller community, Pachomius favoring a larger one. John died not long afterwards, and Pachomius's community gradually began to grow. In 320, he had another vision. At the instigation of his sister, he established a community of women, where she would become the superior. After his own community had grown beyond one hundred monks, he founded another monastery at Phbow just a few miles away from Tabennesis where, in 337, he moved his headquarters. As the communities continued to grow, he continued to found new locations. Palladius reports that, by the end of the fourth century, the different communities may have reached a combined seven thousand monks.[130]

128. Gennadius, *De vir. Inlustr.* 7.

129. Rousseau, *Pachomius*, xiv.

130. Palladius, *Hist. Laus.* 32.1–12; Gennadius, *De vir. Inlustr.* 7; Chitty, *Desert a City*, 7–11; King, *Western Monasticism*, 21–23; Rousseau, *Pachomius*, 58–59.

The physical structures of the communities that he established vaguely resemble what we think of today as typical of a monastery. A wall surrounded the entire compound that contained multiple buildings, including a space for worship, a refectory, a kitchen, an infirmary, a lodge for visitors, and a bakery. The monks lived in cells in houses limited to twenty to forty monks. Early in the life of the community, each individual would have his own cell. They would not be allowed to visit each other's cells, because the cell was the most important place monks would pray. As the community developed over time, as many as three monks came to inhabit one cell. Each house was under the direction of a headmaster (*praepositus*), who was the spiritual director and primary educator of the entire house, and the entire compound would be headed by a superior. Monks may have been grouped together in a house based on a particular skill set that they all shared, although this is not entirely certain.[131]

The daily cycle for the monks was strictly regimented. At daybreak, a gong would signal the beginning of morning prayer in the communal worship space. The monks would go to their designated spaces to listen to the Bible proclaimed, meditate silently, and recite the Our Father. While listening to the Bible, monks silently worked, and penances for infractions against the community's *regula* also were done. After the morning prayer, the monks would return to their cells where they then would be told what labor they would do that day. The monks participated in a variety of types of work, including gardening, basket weaving, matt making, rope making, tailoring, blacksmithing, woodworking, bread making, husbanding, cloth making, and shoe making, to name a just a few. Throughout the day, scriptural recitation, meditation, and discussion about the texts would accompany the work of the monks. During the middle of the day, the main meal, consisting mainly of bread and cooked vegetables, would be eaten silently in the refectory. In the evening, a lighter meal would be eaten, and communal prayer would be held. In each house afterwards, the monks would say more prayers before going to bed.

They were required to fast on both Wednesdays and Fridays. In the evening, they would leave their work and return to their houses where the headmaster would offer a catechetical lecture instead of a meal. Pachomius (or another superior) would deliver a catechetical lecture on Saturdays, and on Sundays he would offer two. The monks would discuss these catecheses in the evening. Also on Saturday evenings, Sunday mornings, and other religious holidays, the monks would antiphonally sing the Psalms, and celebrate the Eucharist. Pachomius did not want any of his monks to be ordained, and not every monastery had its own church, so monks often would be forced to go to a local village to receive communion. On Monday morning, the week would begin all over again.[132]

---

131. Palladius, *Hist. Laus.* 32.2; King, *Western Monasticism*, 21–23; Lawrence, *Medieval Monasticism*, 7–8; Rousseau, *Pachomius*, 78–79.

132. Palladius, *Hist. Laus.* 32.9-12; King, *Western Monasticism*, 24–25; Lawrence, *Medieval Monasticism*, 8; Rousseau, *Pachomius*, 80–86.

PART I: HISTORY

Asceticism was not found only in Egypt, but, most importantly for our purposes, it was also practiced in the city of Rome. The origins of Christian asceticism in Rome are hazy, but pagan forms of renunciation, which undoubtedly helped shape the particular practices of Christian renunciants there, had percolated throughout the Roman aristocracy long before the political winds shifted for Christians at the beginning of the fourth century. The mild renunciation of *otium*, leisured retirement, was one type. More rigorous forms were also practiced. Plotinus, the Neoplatonic philosopher, for example, established a school in Rome at the end of the third century that attracted many Roman senators, including a Senator Rogatianus who gave away all of his property, manumitted his slaves, abandoned all political pursuits, and would only eat one meal every other day.[133]

The rise of Christian asceticism in the city of Rome cannot be attributed simply to the influence of pagans, nor to the change in the political reality of fourth-century Christians.[134] Even with the limited sources available to us, it is clear that Christian asceticism was practiced prior to that time. In the third century, individuals, or groups loosely organized, lived lives of chastity and intense prayer in the city.[135] The schismatic Novatian is the first known ascetic in Rome. He led a group of rigorists, championed chastity, refused penance to those who had succumbed to the pressures of the state during persecution, and, in 249–250, lived in a cell, a decision that Pope Cornelius (251–253) condemned.[136]

During the course of the fourth century, a variety of events happened that increased the awareness and practice of asceticism among the Christian elite in Rome. One was the arrival of Athanasius to the West. During his exiles in 335–337 and 339–346, he went around Italy, to Trier, and to Rome, where he spent a total of seven years,[137] and told stories about Antony and Pachomius, whom he had visited and with whom he may have stayed during another one of his exiles.[138] The *Vita Antonii* was translated into Latin while Athanasius was still alive, but a better translation by Evagrius of Antioch in 374 quickly spread throughout Christian circles in Rome.[139] Another important event for the development of asceticism in Rome was the arrival in 373 of Peter of Alexandria, Athanasius's successor, who brought even more tales of heroic renunciation from the East.[140] A third event, which will be explored later, was the return of Jerome to Rome in 382 after his experience in the Syrian desert,

---

133. Curran, *Pagan City*, 264–68.

134. Brown, "Aspects of Christianization," 164.

135. Rousseau, *Ascetics, Authority*, 80–81; Lavender, "Development," 46.

136. King, *Western Monasticism*, 33; Kelly, *Oxford Dictionary*, 18–19.

137. Jerome, *Epist*. 127.5; Rousseau, *Ascetics, Authority*, 81; Lavender, "Development," 46; Curran, *Pagan City*, 275; Lawrence, *Medieval Monasticism*, 10–12.

138. King, *Western Monasticism*, 28.

139. King, *Western Monasticism*, 33; Lawrence, *Medieval Monasticism*, 10–11.

140. Rousseau, *Ascetics, Authority*, 81–82; Lavender, "Development," 47–51.

and his incorporation into the highest rungs of Roman Christian society—including his relationship with Pope Damasus. Jerome, who will be introduced in detail in a later chapter, already had written his first hagiography of an ascetic, his *Vita Pauli* in 377–379, while he was living in Antioch after he returned from the desert. It would become one of his most popular writings.[141] He also would translate Pachomian works into Latin, probably in 404.[142] Yet another important event that also will be explored in detail later was the return of Rufinus of Aquileia to Rome in 397.[143] Not only did Rufinus bring to Rome his personal experience of asceticism in Palestine, but he translated many important works into Latin, including the ascetic texts of Basil of Caesarea, and the *Historia Monachorum in Aegypto*.[144]

The form of asceticism practiced by Christian aristocrats in the city of Rome was different from both the eremitic form, as epitomized by Antony, and the cenobitic, as epitomized by Pachomius. Although a few aristocrats, as we shall see later, did flee to Palestine to live cenobitic lives, for the most part these aristocratic renunciants in Rome did not abandon society, nor their economic responsibilities, nor did they live in intentional community with each other under a strict *regula*. They often renounced their wealth, but they did not abandon it in the way that Antony had done with his immediate, radical, and grand gesture.[145] Most of them continued to live with their families on their own estates in, or near, the city.[146] Pelagius (and most likely Caelestius) undoubtedly came into contact with this form of genteel asceticism during the decades he lived in Rome.[147]

The most important of these Roman ascetics were women, which is noteworthy because it was uncommon for women to be ascetics (especially desert ascetics),[148] and more uncommon for rich female aristocrats to be so.[149] They were few in number, but their wealth and social prominence made them influential throughout both the Christian and pagan aristocracies.[150] There were multiple women at the heart of this movement whom we could offer as examples, but, for the sake of brevity, only Marcella will be described here, although several others who were in Marcella's circle (such as Paula, Eustochium, and Blesilla) will be discussed later.[151]

141. Kelly, *Jerome*, 60; Rousseau, *Ascetics, Authority*, 81–82; Lavender, "Development," 51–55.

142. Rousseau, *Ascetics, Authority*, 16.

143. Two other important figures for the development of asceticism in the West, although not necessarily in the city of Rome, were Hilary of Poitiers and Martin of Tours. Lawrence, *Medieval Monasticism*, 12.

144. King, *Western Monasticism*, 33–34; Rousseau, *Ascetics, Authority*, 81–82.

145. Brown, *Through the Eye*, 208–322.

146. Brown, "Patrons of Pelagius," 209.

147. Curran, *Pagan City*, 298.

148. Clark, "Women and Asceticism," 40.

149. Clark, "Women and Asceticism," 34.

150. Yarbrough, "Christianization,"151; Curran, *Pagan City*, 319.

151. Other important women in Marcella's circle were Asella, Marcellina, Lea, Felicitas, and Principia. Kelly, *Jerome*, 92–104.

Marcella was the first woman in the city of Rome to become an ascetic.[152] Jerome, who would become a sort of spiritual director for several ascetic women, would eulogize her as "the glory of her native Rome,"[153] "that holy woman,"[154] and "revered Marcella"[155] two years after her death because, he says, he was so distraught that he could not bring himself to write earlier as he could not think clearly.[156] Jerome undoubtedly had a special affection for her because he found his entrance into this circle of women through Marcella's invitation when he had returned to Rome.[157] Little is known about Marcella's lineage,[158] but her ancestry probably consisted of consuls and praetorian prefects.[159] Her father likely died when she was very young, and her husband died less than seven months after they married.[160] Her mother, Albina, attempted to secure for her a second marriage to a distinguished yet much older suitor named Cerealis.[161] Marcella, however, would have none of it. She quipped that "had I a wish to marry and not rather to dedicate myself to perpetual chastity, I should look for a husband and not for an inheritance."[162] Instead, she decided to give up "both wealth and rank; she has sought the true nobility of poverty and lowliness"[163] after hearing about Antony and Pachomius from Athanasius and Peter when they arrived in Rome.[164]

In doing so, she caused a scandal among the aristocracy, because it was seen as "so strange and ignominious and degrading."[165] She dressed in clothes that were intended to keep her warm, rather than to display her figure, and she sold her jewelry to use the money to feed the poor.[166] Her mother and an entourage of serious-minded virgins and widows always would be present anytime she left her home, or anytime she received clergy or monks in her home.[167] When she went out in public (which was

152. Jerome, *Epist.* 127.5.
153. Jerome, *Epist.* 127.1.
154. Jerome, *Epist.* 127.1.
155. Jerome, *Epist.* 127.14.
156. Jerome, *Epist.* 127.1.
157. Jerome, *Epist.* 127.7.
158. Hickey, *Women of Roman*, 38–40.
159. Curran, *Pagan City*, 269.
160. Jerome, *Epist.* 127.2.
161. Jerome claims that Marcella was beautiful, but Hickey has speculated that Marcella may not have been a desirable mate because the only suitor she had was an old man. Jerome, *Epist.* 127.2; Hickey, *Women of Roman*, 39.
162. Jerome, *Epist.* 127.2.
163. Jerome, *Epist.* 127.1.
164. Jerome, *Epist.* 127.5.
165. Jerome, *Epist.* 127.5; see also: Rousseau, *Ascetics, Authority*, 9–11; Yarbrough, "Christianization," 154; Curran, *Pagan City*, 269, 280, 319.
166. For a discussion on modesty, see Wilkinson, "Spectacular Modesty."
167. Jerome, *Epist.* 127.3.

rare), she refused to go to the homes of aristocratic women, so that she would not be forced to see the life that she had forsaken. Her most frequent destinations were to the basilicas of the apostles and martyrs where she would pray privately.[168] She fasted, but only moderately so. She did not eat meat, and imbibed a limited amount of wine—just enough "for her stomach's sake and for her frequent infirmities."[169] She consumed the Bible with a voracious appetite, and she constantly sang the Psalms. Her appreciation of the Bible was not limited to an intellectual exercise, but she knew that she only could understand it fully when she put it into action in her life, and in the world around her.[170] She constantly peppered Jerome with questions about the meaning of the Bible, and became such a master of it that men and priests would come to her for answers.[171] Her education seems not to have been limited to Scripture, as she often quoted Plato, who said that a true philosopher is always preparing for death.[172]

These ascetics, the Pelagians, and Christians who lived out other forms of the gospel all were asking the same general set of questions: what does it mean to be a Christian? How does one live the gospel message? How should Christians relate to the world? How should Christians relate to money? Christians had asked these questions since the first century, but this new era begun by Constantine demanded new answers. Undoubtedly, the ascetic aristocrats helped to shape the Pelagian answers to these questions and, conversely, it is likely that, in his role as a spiritual director in Rome, Pelagius helped to shape their answers. The Pelagians and ascetics, however, did not offer exactly the same answers to these questions, as we shall see.

The Theological Context: The Origenist Controversy

Prior to the Pelagian controversy, a number of controversies addressing trinitarian, christological, anthropological, biblical, and ecclesiastical issues (among others) plagued Christianity. In the second century, for example, the so-called gnostics[173] claimed to have secret knowledge that they had received about Jesus, humanity, and how to obtain liberation. Marcion of Sinope, also in the second century, asserted that the Bible described two Gods: a just God of the Old Testament, and a good God of the New Testament. The God of the Old Testament was not Jesus's Father. Jesus's Father previously had not been known to humanity until Jesus revealed this new God in the first century. The Donatists in North Africa broke away from the church at the beginning of the fourth century after Diocletian's persecution ended, because they

---

168. Jerome, *Epist.* 127.4.
169. Jerome, *Epist.* 127.4.
170. Jerome, *Epist.* 127.4.
171. Jerome, *Epist.* 127.7.
172. Jerome, *Epist.* 127.6; Plato, *Phaed.* 64.
173. Michael Williams has convincingly shown the problems with this term. Williams, *Rethinking "Gnosticism."*

believed that ordination of clergy from bishops who had handed over the Bible to the authorities during the persecution were invalid. Arius of Alexandria, as was mentioned earlier, caused Constantine to call the Council of Nicaea, the first Ecumenical council, because, in his attempt to safeguard the unity of God, he claimed that the Father and the Son are not the same substance. Apollinaris of Laodicea, in the middle of the fourth century, insisted that the Word of God replaced the rational soul of Jesus. He was afraid that if Jesus had a rational soul, it would be impossible for him to resist sin, because the rational soul is the seat of sin.

The theological controversy that had the most important bearing on the Pelagian controversy was the Origenist controversy at the end of the fourth century.[174] Along with Augustine, Origen of Alexandria (184–254)[175] was, as Jean Daniélou has said, one of "the two greatest geniuses of the early church."[176] His theology, however, quickly became suspect in the eyes of many after his death for a variety of different reasons.[177] He was born in Alexandria to a Christian family.[178] His father, Leonides, was beheaded as a martyr during the reign of Septimius Severus (193–211) when Origen was seventeen. Wishing to imitate his father, Origen intended to "come to grips with danger and charge headlong into the conflict,"[179] but he was thwarted when his mother hid his clothing so that he could not leave the house. With seemingly no other options, Origen wrote a letter to his father before he died encouraging him to embrace martyrdom, and not to falter because of his love for his family. When he died, Leonides left Origen's mother, Origen, and his six younger brothers impoverished

---

174. It seems that the exact events that constitute the Origenist controversy are disputed. Banev, for example, relegates the events between Epiphanius, John, Jerome, and Rufinus in Palestine as an "immediate prehistory" of the Origenist controversy, and does not indicate that it actually began until 399. Kim, however, claims that the "first phase" of the Origenist controversy includes the events in Palestine, and marks the beginning of Origenist controversy in 393. I agree with Kim, and believe that, although the Origenist controversy happened over several phases and places, the events in Palestine should not be relegated to a secondary "prehistory." Banev, *Theophilus of Alexandria*, 9–18; Kim, *Epiphanius of Cyprus*, 211–36.

175. Chadwick, *Early Church*, 100.

176. Daniélou, *Origen*, vii.

177. The specific theological reasons why Origen was seen as suspect by Jerome, Epiphanius, and Theophilus varied among them, and are complex. Elizabeth Clark, however, has succinctly summarized their reasons: (1) the Son is subordinate to the Father, and the Holy Spirit is subordinate to both of them; (2) human beings fell from an incorporeal preexistence in heaven, and obtained the "coat of skins" described in Genesis (3:21); (3) Satan can return to his existence as an angel, and be saved by God in the end; (4) demons and humans can be changed into each other; (5) there will be no bodily resurrection; (6) other worlds may have existed in the past, and may exist in the future; (7) hell will not be eternal; (8) Jesus may return a second time to suffer for demons; (9) allegorical exegesis is better than literal exegesis for those people who are spiritually mature; (10) disparagement of reproduction. Clark, *Origenist Controversy*, 11–12.

178. At the end of the third century, Methodius and Eustachius condemned Origen; at the end of the fourth century, Apollinaris, likewise, denounced him, as did Epiphanius of Cyprus. Murphy, *Rufinus of Aquileia*, 65–66.

179. Eusebius of Caesarea, *Hist. eccl.* 6.2.

when his property was confiscated for the imperial treasury. The family only avoided destitution by the generosity of an unnamed rich woman.[180] Also at the age of seventeen, Origen became a teacher of literature, but he quickly concluded that such a vocation ran counter to the Christian life, so he stopped teaching, and sold his library of secular books.[181] Although he never abandoned the world and ran to the desert the way that Antony and Pachomius had done, Gregory Thaumaturgus, Pamphilus, and Eusebius of Caesarea all commented on Origen's life of virtue, singular focus on the philosophical life, and rigid asceticism.[182] Among other behaviors, Origen fasted, rarely slept, did not wear shoes, lived with almost no possessions, did not drink wine, and ate very little.[183] Eusebius also reports that he castrated himself for the sake of the kingdom of heaven (Matt 19:12),[184] but this is unlikely, and hard to imagine that the man who was known—indeed reviled[185]—for his spiritual exegesis would make such an extreme act based on a narrowly literal interpretation of Matthew.[186] In his own studies, Origen would master Hebrew, and compiled a biblical masterpiece, the *Hexapla*, which contained parallel columns of the Hebrew Old Testament, a transliteration of the Hebrew into Greek, the Greek translations from the Septuagint, Aquila, Symmachus, and Theodotion, and two additional translations of the Psalms.[187] He later was ordained to the priesthood in 230 by Palestinian bishops while on a trip to Greece, which resulted in his own bishop, Demetrius, banishing him from Alexandria.[188] He moved to Caesarea where he would spend the rest of his life.[189] While there, Origen was imprisoned and tortured during the Decian persecution, and he died shortly thereafter at the age of 70.[190]

---

180. The majority of our information comes from Eusebius of Caesarea, who should be read with caution as his description of Origen tends more towards hagiography than it does biography. *Hist. eccl.* 6.1–3.

181. Eusebius of Caesarea, *Hist. eccl.* 6.3.

182. Gregory Thaumaturgus, *Orat. Paneg.* 9–15; Pamphilus, *Apol. Orig.* 9; Eusebius of Caesarea, *Hist. eccl.* 6.3.

183. Eusebius of Caesarea, *Hist. eccl.* 6.3.

184. Eusebius of Caesarea, *Hist. eccl.* 6.8.

185. Pamphilus, *Apol. Orig.* 87; Rousseau, *Early Christian Centuries*, 142.

186. Daniélou, *Origen*, 139–73; Chadwick, *Early Church*, 107–9. Indeed, it seems especially unlikely that he would interpret this passage so literally when he condemned such literal interpretations. In his *Princ.* he said "This precept also in the Gospels must be accounted among impossibilities, viz., that if the right eye 'offend' thee, it is to be plucked out; for even if we were to suppose that bodily eyes were spoken of, how shall it appear appropriate, that when both eyes have the property of sight, the responsibility of the 'offence' should be transferred to one eye, and that the right one? Or who shall be considered free of a crime of the great enormity, that lays hands upon himself?" Origen, *Princ.* 1.18.

187. Eusebius of Caesarea, *Hist. eccl.* 6.3; Chadwick, *Early Church*, 102. Jerome would later recall traveling to Caesarea from Jerusalem to consult the text. Kelly, *Jerome*, 135.

188. Eusebius of Caesarea, *Hist. eccl.* 6.23; Chadwick, *Early Church*, 109; Greer, "Introduction," 4.

189. Eusebius of Caesarea, *Hist. eccl.* 6.26.

190. Eusebius of Caesarea, *Hist. eccl.* 6.39–7.1.

The Origenist controversy began in 393 when a monk named Atarbius arrived in Palestine,[191] and accused Rufinus and Jerome of being Origenists, that is, admirers of Origen's theology.[192] Despite having translated several of Origen's works,[193] despite having written in his *De viris inlustribus* of Origen's "immortal genius,"[194] and despite his desire to imitate his literary *persona*,[195] Jerome denounced the Alexandrian to Atarbius's satisfaction. Rufinus, however, refused to meet with him, leading Atarbius to censure him publicly in Jerusalem.[196]

Palladius described Rufinus as "noble," and that "a more learned and reasonable man was never found,"[197] while Gennadius described him as "not the least among the doctors of the church and had a fine talent for elegant translation from Greek into Latin."[198] Modern scholars, however, have been more tempered in their assessment of him. Francis X. Murphy, Rufinus's biographer, said that he "was of a less talented nature than Jerome."[199] Rufinus "cannot be acclaimed as one of the great Christian writers of the fourth century," according to J.N.D. Kelly, but "despite inevitable limitations, his literary achievement ought not to be underrated."[200] While lacking the "colorful personality and brilliant style"[201] of Jerome, as Philip Amidon has said, Rufinus made valuable contributions to the Christian literary tradition through his many translations of Greek Christian authors into Latin and, thereby, making those authors available to the West.

Born in 345 in Concordia,[202] just west of Aquileia in northern Italy, Rufinus came from a family wealthy enough that he was able to go to Rome to be educated.[203] There he met Jerome, who later would say that Rufinus was "inseparably bound to me in brotherly love"[204] during their years in Rome. These men were "joined by a bond of

---

191. Kelly and Kim believe that Atarbius had been an agent for Epiphanius of Cyprus. Although this is possible, there is not definitive evidence to support this claim. Kelly, *Jerome*, 198; Kim, *Epiphanius of Cyprus*, 211.

192. Jerome, *Apol.* 3.33.

193. Jerome translated some of Origen's homilies on the Song of Songs, Ezekiel, Isaiah, Jeremiah, and Luke. He also translated Origen's *Princ.* Kelly, *Jerome*, 86, 77, 143, 237.

194. Jerome, *Vir. Ill.* 54.

195. Vessey, "Jerome's Origen," 135–45.

196. Jerome, *Apol.* 3.33.

197. Palladius, *Hist. Laus.* 46.5–6.

198. Gennadius, *De vir. inlustr.* 17.

199. Murphy, *Rufinus of Aquileia*, 60.

200. Kelly, "Introduction," 7.

201. Amidon, "Introduction," xi.

202. I will be using the dating of Rufinus's life from Francis X. Murphy's biography. Also, the narrative arch of this section is largely dictated by Murphy. Murphy, *Rufinus of Aquileia*.

203. Murphy indicates that Rufinus is from Concordia because Jerome calls him a countryman with a certain Paul of Concordia. Jerome, *Epist.* 5.2; *Vir. ill.* 53; *Apol.* 3.4; Palladius, *Hist. Laus.* 46.5–6.

204. Jerome, *Epist.* 4.2.

friendship known to almost all of the churches,"[205] as Augustine cooed in a letter he wrote to Jerome in 404. This friendship did not last, however, as it collapsed under the weight of their churlish bickering about the orthodoxy of Origen decades after their time there. Although Augustine never met either of them, he lamented the later demise of their friendship, saying that he "was much saddened that so great an evil of discord had emerged between persons so dear and close."[206]

After finishing school and returning to Aquileia, Rufinus became involved in a community of ascetics that had recently begun to flourish there, and was baptized around the age of twenty-five.[207] In the spring of 373, Rufinus left Aquileia for Egypt, and would not return to Italy until 397. During his time in the East, he spent a total of eight years in Alexandria improving his Greek, living an austere life while visiting the anchorites in the desert, and studying under the exegete Didymus the Blind.[208] Sometime after 380, Rufinus moved to Jerusalem where he reunited with Melania the Elder, whom he probably had met in Alexandria.[209] Melania established a monastery for women in Jerusalem, and lived there in charge of fifty consecrated virgins, according to Palladius, for twenty-seven years.[210] When Rufinus arrived, he established a monastery for men as well, presumably with her financial assistance as she came from a prominent and wealthy family from Spain.[211] Eventually, he was ordained to the priesthood (most likely) by John of Jerusalem.[212]

When Rufinus returned to Italy, he was met by a certain Macarius he described as "a man of distinction from his faith, his learning, his noble birth and his personal life."[213] Macarius had been wrestling with the philosophical problem of fatalism, and was unable to resolve the issue. One night, Macarius had a dream of a ship at sea coming to him carrying the solution to his problem. When Macarius awoke, he was unsure of the meaning of the dream, but then realized that the ship in the dream was the ship that had brought Rufinus back to Italy the same day Macarius had his dream. He approached Rufinus and explained his predicament to him, and inquired what Origen had to say on the matter. Rufinus told him that the answer to the problem was complex, but that the martyr Pamphilus (240?–310) had addressed the issue in his *Apologia pro Origene*.[214] Macarius pleaded with Rufinus to translate it, but Rufinus

---

205. Augustine, *Epist.* 73.3.6.

206. Augustine, *Epist.* 73.3.6.

207. Rufinus, *Apol. Hier.* 1.4. See also: Jerome, *Epist.* 4.2.

208. Jerome, *Epist.* 3.3; Rufinus, *Apol. Hier.* 2.12.

209. Murphy, *Rufinus of Aquileia*, 41.

210. Palladius, *Hist. Laus.* 46.5.

211. Palladius, *Hist. Laus.* 46.1.

212. Palladius, *Hist. Laus.* 46.5. Both Murphy and Kelly agree that Rufinus was probably ordained by John. Murphy, *Rufinus of Aquileia*, 55; Kelly, "Introduction," 4.

213. Rufinus, *Apol. Hier.* 1.11.

214. Scheck, "Introduction," 3–31.

hesitated, saying that "I had no practice in this style of composition, and that my power of writing Latin had grown dull through the neglect of nearly thirty years."[215] Macarius persisted, and Rufinus, finally, relented, which began a life dedicated to translation that would continue until his death. He later asked Rufinus to make a translation of Origen's *Peri archon*, which would become one of the main issues to break the friendship between Rufinus and Jerome,[216] and Rufinus would translate a variety of other Greek masters.[217]

In the spring of 399, Rufinus left Rome to return to Aquileia, and a year later Melania returned to Italy. While in Aquileia, Rufinus continued his translations, and also wrote some works of his owns, including an addition of two books to Eusebius of Caesarea's *Historia ecclesiastica*, and a *Commentarius in symbolum apostolorum*. In 407, his good friend Chromatius, the bishop of Aquileia, died, which may have been a direct cause of Rufinus departing Aquileia in October, 408. He went south, and stayed with his friend Ursacius, the Abbot of Pinetum.[218] Rufinus, accompanied by Melania the Younger and her husband Pinianus, fled Italy as Alaric and his horde swept toward Rome in 410.[219] He spent his last days in Sicily, possibly with the intention of returning to Jerusalem, and died in 411. Jerome—ever merciless with his pen—reported shortly after Rufinus's death that "the Scorpion lies beneath the soil of Sicily . . . and the many-headed Hydra has ceased for a time to hiss at us."[220]

Later the same year that Atarbius accused Rufinus and Jerome of being Origenists, Epiphanius, the bishop of Cyprus "renowned for his renown,"[221] came to Jerusalem looking for a fight. Epiphanius was born in Besauduc, Palestine, sometime between 310 and 320.[222] During his childhood, Epiphanius moved to Egypt around 330,[223] for unknown reasons, where he received training from the desert monks there.[224] Returning to Palestine as an adult, he founded and led a monastery in his hometown for almost thirty years.[225] He then was made the bishop of Constantia (Salamis) for thirty-six years, probably from 366/7.[226] Epiphanius was a fierce opponent of Origen, and of anyone who supported Origen's theology. He died in 402/3

---

215. Rufinus, *Apol. Hier.* 1.11.
216. Rufinus, *Prol. ad per.*
217. Gennadius, *De vir. inlustr.* 17.
218. Murphy, *Rufinus of Aquileia (345–411)*, 205.
219. Rufinus, *Prol. ad num.*
220. Jerome, *Comm. Ezech.* 1.
221. Jacobs, *Epiphanius of Cyprus*, 40.
222. Sozomen, *Hist. eccl.* 6.32; Kim, *Epiphanius of Cyprus*, 18.
223. Kim, *Epiphanius of Cyprus*, 18.
224. Sozomen, *Hist. eccl.* 6.32.
225. Kim, *Epiphanius of Cyprus*, 141.
226. Palladius, *Dial.* 16.

on a journey back to Cyprus from Constantinople during his persecution of John Chrysostom.[227] Socrates and Sozomen reported that, before departing Constantinople, Epiphanius snidely said to John that "I hope that you will not die a bishop," and John snarkily retorted that Epiphanius should "expect not to arrive at your own country."[228] The wishes of both men were granted.[229]

Epiphanius was both reviled and revered in his own time. Theophilus of Alexandria called him his "well-beloved lord, brother, and fellow-bishop";[230] Jerome described him as a "venerable" bishop,[231] "saintly,"[232] and "almost the father of the whole episcopate, and a monument of the sanctity of former days";[233] Augustine said he was "highly esteemed for his teaching of the Catholic faith," he was an "eminent scholar," and that he was "saintly";[234] Socrates said of him that he was a man "famous" for his "extraordinary piety" and a man "of simple mind and manners";[235] Sozomen described him as having been "most celebrated in Egypt and Palestine by his attainments in monastic philosophy," that he was "the most revered man under the whole heaven," that he had and became known "to all citizens and every variety of foreigner"[236] for the virtue with which he conducted his civil affairs, and that he was "extremely liberal towards the needy."[237] John of Jerusalem, however, is reported by Jerome to have called Epiphanius a "silly" and "vainglorious old man."[238]

Most modern scholars have shown nothing but "disdain" for Epiphanius.[239] Murphy criticized him as one "of considerable, but ill-digested erudition, joining a certain narrowness of outlook and singleness of purpose to an indisputable piety";[240] Henry Chadwick said that he had "hostility to every sort of intellectual pretension, including theological speculation";[241] Kelly denounced him as a "heretic-hunter," and

227. Kelly, *Golden Mouth*, 203–10.

228. Socrates, *Hist. eccl.* 6.14. See also: Sozomen, *Hist. eccl.* 8.15.

229. We should be cautious of such predictions as the sources of these stories were written years after the events and it is likely that this exchange is apocryphal.

230. Jerome, *Epist.* 90.

231. Jerome, *Apol.* 3.22.

232. Jerome, *Apol.* 3.23.

233. Jerome, *C. Joan.* 12.

234. Augustine, *Epist.* 222.2.

235. Socrates, *Hist. eccl.* 6.10.

236. Socrates, *Hist. eccl.* 6.32.

237. Socrates, *Hist. eccl.* 7.27.

238. Jerome, *C. Joan.* 11.

239. Jacobs, *Epiphanius of Cyprus*, ix. There are some exceptions to this. Riggi, for example, has echoed both Jerome and Augustine and called Epiphanius him a "*santo*," and Kim has said he was not a "simple-minded buffoon or Bible-thumping demagogue," but that he was "eminently fascinating and provocative," and that he "displayed a breadth of secular and sacred knowledge." Riggi, "Catechesi escatologica," 164; Kim, *Epiphanius of Cyprus*, 1, 21.

240. Murphy, *Rufinus of Aquileia*, 66.

241. Chadwick, *Early Church*, 184.

"able but anti-intellectualist, of wide but ill-digested learning and intransigent zeal for 'correct' doctrine, he was inordinately lacking in judgment, tact, and charity, but also inordinately venerated for his force of personality, impressive bearing, and rigorous asceticism";[242] Richard Hanson disparaged him as a "second-rate theologian," and "narrow-minded at best and very silly at worst";[243] Jon Dechow decried him as a "hatchet man," and that he lacked an inherent "philosophical capacity";[244] Aline Pourkier said that "il fait figure d'homme peu cultivé, sachant mal la langue, ignorant et même condamnant la culture païenne";[245] Andrew Jacobs has called him "rigid," a "difficult and harsh figure," and "cantankerous."[246]

While in Jerusalem, Epiphanius preached a sermon against Origen, but, so Jerome tells us, his real target was Bishop John of Jerusalem. John, undoubtedly understanding Epiphanius's meaning, sent an archdeacon to demand that Epiphanius stop his onslaught. Later that day, John turned the tables and preached against the "rustic simplicity" of the anthropomorphites—those who believed that God had a physical form. As with Epiphanius's sermon, John's true object of attack was not the anthropomorphites, but Epiphanius. Epiphanius then requested the opportunity to respond with a few words of his own, and insisted that if the anthropomorphites were to be condemned as having a bankrupt vision of God, so, too, must Origen.[247] Soon after this, John preached another sermon in which he offered a view of the Catholic faith that contented Epiphanius, who then left Jerusalem for Bethlehem, but returned that evening at the urging of all the monks in Jerome's monastery. Apparently unhappy with the way he was treated both in Jerusalem and in Bethlehem, he left Jerusalem that same night at midnight for the monastery he had established in Besanduc.[248]

The following summer, Epiphanius returned to Besanduc from Cyprus. He had been aware of the dearth of priests at the Bethlehem monastery, and when Jerome's brother, Paulinian, and others went to Besanduc, Epiphanius took the opportunity to forcibly ordain him, as we will discuss later. This ordination caused John no small consternation, because Epiphanius had ordained Paulinian in the region of Eleutheropolis, but Jerome's monastery was under the authority of John. John felt that this action was a violation of his sovereignty as bishop.[249] In response, he excommunicated the entire monastery in Bethlehem, and Paulinian was forced to move to Cyprus.[250] In his defense, Epiphanius wrote a letter to John protesting his innocence, and even

---

242. Kelly, *Jerome*, 260, 197.
243. Hanson, *Search for Christian Doctrine*, 658.
244. Dechow, *Dogma*, 13, 254.
245. Pourkier, *L'hérésiologie chez*, 29.
246. Jacobs, *Epiphanius of Cyprus*, 2, 5, 179.
247. Jerome, *C. Joan.* 11.
248. Jerome, *C. Joan.* 14.
249. Jerome, *Epist.* 82.8; *C. Joan.* 44.
250. Jerome, *C. Joan.* 41, 2.

suggested that John should thank him for ordaining Paulinian, who had eluded John's own ordination attempts.[251] This letter was translated by Jerome into Latin at the request of his friend Eusebius of Cremona. Eighteen months later, John and Rufinus obtained a copy of it, and were scandalized that Jerome's translation, in their view, did not convey the meaning of the original as it was not a word-for-word translation, and that Jerome had added his own commentary in the marginalia.[252] Enraged, John secured a decree from the civil authorities to send Jerome into exile, although this was never put into effect because of the invasion of the Huns in 395.[253]

In an attempt to reconcile with his monks, John asked Bishop Theophilus of Alexandria to act as a mediator between the two parties.[254] Theophilus was born circa 345 in Memphis to Christian parents.[255] His parents died when he was a child, and he and his sister found themselves in the care of their Ethiopian slave. According to a legend recounted by John of Nikiu in the seventh century, the slave took them to a temple of Artemis and Apollo to pray, but the statues crumbled when the children entered. The slave became fearful, and fled with the children to Alexandria, and took them to church where they found refuge with Athanasius of Alexandria. After all three were baptized, his sister was placed with consecrated virgins until she married and gave birth to Cyril of Alexandria, the eventual rival of Nestorius. Theophilus grew under Athanasius's tutelage and later became his successor in July 385.[256] He died twenty-seven years later in October 412.

Like Epiphanius, Theophilus was loathed and lauded in his own time, and in ours. Jerome described him as "full of wisdom";[257] Epiphanius called Theophilus the "servant" of the Lord, and "so great a prelate";[258] Vincent of Lérins commended him as "a man illustrious for his faith, his life, [and] his knowledge."[259] Palladius, however, denounced him as a "weathercock," and that he was "by his nature an impetuous person, rash, bold, seeking a quarrel above reason—anything he sees he rushes at in great haste without consideration and allows himself no time for reflection";[260] Socrates reports that the monks of the Egyptian desert charged Theophilus with "impiety" when he initially claimed that God did not have a corporeal form; he also said that the Tall brothers said that the bishop of Alexandria was "devoted to gain, and greedily intent

---

251. Jerome, *Epist.* 51.
252. Jerome, *Epist.* 57.2.
253. Jerome, *Epist.* 82.10. See also: Kelly, *Jerome*, 203–4.
254. Jerome, *C. Joan.* 37.
255. Russell, "Introduction," 3.
256. John of Nikiu, *Chron.* 79; Russell, "Introduction," 4.
257. Jerome, *Epist.* 82.4.
258. Jerome, *Epist.* 91.
259. Vincent of Lérins, *Comm.* 30.
260. Palladius, *Dial.* 6, 9.

on the acquisition of wealth";[261] Socrates himself said that Theophilus was "of a hasty and malignant temperament," that he had "vindictive feelings,"[262] and that he "was held in contempt by all men."[263]

Modern scholars have echoed both interpretations. Norman Russell has said that he is a "neglected figure," that "as far as the Church of Alexandria was concerned, Theophilus was a great pastor and decisive leader of his community, which is how the Copts still remember him"; that he was "politically astute, decisive and ruthless when his authority was challenged. He was also a brilliant orator, an efficient administrator and a capable theologian and canon lawyer"; that he had "integrity," and that he displayed "energy, resilience, and intelligence."[264] But, the majority of scholars view him as nothing more than a shifty power monger bent on maintaining his own interests no matter what the costs. Owen Chadwick described him as "a man of huge ambition, eager to enforce his authority over the Church in Egypt;[265] Kelly decried him as "powerful, ambitious, and entirely ruthless," and that he was "more interested in power politics than in dogmatic truth";[266] Johannes Quasten said that he was "the artful and violent patriarch of Alexandria, a sorry figure of a bishop";[267] Elizabeth Clark denounced him as motivated by nothing other than "political expediency."[268]

At John's request, Theophilus sent a certain priest named Isidore to Jerusalem in hopes of healing the division there, but Isidore only caused more consternation. Three months prior to his arrival, Isidore had sent several letters to John and Rufinus that were intercepted by a presbyter and friend of Jerome named Vincentius. In one of the letters, Isidore had written in support of John, and that "as smoke vanishes in the air, and wax melts beside the fire, so shall they [Jerome and his compatriots] be scattered who are forever resisting the faith of the Church, and are now through simple men endeavoring to disturb that faith."[269] When Isidore arrived in Jerusalem, Jerome demanded to see his credentials, but Isidore refused to provide them, and said that John instructed him not to give them. The negotiations failed even before they began, and Isidore returned to Alexandria carrying a letter (now lost) from John to Theophilus in which John presented his version of the conflagration in Palestine.[270] A copy of this letter also turned up in Rome where it had stoked the smoldering embers

---

261. Socrates, *Hist. eccl.* 6.7.
262. Socrates, *Hist. eccl.* 6.7.
263. Socrates, *Hist. eccl.* 6.17.
264. Russell, "Introduction," vii, 3.
265. Chadwick, *John Cassian*, 34.
266. Kelly, *Jerome*, 243.
267. Quasten, *Patrology*, 100.
268. Clark, *Origenist Controversy*, 38.
269. Jerome, *C. Joan.* 37.
270. Jerome, *C. Joan.* 37–40.

of hatred for Jerome.[271] In his own defense, Jerome composed his *Contra Ioannem Hierosolymitanum*, in which he critiqued John and his letter. Theodosius, however, responded to John's letter with his own letter (also lost) imploring all sides for peace. The letter seems to have been the catalyst needed as it brought Jerome back into communion with John. Even a tenuous rapprochement with Rufinus was achieved.[272] But, the drama was just beginning.

We saw earlier that, when Rufinus arrived back in Rome, Macarius urged him first to translate Pamphilus's *Apologia pro Origene*, and then Origen's *Peri archon*. In his prefaces to his translation of the *Peri archon*, Rufinus made clear that his intention was to follow the precedent set by Jerome in Jerome's earlier translations of Origen's texts by not translating the text word-for-word. First, he fashioned the *Peri archon* so that it did not demonstrate any discrepancies or contradictions from other works by Origen. Second, anything that was theologically suspect concerning the Trinity was either omitted, or was worded in such a way that conformed to orthodox teaching based on other writings of Origen that demonstrated his fidelity to a trinitarian orthodoxy. Third, he expanded the text by including sections found in other writings of Origen that helped clarify the meaning. Fourth, he omitted certain sections of the *Peri archon* that he felt had been interpolations from unnamed sources in an attempt to discredit Origen.[273] Fifth, he excised certain sections of the text for the sake of brevity.[274]

While translating, Rufinus's unfinished draft was either stolen or obtained through bribery by Eusebius of Cremona—the same Eusebius who asked Jerome to translate Epiphanius's letter to John, and who was now in Rome.[275] This draft was handed over to Jerome's friends Pammachius and Oceanus who wrote to Jerome because they perceived a heterodoxy in it that disturbed them, and they suspected that there was even more heterodoxy in the original Greek that Rufinus had omitted, and, therefore, that he was misleading the faithful. They implored Jerome to make his own translation "exactly as it was brought out by the author himself; and we desire you to make evident the interpolations which the defender has introduced."[276] Additionally, Jerome's friends, led by Marcella, publicly took a stand against Origen in

---

271. Jerome, *C. Joan.* 1.

272. Jerome, *Epist.* 82; *Apol.* 3.24–33.

273. Rufinus was so convinced that Origen's works had been interpolated that he included an essay at the end of his translation of the *Peri archon* making his case. Rufinus, *De adult*. Kelly has said that "there is not the slightest reason to believe that Origen's works suffered from them [interpolations] to more than a minimal degree." Kelly, *Jerome*, 230.

274. Rufinus, *Prol. ad per.*

275. Rufinus, *Apol. Hier.* 2.44; Jerome, *Apol.* 3.20. Rufinus said that he and Eusebius had been neighbors in Rome, and who "up to that time we often saw one another, greeted one another as friends and joined together in prayer." Rufinus, *Apol. Hier.* 1.20.

276. Jerome, *Epist.* 83.

Rome, and Eusebius privately attempted to assassinate the reputation of Rufinus, "the scorpion,"[277] throughout Italy.[278]

Jerome immediately responded to the letter from Pammachius and Oceanus. Sensing that Rufinus's prefaces to his translation were attempts to slander him as an Origenist, Jerome defensively claimed that he had only praised Origen in two of his works (in a preface to his translation of Origen's homilies on the Song of Songs, and in the prologue in his book of Hebrew names), and that his praise was restricted to Origen as a commentator, not as a theologian, in his own commentaries on Ecclesiastes and Ephesians.[279] He admits to having read Origen's works; indeed, he has collected so many of Origen's books that they almost have bankrupted him. But, he claims, he has never been a follower of Origen's "poisonous" doctrines.[280] Jerome also obliged Pammachius and Oceanus by making a translation of Origen's *Peri archon*, adhering as closely to the original Greek as he possibly could in an attempt to demonstrate Origen's heresy, and to demonstrate Rufinus's deception. Describing himself as more of an "informer" rather than a translator, he warned his audience in the preface of the heterodoxy the reader must avoid.[281] When Pammachius received this translation, he was so shocked by its contents that he locked it away so as to prevent it being read all over Rome. Pammachius later lent the copy to an unnamed person with the promise that he would read it and quickly return it. This nameless individual made a copy of the text without the permission of Pammachius, but did so with such great haste that the quality of the copy was poor. It then was published without Jerome's consent.[282] At the same time, Jerome dispatched a letter for Rufinus to Rome. In it, Jerome pleaded that, since their reconciliation in Palestine, he has done everything he could to prevent another break in their relationship. He recognized that, even though he was not mentioned explicitly in Rufinus's prefaces to his translation of the *Peri archon*, it is clear to him that Rufinus had intended to harm his reputation. Jerome's tone in the letter is surprisingly sober, and he says that he is willing to show restraint as long as Rufinus and his friends desist from attacking him.[283] Pammachius never forwarded this letter to Rufinus in Aquileia, however, because Rufinus and his associates had been spreading rumors about Jerome.[284] How would this chapter in Christian history have been different had Pammachius forwarded that letter?

This dispute seemed to be coming to an end on its own when it accelerated once again. Theophilus had been of the party that believed that God did not have a

---

277. Jerome, *Epist.* 127.10.
278. Jerome, *Epist.* 127.9; Rufinus, *Apol. Hier.* 1.21.
279. Jerome, *Epist.* 84.2.
280. Jerome, *Epist.* 84.3.
281. Jerome, *Apol.* 1.7.
282. Jerome, *Epist.* 124.1.
283. Jerome, *Epist.* 81.
284. Jerome, *Apol.* 1.12, 3.38.

corporeal form, and he publicly denounced those who held that opposite. Although this may have appeased those who were of the same mind, the majority of the Egyptian ascetics took issue with him, and traveled to Alexandria from their desert cells to threaten to kill him. Theophilus succumbed to their pressure to admit that God has a body, and anathematized Origen's writings. Going a step farther, Theophilus attempted to expel from the desert many monks who were admirers of Origen—including the respected leaders of the monks known for their height called the Tall Brothers (Ammonium, Dioscorus, Eusebius, and Euthymius).[285] Not yet content, he then held a synod in Nitria in order to condemn Origen's writings,[286] and forcibly expelled his adversaries from Egypt.[287] Theophilus then dispatched a letter to Pope Anastasius (399–401) describing what he had done,[288] causing Anastasius to condemn Origen's writings that are contrary to the faith and to dispatch his own letter, via Eusebius of Cremona, to Bishop Simplicianus of Milan, the successor of Ambrose.[289] Recognizing which way the winds were blowing, Rufinus wrote his *Apologia ad Anastasium* in late summer of 400 to defend himself against his attackers. In it, Rufinus insisted that he was unable to visit Anastasius in person since he had recently returned to Aquileia, and he was too weak to journey back to Rome. Rufinus pleaded his case that his orthodoxy was unimpeachable, and offered his profession of faith to prove it.[290] We have no response from Anastatius to Rufinus, but we do have a letter written by Anastasius to John of Jerusalem not long afterwards. Anastasius pleaded ignorance of Origen's works prior to Rufinus's translation (nor does he now have any interest to read more), but it is clear to him that Origen's intent was to destroy (*dissolvere*) the Christian faith.[291] He also says that he is unaware of Rufinus's intention of translating Origen's works; if Rufinus's intention were to unveil Origen's corruption, then the Pope approves; if, however, Rufinus's intention was to propagate Origen throughout the West, then Rufinus is as guilty as Origen.[292] Either way, he icily concluded, Rufinus is "so completely separate from all part or lot with us, that I neither know nor wish to

---

285. Theophilus had ordained Diocorus, the bishop of Hermopolis, and he ordained two others presbyters. Socrates, *Hist. eccl.* 6.7. See also: Sozomen, *Hist. eccl.* 8.11–12.

286. In particular, eight theological points from Origen's *Peri archon* are mentioned: "the Son compared with us is truth, but compared with the Father is falsehood; Christ's kingdom will one day come to an end; we ought to pray to the Father alone, not to the Son; our bodies after the resurrection will be corruptible and mortal; there is nothing perfect even in heaven; the angels themselves are faulty, and some of them feed on the Jewish sacrifices; the stars are conscious of their own movements, and the demons know the future by their courses; magic, if real, is not evil; Christ suffered once for men; he will suffer again for the demons." Jerome, *Epist.* 92.

287. Socrates, *Hist. eccl.* 6.7.

288. Though this letter is no longer extant, it is mentioned by Theophilus in a letter to Simplicianus, the bishop of Milan. Jerome, *Epist.* 95.

289. Jerome, *Epist.* 95.

290. Rufinus, *Anast.* 3–8.

291. Anastasius, *Ad Ioan.* 3.

292. Anastasius, *Ad Ioan.* 4.

know either what he is doing or where he is living. I have only to add that it is for him to consider where he may obtain absolution."²⁹³

Rufinus must have felt he was being assailed on all sides when he received a copy of Jerome's letter to Pammachius and Oceanus. His initial thought was to remain silent, but he felt that his silence would be seen as proof of his guilt, so he responded with his masterpiece, the *Apologia contra Hieronymum*.²⁹⁴ He defended himself, first of all, by insisting that his role as translator must be placed in the proper perspective, and that he should not be viewed as an advocate for Origen.²⁹⁵ Asserting his innocence, he insisted he was only responding to the request of Macarius to act as midwife to birth the Greek author's writings into Latin.²⁹⁶ He also claimed that he never promised that his translation would omit anything in Origen's text that was against the teaching of the church; he only promised that he would not reproduce that which went against claims Origen had made elsewhere.²⁹⁷ Not content only to defend himself, Rufinus went on the attack. He lampooned Jerome for having broken his promise that he would not associate with pagan literature after his terrifying dream where the Judge accused him of being a follower of Cicero, not of Christ. "He not only reads them [pagan authors] and possesses them," Rufinus strikes back, "not only copies them and collates them, but inserts them among the words of Scripture itself, and in discourses intended for the edification of the Church."²⁹⁸ And, in what Jerome must have viewed as the most incendiary part of the entire work, Rufinus disproved Jerome's claim that he had only praised Origen twice in writing by quoting him verbatim. Jerome, Rufinus recounts, called Origen (among other things) "a teacher of the churches second only to the Apostles,"²⁹⁹ a "genius,"³⁰⁰ that he has "surpassed all other men,"³⁰¹ that Origen is "approved not only by us, but by all thoughtful men,"³⁰² he was "the great teacher of the churches next to the Apostles,"³⁰³ he was "so great a man,"³⁰⁴ he was a "man of adamant [a rock],"³⁰⁵ that he had "surpassed those of all pervious writers both Greek and Latin,"³⁰⁶ and that Jerome would "gladly have his knowledge of the Scriptures even

---

293. Anastasius, *Ad Ioan.* 6.
294. Rufinus, *Apol. Hier.* 1.1.
295. Rufinus, *Apol. Hier.* 1.10.
296. Rufinus, *Apol. Hier.* 1.10–11.
297. Rufinus, *Apol. Hier.* 1.14.
298. Rufinus, *Apol. Hier.* 2.8.
299. Rufinus, *Apol. Hier.* 2.13.
300. Rufinus, *Apol. Hier.* 2.13, 2.20.
301. Rufinus, *Apol. Hier.* 2.14.
302. Rufinus, *Apol. Hier.* 2.15.
303. Rufinus, *Apol. Hier.* 2.16.
304. Rufinus, *Apol. Hier.* 2.18.
305. Rufinus, *Apol. Hier.* 2.20.
306. Rufinus, *Apol. Hier.* 2.20.

if accompanied with all the ill-will which clings to his name."[307] This litany must have cut Jerome to his core.

Jerome knew what was coming before Rufinus even published his work, because Jerome's brother had reported to him sections of Rufinus's work he had committed to memory when he visited Rome, causing Jerome to write his own *Apologia adversus libros Rufini* in two books.[308] Jerome's books combined (among other things) a defense of his own translation of the *Peri archon*, an attack on Rufinus for having translated Pamphilus's *Apologia* while, at the same time, stating that he was not advocating for Origen, and, in classic Hieronymian style, he unleashed a torrent of *ad hominem* invective. He said of Rufinus's prose, for example, that "one would think that the man's tongue was in fetters, and bound with cords that cannot be disentangled, so that it could hardly break forth into human speech."[309] When Rufinus received these two books, he wrote a (lost) private letter to Jerome—rather than making a public retort—in an attempt to stem the tide of the vitriol on both sides. Chromatius of Aquileia, their mutual friend, had suggested this course of action to Rufinus, and also had written to Jerome pleading for him to show the same restraint.[310] Rufinus's barbs in his letter, though, were too much for Jerome, and Jerome added a third book to his *Apologia*, insisting (as Rufinus had done earlier) that he had no choice but to respond, or he would appear guilty in the eyes of the public.[311] Rufinus decided not to reply to Jerome's scorn, and this phase of the Origenist controversy came to an uneasy détente. Their friendship never recovered.

The Origenist controversy itself did not end there, but shifted to Constantinople where the Tall Brothers arrived looking for shelter with John Chrysostom, which brought about his demise at the hands of Theophilus and Epiphanius. Although an important event in the history of Christianity, it is outside the scope this study, and will not be explored here.[312]

As Clark has shown, Origen's theological agenda in general was deeply concerned with questions of God's justice, goodness, and human free will—issues that later would become central to the Pelagian controversy.[313] His thought on these issues crystalized in reaction against so-called gnostics, and astral determinists, both of whom called into question the freedom of the human will.[314] Pelagius, as we shall see in a later chapter, was influenced by Origen, although he did not adopt Origen's thought wholesale. Jerome (more than Augustine, Orosius, or Cassian) perceived the

307. Rufinus, *Apol. Hier.* 2.22.
308. Jerome, *Apol.* 1.1–3; 1.21.
309. Jerome, *Apol.* 2.11.
310. Jerome, *Apol.* 3.2.
311. Jerome, *Apol.* 3.3.
312. For an excellent description of the downfall of John, see: Kelly, *Golden Mouth*, 191–290.
313. Clark, *Origenist Controversy*, 194–95.
314. Clark, *Origenist Controversy*, 195–97.

connection between Origen and the Pelagians, and he did not hesitate to sound the alarm. In his letter to Ctesiphon near the beginning of his participation in this controversy, Jerome said that "the new [Pelagian] controversy . . . has taken place of the old [Origenist]," and later in the same letter hypothetically asked Pelagius "would you have me name another of your masters in heresy? Much of your teaching is traceable to Origen."[315] The Origenist controversy is so significant a backdrop for the Pelagian controversy that Gerald Bostock has said that "the history of the attack on Pelagianism is effectively the history of the attack on the implications of Origen's core-doctrine of human free will," Clark has said that the Pelagian controversy "provided an arena in which Origen's questions were answered in new and different ways," and Filip Outrata insisted that the Pelagian controversy "can be seen as one of the phases of the long and twisted Origenist controversy."[316]

---

315. Jerome, *Epp.* 133.1, 3. See also: *In Hier.* 2:6, 25:3, 30:10–11.

316. Bostock, "Influence of Origen," 381; Clark, *Origenist Controversy*, 194–95; Outrata, "Differing Defenders," 490.

Chapter 2

Pelagius: A Man Aflame with Ardent Zeal

The Life of Pelagius

PELAGIUS CAME TO ROME around 384, and became a spiritual mentor to many Roman aristocrats, as Jerome had done years earlier.[1] Often considered to be the founder[2] of Pelagianism,[3] Pelagius was born sometime during the third quarter of the fourth century, and died shortly after 418. Augustine, Prosper of Aquitaine, Orosius, Gennadius, Marius Mercator, and Bede all claimed that he was from Britain. Jerome said he was "*Scotus*," which probably was meant as a slander, and could have meant he was from Ireland.[4] We do not know anything about his family, but he obviously had a good Roman education. We also do not know why he left Britain for Rome—where he lived for many years[5]—but major cultural centers always have an allure for talented people, as can be seen with his contemporaries Augustine and Jerome who were likewise drawn to it. Orosius described him as a physically large Goliath with broad shoulders, a strong neck, portly, and who was "nurtured on baths

---

1. Brown, "Pelagius," 188.

2. Traditionally, Pelagius is described as the founder of the Pelagians. The term "the Pelagians" was first used by Jerome's *Dial.* in 415. Most scholars follow this traditional claim. Brown, *Augustine of Hippo*, 343; Lancel, *Saint Augustine*, 327; Rondet, *Original Sin*, 125; Bardy, "Grecs et Latins," 7; Lamberigts, "Caelestius," 114; Rackett, "What's Wrong?," 223; Chéné, "Saint Augustin," 218; Koopsmans, "Augustine's First Contact," 151; Hwang, *Intrepid Lover*, 70. However, other founders have been suggested. Caelestius, "Rufinus the Syrian," and Rufinus of Aquileia have all been named: Honnay, "Caelestius," 271; Bonner, "Rufinus of Syria," 38; TeSelle, *Augustine*, 280; Refoulé, "Datation," 49; Dunphy makes it clear that he is not sure that Rufinus would have actually agreed with the theological anthropology of Pelagius and his group. However, he believes that Rufinus the Syrian was actually Rufinus of Aquileia and that his translations gave Pelagius and others the courage to proclaim what they did. Dunphy, "Rufinus the Syrian," 157; Rees, "Introduction" 20–25.

3. The idea that "Pelagianism" is a singular and cohesive school of thought has been dismissed by contemporary scholars. Each of the authors who have fallen under the umbrella term "Pelagian" must be read for their own particular modes of thought. Bonner, "Rufinus of Syria," 31; Teske, "Introduction," 11; Rousseau, "Cassian and Perverted Virtue," 14; Ogliari, *Gratia et Certamen*, 230.

4. Augustine *Epist.* 186.1; Prosper of Aquitaine, *Chron.* 2; Orosius, *Lib. apol.*, 12; Marius Mercator, *Sub.* 2.pref; Gennadius, *De vir. Inlustr.* 43; Bede, *Hist. eccl.* 1.10; Jerome, *Com. in Her* 3.pref.

5. Augustine, *Epist.* 177.2; *Grat. Chr.* 2.24.

and sumptuous feasts."[6] Jerome—ever sharp with his tongue—called him a "crazy old woman," a "big, fat Alpine dog," who was "weighed down with Scottish porridge," and walked with the "slow pace of a tortoise."[7] Augustine, the fiercest critic of his anthropology, spoke respectfully of the quality of his character, saying that Pelagius was a "holy man," a "fine and praiseworthy man," an "exemplary Christian," and a "man of circumspection."[8]

The modern scholarly assessment of Pelagius is almost entirely positive. One biographer, B.R. Rees, claimed that Pelagius was "no less orthodox" than Augustine.[9] Making a bolder claim, Clark views the Pelagians as "heroes,"[10] while C.B. Armstrong even went as far as declaring both Augustine and Pelagius equally as "saints."[11] John Ferguson argued that Pelagius had made several important contributions to Christian thought, and that he sides with Pelagius; he looks "with sympathy but ultimately negatively at Augustine's views, and with no sympathy at all at his policies,"[12] and elsewhere he said that "it is not certain that any statement of his [Pelagius] is totally irreconcilable with the Christian faith or indefensible in terms of the New Testament. It is by no means so clear that the same may be said of Augustine."[13] Even Gerald Bonner who, in 1963, said that "it is possible that the pendulum has swung too far and that the heresiarch now enjoys a more favorable reputation than he deserves"[14] changed his mind and, in 2007, said that the Pelagians "deserve more sympathy than they have generally received down through the ages."[15] The list of scholars wishing to "recover" the Pelagians is extensive,[16] and it seems that Pelagian thought has become quite fashionable.[17] This sentiment even spilled out of the academic world when, in 2011, a resolution was proposed by Rev. Benno D. Pattison at the 105th Annual Council of

---

6. Orosius, *Lib. apol.* 2, 31.
7. Jerome, *In Hier.* 17:1, 3.pref, 1.pref; *Dial.* 3.16.
8. Augustine, *Pecc. merit.* 1.1, 3.5, 3.6, 10.18.
9. Rees, "Pelagius," 132. See also 22, 34–35, 83, and 131.
10. Clark, *Origenist Controversy*, 10.
11. Armstrong, "St. Augustine," 155, 164.
12. Ferguson, "In Defence," 114–15.
13. Ferguson, *Pelagius*, 182–83.
14. Bonner, *St. Augustine*, 316.
15. Bonner, *Freedom and Necessity*, ix–x, 72.
16. De Plinval, "L'Heure," 158, 162; Barclift, "In Controversy," 20; Bohlin, *Die Theologie*, 5; Bonner, "How Pelagian?," 351–52; Evans, *Inquiries and Reappraisals*, 66; Ferguson, *Pelagius*, 182–83; Haight, "Notes," 27, 31, 36, 38; Lamberigts, "Le Mal," 111; Lucas, "Pelagius," 73, 84; O'Donnell, *Augustine*, 276; Phipps, "Heresiarch,"133; Rebillard, "Sociologie," 225; Sell, "Augustine Versus Pelagius," 117–18; Wolfson, "St. Augustine," 176. Other scholars wish to place Cassian as a corrective alternative to both Augustine and the Pelagians. Azkoul, "Peccatum Originale," 39–53; Casiday, "Rehabilitating," 270–71; Harrison, "Truth in Heresy?," 82.
17. Lancel, *Saint Augustine*, 342.

The Episcopal Diocese of Atlanta asking for the council to appoint a committee "to honor the contributions of Pelagius and reclaim his voice."[18]

Augustine, the bishops at the Synod of Diospolis of 415, and Mercator labeled Pelagius a "monk" (*monachus*),[19] while Orosius and Pope Zosimus (417–418) described him simply as a layman.[20] This discrepancy points to the complexity of asceticism in Late Antiquity we saw in chapter 1. On the one hand, Pelagius certainly stressed a Christian life that demanded perfection. To one mentee, he said that "the ordering of the perfect life is a formidable matter, formidable, I say, and dependent for its success on a considerable degree of effort and study, and it calls for consummate wisdom to know what is the end which one is pursuing and how to pursue it and, by showing discretion in every act, to do nothing which is likely to make one regret having done it."[21] This perfected life must be obtained by the free will's choice to be righteous. "Righteousness," Pelagius said, "is quite simply, not to sin, and not to sin is to keep the commandments of the law. Keeping these commandments is ensured in two ways, by doing nothing which is forbidden and by striving to fulfil everything which is commanded."[22] Cleary, Pelagius set a high standard.

On the other hand, his message was not just for the spiritual elite like Antony or Pachomius. Although his advice was offered in aristocratic circles, his call for a sinless Christian life was for all Christians. "In the matter of righteousness," Pelagius wrote, "we all have one obligation: virgin, widow, wife, the highest, the middle and the lower stations in life, we are all without exception ordered to fulfil the commandments, nor is a man released from the law if he proposes to do more than it demands."[23] Pelagius never called for a separation of Christians into a class system of professionals and amateurs, nor was he interested in individual achievement, but in an entire church "without spot or wrinkle" (Eph 5:27).[24] Furthermore, Pelagius himself shied away from the term *monachus*. Writing to a nameless addressee, he said that "I can ask of a man of your good sense that you should not suppose that I have uttered these words under the influence of some superstition: I want you to be called a Christian, not a monk

---

18. The Episcopal Diocese of Atlanta 105th Annual Council. "Minutes: 105th Annual Council of the Diocese of Atlanta." https://www.episcopalatlanta.org/Customer-Content/www/CMS/files//Minutes_105th_Council_both_sessions.pdf.

19. Additionally, many contemporary scholars describe him as a monk: Bonner, *St. Augustine*, 316; Harnack has described him as such, and added that he was a eunuch, although there is no evidence for this. Harnack, *History of Dogma*, 170. For a description of the use of the term in antiquity, see Sheridan, "Monastic Terminology," 301–21.

20. Augustine, *Gest. Pelag.* 14.36, 19.43, 20.44, 35.60; Marius Mercator, *Sub.*, 2.2; Orosius, *Lib. apo.*, 5; Zosimus, *Postquam*.

21. Pelagius, *Ad Dem.* 24.1.

22. Pelagius, *Virg.* 6.1. While Pelagius insisted on living a life without sin, he was never interested in detailing the specific means of achieving this goal the way many others had been, such as Cassian.

23. Pelagius, *Ad. Dem.* 10.1.

24. Pelagius, *Virg.* 11.3; Bonner, *Augustine*, 14; Brown, "Pelagius," 194; Barnard, "Pelagius," 193–94; Haight, "Notes," 34.

and to possess the virtue of your own personal claim to praise rather than a foreign name which is bestowed to no purpose by Latins on men who stay in the common crowd, whereas it is given legitimately by the Greeks to those who lead the solitary life."[25] While Pelagius's brand of renunciation has common elements of renunciation and perfection that may be found in other Christian and pagan writers (including the aristocratic tradition of *otium*),[26] it was a Christian program of life that was unique in the ancient world that did not call for the abandonment of society, and it cannot comfortably be described by the umbrella term "asceticism."

Some Christian aristocrats in Rome, like Marcella, embraced a more rigorous asceticism described in chapter 1, while since Constantine most tended towards a more "respectable" Christianity.[27] This change in the Roman aristocracy had less to do with the imperial prohibitions against paganism, and more from a change in the aristocrats themselves. As Peter Brown has said, "by far the most important of these [moves towards a "respectable" Christianity] is the conversion of the Anician family, and, especially, the late baptism of the *doyen* of Roman society, Petronius Probus, celebrated in a grandiose epitaph, and acclaimed by Christian writers as the 'first' conversion among the Roman aristocracy."[28] Like all exclusive aristocracies throughout time, the elite families were connected to each other through marital bonds. This intermarriage of Christians and non-Christians at the highest social echelon, over a brief period of time, was one of the most important reasons for the success of Christianity in Roman high society.[29]

It was under the patronage of such Christian families and their entourages that Pelagius flourished. In fact, Pelagius found himself in the entourage of the *gens* Anicia as a trusted advisor. This relationship did not go unnoticed by Augustine. As we shall discuss in greater detail later, Augustine had written to Juliana Anicia[30] in 417 warning her and her family of the dangers he perceived in a letter from Pelagius[31] to Juliana's daughter, Demetrias, who had recently forsaken an engagement and had consecrated her life to God. Augustine, and his long-time friend and fellow-bishop Alypius, reminded her of their "closeness"[32] to her and that she should receive them, too, as trusted mentors. She should heed their words and disregard Pelagius's guidance. Juliana replied with thinly veiled contempt for their insinuation that her family had been led astray into heterodoxy: "I and my home are far removed from such persons, all our family follows the Catholic faith to the point that it has never strayed into any heresy

---

25. Pelagius, *Div. leg.* 9.3.
26. Brown, *Through the Eye*, 164.
27. Brown, "Aspects," 177.
28. Brown, "Aspects," 177.
29. Brown, "Aspects," 181.
30. Augustine, *Epist.* 188.
31. Pelagius, *Ad Dem.*
32. Augustine, *Epist.* 188.2.

and has never fallen not only into those sects from which it is difficult to free oneself but even into those which are seen to have some small errors."[33]

Pelagius was also under the protection of an "important patron"[34] named Sixtus, a Roman priest and future Pope (432–440).[35] Sixtus had been an influential leader to whom Augustine reported that "those [Pelagian] heretics are accustomed to brag about your friendship."[36] In an abrupt *volte-face*, Sixtus publicly anathematized the Pelagians in front of a large crowd, and included a short letter with Pope Zosimus's *Tractoria* (Zosimus's letter that condemned Pelagius and Caelestius in 418 that will be discussed later) to Aurelius, the bishop of Carthage, which condemned the Pelagians, and ended the first phase of the controversy in 418.[37] He soon afterwards sent a longer letter describing in detail his opposition to the Pelagians.[38] It was this same Sixtus who, as Pope, refused the request of Julian of Eclanum to return to his See in Italy in 439.[39]

A third patron of Pelagius worthy of mention is Paulinus of Nola. Paulinus was influential in the highest Roman circles, and had a burgeoning secular career as suffect consul at Rome, and governor of the province of Campania under the Emperor Gratian (367–383). After a decade of aristocratic *otium* following Gratian's death, he had renounced his immense wealth and career in 394 to live the life of an aristocratic monk.[40] Later that year on Christmas he was ordained,[41] and that following spring or summer Paulinus relocated to Nola where he would live for the rest of his life until he died in 431. Paulinus often would travel to Rome from Nola, including each summer for the Feast of the Apostles on June 29.[42] It must have been on one of his early trips to Rome when Paulinus and Pelagius met. We know little about their relationship, but it is clear that Paulinus was wrestling with the Pelagian ideas of free will and the nature of sin that were circulating in the air in Rome at the end of the fourth century.[43] We

---

33. Augustine, *Epist.* 188.3.

34. Augustine, *Epist.* 191.1.

35. There are a variety of other important Patrons of Pelagius that are not discussed in detail here: Melania the Elder, the "friends of Rufinus and the friends of the friends of Rufinus," Melania the Younger and her husband Pinianus, and the uncle of Melania the Younger, Volusianus, who was the Urban Prefect in 419. Brown, "Patrons of Pelagius," 212–13. It is possible that the future Pope Leo was a supporter. Augustine, *Epist.* 191.1

36. Augustine, *Epist.* 191.2.

37. Augustine, *Epist.* 194.1.1.

38. Neither of Sixtus's letters are extant. Augustine responded (*Epist.* 194) describing his view of the primacy of grace that ignited the turmoil at Hadrumetum, which became part of the so-called Semi-Pelagian controversy.

39. Kelly, *Oxford Dictionary*, 43.

40. For a discussion of Paulinus's understanding of renunciation of wealth, see Brown, *Through the Eye*, 208–40.

41. Trout, *Paulinus of Nola*, 94.

42. Trout, *Paulinus of Nola*, 47.

43. Trout, *Paulinus of Nola*, 230–31.

also know that he and Pelagius had conducted a letter correspondence, presumably when Paulinus was in Nola.[44]

Although he corresponded with Pelagius, Paulinus simultaneously exchanged letters with Augustine, whom he never met, from 394 to the end of Augustine's life.[45] Augustine and Alypius wrote a letter to Paulinus in 416 (six years after Pelagius had left Rome)[46] warning him of the Pelagian danger, and gently probing him to ascertain his sympathies. They recognized that Paulinus had "loved" (*diligere*) Pelagius "as a servant of God," and they claimed that they, too, "still love him."[47] They attempted to discover if he was still in contact with any Pelagians, and hinted that they knew that he may have been supporting some: "some people with you or rather in your city," they said, "at least if what we have heard is true, fight with such stubbornness in defense of this error that they say that it is easier for them to abandon and despise even Pelagius, who condemned the people who hold these views [at the Synod of Diospolis], than to give up the truth, as they see it, of this opinion."[48]

Paulinus "is hard to label."[49] But, it is clear that he never became an avowed Pelagian, as he did not accept entirely the Pelagian program. Like other Roman aristocrats at this time who were struggling to understand how to live a truly Christian life, Paulinus probably was attracted to Pelagius's emphases on moral rigor, excellence, responsibility, and determination.[50] But, as Dennis Trout has said, "Paulinus's frequent assertions of a fundamentally prerequisite divine grace and his public laments of the taint of original sin seem conditionally to distance him from Pelagius."[51] Paulinus's unwillingness to fully embrace Pelagius did not lead him to break relations with him, however, and he also never broke with Augustine, despite Paulinus's patronage of some Pelagians. Disagreements over theological propositions were never significant enough for Paulinus to lead

---

44. Pelagius had written a letter to Pope Innocent (which we will explore later) and prompted him to read a letter (no longer extant) he had written to Paulinus describing his vision of grace, which Pelagius declared was entirely orthodox. Augustine, *Grat. Chr.* 1.35.38.

45. Augustine, *Epist.* 25.

46. Teske claims in the WSA letter series that *Epist.* 186 was written in 416, while Trout claims it was written in 417. It is most important to know that it was written after the Synod of Diospolis in 415 and before the triple condemnation of Pelagius in 418 by the Council of Carthage, the Emperor Honorius, and Pope Zosimus.

47. This love for Pelagius, though, has changed. Augustine says that his earlier love for Pelagius was because he thought Pelagius held "the correct faith," while his current love for Pelagius is rooted in a hope that "God's mercy might set him free from the views which he is said to hold that are hostile and contrary to the grace of God." Augustine, *Epist.* 186.1.1.

48. Augustine, *Epist.* 186.8.29.

49. Trout, *Paulinus of Nola*, 219.

50. Trout, *Paulinus of Nola*, 228.

51. Trout, *Paulinus of Nola*, 233. Augustine also recognized this when he claimed that "you surely see along with us the wicked error that holds them [the Pelagians] captive. For your letters are fragrant with the most pure odor of Christ; in them you are seen to love and confess his grace most sincerely." Augustine, *Epist.* 186.12.39.

him to side with one camp or another, nor to allow them to damage his friendships—something that surely cannot be said of Jerome or Augustine.[52]

Pelagius quickly ingratiated himself with the Roman elite. He may have developed a brief friendship with Jerome, who moved in the same circles as he had, and who left Rome in 385.[53] The extent of their friendship at the time is unclear. Years later in 394, Jerome received a letter (now lost) from a friend, Domnio, in Rome who had warned him about a monk who was disparaging Jerome's books against Jovinian.[54] Around 393, Jerome had written a scathing criticism, his *Contra Iovinianum*, of Jovinian's claims that—among other things—virginity was not superior to marriage.[55] Jerome's friends were so horrified at his merciless invective that his friend Pammachius attempted (but failed) to remove copies of it from circulation to prevent a scandal.[56] Jerome's response to Domnio's letter never mentioned the monk by name, but described him as young, athletically built, lazy, a gossip, philosophically inept, self-taught, self-deluded, that he surrounded himself with uneducated people and weak women, that he had publicly lashed out against Jerome, and that he had inflamed Jerome's anger in many gatherings when he had lived in Rome.[57]

A scholarly debate has arisen speculating if this nameless monk was Pelagius.[58] It is impossible to say with certainty, but I do not believe that it was him. For one, Jerome's anger never relented. He never forgave any adversary for crossing him, and he never forgot any perceived harm done to him.[59] After the break with his own

52. Jerome's break with his friendship with Rufinus is well documented. Elizabeth Clark has discussed the theological differences Augustine had with Melania the Younger, her husband, and Juliana that resulted in the end of their friendships. Clark, "Theory and Practice," 40–45.

53. Writing in 414, Jerome says "If we are obligated to show caution, lest we appear to be wounding an old friendship if we cut off this most arrogant [Pelagian] heresy with our spiritual blade, then we will have to endure these torments to the faith and say along with the prophet, 'I languished in misery as the thorn was driven into me.'" Jerome, *In Hier.* 4.pref.

54. For an excellent discussion of Jerome's fight with Jovinian, see Hunter, *Marriage, Celibacy*.

55. Kelly succinctly describes Jovinian's four arguments that infuriated Jerome: "First, it makes no difference, so far as spiritual perfection is concerned, whether Christians who have been baptized and give proof of the reality of their baptism are married, widowed, or single. Secondly, Christians who have received baptism with full adhesion of faith cannot henceforth fall under the dominion of the devil. If they sin, they can be spared the effects of sin by repentance. Thirdly, Christians who mortify themselves by fasting are in no way superior to those who eat and drink freely while offering thanks to God. Fourthly, on the day of judgment there will be no differentiation of rewards among Christians who have preserved their baptism, but they will all enjoy equal blessings." Kelly, *Jerome*, 181.

56. Jerome, *Epist.* 49.2.

57. Jerome, *Epist.* 50.1–3.

58. De Plinval, *Pélage*, 54; Myres, "Pelagius," 22; Evans, *Inquiries and Reappraisals*, 26–42; Kelly, *Jerome*, 188; Rousseau, "Jerome's Search," 134–35; Ferguson, *Pelagius*, 77; Rees, "Pelagius: A Reluctant Heretic," 5; Cain, *The Letters of Jerome*, 216; Hunter, *Marriage*, 249–50; Duval, "Pélage," 530; Wermelinger, *Rom und Pelagius*, 46–48; Rackett, "Sexuality and Sinlessness," 66. Dunphy says that it could be Ambrosiaster, but he believes that it was Caelestius. Dunphy, "Jerome against Jovinian," 25–48.

59. A notable exception to this would be his change in attitude toward Augustine. Originally, Jerome was deeply suspicious of Augustine but, at the end of his life, he warmed to Augustine. Jerome's

family, for example, he never seemed to have any desire to repair those broken relationships. If the nameless monk in Domnio's letter had been Pelagius, Jerome most certainly would have resurrected their earlier spat during the height of the Pelagian controversy. His silence is telling. Second, when Pelagius wrote his commentary on Paul's letter to the Romans just a few years after Jerome's letter to Domnio, Pelagius did not show zeal for Jovinian that we see in the nameless monk. In fact, Pelagius did not embrace the view of Jovinian that those who fast and those who do not fast are equal; he believed that abstinence was preferable.[60] He also rejected Jovinian's claim of the equality of continence and marriage.[61] Third, although Jerome attempted to associate the thought of Jovinian and the thought of Pelagius during the Pelagian controversy in order to discredit Pelagius,[62] he never identified Pelagius as personally having supported Jovinian.[63]

Pelagius's Commentaries on Paul's Letters

While in Rome, Pelagius wrote a number of texts: a treatise on the Trinity, a collection of biblical passages Augustine referred to as *Liber testimoniorum*, his *De natura*,[64] and a set of commentaries on all of Paul's letters.[65] Only the commentaries survive *in toto*, and are underappreciated by scholars today, most likely because they were begun around the year 405/406, half a decade before the Pelagian controversy. They deserve more attention than they have garnered.[66] Augustine had read Pelagius's commentaries, and they prompted him to add a third book to his *De peccatorum meritis et remissione et de baptismo parvulorum*. Pelagius's rejection of original sin (*peccatum originale*) in his commentary on Romans, furthermore, caused Augustine to exclaim

---

original suspicion was unfounded as Augustine wrote to him with honest intentions. See Squires, "Jerome's Animosity"; White, *Correspondence*; Augustine, *Epist.* 202.

60. De Bruyn, "General Introduction," 51–53. See also: Pelagius, *Expos. (ad Rom.)* 14:13–23; Jerome, *C. Jov.* 1.3.

61. Pelagius, *Ad Cel.* 28.2.

62. Jerome often attempted to associate those whom he considered heretics in an attempt to create scandal. Elm, "Polemical Use."

63. For Jerome's theological connection between Jovinian and Pelagius, see: *Epist.* 133.3; *Dial.* 1.1, 1.2, 2.24, 3.1, 3.15.

64. Scholars disagree when Pelagius's *De natura* was written. Some believe it was written when he was in Sicily in 410–11. Others believe that it was written from Palestine in 413–14. Duval, Teske, and Lancel have argued that it was more likely written 406–10 while in Rome. Duval, "La Date," 274; Rees, "Pelagius," 140; Teske, "Introduction," WSA, 198–99; Lancel, *Saint Augustine*, 326.

65. Orosius called the collection of biblical passages the *Capitulorum liber*, while Gennadius called it the *Eulogiarum liber*. Augustine, *C. du. ep. Pelag.* 4.8.21; Ferguson, *Pelagius*, 47. For a full list of Pelagius's texts, see Rees, "Pelagius," 133–34.

66. Brown, however, has described the commentaries as "the most sure source of his theological views." While this is true, Pelagius's commentaries do not include many of the theological positions that would enrage so many. Brown, *Augustine of Hippo*, 342.

that "it never entered my mind that anyone could think or say such things."⁶⁷ The commentaries rejected any notion of ontological corruption or evil, but they were written primarily against the negative view of human nature of the Manichaeans, as they were Pelagius's initial adversaries.⁶⁸ Pelagius's commentaries were influenced by a number of authors, including Rufinus's translation of Origen's commentary on Romans, Ambrosiaster, the Anonymous Commentator on Paul, Chromatius of Aquileia, and probably Cyprian, Tertullian, and Lactantius.⁶⁹ Theodore de Bruyn also has shown that Pelagius had known and been influenced by several of Augustine's early works on Romans: Augustine's *Expositio quarundam propositionum ex epistula Apostoli ad Romanos*, *Epistulae ad Romanos inchoate expositio*, *De diversis quaestionibus octoginta tribus*, and *Ad Simplicianum*.⁷⁰

The scholarly reaction to Pelagius's commentaries is mixed. Martha Stortz has concluded that "Pelagius was anything but creative, and Jerome's caricatures of him as 'a dolt' and 'that bloated Alpine dog' has a vicious truth in them. Rather, lack of vision causes Pelagius to flounder. His adherence to his sources is slavish; his mind is eclectic without being either integrative or profound. The result is a potpourri of exegetical insights reflecting pluralism in a church that would soon be unable to tolerate pluralism."⁷¹ De Bruyn, on the other hand, detects in the commentaries a "combination of riches and brevity [that] was unprecedented in the west. At first glance, it may suggest that Pelagius approached the epistle to the Romans with no guiding interpretation of his own, but merely provided a synopsis of the comments of others. Such an impression would belie the truth, however. From the many comments one can discern the lineaments of an interpretation born, on the one hand, of Pelagius's attention to the text of the epistle and on the other, of his theological interests."⁷² J.

---

67. Augustine, *Pecc. merit.* 3.1.1.

68. Scheck, *Origen*, 64–67; Bammel, "Rufinus' Translation," 131–42. Bohlin also argues that Pelagius's other main antagonist was Arius. Although Pelagius certainly was against Arius and was fully Nicene, I do not think Pelagius had Arius on his mind as much as the Manichaeans. Bohlin, *Die Theologie*, 10. See also: Pelagius, *Ad Cel.* 28.2.

69. Souter, "Introduction," 185; De Bruyn, "General Introduction," 2–6; Garcia-Allen, "Was Pelagius?," 1252–55; Bostock, "Influence of Origen," 381–93. Pelagius also shows his influences in other texts, such as: Basil, Evagrius, the *Sentences of Sextus*, Hilary of Poitiers, Ambrose of Milan, John Chrysostom, Early Syriac Christianity, and Jerome. See: Augustine, *Nat. grat.* 61.71–66.79; *Grat. Chr.* 1.42.46–50.55. Yamada, "Influence of Chromatius," 661–70; Chadwick, *Sentences of Sextus*; Barnard, "Pelagius," 253.

70. De Bruyn, "General Introduction," 6–7.

71. Stortz, "Exegesis, Orthodoxy," 25.

72. De Bruyn, "General Introduction," 35. Thomas Scheck, likewise, has shown that Pelagius certainly relied on Origen as an important source, but that he departed from Origen on a variety of issues, including a rejection of Origen's claim of the pre-existence of human souls, he avoided Origen's allegories and digressions, rejected ontological consequences to Adam's sin, and overlooked Origen's claim of a fallen condition of infants. Scheck also has noted that "Pelagius's work is literal and terse, whereas Origen's is discursive, speculative, allegorical, and lengthy. Pelagius draws on the entire antecedent tradition, and many tributaries feed into his own independent appropriation of that tradition." Scheck, *Origen*, 65, 83–85.

Albert Harrill has claimed that Pelagius's commentary on Paul's letter to the Romans was a "masterpiece of Latin rhetoric."[73]

My own interpretation is to be more generous than Stortz, as I believe that resurrecting Jerome's abuse is not constructive. Pelagius crafted his interpretation of Paul's letters in such a way as to refute the Manichaeans, rather than simply to regurgitate the thoughts of earlier exegetes.[74] The Manichaeans had a large and disruptive presence in Rome, as the prohibition against them in the Theodosian Code demonstrates.[75] They were often confused with Christian ascetics because of their shared rejection of the world, and disheveled appearance.[76] Because of this rejection, many non-Christians also believed that Christians and Manichaeans shared a belief in the evil of human nature. In his commentaries, Pelagius repeatedly stressed the goodness of nature in opposition to the Manichaeans: "we [humans] presented our [bodily] members to serve sin; it is not the case, as the Manichaeans say, that it was the nature of the body to have sin mixed in."[77] For all of Pelagius's reliance on earlier theologians and all of his theological shortcomings, to say that he slavishly repeated the ideas of his sources is mistaken.

Departure from Rome

Pelagius fled Rome along with many aristocrats shortly before it was sacked in 410 by Alaric, King of the Goths. Christians at the time did not make sense of this event in a singular way. What could it mean, they wondered, that Rome burned just one generation after Christianity became the official religion of the empire? We do not know if Pelagius witnessed any of the destruction, nor how he came to terms with it all. His personal experience fleeing Rome ahead of the invading armies may have been so traumatic that he never could bring himself to write about it. Orosius, though, was not disturbed by the Roman destruction one bit.[78] His interpretation of the sack was twofold: "the enemy was allowed [by God] to do this in order to punish the arrogant, debauched, blasphemy of the town,"[79] while, at the same time, Rome was saved from total annihilation because "it is through his [God's] clemency that we are alive."[80] Melania the Younger, an aristocrat who also had left Italy just ahead of the invading horde, expressed nothing more than relief of having divested her enormous fortune in a turn toward the ascetic life

---

73. Harrill, *Paul the Apostle*, 145.

74. Harrill, *Paul the Apostle*, 145.

75. Huber, "Pelagian Heresy," 113.

76. Lavender, "Development," 73; Jerome, *Epist.* 22.13.

77. Pelagius, *Expos. (ad Rom.)*, 6:19. See also: 1:1, 7:7, 8:7, 9:5; De Bruyn, "General Introduction," 16.

78. Fear, "Introduction," 12.

79. Orosius, *C. pag.* 7.39.18.

80. Orosius, *C. pag.* 2.3.5.

prior to the pillaging: "lucky are the ones who anticipated what was to come and sold their possessions before the arrival of the barbarians!"[81] Jerome was devastated to the point that he says he forgot his own name.[82] "I was so stunned and dismayed," he said safely ensconced faraway in Palestine, "that I could think of nothing else, day or night, but the well-being of all our people. I consider myself captive in the captivity of the saints, and I could not open my mouth until I learned something more definite. Thus, I tortured myself with the afflictions of others, while in my solicitude I hovered between hope and despair. After the most brilliant light of all the world was extinguished . . . the entire world perished in one city."[83] Augustine offered a fourth response. He showed little patience for those who wept over a city that had burned throughout its history, because such distress betrayed a flawed understanding of the Christian vision.[84] Christians must understand that the destruction of an earthly city—even the eternal city—is ultimately meaningless. The heavenly city is the Christian's true home. "The apostle Peter is reigning with the Lord," he rebuked a crowd in Carthage as distraught as Jerome, "the body of the apostle Peter is lying in some place or other. His memorial is meant to stir you to love eternal things, not so that you may stick to the earth, but so that with the apostle you may think about heaven."[85]

Pelagius had known of Augustine prior to his flight from Rome, because he had read Augustine's *Confessiones* during his time there. He was not at all impressed with what he read. Late in his life, Augustine recounted Pelagius's reaction to his now famous prayer to God in Book Ten: "grant what you command, and command what you will."[86] Augustine said that "when these words of mine were cited at Rome by some brother and fellow bishop[87] of mine in Pelagius's presence, he could not tolerate them and, attacking them somewhat emotionally, he almost came to blows

---

81. Gerontius, *Life of Melania*, 19.

82. Jerome, *Epist.* 126.2.

83. Jerome, *Comm. Ezech.* pref. See also: *Epist.* 127.12–13. Rousseau offers an intriguing analysis of Jerome's reaction to the sack of Rome after several years: Rousseau, "Jerome on Jeremiah."

84. Augustine, *Serm.* 296.9.

85. Augustine, *Serm.* 296.7.

86. Augustine, *Conf.* 10.29.40.

87. Brown speculates that this bishop might be Paulinus of Nola. Although this is certainly possible, it is inconclusive. If it were Paulinus, we can see here an example of Paulinus siding with Augustine on original sin that was mentioned earlier. However, Lancel speculates that it may have been Evodius, who had spent some time in Rome during the summer of 404. Another possibility I would offer is that it could be Urbanus of Sicca. Augustine says "my holy brother and fellow bishop, our Urbanus who was a priest here, and is now bishop of Sicca, when he got back from Rome, and there crossed swords with someone [Pelagius] holding such opinions [about "forgive us our debts, as we too forgive our debtors, and do not bring us into temptation" (Matt 6:12–13)]—or rather mentioned that he had crossed swords with him." Urbanus was probably not a bishop at the time of this encounter, but Augustine's recollection of the event was decades later, and he may not have remembered exactly when Urbanus became a bishop. Brown, *Augustine of Hippo*, 343; Lancel, *Saint Augustine*, 326; Augustine, *Serm.* 348A.1.

with the one who had cited them."[88] After fleeing Rome, Pelagius may have spent a brief period in Sicily, but landed in Hippo and left there for Carthage, as Augustine said, "more quickly than one might have expected."[89] Augustine was in Carthage at the time where he saw Pelagius once or twice, but never spoke with him before Pelagius left for the East.[90]

---

88. Augustine, *Persev.* 53.

89. Augustine, *Gest. Pelag.* 22.46.

90. Augustine, *Gest. Pelag.* 22.46. Dunphy offers a revision of the chronology of the year 411 when Pelagius and Caelestius were in Africa. Dunphy, "A Lost Year," 463–64.

Chapter 3

Caelestius: The Commander of the Pelagian Army

Caelestius in Rome and Africa

WE KNOW EVEN LESS about Caelestius than we do about Pelagius, leading Walter Dunphy to describe him as "elusive,"[1] and Guido Honnay to describe him as a "stranger."[2] Scholars have offered a variety of possibilities for the location of his place of birth, ranging from Ireland, Britain,[3] Campania,[4] and Africa,[5] although the most likely candidate is Rome.[6] It is uncertain exactly when he was born, but he certainly was a younger contemporary of Pelagius.[7] Mercator, a little-known layman who had been in Rome around 418, and corresponded with Augustine about their shared fear of the Pelagians,[8] described Caelestius as an aristocrat (*nobilis natu*), leading to the likelihood that Pelagius and Caelestius had met in Rome when Pelagius was a spiritual director there.[9] He also said that Caelestius had legal training, which can be seen on full display as he maneuvered his way around the questions posed to him at the Council of Carthage in 411.[10] Mercator also described Caelestius as a eunuch, but this was most likely just an assassination attempt on his character.[11] Caelestius probably became Pelagius's disciple[12] sometime between 390

---

1. Dunphy, "*De possibilitate*?," 69.

2. Honnay, "Caelestius," 302.

3. Morris believes that Caelestius's family was Irish, but that they may have settled on the west coast of Britain by the time Caelestius was born. Morris, "Pelagian Literature," 41–42.

4. De Plinval, *Pélage*, 212.

5. De Plinval, *Pélage*, 212; O'Donnell, *Augustine*, 254. O'Donnell claims that Caelestius was a "local priest" in Africa, but Caelestius would only later be ordained in Ephesus.

6. Dunphy, "Caelestius," 37.

7. Gennadius, *De vir. inlustr.* 45. We do not know exactly when he was born, but Honnay has guessed he was born around 380. Honnay, "Caelestius," 272.

8. Augustine, *Epist.* 193; Jerome, *Epist.* 154; Bark, "Doctrinal Interests," 210–16; Dunphy, "Marius Mercator," 279–88.

9. Marius Mercator, *Sub.* pref.4.

10. Marius Mercator, *Sub.* pref.4

11. Marius Mercator, *Sub.* pref.4

12. Augustine, for example, says in his *Retractationes* that "Caelestius, his [Pelagius's] disciple

and 400;[13] but, he should not be considered a second-rate copy of his master, as he added his own distinctive flavor to the debate.

Caelestius's foes described him with stinging invective. Jerome claimed he was the "one who is the teacher and commander of his [Pelagius's] whole army,"[14] and "no ordinary blasphemer."[15] Augustine said he was "bloated with the wind of false doctrine,"[16] and that he was "more open," "more stubborn," and "took greater liberties"[17] than his mentor. Vincent of Lérins called him Pelagius's "monstrous" disciple.[18] Modern scholars have described him as "indefatigable,"[19] the "ablest Pelagian leader," a "more impressive personality [than Pelagius]," the "most effective man of action which the movement produced,"[20] an "*enfant terrible*,"[21] "formidable,"[22] "skillful in debate,"[23] a "publicist," a "systematizer," "eloquent," that he "had a keenly analytical mind with a probing intellect,"[24] that he was an "agitator,"[25] "outspoken," "loquacious," "irrepressible,"[26] that he had a "sharper mind than Pelagius for ecclesiastical politics,"[27] a "trouble maker,"[28] "belligerent,"[29] "zealous,"[30] "bold," "stubborn,"[31] and "more Pelagian than Pelagius himself."[32] I would add that Caelestius's legal training formed him to be craftier, wilier, and more evasive than Pelagius.

(*discipulus*), had deserved excommunication before the episcopal tribunal at Carthage [411], at which I myself was not present." Augustine, *Retract.* 2.33.60.

13. Lamberigts speculates that it could have been as early as 390, while Dunphy dates it to roughly 400. However, if Honnay is right that Caelestius was born in 380, then he could not have become Pelagius's student as early as 390 because, if Genndius is right that Caelestius wrote letters to his family *De monasterio*, it would have been unlikely for him to do so at the age of 10. Lamberigts, "Caelestius," 114; Dunphy, "Caelestius," 40–41.

14. Jerome, *Epist.* 133.5.
15. Jerome, *Epist.* 133.6.
16. Augustine, *Grat. Chr.* 2.7.8.
17. Augustine, *Grat. Chr.* 2.12.13.
18. Vincent of Lérins, *Comm.* 24.62.
19. Bonner, *Augustine*, 14.
20. Bonner, "Pelagianism and Augustine," 35, 38; Beatrice, "Pelagian Critique," 28.
21. Harnack, *History of Dogma*, 178; Brown, *Augustine of Hippo*, 343.
22. Brown, *Augustine of Hippo*, 360.
23. Dunphy, "A Lost Year," 400.
24. Ferguson, *Pelagius*, 49.
25. Harnack, *History of Dogma*, 171.
26. Huber, "Pelagian Heresy," 31, 45.
27. Morris, "Pelagian Literature," 43.
28. Lamberigts, "Co-operation," 370.
29. TeSelle, "Rufinus the Syrian," 76.
30. Hwang, *Intrepid Lover*, 70.
31. Beatrice, "Pelagian Critique," 28.
32. O'Donnell, *Augustine*, 254.

The only thing that we know about Caelestius's early life comes from a short description from Gennadius, the fifth-century presbyter and apologist of Marseilles.[33] Gennadius says that "before he [Caelestius] joined Pelagius, while yet a very young man (*adulescens*), wrote to his parents three epistles on monastic life (*de monasterio*), written as short books, and containing moral maxims suited to everyone who is seeking God, containing no trace of the fault which afterwards appeared, but wholly devoted to the encouragement of virtue."[34] Scholars have puzzled over what, exactly, he means that Caelestius had written "*de monasterio*." One possibility is that Caelestius had lived in a monastery as a *monachus* prior to his association with Pelagius, but later left the monastery for unknown reasons. John Morris, for one, believes that Caelestius had been living in a monastery in Britain that had been founded by Victricius of Rouen, who had visited Britain in 396, and founded several monasteries there.[35] Another possibility is that Caelestius was writing to his family about the moral virtues as inspired by the monastic *ethos*. Dunphy and Honnay believe that Caelestius never had been a monk in a monastery, but that he was exhorting his family to live virtuously.[36] My own sense is that Caelestius never lived in a monastery because, outside of Gennadius's passing reference, no other sources point to an early monastic life for him. Furthermore, it is hard to imagine Jerome ignoring the opportunity to take a shot at a man who was unsuccessful at his monastic commitments—despite the fact that he himself had failed at his own ascetic attempt in the desert—the way that he had mocked Jovinian's change of behavior from his earlier strict renunciation. "Although he [Jovinian] boasts of being a monk," Jerome said, "he has exchanged his dirty tunic, bare feet, common bread, and drink of water, for a snowy dress, sleek skin, honey–wine and dainty dishes, for the sauces of Apicius and Paxamus, for baths and rubbings, and for the cook-shops. Is it not clear that he prefers his belly to Christ and thinks his ruddy complexion worth the kingdom of heaven?"[37] Had Jerome known that Caelestius had been a monk, he undoubtedly would have subjected Caelestius to the same sort of treatment.

It is unclear when Caelestius left Rome and arrived in Carthage, but several options present themselves. It is possible that Caelestius went with Pelagius to Africa just before Alaric pillaged Rome.[38] There is no evidence, however, that Caelestius was in Hippo with Pelagius during Pelagius's brief stay there. When Caelestius was in Carthage, he had asked to be ordained at the hands of Bishop Aurelius, but instead was

---

33. Gennadius, *De vir. inlustr.* 99.
34. Gennadius, *De vir. inlustr.* 45.
35. Morris, "Pelagian Literature," 42. See also, Honnay, "Caelestius," 273 n. 16.
36. Dunphy, "Caelestius," 39; Dunphy, "Writings of Caelestius," 26; Honnay, "Caelestius," 273–74. Dunphy believes that these letters were probably written at the end of the fourth century. Dunphy, "Writings of Caelestius," 26.
37. Jerome, *C. Jov.* 1.40.
38. Picard-Mawji, "Le passage," 4.

charged with heresy and put on trial at a council.[39] If Caelestius only had arrived in Carthage at the end of 410, and the Council of Carthage that anathematized him was held in 411,[40] this leaves little time for Caelestius to settle in Carthage, to make connections with the Christian community there, ask for ordination, and for preparations to be made for the council. This possibility, therefore, is unlikely. A second possibility is that Caelestius left Rome and briefly stayed in Sicily (possibly with Pelagius) before continuing his journey to Carthage, although this, too, lacks conclusive evidence, and, as with the first possibility, would leave Caelestius little time to establish himself in Carthage prior to the council.[41] The most likely scenario is that Caelestius left Rome alone several years before Pelagius—possibly when Alaric began terrorizing Rome in 408—and already was established in Carthage by 411.[42]

Caelestius's desire for ordination is noteworthy as it stands in opposition to many of his contemporaries.[43] In the twenty-first century, a young man undergoes an intense process of discernment before entering the seminary. But, this was not the case in the first few centuries of Christianity. Many of the great men during that time were forcibly ordained, and only reluctantly acquiesced to it. Cassian summarizes the prevailing aversion to ordination in the fifth century: "a monk must by all means flee from women and bishops."[44] For monks such as Cassian and Jerome—or others such as Augustine and Paulinus of Nola who desired to live a life of Christian *otium* prior to their ordinations—ecclesiastical politics and administration (as well as the company of women) only sidetrack the serious Christian from his singular focus on God. In order to maintain an undisturbed spiritual practice, one must avoid all unnecessary ecclesiastical and bodily distractions.

Ambrose of Milan, for example, was acclaimed bishop even before he had been baptized.[45] At the urging of Augustine,[46] Paulinus of Milan wrote his *Vita Ambrosii*, in which he recounted Ambrose's reluctant acceptance of the office.[47] Auxentius, the

---

39. Augustine, *Epist.* 157.3.22; Orosius, *Lib. apol.* 3.

40. Scholars debate the exact date when this council was held. Koopsmans believed that it was between July and the first week of September 411. Refoulé believed that it was held sometime during the end of September 411 to the beginning of January 412. Dunphy believes it was held before Lent in early February 411. Koopsmans, "Augustine's First Contact," 152; Refoulé, "Datation," 42–49; Dunphy, "A Lost Year," 436.

41. Harnack, *History of Dogma*, 175; Honnay, "Caelestius," 297; Dunphy, "Caelestius," 41–42; Ferguson, *Pelagius*, 49.

42. Dunphy, "Caelestius," 41–43.

43. Dunphy has conjectured that Caelestius wanted to be ordained because, as a layman, he lacked an authoritative voice. Although this may be the case, there are others, such as Prosper of Aquitaine, who were not ordained and did not seem to feel the need for ordination in order to have an authoritative voice. Pelagius himself did not seem to desire ordination. Dunphy, "Caelestius," 46.

44. Cassian, *Inst.* 11.18.

45. Paredi, *Saint Ambrose*, 116–36.

46. Paulinus of Milan, *V. Amb.* 1.

47. There are two different possible dates for when Paulinus probably wrote the *Vita*, either 412–13

Arian bishop of Milan, died in 374. Ambrose, a Catholic catechumen and governor, entered the church in order to prevent any violence between Catholics and Arians during the selection of Auxentius's successor. "As he was speaking," Paulinus says, "the voice of a small child all at once made itself heard among the people: 'Ambrose for bishop!'"[48] Both the Arians and Catholics agreed, and he was "carried off" (*raptus*)[49] from the seat of judgment by the congregation. In order to change the minds of the people by showing that he was unfit for the office, Ambrose, according to Paulinus, ordered some individuals to be tortured, he attempted to retire to live a life of philosophy, he openly invited prostitutes to visit him, and twice tried to leave the city.[50] When he realized that he would not be able to escape his fate, he reluctantly accepted baptism from a Catholic bishop, and eight days later became the bishop of Milan.[51] He later reflected on his early days as bishop, and said that he was forced "to teach before I began to learn."[52] Although we need not accept every detail from Paulinus, Ambrose's reluctance to be ordained cannot be questioned.

Jerome, as well, had grudgingly accepted ordination at the hands of Paulinus of Antioch. He did not request to be ordained, and he insisted that, if he were ordained, it must be with the understanding that his vocation as a monk would not be impeded by ecclesiastical responsibilities. If Paulinus expected Jerome to abandon his monastic life, Jerome would refuse.[53] After Jerome was ordained, he rarely—if ever—exercised the duties of his office. Years later, in a letter from Epiphanius of Salamis to John of Jerusalem, Epiphanius recounted that "the reverent presbyters, Jerome and Vincent, through modesty and humility, were unwilling to offer the sacrifices permitted to their rank, and to labor in that part of their calling which ministers more than any other to the salvation of Christians."[54] The reasons of "modesty and humility" that Epiphanius gives for Jerome's refusal are overly generous.[55] Because of Jerome's refusal to participate in the life of the church as a presbyter, Epiphanius forcibly ordained Jerome's own brother, Paulinian, so that the monks at Jerome's Bethlehem monastery would have someone there to celebrate the liturgy. Unsurprisingly, Paulinian, like his brother, did not want to be ordained. Epiphanius says that Paulinian "made a hard struggle against it, crying out that he was unworthy, and

---

or 422. Ramsey favors the earlier date, while Paredi favors the later. Paulinus of Milan, "Life of Saint Ambrose," 195–218; Paredi, "Paulinus of Milan," 213.

48. Paulinus of Milan, *V. Amb.* 6.
49. Ambrose, *Off.* 1.1.4.
50. Paulinus of Milan, *V. Amb.* 7–9.
51. Paulinus of Milan, *V. Amb.* 9.
52. Ambrose, *Off.* 1.1.4.
53. Jerome, *C. Joan.* 41.
54. Jerome, *Epist.* 51.1.
55. Andrew Cain points out that when Jerome was ordained by Paulinus, Paulinus was in schism with the church at Antioch, and so the "validity of his ordination in the late 370s was questionable." Cain, *Letters of Jerome*, 141.

protesting that this heavy burden was beyond his strength."⁵⁶ Paulinian felt that this responsibility was more "onerous rather than honourable."⁵⁷

Augustine, who had been baptized by Ambrose,⁵⁸ also accepted ordination only reluctantly. He had gone to Hippo from Thagaste at the invitation of a man who wanted to discuss with Augustine the possibility of entering the monastic life. Augustine had refused to visit any town that did not have a bishop, he says, because he had a growing reputation in Catholic circles, and he feared the possibility of the destiny that eventually befell him. As Hippo already had a bishop, Valerius, Augustine felt confident that it was safe to travel there. But, he miscalculated. The congregation of Hippo "caught"⁵⁹ him and, amidst a stream of tears rolling down his cheeks, he was ordained a presbyter.⁶⁰ In a letter to Valerius shortly after his ordination, Augustine said that there is nothing "more difficult, more laborious, and more dangerous than the office of a bishop, priest or deacon,"⁶¹ and he asked his bishop to give him some time to become better acquainted with the Scriptures.⁶² O'Donnell argues that Augustine needed to write a letter to Valerius to make his request, rather than asking him face-to-face, because Augustine had fled to Thagaste the day after his ordination, and that this letter was a way of reassuring Valerius of his eventual return.⁶³

Paulinus of Nola, too, was forced into presbyterial ordination. Shortly after the public renunciation of his wealth and senatorial rank,⁶⁴ he was "compelled by the crowd with their fingers at my throat"⁶⁵ to accept ordination on December 25, 394 at the hands of Bishop Lampius in Barcelona⁶⁶ He tried to resist, but to no avail.⁶⁷ Reluctantly, he only acquiesced on the condition that he would not be tied to Barcelona, as he was anticipating his move to Nola.⁶⁸ In a letter to his friend Sulpicius Severus, Paulinus recounted the event: "on the day on which the Lord deigned to be born as man, I was ordained into the priesthood. The Lord witnesses that it happened through the sudden compulsion of the crowd, but I believe that I was forced (*corripere*) into it as His [God's] command."⁶⁹ Paulinus admits his unwillingness, but, unlike our previ-

56. Jerome, *Epist.* 51.1.
57. Jerome, *Epist.* 82.8.
58. Augustine, *Conf.* 9.6.14.
59. Augustine, *Serm.* 355.2.
60. Augustine, *Epist.* 21.2.
61. Augustine, *Epist.* 21.1.
62. Augustine, *Epist.* 21.3–4.
63. O'Donnell, *Augustine*, 24–25.
64. Ambrose, *Epist.* 28; Jerome, *Epist.* 58.
65. Paulinus of Nola, *Epist.* 2.2.
66. Trout, *Paulinus of Nola*, 90–103.
67. Paulinus of Nola, *Epist.* 2.2.
68. Trout, *Paulinus of Nola*, 94; Augustine, *Epist.* 31.4.
69. Paulinus of Nola, *Epist.* 1.10.

ous resisters, his hesitation, he says, did not come from fear of the office, but that he did not want to be bound to Barcelona. "I confess that I was unwilling," he said, "not that I despised the rank (for I call the Lord to witness that I longed to begin my holy slavery with the name and office of sacristan), but since I was bound elsewhere and had my mind, as you know firmly intent on another place, I trembled at this strange and unexpected decree of the divine will."[70]

The Council of Carthage of 411

Rather than receive the ordination that he desired, Caelestius was charged with heresy by Paulinus of Milan, the same Paulinus who wrote the *Vita Ambrosii*. Paulinus had been a secretary for Ambrose from 394 to 397 after he had met him when Ambrose was in exile in Florence (393–394), leading to the possible conclusion that Paulinus was from Florence, not Milan. He was a stenographer (*notarius*) for Ambrose, and in charge of his letter correspondence. Paulinus, likely already ordained a deacon, left Milan for Africa for unknown reasons after Ambrose's death, but, while in Carthage, was the caretaker (*defensor et procurator*) of the property of the Milanese church in Africa.[71] He presented Aurelius with a (now lost) *Liber minor* of Caelestius's heresy at a Council in Carthage in 411,[72] which became the first formal action of the Pelagian controversy. It is unclear if the *Liber* was comprised of quotations from Caelestius's texts, teachings that Paulinus had heard directly from Caelestius, or teachings that had been circulating in Carthage that were attributed to him.[73]

Paulinus's examination of Caelestius at the council was bitter and contemptuous.[74] Although it is impossible to state with any certainty, the rancor directed at Caelestius was so noxious that one wonders if there was a personal history between the two men in Italy undergirding Paulinus's accusations. The exchange as recounted by Augustine—who did not participate in the council as he probably was not in Carthage at the time, but reviewed the minutes during a later visit[75]—is worth quoting in its entirety:

> Bishop Aurelius [of Carthage] said, "let the following be read out." And it was read out that the sin of Adam harmed Adam alone and not the human race. After it had been read out, Caelestius said, "I said that I was in doubt about the transmission of the sin, but that I would, nonetheless, agree with one to whom God has given the gift of knowledge, for I have heard differing views from those who have been raised to the priesthood in the Catholic Church." The deacon Paulinus said, "Tell us their names." Caelestius said, "The holy priest

70. Paulinus of Nola, *Epist.* 1.10.
71. Paredi, "Paulinus of Milan," 207–9.
72. Augustine, *Grat. Chr.* 2.3.3.
73. Dodaro, "Carthaginian Debate," 191–92.
74. Augustine, *Grat. Chr.* 2.3.3–4.
75. Augustine, *Retract.* 2.33.60; *Gest. Pelag.* 11.23.

Rufinus, who lived at Rome with the saintly Pammachius. I heard him say that there is no transmission of sin." The deacon Paulinus asked, "is there anyone else?" Caelestius said, "I heard several others say this." The deacon Paulinus said, "state their names." Caelestius replied, "is one priest not enough for you?" After a while at another point, Bishop Aurelius said, "let the rest of the books be read." And it was read out that at their births, infants are in that state in which Adam was before his transgression—and up to the end of the little book that was included above. Bishop Aurelius said, "have you, Caelestius, at any time taught, as the deacon Paulinus claims, that at their birth infants are in that state in which Adam was before his transgression?" Caelestius replied, "I would like him to explain what he means by 'before his transgression.'" The deacon Paulinus said, "you there, go on and deny that you taught this. One thing or the other: either he has to deny that he taught this, or he has now to condemn it." Caelestius replied, "I already said that I would like him to explain what he means by 'before his transgression.'" The deacon Paulinus said, "deny that you taught these things." Bishop Aurelius said, "allow me, I will state what I gather to be the point of this man's objection. When first placed in paradise Adam was said to have been made imperishable. But after his transgression of the commandment he became subject to corruption. Is that what you mean, Paulinus?" The deacon Paulinus said, "exactly, bishop." Bishop Aurelius said, "what Paulinus wants to hear is whether the state of infants before baptism is today the same as Adam's before his transgression or whether it is certain that the infant derives the guilt of the transgression from the same sinful origin from which it is born." The deacon Paulinus said, "did he teach this, and does he refuse to reject it?" Caelestius replied, "with regard to the transmission of sin, I have already said that I heard many within the Catholic Church argue against it and some others defend it, inasmuch as it is open to discussion and not a matter of heresy. I have always said the infants need baptism and must be baptized. What else is he looking for?"[76]

Caelestius's training as a lawyer is evident in this exchange. He is evasive, refuses to say more than is minimally necessary, defers responsibility to others, unnecessarily asks for clarification, and will not admit to anything more than what are already common practices. These tactics increasingly frustrate Paulinus to the point that Aurelius felt compelled to intervene and break the tension. Unfortunately for Caelestius, neither his verbal skills nor his (now lost) *Libellus brevissimus* that he presented to Aurelius in his own defense led to an acquittal.[77] Rather, Caelestius, in Augustine's opinion, "received a sentence worthy of his perversity,"[78] by being anathematized, and, like Pelagius, he left Africa shortly afterwards for the East.

---

76. Augustine, *Grat. Chr.* 2.3.3–4.
77. Augustine, *Pecc. merit.* 1.36.63; *Epist.* 175.6; *Grat. Chr.* 2.19.21.
78. Augustine, *Gest Pelag.* 22.46.

Chapter 4

The "Holy Priest" Rufinus

The Identity of the "Holy Priest" Rufinus

IN THE EXTENDED QUOTATION at the end of the previous chapter, Caelestius said that the "holy priest Rufinus, who lived at Rome with the saintly Pammachius" was one of several people whom he heard deny the idea of the transmission of sin. Caelestius does not mention this Rufinus in any of the other extant quotations we have, nor does Augustine comment about who this person might be. For hundreds of years, scholars have pondered the identity of this obscure figure, because, even though Pelagius is most often described as the progenitor of Pelagianism,[1] Caelestius here hints that there may be someone else from whom he (and maybe even Pelagius) learned at least some of what became classic Pelagian anthropology. Who is this Rufinus? How did he transmit this teaching to Caelestius? When did he live in Rome? Why is he never mentioned again? What happened to him? What teachings did Caelestius learn from him? Is he the true founder of Pelagianism? Scholars have offered a variety of different answers to these questions, and it is safe to say that the identity of Rufinus is one of the most contested aspects of Pelagian scholarship today. Two leading theories attempt to identify this Rufinus.

At the end of the fourth century and the beginning of the fifth, seven men named Rufinus are known through documentation, although there most certainly were many more men with the same name, as it was common at that time.[2] In order to determine the identity of Caelestius's "holy priest," scholars naturally have turned to these seven to see if any connections can be made with them and our mystery man. Four have shown to be promising. The first Rufinus worth mentioning was a little-known monk in Jerome's monastery in Bethlehem. At the end of the fourth century, Jerome sent several presbyters to the West from Bethlehem on business for a variety of private reasons. One of these, Rufinus, was dispatched to aid a certain Claudius, whose life may

---

1. For example: Augustine, *Nupt.* 2.5.16; *C. du. ep. Pelag.* 4.8.21. See also: Antin, "Rufin et Pélage," 793; Rees, "Pelagius," 9.
2. Miller, "Introduction," 3.

have been in danger.[3] In a letter (81) Jerome sent to Rufinus of Aquileia in early 399,[4] we have a reference to this Rufinus when Jerome said that he sent him "on business to Milan by way of Rome, and have requested him to communicate to you [Rufinus of Aquileia] my feelings and respects."[5] This letter was Jerome's attempt at calming the waters between him and Rufinus of Aquileia, but it was suppressed by Pammachius and prevented their reconciliation. This Pammachius—who died in 410 and was the first Roman senator known to have worn the dress of a *monachus*—housed "the holy priest" Rufinus while he was in Rome, according to Caelestius.[6] As Jerome and Pammachius were friends, it is reasonable that the Rufinus from Bethlehem would have lodged with Pammachius when he went to Rome on Jerome's business.

This information alone does not offer any definitive evidence that the Bethlehem Rufinus is the same as the "holy priest" Rufinus known to Caelestius. Mercator, however, supplies additional information that mentions a Rufinus as instrumental in the development of Pelagian thought. Mercator, who was actively writing against the Pelagians around 430,[7] was unknown in the medieval period. It wasn't until a manuscript (*Codex Palatinus Latinus 234*) dated from the ninth century (probably from the Lorsch Abbey) was discovered in the seventeenth century, and editions of his works were published in 1673 by Jean Garnier and Étienne Baluze in 1684 that he came to light.[8] In one of his works found in that manuscript, Mercator mentions a man named Rufinus who had brought Pelagianism from the East and passed on his treachery through Pelagius: "this most stupid but none the less hostile [Pelagian] criticism of the orthodox faith was first introduced into Rome in the papacy of Anastasius (399–401) of sacred memory by a certain Rufinus, at one time of the nation of Syria (*quondam natione Syrus*), who, not daring to promote it on his own, was clever enough to hoodwink (*decipere*) a British monk named Pelagius into doing so, having given him a thorough grounding in the aforesaid holy and foolish doctrine."[9] This quotation from Mercator is noteworthy for two reasons. First, it mentions that this Rufinus had come to Rome between 399 and 401, and we saw earlier that Jerome sent his monk to Rome in 399. This means that both men were in Rome at the same time. Second, Mercator's Rufinus was *quondam natione Syrus*, while Jerome's Rufinus was from Bethlehem. Geographically, these seem

---

3. Jerome, *Apol.* 3.24.

4. Kelly, *Jerome*, 239.

5. Jerome, *Epist.* 81.2; Miller, "Introduction," 5–6; TeSelle, "Rufinus the Syrian," 62–65; Rees, "Introduction," 22.

6. Dunphy, "Rufinus the Syrian," 96–97.

7. Miller, "Introduction," 4; Dunphy, "Rufinus the Syrian," 84.

8. Dunphy, "Rufinus the Syrian," 109.

9. Marius Mercator, *Sub.* pref.2. Translated in Rees, "Pelagius," 9. I have slightly modified Ree's translation from "by a certain Rufinus, a Syrian by race" (*quidam natione Syrus*) to "at one time of the nation of Syria" (*quondam natione Syrus*). Rees is persuaded by the scholarly argument that the original word in the manuscript is *quidam*, rather than *quondam*. I am persuaded by *quondam*. See Dunphy for a description of this scholarly debate. Dunphy, "Rufinus the Syrian," 106–7.

not to be the same location, but Sr. Mary William Miller has noted that "from the time of its establishment, the Seleucid Empire in Asia, which included Syria, Palestine, and Mesopotamia, was commonly referred to simply as Syria, since that country was its center."[10] It is possible, then, that in describing Rufinus *quondam natione Syrus*, Mercator really meant Bethlehem. Based on these two pieces of information from Mercator, identification seems possible that the Rufinus of Bethlehem and the Rufinus *quondam natione Syrus* are the same person.

A third Rufinus who must be considered in our attempt to determine the identity of Caelestius's "holy priest" was the author of a text titled the *Liber de fide*. The only surviving manuscript of this text was copied (possibly in northern Italy) around 600. It was first printed by Jacques Sirmond in 1650.[11] A second manuscript had existed into the seventeenth century, but can no longer be found.[12] It is a text that articulates orthodox teaching, as it sees it, and its primarily opponent is Origenism,[13] although it also refutes Arianism, Eunomianism,[14] Apollinarianism,[15] Helvidius,[16] Jovinian,[17] and Novatianism.[18] This emphasis on refuting Origen supports the possibility that it was written by a monk in Jerome's monastery, as Jerome spent a lot of energy trying to show that he was not an Origenist (despite his obvious debt to the Alexandrian).[19] We could expect any monk living in his monastery would have the same theological bent.

Scholars disagree when the *Liber* was originally written. Miller, following the lead of Berthold Altaner,[20] believes that it was written sometime between 413 and 428. It must have been composed after Augustine's *De peccatorum meritis et remissione et de baptismo parvulorum*, which was written sometime between the summer of 411 and early 412,[21] because, if it had been composed before, Augustine surely would have refuted it, as he never would have let its skewed version of Christianity go unchallenged.[22] Further, they believe that the text is a mature exposition of

10. Miller, "Introduction," 6.
11. Dunphy, "Rufinus the Syrian," 87.
12. Dunphy, "Rufinus the Syrian," 84–85.
13. Rufinus the Presbyter, *Rufini Presbyteri*, 16–22, 27, 36, 51.
14. Rufinus the Presbyter, *Lib. fid.* 3–15, 52–61.
15. Rufinus the Presbyter, *Lib. fid.* 42.
16. Rufinus the Presbyter, *Lib. fid.* 42.
17. Rufinus the Presbyter, *Lib. fid.* 42.
18. Rufinus the Presbyter, *Lib. fid.* 50; Miller, "Introduction," 12–14.
19. Vessey, "Jerome's Origen," 135–45.
20. Altaner, "Der Liber," 448. Miller notes in passing that Sirmond believed that the text was written before 410, while Garnier believed that it was written in Greek before 381. He also believes that it was translated in Rome into Latin before 412. Miller, "Introduction," 8.
21. Dunphy argues for the summer, while Teske suggests that they were written as late as early 412. Dunphy, "A Lost Year," 425; Teske, "Introduction," *WSA*, 20.
22. Altaner and Miller believe that *De peccatorum meritis et remissione et de baptismo parvulorum* was written in 412. Teske says that it was begun shortly after the condemnation of Caelestius at Carthage. The dating of that council was discussed earlier in this chapter. Miller, "Introduction," 8; Teske,

Pelagian thought, and could not have been written earlier when Pelagian thought was still developing. As we shall discuss later, the *Liber* rejects the idea that babies who die without baptism will be consigned to hell.[23] Altaner and Miller conclude that the *Liber* must be a response to Augustine's *De peccatorum meritis et remissione et de baptismo parvulorum*, because this treatise was the first in the history of Christianity make the claim that infants who die and are not baptized go to hell.[24] The latest date that the text could be written is 428 because, while the text demonstrates knowledge of many of the theological controversies of the day, it does not mention Nestorianism, which began in 428 and was condemned at the Council of Ephesus of 431.[25]

Bonner rejects this assessment and offers a different date of composition. Following the lead of François Refoulé,[26] he argues that the *Liber* must have been written earlier than 412, as he concludes that Augustine's *De peccatorum meritis et remissione et de baptismo parvulorum* was a refutation of it, not the other way around. Bonner's first argument is that the *Liber* does not offer a substantive refutation of Augustine's first anti-Pelagian work, and, in fact, it contains very little of what may be considered Pelagian theology. Most of the content of the text addressed a number of heresies that were prominent all over the Mediterranean that had nothing to do with Augustinian anthropology. When it did refute a nameless author—who may (or may not) have been Augustine[27]—the text was, as Bonner stated, "remarkably slow coming to the point,"[28] as this nameless author was only mentioned in passing in the second half of the text.[29] Rather than refuting the *De peccatorum meritis et remissione et de baptismo parvulorum*, Bonner claims that the text's main object of attack was Origen.[30] Bonner posits that the *Liber* was probably written between 399 and 412, and, more specifically, probably around the year 400. Identifying this Rufinus with the Rufinus from Jerome's monastery, Bonner says that it likely was written during the pontificate of Anastasius. When Rufinus arrived in Rome from Bethlehem, he may have felt free to attack Origen because of Anastasius's attitude against Origen.[31] Furthermore, Rufinus of Aquileia, in 400, had written an *Apologia* to Anastasius saying that he knew there

---

vol. 1 "Introduction," 20.

23. Rufinus the Presbyter, *Lib. fid.* 41.
24. Augustine, *Pecc. merit.* 1.28.55.
25. Miller, "Introduction," 8–10.
26. Refoulé, "Datation du Premier," 41–49.
27. Rufinus the Presbyter, *Lib. fid.* 41.
28. Bonner, "Rufinus of Syria," 37.

29. Although Bonner argues that the *Liber* cannot be seen as a reaction against Augustine's *De peccatorum meritis et remissione et de baptismo parvulorum*, he does put forward the possibility that the author of the *Liber* had read Augustine's *De Libero Arbitrio* and his *Ad Simplicianum*. Bonner, "Rufinus of Syria," 43.

30. Bonner, "Rufinus of Syria," 37–38.
31. Bonner, "Rufinus of Syria," 38.

was a debate swirling in Rome about the nature of the soul.[32] The *Liber* had addressed this issue as well, and had condemned Origenist traducianism.[33] Bonner does not insist that the Aquileian's *Apologia* contains a direct reference to the *Liber*. He does say, however, that the *Apologia*, at the very least, points to a conversation in Rome raging at the beginning of the fifth century over a topic that was obviously of concern to the author of the *Liber*.[34]

The first theory, then, of the identity of the "holy priest" Rufinus mentioned by Caelestius, which has become the prevailing theory, claims that the Rufinus from Jerome's monastery in Bethlehem, the Rufinus *quondam natione Syrus* as described by Mercator, the author of the *Liber*, and the "holy priest" Rufinus are all the same person. To summarize this theory: Rufinus was a monk who lived in Jerome's monastery in Bethlehem who had been sent by Jerome to Rome in 399, and then on to Milan, to assist a man by the name of Claudius. When he arrived in Rome during the pontificate of Anastasius, as Mercator tells us, he clandestinely began to spread his teaching to Pelagius. He also had written a *Liber* that was a "source-book"[35] that became important for the development of Caelestius's thought.

Dunphy rejects this theory of the identity of the "holy priest" Rufinus, and presents a second one of his own. He offers the possibility that the "holy priest" Rufinus might have been Rufinus of Aquileia. To review Dunphy's argument in full would be an extensive undertaking, and would lead us on an unnecessary tangent; only the highlights will be offered here. Dunphy says very little about Jerome's Bethlehem Rufinus, but focuses his attention on Mercator's Rufinus *quondam natione Syrus*, and the author of the *Liber*. He believes that Mercator's Rufinus never existed, and the invention of his existence was caused by a corrupted sentence in the lone manuscript from Mercator, which now has fooled scholars for centuries. Surveying Mercator's text, Dunphy has paid close attention to Mercator's usage of the word *quondam*, which we could translate as "formerly," "once," or "at one time."[36] Throughout, Mercator uses the word *quondam* to refer to someone's office or status,[37] and offers several examples to support his point. He shows how Mercator described Nestorius (who was still alive when Mercator was writing) as *quondam* the patriarch of Constantinople, and Theodore (who was already dead) as *quondam* the bishop of Mopsuestia. Mercator also described the status of certain people with the word *quondam*. He described Pelagius as a *monachus*, and Caelestius as *auditorialis scholasticus*. Dunphy concludes

---

32. Rufinus of Aquileia, *Anast.* 6.
33. Rufinus the Presbyter, *Lib. fid.* 27, 28.
34. Bonner, "Rufinus of Syria," 39.
35. Bonner, "Rufinus of Syria," 47.
36. Dunphy notes that there is a scholarly dispute on whether or not *quondam* is the word Mercator originally used, or if it was corrupted to *quidam*. He believes that *quidam* is a legitimate possibility, but retains *quondam*. Dunphy, "Rufinus the Syrian," 106–7.
37. Dunphy, "Rufinus the Syrian," 108.

that it would be inconsistent of Mercator if he were to have used the word *quondam* to describe Rufinus as coming from *natione Syrus*, because *natione Syrus* is a place of origin, not a description of his status.[38] This inconsistency points to the likelihood that *natione Syrus* is actually a transmission error in the manuscript, and something other than *natione Syrus* should follow *quondam*. What we should expect to follow after Rufinus's *quondam* is a modifier describing him, not his place of origin. But, what exactly? Dunphy offers the possibility that what followed *quondam* in the original text was a description of Rufinus of Aquileia as a *monachus*, just as Pelagius had been described as such. While Rufinus of Aquileia is most often labeled a *presbyter*, we also saw that he had spent time as a *monachus* in Palestine. Jerome, who was the source for Mercator's knowledge of Pelagianism being brought to Italy,[39] had described Rufinus as a *monachus* several times. In the only extant letter (3) from Jerome to Rufinus before their notorious split, Jerome addressed his letter to Rufinus *monachus*.[40] He also described Rufinus—as well as his friend Bonosus, and a correspondent Florentius—as *monachi* in his expansion of Eusbeius's *Chronicon*.[41] Even Erasmus of Rotterdam, over a thousand years later, would describe Rufinus as a *monachus*.[42]

How does Dunphy come to the conclusion that it was *monachus*, not *natione Syrus*, that followed *quondam* in Mercator's original text? Admitting that this is only a speculation as there is no way to prove his hypothesis, Dunphy says that in the manuscript

> an end-line division of *mo/nachus* or *monac/hus*, and the frequent interchange of c/t [a common error made by medieval copyists[43]] (also in *Cod. Pal.*!), would readily lend to confusion on the part of the scribe. As a result *quo(n)da(m)mo* was "corrected" [by a copyist] to *quondam*, *nac/nat* was expanded to *natione*, and the remaining enigmatic *hus* (a cursive 'h' being read as 'Syr'?) has become *Syrus* to identify *Rufinus quondam* with the region from which, we have just been informed by Mercator in the same text, the heresy originated [as Mercator learned from Jerome[44]].[45]

Immediately after putting forward this theory, Dunphy admits that this might "appear all too far-fetched to merit consideration, and for its naiveté it will be laughed out of court."[46] Indeed, it is always easy to offer an unusual hypothesis when it is impossible to be either proven right or wrong by the textual evidence. Dunphy, however, has

38. Dunphy, "Rufinus the Syrian," 107–8.
39. Dunphy, "Rufinus the Syrian," 105; Dunphy, "Marius Mercator," 283.
40. Jerome, *Epist.* 3; Dunphy, "Rufinus the Syrian," 107–8.
41. Dunphy, "Rufinus the Syrian," 114. See also: Jerome, *Apol.* 3.12.
42. Dunphy, "Rufinus the Syrian," 115.
43. Dunphy, "Rufinus the Syrian," 110–13.
44. Dunphy, "Rufinus the Syrian," 105.
45. Dunphy, "Rufinus the Syrian," 115.
46. Dunphy, "Rufinus the Syrian," 115.

revealed a plethora of other errors in the extant manuscript.[47] It is reasonable, at the very least, to take his position seriously.

Turning to the *Liber de fide*, Dunphy only vaguely offers the beginning of the fifth century as the date for its composition.[48] Refuting scholarly consensus that the *Liber* was written by one individual, he speculates that it was a "composite work" and, that it was a rough draft that was never finished, nor intended to be published in its current state.[49] It is possible that Rufinus of Aquileia—though not its author—had translated the *Liber* from Greek into Latin, which is how the text came to have the colophon "*exp(licit) Rufini pr(es)b(yter)i prouinciae palestinae / liber de fide translatus de graeco / in latinum sermonem. Amen.*"[50] This speculation is certainly reasonable in light of the Aquileian's prodigious translation output, many of which were read by the Pelagians.[51] These translations, though not articulating a fully Pelagian anthropology, presented a more optimistic vision of the human person than did Augustine, and may have set the foundation for the fully Pelagian worldview as would develop in the second and third decades of the fifth century.[52]

It is impossible to ascertain Rufinus of Aquileia's own anthropology, as he was less of a theologian than a translator. He never explicitly wrote that he rejected the idea of the transmission of sin for which Caelestius was condemned in Carthage, but we must keep in mind that Caelestius merely said that he heard (*audire*) the "holy priest" Rufinus say that he rejected the idea of the transmission of sin, not that he had read a text written by him.[53] Based on what little evidence we have, Dunphy concludes that it is probable that Rufinus would have rejected the idea of the transmission of sin, although he, like all of the Pelagians, accepted the church's practice of infant baptism.[54]

---

47. Dunphy, "Rufinus the Syrian," 105–18.

48. Dunphy, "Ps-Rufinus," 221.

49. Dunphy, "Rufinus the Syrian," 157.

50. Dunphy, "Rufinus the Syrian," 85, 153. Later in 2012, Dunphy says that the *Liber* should remain among the *Pseudo-Rufiniana* until its real author can be established. Dunphy, "The Pelagians," 99.

51. Dunphy, "Rufinus the Syrian," 119. Some of his translations that they may have read include: Origen's *Peri archon*, the *Sententiae Sextiae*, Origen's Homilies on Psalms 36–38, a selection of sermons from Gregory of Nazianzus to Apronianus, homilies of Basil of Caesarea for Apronianus, an abridged version of Origen's commentary on Romans, and Basil's *Regula*. Dunphy, "Rufinus the Syrian," 120–31.

52. Dunphy, "Rufinus the Syrian," 125, 131.

53. Augustine, *Grat. Chr.* 2.3.3; Dunphy, "Rufinus the Syrian," 132.

54. Dunphy, "Rufinus the Syrian," 134, 142.

Chapter 5

Augustine: The Doctor of Grace

The Life of Augustine

THE PRECEDING DESCRIPTIONS ABOUT the lives and events of the authors already discussed are necessarily deficient due to a paucity of sources. Our investigation of Augustine of Hippo (November 13, 354–August 28, 430),[1] however, will not suffer from this problem, because the number of texts from him that have survived surpass those of any other author from Antiquity.[2] In fact, the opposite problem of sifting through the enormous library of Augustine's treatises, letters, and sermons to come to a complete biography of the man is overwhelming.[3] Only the briefest portrait of his life, therefore, will be sketched here, as it would be impossible to distill a comprehensive narrative into a few pages.[4]

Augustine was born in the small town of Thagaste (modern Souk Ahras, Algeria) in the Roman province of Numidia, North Africa. We know very little about his father, Patricius. Possidius, Augustine's younger contemporary and hagiographer, tells us that Patricius was a member of the local town council, and so was partly responsible for municipal governance.[5] To be on the council, Patricius must have been a man of some means, though he certainly was not wealthy. In his *Confessiones*, Augustine said that his father had "very modest resources,"[6] but he preached a sermon in 426 in which he claimed to be "a poor man, born of poor parents."[7] Whatever the exact nature of

---

1. Unless noted otherwise, the dates used here for Augustine's life come from Markus, "Life, Culture," 500–1.

2. Chadwick, *Augustine*, 1.

3. Possidius, *V. Aug.* 28.

4. There are many secondary sources detailing Augustine's life: Bonner, *St. Augustine*; Brown, *Augustine of Hippo*; Chadwick, *Augustine*; Lancel, *Saint Augustine*; O'Donnell, *Augustine*; Chadwick, *Augustine*; Levering, *Theology of Augustine*; Hollingworth, *Saint Augustine of Hippo*; Fox, *Augustine*.

5. Possidius, *V. Aug.* 1.

6. Augustine, *Conf.* 2.3.5.

7. Augustine, *Serm.* 356.13.

his father's wealth, he had enough money for nurses,[8] maidservants,[9] and property;[10] however, he needed patronage from Romanianus, one of the richest men in town (and perhaps a relative),[11] to give Augustine a quality education.[12] Patricius was kind, but ran a hot temper. He was deeply devoted to his wife, Monica, but was unfaithful at the same time.[13] Ambivalent to the Christian faith for most of his adult life,[14] he became a catechumen towards the end of his life,[15] and was baptized shortly before his death when Augustine was sixteen.[16]

We know much more about Monica than we do Patricius, as she is one of the few women from Antiquity described in any detail.[17] Born in 331/332,[18] the root of her name, "Monna," may indicate that her distant ancestors had worshipped a local God, but her immediate ancestors certainly were Christian.[19] It is possible that her family, like most Christians in Africa at the time,[20] was Donatist, although there is no definitive evidence for this.[21] In the late 340s when Monica was a teenager, Christians in Thagaste changed their allegiance from Donatism to Catholicism when the Emperor Constantius sent a legate named Macarius to North Africa, who then proceeded to perseucte the Donatists.[22] Augustine, however, may have indicated in his *Confessiones* that she was raised in a Catholic family when he said that Monica "was trained 'in your fear' (Ps 5:8) by the discipline of your Christ, by the government of your only Son in a believing household through a good member of your Church" (*in domo fideli, bono membro ecclesiae tuae*).[23] It is hard to imagine Augustine describing Monica's family as good members of God's church if they were Donatists.

Monica probably married Patricius in her later teenage years, and gave birth to Augustine, another son named Navigius, and a daughter whose name we never learn. Navigius may have been the eldest son, because Augustine was not born until Monica

8. Augustine, *Conf.* 1.6.7.
9. Augustine, *Conf.* 9.9.20.
10. Possidius, *V. Aug.* 3.
11. Brown, *Augustine of Hippo*, 9.
12. Augustine, *Conf.* 2.3.5.
13. Augustine, *Conf.* 9.9.19.
14. Augustine, *Conf.* 1.11.17.
15. Augustine, *Conf.* 2.3.6.
16. Augustine, *Conf.* 3.4.7, 9.9.22.
17. It is probable that her name was originally spelled Monnica, because most of the earliest manuscripts of *Confessiones* spell it this way. Clark, *Monica*, 8.
18. Fox, *Augustine*, 43.
19. Brown, *Augustine of Hippo*, 21; Lancel, *Saint Augustine*, 5; Clark, *Monica*, 126–27.
20. Possidius, *V. Aug.* 7.
21. O'Donnell, *Augustine*, 56, 212; Clark, *Monica*, 118, 138; Fox, *Augustine*, 43; Willis, *Saint Augustine*, 1–25.
22. O'Donnell, *Augustine*, 211–12.
23. Augustine, *Conf.* 9.8.17.

was twenty-three years old leaving the possibility for Navigius to have been born in the years between her marriage and when Augustine was born.[24] He had several daughters who later would join the convent Augustine had started in Hippo.[25] Monica's daughter (who died around 423)[26] became a widow, and later became the superior of the same convent as Augustine's nieces.[27] Augustine also had one nephew, Patricius,[28] but it is unclear if Patricius was the son of Navigius or Augustine's sister.[29]

A warped description of Augustine that is often disseminated is that he only had come to Christianity in his early thirties after a profound existential crisis. But, this is misleading, as Monica had steeped him in it from the beginning, and he came to believe in Christ from an early age.[30] "This name of my Saviour your Son," he later recollected "my infant heart had piously drunk in with my mother's milk, and at a deep level I retained the memory."[31] As a small child, he had been signed with the cross, and had been exorcised with salt placed on his tongue, but he was not baptized at the time. When he came close to dying after spiking a fever and experiencing a tremendous weight on his chest, he begged to be baptized. Monica, as mentioned in an earlier chapter, was terrified that she might lose her son to death and damnation, and arranged for him to receive the sacrament, but he quickly recuperated, and the baptism was postponed.[32]

From an early age, Augustine prayed to God that he might be spared from the corporal punishments inflicted by the teachers at school for his laziness.[33] Like most children, he hated being forced to learn, and preferred games to the classroom.[34] These games stoked a competitive fire in him, distracted his intellectual progress, and caused him to rebel, which only brought on the cane.[35] He abhorred learning Greek when violence rained down on him as he struggled to learn the vocabulary, and he claims that he never learned it.[36] Was he overexaggerating his ignorance, or was his

24. Augustine, *Conf.* 9.11.28; Clark, *Monica*, 9. Henry Chadwick suggests that since Augustine's father became inebriated after he noticed Augustine's stirrings of adolescence in the bathhouse that this points to Patricius's excitement at the possibility of having his first grandchild, which means that Augustine was older than Navigius. Augustine, *Conf.* 27 n. 8.

25. Possidius, *V. Aug.* 26.

26. Bonner, *St. Augustine*, 41.

27. Possidius, *V. Aug.* 26; Augustine, *Epist.* 211.4.

28. Augustine, *Serm.* 356.3.

29. Bonner, for example, believes that Patricius was the son of Augustine's sister, while Clark believes that Patricius was the son of Navigius: Bonner, *St. Augustine*, 41; Clark, *Monica*, 10.

30. Augustine, *Conf.* 1.11.17.

31. Augustine, *Conf.* 3.4.8.

32. Augustine, *Conf.* 1.11.17.

33. Augustine, *Conf.* 1.9.14.

34. Augustine, *Conf.* 1.11.18.

35. Augustine, *Conf.* 1.9.15–10.16.

36. Augustine, *Conf.* 1.14.23.

Greek as bad as he insisted? Scholars have endlessly debated Augustine's facility with the language as an adult. A variety of answers have been given: Brown suggests that he was "virtually ignorant,"[37] of Greek, and O'Donnell insists that his knowledge of it was "pathetic."[38] Although he certainly never mastered it, Serge Lancel is probably correct that he came to have a working comprehension of it by the end of his life.[39] While he loathed Greek, Augustine came to love studying Latin, and, as it was his first language, he did not struggle to learn it with the cloud of punishment looming over his adolescent head.[40] During his secondary education, in particular, he came to adore Virgil's *Aeneid*—weeping over Dido's love for Aeneas and her death as if he had personally known them both.[41]

Another popular misunderstanding of Augustine is that he was a womanizer as a young man. This misconception is understandable, as his provocative prose lends itself to this conclusion. He said of his early adolescent years that, after returning from a nearby town called Madauros because his father had run out of money to send him to school there, "clouds of muddy carnal concupiscence filled the air. The bubbling impulses of puberty befogged and obscured my heart so that it could not see the difference between love's serenity and lust's darkness. Confusion of the two things boiled within me. It seized hold of my youthful weakness sweeping me through the precipitous rocks of desire to submerge me in a whirlpool of vice."[42] He continued that "sensual folly assumed domination over me, and I gave myself totally to it in acts allowed by shameful humanity but under your [God's] laws illicit."[43] But, Augustine's pubescent indiscretions were not as scandalous as some would like to think. Burning to experience the same pleasures as his friends, he was more talk than action:

> I was ashamed not to be equally guilty of shameful behavior when I heard them [his friends] boasting of their sexual exploits. Their pride was the more aggressive, the more debauched their acts were; they derived pleasure not merely from the lust of the act but also from the admiration it evoked. What is more worthy of censure than vice? Yet I went deeper into vice to avoid being despised, and when there was no act by admitting to which I could rival my depraved companions, I used to pretend I had done things I had not done at all, so that my innocence should not lead my companions to scorn my lack of courage, and lest my chastity be taken as a mark of inferiority.[44]

37. Brown, *Augustine of Hippo*, 24.
38. O'Donnell, *Augustine*, 126.
39. Lancel, *Saint Augustine*, 16.
40. Augustine, *Conf.* 1.13.20, 1.14.23.
41. Augustine, *Conf.* 1.13.21–14.23.
42. Augustine, *Conf.* 2.2.2.
43. Augustine, *Conf.* 2.3.5.
44. Augustine, *Conf.* 2.3.7.

Augustine, chaste at the age of sixteen, was more of a charlatan than a cyprian.[45]

During his year back in Thagaste, Augustine's restlessness got the better of him. He, and a group of friends, stole some pears late one night, though they did not need them as they had access to better pears than those they stole. The superficial reason for the theft was to amuse themselves by throwing them at pigs. But, Augustine, later as a bishop reflecting on the deeper meaning of the event, offers a multilayered insight that details not only his own personal motives, but offers a deeper theological assessment of the human condition. First, the excitement of the illicitness thrilled him. Like any adrenaline junkie pushing the boundaries of the possible, Augustine sought the exhilaration in doing what he knew was forbidden. Second, the sheer wickedness of the act delighted him, not the pears themselves. "It was foul, and I loved it," he said. "I loved the self-destruction, I loved my fall, not for the object for which I had fallen but my fall itself."[46] Third, the pleasure he found was rooted in the intimacy with his group of friends. In fact, he would never have done it if it weren't for them. This is not to say that they pressured him into it. If anything, he was most likely the instigator of the group. But, the communion of the shared indiscretion over food was itself a perverse pleasure.[47]

At the age of eighteen, Augustine went to Carthage to further his education. Diligent and quiet, he was the best student in his school. His oratorical training was intended to lead him to become a lawyer in the courts where, as he sharply put it, "one's reputation is high in proportion to one's success of deceiving people."[48] But, this plan quickly was derailed when Augustine read Cicero's *Hortentius*, a text no longer extant *in toto*. This text changed Augustine's life (as good books often can do to young students) in a way that he never expected by challenging him to reevaluate his fundamental assumptions, and by sparking a desire for wisdom in him, rather than empty sophistry. His enthusiasm for Cicero, however, was dampened because he could not find any reference to Christ in him at all. But, Cicero encouraged him to investigate wisdom in different schools of thought, leading him to read the Bible, which he had never done before. Augustine's intellectual sophistication recoiled from its crude prose, and he contemptuously dismissed it as "unworthy in comparison with the dignity of Cicero."[49]

This pursuit of wisdom led him to become a Manichaean *auditor* for nine years.[50] Manichaeism, as O'Donnell cheekily described it, was a "new-age religion in its time,

---

45. Augustine, *Conf.* 2.3.8.
46. Augustine, *Conf.* 2.4.9.
47. Augustine, *Conf.* 2.4.9–10.18.
48. Augustine, *Epist.* 93.51; *Conf.* 3.3.6.
49. Augustine, *Conf.* 3.5.9.
50. Augustine, *Conf.* 5.6.10.

fashionable, exotic, with an up-to-date brand of humbug."[51] Mani (216–276/277),[52] the founder of the religion, was born in Mesopotamia. He received two revelations of his twin—one at twelve years old, and the other at twenty-four years old. Most importantly, he came to understand that his spirit had existed before he was born; his body was created by his parents, but the preexistent twin came to inhabit the body.[53] He became a peripatetic, wandering through such places as the Indian subcontinent and Persia to spread his teaching. He considered himself to be an apostle of Jesus Christ, the last apostle sent to correct distortions of the message of previous apostles, which had been corrupted by "Judaizers."[54] The Manichaeans did not see themselves as offering an alternative to Christianity, but that they were the "true Christians."[55] After being imprisoned by the Shah of Persia, he died at the age of sixty.[56]

Mani's dualist metaphysical system is far too complicated to reproduce here, and doing so would be an unnecessary tangent. It is enough to know for our purposes that there are two ultimate natures in the universe, the good "Father of Greatness," and the evil "King of Darkness." Jealous of the Father of Greatness, the King of Darkness planned encroachments on his realm of light, but the Father of Greatness responded by emanating the Mother of Life who brought forth the primal human to confront the King. After a long fight, the evil nature defeated the primal human, and obtained his light. But, some of the forces of evil were also captured by the forces of good. Here, we see the beginning of the mixture of goodness (immateriality) and evil (materiality). In short, this dualist mixture of good immateriality and evil materiality is found in all human beings, who are a composite of both the good and evil natures. Evil, then, is baked into our very nature.[57] It was this Manichaean answer to the perennial problem of evil—which haunted Augustine his entire life—that drew him to the religion.

The Manichaeans were divided into two classes or castes: the "Elect" (*electi*), and the "Hearers" (*auditores*). The *electi* practiced a radical form of asceticism, and were required to follow five commandments: (1) the *electi* must immerse themselves entirely in the truth, which means that they may not tell a lie of any kind; (2) they must practice nonviolence. This nonviolence did not rest with abstaining from military service or practicing pacifism, but extended to refraining from killing plants; (3) they were required to refrain from physical pleasure. Of course, this included sexual chastity, but it also included experiences like taking a bath; (4) the *electi* followed strict dietary restrictions, including abstention from fermented beverages, dairy, meat, and certain kinds of vegetables. They only ate fruits and vegetables, such as melons and

---

51. O'Donnell, *Augustine*, 48.
52. Gardner and Lieu, *Manichaean Texts*, 3, 8.
53. Fox, *Augustine*, 93.
54. Gardner and Lieu, *Manichaean Texts*, 10–19.
55. BeDuhn, *Manichaean Body*, 26.
56. Fox, *Augustine*, 91.
57. Baker-Brian, *Manichaeism*, 96–133.

cucumbers, that they considered to have a high concentration of light. Meat, with its density, was deemed laden with darkness, and would pollute and corrupt.[58] They also endured difficult fasts throughout the year; (5) finally, they were required to live lives of poverty, such as abandoning all private possessions.[59]

The *auditores* were not expected to live such strict lives, but they had to follow five commandments of their own: (1) they were required to adhere to ten fundamental articles (reject idolatry, practice "purity of the mouth," abstain from meat and alcohol, right speech, remain faithful to their husband or wife, assist anyone in need and avoid greed, avoid lapsed Manichaeans, not to cause injury, not to steal or commit fraud, and avoid magic); (2) they must pray four times each day. During daily prayers, they must face the sun, and must face the moon during nighttime prayers. Prior to the prayers, they must perform ritualized ablutions before entering sacred space; (3) they must give one tenth of what they own in alms; (4) they must fast each week on Sundays, including abstention from sexual contact, food, and physical labor; (5) the following day, they must confess their sins to a member of the *electi*.[60] The *auditores* were not required to be chaste, but they were not allowed to procreate, as this act would perpetuate the cycle of bringing forth matter into the world. They could eat meat, but the meat must come from a butcher.[61]

Monica sobbed when her son took up with the Manichaeans. Although not physically deceased, he was spiritually dead in her eyes. She dreamt that God had told her not to exclude him from her home, as she had done for a time when he had returned from Carthage. In the dream, she was standing on a wooden rule when an attractive young man inquired why she was despondent. She responded that she feared for her son's salvation, but he said to her that she should not fear. Standing on the rule with her, the young man pointed out, was her son. Later, when Monica recounted this dream to Augustine, he was unimpressed. He tried to warp the meaning of the dream by saying that it was communicating to her to accept his new life, but she shot back that "the word spoken to me was not 'where he is, there will you be also,' but 'where you are, there will he be also.'"[62] Monica also conveyed her dismay to an educated bishop—who had been a Manichaean as a child, and had read almost all of their texts—and implored him to speak with Augustine to show him their errors. The bishop refused to do so, because, he said, Augustine was not ready to listen to anyone else as he was puffed-up with the pride of his own intellect. Left alone, he said, Augustine would come to see their flaws on his own.[63]

58. Gardner and Lieu, *Manichaean Texts from the Roman Empire*, 22.
59. Tardieu, *Manichaeism*, 63–67.
60. Tardieu, *Manichaeism*, 67–71.
61. Fox, *Augustine*, 121.
62. Augustine, *Conf.* 3.11.20.
63. Augustine, *Conf.* 3.11.20.

During this time, Augustine entered a relationship with a woman (*in illis annis unam habebam*).[64] It is hard to define their relationship, because there is no corresponding category in the twenty-first century for her, but she has been described variously as his "concubine,"[65] "companion,"[66] "girl-friend,"[67] "partner,"[68] and even his "wife,"[69] even though they were never legally married.[70] We know nothing about this woman. Even her name is a mystery. She probably was of a lower social standing than he, and may have been a Christian.[71] He deeply loved her, and was devastated when, years later, she was sent away when Monica arranged for a formal marriage for her son that would help advance his career: "my heart," he lamented "which was deeply attached was cut and wounded, and left a trail of blood."[72] They had a son, Adeodatus (gift from God), whom Augustine adored, and who was portrayed as a young man of superior intellectual gifts,[73] but who died of unknown causes sometime between the ages of sixteen and nineteen.[74]

Augustine returned to Thagaste from Carthage to teach. He became friends with an unnamed young man of the same age whom he had known when they were both boys, and with whom he had played games during their schooling. They had many interests in common, and must have engaged in many conversations about religion, because Augustine convinced him to become a Manichaean, which was not particularly difficult as the young man was not dedicated to his Catholic tradition. Augustine's friend—one of the most intimate relationships of his life—contracted a fever and fell unconscious a year into their friendship. At death's door and Augustine at his side, his family had him baptized, but his health improved. Assuming his friend would be as dismissive of the baptism as he was, Augustine joked about this Christian foolishness. His friend, however, had been transformed by the experience, and informed Augustine that, if their friendship were to continue, he must curb his attitude. Baffled, Augustine resolved to remain quiet until his friend fully recuperated, and then he would resume his degradations. Several days later, without Augustine by his side, his health relapsed, and he died. Augustine was destroyed:

---

64. Augustine, *Conf.* 4.2.2.
65. Brown, *Augustine of Hippo*, 27; Fox, *Augustine*, 76.
66. Lancel, *Saint Augustine*, 27.
67. Chadwick, *Augustine*, 11.
68. Fox, *Augustine*, 76.
69. O'Donnell, *Augustine*, 39.
70. Sessa, *Daily Life*, 90–95.
71. Years later when Augustine sends her away, she takes a vow never to be with another man. Augustine, *Conf.* 6.15.25.
72. Augustine, *Conf.* 6.15.25.
73. Augustine, *Conf.* 9.6.14.
74. Brown, *Augustine of Hippo*, 51; O'Donnell, *Augustine*, 24.

"Grief darkened my heart" (Lam 5:17). Everything on which I set my gaze was death. My home town became a torture to me; my father's house a strange world of unhappiness; all that I had shared with him was without him transformed into a cruel torment. My eyes looked for him everywhere, and he was not there . . . I found myself heavily weighed down by a sense of being tired of living and scared of dying. I suppose that the more I loved him, the more hatred and fear I felt for the death which had taken him from me, as if it were my most ferocious enemy.[75]

Haunted, Augustine escaped back to Carthage,[76] because "my soul," he said, "could not be without him."[77] Even twenty years later, Augustine's pain was still so raw that he could not bear to write his friend's name.[78]

After his arrival in Carthage, Augustine reconnected with the Manichaean community there, but doubts quickly began to take shape in his mind. He continued his reading in philosophy, and had turned his attention to the movements of the stars in the heavens. When he compared what he had learned in his studies to the stories of the Manichaeans, Mani's teachings rang hollow.[79] As none of the other Manichaeans there were intellectually capable of answering Augustine's questions, they urged him to wait for Faustus to come to Carthage; he would be able to resolve his queries. A Numidian born in Milevis, Faustus was purported to be an intellectual giant.[80] Arriving in late 382 or early 383, however, Faustus failed to fulfill his billing.[81] Eloquent in speech, he lacked the substance Augustine desired, and was unable to reassure Augustine of the veracity of Mani's truth claims. The luster on the Manichaeans began to fade for Augustine,[82] but he decided to remain with them as there was no better alternative to which he could turn.[83]

This second stint in Carthage did not last long. He heard that the students in Rome were studious and well-disciplined. They entered the classroom in a calm and organized manner, and they did not enter the class of a teacher not their own. This appealed to him, as his own students in Carthage were just the opposite. They were disruptive, vandalic, anarchic, and self-destructive. Monica was dismayed at the prospect of her son going to Rome, and chased him down to the port of Carthage. She begged him to stay, or to allow her to go to Rome with him if he insisted on departing. Lying to his own mother, Augustine told her that he did not want to leave a friend

---

75. Augustine, *Conf.* 4.4.9, 4.6.11.
76. Augustine, *Conf.* 4.6.12.
77. Augustine, *Conf.* 4.4.7.
78. Augustine, *Conf.* 4.4.7–10.15.
79. Augustine, *Conf.* 5.3.3.
80. Lancel, *Saint Augustine*, 54.
81. Fox, *Augustine*, 155.
82. Augustine, *Conf.* 5.7.12.
83. Augustine, *Conf.* 5.7.13.

until that friend had an adequate wind with which to set sail on his own journey. He convinced her to stay that night at a shrine for St. Cyprian, the third century bishop of Carthage. As she prayed and wept there, Augustine slipped away from Africa under the cover of darkness. The next morning, Monica realized his deceit, and crumbled under the weight of her sorrow.[84]

Augustine was greeted at Rome by a crippling illness. He convalesced in a home of a Manichaean *auditor*, and remained connected to the Manichaeans while there, despite his misgivings about their worldview. There were many Manichaeans in Rome at the time, although they were required to live in secret as their religion was outlawed.[85] After he fully recovered from his unspecified illness, Augustine began teaching rhetoric, but found that the students in Rome were even worse than those in Carthage. While they did not commit random acts of violence as had the students in Africa, they would avoid paying tuition to him by transferring *en bloc* to another teacher before it came due. "I cordially detested them," he said, "but not 'with a perfect hatred' (Ps 138:22) . . . Certainly such people are a disgrace and 'commit fornications against you' (Ps 72:27). They love the passing, transient amusements and the filthy lucre which dirties the hand when it is touched. They embrace a world which is fleeing away."[86] When he heard that a teacher of rhetoric was to be appointed by Symmachus, the Prefect of Milan, Augustine used his Manichaean contacts, and took the job when it was offered to him.[87] It was a significant position. He would deliver the official panegyrics of the emperor and the consuls, as Milan had become the primary home of the western emperors since 381.[88] As part of his duties, he gave a panegyric on Valentinian II at the inauguration of a general as a consul in January, 385.[89] Augustine became, as Brown succinctly put it, a "Minister of Propaganda."[90]

Monica joined Augustine in Milan. She had braved a dangerous journey, and had reassured the crew of the ship that they all would make it safely to their destination because God, in a vision, had guaranteed this to her.[91] In Milan, Augustine met Bishop Ambrose, who came to be a channel of wisdom that Faustus had failed to be. There were some similarities between Ambrose and Faustus—both men had good reputations, and both treated Augustine graciously—but were opposites in most respects.[92] Augustine eagerly had anticipated meeting Faustus in Carthage, but had no such similar anticipation

84. Augustine, *Conf.* 5.8.15.
85. Augustine, *Conf.* 5.10.18–19.
86. Augustine, *Conf.* 5.12.22.
87. Augustine, *Conf.* 5.13.23.
88. Fox, *Augustine*, 181.
89. Augustine, *Conf.* 6.6.9; Chadwick, *Augustine*, 17.
90. Brown, *Augustine of Hippo*, 58–59.
91. Augustine, *Conf.* 6.1.1.

92. Faustus had a reputation for being a man trained in the liberal arts, while Ambrose was one of the best and most devout men. Faustus had been generous with Augustine, while Ambrose received Augustine like a father: Augustine, *Conf.* 5.3.3, 5.13.23, 5.6.10, 5.13.23.

of Ambrose;[93] he was only interested in the content of what Faustus had to say, not his rhetoric, but was captured by Ambrose's style while dismissive of his content;[94] Faustus was more engaging, while Ambrose was more educated;[95] after Faustus gave a public discourse (at which Augustine was unable to ask him any questions), Augustine was able to pose his questions to him in private meetings, but after Ambrose gave a public discourse (at which Augustine, again, was unable to ask any questions), Augustine chose not to disturb Ambrose's privacy;[96] Faustus led others down the path of damnation, but Ambrose preached salvation;[97] Augustine and Faustus would read aloud to each other, but Ambrose read alone in silence.[98]

Ambrose's invaluable contribution to Augustine was to help him reorient his understanding of the Bible. Until his encounter with the bishop of Milan, Augustine had retained his earlier belief that the crude Scriptures could never be a font of truth. Ambrose changed all of that. Through Ambrose's preaching, Augustine heard difficult biblical passages interpreted spiritually, not literally. This was nothing short of a revelation. The Old Testament, he now could see, was not an absurdity, and it was entirely defensible.[99] Specifically, he learned that Catholics did not believe that God had a body. He, and other Manichaeans, interpreted the passage from Genesis that humans are created in the image and likeness of God (1:26–27) to mean that God must have a body since humans have bodies. Now, he knew that this was not an assertion of God's physicality. It was difficult for him to conceive of God without a body, and only as a "spiritual substance," but he was relieved to learn that Catholicism was not what he thought it was.[100]

Comforted, he now preferred Catholicism, and became a catechumen, although he was not entirely certain of the church's truth claims.[101] This inability to embrace Catholicism fully—along with the failures of philosophy, love, lust, Manichaeism, astrology, and friendship to bring him to complete happiness—caused an intellectual and existential crisis. He despaired of ever finding that which he sought: "I myself was exceedingly astonished," he said, "as I anxiously reflected how long a time had elapsed since the nineteenth year of my life, when I began to burn with a zeal for wisdom, planning that when I had found it I would abandon all the empty hopes and lying follies of hollow ambitions. And here I was already thirty, and still mucking about in

---

93. Augustine, *Conf.* 5.6.10, 5.13.23.
94. Augustine, *Conf.* 5.3.3, 5.6.11, 5.13.23.
95. Augustine, *Conf.* 5.6.11, 5.13.23.
96. Augustine, *Conf.* 5.6.11, 6.3.3.
97. Augustine, *Conf.* 5.13.23.
98. Augustine, *Conf.* 5.7.13, 6.3.3.
99. Augustine, *Conf.* 5.14.24.
100. Augustine, *Conf.* 5.10.20, 6.3.4.
101. Augustine, *Conf.* 5.14.24, 6.5.7.

the same mire in a state of indecision."[102] It is understandable, then, that, for several years, he found comfort with Skepticism, the only school of thought, he felt, that could bring him a modicum of comfort.[103] Contrary to the popular definition of Skepticism in our own time that is characterized by a radical suspicion of all truth claims, Skepticism, as a philosophical school of thought, recognized the plausibility of the truth claims in all religions or philosophies. For Skepticism, objective truth does exist, but human beings are limited, finite, and flawed creatures who cannot grasp it. As different philosophies and religions often contradict each other, how is truth to be known? Such confusion can lead to overwhelming hopelessness. What is one to do? Skeptics claim that the best thing to do is to suspend judgment by refusing to take sides with any philosophical or religious worldview. This suspension of judgment means that people will cease to dogmatize, which will lead to mental tranquility. In other words, one must refuse to say that one worldview is True while another is False. When this is done, social divisions will no longer be created by stating some are right and others are wrong. The refusal to declare truth will lead to individual and societal peace.

Augustine was a Skeptic for only about three years, and, probably because this period in his life was so brief, it is underappreciated by scholars today.[104] But, he understood the power that Skepticism had had over him, and the danger it posed to anyone seeking truth. This insight led him to write his dialogue against the Skeptics, the *Contra Academicos*, which was his first text written in the months leading to his baptism after he was ready to fully give himself over to Catholicism. The heart of the danger of Skepticism, he came to realize and articulated in this text, was the moral vision at which the Skeptic must arrive. Anyone who refuses to give assent to a truth system is doomed to journey through life without a moral compass.[105] If a Skeptic refuses to assent to the idea that anything is ethically wrong, because we cannot know truth, then what would stop anyone from committing adultery or murder? If one does not agree that it is wrong to seduce another man's wife—either because it is impossible to know if adultery is right or wrong, or that one has constructed an ethical system that does not condemn adultery—what will stop anyone from doing so? If individuals and society refuse to make any truth claims, moral chaos will reign.[106]

Augustine provided three arguments that he felt refuted the claims of the Skeptics. The first may be called logical truths. There are certain statements, he said, that are logically consistent and cannot be denied. There is either one moon or two moons in our night sky; there cannot be one moon and two moons at the exact same time. The soul is either immortal or mortal; it cannot be immortal and mortal at the

---

102. Augustine, *Conf.* 6.6.18.
103. Augustine, *Conf.* 5.10.19, 5.14.25, 6.1.1, 6.4.6.
104. Bonner, *St. Augustine*, 74.
105. Augustine, *Acad.* 3.15.33.
106. Augustine, *Acad.* 3.16.35.

same time.[107] Second, he asserted that there are mathematical truths about which all agree. For example: 3 x 3 = 9. This mathematical certainty is believed by everyone, and is not dependent on geography, time, or culture.[108] Third, the five senses provide a level of certitude that cannot be denied, and lead to what may be called experiential truths. The eyes see what seems to be the color white; the ear hears what seem to be sounds that seem pleasing; the nose smells what seem to be pleasurable scents; the tongue tastes what seem to be rich delicacies; the skin touches what seem to be icy objects. A woman, for example, may taste an apple, and will assert with certainty that it tastes sweet to her. No amount of rhetorical manipulation will ever convince her that it tastes savory.[109]

With Augustine's growing professional success, Monica pressured him to get married. She became the prime instigator of his brief engagement, because she believed that after he got married he would receive the sacrament of baptism.[110] Almost nothing is known about his fiancé, except that she was about ten years old[111]—two years younger than the legal age for marriage.[112] Now engaged, he was forced to exile the mother of his child back to Africa. Augustine was devastated, and she made a vow that she would never have a relationship with another man. Although willing to wait two years for his fiancé because he found her agreeable, he could not stand to wait alone. Just as soon as the mother of his child had left for Africa, Augustine found another (nameless) woman. This new woman, he admitted, was nothing to him other than an object of sexual use for his boundless lust to be discarded as soon as his fiancé was old enough to marry.[113]

While in Milan, an unnamed man "puffed up with monstrous pride"[114] gave Augustine some books of the Platonists (*libri Platonicorum*)[115] that had been translated into Latin from Greek by Victorinus, the polymath and Christian convert.[116] These books, though not explicitly named by Augustine, were most likely from the Neoplatonist Plotinus (204/205–270),[117] the "last great philosopher of antiquity."[118]

---

107. Augustine, *Acad.* 3.9.21–11.25, 3.13.29.

108. Augustine, *Acad.* 3.11.25.

109. Augustine, *Acad.* 3.11.26–28.

110. Augustine, *Conf.* 6.13.23.

111. Augustine, *Conf.* 6.13.23.

112. Chadwick claims that she was ten years old, while Lancel claims that she was twelve. The minimum legal age for girls to get married at the time was twelve. However, this law was often broken, and there were few legal ramifications for breaking the law. Augustine, *Conf.* 108 n.17; Lancel, *Saint Augustine*, 73; Hopkins, "Age of Roman Girls," 313–14.

113. Augustine, *Conf.* 6.15.25.

114. Augustine, *Conf.* 7.9.13.

115. Augustine, *Conf.* 7.9.13.

116. Augustine, *Conf.* 8.2.3–5.12.

117. Wallis, *Neoplatonism*, 37.

118. Henry, "Place of Plotinus," xlii.

Along with the preaching of Ambrose, they would force him to see Catholicism—the same Catholicisim he had assumed was intellectually feeble—in a new way. If he had read the Bible in a serious way before he read the Platonists, he said, he probably would have abandoned his piety (*pietas*) after reading them.[119] But, since he read the Platonists first, they led him towards Paul's letters, and the Gospels.[120] In the Platonists, he saw the same fundamental teaching about the Logos, the incarnation, and the soul, as he came to find in the New Testament, only in a different vocabulary: "there [in the books of the Platonists] I read, not of course in these words, but with entirely the same sense and supported by numerous and varied reasons, 'In the beginning was the Word and the Word was with God and the Word was God. He was in the beginning with God'" (John 1:1–2).[121]

Most importantly, the Neoplatonists finally satisfied for him the question on the nature of evil—the question that had brought him to the Manichaeans, but which had not been answered in his mind after he had abandoned them. Rather than an eternal force that is co-equal with another good God as the Manichaeans had claimed, the Neoplatonists claimed that evil is the absence of the good, in the way that darkness is the absence of light. Light, which is both a particle and wave, can be measured in diverse ways, and felt on the skin. Darkness, on the other hand, cannot be measured or empirically verified, because it is, quite literally, nothing. For the Neoplatonists, then, evil is not a substance, but it is an action that lacks goodness. Neither the trinitarian God nor Jesus are found in their thought, nor is this definition of evil explicitly described in philosophical language in the Bible. But, Augustine saw a natural harmony in this way of conceiving of goodness and evil that is compatible with the fundamental Christian claim, as articulated in the Creeds of the Councils of Nicaea (325) and Constantinople (381), that "we believe in one God," rather than two opposing gods. Augustine, and other Neoplatonic Christians in Milan such as the future bishop of Milan, Simplicianus,[122] married together this Neoplatonic insight with the gospel. "For You [God]," Augustine said, "evil does not exist at all, and not only for you but for your created universe, because there is nothing outside it which could break in and destroy the order which you have imposed upon it."[123] Neoplatonism, he came to see, could be the philosophical language for intellectuals through which the biblical narrative could be expressed.

Intellectually, Augustine now was primed to commit himself fully to his mother's Christianity. But, for ancient philosophers—including Augustine—intellectual assent to a worldview was not sufficient; the philosopher first must yoke his passions to liberate

---

119. Augustine, *Conf.* 7.20.26.
120. Augustine, *Conf.* 7.21.27.
121. Augustine, *Conf.* 7.9.13.
122. Augustine, *Conf.* 8.2.3.
123. Augustine, *Conf.* 7.13.19.

his mind from lower desires.[124] For Augustine, it was his sexual urges that anchored him in place, and prevented him from taking the final step.[125] He often would go to church during his free moments throughout the week, but could not bring himself to forgo the pleasures of the body.[126] This inner conflict produced his famous plea to God: "grant me chastity and continence, but not yet."[127] This prayer was rooted in his fear that God might hear his prayer, and would remove the lust that he enjoyed gratifying.[128] Augustine knew the path he needed to take, but he was unwilling to walk it.

Lust's grip on him began to loosen when he and Alypius were visited by a certain Ponticianus, an African Christian, and holder of an important office at court. Ponticianus noticed a book on a gaming table during their discussion, and was surprised to find that it was Paul's letter to the Romans. Conversation turned towards religion, and Ponticianus told them about Antony of Egypt, monasteries in the deserts, and a monastery outside of Milan under the guidance of Ambrose. Neither Alypius nor Augustine had ever heard about any of this, and were spellbound by Ponticianus, who told them how, years earlier, he and three of his friends were walking in the gardens next to the circus of Trier. The group split into two pairs, and two of his friends discovered Athanasius's *Vita Antonii* in a certain house. They were captivated by it, and decided to imitate Antony by abandoning their careers, and giving themselves entirely to God. Later when the friends reunited and told Ponticianus of their decision, he was delighted, but he did not join them.[129]

This story profoundly moved Augustine. He felt the pull to imitate Pontiacianus's friends, as they had imitated Antony. Stumbling out of the house into the garden where he was staying, he desired to be alone with his inner struggle between what his flesh wanted, sexual gratification, and what his spirit wanted, to turn entirely to God.[130] Weeping, he fell underneath a fig tree, and beseeched God to end his suffering by allowing him to overcome his base desires. Then, he heard a genderless voice nearby chanting "pick up and read, pick up and read" (*tolle lege, tolle lege*).[131] He thought it might have been a chant by children at play, but he had never heard it before, so he assumed that God was speaking to him, and ordering him to return to the house to read from Romans, because he remembered how Antony heard God speaking directly to him when the Gospel of Matthew was proclaimed: "go, sell all you have, give to the poor, and you shall have treasure in heaven; come and follow me"

---

124. Hadot, *Philosophy,* 82–101, 269.
125. Augustine, *Conf.* 8.5.11.
126. Augustine, *Conf.* 8.5.12.
127. Augustine, *Conf.* 8.7.17.
128. Augustine, *Conf.* 8.7.17.
129. Augustine, *Conf.* 8.6.15.
130. Augustine, *Conf.* 8.8.19–11.26.
131. Augustine, *Conf.* 8.11.27–28.

(19:21).[132] Returning to the house, he found Alypius, and he read silently (as Ambrose had done) the first passage his eyes found: "not in riots and drunken parties, not in eroticism and indecencies, not in strife and rivalry, but put on the Lord Jesus Christ and make no provision for the flesh in its lusts" (Rom 13:13–14).[133] This passage was the catalyst he needed to reorient his life. He—and Alypius who had read from the section in Romans immediately after the passage that had changed Augustine's life and was moved by it himself—went to Monica and told her of his decision to give up his engagement and secular ambitions to dedicate himself to God. She was overcome with joy after years of praying to God for him.

This watershed in Augustine's life occurred around August 2, 386, just weeks before the Vintage Vacation began.[134] Begrudgingly, he remained a "salesman of words in the marketplace of rhetoric"[135] until the end of the vacation, then submitted his resignation.[136] He, and a company of close associates,[137] retreated to the country villa of his friend Verecundus the grammarian[138] in Cassiciacum outside of Milan in the fall of 386 where he spent several months reading the Psalms, conversing with his friends, and writing (or dictating)[139] a series of texts; his reading of the Psalms set him ablaze with a love for God, and he yearned to share them with the world; his conversations with his colleagues (when they all were not distracted by domestic duties on the estate) were laboratories through which Augustine could examine his newly adopted philosophy;[140] his books—*Contra Academicos*, *Beata vita*, *Soliloquia*, and *De ordine*—offer us a glimpse into his transitioning mind, although he later dismissed them as reflecting his pre-Christian pride. This period must have been one of the highlights of his life, as he was able to concentrate on making sense of the strange trajectory of his life.[141]

At the end of the vacation, Augustine wrote to Ambrose to ask him to recommend biblical texts to read. Ambrose suggested the prophet Isaiah, because Isaiah's prophesies of the coming Messiah best demonstrate the connection between the Old Testament and the New Testament. He knew of Augustine's Manichaean past, and wanted to prove to Augustine that the Manichaeans were blind in their inability to see that the two testaments belong together. Augustine, however, did not have a strong enough foundation in the Israelite narrative to make any sense of the prophet, so he set it aside for a later

132. Athanasius, *Vit. Ant.* 2.
133. Augustine, *Conf.* 8.12.29.
134. Augustine, *Conf.* 9.2.2–4.
135. Augustine, *Conf.* 9.2.2.
136. Augustine, *Conf.* 9.5.13.
137. This company included Monica, Adeodatus, his brother Navigius, two cousins Lartidianus and Rusticus, Romanianus's son Licentius, Trygetius a native of Thagaste, and Alypius. Lancel, *Saint Augustine*, 100.
138. Lancel, *Saint Augustine*, 99.
139. Augustine, *Acad.* 1.1.4.
140. Augustine, *Acad.* 2.11.25.
141. Augustine, *Conf.* 9.4.7–12.

time. When he returned to Milan, Augustine submitted his name for baptism, along with Adeodatus and Alypius. They were baptized at the hands of the bishop of Milan at the Easter service in April 387.[142] Augustine wept copious tears at the beauty of the hymns that were chanted in the church, and the truth at the heart of the songs caused an overwhelming sense of devotion to God to well up inside him.[143]

Shortly after his baptism, Augustine and his family left Milan to return to Africa. They were stalled outside of Rome in Ostia, however, probably because of the military campaign of the usurper Magnus Maximus rampaging throughout Italy.[144] While there, Monica fell deathly ill, possibly of malaria.[145] In a fevered haze, she surprised her sons by telling them that she wanted to be buried there in Italy, despite having earlier insisted that she be buried next to her husband in Africa. Navigius, trying to lighten her spirits, told her that he hoped that she would not be buried as a stranger in a strange land, but in her home soil. Rebuking him, she told them that it did not matter where she is buried, and that they should not worry about the location of her resting place as it ultimately does not matter. "I have only one request to make of you," she implored her sons, "that you remember me at the altar of the Lord, wherever you may be."[146] Her final resting place was irrelevant, she said, because no one place is more distant from God than any other place, and she was confident that God was able to resurrect her body no matter where she was buried. Nine days after she became sick, she died at the age of fifty-six years old.[147]

Augustine and his retinue returned to Rome, and was forced to remain there for another year until they finally were able to return to Thagaste.[148] When he finally made it across the Mediterranean, Augustine came into possession of a modest amount of property from his father, which his diocese then received from him.[149] Although he did not own the property any longer, he and a group of as many as twelve friends[150] continued to live on the property for the next two to three years.[151] Rather than imitate the monastery in Milan about which he learned from Ponticianus, Augustine was more

142. Possidius, *V. Aug.* 1.

143. Augustine, *Conf.* 9.6.14.

144. Bonner, *St. Augustine*, 104–5.

145. Clark, *Monica*, 17.

146. Augustine, *Conf.* 9.11.27.

147. Augustine, *Conf.* 9.11.28.

148. Augustine, *Epist.* 162.2

149. In 411, Augustine said that the church "took over (*invadere*) the possession of that property," but, in 425, he said that "I had sold (*vendere*) my slender poor man's property and distributed the proceeds to the poor," while Possidius said that Augustine "settled down there [Thagaste] for about three years, selling his property (*ad quos veniens, et in quibus constitutus, ferme triennio, et a se iam alienatis curis saecularibus, cum iis qui eidem ad haerebant*)." Augustine, *Epist.* 126.7; *Serm.* 355.2; Possidius, *V. Aug.* 3, 5.

150. Fox, *Augustine*, 381–82.

151. Brown says that Augustine lived in Thagaste for two years, but Possidius claimed three years. Brown, *Augustine of Hippo*, 128; Possidius, *V. Aug.* 3, 5.

likely trying to recreate the *otium* he experienced at Cassiciacum with its focus on the pursuit of wisdom. Together, Possidius tells us, he and his brothers fasted, prayed, performed good works, conversed, and meditated on the Bible. Augustine also preached and wrote.[152] It would be misleading to call this the first monastery in Africa,[153] as the men living there did not follow a defined *regula*, did not take any vows, did not wear a prescribed habit, nor describe themselves as monks. But, they did live simply, held property in common,[154] and understood themselves as some sort of defined community because they described themselves as the "Servants of God."[155]

In 391, Augustine travelled to Hippo (modern Annaba in Algeria). It was a town of about thirty to forty thousand residents,[156] and probably the second largest diocese in Africa (second only to Carthage).[157] As discussed in an earlier chapter, he went there to talk with a Christian friend of his who was a minor official in the governmental bureaucracy, and who wanted to talk to Augustine about the possibility of living a life of renunciation.[158] Augustine had been looking for a location where he could found a monastery, and live there with his brothers. It is unclear if he had intended to leave Thagaste, or if he was looking for land in Thagaste. Either way, he thought that this man might be interested in joining Augustine in this new endeavor. Augustine had hesitated to visit any other town as he was sure that any place without a bishop would seize him and force him to become their new pastor, but as Hippo already had Bishop Valerius, he did not hesitate to visit.[159] Valerius was an elderly Greek speaker who knew very little of Latin language or literature, and was in desperate need of someone who was better able to relate to the people there.[160] While he was in Hippo, the people—who surely knew of Valerius's needs—held Augustine down, and he reluctantly accepted ordination as a presbyter, bringing with him to the presbyterate nothing other than the clothes on his back. He wept bitter tears at his unavoidable fate, but the people mistook his tears as a sign that he was disappointed that he was not ordained a bishop, and they tried to comfort him.[161] Valerius, possibly in a gesture of consolation, offered to Augustine a plot of land where he was able to build the monastery he had dreamed of building.[162] Five years later, in the summer of 396,[163] Valerius

---

152. Possidius, *V. Aug.* 3.

153. Fox, *Augustine*, 381.

154. Chadwick, *Augustine*, 44. See also: Bonner, *St. Augustine*, 107–8; Brown, *Augustine of Hippo*, 125–30; Fox, *Augustine*, 381–82.

155. Augustine, *Civ.* 22.8.

156. O'Donnell, *Augustine*, 39.

157. Lancel, *Saint Augustine*, 246.

158. Possidius, *V. Aug.* 3.

159. Augustine, *Serm.* 355.2.

160. Possidius, *V. Aug.* 5.

161. Possidius, *V. Aug.* 4.

162. Augustine, *Serm.* 355.2.

163. Fox, *Augustine*, 501.

promoted Augustine as his co-adjutor bishop, despite the fact that this was against the canons of the Council of Nicaea.[164] It was not long after this that the elderly Valerius died, and Augustine became the sole bishop of Hippo.

Augustine would live for more than thirty more years, writing some of his greatest texts (such as his *Confessiones*, *De Trinitate*, and *De civitate Dei*), and getting entwined in some of the most important theological disputes of his day (such as his refutations of the Manichaeans, the Donatists, the Arians, and, of course, the Pelagians). Indeed, it is safe to say that this period of his life contains his most compelling writings—but, for our purposes, it will not be explored here because doing so would be an unnecessary and distracting digression. It is enough to know that, along with his theological writings, sermons, and letters, Augustine lived the multifaceted life of a Late Antique bishop.[165] He never again left Africa, although he travelled to Carthage between fifteen and thirty-three times over a thirty-year period.[166] In 426, he named a priest named Heraclius to succeed him, but he did not promote him as a co-adjutor bishop because he wanted to avoid the mistake that Valerius had made thirty years earlier.[167] Four years later, in 430, Augustine, dying, asked that the Psalms, which had so moved him during his time at Cassiciacum, be written on paper and posted on the wall next to his bed, so that he could read them and weep. Ten days before he died, he requested that no one, except doctors and those assistants bringing food to him, be admitted to his room, which is noteworthy because throughout his life he was an extrovert addicted to the company of friends and colleagues.[168] Just after his death, the Vandals, who had stormed into Africa the year before and had been shaking the gates of Hippo, burst through and burnt the city to the ground.[169]

---

164. Possidius, *V. Aug.* 8; Augustine, *Epist.* 213.4.

165. Rapp, *Holy Bishops*.

166. Brown claims that Augustine went to Carthage thirty-three times, but O'Donnell says that it was only fifteen times: Brown, *Augustine of Hippo*, 423; O'Donnell, *Augustine*, 32.

167. Augustine, *Epist.* 213.

168. Possidius, *V. Aug.* 31.

169. Possidius, *V. Aug.* 28.

Chapter 6

Jerome: The Irascible, Morbidly Sensitive Old Curmudgeon

The Life of Jerome

WE KNOW VERY LITTLE about Jerome's early life.[1] The date of his birth, in particular, is shrouded in mystery, and could range anywhere from 331–347,[2] although his death can be dated more precisely to either 419 or 420.[3] He was born in Stridon, but the exact location of this town is unknown; he indicates that it was on the border of Dalmatia and Pannonia,[4] but this description is of little help. Almost nothing about his family is known, but it certainly was Christian.[5] His father's name was Eusebius,[6] his younger sister became a consecrated virgin,[7] a grandmother and aunt, Castorina, lived with them when Jerome was young,[8] and he had a younger brother, Paulinian, whom we have encountered already. His family's modest wealth (they were at least rich enough to have slaves)[9] allowed him to receive an excellent education in Rome, but was not enough for him to independently finance his scholarly and monastic endeavors later in life, and he was reliant on rich aristocratic women, such as his mentee Paula.[10] During his studies there, Jerome reports spending his Sundays visiting the catacombs: "when I was a youth at Rome studying liberal

---

1. The narrative arc of this section is informed largely by the three biographies on Jerome: Cavallera, *Saint Jérôme*; Kelly, *Jerome*; Rebenich, *Jerome*.

2. Cavallera offers the year 347 and is followed by Murphy, Vessey, Rebenich, and Cain. Kelly offers 331. Cavallera, *Saint Jérôme*, 153; Murphy, "Irascible Hermit," 4; Vessey, "Jerome," 460; Rebenich, *Jerome*, 2; Cain, *The Letters of Jerome*, 1; Kelly, *Jerome*, 1, 337–39.

3. Cavallera and Cain suggest 419, while Vessey, Rebenich, and Kelly suggest 420. Cavallera, *Saint Jérôme*, 165; Cain, *Letters of Jerome*, 3; Vessey, "Jerome," 460; Rebenich, *Jerome*, 28; Kelly, *Jerome*, 331.

4. Jerome, *Vir. ill.* 135.

5. Jerome, *Epist.* 82.3.

6. We know nothing about his mother, but it seems, at the very least, that she was alive during his childhood. Jerome, *Vir. ill.* 135.

7. Jerome, *Epp.* 6, 7.4.

8. Jerome, *Apol.* 1.30; *Epist.* 13.

9. Jerome, *Epist.* 1.30.

10. Jerome, *Epist.* 108; Cain, *Jerome's Epitaph*.

arts, it was my custom on Sundays, along with companions of the same age and same conviction, to make tours of the tombs of the apostles and the martyrs. Often we would enter those crypts which have been hollowed out of the depths of the earth and which, along the walls on either side of the passages, contain the bodies of buried people."[11] It may have been these experiences with the martyrs that led to Jerome's decision to be baptized as a young man.[12]

He bounced around the Roman world for a number of years after his schooling. He and his friend Bonosus, who "were fostered in the bosoms of the same nurses, and carried in the arms of the same bearers,"[13] spent some time in Trier, where he copied two works from Hilary of Poitiers, and where the desire for a more dedicated Christian life began to stir.[14] They eventually left Trier, and returned to the area around Stridon and Aquileia where Jerome reconnected with his family. That connection did not last long. Jerome seems to have become estranged from his family, and was driven out of the region because of an unidentified event, or events, that caused a scandal that left him disgraced in the eyes of the Christian community there.[15]

He intended to journey to Jerusalem, as he put it, "to wage my [ascetic] warfare."[16] The desire to give himself over to the solitary life had been growing in him for several years, but the circumstances of his resolution to live out his desire are unclear.[17] Jerome had become convinced that it was only the hermits who were true Christians, and that those who remained in the world were spiritual zombies. He did not reach the city of David due to some sort of illness from which he suffered during his journey, but took refuge with his friend Evagrius in Antioch[18] in order to recover where he was waylaid for an extended period.[19]

Murphy has said that Jerome became a "true hermit at heart,"[20] but nothing could be farther from the truth. When the time came for Jerome to leave Antioch and begin his life in the desert, he balked. Writing to his friend Florentius, he revealed his inability to bring himself to abandon society, and excused himself because "I am but dust and vile dirt, and even now, while still living, nothing but ashes."[21] No matter how much he wanted to imitate those who had given up everything, like the hermits

---

11. Jerome, *Comm. Ezech.* 40, 5–13, as quoted by Kelly, *Jerome*, 22.

12. The dating of his baptism is unclear. Cavallera speculates that it was probably between 363–367, while Kelly offers that it must have been before the autumn of 366 when Pope Damasus was elected. Cavallera, *Saint Jérôme*,153; Kelly, *Jerome*, 23. See also, Jerome, *Epp.* 15.1, 16.2.

13. Jerome, *Epist.* 3.5.

14. Jerome, *Epp.* 3.5, 5.2.

15. Jerome, *Epist.* 6.2; See also: Cavallera, *Saint Jérôme*, 75–77.

16. Jerome, *Epist.* 22.30.

17. Driver, "Development," 47.

18. Jerome, *Epist.* 3.3. See also *Epp.* 1.15, 3.3, 4.2, 5.3, 15.5; *Vir. ill.* 125.

19. Jerome, *Epp.* 3.1, 6.1.

20. Murphy, "Irascible Hermit," 3.

21. Jerome, *Epist.* 4.2. See also: *Epp.* 2, 7.3.

Paul, Hilarion, and Malchus (whose hagiographies he later would write),[22] he did not have the disposition for seclusion.[23] Jerome's attempt at an eremitic life was probably the worst vocational discernment in the history of Christianity.[24]

During this interior tumult in Antioch,[25] Jerome had a fever-induced vision of the Judge at his judgment. Jerome told the Judge that he was a Christian. "You lie!" the Judge snapped in reply: "You are a follower of Cicero, and not of Christ. Where your treasure is, so also will your heart be."[26] Jerome had preferred refined pagan authors to the vulgar prose of the Bible, describing it as "rude and repellent."[27] Despite Jerome's passion for literature, he did not read any of the great Roman authors for fifteen years after his vision because he was so shaken by the experience,[28] although he later relaxed this strict prohibition.[29]

He finally convinced himself to forsake everything and retreat to the desert of Chalcis, not far from Antioch. This was an unhappy time for Jerome, as he never came to terms with the isolation of his new life. His loneliness comes through in his letter to his friend Niceas in Aquileia when he pleaded that "if you love me, write in answer to my prayer. If you are angry with me, though angry, write. I find my longing soul much comforted when I receive a letter from a friend, even though that friend be out of temper with me."[30] One of his few consolations during this time must have been his explorations of Hebrew under the tutelage of a Jewish convert to Christianity, which became central to his scholarly endeavors later in life.[31]

He lasted in the desert for only a few years, and undoubtedly had mixed feelings when he left.[32] It is not entirely clear why Jerome abandoned Chalcis, but it was probably a combination of several factors, including a realization that he was not fit

---

22. Jerome, *Vit. Paul.*; *Vit. Hil.*; *Vit. Malch.*

23. Driver, "Development," 49.

24. Rebenich has argued that Jerome's life at Chalcis was not as isolated and ascetic as Jerome had led us to believe. Though Rebenich may be correct that Jerome never had fully abandoned the world, I do not think we should diminish the hardship, loneliness, and austerity Jerome underwent, even if he was not living entirely by himself in a cave. Rebenich, *Jerome*, 6–9.

25. Kelly believes that the dream occurred while Jerome was in Antioch, but Rebenich has offered the possibility that this dream happened earlier when Jerome was in Trier. Kelly, *Jerome*, 42; Rebenich, *Jerome*, 4.

26. Jerome, *Epist.* 22.30.

27. Jerome, *Epist.* 22.30.

28. Kelly, *Jerome*, 43.

29. Borrowing an image from Deuteronomy 21, Jerome concludes it is acceptable to appropriate pagan learning if one first shaves the hair and cuts the nails, so to speak, of what is appropriated. In other words, Christians can borrow from pagan culture that which is in harmony with the gospel message, but must also cut away that which is not. Jerome, *Epist.* 70.2

30. Jerome, *Epist.* 8.

31. Jerome, *Epist.* 125.12. Recent scholars have begun to question Jerome's knowledge of Hebrew. Rebenich, *Jerome*, 27.

32. Cavallera speculates 375–377, while Kelly speculates it was late 374 or early 375 and lasted for two to three years. Cavallera, *Saint Jérôme*, 154; Kelly, *Jerome*, 46–48.

for the rigors of the life he had romanticized, less than ideal health, and disquiet from abuse he had received from other monks who had become suspicious of his trinitarian orthodoxy because—though fully in harmony with Nicaea—he hesitated to embrace the language that used the Greek term *hypostasis* (a word that had been used at Nicaea as synonymous with the term *ousios*, which had described the substance, or essence, of God) to express the distinction of the persons of the Trinity.[33]

He returned to Antioch,[34] and reluctantly received ordination from Bishop Paulinus before moving to Constantinople for unknown reasons.[35] While in New Rome, he met Gregory of Nazianzus, whom he described as "my instructor in the Scriptures,"[36] and a "most eloquent man."[37] It is unclear exactly what influence Gregory had on Jerome,[38] although it was most likely through Gregory that Jerome met Gregory of Nyssa,[39] and he may have introduced him to the writings of Origen.[40]

Jerome left Constantinople and returned to Rome in the entourage of Paulinus of Antioch and Epiphanius of Cyprus, who had been summoned to Rome in order to smooth tensions that had arisen between the East and the West.[41] While in Rome, Jerome found himself pulled into the orbit of Pope Damasus (366–384). Damasus was one of the most important and controversial popes of the fourth century.[42] Born in 305, he was chosen to be the bishop of Rome under scandalous circumstances that he was never able to escape entirely. As a deacon, Damasus backed Pope Liberius (352–366), who had been banished from Rome by Constantius II for not supporting his anti-Nicene program, and the Emperor replaced Liberius with an archdeacon named Felix (355–365). Damasus, having been exiled for a brief time with Liberius, returned to Rome, was reconciled to Felix, and resumed his previous clerical life. After Liberius and Felix died within a year of each other, two new popes, Damasus and a deacon under Liberius named Ursinus, were elected on the same day—Damasus from among the supporters of Felix, and Ursinus from among the supporters of Liberius. Violence inevitably followed. For the first time in the history of the Papacy, the civil authority was called upon to act in service of the Pope when Damasus exiled Ursinus and his followers. In addition to his dubious election, Damasus was marked by

---

33. Jerome, *Epist.* 17.

34. Cavallera offers 377–379, while Kelly offers 376/377–379/380. Cavallera, *Saint Jérôme*, 154; Kelly, *Jerome*, 57, 66.

35. Jerome, *C. Joan.* 41.

36. Jerome, *Vir. ill.* 117. See also: *C. Jov.* 1.13; *Epp.* 50.1; 52.8.

37. Jerome, *Apol.* 1.13.

38. Adkin, "Gregory of Nazianzus," 13–24.

39. Jerome, *Vir. ill.* 128.

40. Kelly, *Jerome*, 71.

41. Jerome, *Epp.* 127.7; 108.6.

42. Among other things, Damasus was known for battling heresies, asserting papal primacy, initiated a church building program, arranged the papal archives, wrote poetry, and excavations of the catacombs. Kelly, *Oxford Dictionary*, 32–34; Trout, "Damasus," 519–36.

rumors of sexual impropriety, and by material indulgence. Having seen Damasus's extravagance, the consul Vettius Agorius Praetextatus is reported to have said that if someone were to "make me a bishop of Rome, I will at once be a Christian."[43] Ursinus outlived Damasus, and even attempted to be elected Pope after Damasus's death, but Pope Siricus (384–399) was chosen instead.[44]

Damasus, as Jerome tells us in his preface to his revision of the four Gospels that he dedicated to his new patron, had urged (*cogere*) him to revise (*facere*) the Latin translation of the New Testament[45] (known together with the Old Testament as the *Vetus Latina*) in order to determine where it and the original Greek agree (*consintere*).[46] Jerome knew that his work would cause a backlash for seeming to have tampered with the holy text, but this revision was necessary in order to offer some uniformity to the Gospels because, as Jerome said, "there are almost as many forms of texts as there are copies."[47] Jerome's prediction of the coming disdain for his revision was prescient,[48] just as his later translation of the Old Testament from the Hebrew original possibly garnered even more disdain, as we shall see later.[49]

Jerome left Rome under a dark cloud of scandal similar to his earlier flight from Aquileia. Damasus had died on December 11, 384, and left Jerome vulnerable to the attack from the detractors he had acquired with his insistence on strict asceticism to the circles of rich aristocratic Christian women. Early in 384, Jerome had written his now infamous letter (22) to Eustochium, one of Paula's daughters who had been one of Marcella's proteges,[50] in which he asserted the superiority of virginity.[51] A year earlier, a man named Helvidius had written a treatise arguing that Mary had produced several children with Joseph after the birth and Jesus, and he insisted on the equality of marriage and virginity. Jerome's scathing response, *Adversus Heluidium*, defended Mary's virginity and elevated virginity over marriage.[52]

---

43. Jerome, *C. Joan.* 8.

44. Kelly, *Oxford Dictionary*, 32–35; Trout, *Damasus of Rome*, 1–16.

45. Both Cavallera and Kelly speculate that this revision was completed in 384, just months before Damasus's death. Cavallera, *Saint Jérôme*, 155; Kelly, *Jerome*, 88.

46. Jerome, *Praef. in quat. evang.*

47. Jerome, *Praef. in quat. evang.*

48. Jerome, *Epist.* 27.1.

49. Jerome did not revise the rest of the texts in the New Testament. They were translated by an unknown figure. One theory that has been offered is that it was revised by the so-called Rufinus the Syrian discussed earlier. Dunphy has argued against this theory, however. Rebenich, *Jerome*, 25; Dunphy, "Ps-Rufinus."

50. Jerome, *Epist.* 127.5.

51. Jerome, *Epist.* 22.20.

52. Jerome, *Helv.* 22–24.

While both of these texts won Jerome enemies because of their radicality,[53] it was the death of Blesilla, another of Paula's daughters,[54] that made it impossible for Jerome to remain in Rome after Damasus's death. In her early life, Blesilla's thoughts had been "full of worldly desires and passing pleasures,"[55] as is often the case with young aristocrats, both then and now. Four months prior to her death, however, she "renewed her baptism in her vow of widowhood, and for the rest of her days spurned the world, and thought only of the religious life."[56] Rumors spread after she died that Blesilla's turn to asceticism was not of her choosing, and that overzealous fasting was the cause of her death.[57] Jerome, who proudly called himself Blesilla's "father in spirit, her foster-father in affection,"[58] was accused of being the usher of her demise.[59] Unprotected by his papal patron, and despised by many Christian elites in Rome, Jerome fled after charges were brought against him for some form of inappropriate behavior.[60] Jerome's expulsion from Rome may have been instigated by Paula's own family because of their resentment of Jerome's influence on Paula and her children. The extent of Jerome's punishment may have been banishment from Rome, which is why Paula and Eustochium left Rome for Palestine, without Jerome, just weeks just after his departure.[61]

Jerome, Paula, and Eustochium reunited in Antioch, and then set off for a pilgrimage of the Holy Land, Alexandria, and to the monastic communities of Nitria in Egypt.[62] After visiting Egypt, they returned to Bethlehem and established monasteries there for men and women.[63] Despite never having lived in community, Jerome became the head of his newly constructed cenobium, drawing contempt from Cassian years later because Jerome never had sat at the feet of any master in order to absorb his *experientia*.[64]

While in Bethlehem, Jerome accomplished the task for which he is best known, the translation of the Old Testament from the original Hebrew.[65] Prior to Jerome's version, the *Vetus Latina* translation of the Old Testament had come from the pre-Christian

53. Jerome, *Epist.* 27.2.
54. Jerome, *Epist.* 39.1.
55. Jerome, *Epist.* 39.3.
56. Jerome, *Epist.* 39.3.
57. Jerome, *Epist.* 39.6.
58. Jerome, *Epist.* 39.2.
59. Jerome, *Epist.* 39.6.
60. Jerome, *Epist.* 45.2–6.
61. Cain, *Letters of Jerome*, 99–128.
62. Jerome, *Epist.* 108.
63. Jerome, *Epist.* 108.14.
64. Goodrich, *Contextualizing Cassian*, 78–96.

65. Cavallera believes the project was begun sometime between 389–392, and was completed 405/6. Kelly says Jerome worked on the project from 390 to 405/6. Cavallera, *Saint Jérôme*, 157, 163; Kelly, *Jerome*, 159, 163.

translation of the Old Testament into Greek called the Septuagint. It may seem peculiar to us in the twenty-first century that anyone would place the Septuagint above the Hebrew original, as it is obvious to us that the meaning of any text always gets lost in translation. But, since the beginning of Christianity (and lasting until our present day in the eastern churches), the Septuagint has been considered, as Jaroslav Pelikan has stated, "a true and perfect version"[66] of the original, and was honored since it was the text used by the authors of the New Testament. Just like his revision of the Gospels, Jerome was criticized in his day for his translation of the Old Testament, in particular for his turn to the Hebrew. Augustine wrote to him with less than enthusiasm for the project, saying "I think that they [the translators of the Septuagint] should be given a preeminent authority in this task without controversy."[67] Despite Augustine's protests, Jerome's translation, later to be known as the *Vulgate*, became standard in the church in the medieval period, and was declared "authentic," "approved," and that "no one dare or presume under any pretext whatsoever to reject it" by the Council of Trent in 1546.[68]

In addition to the *Vulgate*, Jerome is infamous for his verbal onslaughts of other Christians of his time. In his *De viris inlustribus*, he curtly dismissed Ambrose of Milan, saying that "I withhold judgment of him because he is still alive, fearing either to praise or blame lest, in one event, I should be blamed for adulation, and, in the other, for speaking the truth."[69] In his fight with Jovinian, Jerome slandered him by saying that "[Peter] more clearly denotes them [the unrighteous], saying, 'in the last days seducing mockers shall come, walking after their own lusts' (2 Pet 3.3). The apostle has described Jovinian speaking with swelling cheeks and nicely balancing his inflated utterances, promising heavenly liberty, when he himself is a slave of vice and self-indulgence."[70] Even after the death of Rufinus of Aquileia, his fiercest opponent and one-time friend, Jerome could not resist taking one last shot at him by calling him a "pig" (*grunnius*).[71]

It is these types of comments that have led scholars to declare Jerome an "irascible, morbidly sensitive old curmudgeon,"[72] that he "resented adverse criticisms,"[73] that he was "sensitive and easily offended," [74] that he had a "prickly character,"[75] and that he was "unbalanced."[76] Although these criticisms may not be far from the mark,

66. Pelikan, *Whose Bible?*, 64.
67. Augustine, *Epist.* 28.2.
68. Council of Trent, *Canons and Decrees*, 18.
69. Jerome, *Vir. ill.* 124.
70. Jerome, *C. Jov.* 1.39–40.
71. Jerome, *In Hier.* 1.pref, 4.pref, 22:24–27, 28:12–14, 29:14–20.
72. Cannon, "Jerome-Augustine," 39.
73. Hellenga, "Exchange of Letters," 177.
74. Bonner, *St. Augustine*, 147.
75. O'Connell, "When Saintly Fathers," 346–47.
76. McGuckin, *Gregory of Naziansus*, xxvii.

it is precisely this side of Jerome—the deeply flawed side—that has fascinated readers through the centuries. He was not the stoic Athanasius who courageously shouldered his burdens when he was exiled from Alexandria five times because of his fights with Arians. When Jerome experienced his own sort of exile after the death of Damasus, he venomously hissed at the "Senate of Pharisees"[77] for having driven him from his beloved Rome. He was not the continent Augustine who never hinted at struggles with concupiscence after his famous moment in the garden that brought him the chastity for which he had been praying. In his mid-seventies, Jerome tells us that it was only when his body was broken by age that he was freed from his disordered desires.[78] He was not the disciplined Antony of Egypt who spent twenty years alone pursuing a life of renunciation and who perfected the art of self-mastery.[79] He completely failed at his own desert experiment, even though he had dragged his sizeable library across the Mediterranean to keep him company. Years later, he said of his time there that "when I was living in the desert, in the vast solitude which gives to hermits a savage dwelling-place, parched by a burning sun, how often did I fancy myself among the pleasures of Rome. I used to sit alone because I was filled with bitterness."[80]

Jerome's years in Bethlehem were replete with literary activity in addition to his translation of the Old Testament. He wrote numerous biblical commentaries; he engaged in polemical work against Jovinian and Vigilantius; he was drawn into the Origenist controversy; he translated the works of other writers (including his controversial translation of Origen's *Peri archon*); he corresponded with many of the leading Christians of the day, including Paulinus of Nola,[81] Pope Innocent I (401–417),[82] and Bishop Theophilus of Alexandria.[83] By far, Jerome's most intriguing letter correspondence was with Augustine.[84] For twenty-five years (394–419), the two sporadically traded letters, but were never quite able to establish a fruitful relationship.[85] Augustine had written to Jerome (the only man from whom he would ever seek advice),[86] saying "I desire very much to know you in every respect,"[87] and continued to write to Jerome—even when Jerome had failed to respond—in hopes of making a connection.[88] Jerome, when he

77. Jerome, *Int. Did.* pref.
78. Jerome, *Comm. Am.* pref. See also: Kelly, *Jerome*, 295.
79. Athanasius. *Vit. Ant.*14.
80. Jerome, *Epist.* 22.7.
81. Jerome, *Epist.* 53, 58, 85.
82. Jerome, *Epist.* 135, 136, 137.
83. Jerome, *Epist.* 63, 82, 86, 87, 88, 89, 90, 92, 93, 94, 96, 98, 99, 100, 113, 114.
84. Jerome, *Epist.* 56, 67, 101, 102, 103, 104, 105, 110, 111, 112, 115, 116, 131, 132, 134, 141, 142, 143, 144.
85. See: O'Connell, "When Saintly Fathers," 344–64; Cannon, "Jerome-Augustine," 35–45; White, *Correspondence*; Duval, "La correspondance," 363–84.
86. O'Donnell, *Augustine*, 299.
87. Augustine, *Epist.* 28.1.1.
88. Augustine had written *Epp.* 28, 40, 67, and 71. Jerome had written two letters (Augustine, *Epp.*

finally responded, felt he was under attack by Augustine's concern about Jerome's interpretation of the dispute between Peter and Paul at Antioch (Gal 2:11–14),[89] and, as we saw earlier, Augustine's dissatisfaction that Jerome prized the Hebrew Old Testament over the Septuagint.[90] Jerome responded to Augustine saying that "you provoke an old man; you goad a silent one; you seem to boast of your learning."[91] It was only at the end of Jerome's life when he was unable to continue his own attack on the Pelagians that he wrote to Augustine with affection and admiration.[92]

Around 416, a group of individuals had committed acts of violence against Jerome, his company, and his monasteries that so traumatized him that he never would recover.[93] Surprisingly, we learn more of the details about the horror from Augustine than we do from Jerome. Augustine recounts that "women and men servants of God under the care of the holy priest, Jerome, were criminally slaughtered, a deacon was killed, and their monastic buildings were burned. By God's mercy, a better fortified tower was just able to protect Jerome himself from the attack and assault of these godless persons."[94] Jerome, Eustochium, and Paula all had written to Pope Innocent to inform him of the devastation from the "ravages, murders, fires and outrages of all kinds."[95] Innocent wasted no time writing to Bishop John of Jerusalem to scold him for not protecting them better. "It speaks ill of your capacity as a priest (*sacerdos*)," Innocent said, "that a crime so terrible should have been committed in the pale of your church. Where were your precautions? Where, after the blow had been struck, were your attempts at relief? Where, too, were your words of comfort?"[96]

The identity of the perpetrators of the carnage is unknown. Augustine had no doubt that it was "a band of depraved persons who were reputed to side with Pelagius in this evil,"[97] but Pelagius was not necessarily the culprit. Innocent, like Augustine, believed that "there can be no doubt as to who is the guilty person,"[98] but, at the same time, he hesitated to name the "devil"[99] because Jerome, Eustochium, and Paula had

---

39, 68) to Augustine before his substantive response (Augustine, *Epist.* 72), but those two letters did not respond to Augustine's inquiries.

89. Augustine, *Epist.* 40.3.3.

90. Augustine, *Epist.* 71.2.4. I have written elsewhere that I believe that, aside from the content of Augustine's letter that Jerome did not like, Jerome disliked Augustine because of Augustine's past relationship with Ambrose of Milan. It is well known that Jerome detested Ambrose. Squires, "Jerome's Animosity," 181–99. See also: Adkin, "Ambrose and Jerome," 364–76.

91. Augustine, *Epist.* 72.3.5.

92. Jerome, *Epist.* 141.

93. Lössl, "Who Attacked?," 94.

94. Augustine, *Gest. Pelag.* 66.

95. Jerome, *Epist.* 137.

96. Jerome, *Epist.* 137.

97. Augustine, *Gest. Pelag.* 66.

98. Jerome, *Epist.* 137.

99. Jerome, *Epist.* 137.

refrained from telling him who he was, and they did not bring any specific criminal charges against the guilty party.[100] While Jerome never named the instigator, he does hint that the attacks were theologically motivated. In a letter to a certain Riparius, Jerome tells him that "I myself have thought it better to change my abode than to surrender the true faith; and have chosen to leave my pleasant home rather than to suffer contamination from heresy. For I could not communicate with men who would either have insisted on my instant submission or would have summoned me to support my opinions by the sword."[101]

We hear very little from Jerome after this, as his scholarly activities ground to a complete halt. He died a few years later.

---

100. Jerome, *Epist.* 136, 137.

101. Jerome, *Epist.* 138. Josef Lössl has argued that there is not enough evidence provided to reach a definitive conclusion about the identity of Jerome's attackers. He is sure, however, that Pelagius should not be held responsible, and that there are several possible suspects, including disgruntled ascetics angry with Jerome who had been angry with him when he was in the desert in Chalcis, and possibly some locals who resented his presence in their land. Although Lössl's speculations may be accurate, Jerome's statement here about heresy indicates to me that the crime came out of a theological disagreement, which points to the Pelagians. Lössl, "Who Attacked?," 91–112.

Chapter 7

Orosius: A Useful Vessel in the House of the Lord

Orosius in Spain and Africa

BONNER HAS STATED CORRECTLY that Orosius, "despite his relatively small part in the drama, is one of the key-figures in the Pelagian controversy."[1] Orosius's contribution to this fight, however, is too often overlooked by modern scholars, and his role needs to be appreciated more. Little is known about him, as even his name is uncertain. Augustine and Jerome—his contemporaries who knew him personally—simply called him Orosius, but the name "Paulus" has been attributed to him since the medieval period.[2] Augustine's description of him in 415 as a young man[3] indicates that he probably was born sometime between 375–390.[4] We should not take his false humility seriously when Orosius described himself as "not a quick-witted man,"[5] because he clearly received a first-rate Roman and Christian education, which points to the likelihood that he came from a family of means.[6] Undoubtedly, he was from Spain as both Augustine and Gennadius mentioned it as his homeland,[7] and at some point while there was ordained to the priesthood.[8] The exact city of his home remains obscure, but three locations are the most likely possibilities: Tarragona,[9]

---

1. Bonner, "Pelagianism Reconsidered," 238.

2. Fear suggests that the name Paulus can be traced to the sixth century, but Hamman says it can be traced only to the eighth century. Fear "Introduction," 1; Hamman, "Orosius de Braga," 346 n. 1. Some modern scholars, such as Rees, continue to call him Paulus, or even Paul. Rees, "Pelagius," 82.

3. Augustine, *Epist.* 166.1.2.

4. Ferguson says that Orosius was born in the 380s; Lacroix offers 375–380; Bogan suggests 380–390; Hanson says 380–390; Teske believes 380; Frend offers 380–385; Fear says 385. Ferguson, *Pelagius*, 81; Lacroix, *Orose et*, 34; Bogan, "Introduction," 215; Hanson, "Introduction," 97; Teske, "Introduction," *Arianism*, 92; Frend, "Orosius," 615; Fear, "Introduction," 2.

5. Orosius, *C. pag.* 4.23.8.

6. Lacroix, *Orose et*, 30.

7. Augustine, *Epist.* 166.1.2, 169.13; *Retract.* 2.70; Gennadius, *De vir. Inlustr.* 40.

8. Augustine, *Epist.* 166.1.2, 169.13, 175.1, *19.1; *Gest. Pelag.* 16.39; *Retract.* 2.70; Jerome, *Epist.* 134.1.1; Gennadius, *De vir. Inlustr.* 40.

9. Ferguson believes that Orosius was from Tarragona, while Lacroix believes that it is as likely a possibility as Braga. Ferguson, *Pelagius*, 81; Lacroix, *Orose et*, 33.

Braga,[10] and Corunna.[11] In his *Historiae adversum paganos*, Orosius's best known text, he inserted a clue into a list of towns that had been sacked by the Goths that might point to Tarragona as his home: "among these [towns], we too in Spain can show our town of Tarragona to reconcile us to our recent troubles."[12] Orosius's description of Tarragona as "our town" may point to the possibility that he was from there, although this is not certain. In his *Commonitorium*, Orosius opened the possibility that he was from Braga, which is considered by most scholars to be the most likely location of his birth.[13] In it, he says that "two of my fellow citizens, Avitus and another man named Avitus, sought out foreign ideas although the truth alone had already exposed by itself such shameful misunderstanding."[14] Orosius's description of "my fellow citizens" may point to Braga as his home, because elsewhere Avitus of Braga wrote in a letter to a certain Pachonius that Orosius was "my son and fellow-priest,"[15] leading to the likelihood that Avitus of Braga is one of the men to whom Orosius refers. Corunna in Galicia, on the northwest coast of Spain, may also be Orosius's hometown, as he had demonstrated an intimate knowledge of a lighthouse there facing Britain, which he described as "a work with which few can be compared."[16] Furthermore, Augustine mentioned in passing that Orosius "came to us from the furthest reaches of Spain, that is, from the shore of the ocean."[17] These two pieces of information together point to Corunna as a possibility, though, it too, cannot be confirmed.[18]

Orosius was respected and admired in his own time by his associates: Augustine called him his "dear son,"[19] and described him to Jerome in a letter (166) as a "pious young man, a brother in Catholic peace, a son in terms of age, our fellow priest in terms of dignity"[20] who was "alert in mind, ready in speech, afire with zeal, a man who desires to be a useful vessel in the house of the lord."[21] He also wrote to his friend Evodius, the bishop of Uzalis, describing Orosius as a "very holy and enthusiastic young man" who was "ablaze with the love of the holy scriptures."[22] Jerome responded to Augustine in

---

10. Frend, Hanson, and Van Nuffelen, believe the most likely candidate is Braga. Frend, "Orosius," 615; Hanson, "Introduction," 97; Van Nuffelen, *Orosius*, 3.

11. Fear offers that Orosius was most likely from Corruna. Fear, "Introduction," 3.

12. Orosius, *C. pag.* 7.22.8.

13. Fear, "Introduction," 3.

14. Orosius, *Prisc. et Orig.* 3.

15. Fear, "Introduction," 3.

16. Orosius, *C. pag.* 1.2.71

17. Augustine, *Epist.* 169.13. See also 166.1.2.

18. See Fear, "Introduction," 2–3.

19. Augustine, *Priscill.* 1.1.

20. Augustine, *Epist.* 166.1.2.

21. Augustine, *Epist.* 166.1.2.

22. Augustine, *Epist.* 169.13.

his own letter and called Orosius an "honorable man,"[23] while Gennadius labeled him "a man most eloquent and learned in history."[24]

Modern scholars, however, have given Orosius mixed reviews. Bonner called him a man whose "burning zeal for the Faith was united with a narrow and ungenerous nature, and the whole allied to an impetuous temperament, and a remarkable naivety," that Orosius was "the most bitter and violent enemy of Pelagius and his supporters,"[25] he was "aggressive," and that he lacked "tact";[26] Benoît Lacroix said he was "plutôt remarquable" and that "il est cultivé, assez en tout cas pour attire l'attention des siens et gagner la confiance de deux grands écrivains chrétiens de son époque." Orosius was also "soucieux de s'instruire, prêt à obéir, préoccupé de l'orthodoxie chrétienne";[27] Brown labeled him a "superficial man"[28] who was "incapable of getting on with foreigners";[29] Kelly regarded him as a "talented, opinionated, narrowly orthodox, impetuous young man," and "aggressive and tactless";[30] Dunphy branded him as "a man with an impetuous character";[31] Frend considered him "bold," but "impetuous and tactless."[32]

Orosius left Spain for Africa sometime between 409 and early 415, but it is not entirely clear why he left.[33] Orosius wrote to Augustine telling him that

> I have been sent to you by God. Through him I place my hope in you, while I ponder how it happened that I have come here. I do recognize why I have come. It was not by choice, not by necessity, and not by common agreement [*sine voluntate, sine necessitate, sine consensu*] that I departed from my native land. Rather, I was prompted by some hidden force, until I was delivered to the shores of this land. Here, at last, I have come to the realization that I was being ordered to come to you.[34]

23. Jerome, *Epist.* 134.1.1
24. Gennadius, *De vir. Inlustr.* 40.
25. Bonner, *St. Augustine*, 332.
26. Bonner, "Pelagianism Reconsidered," 238.
27. Lacroix, *Orose et*, 30.
28. Brown, *Augustine of Hippo*, 321.
29. Brown, *Augustine of Hippo*, 358.
30. Kelly, *Jerome*, 317–18.
31. Dunphy, "A Prelude," 128.
32. Frend, "Orosius," 615–17.

33. Fear says that it is possible he left Spain in 409, but believes it is more likely that he left in 411. Frend and Hanson suggest 414. Dunphy believes it was early 415 or soon before that. Fear "Introduction," 3; Frend, "Orosius," 615; Hanson, "Introduction," 98; Dunphy, "A Prelude," 126.

34. Orosius, *Prisc. et Orig.* 1. See also: Bonner, *St. Augustine*, 332. Fear has suggested that before Orosius arrived in Africa that he had never heard of Augustine. This does not seem likely, however, in light of the fact that in his *Historiae* Orosius seems to be aware of Augustine's well-known reputation throughout the Roman world. Furthermore, Augustine says of Orosius that, arriving in Africa, Orosius "ceased to believe much of what was said about me." This seems to suggest that Augustine is saying that Orosius had an inflated knowledge of Augustine, and that Orosius no longer had an

Augustine echoed this justification when he said that Orosius "hastened to us from there [Spain], almost from the very shore of the ocean, stirred by the idea that he could learn from me whatever he wanted concerning those matters he wanted to know."[35] Later in his *Historiae*, however, Orosius indicates that his flight had less to do with a divine command, but more to do with fleeing the invading gothic hordes: "I escaped from their hostility, flattered those in power, guarded myself against those I could not trust, outwitted those who lay in wait for me, and finally, how, when they pursued me by sea with their rocks and spears, and had almost laid hands upon me, I escaped them when I was covered by a fog which suddenly arose."[36]

Scholars have offered several other theories about why Orosius went to Africa. Rees has suggested that Orosius was sent by Spanish bishops to consult with Augustine about how to defeat Priscillianism, which was rampant in Spain at that time. The bishops viewed Priscillianism as a new manifestation of Manichaeism, and thought that Augustine would be able to advise them on how to defeat it because of his personal history and knowledge of Manichaeism.[37] There is no indication in any of Orosius's or Augustine's writings, however, that suggests that Orosius was following orders from any bishop. In a second theory, Peter Van Nuffelen has suggested the exact opposite— Orosius left Spain for dubious reasons without the permission of his superiors. In the above quotation in which Orosius explained to Augustine the divine command that sent him to Africa, Van Nuffelen says that the passage suggests that Orosius's departure from Spain was controversial. By saying *sine voluntate*, Orosius lays himself open to the charge of *akedia*, the accusation of spiritual lethargy; *sine necessitate* suggests that he absconded without there being a pressing cause, whereas *sine consensu* points to the fact that presbyters were not supposed to travel without permission. Orosius had clearly taken leave without asking. His departure from Spain was thus at least a breach of decorum, and without proper justification.[38]

Although Van Nuffelen has an intriguing theory, it is unconvincing because every indication points Orosius's intention to return to Spain.[39] In fact, Orosius did make a return effort to Spain, but only made it as far as Minorca, and was forced to return to Africa.[40] It is hard to imagine Orosius wanting to return to Spain if he were in trouble with the bishops there, and might be punished.

---

unreasonable view of Augustine. Van Nuffelen has argued that Orosius was trying to cash-in on that reputation. Fear, "Introduction," 4; Van Nuffelen, *Orosius*, 3; Augustine, *Epist.* 166.1.2. for Augustine's reputation, see O'Donnell, "Authority of Augustine," 7–35.

35. Augustine, *Epist.* 166.1.2.

36. Orosius, *C. pag.* 3.20.6–7. See also: Augustine, *Epist.* 166.1.2; Dunphy, "A Prelude," 126; Frend, "Orosius," 615; Hamman, "Orosius de Braga," 347; Hanson, "Introduction," 99.

37. Rees, "Pelagius," 25.

38. Van Nuffelen, *Orosius*, 27–28.

39. Orosius, *Prisc. et Orig.* 1; Augustine, *Epist.* 166.1.2.

40. Fear, "Introduction," 5.

While in Africa this first time in late 414 or early 415,[41] Orosius penned the first of his three works, his *Commonitorium de errore Priscillianistarum et Origenistarum*. He already had spoken with Augustine, but waited for Augustine's mind to be freed from other distractions before formally writing to him.[42] When satisfied that he had Augustine's full attention, Orosius wrote this short text summarizing their previous conversations,[43] and asked him to refute Priscillianism and Origenism, which, as the bishop of Hippo said, had "slain the souls of Spaniards much more tragically then the barbarian sword has slain their bodies."[44] He then proceeded to offer a brief summary of the errors of them both, pleading to Augustine to "quickly employ the medicine after examining the illness."[45] Priscillianism had been in Spain already for some time, but Origenism was brought to Spain by the two men named Avitus mentioned earlier. They left Spain—one traveled to Jerusalem and the other to Rome—in an attempt to learn how to refute Priscillianism. When they returned, one brought back Origenism, while the other brought back Neoplatonism learned from a man named Victorinus,[46] who may well be the same Marius Victorinus who had influenced Augustine's turn to Neoplatonism.[47] Not long afterwards, the one Avitus who brought Neoplatonism to Spain switched his allegiance to Origenism, and now, much to Orosius's dismay, both Priscillianism and Origenism flourished.[48] Augustine promptly responded to Orosius's request with his own short work, the *Ad Orosium contra Priscillianistas et Origenistas*. He explicitly stated that he knew nothing about Priscillianism prior to Orosius's arrival,[49] and even though he already had heard about Origen and Origenism (indeed had asked Jerome to translate more of Origen's writings for a Latin audience),[50] it is likely that he learned about Origenism from Orosius.[51] Augustine did not respond point-by-point to each of Orosius's concern. Rather, he directed Orosius to some of his "little works" (*opusculum*) against the Manichaeans that, he said, apply to many of the problems of Priscillianism, even though Priscillianism is not discussed in them.[52]

41. Hanson, "Introduction," 106.

42. Frend states that Orosius had brought to Africa with him his *Commonitorium*, but Orosius is clear that he wrote it after having arrived in Africa: "I had, indeed, broached the subject to your Holiness earlier, but even then I was intending to present a memorandum on the subject I spoke of—once I was aware that had been freed from other matters demanding your attention." Frend, "Orosius," 615; Orosius, *Prisc. et Orig.* 1.

43. O'Connell, "St. Augustine's Criticism," 84–85.

44. Augustine, *Epist.* 166.1.2.

45. Orosius, *Prisc. et Orig.* 4.

46. Orosius, *Prisc. et Orig.* 3.

47. Augustine, *Conf.* 8.2.3–5.10.

48. Orosius, *Prisc. et Orig.* 1.

49. Augustine, *Priscill.* 1.1. See also: *Epist.* 166.3.7.

50. Augustine, *Epist.* 28.2.2.

51. O'Connell, "St. Augustine's Criticism," 84–85.

52. Teske's translation of *opusculum* is "shorter works," but I believe "little works" is more accurate, because I think that Augustine is trying to convey a sense of humility. Augustine, *Priscill.* 1.1.

Chapter 8

Texts, Councils, Popes, and an Emperor

Augustine's De peccatorum meritis et remissione et
de baptism parvulorum *and* De spiritu et littera

DURING THE FIRST PHASE of the Pelagian controversy, a flurry of letters and texts were written (or dictated) by individuals on both sides of the fight; a number of councils were held either condemning Pelagius (and the Pelagians), or declaring him to be in harmony with Christian teaching; two popes gave conflicting messages that caused a swarm of activity; and an emperor brought the might of the state down on the heads of the Pelagians. All of this happened in a very brief amount of time (411–418) all over the Mediterranean world in two different languages (Latin and Greek). It is difficult, therefore, to disaggregate all of this activity, and discuss it in an organized way. But, that is the goal of this chapter.

Augustine's textual entrance into the Pelagian controversy were the first two books of his *De peccatorum meritis et remissione et de baptism parvulorum*,[1] written sometime between the summer of 411 and early 412,[2] in response to a letter, no longer extant, from a certain tribune[3] named Flavius Marcellinus.[4] Little is known about Marcellinus prior to his appointment by the Emperor Honorius in an edict on October 14, 410 to adjudicate the dispute between the Donatists and the Catholics in Africa at a synod in Carthage the following June.[5] Orosius, who may have gotten to know him during his own stay in Africa, described him as "a prudent, energetic man

---

1. In his *Retractiones* on his *De peccatorum meritis et remissione et de baptismo parvulorum*, he tells us that he had been refuting the Pelagians "in sermons and conferences" before he ever wrote any texts against them. Augustine, *Retract.* 2.59.

2. Dunphy argues for the summer, while Teske suggests that they were written as late as early 412. Dunphy, "A Lost Year," 425; Teske, vol. 1 "Introduction," *WSA*, 20.

3. Orosius, *C. pag.* 7.42.16.

4. Augustine, *Pecc. merit.* 1.1.1, 3.1.1; *Gest. Pelag.* 11.25.

5. Dunphy, "Who Was?," 233, 237–38.

and most eager to pursue everything that was good."[6] A younger contemporary of Augustine,[7] Marcellinus was well-versed in the theological issues of his day.[8] During this time, he became "a friend most dear" to Augustine—a friendship that lasted beyond the synod until his Marcellinus's death.[9] In a letter (151) to a certain Caecilian, Marcellinus's successor, shortly after Marcellinus's death, Augustine lauded his friend as a man of virtue. Marcellinus, he said,

> lived according to his religion with a very Christian heart and life. This reputation preceded him so that it was thus that he came on a matter of Church business, and stayed with him after he came. But what goodness he had in conduct, what loyalty in friendship, what eagerness in learning, what sincerity in religion, what chastity in marriage, what self-control in judgment, what patience toward enemies, what affability towards friends, what humility toward the saints, what love toward all! What readiness he had in offering favors, what modesty in asking for them, what love for correct actions, what sorrow over sins! What great beauty of morality, what splendor of grace, what concern for piety! What mercy in helping, what benevolence in pardoning, what confidence in praying! How modestly he spoke what he knew was useful for salvation! How cautiously he searched for what it was harmful not to know! What great scorn he had for things of the present, what great hope and desire he had for eternal goods! The bond of marriage by which he was already bound when he began to desire better things prevented him from abandoning all worldly pursuits and taking up the belt of a soldier of Christ, for it was not permissible to abandon those circumstances in which he was, although they were inferior.[10]

Augustine clearly admired Marcellinus as an administrator, Christian, friend, and husband, which is why he was wounded deeply when Marcellinus and his brother, the Proconsul Arpingius, were executed on September 13, 413.[11] Several reasons for their arrest and execution have been offered. Orosius claimed that Marinus, a friend and colleague of Caecilian, had them killed either because of jealousy, or because he was bribed by someone with gold.[12] Jerome mentioned in passing that some unspecified "heretics" (*haeretica*) executed Marcellinus for participating in the attempted revolt of Heraclian, the military commander of Africa.[13] Augustine, in his letter to Caecilian, admitted that Caecilian had "suffered a very serious injury" at the hands of either Marcellinus or

---

6. Orosius, *C. pag.* 7.42.16.
7. Dunphy, "Who Was?," 238.
8. Augustine, *Epist.* 190.6.20; Dunphy, "Who Was?," 238.
9. Augustine, *Epist.* 190.6.20.
10. Augustine, *Epist.* 151.8.
11. Augustine, *Epist.* 151.6.
12. Orosius, *C. pag.* 7.42.16.
13. Jerome, *Dial.* 3.19; *Epist.* 130.7.

Arpingius, but that Augustine was convinced that Marcellinus was innocent, although Arpingius may have been guilty.[14] Regardless of the motivation for the execution, Honorius was furious at Marinus's actions (actions that Augustine described as "impious," "cruel," and "wicked"),[15] and swiftly punished him. According to Orosius, Honorius immediately recalled Marinus from Africa, and stripped him of his rank.[16]

In his letter to Augustine, Marcellinus asked Augustine to respond to three propositions he had heard some unspecified individuals make:[17] (1) even if Adam had not sinned he would have died, (2) that sin was not transmitted to Adam's offspring by propagation, and (3) that there have been, are, and will be humans without sin.[18] Note that here, at the beginning of Augustine's contribution to this fight, that the issue of grace, for which Augustine later would say was the heart of the dispute,[19] and for which Augustine later would receive the title the "Doctor of Grace," is not mentioned at all. Marcellinus was primarily concerned with Adam, and the effects of his transgression. The issue of the proper definition of grace would come only later.

Augustine had not yet encountered any texts from Pelagius, but he did reference several quotations or paraphrases in his response to Marcellinus from an unnamed Pelagian or Pelagians[20]—unnamed, he later said in his *Retractiones*, because he hoped that they might be open to correction, and he did not want to embarrass them.[21] Scholars have disagreed over the source or sources of these quotations, but most are divided between the author of the *Liber de fide* and Caelestius.[22] Augustine's refutation of these claims about Adam by these nameless shadows, as we shall investigate in more depth later, was to insist that if Adam had not sinned his body would have been changed to a spiritual body, "and pass into the state of incorruption, which is promised to believers and saints, without suffering the punishment of death,"[23] that Adam did indeed pass his sin to his offspring through propagation,[24] and that a sinless life is theoretically possible because God is able to do all things, but that sinlessness has not

---

14. Augustine, *Epp.* 151.4; 151.9.
15. Augustine, *Epp.* 151.3.
16. Orosius, *C. pag.* 7.42.16.
17. Augustine, *Gest. Pelag.* 11.25.
18. Augustine, *Pecc. merit.* 3.1.1.
19. Augustine, *Gest. Pelag.* 30.55.
20. Augustine, *Pecc. merit.* 1.2.2, 1.18.23, 1.30.58, 1.34.63–64, 2.3.3, 2.9.11, 2.10.13, 2.15.22–16.24, 2.25.39–41, 2.27.44, 2.30.49, 2.33.53, 2.36.58.
21. Augustine, *Retract.* 2.59.
22. Refoulé and Wermelinger believe the quotations or paraphrases come from the author of the *Liber de fide*, while TeSelle and Dunphy believe they come from Caelestius. Dodaro believes that there is not enough evidence to reach any conclusion. Refoulé, "Datation du Premier," 49; Wermelinger, *Rom und Pelagius*, 18–22; Dunphy, "A Lost Year," 416–25; TeSelle, "Rufinus the Syrian," 75–76; Dodaro, "Carthaginian Debate," 197.
23. Augustine, *Pecc. merit.* 1.2.2.
24. Augustine, *Pecc. merit.* 1.9.9–10.11.

been achieved by anyone in this life.²⁵ When Augustine completed the first two books, he sent them to Marcellinus, but received them back from him for reasons he cannot remember. Augustine speculated in a letter (139) that it may have been because he wanted to make revisions to the books,²⁶ but there is no indication in the text itself that he ever intended to make any revisions.²⁷

Just a few days after completing these first two books, Augustine received a copy of Pelagius's commentaries on Paul, which prompted him to write a letter to Marcellinus that has come down to us as book three of his *De peccatorum meritis et remissione et de baptism parvulorum*.²⁸ It is possible that it was Marcellinus who sent Pelagius's commentaries to Augustine,²⁹ and if Mercator is correct that they were shared only with Pelagius's friends, then it is possible that Marcellinus had befriended Pelagius, and been influenced by him in Rome or during Pelagius's short stay in Carthage, which would explain Marcellinus's dissatisfaction with Augustine's first two books, and why he returned them back to him.³⁰

Unlike the first two books where he refused to name the person or persons with whom he took issue, Augustine identified Pelagius in book three, and he did so, as he would later claim in his *Retractiones*, "not without some praise"³¹ of Pelagius, because he had not yet come to view Pelagius as a heresiarch. Augustine's minimization of his praise of Pelagius fifteen years later obfuscates the degree to which he showered him with commendation at the time, saying, among other things, that Pelagius was "a Christian of considerable religious development."³² Augustine, furthermore, insisted that it was unlikely that Pelagius was the source of the rejection of the transmission of sin,³³ which he had read in Pelagius's commentary on Romans, and which became the central issue addressed in book three.³⁴ "Do you see, then, I ask you," he asked Marcellinus, "how Pelagius introduced all this [rejection of original sin] into his writings, not in his own name, but in the name of others? He knew full well that this was some sort of innovation that had already begun to sound contrary to the ancient view of the Church. And

---

25. Augustine, *Pecc. merit.* 2.6.7–20.34.

26. Augustine, *Epist.* 139.3. Dunphy suggests that Marcellinus sent them back to Augustine because he was dissatisfied with Augustine's answer that it is theoretically possible to be sinless, though no one has been so in reality. Dunphy, "A Lost Year," 404–5.

27. Dunphy, "A Lost Year," 423 n. 112.

28. Augustine, *Pecc. merit.* 3.1.1.

29. Dunphy, "A Lost Year," 423.

30. Dunphy, "Unexplored Paths," 47; Dunphy, "A Lost Year," 405. It should be noted, however, that Pelagius was in Carthage only for a brief time, so he and Marcellinus may not have had enough time to develop a meaningful relationship. Augustine, *Gest. Pelag.* 22.46.

31. Augustine, *Retract.* 2.59.

32. Augustine, *Pecc. merit.* 3.1.1.

33. Augustine, *Pecc. merit.* 3.1.1.

34. Augustine, *Pecc. merit.* 3.3.5.

as a result, he was either ashamed or afraid to make it his own."³⁵ Augustine's insistence that Pelagius was not the originator of the idea that Adam's sin was not passed to his offspring through propagation, along with his repeated praise of Pelagius, increases the likelihood that Augustine knew Marcellinus had befriended Pelagius, and that Augustine was trying to balance his critique of the ideas while, at the same time, trying not to offend Marcellinus by making accusations against his friend.

Marcellinus was not satisfied. After having read Augustine's books, he wrote a letter to him protesting the second book—specifically, that he was disturbed that Augustine would claim that it is theoretically possible to be sinless, but that no one ever has been so. It is absurd (*absurdum*), he insisted, to say that something is possible when there are no historical examples of it.³⁶ As Marcellinus's letter is no longer extant, it is unclear if Marcellinus genuinely was perplexed by Augustine's claim about the theoretical possibility of sinlessness and simply wanted Augustine to elaborate further, or if he was challenging Augustine because he was convinced by the Pelagians that sinlessness is not only theoretically possible, but that there have been some in the past who have been sinless. This may be another example demonstrating his sympathy for the Pelagians.

Marcellinus's letter prompted Augustine to compose his second anti-Pelagian work, his *De spiritu et littera*, written sometime between late 412 and the spring of 413.³⁷ Using gentle language because he did not want to alienate Marcellinus,³⁸ Augustine offered multiple examples to show that some things are theoretically possible, but have never occurred. A camel, he wrote, has never passed through the eye of a needle, even though Jesus said that it was theoretically possible (Matt 19:24–26); twelve legions of angels could have prevented Jesus from being arrested in the garden (Matt 26:53), even though this did not happen; God immediately could have eliminated all the gentiles in the promised land as the Israelites emerged from the desert (Deut 31:3), but this did not happen. Thousands of examples could be given to show that theoretical possibility does not necessitate historical reality, but these three, Augustine hoped, would be convincing.³⁹

Augustine's main concern in this text was not to dwell on the theoretical possibility of sinlessness, but to show that any righteousness will not be gained by the movement of the free will alone. The will must be aided by God's assistance: "the human will is helped to achieve righteousness in this way: besides the fact that human beings are created with free choice of the will and besides the teaching by which they are commanded how they ought to live, they receive the Holy Spirit so that there arises in their minds a delight in and a love for the highest and immutable good that is God, even

---

35. Augustine, *Pecc. merit.* 3.3.6.
36. Augustine, *Spir. et litt.* 1.1.
37. Teske, vol. 1 "Introduction," WSA, 136.
38. Augustine, *Spir. et litt.* 35.61.
39. Augustine, *Spir. et litt.* 1.1.

now while they walk by faith, not yet by vision."⁴⁰ His unnamed Pelagian opponents (the "enemies of grace" as he calls them for the first time, but not for the last),⁴¹ he insists, do not believe that the will is infused with God's assistance, but that they are only aided by the gift of the free will, the commandments, and God's teachings.⁴² He then proceeds to offer an exegesis of Paul's meaning when he claims that "the letter kills, but the Spirit gives life" (2 Cor 3:6). It is true that this passage is often understood to mean that passages in Scripture that are expressed figuratively should not be interpreted literally,⁴³ but Augustine has a different meaning in mind. Here, he takes the "letter" to refer to the commandments of the law, while the "Spirit" refers to the indwelling of God that allows the individual to accomplish what the law demands. "The letter of the law," he says, "which teaches that we should not sin, kills, if the life-giving Spirit is not present."⁴⁴ Without the grace of the Spirit, the law cannot bring the Christian into a rightly ordered relationship with God. In light of this understanding of the relationship between commandment and grace, he concludes, it theoretically may be possible to be sinless, but all righteousness ultimately comes from God's active agency.⁴⁵

Jerome's *Commentarii in Ezechielem* and his Letter (133) to Ctesiphon

The first foray for Jerome into battle with the Pelagians was in his *Commentarii in Ezechielem*, which he began writing in 410 and completed around 414, although it wasn't until book six, probably written around 412 (roughly the same time Augustine began writing against the Pelagians), that he attacked the Pelagians.⁴⁶ Without identifying his opponents by name, he said that

> I thought that when the serpent was hacked through its middle, the shoots of a new hydra would not sprout up again; and according to the tales of the poets, the dogs of Scylla would not in any way rage against me, after Scylla was dead, even though they never stop barking. Likewise, when the heretics are struck by the hand of God, lest they tempt, "were it possible, even the elect of God" (Matt 14:24), the heresy itself does not die, since it has bequeathed the hereditary cubs [*catuli*] of its hatred against us. And these cubs, who imitate the poison of the ancient Mother and of wily Ulysses, do not abandon our destruction. Their lips alone are speared with honey; and according to the expression of Scripture: "they softened their words more than oil" (Ps 54:21),

40. Augustine, *Spir. et litt.* 3.5.
41. Augustine, *Spir. et litt.* 35.63.
42. Augustine, *Spir. et litt.* 2.4.
43. Augustine, *Spir. et litt.* 4.6.
44. Augustine, *Spir. et litt.* 5.8.
45. Augustine, *Spir. et litt.* 5.7.
46. Cavallera, *Saint Jérôme*, 164; Kelly, *Jerome*, 311.

but they themselves are darts, fiery darts, which must be repelled and extinguished by the shield of faith.[47]

The serpent in this cryptic image represents Rufinus of Aquileia, while the cubs represent the Pelagians. This assault initiates a theme that will weave its way throughout all of Jerome's attacks on the Pelagians, for, as we shall discuss in detail later, Jerome's chosen method of attack against the Pelagians is to genealogically associate them with men whom he considerd to be of dubious orthodoxy.

Sometime in 414,[48] Jerome also wrote a letter (133) in response to one he received from a certain man named Ctesiphon. We know almost nothing about Ctesiphon, but it seems that he was living in the West (possibly Rome)[49] in a "holy and illustrious house" that was "famous for virtue and holiness."[50] Jerome warmly received his letter, saying that "your conduct has been prompted by zeal and friendship."[51] But, Jerome's reply, which is his second most important contribution to this controversy, was anything but warm, as he warned Ctesiphon and his friends that they should not associate with the Pelagians, or financially support them, as it seems that Ctesiphon and his associates had been doing.[52] One peculiar theme introduced in this letter, and continued throughout the rest of his writings against the Pelagians, was his conviction that the Pelagians, like other groups in antiquity such as the gnostics, held secret teachings known only to an elite inner circle.[53] "You [Pelagians] know very well what it is that you teach your pupils in private," he wrote, "and that while you say one thing with your lips you engrave another on your heart. To us, ignorant outsiders you speak in parables; but to your own followers you avow your secret meaning."[54] It is possible that this was just a gambit employed to discredit his opponents in the eyes of Ctesiphon and his circle, and Jerome knew that the Pelagians did not have any secret doctrines. Another possibility might be that Jerome knew that Pelagius, like he himself, was a spiritual director for aristocratic women, and he was genuinely concerned that Pelagius was disclosing some teachings to them in private not disclosed to others. In either case, Jerome's charge is perplexing,

---

47. Jerome, *Comm. Ezech.* 6.pref. I have modified Nugent's translation slightly. She translated the word *catuli* to mean "whelps," where I have translated here as "cubs."

48. Cavallera, *Saint Jérôme*, 164.

49. Jerome says that "before the arrival of your letter many in the East have been deceived into a pride which apes humility." This indicates that Ctesiphon was living in the West. Although it is impossible to say where exactly, it is unlikely that he lived in Africa as it is clear that Ctesiphon did not inform him about what had happened to Caelestius in Carthage. The most likely possibility, then, would be Rome. It is also likely that Ctesiphon and Jerome had become friends when Jerome had lived in Rome. Jerome, *Epist.* 133.1.

50. Jerome, *Epist.* 133.13.

51. Jerome, *Epist.* 133.1.

52. Jerome, *Epist.* 133.13.

53. Jerome earlier had accused Rufinus as well of being part of a group that had secret teaching. Rufinus, *Apol. Hier.* 2.1.

54. Jerome, *Epist.* 133.3. See also: 133.11–12; *In Hier.* 4.pref; *Dial.* 3.16.

as there is no indication that they ever held any secret doctrines, and none of the other opponents of the Pelagians made this claim.

Letters to the Virgin Demetrias

Pelagius settled in Jerusalem after he left Carthage.[55] Roland Teske has suggested that he moved into Rufinus of Aquileia's former monastery.[56] Although this might explain why the bishops as the Synod of Diospolis described Pelagius as a *monachus*, there is no evidence to support this assertion, and he never showed any inclination to the cenobitic life in Rome.[57] While in Jerusalem, Pelagius received an invitation from Anicia Juliana to write a letter of spiritual direction to her teenage daughter, Demetrias, because Demetrias had recently broken her engagement shortly before her wedding[58] in 412 in order to take the veil as a consecrated virgin[59] at the hands of Aurelius, the bishop of Carthage.[60] Demetrias's family, as we have already seen, was one of the richest and noblest families in all of Rome. Her paternal grandfather, Sextus Petronius Probus, had been Proconsul of Africa at twenty-two years old. He had been the Praetorian Prefect four times, and Consul with Gratian in 371. He also had been Regent for Valentinian II, and married Anicia Faltonia Proba, Demetrias's grandmother, before being baptized on his deathbed around 390.[61] His mausoleum was constructed adjacent to an apse of the shrine of St. Peter on the Vatican.[62] Their daughter, Juliana,[63] born around 380,[64] married Anicius Hermogenianus Olybrius, who had been consul and senator, and who had died shortly before the sack of Rome in 410.[65] Proba and Juliana, now both widows, fled Rome with Demetrias just before Alaric's arrival in Rome and, as Jerome reports, Proba, in a "fragile boat," could see "the smoke of her native city"[66] as it burned. When they arrived in Africa, they found themselves still in danger. The same Heraclian who was associated with Marcellinus and was executed

---

55. Harnack offers the possibility that Pelagius left Carthage when he realized that his presence there would only bring him problems. Though this is a possibility, there is no conclusive evidence for this hypothesis. Harnack, *History of Dogma*, 175.

56. Teske, vol. 1 "Introduction," *WSA*, 310.

57. Augustine, *Gest. Pelag.* 20.44.

58. Jerome, *Epist.* 130. 5. It is probable that her fiancé was an exile from Italy. Pelagius, "To Demetrias," 29.

59. McWilliam, "Letters to Demetrias," 131.

60. Jerome, *Epist.* 130.2.

61. Krabbe, *Epistula*, 1–2.

62. Brown, *Through the Eye*, 286.

63. A suggestion has been made that Julian of Eclanum was Demetrias's uncle: Krabbe, *Epistula*, 5. But there is no proof for such a claim: Dunn, "Christian Networks," 64.

64. Dunn, "Christian Networks," 56.

65. Krabbe, *Epistula*, 2.

66. Jerome, *Epist.* 130.7.

for an attempted *putsch*,[67] forced Proba to pay large sums of money to purchase "the chastity of her numerous companions."[68]

Pelagius responded to Juliana's request and wrote to Demetrias—a girl whom he probably knew from his time in Rome—in 414.[69] Or, to put it more accurately, Pelagius responded to Juliana's demand. "Even if I could claim to possess natural talent of a high quality," he says, "and an equally high degree of artistic skill and believed myself for that reason to be capable of fulfilling with ease the obligation of writing, I would still not be able to enter upon this arduous task without considerable fear of the difficulties involved."[70] Setting aside Pelagius's false humility—a commonplace in the antique epistolary tradition[71]—we should not take his complaint that this was an "appointed task"[72] too seriously, as he would have seen this opportunity as a great honor.[73]

Pelagius's letter to Demetrias has been called a "manifesto,"[74] a "real showpiece,"[75] and one "*des joyaux de la littérature chrétienne*."[76] It is, without a doubt, the best unmediated picture we have of Pelagius's theology. Several other letters from Pelagius are extant as well, but none of them give quite the insight into Pelagius's mind as this letter.[77] With the Pelagian controversy well under way at this point, we hear him speak for himself, rather than receive his voice from a selection of quotations found in Augustine's *oeuvre*, which constitute the bulk of our knowledge of his contested theology. The letter was a set of instructions for how to live the life of a consecrated virgin. In the twenty-first century, the daily life of consecrated women has been established and refined over the centuries. But, in the early fifth century, female renunciation was still fairly new. As we saw earlier with Marcella, aristocratic women living in Rome did not retreat to convents after consecration—as had Augustine's sister, who had become the superior of a convent in Hippo,[78] Melania the Elder, who founded a monastery on the Mount of Olives,[79] or Paula, who established a monastery in Bethlehem.[80] Pelagius's

---

67. Rees, "Pelagius," 29.

68. Jerome, *Epist.* 130.7.

69. McWilliam, "Letters to Demetrias," 132.

70. Pelagius, *Ad. Dem.* 1.1.

71. Jerome also begins his letter to Demetrias with the same false humility: "I am unequal to the task before me." Jerome, *Epist.* 130.1.

72. Pelagius, *Ad. Dem.* 1.2.

73. Jerome, too, makes it clear that his letter to Demetrias was also demanded: "her grandmother and her mother are both women of mark, and they have alike authority to command, faith to seek and perseverance to obtain that which they require." Jerome, *Epist.* 130.1.

74. Brown, "Pelagius," 185.

75. Rees, "Pelagius," 32.

76. De Plinval, *Pélage*, 245.

77. See: Pelagius, *Div. leg; Ad Cel; Virg; Vit. Christ*.

78. Augustine, *Epist.* 211.4.

79. Brown, *Through the Eye*, 276.

80. Jerome, *Epist.* 108.14.

letter, then, was a guide to help Demetrias understand how to live her new life beneath the veil. In it, he discussed the "power and quality of human nature,"[81] his understanding of the liberty of the free will,[82] his claim that sin happens out of habit (not out of an inclination to sin because of original sin),[83] his belief of Christ as an example,[84] his vision of marriage,[85] the necessity of fulfilling all of the commandments,[86] the pursuit of the perfect life,[87] and the merit of divine grace.[88] He also made sure to warn Demetrias of the corrupting influence of Augustine:

> we accuse God of a twofold lack of knowledge, so that he appears not to know what he has done, and not to know what he has commanded; as if, forgetful of the human frailty of which he is himself the author, he has imposed on man commands which he cannot bear. And, at the same time, oh horror!, we ascribe iniquity to the righteous and cruelty to the holy, while complaining, first, that he has commanded something impossible, secondly, that man is to be damned by him for doing things which he was unable to avoid, so that God—and this is something which even to suspect is sacrilege—seems to have sought not so much our salvation as our punishment![89]

Although the bishop of Hippo is not mentioned explicitly by name here, Pelagius clearly had Augustine in mind.[90] Augustine had met the family when they arrived in Africa, and Pelagius undoubtedly was worried about Augustine's influence over his former patrons.[91]

Jerome also received a directive from Proba and Juliana to write to Demetrias.[92] Jerome's epistle (130), also written in 414 around the same time Jerome wrote to Ctesiphon,[93] is his last extant letter to noblewomen.[94] It comes as a surprise that his advice was solicited, despite the fact that he had carefully constructed his reputation

81. Pelagius, *Ad. Dem.* 2.1.
82. Pelagius, *Ad. Dem.* 3.1–2, 8.1.
83. Pelagius, *Ad. Dem.* 8.3, 17.3.
84. Pelagius, *Ad. Dem.* 8.4.
85. Pelagius, *Ad. Dem.* 9.2.
86. Pelagius, *Ad. Dem.* 10.1, 16.1.
87. Pelagius, *Ad. Dem.* 24.1.
88. Pelagius, *Ad. Dem.* 25.3.
89. Pelagius, *Ad. Dem.* 16.2.
90. McWilliam, "Letters to Demetrias," 135.
91. Augustine, *Epist.* 188.1.

92. It has often been repeated that Pope Innocent I (*PL* 20 518–19) had also written a letter to Demetrias, but Dunn has argued that Innocent's short letter seems to be directed towards Juliana. Dunn, "Christian Networks," 54–71. An anonymous letter also was written to Demetrias, many years later around the year 440, which may have been written by Pope Leo or by Prosper of Aquitaine. Jacobs, "Writing Demetrias," 744; Krabbe, *Epistula*, 138–214.

93. McWilliam, "Letters to Demetrias," 132.
94. Wilkinson, "Spectacular Modesty," 24.

as an ascetic master and that, as he said, "it is not indeed anything very new or special they ask of me; my wits have often been exercised upon similar themes."[95] Although he had written before to other nobles instructing them on the life of renunciation, including his famous letter to Eustochium thirty years earlier,[96] Jerome had not known these three women prior to their "command"[97] to write to Demetrias.[98] Furthermore, the Anicia had moved in the same circle as Rufinus,[99] and Jerome certainly knew of the relationship between the Anicia and Pelagius.[100] As they were both in Palestine, it is likely that Pelagius and Jerome knew that the other was writing to Demetrias at the same moment, which should color the way that we read their letters.[101]

Despite all of this, Jerome took to the task with gusto. He states right from the beginning that he has "high esteem" for Demetrias, despite writing "as a stranger to a stranger."[102] His letter is the best source we have detailing Demetrias's decision to take the veil, and of the perilous flight of the women from Rome to Africa. After Demetrias had made her decision to reject the married life, Jerome says that she

> cast from her as so many hindrances all her ornaments and worldly attire. Her precious necklaces, costly pearls, and glowing gems she put back in their cases. Then dressing herself in a coarse tunic and throwing over herself a still coarser cloak she came in at an unlooked for moment, threw herself down suddenly at her grandmother's knees, and with tears and sobs showed her what she really was. That staid and holy woman was amazed when she beheld her granddaughter in so strange a dress. Her mother was completely overcome for joy. Both women could hardly believe that which they had longed to be true. Their voices stuck in their throats, and, what, with blushing and turning pale, with fright and with joy, they were a prey to many conflicting emotions.[103]

Although his lack of personal knowledge of Demetrias, and his exaggerated rhetorical panache must make us hesitate to believe every detail of his description, we still must appreciate the difficulty of her decision at the same time. We have seen that the

---

95. Jerome, *Epist.* 130.1.

96. Jerome, *Epist.* 22.

97. Jerome, *Epist.* 130.1.

98. Dunphy has argued that Jerome had never had any contact with anyone from the *gens* Anicia, but Dunn has shown that Jerome had corresponded with Probus's daughter-in-law, Furia. Dunphy, "Saint Jerome," 139; Dunn, "Christian Networks," 65; Jerome, *Epist.* 54 and 123.17.

99. Dunphy discusses several other contrasting points between the Anicia and Jerome: Dunphy, "Saint Jerome," 142.

100. Dunphy, "Saint Jerome," 143; Dunn, "Christian Networks," 66.

101. Dunphy suggests that Jerome was eager to make a good impression because he had lost the support of Pammachius and Marcella and was in need of a new source of support. Dunphy, "Saint Jerome," 143. Kelly suggests that Jerome had read Pelagius's letter before he wrote his own. Kelly, *Jerome*, 313.

102. Jerome, *Epist.* 130.2.

103. Jerome, *Epist.* 130.5.

Christian ascetic life had been increasing in popularity among Roman aristocrats for several decades, but such a step by a girl of approximately fourteen years of age from such an important family makes her decision remarkable, and everyone knew it. Jerome was sure to let her know that "every church in Africa danced for joy. The news reached not only the cities, towns, and villages, but even the scattered huts. Every island between Africa and Italy was full of it, the glad tidings ran far and wide, disliked by none. Then Italy put off her mourning and the ruined walls of Rome resumed in part their olden splendor."[104] He even took some credit for her glory. "The grandmother and the mother have planted," he said, "but it is I that water and the Lord that giveth the increase."[105]

The picture of the day-to-day life of a virgin that Jerome sent to Demetrias is not radically different from what he had offered Eustochium, nor, in fact, radically different from Pelagius's letter.[106] Like his earlier letter and Pelagius's letter, he emphasized, among other things, the reading of Scripture,[107] fasting,[108] avoiding flatterers,[109] wearing modest garments,[110] and prayer.[111] He also told her that she must never look at men (especially young men),[112] she should not be covetous,[113] and that she should avoid married women.[114] He further urged her to recognize that her vast wealth no longer belonged to her, and after her grandmother and mother die that she must use the money for the poor and refrain from building churches.[115] Decades later as an adult during the pontificate of Leo the Great (440–461)—well after Proba and Juliana

---

104. Jerome, *Epist.* 130. 6. Pelagius also notes the public acclaim for Demetrias's decision: "the glorious news of your act of pubic profession has spread abroad and become common talk among all men, and the whole world has become so exultant at your conversion that people seem to have wanted all along for something to happen which, now that is has happened, they are still scarcely able to credit for all their great joy." Pelagius, *Ad Dem.* 14.2.

105. Jerome, *Epist.* 130.2.

106. Bonner, "Manuscript Transmission," 626–28.

107. Jerome, *Epist.* 130.7.

108. Jerome, *Epist.* 130.10.

109. Jerome, *Epist.* 130.4. Although he encouraged fasting, he also insisted that her fasting must not be "extreme fasting or abnormal abstinence from food." Jerome, *Epist.* 130.11. His insistence on moderation on this point may come as a result of the death of the young Blesilla three decades earlier. His advice here is certainly less demanding than what he wrote to Eustochium: "let your fasts be of daily occurrence and your refreshment such as avoids satiety." Jerome, *Epist.* 22.17.

110. Jerome, *Epist.* 130.4.

111. Jerome, *Epist.* 130.15. Jerome earlier instructed Eustochium on the same practices: Scripture (22.35); fast (22.17); flatterers (22.2.); garments (22.27); prayer (22.37). Pelagius, too, instructs Demetrias on these behaviors: Pelgaius, *Ad Dem.* Scripture (23.2.); fasting (21.2); flatterers (22.1.); garments (20.1.); prayer (23.1.).

112. Jerome, *Epist.*130.12.

113. Jerome, *Epist.* 130.14.

114. Jerome, *Epist.* 130.18.

115. Jerome, *Epist.* 130.14.

had died—Demetrias endowed a church built in Rome in honor of St. Stephen,[116] disregarding at least some of Jerome's advice, and leaving us to wonder what other advice from him that she would ignore.[117]

At the end of his letter, Jerome came to "the most important point of all."[118] Just as Pelagius had warned Demetrias about the dangers of Augustine, Jerome warned her of the dangers of Pelagius. Not mentioning Pelagius by name, he alerted Demetrias to his belief that Pelagius is a successor of Origen. "The poisonous germs of this heresy [Origenism]," he cautioned, "still live and sprout in the minds of some to this day."[119] Jerome encouraged Demetrias to remain faithful to the teachings of Innocent I, the bishop of Rome, whom he described as the successor of Pope Anastasius, who "smote the noxious thing on the head, and stayed the hydra's hissing."[120] He is concerned specifically with Pelagius's beliefs about the human soul. He says that Pelagius questioned the justice of God's decision to allow one soul to be born to Christian parents, while others are born "among wild beasts and savage tribes who have no knowledge of God,"[121] although there is no indication in Pelagius's extant writings that he was haunted by this question.[122] Jerome, however, correctly recognized the Pelagian rejection of the brokenness of humanity at birth: "is it for nothing . . . that a little child scarcely able to recognize its mother by a laugh or a look of joy which has done nothing either good or evil is seized by a devil or overwhelmed with jaundice or doomed to bear afflictions which godless men escape, while God's servants have to bear them?"[123] But, Jerome's depiction of the Pelagian alternative is perplexing: "we are compelled by reason to believe that our souls have preexisted in heaven, that they are condemned to and, if I may say so, buried in human bodies because of some ancient sins, and that we are punished in this valley of weeping for old misdeeds."[124] Certainly, we already have seen that Origen had influenced Pelagius's Pauline commentaries. But, there is no indication in Pelagius's writings that he agreed with Origen on the preexistence of the soul.[125] Jerome's perception of Pelagian teaching, though confused at this point, would soon come more clearly into focus.[126]

---

116. Brown, *Through the Eye*, 463–65.

117. Jacobs, "Writing Demetrias," 744.

118. Jerome, *Epist.* 130.16.

119. Jerome, *Epist.* 130.16.

120. For a description of the relationship between the *gens* Anicia and Innocent I, see: Dunn, "Christian Networks," 68–71.

121. Jerome, *Epist.* 130.16.

122. Jerome, *Epist.* 130.16.

123. Jerome, *Epist.* 130.16.

124. Jerome, *Epist.* 130.16.

125. For example, Pelagius says that we are "begotten without virtue, so we are begotten without vice." Augustine, *Grat. Chr.* 2.13.14.

126. A recent minority report argues that this warning from Jerome had nothing to do with Pelagius. Van Egmond, "Pelagius," 637.

Scholars have received Jerome's letter to Demetrias differently. Kelly has stated that he believes that it is "one of his most impressive literary productions,"[127] and Joanne McWilliam believes that it is more interesting than Pelagius's letter because of its "vivid descriptions"[128] of the dangerous journey the women had to Africa, and Demetrias's agonizing decision to take the veil. Rees, on the other hand, dismisses it as "an unexceptional but quite unremarkable piece of moral instruction, which an old hand like its writer would be able to turn out on demand every day of the week, and I would rate no higher than beta plus."[129] My own reaction is somewhere in the middle. Compared to his letter to Eustochium, I find his letter to Demetrias less compelling, as it is a more moderate rehash of much of the same advice from three decades earlier. But, to disregard it as "unremarkable" does not do Jerome justice. Despite the fact that he does not seem to offer any profoundly new insights into the ascetic life, we must not forget that Jerome's vision of the consecrated life was still considered dangerous by many, and it never ceased to generate new detractors.[130]

Like Pelagius and Jerome, Augustine had written concerning Demetrias on two occasions. At roughly the same time as Pelagius and Jerome, at the end of 413 or the beginning of 414, Augustine wrote a short letter (150) to Proba and Juliana, lukewarmly praising Demetrias's decision, and thanking Proba for a gift she sent to him in celebration. Several years later, at the end of 417 or the beginning of 418, Augustine (and Alypius) wrote a longer, anxious letter (188) to Juliana after Augustine had read the letter that Pelagius had sent to Demetrias.[131] They clearly were trying to make amends for not having written in detail earlier, and were hoping to repair any damage Augustine's neglect may have caused.[132] Although Augustine and Alypius had written to Proba and Juliana concerning Demetrias, they did not write a letter directly addressed to Demetrias—as had Pelagius and Jerome—nor do we have any explicit mention of an invitation or command from Proba or Juliana.[133] There are, however, multiple reasons to believe that he and Alypius were invited to do so. First, unlike Jerome, Augustine and Alypius knew these women personally after their arrival in

127. Kelly, *Jerome*, 312.
128. McWilliam, "Letters to Demetrias," 132.
129. Rees, "Pelagius," 32.
130. Jerome, *Epist.* 130.19.
131. Augustine, *Epist.* 188.3.14.

132. Clark notes that this is the last letter that Augustine wrote to Proba or Juliana and she suspects that the friendship they had had could not withstand any support that Proba and Juliana gave to Pelagius. Clark, "Theory and Practice," 416.

133. Andrew Jacobs suspects that Augustine and Alypius did not direct their letter to Demetrias because "Augustine does not construe Demetrias as the governing principle of her own ascetic life, and the worried letter to Juliana reinforces the inability and lack of authority in the daughter by instead focusing on the mother." Jacobs, "Writing Demetrias," 732.

Africa,[134] and, as we saw earlier, they wrote of their "closeness" to them.[135] Second, they had played an important role in Demetrias's decision to take the veil. Demetrias had abandoned her engagement shortly after Augustine and Alypius had ministered to her in her home.[136] Like Jerome, they alluded to Paul's agricultural image to describe how they had contributed to Demetrias decision: "[God] plants and waters through his servants [Augustine and Alypius] but gives through himself" (1 Cor 3: 5–7). Third, a precedent already had been established by Proba and Juliana asking Augustine to write to them two other times.[137] Fourth, because Augustine's reputation was as highly esteemed as Pelagius's and Jerome's, it would be logical for Proba and Juliana to have asked him for a letter.[138] Fifth, although their second letter (188) to Juliana was not addressed to Demetrias, Demetrias was clearly as much of the intended audience as Juliana. Sixth, Augustine and Alypius tells us that their letter (188) was a response to a letter (no longer extant) written to them from Juliana.[139] It is likely that Juliana had made her request in that letter.

Augustine and Alypius had a different agenda than Pelagius and Jerome. While Pelagius and Jerome offered a detailed spiritual program for the young Demetrias, the Africans were only interested in showing the error of Pelagius's letter, and of warning the women of that error. They do not stress the reading of scripture, fasting, or instruct her on the types of clothes she should wear. Nor do they dictate the type of company she should keep or to guard against a wandering eye. They do tell her to pray, but their directive has less to do with encouraging a robust life of prayer, and more about reminding her to offer prayers of thanksgiving for her perseverance and progress in her spiritual life, which, they stress, do not come from her but come from God.[140]

Augustine and Alypius are mainly concerned that these women "should carefully avoid what does not pertain to sound doctrine."[141] The women were offended that Augustine would even hint that they had strayed from orthodoxy, and insisted that everyone in their family always had been orthodox Christians.[142] To them, being faithful to "sound doctrine" means that they believe the trinitarian claims defined at

134. Augustine, *Epist.* 188.1.1.

135. Augustine, *Epist.* 188.1.2.

136. Augustine, *Epist.* 188.1.1. Clark has stated that Demetrias had read Augustine's *De sancta virginitate* written thirteen years earlier, but I cannot find any evidence of this.

137. Augustine had written to Proba in 411: "recalling that you asked and that I promised that I would write something for you on praying to God" (130.1.1). He also had written to Juliana in 414 "Not any longer to be in debt of my promise to your [Juliana] request and love in Christ, I have seized the occasion as I could, amid other very pressing engagement, to write to you somewhat concerning the profession of holy widowhood." (*B. vid.* 1).

138. For a discussion on Augustine's authority in his own time, see: O'Donnell, "Authority of Augustine," 14.

139. Augustine, *Epist.* 188.1.1.

140. Augustine, *Epist.* 188.2.7.

141. Augustine, *Epist.* 188.1.2.

142. Augustine, *Epist.* 188.1.3.

the Council of Nicaea (325) and the Council of Constantinople (381).[143] The Africans recognize the faithfulness of the women to these conciliar pronouncements, but, they say, "human error does not sneak up on one on this point alone ... for there are other doctrines on which one errs in a most destructive way."[144] In addition to faithfulness to theological claims, the women also need to "avoid teachings opposed to the grace of God."[145] Today, we might agree with Augustine and Alypius that heterodoxy may be manifest in a variety of ways, but the Anician women were correct that a precise definition of the grace of God had not been defined definitively by a council at this point, nor had it been a locus of serious theological disagreement in the way that the trinitarian and christological fights had been for decades.

Jerome's *In Hieremiam prophetam* and *Dialogi contra Pelagianos*

Jerome's next attack on the Pelagians came in his biblical commentary *In Hieremiam prophetam*, in which he called the Pelagians "dumb dogs."[146] Dedicated to his friend Eusebius of Cremona, to whom he had dedicated his *Commentaria in Matthaeum* in 398,[147] Jerome began dictating this biblical commentary to his secretaries in 414,[148] but never completed it as his monastery was burned two years later.[149] It is important for our purposes because it reveals that Pelagius resurrected two charges that had been brought against Jerome decades earlier, although there are no extant texts from Pelagius leveling these charges directly against him. Either the texts have been lost, or Jerome only had heard Pelagius make them in person when Pelagius was in Jerusalem.

The first resurrected charge against Jerome was his use of Origen in his *Commentaria in Epistolam ad Ephesios*, against which Jerome already defended himself in his fight with Rufinus. During the height of the Origenist controversy, Rufinus had taken up Jerome's challenge to read through his *Commentaria in Epistolam ad Ephesios*, written between 386 and 388,[150] where, so Jerome claims, Rufinus can see him refuting Origen's heterodoxy.[151] Rufinus retorts that just the opposite is true, and that Jerome's commentary is marinated in the influence of Origen, whom Rufinus calls

---

143. For example, Pelagius declares his belief in the Nicene Trinity while defending himself at the Synod of Diospolis despite the fact that none of the charges brought against him had anything to do with the Trinity. Augustine, *Gest. Pelag.* 19.43.

144. Augustine, *Epist.* 188.3.10.

145. Augustine, *Epist.* 188.1.2.

146. Jerome, *In Hier.* 4.pref.

147. Jerome, *In Hier.* 1.pref; Graves, "Introduction," xxix.

148. Jerome, *In Hier.* 1.pref.

149. Cavallera, *Saint Jérôme*, 164.

150. Heine, "Introduction," 7.

151. Jerome, *Epist.* 84.2; Rufinus, *Apol. Hier.* 2.28.

Jerome's "partner," and his "brother mystic."[152] If Origen must be condemned for his diversion from orthodoxy as Jerome claims, so, too, must Jerome: "but it may be said," Rufinus insists, "that the works themselves ought to be condemned and their author [Origen] as well. If that be so, what is to happen to the other author [Jerome] who writes the same things, as I have shown most fully above? He must receive a similar judgment."[153] In fact, Rufinus says, Jerome's commentary is riddled with even more extreme doctrines than are contained in Origen's works.[154]

Jerome's defense against these accusations was to explain his method of writing biblical commentaries.[155] He said that his commentary had multiple objectives. First, he was trying to render into clear and concise language what Paul had written obscurely in his letter. Second, he offered his own interpretation of Paul's meaning. Third, he offered interpretations from Origen, Didymus the Blind, and Apollinaris of Laodicea, saying that he "partly followed" Origen's interpretation, and that he "culled some things, though but few" from Didymus and Apollinaris.[156] Fourth, he insisted that he always made it clear when he was offering his own interpretation, and when he was offering the interpretations of others; he also insisted that he always made it clear which doctrines from these other interpreters were heretical, and which were orthodox. Fifth, it is the responsibility of the reader to decide which interpretations he feels most authentically reflects the meaning of the author, and Jerome cannot be held responsible for the interpretations of others. This method of textual interpretation, he maintains, is accepted by all men of letters, Christian and non-Christian, of both scriptural and secular texts.[157]

When Pelagius revived this accusation against him years later, Jerome responded that he was an "unlearned detractor" who snores "in extreme dementia," and does not understand the rules of biblical exegesis.[158] He then repeated a similar defense that he had given to Rufinus that his role as an exegete was to offer the opinions of various authors, and that the reader must decide his preferred interpretation.[159]

The second resurrected charge against Jerome—from his earlier fight with Jovinian—addressed the contentious issue of virginity, marriage, and remarriage.[160] Specifically, Jerome said that Pelagius, following Jovinian, was disturbed that Jerome believed that "virginity is preferable to marriage, that marriage is preferable to bigamy and that

---

152. Rufinus, *Apol. Hier.* 1.23.
153. Rufinus, *Apol. Hier.* 2.28.
154. Rufinus, *Apol. Hier.* 2.28.
155. For an expanded description of see: Evans, *Inquiries and Reappraisals*, 6–25.
156. Jerome, *Apol.* 1.21.
157. Jerome, *Apol.* 1.15–16, 21, 3.11. See Heine for a review of the debate between these two over Jerome's commentary, and Jerome's use of Origen. Heine, "Introduction," 10–18.
158. Jerome, *In Hier.* 1.pref.
159. Jerome, *In Hier.* 1.pref.
160. Evans, *Inquiries and Reappraisals*, 26–42.

bigamy is preferable to polygamy."[161] Pelagius's problem with Jerome seems to rest on the question of the remarriage of widows, which is what he meant by "bigamy," and "polygamy."[162] Jerome defended himself by repeating what he had said in his *Contra Iovinianum* that he does not condemn remarriage.[163] But, this defense fails to address the charge itself, because the charge is not that Jerome condemns marriage, but that he hierarchically places first marriages over second marriages. To this charge, Jerome is guilty. Jerome was disgusted by the thought of remarriage, and likened it to a dog returning to its own vomit.[164] Against Jovinian, he was convinced that as Paul "subordinated marriage to virginity, so he makes second marriages inferior to first, and he says 'a wife is bound for so long [a] time as her husband lives; but if the husband be dead, she is free to be married to whom she will; only in the Lord. But she is happier if she abide as she is, after my judgement: and I think that I have the Spirit of God'" (1 Cor 7:39–40).[165] Later in the same text, he said that "what the holiness of second marriage is appears from this—that a person twice married cannot be enrolled in the ranks of the clergy, and so the apostle tells Timothy, 'let none be enrolled as a widow under threescore years old, having been the wife of one man'" (1 Tim 5:9).[166] Jerome—while allowing remarriage of widows as lawful—relegates second marriage to a second-class status.

Pelagius's vision of marriage was a *via media* between Jerome and Augustine.[167] Along with Jerome, Pelagius rejected the Manichaeans who dismissed marriage, and rejected Jovinian who equated marriage and virginity;[168] both men, furthermore, favored virginity over marriage. But, Pelagius was not as critical of marriage as Jerome, who said that the only good of marriage is that the fruit of the sexual union may lead to future virgins.[169] Pelagius was more in harmony with Augustine than Jerome on marriage, but differed from Augustine in that Pelagius believed that sex within marriage was not sinful,[170] whereas Augustine said that sex for the purpose of procreation was without sin, but that sex within marriage for the pleasure of the flesh is a sin, though pardonable.[171] Pelagius's opinion on remarriage also differed from Jerome, prompting Jerome's touchy response in this commentary. Although Pelagius, like Jerome, preferred widows to remain single (he encouraged them to remain as they are by saying

161. Jerome, *In Hier.* 1.pref. See also: 16:1–4.
162. Evans, *Inquiries and Reappraisals*, 27.
163. Jerome, *In Hier.* 1.pref. See also: *C. Jov.* 1.15.
164. Jerome, *Epist.* 54.4.
165. Jerome, *C. Jov.* 1.14.
166. Jerome, *C. Jov.* 1.15.
167. Rackett, "Sexuality and Sinlessness," 51–132; Hunter, *Marriage, Celibacy*, 259–68.
168. In his *Libellus fidei* written to Innocent, Pelagius rejected those who condemn marriage (Manichaeans) and those who condemn remarriage (Cataphrygians). Pelagius, *Lib. fid.* 10.
169. Jerome, *Epist.* 22.20.
170. Rackett, "Sexuality and Sinlessness," 78.
171. For example: Augustine, *Nupt.* 1.15.17.

that widowhood is superior to even chaste married women, and insisted that widows receive a greater reward than those who remarry), he did not disparage those who wanted to remarry, as Jerome had done.[172] If any widow wavered and did not want to remain in widowhood, Pelagius encouraged them to marry (as long as it was to a Christian),[173] because it is better to marry than to fall prey to temptation.[174]

Jerome's final attack on the Pelagians was his *Dialogi contra Pelagianos*, which fulfilled his promise to Ctesiphon to offer a full explanation of his mind on the Pelagians.[175] They are his most important and most sustained work from which the majority of his refutation against them comes. Begun in middle of 415, he completed at least a working draft—or an entire final draft—immediately before the Synod of Diospolis. Heros and Lazarus used them as the main source for their charges against Pelagius at the synod, as we shall see later.[176] Written in three books, they were a fictionalized discourse between two *personae*: Atticus was the character representing Jerome, while Critobulus was the voice of the Pelagians. These books, for the most part, presented Pelagian arguments fairly and evenhandedly, which is noteworthy as most of his assaults on other opponents twisted their positions beyond caricature. Within a year after finishing his third book, Jerome's monastery was burned to the ground, and he ceased his onslaught of his last enemies. In one of his final letters shortly before his passing, he praised Augustine and Alypius for their contributions in bringing about the triple condemnation of the Pelagians in 418, and informed them of his inability to continue writing based on the unfortunate cocktail of physical illness, grief over the death of Eustochium, and a paucity of secretaries.[177]

Augustine's *De natura et gratia* and *De perfectione iustitiae hominis*

Sometime between January 415 and 416,[178] Augustine wrote his *De natura et gratia* in response to Pelagius's *De natura*,[179] which he had received from Timasius and James,

---

172. Pelagius, *Expos. ad 1 Cor.* 7:40.

173. Pelagius, *Expos. ad 1 Cor.* 7:39. Rackett notes that "it is significant that Pelagius says that widows may remarry 'if they do not *wish* to be continent' (*si nec tunc se continere uolerit*) rather than 'if they are not *able* to be continent.'" Rackett, "Sexuality and Sinlessness," 98 n. 166.

174. Pelagius, *Expos. ad 1 Tim.* 5:14. See also: 3:2, 3:12; *Expos. ad Tit.* 1:6.

175. Jerome, *Epist.* 133.13; *Dial.* 1.1.

176. Cavallera, *Saint Jérôme*, 164; Kelly, *Jerome*, 321; Burnett, "Dysfunction," 160–64.

177. Jerome, *Epist.* 143.

178. Teske, vol. 1 "Introduction," 198.

179. As mentioned in a previous chapter, scholars disagree when Pelagius's *De natura* was written. Some believe it was written when he was in Sicily in 410–411. Others believe that it was written from Palestine in 413–414. Duval, Teske, and Lancel have argued that it was more likely written 406–410 while in Rome. Duval, "La Date," 274; Rees, "Pelagius," 140; Teske, vol. 1 "Introduction," 198–99; Lancel, *Saint Augustine*, 326.

two of Pelagius's former disciples who asked him to respond to it.[180] Little is known about these two men, or their relationship with Pelagius, but they had been so moved by Pelagius's teaching that they had abandoned their worldly (*saeculum*) pursuits to become servants of God (*ad Dei servitium*),[181] although there is no indication that they had desired to be ordained as had Caelestius. Augustine described them as "good and honest men"[182] to Aurelius, and in a letter (179) to John of Jerusalem he described them as "sons of the finest families and well educated in the liberal arts."[183] If they had met Pelagius during his years in Rome (and possibly came to Africa with him), they may have abandoned significant administrative careers to follow Pelagius's path. Pelagius's influence on them may not have lasted very long, as they turned away from his teaching because of Augustine. In a letter (168) they both wrote to Augustine, they said that they "cast off our subjugation to this [Pelagian] error, after having been instructed by the spirit of love, which is present in you."[184]

When Augustine received Pelagius's *De natura* from them, he put down other work he had been writing and quickly read it.[185] What he found appalled him. Pelagius was a man "aflame with ardent zeal,"[186] he claimed, but not a man of much knowledge. Pelagius passionately railed against "those who look for an excuse for their sins in the weakness of human nature,"[187] and posited a vision of an unblemished humanity.[188] Despite this error about nature (as Augustine understood it), Augustine was not willing to attack Pelagius openly. In a letter (186) written to Paulinus of Nola shortly after completing his *De natura et gratia*, Augustine indicated that—like the first two books of *De peccatorum meritis et remissione et de baptism parvulorum* where he hesitated to name his interlocutors in hopes that they might be open to correction—he hesitated to mention Pelagius by name (even though he had already done so in book three of his first anti-Pelagian text),[189] because he wanted to believe that Pelagius was not misleading the faithful on purpose, but that he ignorantly did not know what he was doing. "I do not want to say that what he [Pelagius] does in this book [*De natura*] he does knowingly," Augustine said, "because I want to avoid the judgment that its author should not be regarded even as a Christian. Rather, I believe that he does this without knowledge, but with great strength. But I want that

---

180. Augustine, *Nat. grat.* 1.1; *Epist.* 179.2.
181. Augustine, *Epist.* 179.2.
182. Augustine, *Gest. Pelag.* 23.47.
183. Augustine, *Epist.* 179.2.
184. Augustine, *Epist.* 168.
185. Augustine, *Nat. grat.* 1.1.
186. Augustine, *Nat. grat.* 1.1, 7.7; see also *Epist.* 186.1.
187. Augustine, *Nat. grat.* 7.7.
188. Augustine, *Nat. grat.* 19.21.
189. Augustine, *Epist.* 186.1.

strength to be healthy, not the sort found in lunatics."[190] Even now after he had written three texts against the Pelagians over approximately a four-year span, Augustine still wanted to give Pelagius the benefit of the doubt.

Although the *De natura* is no longer extant, the organization of Augustine's *De natura et gratia*, and the extensive quotations from it, likely reveal much of Pelagius's project.[191] After the introductory sections, Augustine returns to the issue discussed primarily in book two of *De peccatorum meritis et remissione et de baptism parvulorum*, the possibility of living a life without sin. Pelagius clearly agreed with the unnamed Pelagians in that book that it is possible to be sinless in this life.[192] Next, Augustine circles back to the issue primarily discussed in book one of *De peccatorum meritis et remissione et de baptism parvulorum*, that Adam's sin did not injure anyone other than himself.[193] Third, the issue of sinlessness is once again discussed,[194] and Augustine responded to a list of people Pelagius included whom he concluded were sinless.[195] Fourth, sinlessness, nature, and original sin continued to be explored.[196] Finally, Augustine responded to the quotations from the variety of ecclesiastical authorities (such as Lactatnius, Hilary of Poitiers, Ambrose, John Chrysostom, a man named Xystus whom both Pelagius and Augustine thought was Pope Xystus II but was a Pythagorean named Sextus,[197] Jerome, and even Augustine himself).[198] These authorities, Augustine insisted, neither helped nor hurt Pelagius's arguments, because the quotations Pelagius chose from them were "neutral" (*media*).[199]

Augustine also received a request from two bishops, Eutropius and Paul, to reply to a text, *Definitiones, ut dicitur Caelestii*. Nothing about the bishops is known, other than that they were mentioned in Orosius's *De errore Priscillianistarum et Origenistarum*, leading to the possibility that they were from Spain, like Orosius.[200] The bishops, who may have been in Africa at the time, had received the *Definitiones* from some unnamed individuals who had brought the text from Sicily and gave it to them.[201] The text itself was not named the *Definitiones* by the author, but probably was given that

---

190. Augustine, *Nat. grat.* 7.7.

191. Teske, vol. 1 "Introduction," *WSA*, 201.

192. Augustine, *Nat. grat.* 7.8–18.20.

193. Augustine, *Nat. grat.* 19.21–32.36.

194. Augustine, *Nat. grat.* 33.37–44.51.

195. Abel, Henoch, Melchizedek, Abraham, Isaac, Jacob, Joseph, Joshua the son of Nun, Phinehas, Samuel, Nathan, Elijah, Elisha, Micah, Daniel, Hananiah, Azariah, Mishael, Ezekiel, Mordecai, Simeon, Joseph, Deborah, Anna the mother of Samuel, Judith, Esther, another Anna the daughter of Phanuel, Elizabeth, and Mary. Augustine, *Nat. grat.* 36.42.

196. Augustine, *Nat. grat.* 44.52–60.70.

197. Chadwick, *Sentences of Sextus*, 121–37.

198. Augustine, *Nat. grat.* 61.71–67.81.

199. Augustine, *Nat. grat.* 61.71.

200. Orosius, *Prisc. et Orig.* 1.

201. Teske, vol. 1 "Introduction," *WSA*, 269.

title by the men who brought it to Africa. Augustine said that the text was written either by Caelestius, or by some of his companions, because the content of the *Definitiones* is remarkably similar to an unnamed text Augustine knew that certainly was written by Caelestius.[202]

Augustine's response to these two bishops, his *De perfectione iustitiae hominis* written in 415,[203] was the only text he wrote exclusively against Caelestius. Although the *Definitiones* are no longer extant, it seems that the *De perfectione iustitiae hominis* reflected both the substance and organization of Caelestius's text. Substantively, it was primarily about the possibility of a sinless life. Augustine was forced to respond to Caelestius's definition of sin, his claims for the responsibility of living a life without sin, the possibility of a sinless life, that God has commanded that we live without sin, and how God's commandments to be sinless are not difficult.[204] Organizationally, it mirrored the *Definitiones* by first responding to Caelestius's philosophical arguments, then responding to both the scriptural passages in support of the claims of the Pelagians and the scriptural passages that seemed to support the arguments of their interlocutors.[205] Unlike his previous text in which he refused to mention Pelagius by name because he did not want to embarrass him and inhibit any chance of reform, Augustine does mention Caelestius by name in this work.[206] Apparently, he was not as concerned with Caelestius's anonymity, possibly because Augustine had not heard the same high praise about his character as he had heard about Pelagius's character, or because Caelestius did not have the same social connections as Pelagius.[207]

The *Conventum* of Jerusalem and the Synod of Diospolis of 415

In the spring or early summer of 415,[208] Augustine sent Orosius to Bethlehem "to learn the fear of the Lord by sitting at the feet of Jerome."[209] Along with Orosius,

---

202. A scholarly debate has arisen over whether Augustine truly believed that the *Definitiones* were written by Caelestius, or only by his companions. Most scholars, including Ferguson, conclude that Augustine believed that Caelestius was the author. Robert Dodaro is uncommitted, although he seems to lean to the probability that Augustine believed Caelestius was the author. Honnay does not believe that Augustine was convinced that Caelestius wrote the text. I would argue that Augustine did not decisively conclude that Caelestius was the author because he could not be entirely sure, but he strongly suspected that Caelestius was the author. Ferguson, "In Defence," 116. See Honnay for the list of the different opinions of scholars: Honnay, "Caelestius," 281–82 n. 69; Dodaro, "Carthaginian Debate," 195–96; Honnay, "Caelestius," 281.

203. Teske, vol. 1 "Introduction," 269.

204. Augustine, *Perf.* 2.1–11.28.

205. Teske, vol. 1 "Introduction," 270.

206. Augustine, *Perf.* 1.1.

207. Brown, "Pelagius," 183–207; Brown, " Patrons of Pelagius," 208–26.

208. Kelly suggests he left Africa in the spring or summer of 415, while Hanson suggests it must have been the spring of that year. Kelly, *Jerome*, 317; Hanson, "Introduction," 99.

209. Orosius, *Lib. apol.* 3.

Augustine sent to Jerome two letters (166, 167), a copy of the letter (157) that he had written to a layman from Syracuse in Sicily named Hilary, and, most likely, provided both his *De peccatorum meritis et remissione et De baptismo parvulorum* and *De spiritu et littera*.[210]

In 414 or 415, Hilary wrote a letter (156) to Augustine asking for clarity because some Christians were teaching five propositions of the Christian faith that perplexed him. These propositions were: "human beings can be without sin and easily keep the commandments of God if they will; an infant who was not baptized because prevented by death cannot deserve to perish because it is born without sin; a rich man who remains in his riches cannot enter the kingdom of God unless he has sold all his possessions, and it does not profit him if he has perhaps observed all the commandments by the use of his riches; one ought not to swear an oath at all; the Church does not have a wrinkle or a spot."[211] Concerning the last proposition, Hilary asked the Christians teaching this if the spotless church is the church present on earth now, or the future church at the eschaton. He said that an unnamed "certain man" insisted that the spotless church is here and now,[212] and can be sinless. We will explore in detail later that, at the Synod of Diospolis, Pelagius was accused of repeating teachings for which Caelestius had been anathematized, three of which are important for our purposes here: human beings can be without sin if they want; infants attain eternal life, even if they are not baptized; if wealthy persons who have been baptized do not renounce all their possessions, they have no merit, even if they seem to do something good, and they cannot possess the kingdom of God.[213] Although the list provided by Hilary and the accusations from Diospolis are not exactly the same, Augustine said in his *De gestis Pelagii* that these three charges from Diospolis had been brought to his attention earlier by Hilary, which points to the likelihood that Caelestius had been in Sicily for a time.[214]

In his response to Hilary (*Epist.* 157), Augustine says that he suspects that the unnamed man was Caelestius. He reported to Hilary that there are many in Carthage who still hold similar positions to the ones described by Hilary, although they "now whisper in hiding, fearing the most well-founded faith of the Church."[215] He says that Caelestius had been "found guilty and detested by the Church rather than corrected

---

210. Orosius, *Lib. apol.* 3; Jerome, *Dial.* 3.19. Kelly says that Orosius brought Augustine's *De natura et gratia*, but Orosius tells us that Augustine had not yet completed it. Augustine did not send Jerome *De natura et gratia* until the summer of 416 by a courier named Luke, but by then Jerome's monastery may have been burned. Augustine, *Epist.* 19*.3; Kelly, *Jerome*, 317–18.

211. Augustine, *Epist.* 156.

212. Augustine quotes Caelestius saying this in his report to Aurelius about the Synod of Diospolis. Augustine, *Gest. Pelag.* 35.63.

213. Augustine, *Gest. Pelag.* 11.23.

214. Augustine, *Gest. Pelag.* 11.23.

215. Augustine, *Epist.* 157.3.22.

and subdued,"[216] and mentions this to Hilary to warn him.[217] If Caelestius had been in Sicily,[218] he most likely did not remain for more than a few years, and had left before the end of 415.[219] In his *De perfectione iustitiae hominis*,[220] Augustine reports that Caelestius was not in Sicily then, although he does not say when he had left or where he went.[221] Jerome mentions that, on the islands of Sicily and Rhodes, Pelagianism was "growing daily and defiling many, as they teach this heresy in secret but deny everything in public."[222] Although Jerome does not indicate that there is a direct link between Caelestius and these islands, the possibility arises that Caelestius may have been in Sicily and left there for Rhodes. Aside from the exact identity of the "certain man," Augustine is gravely concerned that the teachings of Pelagius and Caelestius are becoming more popular than he would have expected, and "becoming so numerous that I do not know where they will turn up."[223]

Several theories have arisen why Augustine would dispatch Orosius to Palestine. One theory holds that Orosius was "hunting Pelagius"[224] in Jerusalem, and that Augustine wanted to warn Jerome of the danger of the Pelagians. This is unlikely, however, because Orosius had shown no interest in the Pelagians prior to his journey to the East. Furthermore, it is hard to imagine that Augustine, who had the highest regard for Jerome's intellect, would think that Jerome was incapable of sussing out the Pelagian threat for himself.[225] Another theory holds that Augustine[226] wanted Orosius to collect information from Jerome, so that Orosius might compose his *Historiae adversum paganos*,[227] which he hastily completed in a year or year and a half sometime from 416 and 418.[228] While Orosius did consult Jerome's translation of Eusebius's *Chronicon*, and Jerome's addition to that text, there is no indication that this was Augustine's primary motivation for Orosius's journey.[229] In one of the letters

---

216. Augustine, *Epist.* 157.3.22.
217. Augustine, *Epist.* 157.3.22.
218. Augustine, *Perf.* 1.1.
219. Honnay, "Caelestius," 279–80.
220. Teske, "Introduction," *WSA*, 269.
221. Augustine, *Perf.* 1.1.
222. Jerome, *In Hier.* 4.pref.
223. Augustine, *Epist.* 157.3.22.
224. Brown, *Augustine of Hippo*, 358. See also: Kelly, *Jerome*, 318; Hanson, "Introduction," 101.
225. Augustine always heaped praise and admiration on Jerome for his intellectual abilities. For example: Augustine, *Epist.* 28.1.1.
226. Orosius, *C. pag.* 1.pref.
227. Dunphy, "A Prelude," 126–27.
228. Fear argues that it was finished by 418 and completed under one year. Van Nuffelen says that it was written in 416/17. Hanson says that is was finished in late 417 or early 418, and it took a year and a half. Fear, "Introduction," 6–7; Van Nuffelen, *Orosius*, 1; Hanson, "Introduction," 105–6.
229. For a discussion of the sources that Orosius used for his *Historiae*, see: Fear, "Introduction," 15–6.

he sent to Jerome, Augustine himself indicates several reasons why he felt it prudent to send Orosius to meet him:

> I taught him [Orosius] what I could and advised him where he could learn what I could not and encouraged him to go to you [Jerome] . . . I believe that the Lord had granted me an opportunity to write to you about these matters that I want to know from you. For I was looking for someone to send to you, but I did not easily find someone suitable who would act with reliability, obey quickly and was experienced in traveling. And so, when I learned that this young man was the very sort of person for whom I was asking the Lord, I could not hesitate. Listen, then, to what I ask you to disclose to me, and do not be slow to discuss it. The question of the soul troubles many people, and I confess that I am among them.[230]

This selection shows that Augustine had several motives: first, when he said that he taught Orosius everything that he could teach him, he most likely meant that he felt as if he inadequately responded to Orosius's request to refute the Priscillianists and Origenists, because of the paucity of information he had about both. Second, when he said that he was sending Orosius to Jerome to learn from him, he most likely did not have in mind Eusebius's *Chronicon* or Jerome's addition to it, but that Augustine wanted Orosius to learn about Origenism from Jerome, so that Orosius could better refute it. Third, Augustine's letter (166) continued to discuss the thorny issue of the origin of the soul (which he had discussed in his *Ad Orosium contra Priscillianistas et Origenistas*), and asked Jerome to write back to him with his assessment of the question.[231]

In his other letter he sent to Jerome (167), Augustine again asked Jerome for assistance. In the introduction, he says that "a question that is more urgently pressing ought much less to be neglected. Hence, I ask and beg you by the Lord to explain to me something that I think will be of profit to many or, if you have or someone else has already explained this question, send it on to us, namely, how one should interpret what is found in the Letter of the apostle James, 'for whoever has observed the whole law, but offends on one point, has become guilty of all'" (Jas 2:10). Augustine was perplexed by the meaning of this, and asked Jerome for his own exegesis of the passage, saying "for he is an unfortunate man who does not worthily honor the very important and very holy labors of your studies and does not, on their account, thank the Lord our God by whose gift you are such a man."[232] Augustine, then, sent Orosius to Palestine for Orosius's education, but also out of his own desire to learn from Jerome.

Orosius seems to have stayed for a short time in Egypt on his way to Palestine, because, as he mentioned in passing in his *Historiae*, he saw with his own eyes the tracks left by the Pharaoh's army as it chased the Israelites through the Red Sea, and

---

230. Augustine, *Epist.* 166.1.2.

231. For a discussion of Augustine and the origin of the soul, see: O'Connell, "Augustine's Rejection," 1–32; Penaskovic, "Fall of Soul," 135–45; Lamberigts, "Julian and Augustine," 243–60.

232. Augustine, *Epist.* 167.21.

saw the destruction of Alexandria's libraries brought on by Caesar's armies.[233] For the brief time that he was in Palestine, he hinted that he lived in Jerome's monastery in Bethlehem,[234] and shortly after his arrival, Orosius, "in obscurity at Bethlehem, a foreigner, penniless and unknown,"[235] as he claimed, was summoned to appear before John of Jerusalem and a group of bishops in July 415.[236] He called this event a *conventum*,[237] which scholars have described in different ways as a "synod,"[238] a "conference,"[239] an "informal conference,"[240] a "*colloque*,"[241] a "meeting of an ecclesiastical assembly,"[242] and a "meeting of a standing committee of priests entrusted with the affairs of Western residents and pilgrims in Jerusalem."[243] According to Orosius's summary of events, which is the only record extant, the bishops asked Orosius to tell them whatever he knew about what had occurred when Pelagius (whom he called "dust and ashes," "puffed up," a "blind and wicked man," an "evil and wicked slave," a "wretched man," and a "conceit-filled but empty man"[244]) and Caelestius were in Africa. He informed them that Caelestius had been given a hearing before many bishops, and he had "been found guilty, confessed, been denounced by the Church and made his escape from Africa."[245] Augustine, Orosius continued, was writing a response to a book written by Pelagius.[246] At the request of the bishops, Orosius read aloud Augustine's letter (157) to Hilary of Syracuse.

233. Orosius, *C. pag.* 1.10.17, 6.15.32.
234. He said that "I lay in obscurity at Bethlehem." Orosius, *Lib. apol.* 3.
235. Orosius, *Lib. apol.* 3, 8.
236. Most scholars (Ferguson, Bonner, Kelly, Dunphy, Frend, Hanson, Lancel, and Fear) have said that this meeting took place on July 28th; several scholars (Hamman, Teske) have said that it took place on July 30th. Orosius himself says that the event took place forty-seven days prior to the first day of the Feast of the Dedication of the Church of the Resurrection in Jerusalem (Holy Sepulchre). There is a disagreement over the date of the dedication of the Holy Sepulchre by Constantine in 335. Dates range for this event from September 12th to the 14th. Ferguson, *Pelagius*, 82; Bonner, *St. Augustine*, 332; Kelly, *Jerome*, 318; Dunphy, "A Prelude," 128; Frend, "Orosius," 615; Hanson, "Introduction," 102; Lancel, *Saint Augustine*, 335; Fear, "Introduction," 5; Hamman, "Orosius de Braga," 348; Teske, "Introduction," WSA, 369 n. 65; Orosius, *Lib. apol.* 7.
237. Orosius, *Lib. apol.* 3. It should be noted that no minutes seem to have been taken at this *conventum*.
238. Ferguson, *Pelagius*, 82; Bonner, *St. Augustine*, 332; Frend, "Orosius," 615; Fear "Introduction," 5.
239. Teske, vol. 1 "Introduction," 369 n. 65; Hanson, "Introduction," 102.
240. Kelly, *Jerome*, 318.
241. Hamman, "Orosius de Braga," 348.
242. Lancel, *Saint Augustine*, 335.
243. Dunphy, "A Prelude," 128.
244. Orosius, *Lib. apol.* 10, 13, 29, 30, 31.
245. Orosius, *Lib. apol.* 3.
246. It is not entirely clear which of Augustine's anti-Pelagian texts he means. Most scholars suggest that it was probably *De natura et gratia*, although Ferguson contends that it was his *De perfectione iustitiae hominis*. Ferguson, *Pelagius*, 80.

After hearing this, John demanded that Pelagius be summoned immediately. The bishops approved of John's demand out of respect for his office, for the good of the proceedings, and because it would be more appropriate to condemn Pelagius to his face, according to Orosius.[247] When Pelagius arrived, the bishops asked him if he was aware that Augustine was against some of his teachings. To the shock of all those who were present, Pelagius asked "and who is Augustine to me?"[248] This sent everyone into an uproar, shouting that Pelagius had blasphemed against the famous bishop who had brought unity to Africa (a reference to Augustine's efforts to quash the Donatists), and demanded that Pelagius be expelled not only from the *conventum*, but from the church. John, not missing a beat, ordered Pelagius to sit down, and exclaimed "I am Augustine,"[249] placing himself in the role of Augustine so that he might more easily pardon Pelagius, Orosius said, and to calm the passions of those aggravated by Pelagius's dismissal of the bishop of Hippo. Orosius, displeased with John's intention, snapped in reply: "if you are going to assume the role of Augustine, then follow the sentiments of Augustine!"[250]

John deftly changed the direction of the conversation by stating that Augustine's letter discussed individuals other than Pelagius, and asked if Orosius had problems with Pelagius himself. Orosius responded that Pelagius had told him that he was teaching that people can be without sin, and can easily observe God's commandments, which, it should be noted, was the only accusation brought against Pelagius at this *conventum*. Pelagius confirmed that he had been teaching this. Orosius declared that this was the teaching that had been condemned in Carthage in 411,[251] had been denounced by Augustine in his writings, had been refuted in Jerome's letter (133) to Ctesiphon, and, he said, about which the West was eagerly awaiting Jerome's further refutation in his *Dialogi contra Pelagianos*.[252] John was not paying any attention to what Orosius was saying, and tried to place Orosius in the role of the accuser and John himself in the role of the judge. Orosius repeatedly refused the label, and said he was not there as an accuser, but was the messenger conveying to John and the other bishops what had happened in Africa. Dissatisfied with this response, John attempted to entice Orosius to make a formal charge against Pelagius by quoting Genesis when God told Abraham "walk before me and be without sin" (Gen 17:1), and that Zechariah and Elizabeth had been declared "both righteous before the Lord, walking in all of the just commandments of the Lord without blame" (Luke 1:6).[253] This attempt on John's part reveals that the *conventum* was not

---

247. Orosius, *Lib. apol.* 3.
248. Orosius, *Lib. apol.* 4.
249. Orosius, *Lib. apol.* 4.
250. Orosius, *Lib. apol.* 4.
251. Augustine, *Gest. Pelag.* 11.23.
252. Orosius, *Lib. apol.* 4.
253. This attempt on John's part reveals that, however we want to conceive of the nature of this

a formal synod or trial summoned for the express purpose of charging Pelagius with heresy, as no charges had been brought against him.

Repeating himself, Orosius insisted that he would not overreach his role as a presbyter to act as a teacher and judge. The bishops in Africa made their judgement about the heresy of Pelagius's teachings.[254] John sat in silence contemplating Orosius's claims after the interpreter had translated Orosius's Latin into Greek. The translator was unknown to Orosius. He was inexperienced, and, according to a certain Passerius, a certain Avitus (possibly Avitus of Braga), and a man named Domnus who were there, proven to have made translation errors. The translator also had omitted translating some of what Orosius had said, or had suggested to John different implications for some of Orosius's claims. After some time, John said that if Pelagius had said that it is possible to be sinless without God's assistance, then that would deserve to be condemned. He then asked Orosius to respond to Pelagius's claim that God's grace is indeed necessary, to which Orosius replied that anyone who denies God's assistance should be anathematized. Probably sensing that he was fighting a losing battle, Orosius insisted that, because Pelagius's theology is better known in the West, the case should be adjudicated by Latin-speaking judges. Other issues were addressed at the *conventum*, indicating that it was not called to address the problem of Pelagius alone. After the other issues were addressed, John declared that several unnamed brothers (possibly bishops) and letters were to be sent to Pope Innocent I, and that everyone agreed to obey whatever he decreed. But, there is no indication that anyone or any letters were sent to Innocent in Rome.[255] Pelagius, in the meantime, must remain silent, keep to himself, and Orosius must stop his "mockery of John, who had been proven to be wrong and who had admitted as much."[256] Mass was celebrated, peace was made, and a final prayer was offered as a gesture of reconciliation.

The conflict between Orosius and John did not end there, as John confronted him forty-seven days later on September 12, the first day of the Feast of the Dedication of

---

conventum, it was not a formal synod or trial summoned for the express purpose of charging Pelagius with heresy.

254. Orosius, *Lib. apol.* 5.

255. Dunphy offers some possible explanations why this case was not taken to Rome as was decreed: "John is actively lending support to Pelagius. As bishop he harbours a heretic in his church. As priest he abuses the priestly office. John's counter-accusation of sacrilege, an equivalent of heresy, against Orosius explains why the case was not brought to Rome after the meeting in July. Orosius implicates others in John's accusation indicating an ongoing debate at the time. A number of factors that would militate against recourse to Rome being pursued should be noted. The anti-Pelagians had refused to bring a formal charge of heresy against Pelagius, and in the ensuing debate they were themselves suspected of heresy, even by the bishop of Jerusalem. This would greatly weaken their case in Rome. In Rome, in fact, there is little indication that a case against Pelagius would have found a sympathetic hearing. Pope Innocent apparently took no side when the debate started a decade earlier in Rome. When, eventually, he was directly petitioned by the African bishops, he took a very independent stance and refused to condemn Pelagius *tout court*." Dunphy, "A Prelude," 139–40.

256. Orosius, *Lib. apol.* 6.

the Church of the Resurrection in Jerusalem.[257] When Orosius went to Jerusalem from Bethlehem to pay his respects, as he often had done since his arrival in Palestine a few months earlier, John demanded to know why Orosius, who had blasphemed, had presented himself to him, which Orosius interpreted to mean that he should not touch John as John was without sin. Orosius was confused by this, and asked what he had said that would lead to this accusation. John said that he had heard Orosius say that not even with God's help can a person be sinless. Orosius immediately responded that he had never said such a thing, and was baffled why John did not make this accusation at the *conventum* when he supposedly said it, or, at the very least, warn him.[258] Orosius was convinced that the problem originated from an error in translation during the *conventum*, but he left it up to God to determine whether John carelessly believed Orosius had made this claim, whether Orosius had been purposely misrepresented by the translator, or whether John misunderstood through ignorance. It is unclear how this confrontation was resolved as Orosius did not say, but he did mention that he would never challenge a bishop—certainly not the bishop of Jerusalem—in front of a group of other bishops.[259] This tense moment probably dissipated awkwardly, but it does not seem to have had any negative formal consequence for him, as the focus quickly shifted back to Pelagius at the Synod of Diospolis.[260]

The story of the *conventum* and the encounter with John in September were recounted by Orosius in the second text he wrote, his *Liber apologeticus contra Pelagianum*, which was addressed to an anonymous group of priests who had been present at the *conventum*. He wrote it while still in Bethlehem, because he felt the need to exonerate himself, and to draw attention to the Pelagians, whom he described as "wolves caught within the flock of sheep," and "imperious serpents, licking their putrid mouths with their darting tongues while taking up residence at the holy and inviolable episcopal see unto which they stealthily crept."[261] It has been suggested that Orosius wrote it shortly after his September confrontation with John,[262] but a passing reference to the blood of St. Stephen points to the likelihood that it was written sometime between the Synod of Diospolis in December 415[263] and his departure from

---

257. Orosius, *Lib. apol.* 7.
258. Orosius, *Lib. apol.* 7.
259. Orosius, *Lib. apol.* 8.
260. Augustine, *Gest. Pelag.* 16.39.
261. Orosius, *Lib. apol.* 1, 3.
262. Hanson, "Introduction," 104.

263. Brown and Frend state that the exact date was December 20th; Teske and Lancel say that it was late December; Burnett does not offer a more specific date; Dunphy refuses to be more specific than late December; Fear offers the dates of December 20th–23rd. Brown, *Through the Eye of a Needle*, 370; Frend, "Divjak Letters," 501; Teske, vol. 1 "Introduction," 310; Lancel, *Saint Augustine*, 335; Burnett, "Dysfunction at Diospolis," 153; Dunphy, "Concerning the Synod of Diospolis and its Acts," 104; Fear, "Introduction," 5.

Palestine sometime between spring and summer 416.[264] During the synod,[265] the relics of St. Stephen were discovered not far from Jerusalem in Kaphar Gamala by a certain priest named Lucianus.[266] Lucianus had had some visions in early December pointing him to the location of the relics. When he found them, he informed John of the discovery, who then left before the closing of the synod to return to Jerusalem to inspect the discovery. Somehow, Avitus of Braga obtained some (although not all) of the bones, and gave them to Orosius to take to Palchonius (or Balchonius), the bishop of Braga.[267] He also sent along a cover letter and a Latin translation of a public letter written by Lucianus that described his visions.[268]

The Synod of Diospolis (modern Lydda) included fourteen bishops under the leadership of Eulogius, the bishop of Caesarea and Metropolitan of Palestine.[269] The accusations against Pelagius were brought by two Gallic bishops, Heros of Arles and Lazarus of Aix.[270] Heros had been a follower of St. Martin of Tours, had been a bishop in Spain, and had been a supporter of the usurper Constantine III. He left Spain under political pressure, and arrived in Gaul where he was installed by Constantine as the bishop of Arles, against the outcry of the entire Catholic community. After Constantine's death in 411, Heros once again fled, this time to Palestine. Lazarus had been the bishop of Veseo, and was installed by Constantine as the bishop of Aix. He, too, resigned under pressure, and sailed for Palestine.[271]

Our knowledge of this synod mainly comes from Augustine's *De gestis Pelagii*, written in late 417, which he wrote to explain to Aurelius, the bishop of Carthage, why Pelagius had been deemed orthodox by the bishops there. Augustine had received a report from Pelagius about his exoneration at Diospolis (sophomorically

---

264. Orosius, *Lib. apol.* 8. Bonner said he left "early" in 416; Kelly believes that he left "as soon as the sea route opened" in 416; Hanson suggests that Orosius left in spring 416, while Fear suggests mid-summer, and Brown suggests September. It could not be as late as September, however, because Orosius was already back in Carthage during the summer for the synod there. Bonner, *St. Augustine*, 340; Kelly, *Jerome*, 321; Hanson, "Introduction," 104; Fear, "Introduction," 5; Brown, *Augustine of Hippo*, 358.

265. Several dates have been suggested for when the relics of St. Stephen were found. Frend suggests, July 415, which is too early. Fear suggests December 3rd, and Hanson is not more specific than December. As we saw in an earlier chapter, the exact date for the Synod of Diospolis cannot be dated more specifically than December 415. Frend, "Orosius," 616; Fear, "Introduction," 5; Hanson, "Introduction," 104–5.

266. Gennadius, *De vir. Inlustr.* 47.

267. Gennadius, *De vir. Inlustr.* 40.

268. Gennadius, *De vir. Inlustr.* 47; Dunphy, "Concerning the Synod," 103–4; Fear, "Introduction," 5; Hanson, "Introduction," 105.

269. Dunphy believes that Diospolis was chosen because it was a geographical intersection between Caesarea and Jerusalem (who feuded over primacy) and because it "had a flourishing Christian community that could boast of a history dating back to Apostolic times" (Acts 9:32). Dunphy, "Concerning the Synod," 104.

270. Augustine, *Gest. Pelag.* 1.2.

271. Ferguson, *Pelagius*, 86.

taunting Augustine by not providing an accompanying letter), which left Augustine skeptical about the entire affair. He wrote to John of Jerusalem asking him for the official proceedings from the synod so that he could make his own interpretation of the events.[272] Augustine never received them from John—possibly because of John's esteem that he had for Pelagius, which Augustine recognized.[273] But, the recent discovery in 1981 by Johannes Divjak of thirty-one letters by Augustine reveals that he received a copy from Cyril of Alexandria.[274] After reading the proceedings, Augustine concluded that the bishops were correct in exonerating Pelagius based on his verbal testimony, but that Pelagius had lied to the bishops about the content of the texts he had written.[275] His texts had been written in Latin, but, as Pelagius had been living in Palestine for several years at this point, he was able to provide his testimony in Greek. Augustine believed that, in addition to Pelagius's duplicity, a language barrier caused the failure of the bishops to condemn Pelagius because a translator was used by the bishops when examining Pelagius's texts.[276] The case against Pelagius was further hampered by the fact that neither Heros nor Lazarus attended the synod because one had fallen ill, and the other refused to be present without the other.[277] Jerome had nothing to do with the synod (which he decried as "wretched"),[278] most likely because of his disdain for John.[279] Orosius, too, was absent.[280]

272. Augustine, *Epist.* 179.7. Augustine also sent John copies of Pelagius's *De natura* and his own *De natura et gratia* (179.5).

273. Augustine, *Epist.* 179.1.

274. Augustine, *Epist.* 4*.2. While most scholars believe that Augustine asked Cyril for the proceedings only after John failed to provide them, Dunn has argued that Augustine wrote both of them at the same time in order to get copies from both of them. Dunn, "Augustine," 72. For more information on the Divjak letters, see Frend, "Divjak Letters." Dunphy believes that the copy of the proceedings Augustine received from Cyril "was in Latin, and was part of the Pelagian campaign intended to inform the Latin community in Alexandria, and elsewhere, of Pelagius's acquittal at Diospolis. When, then, we read the account of the Acts of the Synod of Diospolis as presented by Augustine we would seem to be presented with a Pelagian version of those Acts." Dunphy, "Concerning the Synod," 111–12. Although Dunphy offers a compelling argument, the discrepancy that Augustine noticed between the copy of the proceedings he received from Pelagius, and the copy he received from Cyril, indicates to me that the copy that Augustine received from Cyril did not have any overt bias for Pelagius.

275. Augustine states several times that Pelagius had lied to the bishops: *Gest. Pelag.*, 6.19; *Grat. Chr.* 2.8.9–22.25; *Epist.* 4*.2. See also: Evans, "Pelagius' Veracity," 21.

276. Augustine, *Gest. Pelag.* 1.2. Beatrice recently has argued, however, that two of the bishops, Chromatius of Ascalon and Jovinus of Aquileia, could read Latin and therefore would not have fallen prey to any linguistic deception. Beatrice, "Chromatius and Jovinus," 9.

277. Augustine, *Gest. Pelag.* 1.2.

278. Augustine, *Epist.* 202.2.

279. Burnett, "Dysfunction," 155–56.

280. Ferguson believes that Orosius was still in Palestine during the synod; Burnett, too, believes that Orosius was still in Palestine; Teske believes that Orosius had left Palestine before the synod began; Augustine said that "for whatever bishop John said concerning our absent brothers, whether his fellow bishops Heros and Lazarus, or the priest Orosius, or others whose names are not mentioned there [Jerome?], I believe that he understands that it did not count against their complaint." To me,

A number of different charges were leveled against Pelagius. The initial set of accusations was purported to come out of Pelagius's own texts, but Carole Burnett has shown that the selections[281] came from second-hand material—a draft of Jerome's *Dialogi Contra Pelagianos*—rather than directly from Pelagius's own writings, further weakening the case against him.[282] The first accusation from this set was that "only one who has knowledge of the law can be without sin." Pelagius stated that what he actually said was that "a person is helped through knowledge of the law not to sin."[283] The second accusation was that "all are governed by their own will." The bishops approved this in light of Pelagius's clarification: "I said that on account of the free choice, which God assists when it chooses what is good, but sinners are themselves at fault because of their free choice."[284] Third, it was read out loud that "on the day of judgment the wicked and sinners are not to be spared; rather, they are to be burned with eternal fire." The bishops initially were agitated (*movere*) by this claim, but, when Pelagius said that anyone who believed the contrary was an Origenist (an accusation still raw to many in Palestine), the bishops approved. Fourth, the accusation was raised that Pelagius said that "evil does not even enter one's thoughts." Pelagius corrected them by saying that "we did not state it in that way; rather, we said that a Christian ought to strive not to think evil."[285] Fifth, another proposition that was raised but that the bishops approved was that "the kingdom of heaven was promised even in the Old Testament."[286] The sixth charge was that Pelagius claimed that "human beings can be without sin, if they want." Pelagius admits to these words, but says that he did not mention that anyone had ever been sinless in this life, and the bishops approved.[287] Seventh, the objection was raised that "the Church on earth is without stain or wrinkle," which Augustine immediately had associated with the Donatist schism that had just been legally repressed by the state. Pelagius replied that "we said this, but we said it in the sense that by the baptismal bath the Church is cleansed from every spot and winkle and that the Lord wants her to remain that way."[288] Once again, the bishops agreed. Three other charges[289] were leveled against

---

this indicates that Orosius was still in Palestine. Ferguson, *Pelagius*, 93; Burnett, "Dysfunction," 171; Teske, "Introduction," WSA, 312; Augustine, *Gest. Pelag.* 16.39.

281. The quotations in this text have become known by a variety of titles: *Liber ecolagrum, Liber capitulorum,* or *testimoniorum.* Teske, vol. 1 "Introduction," 367 n. 3.

282. Burnett, "Dysfunction," 155.

283. Augustine, *Gest. Pelag.* 1.2.

284. Augustine, *Gest. Pelag.* 3.5.

285. Augustine, *Gest. Pelag.* 4.12.

286. Augustine, *Gest. Pelag.* 5.13.

287. Augustine, *Gest. Pelag.* 6.16. Augustine claimed that Pelagius had stated that Abel "never sinned in the slightest" (*Gest. Pelag.* 10.22.). See also: *Nat. grat.* 36.42–45; *Epist.* 179.8.

288. Augustine, *Gest. Pelag.* 12.27–28.

289. The three charges were: "may piety, which has nowhere found home, find a home with you; may righteousness, which is everywhere a wayfarer, find its abode in you; may truth, which no one now recognizes, become a member of your household and your friend, and let the law of God, which

Pelagius from a letter and a treatise he wrote to a widow,[290] but he denied that he had written them.[291] Augustine, however, stated that Pelagius had lied about this denial,[292] and Robert Evans has shown that Augustine was correct.[293]

The second set of accusations came from six statements from Caelestius at the Council of Carthage of 411. These statements were: (1) Adam was created mortal so that he would die whether he sinned or did not sin; (2) the sin of Adam harmed him alone and not the human race; (3) the law leads to the kingdom just as the gospel does; (4) before the coming of Christ there were human begins without sin; (5) newly born infants are in the same state in which Adam was before his transgression; (6) the whole human race does not die through the death or transgression of Adam, nor does the whole human race rise through the resurrection of Christ.[294]

The third set of accusations came from three statements from Caelestius: human beings can be without sin if they want; infants attain eternal life, even if they are not baptized; if wealthy persons who have been baptized do not renounce all their possessions, they have no merit, even if they seem to do something good, and they cannot possess the kingdom of God.[295] Augustine, as mentioned earlier in this chapter, noted a connection between these charges and the letter he received from Hilary.[296]

Pelagius had little to say to the six charges that came from the Council of Carthage that anathematized Caelestius, or the three charges from Caelestius's statements. To the charge that humans can be sinless if they want, he deferred to his earlier statement that humans can be without sin and observe God's commandments if they want.[297] To the charge that before Christ there were human beings without sin, Pelagius declared that "some people lived holy and righteous lives."[298] But, to the other charges, Pelagius dismissed them out of hand because he was not Caelestius, and should not be responsible for them. He then anathematized anyone

---

is overlooked by almost all, be honored by you; O happy and blessed are you, if the righteousness, which one should believe exists only in heaven, is found with you alone on earth; they [the saints] raise their hands to God in a worthy manner; they pour forth a prayer in good conscience, if they can say, 'you know, O Lord, how holy and innocent and clean of all malice, wickedness, and greed are the hands I extend to you. You know how righteous and clean and free from every lie are the lips by which I offer my prayer to you that you may have mercy on me.'" Augustine, *Gest. Pelag.* 6.16.

290. Harnack claims that the woman's name was Livania. Teske argues that the woman was named Livania or Liviana, while Ferguson believes her name was Juliana. Harnack, *History of Dogma*, 177 n. 2. Teske, "Introduction," *WSA*, 368 n. 18; Ferguson, *Pelagius*, 88. Evans has shown that the text was Pelagius's *Liber de vita christiana*, and proves Augustine's claim that Pelagius was lying.

291. Augustine, *Gest. Pelag.* 6.16.

292. Augustine, *Gest. Pelag.* 6.19.

293. Evans, "Pelagius' Veracity," 21.

294. Augustine, *Gest. Pelag.* 11.23.

295. Augustine, *Gest. Pelag.* 11.23.

296. Augustine offered an extensive response to Hilary in his letter 157.

297. Augustine, *Gest. Pelag.* 6.16.

298. Augustine, *Gest. Pelag.* 11.24.

who ever currently holds such positions, or who had ever held such positions. The bishops were satisfied with this response.

The final set of accusations comes from Caelestius's *Liber definitionum*.²⁹⁹ First, Pelagius was charged with saying that people do more than is prescribed in the law and the gospel. Pelagius responded that "they [Heros and Lazarus] set that forth as if it were our statement, but we said it in the sense of the apostle speaking on virginity. He says of it, 'I do not have a command of the Lord'" (1 Cor 7:25).³⁰⁰ This exchange refers to Paul's claim that virginity is superior to marriage, but that virginity is not a requirement from God. If one does not have the control to remain a virgin, one is permitted to marry (1 Cor 7:9). The bishops approved of this clarification. Second, Pelagius was charged with the claim that God's grace and help is not given for individual actions, but consists in free choice or in the law and teaching. As he did earlier, Pelagius stated that it was Caelestius who had made this claim, and that Pelagius should not be held responsible for the claim of someone else. Further, Pelagius says that he never held this view, and anathematizes anyone who believes so.³⁰¹ The third and final charge of this set was that everyone can have all the virtues and graces, and that Caelestius and Pelagius destroy the diversity of graces Paul teaches. Pelagius clarifies the statement by saying that "God gives all the graces to one who is worthy to receive them, as he gave them to the apostle Paul."³⁰² The bishops responded that "your views on the gift of graces found in the holy apostle are reasonable and in accord with the mind of the Church."³⁰³

To further his defense, Pelagius produced a letter Augustine had written to him³⁰⁴ in response to a letter he had written to Augustine in order to show that he was on good terms with the bishop of Hippo.³⁰⁵ The short letter to Pelagius, written around 410 shortly after Pelagius arrived in Africa, reads as follows:

> I am very grateful that you were so kind as to bring me joy by your letter and assure me of your good health. May the Lord reward you, my beloved lord and brother for whom I long very much, with the good tidings by which you may be good forever and live eternally with the eternal God. Though I do not find

---

299. This text is no longer extant *in toto*, but is quoted in Augustine's *De perfetione iustitiae hominis*.

300. Augustine, *Gest. Pelag.* 13.29.

301. Augustine, *Gest. Pelag.* 14.30.

302. Augustine, *Gest. Pelag.* 14.32.

303. Augustine, *Gest. Pelag.* 14.32.

304. Although this is the only extant letter we have from Augustine to Pelagius, Augustine tells us that he was "in the habit of writing to him in a friendly way as a servant of God, as he has done to me, and so last year, when my son the priest Orosius, who is a servant of God with us from Spain, had gone to the East with letters of mine, I wrote by him to the same Pelagius, not branding him in my letter as a heretic, but urging him to hear from the priest what I had commissioned him to say." Augustine, *Serm.* Dolbeau 30.6 (348A). For a description of the letter correspondence between Augustine and Pelagius, see: Duval, "La correspondance," 363–84; Den Boeft, "Augustine's Letter," 73–84.

305. Pelagius had produced some letters from others in an attempt to achieve the same effect, although Augustine does not mention who wrote those letters. *Gest. Pelag.* 29.53.

in myself the grounds for that praise for me that your kind letter contains, I cannot fail to be grateful for your good will toward the slight goodness I have. At the same time I admonish you rather to pray for me so that the Lord might make me the sort of person you think me already to be.[306]

Although Augustine does not tell us how the bishops reacted to his letter, he clearly was not pleased with Pelagius for using his words, and he offered several explanations of what he considers to be the true meaning of his letter, some of which are more convincing than others. First, he argues that he, in fact, did not praise Pelagius, but that he admonished (*admonere*) him "to hold sound doctrines, as much as I could, without raising any question about the grace of God."[307] Second, he acknowledged that he called Pelagius "lord," but that this should not be understood as anything other than standard epistolary convention, a courtesy offered even to non-Christians.[308] Third, he explained his use of the term "beloved" that it is his Christian duty to love Pelagius, and that he had wished to meet Pelagius because he had heard a rumor that Pelagius was opposing grace. Fourth, the curt tone of his letter should indicate his true displeasure with Pelagius. Fifth, Augustine asked Pelagius to pray for him to become the type of person Pelagius had perceived him to be. In asking for Pelagius's prayers, Augustine says that he was trying to show Pelagius that people need God's active agency working in their lives, and that the gift of the free will alone was not enough.[309]

After all of the scrutiny of Pelagius at the Synod of Diospolis, the bishops declared him to be in full communion with the church, and Pelagius, at least for a little while, triumphed over his detractors.[310]

After the Synod of Diospolis

The Africans wasted no time in their response to Diospolis.[311] In the summer of 416, sixty-eight bishops (including Aurelius) held a council in Carthage, and fifty-nine bishops (including Augustine and Alypius) held a council in Milevis in Numidia. The bishops in Carthage met for a variety of reasons unrelated to Pelagianism, but, when Orosius arrived and presented them with letters from Heros and Lazarus, they turned their attention to Pelagius and Caelestius, and anathematized them.[312] The Council of Milevis did not explicitly anathematize Pelagius and Caelestius as the

---

306. Augustine, *Epist.* 146. See also: *Gest. Pelag.* 21.45, 27–28.52.
307. Augustine, *Gest. Pelag.* 26.51.
308. Augustine, *Gest. Pelag.* 26.51.
309. Augustine, *Gest. Pelag.* 26.51.
310. Augustine, *Gest. Pelag.* 20.44.
311. Wermelinger, *Rom und Pelagius*, 88–133.
312. Augustine, *Epist.* 175.1.

Council of Carthage had done, but it strongly denounced the "authors of this most destructive heresy."[313]

Orosius intended to return to Spain from Palestine, but he had promised Augustine before he had left Africa that he would return there on his journey home.[314] It is likely that he told the bishops in Carthage everything that he knew about the *conventum* in Jerusalem in July, 415, the Synod of Diospolis in December, and even may have provided them a copy of his *Liber apologeticus*, his work detailing the *conventum*, although there is no explicit evidence of this. He also brought with him a short letter (134) from Jerome to Augustine in which he hinted at the destruction of his monastery that impeded him from responding to Augustine's letters (166, 167) about the origin of the soul and how to interpret James's statement that "for whoever has observed the whole law, but offends on one point, has become guilty of all" (Jas 2:10).[315] Augustine learned "many things" about Jerome from Orosius,[316] and it even is possible that Orosius brought Augustine a copy of Jerome's *Dialogi contra Pelagianos*.[317]

Both the council in Carthage and the council in Milevis wrote to Pope Innocent I, whom Brown described as "an old man, confident of his authority,"[318] informing him of their actions, and asked him to add his own voice to their denunciations, deferring to the "greater grace"[319] of the apostolic see, and hoping that Pelagius and Caelestius "will more easily yield to the authority of Your Holiness, which is derived from the authority of the holy scriptures."[320] In addition to these letters from these two councils, five bishops (Aurelius, Alypius, Augustine, Evodius, and Possidius) sent a letter of their own to Innocent. It is unclear why they felt the need to supplement the letters from the councils. Perhaps they felt that the letters from the councils did not adequately portray the dangers of Pelagian thought, as their letter is much longer than that of the letters from the councils, and it goes into greater detail about their errors. They also warned Innocent that Pelagianism was present in Rome (and

---

313. Augustine, *Epist.* 175.4.

314. Augustine, *Epist.* 166.1.2.

315. Jerome, *Epist.* 134.

316. Augustine, *Epist.* 19*.1.

317. There are two pieces of evidence that point to the possibility that Orosius brought Jerome's *Dialogi* to Augustine. First, Jerome wrote to Augustine and mentioned his *Dialogi*, saying that "even in the dialogue that I recently published, I was mindful, as was proper of Your Beatitude." Although this does not explicitly state that Jerome sent him a copy to Augustine here, it does make clear that the *Dialogi* were completed before Orosius left Palestine. Second, Augustine later wrote to Jerome that several people, including Orosius, who had brought him news from Jerome. Augustine also mentioned in passing Jerome's *Dialogi*. I would speculate that, since Augustine did not ask for a copy of it, he already possessed a copy. It is not certain that Orosius was the one who brought it to him, but it is likely. Jerome, *Epist.* 134; Augustine, *Epist.* 19*.

318. Brown, *Augustine of Hippo*, 360.

319. Augustine, *Epist.* 175.3.

320. Augustine, *Epist.* 176.5.

was well known in Carthage),[321] perhaps trying to provoke a response from Innocent by stoking his fear.[322] These bishops sent Innocent copies of Pelagius's *De natura*, so that he could get a taste for Pelagius's errors, and also sent a copy of Augustine's reply, *De natura et gratia*.[323] They also asked Innocent to summon Pelagius to Rome to question him, or to correspond with him (recommendations that neither Carthage nor Milevis had made).[324]

Innocent promptly responded on January 27, 417 with three letters. To the councils, he began by acknowledging and praising their deference to the authority of the apostolic see, saying to the bishops at the council in Carthage that "one should not regard as settled, whatever questions are dealt with, even in distant and remote provinces, before it comes to the knowledge of this see."[325] This declaration of primacy from Innocent may not be surprising to us as such claims of papal authority, in matters of faith and morals that have developed over the centuries culminating at Vatican I, are well known.[326] But, we should not forget that it is only since the middle of the fourth century that this authority began to take shape,[327] and Innocent's letters to the Africans should be read not simply as a reminder of that authority, but also as an assertion of it. Innocent also echoed their excommunications of Pelagius and Caelestius[328] (and anyone else who defended their teachings),[329] causing Pelagius to leave Jerusalem for a short time once this news got back to him.[330] But, in a pastoral tone not found in the councils themselves, Innocent stressed the possibility that they could return to the church if they condemn their own teachings.[331]

In his personal letter to the five bishops who had written to him, Innocent claims that he is unaware of any Pelagians in Rome and, even if they were there, he is

---

321. A year after the bishops wrote to Innocent, Augustine preached a sermon in Carthage saying that Pelagianism was "better known" in Carthage than other heresies, such as Arianism, Eunominaism, Sabellianism, and Photinianism. Augustine, *Serm*. 183.1, 12. See also: *Serm*. Dolbeau 30.5. (348A); *Epist*. 157.3.22.

322. Augustine, *Epist*. 177.2. The Council of Carthage had also sent Innocent a copy of the decision of the earlier Council of Carthage of 411, which anathematized Caelestius, and also sent a copy of the letter Orosius brought from Heros and Lazarus (Augustine, *Epist*. 175.1.).

323. Augustine, *Epist*. 177.6.

324. Augustine, *Epist*. 177.3.

325. Augustine, *Epist*. 181.1. To the bishops of the council in Milevis, Innocent wrote "all our brothers and fellow bishops ought to refer it [a question of faith] only to Peter, that is, to the source of their title and dignity, as Your Charity has now referred this question, which could benefit all the churches in common throughout the world" (182.2.).

326. O'Malley, *Vatican I*, 180–225.

327. Chadwick, *Early Church*, 237.

328. Augustine, *Epist*. 181.8, 182.6.

329. Augustine, *Epist*. 181.8, 182.6.

330. Jerome, *Epist*. 138.

331. Augustine, *Epist*. 181.9, 182.7. Innocent was also optimistic about the correction of Pelagius and Caelestius in his personal letter to the five bishops who had written to him (183.2).

unperturbed by their presence, as he is confident that they will be corrected after they learn of Pelagius's excommunication.[332] Innocent also says that he is unclear about the happenings at Diospolis. He had received copies of the proceedings of Diospolis from some lay people, but they were not accompanied by any formal statement from the synod, nor had the bishops written directly to him. Innocent, who had by now read the copy of Pelagius's *De natura* that Augustine and the other four bishops had sent to him,[333] suspected that Pelagius was able to escape condemnation either by avoidance, or confusing the bishops by "heaping many words upon them."[334] But, because Innocent was unsure of the legitimacy of the documents he had received, he was unwilling to cast aspersions on the bishops of the synod. It is noteworthy that Innocent does not write to the bishops of Diospolis to inquire what actually had happened, nor does he hesitate to excommunicate Pelagius and Caelestius solely based on the information at hand. He was unwilling, however, to summon Pelagius to Rome or question him by letter, as the five bishops had requested, because he believed that Pelagius should present himself before him if he was confident enough in his own orthodoxy.[335] After receiving these letters from Innocent, Augustine—confident that the victory over the Pelagians finally had been won—preached a sermon on September 23, 417 declaring that the "*causa finita est.*"[336]

Pope Zosimus

But, it was not finished. Innocent died on March 12, 417 just weeks after the excommunications of Pelagius and Caelestius, and Pope Zosimus, elected on March 18, 417, had other ideas.[337] Zosimus's name indicates that he might have had an eastern background, and probably would have been sympathetic to the eastern Synod of Diospolis. He has not been received well by modern scholars, who have described him as "indecisive,"[338] "*impulsif, cassant, plus autoritaire que vraiment énergique,*"[339] a "new bishop in a hurry to get things done,"[340] a "man who hated muddles . . . a weak man

---

332. Augustine, *Epist.* 183.2.

333. Augustine, *Epist.* 183.5.

334. Augustine, *Epist.* 183.3. Augustine will state that he believes that Pelagius was able to avoid condemnation because of a language problem as the bishops at Diospolis did not speak Latin. Augustine, *Gest. Pelag.* 1.2.

335. Augustine, *Epist.* 183.4.

336. Augustine, *Serm.* 131.10.

337. Wermelinger, *Rom und Pelagius*, 134–64.

338. Markus, "Legacy of Pelagius."

339. De Plinval, *Pélage*, 313.

340. Brown, *Through the Eye*, 370.

who was determined to get his way, even by gross favouritism and rudeness,"[341] and replete with "fussy authoritarianism."[342]

Caelestius returned to Rome[343] armed with a *Libellus fidei*[344] to defend himself, and Pelagius had sent his own *Libellus* accompanied by a letter from Praylius, who became the bishop of Jerusalem after John died.[345] Caelestius had already received the ordination he sought in Ephesus no later than the summer of 416 when the Council of Carthage that year anathematized him.[346] From there we know that he went to Constantinople, but he was exiled by Bishop Atticus (406–425). He then headed to Rome, and, on his way to there, he met with Heros (and maybe Lazarus), possibly in Palestine.[347] There is no indication of what happened when they met.

Both Pelagius and Caelestius hoped that Zosimus would recognize their fidelity to the church. Zosimus held a conference in the basilica of St. Clement at which Caelestius declared that he was willing to condemn any heresy,[348] and the Roman clergy was confused why the Africans would accuse Pelagius of heterodoxy.[349] Afterwards, Zosimus wrote to Africa. Paulinus of Milan, the deacon who had brought charges against Caelestius at the Council of Carthage of 411, was summoned by Zosimus to go to Rome within two months to defend himself,[350] and Heros and Lazarus were excommunicated for their behavior.[351] Zosimus exonerated Pelagius and Caelestius,[352] instructed the African bishops to reassess their position, and criticized them for condemning Pelagius and Caelestius without giving them the opportunity to defend themselves in person.[353] These letters arrived in Africa on November 2, 417. Paulinus wrote a response just six days later refusing to go to Rome,[354] and the African bishops

---

341. Brown, *Augustine of Hippo*, 360.

342. Bonner, *Augustine*, 49.

343. Marius Mercator, *Sub.* pref.4; Augustine, *C. Iul.* 3.1.4.

344. For a discussion of Caelestius's *Libellus fidei*, see: Van Egmond, "Confession of Faith," 317–39.

345. Zosimus, *Posteaquam* 1.

346. Augustine, *Epist.* 175.1, 176.4; Marius Mercator, *Sub.* pref.4.

347. Zosimus tells us that they met, but scholars disagree about the meaning of this. Ferguson believes that Caelestius went to Palestine on his way to Rome in order to take refuge under the bishops who had exonerated Pelagius at Diospolis, and that he only met with Heros. De Plinval also believes that Caelestius only met with Heros. Honnay believed that Caelestius met with both Heros and Lazarus. Zosimus, *Magnum Pondus* 4–5; Ferguson, *Pelagius*, 101–2; De Plinval, *Pélage*, 313; Honnay "Caelestius," 286.

348. Zosimus, *Magnum pondus*, 2; Augustine, *Grat. Chr.* 2.7.8.

349. Zosimus, *Posteaquam* 3.

350. Zosimus, *Magnum pondus* 8.

351. Zosimus, *Magnum pondus* 3–6; *Posteaquam*, 4–7.

352. Dunn, "Did Zosimus?," 656.

353. Zosimus, *Magnum pondus* 5,6; *Posteaquam* 7, 17.

354. Paulinus of Milan, *Libellus Paulini* 1–15. Augustine, *Grat. Chr.* 2.7.8.

made it clear that they were not going to change their minds.³⁵⁵ Clearly, the deference that the African bishops showed earlier to Rome during the pontificate of Innocent was based primarily on the Pope's willingness to agree with them. When Zosimus came to a different conclusion, the African bishops had no misgivings about ignoring him, and holding their ground. Zosimus, in turn, responded in March of 418,³⁵⁶ and the letter arrived in Carthage on April 29, reasserting his position and, like Innocent had done, emphasized the prerogative of Rome in this matter.³⁵⁷

This impasse was overcome quickly when, on April 30, the Emperor Honorius issued a rescript from Ravenna to the Roman Prefect Palladius condemning Pelagius and Caelestius, and banishing them from the city of Rome (even though Pelagius was not there). This did not achieve its desired goal because a year later, on June 9, 419, Honorius was forced to issue a new rescript, "because of persistent evil of their obstinate error,"³⁵⁸ banishing them from the provinces. The Africans most likely lobbied the Emperor for his support in this matter; but, it is unclear whether the pressure came after Innocent's excommunications (in order to obtain a harmony between church and state), or if it came after Zosimus's exonerations (in order to undermine Zosimus).³⁵⁹ Regardless, the very next day, May 1, 418, yet another council was held in Carthage and, once again, over two hundred bishops condemned Pelagius and Caelestius, showing Zosimus that they would stand firm in their opposition.³⁶⁰ Zosimus was in a difficult position, and summoned Caelestius, but Caelestius had already left town.³⁶¹ Seemingly without any more options, Zosimus wrote his *Tractoria*³⁶² condemning Pelagius and Caelestius in the summer of 418, and required other bishops to subscribe to it.³⁶³ Shortly afterwards, Theodotus of Antioch held a council that prohibited Pelagius from visiting the holy sites in Jerusalem, and Praylius confirmed the decision.³⁶⁴ Pelagius left Palestine soon thereafter, and there is speculation that he went to Egypt, although this is not certain.³⁶⁵

---

355. Zosimus, *Quamvis partum* 5.

356. Burns believes that it was on March 23rd, while Lamberigts believes that it was on either March 18th or 21st. Burns, "Augustine's Role," 72–73; Lamberigts, "Co-operation," 367.

357. Zosimus, *Quamvis partum* 1.

358. Augustine, *Epist.* 201.1.

359. Burns, "Augustine's Role," 77. See also: Lamberigts, "Co-operation," 368–69.

360. For a list of the nine canons of the council, see: Teske, "Introduction," *WSA*, 378–80.

361. Augustine says that Caelestius refused to respond to Zosimus's summons, but Lamberits has argued that Caelestius had left town because of Honorius's forced exile. Augustine, *C. du. ep. Pelag.* 2.3.5; Lamberigts, "Co-operation," 371.

362. For the extant fragments of the *Tractoria*, see Wermelinger, *Rom und Pelagius*, 307–8. See also PL 48 509–526 for the *Libellus fidei* of the Italian bishops to Zosimus; Beatrice, "Pelagian Critique," 31; Lamberigts, "Recent Research," 187–88.

363. Wermelinger, *Rom und Pelagius*, 209–18.

364. Ferguson, *Pelagius*, 114.

365. Ferguson, *Pelagius*, 114.

After leaving Rome in haste, history reports only a few more sightings of Caelestius. He later returned to Rome from an unknown location—after Zosimus and his successor Boniface (418–422) both had died—in attempt to petition Celestine (422–432) to allow him back into good standing with the church, probably around 423/424.[366] Celestine, as Prosper of Aquitaine reported, "gave orders to ban him [Caelestius] from the territory of Italy. So convinced was he that the decisions of his predecessors and the decrees of the councils were to be kept inviolate that he in no way allowed a new trial of what had once been judged and condemned."[367] Later in 428/9, Caelestius again returned to Constantinople, in an attempt to gain favor with Nestorius. Nestorius listened, but he, along with the Emperor Theodosius II, cast all the Pelagians out of Constantinople after Mercator, who had left Rome at some point and now was in Constantinople, brought charges against them, including Pelagius and Julian of Eclanum.[368] Along with several other Pelagians, Caelestius received one more condemnation at the Council of Ephesus in 431, and then he is never heard from again.[369]

Augustine's *De gratia Christi et de peccato originali*

There was reason for Augustine to hope that the entire nightmare might be over with the triple condemnation of the Pelagians in 418. But, he received a (now lost) letter in the early summer of 418[370] while in Carthage[371] from three aristocrats of the Valeria family, Albina, Pinianus, and Melania the Younger, who claimed that Pelagius said in writing that "I declare anathema anyone who thinks or says that the grace of God by which 'Christ came into this world to save sinners' (1 Tim 1:15) is not necessary, not only at every hour and at every moment, but also for every act of ours. And those who attempt to do away with this doctrine deserve eternal punishment."[372] Although these three were satisfied—indeed overjoyed—with Pelagius's condemnation, Augustine was suspicious, prompting him to write his *De gratia Christi et de peccato originali* sometime between late July and early September of 418.[373]

The first book of *De gratia Christi et de peccato originali* was written not only in response to the letter from the Valeria family, but also indirectly against Pelagius's

---

366. Honnay "Caelestius," 295.

367. Prosper, *C. coll.* 21.2.

368. Marius Mercator, *Sub.* pref.4; Honnay "Caelestius," 295–96.

369. Council of Ephesus, *Epist.* 20.

370. Teske, "Introduction," *WSA*, 374.

371. Augustine, *Grat. Chr.* 1.1.1.

372. Augustine, *Grat. Chr.* 1.2.2. For other places where Pelagius offered a vague definition of grace, see: *Nat. grat.* 44.52–45.53; *Grat Chr.* 1.6.7, 1.37.40; *Grat. Chr.* 1.35.38.

373. Teske, "Introduction," *WSA*, 374.

letter sent to Paulinus of Nola,[374] his (lost) four books titled *Pro libero arbitrio* (written shortly after the Synod of Diospolis),[375] his letter to Pope Innocent,[376] and his letter to Demetrias.[377] It demonstrates that, despite Pelagius's emphasis on grace, his definition is both ambiguous[378] and deficient, because, according to Augustine, he denies the necessity of God's assistance in every action.[379] In the second book, Augustine turns his attention to contesting the Pelagian rejection of original sin. Here, he not only took on Pelagius, but he also refuted Caelestius's statements at the Synod of Carthage of 411,[380] and Caelestius's *Libellus* given to Pope Zosimus.[381] Towards the end of the text, he cited a quotation from a nameless author—which probably is the first reference to the writings of Julian of Eclanum—in which he defends the goodness of marriage.[382] Although he did not know it at the time, this short section transitions Augustine's focus to marriage, which would become a central theme for much of the rest of the Pelagian controversy in his later writings against Julian.[383]

374. Zosimus, *Posteaquam* 1; Augustine, *Grat. Chr.* 1.35.38.

375. Augustine, *Grat. Chr.* 1.3.3.

376. Augustine, *Grat. Chr.* 1.34.37.

377. Augustine, *Grat. Chr.* 1.37.40.

378. Augustine discusses the ambiguity of the language of both Pelagius and Caelestius in several places in this text: *Grat. Chr.* 1.2.2, 1.33.36, 1.37.40, 1.39.43, 1.41.45, 2.17.20–21.24.

379. Augustine, *Grat. Chr.* 1.3.3–9.10.

380. Augustine, *Grat. Chr.* 2.2.2–4.4, 2.23.26.

381. Augustine, *Grat. Chr.* 2.5.5–7.8, 2.23.26.

382. Augustine, *Grat. Chr.* 2.33.38.

383. The goodness of marriage was briefly discussed by Augustine at the beginning of his *De peccatorum meritis et remissione et de baptism parvulorum* (1.59.57.), but it failed to materialize as a significant point of contention until Julian.

Chapter 9

Julian of Eclanum: The Architect of Pelagian Doctrine

The Life of Julian of Eclanum

AFTER THE TRIPLE CONDEMNATION of Pelagius and Caelestius by Honorius, the Council of Carthage of 418, and Pope Zosimus, the first phase of the Pelagian controversy came to an end. The second phase began when Julian, the bishop of Eclanum, and eighteen other Italian bishops[1] refused to sign Zosimus's *Tractoria*. After Julian wrote two letters to Zosimus in protest,[2] he and the other bishops were deposed, and soon were sent into exile.[3] This second phase—which would last until the Council of Ephesus (431) condemned the Pelagians—was comprised of two facets: Augustine's seemingly endless fight with Julian, and Cassian's refutation of Pelagius, and correction of Augustine.

Mathijs Lamberigts has viewed the battle between Augustine and Julian as positive, saying that "Julian was in several respects more important than some of his predecessors in the context of the Pelagian controversy. Indeed he engaged in discussion with Augustine in a much more direct and thorough manner."[4] Most scholars, however, have seen it as an ugly affair, displaying the worst of both men. Bonner said that "the polemical writings which passed between him [Julian] and Augustine were neither edifying nor conducive to the establishment of truth,"[5] and that "one could wish indeed that the whole episode had been omitted from the history of the Church."[6] Brown described it as "an unintelligent slogging-match."[7] Joanne Dewart deemed it "one of the most tedious of the patristic age."[8] Lenka Karfíková has lamented that reading the exchange between

---

1. Augustine, *C. du. ep. Pelag.* 1.1.3.
2. Augustine, *C. Jul. op. imp.* 1.18.
3. Teske, "Introduction," *WSA*, 13–14; Wermelinger, *Rom und Pelagius*, 209–11.
4. Lamberigts, "Recent Research," 185.
5. Bonner, *St. Augustine*, 347.
6. Bonner, *St. Augustine*, 347.
7. Brown, *Augustine of Hippo*, 389.
8. Dewart, "Christology," 1233.

them is "disconcerting and tiring,"[9] because "the positions of both sides are given in advance, the arguments have more or less been presented already, and their constant repetition does not quite reveal any new depths even if one regards them as two spirals of parallel monologues. It is actually a 'conversation of the deaf.'"[10]

In his own century, Julian was seen by most of his contemporaries, or near contemporaries, as a man of virtue and intelligence, although Prosper of Aquitaine couldn't resist calling him "insolent."[11] Paulinus of Nola, Julian's friend and mentor, said he was "saintly,"[12] and a "handsome soul."[13] Gennadius—who had no sympathy for Julian's theological assumptions—said that he was "a man of vigorous character," and "distinguished among the doctors of the Church."[14] Even Augustine had some positive words for him, calling him an "excellent logician,"[15] "intelligent,"[16] a "mighty" and "chaste" man,[17] a man "free from foolishness,"[18] an "outstanding" man,[19] and "eloquent with a stupendous wealth of words."[20]

Despite these few warm sentiments, the fight took a nasty turn when Augustine unleashed a torrent of *ad hominem* invective against his opponent, calling him "bereft of truth,"[21] with a "stubbornness of heart,"[22] a "youngster,"[23] "inept and uneducated,"[24] "thoughtless,"[25] a "madman,"[26] a "blind man,"[27] "bull-headed,"[28] a "heretic,"[29] an "insulting lout,"[30] "Tullian,"[31] with a "foul mind,"[32] a "pitiful man,"[33]

9. Karfíková, *Grace and Will*, 298.
10. Karfíková, *Grace and Will*, 298.
11. Prosper of Aquitaine, *C. coll.* 21.
12. Paulinus of Nola, *Poe.* 25.82, 25.91.
13. Paulinus of Nola, *Poe.* 25.94
14. Gennadius, *De vir. Inlustr.* 46.
15. Augustine, *C. Jul.* 3.6.13.
16. Augustine, *C. Jul.* 5.4.16.
17. Augustine, *C. Jul.* 5.7.29.
18. Augustine, *C. Jul.* 6.1.2.
19. Augustine, *C. Jul.* 6.11.34.
20. Augustine, *C. Jul. op. imp.* 4.5.
21. Augustine, *C. Jul.* 1.1.3.
22. Augustine, *C. Jul.* 2.5.14.
23. Augustine, *C. Jul.* 3.1.2.
24. Augustine, *C. Jul.* 3.7.16.
25. Augustine, *C. Jul.* 3.7.16.
26. Augustine, *C. Jul.* 5.1.1, 5.15.52; *C. Jul. op. imp.* 2.1.2, 2.31.
27. Augustine, *C. Jul.* 5.1.1; *C. Jul. op. imp.* 3.95.1, 4.73.
28. Augustine, *C. Jul.* 6.26.83; *C. Jul. op. imp.* 3.187.5.
29. Augustine, *C. Iul.* 1.2; *C. Iul. imp.* 3.101.2.
30. Augustine, *C. Iul. imp.* 1.11.
31. Augustine, *C. Iul. imp.* 1.22.4.
32. Augustine, *C. Iul. imp.* 1.58.
33. Augustine, *C. Iul. imp.* 1.63.2.

who is "overwhelmed by the desire to speak evil,"[34] replete with "foolish insolence,"[35] "silly,"[36] a "contentious rascal,"[37] a "slanderer,"[38] a "blabbermouth,"[39] a "deceiver,"[40] a "braggart,"[41] "raving mad,"[42] a "complete liar,"[43] "stupid,"[44] a "quarrelsome fellow,"[45] "loquacious,"[46] "deceptive,"[47] a "wretch,"[48] an "ass,"[49] with a "brash mouth,"[50] a "man of many words and little wisdom,"[51] "insane,"[52] "eloquent with a river of nonsense,"[53] a "great magician,"[54] a "clever dialectician,"[55] an "idiot"[56] with "viperous shrewdness,"[57] and a "facile mind."[58] Clearly, Julian, in Augustine's mind, had become not just an opponent to be refuted, but became his "punching bag."[59]

Julian, Pelagianism's doctrinal "architect,"[60] has had a mixed reception among modern scholars. Some have neutrally stated that he was "the most relentless of Augustine's many critics,"[61] that "no one else pressed Augustine so hard as he,"[62] that he was Augustine's "last bitter foe,"[63] and that he was "quite a complex, multi-faceted

---

34. Augustine, *C. Iul. imp.* 1.68.3.
35. Augustine, *C. Iul. imp.* 2.33.
36. Augustine, *C. Iul. imp.* 2.154.
37. Augustine, *C. Iul. imp.* 2.164.1, 2.224.
38. Augustine, *C. Iul. imp.* 2.164.2, 2.202.1, 4.50.3.
39. Augustine, *C. Iul. imp.* 2.202.1, 2.208.
40. Augustine, *C. Iul. imp.* 2.232, 3.188.1.
41. Augustine, *C. Iul. imp.* 3.32.2.
42. Augustine, *C. Iul. imp.* 3.92.
43. Augustine, *C. Iul. imp.* 3.106.1, 3.134.
44. Augustine, *C. Iul. imp.* 3.202.
45. Augustine, *C. Iul. imp.* 4.25.2, 4.101.
46. Augustine, *C. Iul. imp.* 4.50.3.
47. Augustine, *C. Iul. imp.* 4.50.3.
48. Augustine, *C. Iul. imp.* 4.54.2.
49. Augustine, *C. Iul. imp.* 4.56.
50. Augustine, *C. Iul. imp.* 4.73.
51. Augustine, *C. Iul. imp.* 4.87, 4.128.
52. Augustine, *C. Iul. imp.* 4.122.
53. Augustine, *C. Iul. imp.* 4.128.
54. Augustine, *C. Iul. imp.* 5.9.
55. Augustine, *C. Iul. imp.* 5.23.
56. Augustine, *C. Iul. imp.* 5.36.
57. Augustine, *C. Iul. imp.* 6.28.
58. Augustine, *C. Iul. imp.* 6.29.8.
59. O'Donnell, *Augustine*, 283.
60. Augustine, *C. Jul.* 6.11.36; Beatrice, "Pelagian Critique," 30.
61. Brown, *Body and Society*, 408.
62. Harnack, *History of Dogma*, 187.
63. O'Donnell, *Augustine*, 49.

figure, whom one cannot do justice by reducing him to a deposed bishop who seeks restitution. There are many sides to his character."[64]

Other scholars have found him unpalatable. They view him as a "hothead youngster who could have been [Augustine's] son,"[65] "naïve and unrealistic in his own expectations of the working of Christian morality,"[66] and "one of the tragic figures" of the Pelagian controversy whose "character has appealed to many historians but it is not easy to see why," because there is in Julian "an arrogance of a most unattractive nature."[67]

Still others have admired him as the only real intellectual equal Augustine ever encountered,[68] claiming that he was the most brilliant of all the Pelagian authors.[69] He was "clever,"[70] "tenacious,"[71] a "blistering polemicist,"[72] Augustine's "bugbear,"[73] "learned and eloquent and stood more nearly in the mainstream of the Christianities of his time than Augustine did,"[74] "a bonny fighter who had no compunction about delivering a few blows below the belt,"[75] "the system builder and the tireless spokesman of the movement,"[76] someone whom we "have only begun to appreciate the extent of his learning and originality,"[77] and "is generally characterized as a hot-headed young man, but he may very well have been one of those people who come across very differently in their writings than in everyday dealings with people."[78]

Julian was born sometime between 380–386[79] to an aristocratic Italian family.[80] Augustine mentions in passing his birthplace as "Apulia,"[81] but the precise meaning of this is not clear. Scholars have proffered several different cities without coming to any

64. Lössl, "Augustine," 143.
65. Lancel, *Saint Augustine*, 418.
66. O'Donnell, *Augustine*, 283.
67. Bonner, *St. Augustine*, 347.
68. Chadwick, *Augustine,* 149; Clark, *Origenist Controversy*, 216; Trout, *Paulinus of Nola*, 232; Karfíková, *Grace and Will*, 211, 297; Teske, "Introduction," *WSA*, 13; Hwang, *Intrepid Lover*, 72.
69. Teske, vol. 3 "Introduction," 13, 15; Chadwick, *Augustine*, 149; Lamberigts, "Recent Research," 193; Lössl, "Augustine," 129.
70. Brown, *Augustine of Hippo*, 388.
71. Brown, *Ransom of Soul*, 105.
72. O'Donnell, *Augustine*, 281.
73. O'Donnell, *Augustine*, 50.
74. O'Donnell, *Augustine*, 283.
75. Chadwick, *Augustine*, 149.
76. Beatrice, "Pelagian Critique," 30.
77. Brown, *Augustine of Hippo*, 389.
78. O'Donnell, *Augustine*, 281.
79. Lamberigts said that he was probably born around 380, Teske has said he was probably born between 380–386, and Lössl has said that he was born between 380–383. Lamberigts, "Julian of Aeclanum," 5; Teske, "Introduction," *WSA*, 13; Lössl, *Julian*, 19.
80. Brown, *Through the Eye*, 374.
81. Augustine, *C. Jul. op. imp.* 6.18.

consensus, including Atella, Capua, Eclanum, and, generally, someplace in southern Italy. Apulia even may have less to do with a geographic location, and may point more to Julian's ethnic or cultural heritage. Regardless of his exact birthplace, he undisputedly was from somewhere in southern Italy.[82] His father, Memorius, was ordained bishop of an unknown see sometime after Julian's birth.[83] His mother, Juliana,[84] also gave birth to two sisters, who would eventually become consecrated virgins.[85] Augustine later would praise Julian's parents as "good Catholic Christians" who had died before "they saw you [Julian] a heretic," which means they probably died between 409 and 418.[86] Little is known about Julian's childhood, although he received an excellent education,[87] likely in Rome, and he became fluent not only in Latin but also in Greek[88] (something that was increasingly uncommon in the West, as Augustine's own education demonstrates). In addition to the Roman education he received, he also became steeped in the Bible,[89] and developed a life-long dedication to it.[90]

Sometime between 400–408,[91] Julian, now a lector,[92] married a young woman named Titia, who probably was the daughter of Bishop Aemilius of Beneventum.[93] For the occasion, Paulinus of Nola penned an *epithalamium*, a marriage poem, in which he offered advice to the couple about how to celebrate properly on the day of the wedding, and how, as Christians, they should live their marriage.[94] Their wedding celebration, he said, must be set apart from the rude celebrations of the masses. Pagan influences, including the "symbols of lust"[95] of Juno, Cupid, and Venus, must be banned. The atmosphere must be one of peace, modesty, holiness, sober joy, and unimpassioned prayer, because it is the chaste offspring of holy bishops who are being joined in matrimony. Christ's name must be ever present. Indecent dancing in

82. Bede said that he was from Campania, but this does not necessarily mean that Julian was born there. Bede, *Hist. eccl.* 1.10; Lössl, "'Te Apulia Genuit,'" 223–37. See also Bruckner, *Julian*, 13–14; Rackett, "Sexuality and Sinlessness," 201–2.

83. Teske, vol. 2 "Introduction," 13; Lamberigts, "Julian of Aeclanum," 5.

84. Marius Mercator, *Sub.* 1.4.4.

85. Marius Mercator, *Sub.* 1.4.5.

86. Augustine, *C. Jul. op. imp.* 1.68. See also: *C. Jul.* 1.4.12.

87. Bruckner, *Julian*, 82–86.

88. Gennadius, *De vir. Inlustr.* 46.

89. Gennadius, *De vir. Inlustr.* 46.

90. Paulinus of Nola, *Poe.* 25.91.

91. Brown claims that the wedding occurred 400–403; Clark says it was probably before 404; Rackett says that it was around 403; Trout said that it was between 400 and 408; Brown, *Body and Society*, 409; Clark, *Origenist Controversy*, 35; Rackett, "Sexuality and Sinlessness," 203; Trout, *Paulinus of Nola*, 215–16 n. 103; See also Bruckner, *Julian*, 18–20; Lössl, *Julian*, 56–73.

92. Paulinus of Nola, *Poe.* 25.141–52.

93. Paulinus of Nola, *Poe.* 25.213–30. For the claim that he was only her spiritual father, see n. 51 in Walsh translation.

94. Trout, *Paulinus of Nola*, 215–17.

95. Paulinus of Nola, *Poe.* 25.9–38.

ornamented streets should be forbidden. The ground must not be strewn with leaves, nor the threshold with foliage. An immodest procession through the streets must be avoided, as well as any other celebration that smacks of pagan ritual. The ceremony must properly reflect Christian chastity, and unnecessary gifts should be shunned because character is the true value.[96]

Paulinus then turned his attention toward Titia. A Christian bride must only receive the dowry of Christ, the light of life. She must reject ostentatious clothing adorned with purple or gold, because Christ's shimmering grace is her golden garment. She must not wear necklaces bedecked with jewels, so that she may become a shining jewel for Jesus. Her time must be spent on her interior grooming, rather than exterior. She must not waste her money on superficialities like gems or silks, but her soul should be bejeweled with the virtue of chastity for her husband. Displays of physical and sartorial grandiosity diminish her dignity. "The shameless individual," he said, "fails to realise the foulness of the adornment thus put on, which makes the wearer delighting in such garments cheaper than the clothing itself."[97] Titia should avoid rouge, mascara, and highlighting her hair, because distorting her natural beauty betrays the sin of pride. Perfumed clothing and hair must be eschewed, and elaborately coifed hair—even for the delight of her groom—must be shunned. All such follies display an empty mind, and they distract from her true inner beauty that has been clothed in Christ.[98]

Paulinus also advised Julian to show a similar amount of restraint and circumspection. Like Titia, Julian must cultivate an internal life of beauty by scorning the pursuit of physical attractiveness. Christ has adorned Julian's soul with riches, including the wedding gifts of hope, devotion, fidelity, peace, and chastity. The gift of silver is God's word, while the gift of gold is the Holy Spirit. His jewels are the incandescent good works shining in his heart. The simplicity of Adam, Eve, and Rebecca with their rejection of high fashion and gaudy accessories is the model for Julian to imitate in his own life. The daughter of Herodias, with her enticing dress and gyrating frame, is the antithesis of Christian comportment.[99]

Paulinus also had advice for their marriage. Echoing Paul's instruction about husband and wife (Eph 5:22–33), Julian must love his wife, while Titia must allow her husband to become her head, just as Christ is Julian's head. If the couple were to find this marital harmony, they will be aided by Mary. He also encouraged them to live chastely.[100] During this period of Christian history, it was required for deacons and bishops to live with their wives as brothers and sisters,[101] just as Paulinus and his wife

---

96. Paulinus of Nola, *Poe.* 25.9–60.
97. Paulinus of Nola, *Poe.* 25.39–60.
98. Paulinus of Nola, *Poe.* 25.39–90.
99. Paulinus of Nola, *Poe.* 25.91–102.
100. Paulinus of Nola, *Poe.* 25.141–240.
101. Callam, "Clerical Continence," 3–50.

had done.[102] Rather than turning their attention towards each other, the couple should direct their lives towards Christ, so that they may become one flesh with him in the eternal body. If they are unable to live chastely, Paulinus prayed that their children will become consecrated virgins when they mature. If this, too, were not possible, he prayed that they will grow to become priests.[103] Paulinus's poem may have had its desired effect. Julian and his wife never had any children, and even if they had spent several years trying to reproduce, by the time Augustine wrote his *Contra Iulianum* in 422 (at the very latest), Julian was continent.[104] Titia's fate is unclear. It is possible that Julian became a widower,[105] or she may have joined a religious community of women by the time he was ordained a deacon.[106]

Julian's father showed a keen interest in the intellectual development of his son, even after Julian was married. Around 408, Memorius wrote a (no longer extant) letter to Augustine—possibly after having come to know of him through their mutual acquaintance Paulinus of Nola—requesting that Augustine send him a copy of his *De musica* for Julian's edification. Augustine responded with a letter (101) in late 408 or early 409 that he sent to Italy with Possidius, and affectionately praised Memorius as one "filled with holy charity," and a "priest [*sacerdos*] of the Lord whom I perceive to be so pleasing to God."[107] But, Augustine was less effusive about his request, or, rather, the "burden,"[108] as he described it. His initial response was to claim that he did not send the books with Possidius because they had not yet been corrected, and that he was too busy with "many serious concerns"[109] to correct them. He then dismissed as vain the types of books that constitute a liberal education that Memorius requested. "Those countless and impious stories," he lamented, "with which the poems of pagan poets are filled are in no way consonant with our [Christian] freedom, nor are the proud and polished lies of the orators, nor, finally, are the wordy sophistries of those philosophers who either have not known God at all or, 'though they knew God did not glorify him as God or thank him. Rather they became vain in their thoughts and their foolish heart was darkened'" (Rom 1:21).[110]

---

102. Brown, *Body and Society*, 409; Trout, *Paulinus of Nola*, 78–103.

103. Paulinus of Nola, *Poe.* 25.141–240.

104. Augustine, *C. Jul.* 3.14.28, 5.12.46. Rackett, "Sexuality and Sinlessness," 212. Julian's continence may have begun even before Augustine's *Epist.* 101 written at the end of 408 or the beginning of 409. In that letter, Augustine claimed that Julian was "now fighting with us in Christ's army," that is, that he was continent like Augustine and Memorius. Augustine *Epist.* 101.4. Rackett speculates that Julian was sexually active between one and nine years. Rackett, "Sexuality and Sinlessness," 211.

105. Chadwick, *Augustine*, 161.

106. Brown, *Body and Society*, 409; Rackett, "Sexuality and Sinlessness," 211–12; Lancel, *Saint Augustine*, 414.

107. Augustine, *Epist.* 101.1.

108. Augustine, *Epist.* 101.1.

109. Augustine, *Epist.* 101.1. He may have in mind his fight with the Donatists.

110. Augustine, *Epist.* 101.2.

Pivoting, Augustine recalled that at the beginning of his life of *otium* around 387 while still at Cassiciacum, he had begun writing six books on rhythm, and had intended to write another six books on melody, but the office of priest "was imposed [*imponere*] on me," such that those "trifles"[111] had disappeared, and Augustine cannot seem to recall where he put them. Immediately after saying this, however, he felt compelled to acquiesce to Memorius's request, and sent the sixth book with Possidius because he found it already corrected, and that it contains the "fruit" of the previous five books, which are difficult to comprehend without a guide.[112] Furthermore, the first five, he said, are worthless.

He hoped that the sixth book would be beneficial to "our son and fellow deacon, Julian, since he is now fighting with us in Christ's army."[113] Augustine then requested that Memorius send Julian to visit him in Africa while still a young man before Julian becomes overburdened with ecclesiastical responsibilities. "I do not dare to say that I love him more than you [Memorius]," he said, "because I would not say this truthfully, but I still venture to say that I desire his presence more than yours. It can seem strange that I should desire his presence more though I love him equally."[114] Julian eventually would go to Carthage, possibly after Alaric's pillaging of Rome in 410,[115] although he and Augustine did not meet then, nor at any time in the future.[116] During his time in Carthage, he met Honoratus, Augustine's childhood friend, to whom Augustine dedicated his *De utilitate credendi* written between 391 and 392 in his attempt to draw Honoratus away from Mani's philosophy.[117]

Julian was ordained a bishop by Pope Innocent, probably around 416 or 417.[118] Either just before his ordination while armies of the Visigoths rampaged across Italy in 411 or 412 causing a famine in the land,[119] or just after his ordination, Julian generously gave significant alms to the poor to help alleviate their suffering.[120] But, at no point during this period—the height of drama of the first phase of the Pelagian controversy—is Julian's voice heard. Why was he silent? It is not entirely clear when Julian began to have Pelagian sympathies. Prosper of Aquitaine claims that Julian had fallen

---

111. Augustine, *Epist.* 101.3.
112. Augustine, *Epist.* 101.3–4.
113. Augustine, *Epist.* 101.4.
114. Augustine, *Epist.* 101.4.
115. Lancel, *Saint Augustine*, 414.
116. Augustine, *C. Jul. op. imp.* 5.26.

117. It is also possible, though not definite, that this is the same Honoratus mentioned in *Epist.* 83, or to whom he wrote *Epp.* 140, or 228.

118. Marius Mercator, *Comm.* 3.2. Brown says that Julian was ordained in the mid-410s; Teske and Lancel claim around 416; Lössl and Rackett claim it occurred around 417. Brown, *Through the Eye*, 375; Teske, "Introduction," *WSA*, 13; Lancel, *Saint Augustine*, 414; Lössl, *Julian*, 19; Rackett, "Sexuality and Sinlessness," 203.

119. Brown, *Through the Eye*, 375.
120. Gennadius, *De vir. Inlustr.* 46.

in with Pelagius and Caelestius as early as 413, but Mercator said that Julian was still in communion with Rome in 417 when Innocent condemned the Pelagians.[121] Julian may never have known either Pelagius or Caelestius personally.[122] He only mentions Pelagius's name a few times in passing,[123] and an intimate familiarity with their writings is dubious. He knew of Pelagius's *De natura* and *Pro libero arbitrio*, but he only may have become acquainted with *De natura* through reading Augustine's *De natura et gratia*, and there is no indication that he had actually read Pelagius's *Pro libero arbitrio*.[124] It seems that he had read Jerome's *Dialogi*,[125] and Augustine's *Confessiones*,[126] as well as his anti–Pelagian writings *De peccatorum meritis et remissione et de baptismo parvulorum*,[127] *De natura et gratia*,[128] *De gratia Christi et de peccato originali*,[129] and *Contra duas epistulas Pelagianorum*.[130]

Considering this apparent absence of any personal relationship with the Pelagians, and his scant knowledge of their writings, it is perplexing why Julian would so vigorously defend their cause, and be willing to be sent into exile for it. But, before Julian departed to the East, Pope Zosimus died in December 418, sending Julian and the other Italian bishops into a letter writing frenzy hoping to muster support. The first was to Zosimus's successor,[131] but the election was contested, and Boniface (December 28, 418–September 422) was not universally recognized as Pope until Easter of 419, at which time he read Julian's letter.[132] Julian also wrote to a certain Valerius, an important military official at the imperial court in Ravenna,[133] begging him to assign some impartial judges to adjudicate their case.[134] Yet another letter was written by the bishops to Bishop Augustine of Aquileia calling for a synod to be held.[135] Still another letter was written by the bishops to Bishop Rufus of Thessalonica, as Augustine put it, "to tempt him with their cleverness, and, if possible, to draw him to their side."[136] Rather than honoring Julian's request for judges,[137] Valerius sent three letters

---

121. Rackett, "Sexuality and Sinlessness," 205; Lamberigts, "Les évêques," 273–74 n. 37.
122. Lamberigts, "A Plea," 7; Rackett, "Sexuality and Sinlessness," 205–6.
123. Augustine, *C. Jul. op. imp.* 4.88, 4.112.
124. Rackett, "Sexuality and Sinlessness," 206–7.
125. Augustine, *C. Jul. op. imp.* 4.88.
126. Augustine, *C. Jul. op. imp.* 1.25.
127. Augustine, *C. Jul. op. imp.* 2.178, 4.104.
128. Augustine, *C. Jul. op. imp.* 5.10.
129. Augustine, *C. Jul. op. imp.* 4.47.
130. Augustine, *C. Jul. op. imp.* 2.178; Clark, "Vitiated Seeds," 390.
131. Augustine, *C. du. ep. Pelag.* 1.1.2–3.
132. Kelly, *Oxford Dictionary*, 40.
133. Augustine, *Nupt.* 1.2.2, 2.1.1.
134. Augustine, *C. Jul. op. imp.* 1.10, 2.1.
135. The letter may be found in *PL* 45 1732–37, 48 508–26.
136. Augustine, *C. du. ep. Pelag.* 1.1.3.
137. Augustine says that Valeirus had "scorned them [Pelagians] with a robust faith." *Nupt.* 1.2.2.

to Augustine, one letter, which was not addressed specifically to him, was sent by a certain Bishop Vindemialis, and two letters, which were addressed specifically to him, by a certain priest Firmus.[138] Augustine had written several times to Valerius sometime earlier, and he was irritated that he had not received any response from him.[139] When he received the three letters, Augustine wrote a letter (200), which he attached as a preface to the first book of his *De nuptiis et concupiscentia*, written during the winter of 418/419.[140] In that letter, Augustine flattered Valerius as "my illustrious lord and my deservedly most excellent and most dear son,"[141] and saying, among other things, that Valerius had "a sound Catholic faith, your pious expectation of things to come, your love for God and the brethren, and your humble attitude amid your high honors,"[142] and that he had lived "an exemplary life of marital chastity."[143]

Augustine did not hesitate to send him the first book of *De nuptiis et concupiscentia*, even though Valerius was a layman, because he had heard that Valerius had read some of his other works and was pleased by them.[144] Julian obtained a copy of it, possibly the same one that Augustine sent to Valerius, and quickly responded in the summer of 419 with his *Ad Turbantium*,[145] a treatise in four books[146]—no longer extant in its entirety but extensively quoted by Augustine in book two of his *De nuptiis et concupiscentia*, *Contra Iulianum*, and *Contra Iulianum opus imperfectum*—written to Turbantius, whom he "converted" (*convertere*)[147] to Pelagianism, and who was one of the Italian bishops who refused to sign the *Tractoria*. A nameless individual then copied select excerpts from it titled *Capitula de libro Augustini quem scripsit, contra quae de libris pauca decerpsi*, and gave them to Valerius. Valerius then gave them to Alypius (and also sent a copy to Rome)[148] when Alypius had been in Ravenna to give to Augustine, asking Augustine to write a response quickly.[149] While in Italy, Alypius also had been welcomed by Pope Boniface, who had provided him with copies of the letter Julian sent to Rome after Zosimus had died, and the letter the Italian bishops sent to Rufus of Thessalonica.[150] These letters sent Augustine to work immediately. In response to Valerius's request, he wrote book two of his *De nuptiis et concupiscentia* in

---

138. Augustine, *Epist.* 200.1.
139. Augustine, *Epist.* 200.1.
140. Teske, "Introduction," *WSA*, 14.
141. Augustine, *Epist.* 200.1. See also: *Nupt.* 1.1.1; *Retract.* 2.79; *Epist.* 207.
142. Augustine, *Epist.* 200.2.
143. Augustine, *Nupt.* 1.2.2. See also *Epist.* 200.3.
144. Augustine, *Epist.* 200.3.
145. Teske, "Introduction," *WSA*, 14.
146. Augustine, *Nupt.* 2.2.2.
147. Augustine, *C. Jul. op. imp.* 5.4.
148. Augustine, *Nupt.* 2.1.1.
149. Augustine, *Nupt.* 2.2.1–2; *Epist.* 207; *Retract.* 2.79; *C. Jul. op. imp.* pref.
150. Augustine, *C. du. ep. Pelag.* 1.1.1–3.

420 or 421,[151] sending it to him via Alypius.[152] For Boniface, Augustine composed his *Contra duas epistulas Pelagianorum*, also in 420 or 421.[153]

Around this time, between 419 and 421,[154] when it was clear that Boniface would not reverse Zosimus's decision, Julian (and some of the other Italian bishops) took refuge with Theodore of Mopsuestia[155] (350–428)[156] in Cilicia until around 428 when Theodore died.[157] In his own time, Theodore was considered the leader of the Antioch school, and a highly respected exegete.[158] But, he came to be known as the father of Nestorianism,[159] which led, in part, to his condemnation at the Second Council of Constantinople in 553. Although this condemnation did not occur until over a century after both Julian and Theodore were dead, Julian's association with this condemned figure certainly would not have boosted his reputation in the eyes of Christians down the centuries.

Theodore was born into a rich family in Antioch. He studied with John Chrysostom, and later entered a monastery led by Diodore, the founder of the School of Antioch.[160] At some point, Theodore left the monastery in hopes of marrying, but was persuaded by Chrysostom to return. Eventually, he was ordained a priest in 383, and the bishop of Mopsuestia in 392.[161] Theodore (and the Antioch School) is best known for his literal exegesis that focused on the historical sense of the Bible, as a fierce opponent of Origen's allegorical exegesis, and his emphasis on the humanity of Christ.[162]

When Julian arrived in Cilicia, he probably informed Theodore of the tumult over Pelagian ideas in the West, as there is no indication that Theodore had any prior knowledge of what had transpired during the previous years.[163] A friendship developed between the two men as evidenced by Julian's translation of a commentary into Latin

---

151. Teske, "Introduction," WSA, 14.
152. Augustine, *C. Jul. op. imp.* 1.7.
153. Teske, "Introduction," WSA, 100.

154. Malavasi claims 418. Brown first claims 419 and then says late 418; Teske claims 419; Lancel claims 420 or 421; O'Donnell claims summer of 419. I would speculate that Julian did not leave any earlier than the summer of 419 because he would have wanted to wait to see if Boniface would reverse Zosimus's decision. Malavasi, "Involvement," 228; Brown, *Body and Society*, 408; Brown, *Through the Eye*, 375; Teske, vol. 2 "Introduction," 223; Lancel, *Saint Augustine*, 417; O'Donnell, *Augustine*, 282.

155. Julian's decision to stay with Theodore was sensible because Theodore was friends with Chrysostom, as was Julian's father-in-law, Aemilius, as well as Melania the Younger, who was friends with Paulinus of Nola. Rackett, "Sexuality and Sinlessness," 207–8.

156. Malavasi, "Involvement," 227.
157. Lössl, *Julian*, 292–98.
158. Kelly, *Golden Mouth*, 18.
159. McLeod, "Introduction," 64. See also 3–4.
160. Kelly, *Golden Mouth*, 6.
161. McLeod, "Introduction," 3–4.
162. McLeod, "Introduction," 3, 18–20.
163. Malavasi, "Involvement," 227.

JULIAN OF ECLANUM: THE ARCHITECT OF PELAGIAN DOCTRINE

on the Psalms that Theodore had written.[164] Mercator claimed that Theodore condemned Julian at a synod around 425.[165] But, scholars have disputed this assertion,[166] and it would be strange for Theodore to do so after Julian seems to have prompted him to write one of the last treatises he ever wrote (titled by Mercator as *Contra defensores peccati originalis*),[167] which sided with Julian.[168] Extant now only in fragments,[169] it was the lone treatise written in Greek during the Pelagian controversy.[170]

It is not clear whom Theodore was attacking in it. Some scholars have argued he had learned about Augustine's arguments from Julian, and had him in mind as his opponent;[171] others believe that his target was Jerome;[172] still others are undecided.[173] Photius (ca. 810–ca. 893),[174] the Byzantine Patriarch of Constantinople and "most learned man of his time"[175] who possessed an entire copy of Theodore's treatise, claimed in his *Bibliotheca* that Theodore was assailing Jerome, not Augustine. His description of Jerome was unmistakable, even though he said that Theodore named him (or nicknamed him) "Aram." Aram, he said, was the founder of the heresy who came from the West, but lived in the East, and created a fifth Gospel that he claimed to have found in the library of Eusebius of Caesarea; he rejected the Old Testament translations of the Septuagint, Symmachus, and Aquila to make his own translation, despite not having learned Hebrew as a child nor, he said, had he mastered the meaning of the Bible.[176] Photius's description of Theodore's listing of the teachings of Aram, which he described as "repulsive [and] blasphemous,"[177] were: (1) people sin by nature, rather than by intention. This sinful, mortal nature was acquired in an exchange after Adam's sin of an immortal, good nature; (2) newborn babies are not free from sin; (3) no human being

---

164. Clark, *Origenist Controversy*, 216.

165. ACO 1.5.1.2.3; Lössl, "Augustine," 142.

166. Kavvadas has said that Mercator's claim is of "very questionable reliability"; Wickham, however, seems to take Mercator's claim at face value. Lössl said that Mercator's statement is "spurious"; Kavvadas, "An Eastern View," 274; Lössl, "Augustine," 142; Wickham, "Pelagianism in East," 207.

167. Kavvadas, "An Eastern View," 284, n. 5.

168. Theodore of Mopsuestia, *C. def.* 1005:1–3.

169. Kavvadas, "An Eastern View," 272–73.

170. Kavvadas, "An Eastern View," 272.

171. Wickham, "Pelagianism in East," 206–7.

172. Malavasi has argued that Theodore did not have a direct knowledge of Jerome's works, but that he learned from Julian to oppose Jerome. Kavvadas first said it was "probably" against Jerome, then, in the same text, said Jerome was "no doubt" the target. Malavasi, "Involvement," 227, 258; Kavvadas, "An Eastern View," 272, 275.

173. McLeod, "Introduction," 24.

174. Wilson, "Introduction," 1.

175. Wilson, "Introduction," 1.

176. Photius, *Bibliotheca* 177.121b–123a.

177. Photius, *Bibliotheca* 177.122a.

is just; (4) not even Christ was free from sin, and that Christ's incarnation was only in appearance; (5) marriage, sexual desire, and the emission of semen are all evil.[178]

From Theodore's own fragments we can get a sense of the treatise, although a full appreciation of the entirety of the text is not possible. Theodore criticized his opponent on several points. First, he claimed that his adversary believed that God did not know that Adam was going to sin, which he described as insane because God knew he would sin and then die. Second, Theodore said that he asserted that God first made Adam immortal, then, six hours later, Adam disobeyed God causing him to be expelled from the garden and to become mortal. Theodore rhetorically asked if God wanted Adam to be immortal, why did God not impede his sin? Why, furthermore, did he not make the devil mortal?[179] Third, he said that his adversary claimed that God sentenced Adam, and all of Adam's descendants, to death because of Adam's one sin. This, Theodore scoffs, shows a lack of knowledge of the Bible, resulting in a concoction of theological opinion conjured out of ineptitude. God does not punish anyone for the sin or sins of another. Everyone will be judged in the end on their own merits.[180] Furthermore, the claim that everyone is equally condemned in Adam's sin ignored the reality of the incalculable men and women throughout history who were "righteous," including Noah, Abraham, David, and Moses. God, he said, would be unjust if he were to ignore the many virtuous works of the faithful in favor of Adam's lone transgression.[181]

Photius's description of Theodore's text, and the extant fragments of the text itself, seem to be pointing to two different intended interlocutors. Photius, without question, assumed that Theodore was attacking Jerome. Theodore's own fragments, however, are not as conclusive. Theodore's first accusation (that God did not know Adam would sin) is strange. Neither Augustine nor Jerome ever made such a bizarre claim. It is especially puzzling why Theodore would make such an accusation considering his personal relationship with Julian, as Julian never made this accusation in any of his works against Augustine. Theodore's second accusation (that God made Adam briefly immortal and then Adam became mortal after his sin) is not exactly what Augustine asserted, but as Theodore did not have access to Augustine's writings in Greek, his confusion is understandable. At the very beginning of his *De peccatorum meritis et remissione et de baptismo parvulorum*, Augustine claimed that if Adam had not sinned, "he was going to be changed into a spiritual body and pass into the state of incorruption, which is promised to believers and saints, without suffering the punishment of death," and that "if Adam had not sinned, he was not going to be stripped of his body; rather, he was going to be clothed over with immortality and incorruption so that what was mortal might be swallowed up by this life, that is, that he might

---

178. Photius, *Bibliotheca* 177.122a–123a.
179. Theodore of Mopsuestia, *C. def.* 1005: 1–3.
180. Theodore of Mopsuestia, *C. def.* 1007: 1.
181. Theodore of Mopsuestia, *C. def.* 1008: 3.

pass from an animal to a spiritual body."[182] It is likely that this was the teaching from Augustine that Theodore had in mind, although Theodore did not understand entirely what Augustine meant. Jerome, however, never made any claim about Adam's mortality or immortality that remotely resembles Theodore's accusation. Theodore's third accusation (that God sentenced Adam and all his descendants to death because of his one sin) could possibly be leveled against both Augustine and Jerome. As we will explore more in depth later, both Augustine[183] and Jerome[184] asserted that Adam's punishment of death was passed to his descendants, although they did not share the exact same understanding of how this happens. While these extant fragments from Theodore offer us only a small slice of the entire text, it seems more likely that Theodore had Augustine on the brain, not Jerome, when writing his tract.

Around 421,[185] Augustine received a complete copy of Julian's *Ad Turbantium* from Bishop Claudius, an Italian who was sympathetic to Augustine's cause against the Pelagians. When Augustine read it, he saw that the excerpts of it he had received earlier, which had been passed to him from Valerius, did not accurately represent Julian's original work. In a letter (207) back to Claudius, Augustine said that the person who made the excerpts did not cite everything as it is found in the text.[186] A few years later in his *Retractiones*, Augustine again said that the excerpts he received from Valerius were not accurate, but this time he more specifically said that the person who had made the excerpts did not simply leave out important sections of the original, but that he had altered them in some way.[187] Regardless whether the excerpts simply were missing crucial sections, or if the original text had been purposely changed, Augustine's book two of his *De nuptiis et concupiscentia* did not accurately portray Julian's arguments. When Julian read it, he spotted the distortion, and later in his *Ad Florum* angerly blamed Augustine for twisting his words.[188] Recognizing that he needed to respond to *Ad Turbantium* itself, not just the excerpts from it, Augustine composed his *Contra Iulianum* in 421 or 422, which Teske called "perhaps the most important of the anti-Pelagian works,"[189] and immediately sent it to Claudius.[190]

While still in Cilicia with Theodore, probably between 423 and 426,[191] Julian wrote his *Ad Florum*, prompted by his reading of book two of Augustine's *De nuptiis*

---

182. Augustine, *Pecc. merit.* 1.2.2.
183. Augustine, *Pecc. merit.* 1.4.4–8.8.
184. Jerome, *Dial.* 3.18.
185. Teske, vol. 2 "Introduction," 223.
186. Augustine, *Epist.* 207.
187. Augustine, *Retract.* 2.88.
188. Augustine, *C. Jul. op. imp.* 4.4, 4.77, 5.15.
189. Teske, vol. 2 "Introduction," 223.
190. Augustine, *Epist.* 207.
191. Teske, vol. 3 "Introduction," 14.

et concupiscentia,[192] as well as the encouragement of his "blessed father"[193] Florus, a bishop who, along with Julian, later would be anathematized at the Council of Ephesus.[194] While in Rome in 427,[195] Alypius came across a copy of all eight books; he copied the first five and sent them to Augustine—insisting that he respond to them immediately—with the promise that he would send the last three as soon as possible. Julian's *Ad Florum* deeply disturbed Augustine, causing him to slow the progress he had made writing his *Retractiones*, crafting it, and his response to Julian, one by day and the other by night.[196] Augustine also was forced to postpone starting a text on heresies[197] that had been requested by Quodvultdeus, a deacon in Carthage who would later become the bishop there.[198]

Augustine's response, the onerous *Contra Iulianum opus imperfectum* begun around 428, is a text that makes the eyes cross of even the most enthusiastic student of Augustine. It was his last, responding only to Julian's first six books because he died before being able to complete it.[199] He wrote in a new style different from his previous anti–Pelagian writings. As if writing a biblical commentary, he quoted a paragraph or more of Julian's text, and then refuted Julian's claims point by point, alternating sections between quotations from Julian and his own response. Augustine may have adopted this method to avoid the accusation that he was misquoting Julian's writings, an accusation to which Augustine seemed sensitive.

In addition to his theological attacks on Augustine, Julian accused him of thwarting him in other ways. Augustine, he said, paid people to cause rebellions in Rome, bribed civil authorities with gifts from the inheritances of unnamed matrons, caused discord in churches, and corrupted the emperor.[200] Through Alypius, Julian claimed, Augustine also sent "fattened herds"[201] of more than eighty horses[202] that had been paid for "at the expense of the poor"[203] to certain tribunes and centurions in Italy (probably meaning Valerius).[204] Augustine flatly denied these accusations, claiming that Julian was either rashly ignorant, or a liar. [205]

---

192. Augustine, *C. Jul. op. imp.* 1.16–19.
193. Augustine, *C. Jul. op. imp.* 1.2, 1.7
194. Council of Ephesus, *Ad Coel.* 6.
195. Teske, vol. 3 "Introduction," 14.
196. Augustine, *Epist.* 224.2.
197. Augustine would eventually write *De haeresibus* for Quodvultdeus. *Haer.* pref.1.
198. Augustine, *Epist.* 224.1–2.
199. Julian's final two books of his *Ad Florum* are no longer extant.
200. Augustine, *C. Jul. op. imp.* 3.35.
201. Augustine, *C. Jul. op. imp.* 3.35.
202. Augustine, *C. Jul. op. imp.* 1.42.
203. Augustine, *C. Jul. op. imp.* 3.35. See also: 1.42, 1.74.
204. Brown, *Through the Eye*, 376.
205. Augustine, *C. Jul. op. imp.* 1.42. See also: 1.74, 3.35.

After Theodore died in 428, Julian moved to Constantinople where he may have met Caelestius for the first time.[206] He chose Constantinople in hopes of finding refuge with Nestorius, who had been taught briefly by Theodore,[207] and had been an "eloquent and austere superior"[208] of a monastery in Antioch when he had become patriarch of Constantinople the same year Theodore died. While Julian's association with Theodore during his life had not been suspect because of Theodore's pristine reputation, his association with Nestorius quickly became problematic, especially in the eyes of Cassian, as we shall explore later.

When he arrived in Constantinople, Nestorius found himself caught in a conflict about Mary that had already been percolating for some time.[209] The controversy concerned a dispute over the description of Mary as either *Christotokos*, best translated as "the one who gave birth to Christ,"[210] or *Theotokos*, best translated as "the one who gave birth to the one who is God."[211] The title *Theotokos* may or may not have been employed by the faithful prior to the fourth century,[212] but it certainly had been used by Athanasius in the early fourth century, and later by Eusebius of Caesarea, Cyril of Jerusalem, and Gregory of Nazianzus.[213] Nestorius, however, loathed the title, and began preaching against it, publishing his sermons, and even sending them to Pope Celestine (422–432).[214] The import of the disputed title of Mary is ultimately christological, because of the intimate relationship between Mary and Jesus. Whatever is said about Mary ultimately speaks of Jesus. Nestorius felt that *Theotokos* was haunted either by Arianism, because it sounded as if it claimed that Jesus was part of creation, or Apollinarianism, because it sounded as if Jesus's humanity was completed by the Logos. He preferred the title *Christotokos*, because he felt that it more clearly described Mary as the one who gave birth to Christ who was a human, and a "vehicle for divinity."[215] Nestorius, furthermore, was primarily concerned with emphasizing the distinction between Jesus's two natures,[216] while his critics, including Cyril of Alexandria, accused

---

206. Bonner, Brown, and Lamberigts all say that Julian and Caelestius were in Constantinople together. Lössl and Rackett are unclear about their relationship at that time. Bonner, *St. Augustine*, 346; Brown, *Augustine of Hippo*, 384; Lamberigts, "Recent Research," 194; Lössl, *Julian*, 298 n. 274; Rackett, "Sexuality and Sinlessness," 209.

207. Rousseau, *Early Christian Centuries*, 274.

208. Davis, *First Seven*, 139.

209. Grillmeier, *Christ*, 451.

210. Pelikan, *Mary through Centuries*, 56.

211. Pelikan, *Mary through Centuries*, 55.

212. Pelikan says that there is no evidence that *Theotokos* was a titled used before the fourth century, but O'Collins says that it probably had been used by Origen, and Davis claims that it can be traced to the oldest Greek prayer to Mary in the third century. Pelikan, *Mary through Centuries*, 57; O'Collins, *Christology*, 187; Davis, *First Seven*, 140.

213. O'Collins, *Christology*, 187; Davis, *First Seven*, 140.

214. Davis, *First Seven*, 140.

215. Davis, *First Seven*, 145.

216. Grillmeier, *Christ*, 444, 457.

him of separating Christ's two natures, and describing their relationship as nothing more than a moral unity.[217] This fight came to a climax at the Council of Ephesus, after which Nestorius resigned his office, and returned to his monastery near Antioch. In 435, imperial decrees demanded the destruction of his texts, and sent him into exile to Oasis in Upper Egypt until his death in 451.[218]

Like Theodore before him, Nestorius had not heard of Julian, nor the controversy swirling around him, when Julian arrived in Constantinople. He wrote a letter, *Fraternas nobis invicem*,[219] to Pope Celestine asking him for clarification about what had unfolded in the West. While Nestorius was waiting for a response, in 429[220] Mercator informed the Emperor Theodosius II about the Pelagians, who then banished Julian from Constantinople.[221] After several more letters of inquiry from Nestorius, Celestine finally responded on August 10, 430 causing Nestorius to withdraw his support of Julian.[222] The final blow for Julian and the Pelagians came at the Council of Ephesus at which Julian and his companions were denied the opportunity to have their voice heard.[223] Pelagius (who probably was dead at this point), Caelestius, Julian, Florus, and three other bishops, Praesidius, Marcellian, and Orontius, who probably were some of the bishops from Italy who refused to sign the *Tractoria*, were anathematized. Any cleric who held the same beliefs as they held were also deposed.[224] Almost nothing of Julian's fate is known after this. He may have returned to Rome around 439[225] during the pontificate of Sixtus III (432–440), and later died sometime before 455.[226]

---

217. O'Collins, *Christology*, 186.

218. Young, *From Nicaea*, 290.

219. This letter also included information about his issues with Arians, Apollinarians, and their followers. He also wrote of his distaste for the title *Theotokos*.

220. Lamberigts, "Les évêques," 272–73.

221. *ACO* 1.5.1.65; Lössl, "Augustine," 142.

222. *ACO* 1.2.12–14; Grillmeier, *Christ*, 467.

223. Lamberigts, "Recent Research," 194; Lamberigts, "Les évêques," 279–80.

224. For the relevant texts from this Council in English, see *NPNF* Second series. Vol. 14 pp. 191–242, esp. 225, 229–30, 238–39.

225. Prosper of Aquitaine, *Chron.* PL 51 col. 598.

226. Gennadius, *De vir. Inlustr.* 46; Lössl, *Julian*, 326. Some scholars, such as Brown and Lancel, have claimed that he may have spent the remainder of his days as a teacher in Sicily. This, however, is not definitive. Brown, *Augustine of Hippo*, 384–85; Lancel, *Saint Augustine*, 418; Lössl, *Julian*, 327–29.

Chapter 10

John Cassian: Master of the Inner Life

Cassian's Early Life

SINCE THE LATE SIXTEENTH century,[1] John Cassian's anthropological writings—along with the writings of several others from southern Gaul,[2] and Augustine's writings that were written in response to them and to the monks of Hadrumetum in North Africa who were perplexed by Augustine's seeming dismissal of monastic effort[3]—have been consigned to a secondary debate called the "Semi-Pelagian Controversy,"[4] which has been seen as historically and theologically distinct enough from the Pelagian controversy that it necessitated its own designation.[5] Because of this, Cassian is rarely discussed by scholars as part of the Pelagian controversy. But, the relegation of Cassian to another controversy is mistaken, as he was not fighting a different battle, nor did he view himself as doing so. Rather, like Augustine, Jerome, and Orosius before him, he offered his own direct response to the Pelagian understanding of the human person, grace, free will, sinlessness, and Christ. He also offered a corrective—as he saw it—to Augustine's thought on the relationship between grace and free will.[6] Therefore, it is necessary to include his voice as part of this discussion of the Pelagian controversy.

---

1. Leyser claims the late sixteenth century, while Chadwick, Markus, Rea, Stewart, and Hanby all claim the seventeenth century. Backus and Goudriaan have recently argued that the term "semipelagianism" began to describe the teachings of the monks of Hadrumetum and Gaul in 1571 by Nicholas Sanders. Leyser, "Semi-Pelagianism," 761; Chadwick, *Primitive Monasticism*, 113; Chadwick, *John Cassian*, 127; Markus, *End of Ancient Christianity*, 178; Rea, "Grace and Free Will," 217; Stewart, *Cassian the Monk*, 19; Hanby, *Augustine and Modernity*, 107; Backus and Goudriaan, "'Semipelagianism,'" 42–46.

2. This includes a variety of sources such as Prosper of Aquitaine, Vincent of Lérins, Faustus of Riez, Fulgentius of Ruspe, Caesarius of Arles, and the Second Council of Orange (529).

3. See *Grat; Corrept; Praed; Persev.*

4. For introductions to the Semi-Pelagian controversy, see: Weaver, *Divine Grace*; Ogliari, *Gratia et Certamen*.

5. Casiday, "Rehabilitating," 272.

6. Chadwick, *John Cassian*, 120.

Cassian, who was one of the most important writers for the development of monasticism in the West,[7] was both admired and criticized in his day, as well as our own. In Cassian's own time, Prosper of Aquitaine[8] was Cassian's most hostile rival, but wrote a letter to Augustine in which he praised Cassian and other Gallic "servants of Christ"[9] who had rallied to Cassian's side as "holy men"[10] who were "so renowned and so outstanding in the pursuit of all the virtues."[11] Elsewhere, he said that Cassian was "admittedly more competent than any other in the knowledge of Holy Scripture."[12] Later, Benedict of Nursia in his *Regula* encouraged his monks to read "father" Cassian, whose writings "are nothing less than tools for the cultivation of virtues."[13] At the end of the sixth century, Gregory the Great wrote a letter to a certain Abbess Respecta in Marseilles describing Cassian as a "saint."[14]

Despite his positive sentiments of Cassian and the other Gallic monks, Prosper planted the seed of suspicion that Cassian taught a warped relationship between grace and free will when he said that Cassian "invented some hybrid third system" that agreed "neither with the heretics [Pelagians] nor with the Catholics."[15] Prosper scathingly labeled Cassian a "crafty inquisitor,"[16] and accused him and the other Gallic monks of putting on an appearance of piety "which their inner conviction belies,"[17] that they were "deceitful slanderers,"[18] that they were "new geniuses,"[19] that they were followers of "madness,"[20] and that as "opponents of Augustine" they were fighters "against truth" and defenders of "falsehood."[21]

Overall, modern scholars have viewed Cassian in a much more positive light, and a deeper appreciation for his writings and influence has taken hold in the scholarly community over the past few decades. Despite Prosper's warnings, the cloud of suspicion around Cassian seems to be evaporating.[22] Owen Chadwick, for one, insisted that

---

7. Chadwick, *Primitive Monasticism*, 5.
8. For an excellent introduction to Prosper, see Hwang, *Intrepid Lover*.
9. Augustine, *Epist.* 225.2.
10. Augustine, *Epist.* 225.
11. Augustine, *Epist.* 225.2.
12. Prosper of Aquitaine, *C. coll.* 2.1.
13. Benedict, *Reg.* 73.
14. Gregory the Great, *Epistulae*, Book 7 *Epist.* 12.
15. Prosper of Aquitaine, *C. coll.* 3.1.
16. Prosper of Aquitaine, *C. coll.* 1.2.
17. Prosper of Aquitaine, *C. coll.* 1.1.
18. Prosper of Aquitaine, *C. coll.* 1.1.
19. Prosper of Aquitaine, *C. coll.* 1.2.
20. Prosper of Aquitaine, *C. coll.* 21.1.
21. Prosper of Aquitaine, *C. coll.* 22.1.
22. Colish, *Stoic Tradition*, 116; Rea, "Grace and Free Will," 218; Pristas, "Theological Anthropology," 370; Casiday, *Tradition and Theology*, 9.

Cassian should be "regarded as a saint,"[23] and Roland Teske has echoed this by calling him "saintly."[24] Augustine Casiday has praised him as a "brilliant synthetic thinker who translated eastern asceticism into forms intelligible to his western audience."[25] Donald Fairbairn claimed that "one may rate Cassian's theological acumen considerably more favourably than most scholars have,"[26] and Boniface Ramsey described him as a "master of the inner life."[27]

Modern scholars do read Cassian with a critical eye, however. Criticisms of Cassian generally fall into two categories: first, it is said (often with a hint of regret) that Cassian was not a systematic thinker or writer.[28] Rousseau has even gone as far as saying that "he's also self-contradictory, repetitive, and even confused. I rather fear we don't admit this of the man often enough."[29] It is true that, compared to someone like Thomas Aquinas or other medieval scholastics, Cassian cannot be described as systematic. But, I do not think that his lack of orderliness should be considered a serious defect. Second, it is often claimed that Cassian, as Peter Munz said, "was never given to metaphysical speculation,"[30] and, relatedly, as Aloys Grillmeier stated, Cassian was "no great theologian."[31] This is true, especially compared to the great Christian metaphysicians like Origen, Augustine, and Aquinas. But this, too, is unfair to Cassian, because some of the most influential Christian writers in the history of tradition—such as Thomas à Kempis, Ignatius of Loyola, and Theresa of Avila—were not philosophers. It would be better to liken Cassian to other monastic or spiritual writers such as Benedict, Bernard of Clairvaux, or even Thomas Merton than it would be to compare him to the great logicians.[32]

We know very little about this "elusive"[33] man. Unlike other authors like Pelagius, Caelestius, and Orosius we have discussed whose elusiveness rests in a scarcity of sources that attest to their character and thought, Cassian's obscurity rests in an intentional obfuscation born out of monastic humility.[34] What little we do know of

---

23. Chadwick, *John Cassian*, 158. For a discussion of Cassian's status as a saint, see Stewart, *Cassian the Monk*, 21 n. 196.

24. Teske, "1 Timothy 2:4," 15.

25. Casiday, "Cassian, Augustine," 44.

26. Fairbairn, *Grace and Christology*, 197.

27. Ramsey, "General Introduction," 24.

28. Rousseau, "Cassian, Contemplation and the Coenobitic Life," 113; Stewart, *Cassian the Monk*, 37; Ogliari, *Gratia et Certamen*, 152; Rea, "Grace and Free Will in John Cassian," 50.

29. Rousseau, "Cassian and Perverted Virtue," 2.

30. Munz, "John Cassian," 9.

31. Grillmeier, *Christ*, 468. See also: Chadwick, *Primitive Monasticism*, 158; Ramsey, "General Introduction," in *The Conferences*, 23; Hanby, *Augustine and Modernity*, 107.

32. For an excellent discussion of monastic culture, see: Leclercq, *The Love of Learning and the Desire for God*.

33. Stewart, *Cassian the Monk*, vii.

34. Chadwick, *Primitive Monasticism*, 6–7.

him is disputed at every turn, including his name.[35] In his own works, he called himself "Iohannes" two times,[36] but Prosper called him "*Ioannes Monachus cognomento Cassianus Massiliae insignis et facundus scriptor habetur*,"[37] while Gennadius[38] and Cassiodorus[39] both called him "Cassianus." Scholars have proposed a date of birth anywhere from 355 to 375, and a date of death from the early 430s until 435.[40] He was born into a family for whom he felt great affection,[41] including a sister who may have become a consecrated virgin.[42] Presumably, they were wealthy, as he had a teacher who taught him Roman literature, which he later lamented by saying that "my mind, infected as it were with those [pagan] poems, meditates even during the time for prayer on the silly fables and narratives of wars with which it was filled when I was a boy and had begun my studies. The shameless recollection of poetry crops up while I am singing the psalms or asking pardon for my sins or a vision of warring heroes passes before my eyes."[43] An important part of his education was that he became fluent in both Latin and Greek, which allowed him to navigate both intellectual and cultural worlds, and which disposed him to translate the Greek ascetic world into something palatable to the West.

The place of his birth is even more disputed than the dates of his birth and death, and has received excessive scholarly attention as it has no relevance to the important role he played in the history of Christianity.[44] In his last *Collatio*, he described the "pleasant and delightful nature" of his homeland, and how "graciously and agreeably it stretched out to the reaches of the wilderness, so that the recesses of the forests might not only gladden a monk but also provide sufficient supplies of food,"[45] but this description does not reveal anything about its exact location. Elsewhere, he addressed

35. Rousseau, *Ascetics, Authority*, 175.
36. Cassian, *Inst.* 5.35; *Coll.* 14.9.4.
37. Prosper of Aquitaine, *Chron.* PL 51 596.
38. Gennadius, *De vir. Inlustr.* 62.
39. Cassiodorus, *De div.* 29.
40. For the date of his birth, Sillem suggests 355–365, Stewart suggests in the early 360s, Ogliari proposed 360–365, Ramsey proposed about 360, Casiday proposed around 360, Rea proposed about 365, and Frank between 370 and 375. Sillem, "A New Study," 334; Stewart, *Cassian the Monk*, 4; Ogliari, *Gratia et Certamen*, 119; Ramsey, "General Introduction," 5; Casiday, *Tradition and Theology*, 1; Rea, "Grace and Free Will," 8; Frank, "John Cassian," 421. For the date of his death, Gennadius said that Cassian "made an end, both of writing and living, at Marseilles, in the reign of Theodosius and Valentinianus." Ramsey proposed the date of the early 430s, Chadwick proposed 433 or soon afterwards, Stewart and Ogliari proposed the mid-430s, while Weaver and Casiday proposed 435. Gennadius, *De vir. Inlustr.* 62; Ramsey, "General Introduction," 6; Chadwick, *Primitive Monasticism*, 168; Stewart, *Cassian the Monk*, 24; Ogliari, *Gratia et Certamen*, 124; Weaver, *Divine Grace*, 115; Casiday, *Tradition and Theology*, 1.
41. Cassian, *Coll.* 24.1.2.
42. Cassian, *Inst.* 11.18.
43. Cassian, *Coll.* 14.12.
44. Chadwick, *Primitive Monasticism*, 190; Driver, *John Cassian*, 14.
45. Cassian, *Coll.* 24.1.3.

those "who live within the circuit of Constantinople, and who are my fellow-citizens through the love of my country, and my brothers through the unity of faith,"[46] although this does not necessarily mean that he originated from New Rome. Other possible options that scholars have suggested (among other places) are Gaul, Athens, Palestine, Serdica, Rome, Afer, and Sert in Kurdistan.[47] But, the most likely possibility is that Cassian was born in Scythia (*natione Scythe*), as claimed by Gennadius,[48] which is a region between the Danube and the Black Sea today known as Dobrudja in Romania and Bulgaria.[49] All of this, however, is conjecture, and there is no way of knowing with any certainty where he was born.

At some point during his youth,[50] Cassian and his older[51] friend[52] Germanus[53] went to Bethlehem to begin a life of ascetic abandonment at a monastery that was close to the spot where Jesus was born.[54] Like the date of his birth, scholars have offered a wide spectrum of possibilities for the date of their arrival in Palestine, anywhere from 378 to 392.[55] Ramsey has speculated that Cassian may have been in his twenties or thirties when he arrived,[56] but it is impossible to know his exact age at the time.[57] There is no indication that they had gotten to know Jerome personally when he arrived in Bethlehem, and they may have left even before his arrival, but an acquaintance with him cannot be ruled out.[58] It is likely that they left after only several years,[59] because they felt

---

46. Cassian, *De inc.* 7.31.

47. Frank, "John Cassian," 423; Stewart, *Cassian the Monk*, 142 n. 19; Rea, "Grace and Free Will," 3–7; Chadwick, *Primitive Monasticism*, 190–99; Damian, "Critical Considerations," 275–76.

48. Gennadius, *De vir. Inlustr.* 62.

49. Stewart, *Cassian the Monk*, 5; Rea, "Grace and Free Will," 3–7; Chadwick, *Primitive Monasticism*, 7, 190–99; Damian, "Critical Considerations," 264–77; Ogliari, *Gratia et Certamen*, 119; Chadwick, *Early Church*, 181; Marrou, "Jean Cassien," 6; Rousseau, *Ascetics, Authority*, 169; Ramsey, "General Introduction," 3.

50. Cassian, *Coll.* 17.7.

51. Cassian, *Coll.* 14.9.4.

52. Cassian, *Coll.* 16.1.

53. Germanus was Cassian's traveling companion in Bethlehem, Egypt, Constantinople, and Rome. Stewart speculates that he died before Cassian arrived in Gaul, but Dunn has proposed the possibility that Germanus went to Africa when Cassian went to Gaul. Stewart, *Cassian the Monk*, 5; Dunn, "Cassian in Syria?," 15.

54. Cassian, *Inst.* 4.31.

55. Ogliari has speculated that their arrival was between 378 and 380; Chadwick first suggested sometime between 378 and 388, but later said that it was no later than 392, and possibly several years earlier; Stewart has suggested around 380. Ogliari, *Gratia et Certamen*, 120; Chadwick, *Primitive Monasticism*, 8; Chadwick, *John Cassian*, 10; Stewart, *Cassian the Monk*, 6.

56. Ramsey, "General Introduction," in *The Conferences*, 5.

57. Driver, *John Cassian*, 14.

58. Chadwick, *Primitive Monasticism*, 10–11. Frank, "John Cassian," 428–29.

59. Stewart, *Cassian the Monk*, 6.

that the monastic life there was inferior[60] to that of the life in the Egyptian desert,[61] and because they were inspired by an encounter with Abba Pinufius.[62]

Pinufius was an elderly abba of a large cenobium in Egypt close to the town of Panephysis. He was so highly respected and admired that he felt that his position did not allow him to pursue the humility he desperately desired, so he fled to the cenobium of Tabennesis in Upper Egypt, which practiced the most severe austerities of all of the desert communities. There, he begged to be welcomed, and, when he finally was permitted to enter, he was only begrudgingly embraced because the other monks felt that he wanted to be admitted for the safety and security of a community in his old age. He was placed under the charge of a younger monk, and was given the responsibility of caring for the garden. After living there for three years, a monk from his original cenobium had been visiting Tabennesis, and eventually recognized him—despite a change in his physical appearance and lowliness of his task. His own monks, in fact, had been looking for him, and had dispatched brothers in all directions to find him. When the monks at Tabennesis learned of Pinufius's identity, they all asked for his forgiveness for their ill treatment of him. Pinufius, bitterly weeping, was carted back to his original cenobium where he stayed for only a short time until he was able to escape yet again by boarding a boat to Palestine. Cassian and Germanus met him there as he took up residence in their monastery in Bethlehem, and the abba assigned him to their cell. Not long afterwards, however, some brothers from his first cenobium were in Palestine to pray at the holy shrines. Immediately recognizing him, they took him back to Egypt. "When," Cassian recounted, "therefore, after a short while a desire for holy instruction had compelled us to come to Egypt ourselves, and we had sought out this man with great longing and desire, we were received with such graciousness and hospitality that he even honored us, as former sharers of the same cell, with lodging in his own cell, which he had built at the far end of his garden."[63]

Egypt, Constantinople, and Rome

Cassian and Germanus may have arrived at the Egyptian town Thennesus[64] sometime between the mid-380s and 390,[65] and met Bishop Archebius, who had lived in a community of anchorites for thirty-seven years, but was forced to become the bishop of Panephysis.[66] He generously showered them with hospitality when he

---

60. Cassian, *Coll.* 17.2.1–2, 17.7, 17.10.
61. Cassian, *Coll.* 11.1.
62. Cassian, *Inst.* 4.30–35; *Coll.* 20.1.1.1–3.1.2.
63. Cassian, *Coll.* 20.2.1.
64. Cassian, *Coll.* 11.1.
65. Stewart suggests the mid-390s; Chadwick suggests it was sometime between 385 and 390. Stewart, *Cassian the Monk*, 8; Chadwick, *Primitive Monasticism*, 11–13.
66. Cassian, *Coll.* 7.26.

learned of their intention to visit monks in every corner of the desert, and took them to meet some who lived close to Panephysis, which had been ravaged by the sea after an earthquake.[67] It was during this exploration of Egypt—which may have lasted anywhere from a few months to fifteen years[68]—that Cassian met many of the great abbas of the desert, and he acquired the material that would later constitute his teachings to the Gallic monks. Although he is not mentioned by name in any of his writings because he became a controversial figure, Cassian may have met Evagrius Pontius,[69] the "philosopher of the desert,"[70] who conveyed Origen's teachings to him, and who became his most important intellectual influence.[71] During their time there,[72] Cassian and Germanus traveled throughout the great monastic communities in the Nile Delta, Scetis, and Kellia.[73]

While in Egypt, they had a crisis of conscience. They had found there among the "examples of these great men"[74] a monastic life that filled them "with spiritual joy," and that allowed them to "make great progress."[75] The life that they led in the cenobium in Bethlehem was "lukewarm,"[76] "unsuitable,"[77] and was filled with elders with "rigidly obstinate"[78] minds that led to "mediocrity."[79] Problematically, while still in Palestine, Cassian and Germanus had made a vow to return as quickly as possible after having taken a tour of the desert.[80] They did not want to break their vow, but,

67. Cassian, *Coll.* 11.2.1–4.1.

68. Driver argues that they may have been in Egypt "for a period that could be measured either in decades or in months"; Franks argues that "his stay among them was considerably shorter and less intense than has often been argued"; Rousseau argues that "he lived as an ascetic in Egypt for two years at least, if not longer"; Ramsey argues that he spent "perhaps as long as ten years there"; Sillem argues that they remained there "ten or twelve years in all"; Chadwick argues that for fourteen years "from 385 to 399, [were] the years covering Cassian's stay in Egypt"; Stewart argues that he spent "fifteen years or so" in Egypt. Driver, *John Cassian*, 16; Frank, "John Cassian," 431; Rousseau, *Ascetics, Authority*, 169; Ramsey, "General Introduction," 5; Sillem, "A New Study," 334; Chadwick, *Primitive Monasticism*, 26; Stewart, *Cassian the Monk*, 8.

69. Chadwick and Ogliari suggest that they had met Evagrius, but Driver suggests that they had never met. Chadwick, *Primitive Monasticism*, 26; Ogliari, *Gratia et Certamen*, 120; Driver, *John Cassian*, 16.

70. Ogliari, *Gratia et Certamen*, 120.

71. Chadwick, *Primitive Monasticism*, 25; Stewart, *Cassian the Monk*, 4, 11–12, 36; Weaver, *Divine Grace*, 71–73; Hanby, *Augustine and Modernity*, 120.

72. For suggested itineraries of their travels throughout Egypt, see Chadwick, *Primitive Monasticism*, 27; Stewart, *Cassian the Monk*, 9.

73. Stewart suggests that Scetis was Cassian's "Egyptian monastic base," but Driver suggests they "settled at Nitria." Stewart, *Cassian the Monk*, 10; Driver, *John Cassian*, 13.

74. Cassian, *Coll.* 17.2.1.

75. Cassian, *Coll.* 17.5.1.

76. Cassian, *Coll.* 17.8.3.

77. Cassian, *Coll.* 17.9.

78. Cassian, *Coll.* 17.23.1.

79. Cassian, *Coll.* 17.10.

80. Cassian, *Coll.* 17.2.1–2.

at the same time, they did not want to return to a life that they knew was inferior. They thought that it might be possible to return to Palestine for a brief time to fulfill their promise, and to hastily return back to Egypt; but, they worried that their elders would not give them permission to leave their cenobium permanently after they had returned from Egypt.[81] Unable to decide how to proceed, they approached Abba Joseph for his wisdom.[82]

Abba Joseph advised them—probably to the surprise of many modern readers—that they should break their promise and stay in Egypt. If they were to profit by remaining there, they "should not cling stubbornly"[83] to the promise that they had made, because, in the end, their souls would suffer spiritually if they returned. They should always choose whatever is best for the pursuit of purity of heart.[84] Cassian and Germanus seem to be convinced by Joseph's advice as they stayed in Egypt.[85] Cassian's audience, furthermore, is left with the impression that, under circumstances when a spiritual good may be obtained, it is acceptable to break a promise—and even, sometimes, to tell a lie.[86] Curiously, however, Cassian and Germanus later returned to Palestine. Despite having found peace with their decision, they "gladly"[87] fulfilled their promise after they were sure that they would be allowed to return to Egypt.[88] Perhaps their consciences were not as clear as Cassian suggested, and they may have been disturbed that many of the elders in Bethlehem were not convinced by their explanations. They seem to have felt the nagging urge to restore the "former love to the souls of those who, out of an ardent love, had not in the least been appeased by the frequent excuses contained in our letters."[89] After they had soothed any hurt feelings that their *volte-face* may have caused, they once again returned to Scetis with the joyful approval of their Palestinian superiors.

Cassian and Germanus did not remain permanently in the desert, however. They were still in the Egypt when Theophilus wrote his letter in 399 that condemned the Anthropomorphites,[90] the monks who imagined God with a corporeal form, but they left after Theophilus changed his mind and drove out the monks there who were influenced by Origen.[91] Many scholars have speculated that Cassian and his com-

81. Cassian, *Coll.* 17.5.2–3.
82. Cassian, *Coll.* 17.3.
83. Cassian, *Coll.* 17.15.14.
84. Cassian, *Coll.* 17.14.1.
85. Cassian, *Coll.* 17.30.2.
86. Cassian, *Coll.* 17.17.1.
87. Cassian, *Coll.* 17.30.2.
88. Cassian claims that he went back to Palestine after seven years in Egypt, but, as discussed earlier, many scholars are not convinced that he and Germanus were not in the desert for as long as Cassian claimed. Cassian, *Coll.* 17.30.2.
89. Cassian, *Coll.* 17.30.2.
90. Cassian, *Coll.* 10.2.2.
91. Socrates, *Hist. eccl.* 6.7; Kelly, *Golden Mouth*, 193–94.

panion had fled with all of the other students of Origenist thought,[92] but, this is not necessarily the case.[93] Although he certainly left Egypt around this same time as the Anthropomorphites, Cassian himself tells us that he and Germanus were haunted by the memory of their families, and longed to see them again.[94]

Regardless of the reason why, they left the desert and soon arrived in Constantinople, which may or may not have been their intended final destination.[95] While there, Cassian was ordained a deacon (against his will)[96] by John Chrysostom,[97] and Germanus, at some point, was ordained a presbyter, also possibly by Chrysostom.[98] Cassian claims to have been his student, and that his christological insights ultimately may be traced back to Chrysostom: whatever "belongs to the disciple," he later wrote to the faithful in Constantinople, "ought all to be referred to the honour of the master."[99] But, there is no evidence that Chrysostom had any direct influence on his intellectual development.[100] Cassian's deep admiration for Chrysostom cannot be denied, however, for he declared him a man of "holiness," a "marvel of faith and purity," and "a disciple of Jesus and an Apostle; and so to speak ever reclined on the breast of the heart of the Lord."[101]

He and Germanus remained in Constantinople for only a few years,[102] and soon left for Rome on a mission for Chrysostom. In late 404, or even 405,[103] they carried letters to Pope Innocent from Chrysostom and all of his clergy, and they described to him the "scenes of evil"[104] that led to Chrysostom's second exile from Constantinople.[105] They also deposited gold, silver, and clothing with the magistrates of the city in order to clear Chrysostom of the charges brought against him that he had taken possessions from the church.[106] At some point, Cassian was ordained a presbyter (once

---

92. For example: Chadwick, *Primitive Monasticism*, 36; Stewart, *Cassian the Monk*, 12.

93. Rousseau, *Ascetics, Authority*, 171–72; Ramsey, "General Introduction," in *The Conferences*, 5.

94. Cassian, *Coll.* 24.1.2.

95. Rousseau and Ramsey have speculated that on his way home, which they believe was in Scythia, they may have stopped in Constantinople because of the reputation of Chrysostom. Rousseau, *Ascetics, Authority*, 172; Ramsey, "General Introduction," in *The Conferences*, 5.

96. Cassian, *Inst.* 11.18.

97. Cassian, *De inc.* 7.31; Gennadius, *De vir. Inlustr.* 62.

98. Palladius *Dial.* 3; Sozomen *Hist. eccl.* 8.26.

99. Cassian, *De inc.* 7.31.

100. Rousseau, *Ascetics, Authority*, 172.

101. Cassian, *De inc.* 7.31.

102. They may have been in Constantinople around 400 and 404. Chadwick, *Primitive Monasticism*, 36; Stewart, *Cassian the Monk*, 12–13.

103. Rousseau and Stewart claim 404; Chadwick claims 405; Rousseau, *Ascetics, Authority*, 169; Chadwick, *Primitive Monasticism*, 40; Stewart, *Cassian the Monk*, 14.

104. Sozomen *Hist. eccl.* 8.26. See also: Innocent, *Epist.* 7.1.

105. Palladius, *Dial.* 3; Sozomen *Hist. eccl.* 8.26.

106. Palladius, *Dial.* 3; Kelly, *Golden Mouth*, 252–53, 275–76.

again, probably against his desires), and it may have been in Rome at the hands of Innocent, although it may have occurred later after he left.[107] While still in Rome, he may have met and befriended a young deacon and future Pope Leo,[108] who later would ask Cassian to write a response to Nestorius, which would result in Cassian's *De incarnatione Domini contra Nestorium*.[109] What is often overlooked is that it is also likely that at this time Cassian probably had met Pelagius (and possibly Caelestius), and become acquainted with his thought—although there is no indication that a friendship developed between the two. This depends, of course, on how long Cassian stayed in Rome, which is of no little dispute among scholars. Some scholars say that Cassian remained in Rome for several years, and left after the devastation brought on by Alaric in 410.[110] Others believe that he may have been the messenger who took Innocent's reply to Chrysostom back to Constantinople.[111] Still others believe that Cassian was the same Cassian mentioned in two letters[112] from Innocent to Bishop Alexander of Antioch written around 413 in which Innocent indicates that Cassian was important in the reconciliation between Rome and Antioch after the Melitian schism.[113] A return to Palestine is yet another possibility.[114] All of this is supposition.

Gaul

What we do know for certain is that Cassian went to Gaul at some point between 405–426,[115] although his reason for going there, rather than some other destination,

107. Gennadius says that he was ordained a deacon by Chrysostom in Constantinople, and a "presbyter at Marseilles." This may mean he was ordained a presbyter while in Gaul, or that he already had been ordained by the time he arrived in Gaul. Ogliari, Frank, and Ramsey believe that he was ordained a presbyter in Rome. Griffe believes that he was ordained in Antioch, and Rousseau suspects he was ordained in Gaul. Stewart seems to be divided between Rome and Antioch. Gennadius, *De vir. Inlustr.* 62; Ogliari, *Gratia et Certamen*, 122; Frank, "John Cassian," 421; Ramsey, "General Introduction," in *The Conferences*, 6; Griffe, "Cassien," 241; Rousseau, "Monastery and World," 68–69; Stewart, *Cassian the Monk*, 14–15.

108. Gennadius says that "at the request of Leo the archdeacon, afterwards bishop of Rome, he [Cassian], wrote seven books against Nestorius." Stewart allows the possibility of them meeting; Chadwick is positive they met; Frank says that it is unlikely that a friendship developed; Rousseau is skeptical. Gennadius, *De vir. Inlustr.* 62; Stewart, *Cassian the Monk*, 14; Chadwick, *Primitive Monasticism*, 40; Stewart, *Cassian the Monk*, 41; Frank, "John Cassian," 421; Rousseau, *Ascetics, Authority*, 173.

109. Cassian, *De inc.* pref.

110. Chadwick, *Primitive Monasticism* 41; Stewart, *Cassian the Monk*, 15; Ogliari, *Gratia et Certamen*, 122; Frank, "John Cassian," 421.

111. Sozomen *Hist. eccl.* 8.26. See also: Innocent, *Epist.* 7.1; Marrou, "Jean Cassien," 18; Griffe, "Cassien," 241; Rousseau, *Ascetics, Authority*, 173.

112. Innocent, *Epp.* 19, 20.

113. Ramsey, "General Introduction," in *The Conferences*, 6; Rousseau, *Ascetics, Authority*, 174. Dunn has argued that the Cassian mentioned in these two letters is not John Cassian. Dunn, "Cassian in Syria?," 5.

114. Driver, *John Cassian*, 11, 16–17; Marrou, "Jean Cassien," 18–19.

115. Dunn says he may have arrived as early as 405; Stewart suggests the mid-to-late 410s; Weaver

is not entirely clear.[116] Shortly after his arrival, he established two monasteries (one for men, and one for women),[117] but he did not start the monastic movement there. The extent of the inroads that monasticism had made in Gaul at the beginning of the fifth century is disputed. Owen Chadwick has argued that by 410 asceticism "had made little progress"[118] there, but Donato Ogliari has claimed that at that time already there was a "decisive spread of monastic ideals."[119] However deeply entrenched it had become (or the exact forms that it had taken)[120] among the aristocrats and the masses when he disembarked at the port city Massilia,[121] Cassian was appalled by what he found.

Richard Goodrich has written an excellent study detailing Cassian's criticisms of the troubled monastic scene in Gaul, the causes of the problems, and the cure that Cassian prescribed.[122] As he has pointed out, the primary problem in Gaul was the lack of experience of the monastic superiors who had placed themselves in leadership roles without first having been obedient beginners. Rather than passing on to the next generation what they themselves had learned as novices, they devised something entirely novel based on nothing other than their own personal judgment. Novelty and individual creativity may seem preferable in our postmodern context, but to Cassian—and to the Egyptian monastic culture in general—this was a tragic mistake that inevitably would lead to the destruction of monastic life there, because the foundation of Gallic monastic culture was based on the arrogant pride of the superior.[123]

This self-reliance could not have surprised Cassian because the authors of the monastic literature that were popular in Gaul at that time all had vaulted past studying to teaching. Sulpicius Severus and Paulinus of Nola, for example, chose to dispense their own flavors of renunciation without having gone through the stages of apprenticeship. It was Jerome, more than any other, on whom Cassian seemed to focus his criticism. Jerome never sat at the feet of any established master. Indeed, with

---

believes 414–417; Markus, Rousseau, and Hwang assert it was around 415; Driver puts the date possibly as late as 426. Dunn, "Cassian in Syria?," 16; Stewart, *Cassian the Monk*, 16; Weaver, *Divine Grace*, 77; Markus, *End of Ancient Christianity*, 163; Rousseau, "Monastery and World," 68; Hwang, *Intrepid Lover*, 84; Driver, *John Cassian*, 14.

116. Chadwick offers the possibility that Cassian went to Gaul because the church there was ruled by Proculus, who was a bishop interested in the monastic movement. Ogliari cannot trace any personal or professional reason for going there. Rousseau says that he may have gone to Gaul from the East with Lazarus of Aix. Chadwick, *John Cassian*, 41; Ogliari, *Gratia et Certamen*, 122; Rousseau, *Ascetics, Authority*, 174.

117. Gennadius, *De vir. Inlustr.* 62.

118. Chadwick, *Primitive Monasticism*, 46.

119. Ogliari, *Gratia et Certamen*, 110. See also: Rousseau, "Monastery and World," 69; Goodrich, *Contextualizing Cassian*, 32; Stewart, *Cassian the Monk*, 16–17.

120. Rousseau has argued that by the time Cassian arrived, the asceticism in Gaul had become increasingly cenobitic. Rousseau, *Ascetics, Authority*, 177.

121. Stewart, *Cassian the Monk*, 15.

122. Goodrich, *Contextualizing Cassian*, 32–115.

123. Goodrich, *Contextualizing Cassian*, 49–55.

our knowledge of Jerome's personality, it is hard to imagine him ever being obedient to someone else. He, rather, relied on his own ingenuity (*ingenium*) and eloquence (*eloquentia*)—which together were suspect for being a "mask for untruthfulness"[124]— to devise an ascetic program, a "Syrian version of *otium*,"[125] that he disseminated to others as if he were an expert.[126]

Several symptoms pointed to the flawed Gallic monastic practice caused by a lack of experience. First, the rules for the nocturnal psalmody were not uniform throughout Gaul, because each superior devised them anyway he saw fit. Gallic communities did not chant twelve psalms in the evening as was the practice in Egypt, but varied in number from community to community. Second, the Gallic communities did not chant the psalms properly. Cassian criticized their chanting as wrongly focused on the external gestures, and inattentive to internal transformation because, at the end of chanting, many Gallic monks fell to their knees. This led to a disordered understanding of the objective of the monastic life, which should be focused on the interior life. The Egyptian monks, by contrast, prayed standing for a time after chanting, then placed their faces to the ground, stood up, and resumed praying with their arms extended. Third, this interior disorder led to a hollow spiritual practice that led to apathy, which was demonstrated by the vulgar spitting, coughing, yawning, groaning, sighing, and throat clearing that were common among the Gallic monks. Egyptian monks, contrarily, remained silent after chanting. Fourth, the practice that monks engage in manual labor, as demonstrated by the later Benedictine motto of "pray and work" (*ora et labora*), had yet to become a commonplace everywhere. Gallic monks did not regularly engage in work, which was necessary both practically and spiritually. Egyptian monks always engaged in some form of labor, such as basketmaking. Fifth, Gallic monks assumed that God's anger, which can be found throughout the Old Testament, sanctions human anger. They did not strive to eradicate it in their own lives, therefore. An important goal of the monastic life, Cassian insisted, was to eliminate anger so as not to impede progress towards purity of heart. The Gallic disinterest in purging this bad *habitus* spoiled any further spiritual development.[127]

The *De institutis coenobiroum,* Collationes, *and* De incarnatione Domini contra Nestorium

The solution to Gallic inexperience was the wisdom of the Egyptian monks forged in the crucible of experience in the desert. Since Cassian could not bring the Gallic monks to the desert, he brought the desert to them with his *De institutis coenobiroum* and *Collationes.* The *De institutis coenobiroum,* simply referred to as the *Institutiones,*

---

124. Goodrich, *Contextualizing Cassian,* 70.
125. Goodrich, *Contextualizing Cassian,* 83.
126. Goodrich, *Contextualizing Cassian,* 52, 78–97.
127. Goodrich, *Contextualizing Cassian,* 55–59.

was written sometime between 419 and 426.[128] It was the first of his two great manuals instructing Gallic monks how to live a rightly ordered exterior and interior life in order to pursue purity of heart.[129] It was written at the request of Bishop Castor of Apt,[130] approximately forty miles north of Marseilles.[131] Cassian described Castor as an "unparalleled model of devotion and humility."[132] There were no monastic foundations in Apt at that time,[133] but Castor wanted to "construct a true and spiritual temple for God not out of unfeeling stones but out of a community of holy men"[134] that would be influenced by eastern—particularly Egyptian—cenobia. Cassian protested that he was not intellectually up to the challenge, that he could not remember every detail of his life in Palestine and Egypt since it had been so many years earlier, and that he did not have the requisite skills to communicate articulately.[135] Despite these protestations, Cassian acquiesced, saying that he would use simple language, and, without resorting to titillating stories of miracles, to convey as best he could what Castor requested.[136] Although he wrote about the practices of the desert monasteries, Cassian clearly was sensitive to the behavioral and climatic differences between Gaul and Egypt. "What I discern in the rule of the Egyptians to be impossible or hard or arduous for this country," he said, "I shall temper somewhat by recourse to the customs of the monasteries in Palestine and Mesopotamia, for, if reasonable possibilities are offered, the same perfection of observance may exist even when there is unequal capability."[137] We see here Cassian's recognition that his job was not to write hagiographies of the abbas he had met, a stilted history of the desert, nor rigid rules to be imposed thoughtlessly in any cultural context. His task was to make the Egyptian experience meaningful to a Gallic environment.

The *Collationes* was Cassian's monastic masterpiece. Written sometime between 420 and 429,[138] he had hinted in his *Institutiones* that he had intended to write it as a

---

128. Stewart asserts that they were begun by at least 419; Weaver says that they were written between 419 and 425, but probably were written in 424; Marrou, Ogliari, and Hwang all posit 419–426. Stewart, *Cassian the Monk*, 16; Weaver, *Divine Grace*, 88; Marrou, "Jean Cassien," 6; Ogliari, *Gratia et Certamen*, 124; Hwang, *Intrepid Lover*, 86.

129. Weaver, *Divine Grace*, 89; Stewart, *Cassian the Monk*, 29; Ogliari, *Gratia et Certamen*, 124–25.

130. Cassian, *Inst.* pref.2.

131. Chadwick, *John Cassian*, 37.

132. Cassian, *Inst.* pref.7.

133. Cassian, *Inst.* pref.3.

134. Cassian, *Inst.* pref.2.

135. Cassian, *Inst.* pref.4–5.

136. Cassian, *Inst.* pref.3, 7.

137. Cassian, *Inst.* pref.9.

138. Marrou suggests 420–429; Stewart says they were begun in the middle 420s; Chadwick says they were begun in 425; Ogliari claims 425/6–428; Ramsey says 426–429; Weaver is not clear. At first, she says that they were written between 425 and 427, with the first two groups completed by the end of 426 and the third group composed in 427. Later in the same book, however, she says that they were completed two years later in 429. Marrou, "Jean Cassien," 6; Stewart, *Cassian the Monk*, 16;

companion volume.[139] This text was more widely read and copied during the medieval period than Cassian's others.[140] In it, Cassian passed on the teachings of the abbas he and Germanus had met in Egypt. Scholars have long debated the historicity of the portraits painted of the Egyptian desert and of these conversations.[141] It must be admitted that it would be next to impossible for Cassian to reproduce every conversation word-for-word that he had with these renunciants, and there is no indication that he had taken short-hand notes as a *notarius* while they were speaking, as was often the case when a bishop preached.[142] Nevertheless, it is safe to say that, at the very least, Cassian transmitted to his audience the substance of the desert wisdom he had absorbed while there. The dialogues transpired between multiple abbas and Germanus, while Cassian remained largely silent, and in the background. They were written in three parts: the first part, *Collationes* 1–10, were conversations with the monks of Scetis; the second part, *Collationes* 11–17, were conversations with the monks around Thennesus; the third part, *Collationes* 18–24, were conversations with monks around Diolcos. Cassian indicates that his original intention was to write only the first ten, but then added the last fourteen in order to expand on those topics that "were perhaps treated rather obscurely or passed over in our previous works."[143]

The first part, which he says was put together "haphazardly,"[144] was dedicated to Bishop Leontius,[145] who probably was the bishop of Fréjus,[146] and to Helladius,[147] who would become a bishop by the time the second group of *Collationes* had been written,[148] even though Castor had requested it. Castor, at some point, had died between the completion of the *Institutiones* and the beginning of the *Collationes*.[149] Cassian's intent was to shift his discussion from "the external and visible life of the monks," that is, from a discussion of such topics as the monk's belt, hood, cord, staff, and footwear that had been discussed in the *Institutiones*, to a discussion on

---

Chadwick, *Primitive Monasticism*, 29; Ogliari, *Gratia et Certamen*, 125; Ramsey, "General Introduction," 8; Weaver, *Divine Grace*, 93–94, 115.

139. Cassian, *Inst.* 2.1, 2.9, 2.18, 5.4.

140. Rea, "Grace and Free Will," 52.

141. For example, Chadwick claimed that "it must be admitted that a fairly weighty case can be indited in favour of treating the *Conferences* with some caution." Chadwick, *Primitive Monasticism*, 28. See also: Ogliari, *Gratia et Certamen*, 126–27.

142. See, for example, Cardinal Pellegrino's discussion of the transmission of Augustine's sermons: Pellegrino, "Introduction," 15–19.

143. Cassian, *Coll.* 11.pref.2.

144. Cassian, *Coll.* 11.pref.2.

145. Cassian, *Coll.* 1.pref.2.

146. Weaver, *Divine Grace*, 94.

147. Cassian, *Coll.* 1.pref.2.

148. Cassian, *Coll.* 11.pref.2.

149. Cassian, *Coll.* 1.pref.2.

the subject of the "invisible character of the inner man,"[150] such as discretion, the changeableness of the soul, and the life or prayer.

The second part was dedicated to Honoratus and Eucherius, both of whom swelled with admiration for the men of the desert. Cassian said that Honoratus presided over a large cenobium of brothers,[151] which points to the probability that this was the same Honoratus who had founded a monastery at Lérins, and who later would become the bishop of Arles in 426 after the death of Patroclus.[152] Honoratus, Cassian claimed, wanted his community of monks to be instructed in the ways of the elders. Eucherius, moreover, burned with desire to leave Gaul because it spiritually was "sluggish with the numbness of a Gallic frost,"[153] and to travel to Egypt to see for himself the heat of the monastic training grounds. In order to bolster Honoratus's authority by providing him with the weight of the desert fathers, and to save Eucherius from the burdensome journey across the Mediterranean, Cassian wrote for both of them seven *collationes* on a variety of topics, including chastity, friendship, and his infamous *Collatio* 13, *De protectione Dei*, that explores the relationship between grace and free will.

The third part was dedicated to four "holy brothers."[154] The first three, Jovinianus, Minervus, and Leontius, are unknown figures other than Cassian's description that they taught and inspired not only new monastic professions to the cenobitic life, but those who longed for the solitary life. The fourth dedicatee, Theodore, had established cenobia throughout Gaul that Cassian admired for their strict adherence to the "ancient virtues,"[155] and who probably succeeded Leontius as the bishop of Fréjus in 432.[156] These final seven *collationes* transmitted teachings that were balanced to be fruitful for both a cenobitic audience and an anchoritic one, and should be received more easily by them because of the foundation the four dedicatees already had laid. Armed with the teachings of these four men, along with Cassian's writings of Egyptian wisdom on such topics as mortification, sinlessness, and repentance, these cenobites and anchorites need not rely on themselves to blaze their own ascetic paths, but to follow the examples of the ancient tradition that Cassian has handed on to them.[157]

Cassian's third and final text was his "little-read" *De incarnatione Domini contra Nestorium*, written[158] sometime between 428 and 431.[159] It was primarily a

150. Cassian, *Coll.* 1.pref.2.
151. Cassian, *Coll.* 11.pref.1.
152. Weaver, *Divine Grace*, 74, 94.
153. Cassian, *Coll.* 11.pref.1.
154. Cassian, *Coll.* 18.pref.1.
155. Cassian, *Coll.* 18.pref.1.
156. Weaver, *Divine Grace*, 94.
157. Cassian, *Coll.* 18.pref.3.
158. Stewart, *Cassian the Monk*, 4.
159. Marrou offers the largest window between 428 and 431; Chadwick claims 430; Stewart claims late 429 to early 430; Casiday suggests 429 or 430; Ramsey suggests shortly before his death in the early 430s; Rea says 430; Marrou, "Jean Cassien," 6; Chadwick, *Primitive Monasticism*, 153; Stewart,

christological response to Nestorius, but it also criticized the Pelagians, which is often overlooked by modern scholars. It never made a significant christological contribution to the tradition as evidenced by the fact that only seven manuscripts of it survive,[160] and it is repeatedly disparaged by modern scholars for either a deficient Christology, or that it failed to respond to Nestorius in any meaningful way.[161] Owen Chadwick skewered it by calling it "pathetic reading," that it is not a "salient work of history of Christology,"[162] that it is "marred by carelessness and by a controversial tone, by immature phrases, by obscure construction and bludgeoning argument," it is a "bad book,"[163] and that Cassian's language "is so careless."[164] Rousseau called it "an essay in bitter polemic," that it displayed "ineptitude," and that "its chief significance is its very existence."[165] Grillmeier says that Cassian "betrays some uncertainty in his Christology,"[166] that he is "extremely unclear in parts,"[167] that he "draws a very empty picture of the humanity of Jesus,"[168] and that Leo "may have shaken his head"[169] when he had read parts of it. Ogliari called it a "somewhat inaccurate work,"[170] while Stewart pronounced it "rather wearying,"[171] that it suffered from a "lack of sparkle,"[172] that it is "for the most part a fairly dull example of polemical Christology,"[173] that "a great work of Christology this is not," that Cassian's "grasp of the finer points of the [Nestorian] controversy was, to put it kindly, imprecise," and that "if the *Institutes* and *Conferences* had been lost, and Cassian were judged solely on the basis of this treatise, he would be dismissed as a second-rate theologian."[174]

Not all scholars, however, have been quite so negative. Fairbairn has said that "this gloomy assessment of Cassian is harsher than the evidence warrants," that "there is a fundamental consistency underlying his [christological] thought," and that

---

Cassian the Monk, 22; Casiday, *Tradition and Theology*, 229; Ramsey, "General Introduction," in *The Conferences*, 8; Rea, "Grace and Free Will," 25.

160. Chadwick, *Primitive Monasticism*, 162–63.
161. Casiday, *Tradition and Theology*, 216–20.
162. Chadwick, *Primitive Monasticism*, 157.
163. Chadwick, *Primitive Monasticism*, 163.
164. Chadwick, *Primitive Monasticism*, 157.
165. Rousseau, "Monastery and World," 84.
166. Grillmeier, *Christ*, 468.
167. Grillmeier, *Christ*, 470.
168. Grillmeier, *Christ*, 471.
169. Grillmeier, *Christ*, 469. Casiday assesses Grillmeier's pages on Cassian's Christology to be "more truculent than they are learned." Casiday, *Tradition and Theology*, 223.
170. Ogliari, *Gratia et Certamen*, 123.
171. Stewart, *Cassian the Monk*, 22.
172. Stewart, *Cassian the Monk*, 23.
173. Stewart, *Cassian the Monk*, 109.
174. Stewart, *Cassian the Monk*, 23.

scholars should "reconsider"[175] their negative assessment. Casiday has exerted a significant amount of effort trying to rehabilitate the reputation of Cassian's christological treatise.[176] He has described it as "a work of genuine interest," that should be seen as "the apex of Cassian's literary career,"[177] that it is "theologically sound,"[178] that it is "attractive for its warm piety and its robust appreciation of the astounding humility of God," that it is "meaningful,"[179] that it is "consistent and coherent,"[180] and that it "should not be summarily dismissed."[181]

After having finished his *Collationes*, which he described as "rude utterances [that] were unequal to the deep thoughts of the saints,"[182] Cassian had hoped to "remain in the obscurity of silence,"[183] but was forced (*compellere*) by Leo to condemn the Christology of Nestorius,[184] who was still the bishop of Constantinople at that time.[185] He described Nestorius as a "new enemy of the faith," and a "dragon now rising up with sinuous course against the Churches of God."[186] Cassian attacked him both personally and theologically, but probably had little knowledge of Nestorius's thought, as few traces of his Christology can be found in his *De incarnatione*.[187] In his attempt to discredit Nestorius, Cassian associated him with Pelagius, who had been anathematized for at least a decade by that time. Nestorius, he said, "encourages the complaints of the Pelagians by his intervention, and introduces their case into his writings, because he cleverly or (to speak more truly) cunningly patronizes them and by his wicked liking for them recommends their mischievous teaching which is akin to his own, for he is well aware that he is of the same opinion and of the same spirit."[188] Cassian's attempt to connect Nestorius and Pelagius is puzzling, as no theological connection between

---

175. Fairbairn, *Grace and Christology*, 134.

176. He says scholarship on Cassian's Christology is "currently in a dismal state," and that it is "despised as an effort at theology, it has been relegated to the unhappy heap where we keep texts that are only useful (if at all) because we occasionally find it convenient to extract an interesting fact or a curious phrase from them." Casiday, *Tradition and Theology*, 226, 228.

177. Casiday, *Tradition and Theology*, 13.

178. Casiday, *Tradition and Theology*, 254.

179. Casiday, *Tradition and Theology*, 257.

180. Casiday, *Tradition and Theology*, 225.

181. Casiday, *Tradition and Theology*, 254.

182. Cassian, *De inc.* pref.

183. Cassian, *De inc.* pref.

184. Gennadius, *De vir. Inlustr.* 62.

185. Casiday, *Tradition and Theology*, 229.

186. Cassian, *De inc.* pref.

187. Grillmeier, *Christ*, 468.

188. Cassian, *De inc.* 1.3. See also: 5.1–2.

the two is evident;[189] but, his criticisms of Pelagius in this text need to be taken more seriously. We will explore these criticisms closely in a later chapter.[190]

Cassian and the Pelagian Controversy

By the time Cassian began writing his *Institutiones*, the triple condemnation of the Pelagians in 418 already had ended the first phase of the controversy. But, these condemnations did not make Pelagianism magically disappear, and it persisted in Gaul as evidenced by the imperial edict from Theodosius II and Valentinian III who, in 425, demanded that all bishops there must proclaim their orthodoxy to Bishop Patroclus of Arles against the "nefarious"[191] Pelagius and Caelestius. When Cassian wrote his three texts, therefore, he surely considered the Pelagians to be a continuing threat, and that his literary contributions were part of an ongoing fight, not a fight that had already reached its conclusion.

All three of Cassian's texts at one point or another exhibit concern either explicitly or implicitly with Pelagianism, not just his writing on grace and free will in his *Collatio* 13, which is the text on which scholars too often narrowly focus their attention. As stated earlier, he may have known Pelagius personally at the beginning of the fifth century in Rome, and likely had conversations or fights about Pelagius's theological preoccupations. Although Cassian does not quote verbatim from any Pelagian author, Cassian's writings clearly indicate an intimate knowledge of Pelagian thought.[192] It is likely, at the very least, that he had read some of Pelagius's instructional letters on the ascetic life, such as his letter to Demetrias.[193]

While Cassian was a firm critic of Pelagius, his intellectual relationship with Augustine was more complicated.[194] At the end of his *De incarnatione*, Cassian described him as "Augustine the bishop (*sacerdos*) of Hippo Regiensis,"[195] which may sound innocuous enough, but immediately before and after this description Cassian wrote effusively about other great theologians of the era. He called Hilary of Poitiers a man "endowed with all virtues and graces, and famous for his life as well as for his eloquence";[196] he described Ambrose of Milan as "that illustrious priest of God, who never leaving the Lord's hand,

---

189. Julian and some of the other Pelagians had taken refuge in Constantinople after their exile. Cassian may have this in mind. Chadwick, *Primitive Monasticism*, 156–59; Stewart, *Cassian the Monk*, 22.

190. Cassian's assessment of Nestorius's christology is well outside the scope of this study, and will not be addressed here.

191. *PL* 45.1751; Stewart, *Cassian the Monk*, 22.

192. Rousseau, "Monastery and World," 82; Rea, "Grace and Free Will," 107; Casiday, *Tradition and Theology*, 129; Ogliari, *Gratia et Certamen*, 107; Hwang, *Intrepid Lover*, 87.

193. Work remains pinpointing exactly which Pelagian texts Cassian had read.

194. Casiday, "Cassian, Augustine," 47; Ramsey, "General Introduction," in *The Conferences*, 10.

195. Cassian, *De inc.* 7.27.

196. Cassian, *De inc.* 7.24.

ever shone like a jewel upon the finger of God";[197] he called Rufinus of Aquileia, whose reputation had been stained after his fight with Jerome, a "Christian philosopher, with no mean place among Ecclesiastical Doctors";[198] he called Gregory of Nazianzus "that most grand light of knowledge and doctrine";[199] he described Athanasius as "a splendid instance of constancy and virtue";[200] he even lavished praise on Jerome by saying his writings "shine like divine lamps throughout the whole world."[201] Cassian's description of Augustine merely as "the bishop of Hippo Regiensis" in light of this praise has caught the attention of many scholars. Although Casiday has argued that Cassian's description simply demonstrates that Augustine was still alive when everyone else listed already had died,[202] most scholars view it as a snub.[203] Cassian, it seems, was subtly indicating that he viewed Augustine with at least a little suspicion.

On the other hand, however, Cassian clearly had been influenced by Augustine, and had intimate knowledge of both his non-Pelagian and anti-Pelagian writings. Ramsey has published an important study investigating which texts from Augustine that Cassian probably had read.[204] Of his pre-Pelagian texts that are worth mentioning, Cassian seems to have read Augustine's *De libero arbitrio*,[205] *Confessiones*, and *Epist.* 130 to Proba.[206] He also may have read *De gratia et libero arbitrio* and *De correptione et gratia*, which are usually classified as part of Augustine's "Semi-Pelagian" corpus.[207] It is also likely that he had read the anti-Pelagian *De peccatorum meritis et remissione et de baptismo parvulorum*,[208] and he almost certainly read his *Contra Iulianum*.[209] Ramsey also says that Cassian "was familiar with more than just some of Augustine's anti-pelagian works and that, indeed, he seems to have read more widely in Augustine";[210] disappointingly, however, Ramsey is not more specific about which other texts he had in mind. It is clear, in the end, that Cassian was well-versed in Augustinian literature.[211]

197. Cassian, *De inc.* 7.25.
198. Cassian, *De inc.* 7.27.
199. Cassian, *De inc.* 7.28.
200. Cassian, *De inc.* 7.29.
201. Cassian, *De inc.* 7.26.
202. Casiday, "Cassian, Augustine," 47.
203. John Cassian, "Seven Books," 191 n. 3; Chadwick, *John Cassian*, 146.
204. Ramsey, "Student of Augustine," 5–15.
205. Augustine, *Epist.* 226.8.
206. Ramsey, "Student of Augustine," 9–13.
207. Ramsey, "Student of Augustine," 6 n. 6; Rea, "Grace and Free Will," 154–55.
208. Ramsey, "Student of Augustine," 6 n. 6.
209. Augustine, *Epist.* 225.3.
210. Ramsey, "Student of Augustine," 14.
211. Unfortunately, it is impossible to know when Cassian had read these texts. For example, it is not clear if Cassian read Augustine's *De correptione et gratia* before or after he began writing his *Collatio* 13.

Cassian's attitude toward Jerome was equally complex. At the end of his *De incarnatione*, as mentioned above, Cassian claimed that Jerome's writings illuminated the world. He also called him "a man of the greatest knowledge and also of the most pure and approved doctrine."[212] In the Preface to his *Institutiones*, furthermore, Cassian said that he "not only wrote books springing from his own genius but even made translations from Greek into Latin," and that his writings were "overflowing rivers of eloquence."[213] But, Cassian saw Jerome as one of the root causes of the monastic failures in Gaul. As discussed earlier, Goodrich has pointed out that Cassian's purported esteem for Jerome was in fact an (almost imperceptible) animus towards his contemporary.[214] Jerome's refusal to be trained by experts, his self-presentation as an ascetic expert who had spent time in the Syrian desert (despite his inability to remain there), and his leadership in his cenobium without first having been an apprentice, were all unforgiveable to Cassian.

Despite these misgivings, there is evidence that Cassian knew several of Jerome's writings and translations, and even incorporated them into his own texts;[215] he knew Jerome's letter to Eustochium (22), his *Commentaria in Isaiam*,[216] his translations from Pachomius, his *Vita Pauli*, probably his *Vita Hilarionis* and *Vita Malchi*,[217] and possibly even his *Contra Iovinianum*.[218] Unfortunately, there is no concrete evidence that he had read any of Jerome's anti-Pelagian writings, although Stewart has claimed that Jerome's letter (133) to Cteisphon was the instigator of Cassian's *Collatio* 23, *De anamarteto*, which was his refutation of the Pelagian claim for the possibility of a life free of sin.[219]

---

212. Cassian, *De inc.* 7.26.

213. Cassian, *Inst.* pref.5–6.

214. Goodrich, *Contextualizing Cassian*, 78–96.

215. Stewart argues that Jerome's *Epist.* 22.34–37 was incorporated into Cassian's *Coll.* 18.4–7, and it is possible that *Epist.* 22.35.1–2 had informed *Inst.* 4.10 and 4.17, and *De inc.* 7.26. Stewart, *Cassian the Monk*, 163 n. 64.

216. Cassian, *De inc.* 7.26.

217. Stewart, *Cassian the Monk*, 36.

218. Rebillard, "*Quasi Funambuli*," 215.

219. Stewart, *Cassian the Monk*, 163 n. 64.

Part II: **Theology**

Chapter 11

The Theology of Pelagius

Rejection of Original Sin

Now that we have surveyed the biographies of the main characters in this drama, the texts that they wrote, the councils that were convened, and the popes who asserted their authority, we may turn our attention to the ideas that these men taught.

Pelagius has often been described simply as a moralist,[1] but he should be taken seriously as a theologian.[2] We will begin with his fundamental theological proposition, which rests underneath all of his other anthropological assertions, that the human person is good because it is the creation of the good God.[3] In his letter to Demetrias, he asks her "if it is he [God] who, as report goes, has made all the works of and within the world good, exceedingly good, how much more excellent do you suppose that he has made man himself, on whose account he has clearly made every thing else? And before actually making man, he determines to fashion him in his own image and likeness and shows what kind of creature he intends to make him."[4] The Biblical foundation to which Pelagius hints here is, of course, the beginning of Genesis: "let us make human beings in our image, after our likeness" (Gen 1:26). If God is good, and God created humanity in his image and likeness, the conclusion must be that humanity is good.

Pelagius continues by stating that the dignity of the human person clearly becomes manifest in the dominion over the rest of God's creation. "For he [God] did not leave man naked and defenseless," Pelagius says, "nor did he expose him in his weakness to a variety of dangers; but, having made him seem unarmed outwardly, he provided him with a better armament inside, that is, with reason and wisdom, so that by means of his intelligence and mental vigour, in which he surpassed the other animals, man alone was able to recognize the maker of all things and to serve God by using those same faculties

---

1. Bonner, *St. Augustine*, 316; Rees, "Pelagius," 3; Rousseau, *Early Christian Centuries*, 253; Ryan, "Pelagius' View," 188.
2. Evans, *Inquiries and Reappraisals*, 91.
3. Evans, *Inquiries and Reappraisals*, 92.
4. Pelagius, *Ad Dem.* 2.2. See also: 4.1, 8.1, 17.3.

which enabled him to hold sway over the rest."[5] Pelagius's emphasis on the goodness of humanity predated his battles with his Christian opponents,[6] and originally was stressed in his attacks on the Manichaeans for saying that the human person is evil in its materiality.[7] Later, when Pelagius turned his attention to his fellow Christians who insisted that humanity had been corrupted, he repeated his claim, without modulation, that God's creation is exceedingly good.[8]

Pelagius was not naïve, and he recognized the ugly underbelly of the human condition. If humans were not created evil, Pelagius needed to account for the root of sin. If we are created good by the good God, why do we sin? His answer was that we sin out of "imitation" (*imitatio*),[9] "obedience," and "consent"[10] to the "example or pattern"[11] of Adam and Eve. He did not mean that we read Genesis and consciously decide to follow their example of disobedience, but that they were a "model of transgression."[12] As he said in one of his letters,[13] "Adam was created as the first man at the first foundation of the world; was he condemned because of faithlessness or sin? I find that there was no disbelief in him but only disobedience, which was the reason why he was condemned and why we are all condemned for following his example."[14] Every sin we commit repeats the same act as Adam,[15] not because we are compelled to do so by a weakened nature, but in the way that children intuitively adopt the gait, mannerisms, and speech patterns of their parents. Imitation of sin, like imitation of any familial or cultural norm, can permeate our entire being even without our knowledge, such that it may seem to be part of our nature.

The problem of sin does not remain at the level of our imitation of Adam and Eve, however. Individual acts of sin begin to accumulate until a pattern takes shape and a habit (*habitus*) forms. Pelagius did not invent the moral category of habits,[16] which William Mattison has succinctly defined as "an abiding quality a person has that characterizes who he is,"[17] but it had been crucial for the western moral life long

---

5. Pelagius, *Ad Dem.* 2.2.

6. We can see Pelagius discussing the goodness of humanity in his Pauline commentaries: *Expos. (ad Rom.)* 5:15.

7. For a nuanced understanding of Manichaean anthropology, see: BeDuhn, *Manichaean Body*.

8. Augustine, *Nat. grat.* 9.10; *Grat. Chr.* 1.35.38–39.43, 2.26.30.

9. Augustine, *Nat, grat.* 9.10.

10. Pelagius, *Expos. (ad Rom.)* 6:12.

11. Pelagius, *Expos. (ad Rom.)* 5:12, 5:19.

12. Pelagius, *Expos. (ad Rom.)* 5:16.

13. Pelagius, *Vit. Christ.* pref.

14. Pelagius, *Vit. Christ.* 13.2.

15. Augustine, *Nat. grat.* 29.33–30.34.

16. It is likely that Pelagius was influenced by Origen on the issue of habits. Bostock, "Influence of Origen," 388–89.

17. Mattison, *Moral Theology*, 58.

before Pelagius, as best demonstrated by Aristotle's *Nichomachean Ethics*.[18] It is these habits—not a corruption of our nature—that drag us into repeated sinful acts time and again. "Nor is there any reason why," Pelagius said, that

> it is made difficult for us to do good other than that long habit of doing wrong which has infected us from childhood and corrupted us little by little over many years and ever after holds us in bondage and slavery to itself, so that it seems somehow to have acquired the force of nature. We now find ourselves being resisted and opposed by all that long period in which we were carelessly instructed, that is, educated in evil, in which we even strove to be evil, since, to add to the other incentives to evil, innocence itself was held to be folly. That old habit now attacks our new-found freedom of will, and, as we languish in ignorance through our sloth and idleness, unaccustomed to doing good after having for so long learned to do only evil, we wonder why sanctity is also conferred on us as if from an outside source.[19]

Any smoker trying to quit smoking, or alcoholic trying to quit drinking, knows that ingrained habits are painfully difficult to eradicate, and often seem impossible ever to do so. In a similar way with sin, Pelagius recognized the difficulty of arresting the painful patterns of our lives. But, it is possible, he believes, to overcome them: "even those people who have become hardened, as it were," he says, "by having sinned for a long time can be restored by penance."[20]

Free Will and Predestination

Overcoming our bad habits is precipitated by the movement of our unadulterated free will.[21] Pelagius defines the free movement of the will to be "on this choice between two ways [good actions or evil actions], on this freedom to choose either alternative, that the glory of the rational mind is based, it is in this that the whole honour of our nature consists."[22] As we are created in the image and likeness of God, we, like God, must have a free will, and our will is one of the fundamental differences that sets humans apart from the animals. If our will were hampered by original sin such that we are unable to resist evil or to choose the good, then our actions cannot be attributed

---

18. Aristotle, *Nicomachean Ethics*. See, in particular, books II and III. In the scholarly literature about Pelagius's influences, there is almost no mention about a direct or indirect influence from Aristotle. Perhaps there is room for more research on this front.

19. Pelagius, *Ad Dem.* 8.3. See also, *Expos. (ad Rom.)* 7:15, 7:17. Augustine, *Grat. Chr.* 1.39.43.

20. Augustine, *Grat. Chr.* 1.37.41. See also, Pelagius, *Ad Dem.* 17.3.

21. Origen was a great influence on Pelagius's understanding of the will. Bostock, "Influence of Origen," 386.

22. Pelagius, *Ad Dem.* 3.1. Julian later refines this definition by stating that it is "nothing but the possibility of sinning and of not sinning, which is not subject to any violence from either side, but which has the ability to move by its spontaneous judgment to the side which it wills." Augustine, *C. Jul. op. imp.* 6.9.

to us,²³ but ultimately must be attributed to God.²⁴ As we can never blame God for our misdeeds, and we must be held responsible for all of our actions (otherwise God's punishment of our sins must be unjust), Pelagius concludes that our will must be free to choose either good or evil.²⁵ Certainly, God hopes that we will choose to be in harmony with his will, but the ability to choose evil, in the end, is good because "it makes the good part better by making it voluntary and independent, not bound by necessity but free to decide for itself."²⁶

The Pelagians had very little interest in the question of predestination, and it only became a pressing issue in the so-called Semi-Pelagian controversy.²⁷ Pelagius's few comments about predestination are centered in chapters 8 and 9 of his commentary on Romans, specifically Paul's vexing statement that "from those he [God] foreknew he also predestined to be conformed to the image of his son, so that he might be the firstborn among many brothers. And those he predestined he also called; and those he called he also justified; and those he justified he also glorified" (Rom 8:29–30). For Pelagius, predestination and foreknowledge are synonymous.²⁸ God's judgment is always in response to our actions. If we sin, we will be judged accordingly. If we repent, likewise we will be judged accordingly.²⁹ Pelagius does not entertain the thought that God elects those whom he chooses based on his will. Rather, God elects based on the virtuous actions of the individual. God will choose to glorify those who, through the movement of their own free will, work towards salvation.³⁰ It is precisely this idea of working toward salvation that has made the term "Pelagian" a slander. When someone is accused of being a Pelagian even today, it is an accusation that the person believes that salvation can be earned through good works.

Sinlessness

Building off of his assertions that we have an uncorrupted nature, and that we have a will that is free to choose either good or evil, Pelagius concludes that we can live a life entirely free of sin if we want it badly enough.³¹ Pelagius understood sin in contrast with the Manichaeans, who claimed that sin is a substance. For Pelagius, sin was an

---

23. Augustine, *Nat. grat.* 34.38.
24. Pelagius, *Ad Dem.* 2.2.
25. For more discussion from Pelagius on free will, see: Pelagius, *Expos. (ad Rom.)* 6:13, 8:32; *Div. leg.* 1.2; Augustine, *Nat. grat.* 43.50; *Grat. Chr.* 1.22.24, 1.28.29–33.36.
26. Pelagius, *Ad Dem.* 3.2.
27. Wetzel, "Predestination, Pelagianism," 51.
28. Pelagius, *Expos. (ad Rom.)* 8:29.
29. Pelagius, *Expos. (ad Rom.)* 9:12–15.
30. Pelagius, *Expos. (ad Rom.)* 8:29, 9:10.
31. Pelagius, *Expos. (ad Rom.)* 6:20; *Ad Dem.* 17.1–3; *Virg.* 15; *Lib. fid.* 27; Augustine, *Nat. grat.* 46.54–52.60. See also: Rackett, "Sexuality and Sinlessness," 251–63.

"act of wrongdoing";[32] it is ingratitude towards God's love and grace. Any sin against another Christian is also a sin against Christ, and sin causes the Holy Spirit to depart from the sinner.[33] To be sinless is to show gratitude to God by keeping the commandments, by avoiding what is forbidden, and fulfilling everything that God demands.[34] Pelagius recognizes that to live a sinless life is difficult, but to allow for the possibility of sinlessness, he says, one also must allow for the means of achieving the goal,[35] which he enumerates as effort, study, wisdom, and discretion.[36]

While asserting the possibility of a sinless life, Pelagius confesses that he himself was not sinless,[37] and everyone should be wary of assuming that they have reached that state of perfection.[38] He is less clear, however, if anyone else has ever achieved such a state. At the beginning of his *De natura et gratia*, Augustine quotes Pelagius's claim that it is possible to be sinless, but that no one who is currently living (in the fifth century) is so.[39] Later in the same text, Pelagius stated that there were people in the past who were without sin. Despite his initial disobedience of eating the fruit of the tree of the knowledge of good and evil, Adam was sinless after that first transgression.[40] Pelagius posits that we can be sure that Adam was sinless after his first sin, and that Abel was sinless throughout his life, because Genesis did not mention any of their sins.[41] As there were only four people alive at that time, the Bible most certainly would have noted any transgression from Adam or Abel. As the Bible did not do so, we can be assured of their perfection.[42] Pelagius also provided a laundry list of people that the Bible "reports, not only did not sin, but lived righteously: Abel, Henoch, Melchizedek, Abraham, Isaac, Jacob, Joseph, Joshua the son of Nun, Phinehas, Samuel, Nathan, Elijah, Elisha, Micah, Daniel, Hananiah, Azariah, Mishael, Ezekiel, Mordecai, Simeon, Joseph, to whom the Virgin Mary was betrothed, and John." Many women also were sinless: "Deborah, Anna the mother of Samuel, Judith, Esther, another Anna the daughter of Phanuel, Elizabeth, and also the mother of our Lord and Savior. Piety demands . . . that we admit that she was without sin."[43]

---

32. Augustine, *Nat. grat.* 19.21.

33. Pelagius, *Expos.* (*ad Eph.*) 1:1–2, 2:11; *Vit. Christ.* 2; *Ad Cel.* 4; *Expos.* (*ad 1 Cor.*) 8.12. García-Sánchez, "Pelagius," 133–36.

34. Pelagius *Virg.* 4.2., 6.1; *Ad Dem.* 10.1., 16.1; *Div. leg.* 7.1–2., *Vit. Christ.* 14.1. Augustine, *Nat. grat.* 69.83.

35. Augustine, *Nat. grat.* 10.11.

36. Pelagius, *Ad Dem.* 24.1.

37. Augustine, *Nat. grat.* 13.14.

38. Pelagius, *Ad Dem.* 27.3.

39. Augustine, *Nat. grat.* 7.8.

40. Augustine, *Nat. grat.* 21.23.

41. Augustine, *Nat. grat.* 37.43–39.46.

42. Augustine, *Nat. grat.* 37.44, 21.23.

43. Augustine, *Nat. grat.* 36.42, 37.44.

Later in Augustine's *De natura et gratia*, however, Pelagius contradicts his earlier list of sinless men and women by stating that "I will agree that scripture testifies that all were sinners. After all, it states what people were, not that they could not be different. Hence, even if it could be proved that all human beings are sinners, that would present no problem for our thesis, since we are defending, not so much what human beings are, but what they can be."[44] At the Synod of Diospolis, furthermore, when Pelagius was charged with claiming that humans can be without sin, he reaffirmed his position of the possibility of sinlessness, but said that "we did not, however, say that there is anyone who never sinned from infancy to old age, but that those who have turned away from sin can by their own effort and by the grace of God be without sin. But that does not mean that they cannot return to sin in the future."[45] In the end, it is unclear if Pelagius believed that sinlessness only remained in the realm of possibility, if he believed there were a select few individuals who had achieved it, and that he was lying to the bishops about his list of sinless individuals, or whether he had believed in the past that there had been sinless individuals but later changed his mind. In light of Pelagius's lie to the bishops about his letter to a widow discussed in an earlier chapter, it is likely that he was lying in this instance as well.

Grace

Pelagius's definition of grace is, without a doubt, his most controversial and misunderstood theological proposition. This misunderstanding is due largely to Augustine's rhetorical skills,[46] branding Pelagius and the Pelagians as "enemies of the grace of God" (*inimici gratia Dei*),[47] which is not entirely fair because they did believe in grace. If Pelagius entirely rejected grace, he would have been dismissed easily by all Christians, and would be a minor footnote in the history of Christianity. Pelagius did trumpet the importance of grace, but he offered a definition of grace that, for Augustine, was inadequate and dangerous.

Another reason why Pelagius's definition of grace is misunderstood is because the definition he offers at times lacks precision.[48] After the Synod of Diospolis, as we have already explored, Albina, Pinianus, and Melania the Younger excitedly wrote to Augustine that they were able to secure from Pelagius a written condemnation of the theology purported to be his, and that he said that grace is necessary for every moment of life.[49] Squelching their enthusiasm, Augustine responded that "anyone who

---

44. Augustine, *Nat. grat.* 41.48.
45. Augustine, *Gest. Pelag.* 6.16.
46. For a discussion about rhetoric in the Pelagian controversy, see: Toczko, "Heretic," 211–31.
47. Augustine, *Spir. et litt.* 35.63; *C. du. ep. Pelag.* 7.12; *C. Jul.* 14.44; *C. Jul. op. imp.* 1.68.3, 1.134.
48. Augustine, *Gest. Pelag.* 6.20–10.22.
49. Augustine, *Grat. Chr.* 1.2.2. For other places where Pelagius offered a vague definition of grace, see: *Nat. grat.* 44.52–45.53; *Grat. Chr.* 1.6.7, 1.37.40; *Grat. Chr.* 1.35.38.

hears this without understanding his meaning . . . is going to think that he is in complete agreement with the truth . . . Anyone who pays attention to his clear statements in them [his books] ought to hold even these words of his suspect."[50]

Pelagius defined grace in several different ways. First, God gives the gifts of divine revelation[51] in the law,[52] and the teaching[53] of Jesus in the Bible. Originally, God wrote the law of nature on our hearts. However, that law of nature was tarnished due to sin, so God provided the written law as a guide. There is no indication that Pelagius believed that Christians need to follow the Mosaic laws such as circumcision and dietary restrictions, but that he gleaned the goodness of the law from his reading of Paul. Paul asked:

> What can we say? That the law is sin? Of course not! Yet I did not know sin except through the law, and I did not know what it is to covet except that the law said, "You shall not covet." But sin, finding an opportunity in the commandments, produced in me every kind of covetousness. Apart from the law sin is dead. I once lived outside the law, but when the commandment came, sin became alive; then I died, and the commandment that was for life turned out to be death for me. For sin, seizing an opportunity in the commandment, deceived me and through it put me to death. So then the law is holy, and the commandment is holy and righteous and good (Rom 7:7–12).

The law is helpful, then, so that humans know how to live a flourishing life.[54]

The second level of grace that God offers is the gift of the incarnate Word. The law and teaching of the Bible, though helpful, are abstract and insufficient,[55] while Jesus is concrete. Mirroring his claim that we sin out of imitation (*imitatio*) of Adam, Pelagius claims that we must imitate[56] the example (*exemplum*)[57] of Christ in our daily lives. By imitating Christ, we are better able to comprehend and internalize the instructions of the law and teaching so that we may live righteous lives. In his *Expositiones*, which contain the majority of Pelagius's christological insights, he says that "just as by the example of Adam's disobedience many sinned, so also many are justified by Christ's obedience."[58] Pelagius's claim that Christ is a moral exemplar to be imitated is not a

---

50. Augustine, *Grat. Chr.* 1.2.2.

51. Augustine, *Grat. Chr.* 1.10.11.

52. Pelagius, *Expos. (ad Rom.)* 7:12, 7:21, 8:2; *Div. leg.* 3.1; Augustine, *Grat. Chr.* 1.6.7; Jerome, *Epist.* 133.5.

53. Pelagius, *Expos. (ad Rom.)* 6:18; Augustine, *Grat. Chr.* 1.6.7.

54. De Bruyn notes that Pelagius's insistence on the goodness of the law was in reaction to the Marcionites and the Manichaeans. Pelagius, *Expos. (ad Rom.)* 8:1 n. 1.

55. Augustine, *Grat. Chr.* 2.26.30.

56. Pelagius, *Expos. (ad Rom.)* 5:10; *Vit. Christ.* 14.1–2; *Ad Cel.* 12.

57. Pelagius, *Expos. (ad Rom.)* 5:15, 5:16, 5:19, 6:14, 6:18, 8:4, 16:25; *Ad Dem.* 8.4; *Virg.* 15; *Vit. Christ.* 14.1; *Ad Cel.* 12; Augustine, *Grat. Chr.* 1.38.42. Yamada conjectures that Pelagius learned the idea of Christ as *exemplum* from Chromatius: Yamada, "Influence of Chromatius," 662–63.

58. Pelagius, *Expos. (ad Rom.)* 5:19.

new idea as it reaches back as far as Paul's command to the community in Corinth that they "be imitators of me, as I am of Christ" (1 Cor 11:1). His almost singular emphasis on *imitatio* and *exemplum*, however, forces us to inspect his Christology more closely. Pelagius vehemently rejected Arianism[59] and viewed himself to be in harmony with the councils of Nicaea (325) and Constantinople (381). He did not see Jesus as merely a prophet and moral teacher, but that the Logos is consubstantial (*homoousios*) with the Father.[60] Furthermore, he said that we are "saved by Christ's death,"[61] that Jesus "discharged the sins of many . . . and . . . forgave sins freely,"[62] that he "carried our sins and suffered,"[63] that we have been "purified and cleansed by his blood,"[64] and that we have been "restored through the grace of Christ and have been reborn into a better human being; having been reconciled and purified by his blood."[65] But, all this is secondary for Pelagius, and, when read in the context of his description of Jesus as *exemplum*, these comments fade in importance. What is most important for Pelagius is that Christ acts as our lighthouse leading us to the sinless life—as Christ had been sinless—through the movement of our own free will.

Pelagius's Christology largely has been neglected by modern scholars and deserves much more attention.[66] In what little that has been written, scholars disagree on how Pelagius's Christology should be received. Joanne Dewart, on the one hand, has declared that Pelagius held an "accepted late fourth and early fifth century western christology"[67] as understood prior to the Council of Chalcedon (451), and that "Christology and soteriology were not issues [in the thought of the Pelagians]. Augustine knew this, and yet he tried to make them so."[68] Michael Hanby, on the other, has said that Pelagianism "is a threat to orthodox Christology,"[69] because it "institutes a rupture in this christological and trinitarian economy, and, insofar as it determines the direction of subsequent Christian thought, creates the possibilities for human nature 'outside' the Trinity and the mediation of Christ."[70] My interpretation is much closer to the analysis offered by Hanby than Dewart. Pelagius's stress on Christ as *exemplum*, paired with his belief in the unrestricted free will to choose either good or evil actions, in my estimation, results in a flattened, low Christology that casts a shadow on the necessity of Christ's

59. Pelagius, *Lib. fid.* 6.
60. Pelagius, *Lib. fid.* 2.
61. Pelagius, *Expos. (ad Rom.)* 5:10.
62. Pelagius, *Expos. (ad Rom.)* 5:16.
63. Pelagius, *Expos. (ad Rom.)* 6:10.
64. Pelagius, *Ad Dem.* 8.4.
65. Augustine, *Grat. Chr.* 1.38.42.
66. Some notable exceptions to this are: Dewart, "Christology," 1221–44; Dodaro, "*Sacramentum Christi*," 274–80; Hanby, *Augustine and Modernity*, 72–105; Keech, *Anti-Pelagian Christology*.
67. Dewart, "Christology," 1223.
68. Dewart, "Christology," 1240. See also: Keech, *Anti-Pelagian Christology*, 15.
69. Hanby, *Augustine and Modernity*, 77.
70. Hanby, *Augustine and Modernity*, 73.

saving action on the cross. As Dominic Keech has succinctly put it: "Pelagius draws into question the purpose of the Incarnation, by reducing the effectiveness of Christ's death to a sign that humans may or may not choose to inspire their moral choices. Likewise, for Pelagius prayer is nothing more than an internal reflection on the example of Christ and the commandments, and ceases to be a true petition for grace."[71] Although Pelagius may not have intended to diminish the significance of Christ's sacrifice, his two-dimensional Christology, nevertheless, fails to adequately safeguard Christ as the mediator through whom salvation is received.

The third level of grace for Pelagius is the gift of our nature. We did not create ourselves, nor did we ask to be created. God gratuitously chose to create us. Pelagius divides his discussion of our nature into three parts: ability (*posse*), willing (*velle*), and being (*esse*).[72] The first part, *posse*, is the ability to choose either good actions or evil actions. As we are not burdened by original sin, our ability is not hampered in any way. This *posse* is entirely a gift from God, and we did nothing to merit it. The second part, *velle*, is the movement of the will in choosing either good or evil actions. The third part, *esse*, is the action that is the result of the *velle*. While *posse* entirely comes from God's graciousness, *velle* and *esse* rest solely in the purview of the individual.[73] Pelagius offers several easy examples to help clarify. He says that our *posse* to see does not come from us, as God gave us our eyes and the power to see. However, the *velle* and *esse* in seeing either good or evil sights is entirely with us. A second example rests with our speech. The *posse* to speak is given to us from God, but the *velle* and *esse* to speak well or ill is entirely in our power. "And to sum up everything in a general statement," he says "our being able to do, say, or think anything good comes from him who gave us this ability and who helps this ability, but our doing or speaking or thinking anything good is due to us, since we can also turn all these toward something evil."[74] As we have seen, Pelagius's ultimate concern is in the *posse*, *velle*, and *esse* of sinlessness. We have the *posse* to not sin from God, but the *velle*, and *esse* of a sinless life come from us.[75] It is this understanding of nature, in particular his description of *posse*, that allows Pelagius to say to Albina, Pinianus, and Melania—and which leads Augustine to declare Pelagius's conception of grace is deficient—that God's grace is instrumental for every action because it is necessary "not only at every hour and at every moment, but also for every act of ours."[76]

---

71. Keech, *Anti-Pelagian Christology*, 90, 98.
72. Augustine, *Grat. Chr.* 1.4.5; Dupont and Malavasi, "Question of Impact," 542–48.
73. Augustine, *Grat. Chr.* 1.6.7, 1.6.7–25.26.
74. Augustine, *Grat. Chr.* 1.4.5; *Nat. et gr.* 45.53.
75. Augustine, *Nat. et gr.* 45.53–51.59.
76. Augustine, *Grat. Chr.* 1.2.2.

Baptism

In the first few centuries of Christianity, baptism could have been received during a variety of different stages of life. Deathbed baptism, as demonstrated by the Emperor Constantine who was baptized in 337 at the hands of Eusebius of Nicomedia, was one common time when baptism was received.[77] A second was after a conversion experience, as demonstrated by Augustine in 387 at the hands of Ambrose of Milan.[78] The third, which became the most common way until the Protestant Reformation in the sixteenth century, was infant baptism. Although the baptismal action can be traced back to the first century, the theological meaning of baptism took centuries to develop.[79]

The baptismal action operates on two different levels, according to Pelagius. The first is the water itself, which is of little importance for Pelagius as it does not change the body,[80] nor does it "reach the soul of the believer in his heart."[81] The second, which is more important, is that the soul must be cleansed by the *verbum* simultaneously with the water.[82] The *verbum*, as Carlos García-Sánchez has said, is "nothing else but the living Word of God, Christ; it is Christ himself who cleanses the soul at baptism." [83] This cleansing of the soul from the *verbum* is only possible, however, if the baptized internally consents. "Grace indeed freely discharges sins," Pelagius says, "but with the consent and choice of the believer, as Philip proves to the eunuch in the Acts of the Apostles, saying: if you believe with all your heart, you can (Acts 8:37). By this testimony it is understood that there is no less danger if an unbeliever is baptized than if a baptism is refused to a true believer."[84] We see here that the operation of grace can be frustrated by the internal disposition of the individual. If the will of the baptized accepts the gift of regeneration, then the gift is received. But, Pelagius's emphasis on the autonomy of the individual necessitates the superiority of the will over the divine action.[85]

The effects of baptism are numerous. The baptized receive the gift of the Holy Spirit,[86] become adopted sons and daughters of God,[87] become members of the

---

77. Socrates, *Hist. eccl.* 1.39.
78. Augustine, *Conf.* 9.6.14.
79. For an excellent survey of baptismal practices in the first few centuries of Christianity, see: Ferguson, *Baptism*.
80. Pelagius, *Div. leg.* 2.1.
81. Pelagius, *Div. leg.* 2.3.
82. Pelagius, *Div. leg.* 1.2; *Vit. Christ.* 13.4.
83. García-Sánchez, "Pelagius," 211. See also: Evans, *Inquiries and Reappraisals*, 115.
84. Pelagius, *Div. leg.* 2.3. See also: 13.4; Augustine, *Nat. grat.* 41.48.
85. García-Sánchez, "Pelagius," 212–13.
86. Pelagius, *Expos. (ad Rom.)* 1:5; *Vit. Christ.* 13.4.
87. Pelagius, *Expos. (ad 1 Tim.)* 2:15.

church,[88] are absolved of previous sins,[89] and receive the grace of sanctification.[90] After baptism, the baptized must have a conversion or transformation away from the old self and turn towards a new self that glorifies God, rather than his or her own desires.[91] This new self is not "permitted to sin, and it befits all without exception who have been purified by the sanctification of spiritual water to pass a spotless life and thus be allowed entry into the very heart of the Church, which is described as 'without spot or wrinkle or anything of that kind'" (Eph 5:27).[92]

Pelagius supported infant baptism in addition to adult baptism, but he was less interested in it than adult baptism, and there is no indication that he actively encouraged it.[93] This ambivalence is certainly consistent with his vision of the human person at birth. As Pelagius did not believe in original sin, baptism did not wash away the guilt (*reatus*) of original sin, as it did in Augustine's theology. There is no pressing need for babies to be baptized—even in an era with high infant mortality—if there is no existential ailment in need of medicine.[94] Pelagius knew that Christians baptized their infants, and he did not protest against it. He repeatedly stated that infants need to be baptized with the same words as those said during adult baptisms.[95] But, it is here with infant baptism that Pelagius's thought begins to show cracks, as it becomes incoherent in light of the above description of baptism that demands the willful acceptance of the individual. Such a reception obviously would be impossible for any infant, as the infant would be uncomprehending of the meaning of the action. This flaw in Pelagius's logic has led Evans to say that Pelagius's baptismal theology "makes scarce sense,"[96] García-Sánchez has said that it was "insufficient,"[97] and Rees has said that it was "ambiguous."[98]

---

88. Pelagius, *Expos. (ad 1 Cor.)* 6:14.
89. Pelagius, *Div. leg.* 2.3; *Vit. Christ.* 13.4; Augustine, *Grat. Chr.* 1.39.43.
90. Pelagius, *Vit. Christ.* 13.4; *Virg.* 11.3; Augustine, *Nat. grat.* 41.48; *Grat. Chr.* 1.39.43.
91. Pelagius, *Expos. (ad Rom.)* 6:4.
92. Pelagius, *Virg.* 11.3.
93. García-Sánchez, "Pelagius," 201.
94. Augustine reports that Pelagius said that babies who die unbaptized do not go to heaven, but he does not necessarily think that they go to hell: "I know where little ones who die without baptism do not go; I do not know where they go." Augustine, *Grat. Chr.* 2.21.23. See also: Ferguson, *Baptism*, 814.
95. Augustine, *Grat. Chr.* 1.32.35, 2.1.1, 2.18.20–21.24.
96. Evans, *Inquiries and Reappraisals*, 118.
97. García-Sánchez, "Pelagius and Christian Initiation," 387.
98. Rees, "Pelagius," 79.

Chapter 12

The Theology of Caelestius and the Theology of the Author of the *Liber de Fide*

Adam and the Rejection of Original Sin

AS MENTIONED IN AN earlier chapter, the Council of Carthage of 411 leveled six charges against Caelestius:[1] (1) Adam was created mortal so that he would die whether he sinned or did not sin; (2) the sin of Adam harmed him alone and not the human race; (3) the law leads to the kingdom just as the gospel does; (4) before the coming of Christ there were human begins without sin; (5) newly born infants are in the same state in which Adam was before his transgression; (6) the whole human race does not die through the death or transgression of Adam, nor does the whole human race rise through the resurrection of Christ.[2] It quickly becomes apparent reading this list that the primary concern of the council had nothing to do with grace—although grace became the overriding preoccupation with Augustine later in the controversy—but with sin, as four of the six accusations dealt with Adam and the implications of his transgression.[3] The council does not use the exact Augustinian phrase "original sin," nor does that phrase appear in the quotations we have from Caelestius. But, it is clear that the anthropological issue at stake here is whether or not the sin of Adam infected his descendants. As we saw earlier, Caelestius did not take responsibility for having put forth the ideas with which he was charged. It was the "holy priest" Rufinus from whom Caelestius had heard these teachings. At the same time, Caelestius never repudiated any of the charges brought against him, nor attempted to interpret his way out of the charges in the way that Pelagius did with the indictments brought against him at Diospolis.

It is nearly impossible to give a full account of the similarities and differences between Caelestius and Pelagius on this issue, as we have no quotations from Caelestius

---

1. For a discussion of this council and the beginning of the controversy, see: Dodaro, "Carthaginian Debate," 187–202; Dunphy, "A Lost Year," 389–466.

2. Augustine, *Gest. Pelag.* 11.23. Augustine would address the question of the relationship between law and the gospel in his *Spir. et litt.* The topic of sinlessness will be discussed later.

3. Rackett, "What's Wrong?," 224–29.

on this topic other than those at the Council of Carthage and the Synod of Diospolis.[4] A clear similarity, however, rests in their exegesis of Genesis. Both men interpret the story of the garden in such a way as to prohibit any sinful consequence to anyone other than the offenders themselves. What cannot be confirmed, because of a lack of evidence, is whether or not Caelestius has the same view of the force of imitation and the development of habits to explain the persistence of sin in the same way that Pelagius did. One can reasonably surmise that he did, but it is impossible to prove. The message from Caelestius is evident that he believed that humanity, created good by a good God, has not been harmed in anyway by the sin of Adam.

Sinlessness

Of the few extant excerpts from Caelestius we have, sinlessness is the topic most often quoted from him in Augustine's writings. This does not necessarily mean that Caelestius felt that sinlessness was the most important theological issue. It is possible that Augustine focused on this particular subject, and magnified, or distorted, its importance for Caelestius. This is not likely, however, because Augustine informs us at the beginning of his *De perfectione iustitiae hominis* (which contains the majority of the extant quotations from Caelestius) that he must quote his opponent verbatim extensively in order for his readers to make sense of his own argument.[5] Because of Augustine's careful quotations, Teske has speculated that it is possible that we have most, if not all, of Caelestius's *Definitiones*.[6] If Teske is right, then it is safe to say that sinlessness is of central importance to Pelagius's protégé.

The substance of Caelestius's argument for the possibility of sinlessness is not fundamentally different from Pelagius's own argument. Like Pelagius, Caelestius believes in an uncorrupted nature and an uninhibited free will to choose sinlessness;[7] like Pelagius, he claims that sin is not a substance but an act of the will;[8] like Pelagius, he states that sinlessness is not only possible, but it is the duty of the Christian life to pursue it;[9] like Pelagius, he admits that he himself cannot claim to be sinless;[10] like Pelagius, he points to Zechariah and Elizabeth as having been sinless,[11] but he also says

---

4. The one exception comes from the beginning of Augustine's *Pecc. merit.* 2.2. where a nameless author is cited saying "Adam was created so that he would die, even if he did not sin, not as a punishment for his guilt, but by the necessity of his nature," which can be clearly identified as Caelestius because of the nearly identical phrasing with that of the charges against Caelestius laid out in *Gest. Pelag.* 11.23. See also, *Grat. Chr.* 2.3.3.

5. Augustine, *Perf.* 1.1.

6. Teske, vol. 1 "Introduction," 270.

7. Augustine, *Perf.* 4.9, 6.14, 11.23; *Gest. Pelag.* 14.30, 18.42;

8. Augustine, *Perf.* 4.9.

9. Augustine, *Perf.* 3.5.

10. Augustine, *Perf.* 7.16.

11. Augustine, *Perf.* 17.38. We saw in an earlier chapter that Pelagius offered an extensive list of

that Job was sinless (whom Pelagius did not mention).[12] He does not mention Abel, Enoch, Elijah, and Noah (as did the *Liber de fide*).[13]

It is the differences between Pelagius and Caelestius that are noteworthy. First, we saw that Pelagius's understanding of the human person, sin, and the possibility of sinlessness came out of a strong rejection of Manichaeism. Caelestius is not overly concerned with Manichaeism in the same way. Second, we saw that Pelagius was not entirely forthcoming if he believed that there were some individuals who had been sinless, and he very well may have misled the bishops at Diospolis on this point. Caelestius, on the other hand, is confident that sinlessness is both theoretically possible, and has been lived in the lives of several biblical figures. There is no duplicity on his part. Third, Caelestius's style of argumentation is quite different from Pelagius, which is most likely a result of his legal training. While both men quote Scripture to support their claims, Caelestius used logic and philosophical jargon in a way that is not paralleled in Pelagius's writings. He poses the same sort of questions in a variety of different ways, trying to get to the heart of the matter from different perspectives—circling around the issue of sin as if it were a defendant on the witness stand. He questions if sin can be avoided, or cannot be avoided. If something cannot be avoided, it cannot be a sin. But, if sin can be avoided, then it is possible to be sinless.[14] Asking from a different angle, he inquired if sin comes from necessity, or the movement of the will. If from necessity, it cannot be avoided; if from the will, it may be avoided.[15] He then ponders if sin is something in our nature, or "accidental"[16] to our nature. In this question, we can see Caelestius's philosophical background come into the light.[17] The extent of Caelestius's formal philosophical training is unclear, as we know so little about his educational background, but it does seem that he had more of a philosophical background, formal or informal, than did Pelagius. Caelestius most likely did not have a direct knowledge of Aristotle and his categories of substance and accident. But, these two categories easily could have filtered down to Caelestius through Latin intermediaries. He then continues to ask if sin is a thing or an action. His answer is that it must be an action because if it were a thing, it would have an author. As sin lacks goodness, the author would be something other than God. As there is no author other than God, sin must

---

sinless biblical figures: "Abel, Henoch, Melchizedek, Abraham, Isaac, Jacob, Joseph, Joshua the son of Nun, Phinehas, Samuel, Nathan, Elijah, Elisha, Micah, Daniel, Hananiah, Azariah, Mishael, Ezekiel, Mordecai, Simeon, Joseph, to whom the Virgin Mary was betrothed, and John . . . Deborah, Anna the mother of Samuel, Judith, Esther, another Anna the daughter of Phanuel, Elizabeth, and also the mother of our Lord and Savior." Augustine, *Nat. grat.* 36.42, 37.44.

12. Augustine, *Perf.* 12.29–30, 16.37, 17.38.
13. Rufinus the Presbyter, *Lib. fid.* 39.
14. Augustine, *Perf.* 2.1.
15. Augustine, *Perf.* 2.2.
16. Augustine, *Perf.* 2.3.
17. Teske, vol. 1 "Introduction," 304 n. 3.

be an action. If sin is an action, then, it may be avoided.[18] Continuing, he inquires if one ought to be without sin. He concludes that one ought to be sinless, and, if one ought to be sinless, then one is able to be sinless. If one ought not to be sinless, then one ought to be sinful. If one ought to be sinful, then there is no sin.[19] Furthermore, he asks if there is a commandment from God to be without sin, or not. Either one cannot be without sin and there is no commandment, or one can be sinless and there is a commandment.[20] And, sinlessness must be possible because it is something that God wills. "Who is so insane," he asks "as to doubt that something is possible, if one has no doubt that God wills it?"[21] He then states that God created human beings good and commanded them to do good.[22] Caelestius continues to inquire about the forms of sin; he says that there are two forms: doing those actions which are forbidden, and abstaining from certain actions as commanded by God. Both forbidden and commanded actions, he says, must be possible because if they were not possible it would be futile to forbid or command anything. He concludes his line of questioning with a statement that God is righteous, as everyone agrees, and that "God also imputes to human beings every sin. I think that we must admit this too, for whatever will not be imputed as sin is not a sin. And if there is a sin that cannot be avoided, how is God said to be righteous if he is thought to impute to anyone what cannot be avoided?"[23]

Baptism

We have few quotations from Caelestius about baptism, but what we have suggest both similar and different visions of baptism from Pelagius. In his *De gratia Christi et de peccato originali*, Augustine quotes several sections from the *Libellus fidei* that Caelestius presented to Pope Zosimus in his defense when he arrived in Rome after having been exiled from Constantinople. Several discrepancies between Pelagius and Caelestius are noticeable. Caelestius does not mention several points we saw in the last chapter concerning how Pelagius understood baptism, including: the necessary dual movement of water and *verbum*, the ability of the individual to resist the grace received, nor a detailed list of the effects of baptism. These absences do not necessarily mean that Caelestius rejected these ideas from Pelagius. It is possible that Caelestius was in perfect harmony with Pelagius on these points. It is also possible, however, that Caelestius either rejected the details of Pelagius's baptismal theology, or had not developed his own baptismal theology with such detail.

18. Augustine, *Perf.* 2.4.
19. Augustine, *Perf.* 3.5.
20. Augustine, *Perf.* 3.6.
21. Augustine, *Perf.* 3.7–8.
22. Augustine, *Perf.* 4.10.
23. Augustine, *Perf.* 6.15.

As neither Pelagius nor Caelestius believed in original sin, neither held that baptism washed it away, nor washed away the guilt (*reatus*) of original sin. Caelestius said that baptism is not "for the forgiveness of sins in such a way that we should be thought to affirm a sin derived from generation."[24] For Caelestius, baptism is necessary because the kingdom of heaven (*regnum coelorum*) can be received only by those who have been baptized.[25] He does not explain clearly what he means by this. Because he rejected the idea that babies were born with original sin, why would a baby need to be baptized for the kingdom of heaven if it has committed no sins? Augustine preached a sermon (294)[26] that helps shed some light on Caelestius's meaning. To his audience in Carthage, he said that

> they [the Pelagians] say that it [baptism of infants] is not for the sake of salvation, not for the sake of eternal life, but for the sake of the kingdom of heaven. Pay attention, please for a moment or two, while I explain as best I can what this may mean. A baby, they say, even if it isn't baptized, on the strength of its innocence, in that it has no sin at all, neither its own nor original; neither coming from itself nor derived from Adam; must necessarily have salvation and eternal life, even if it isn't baptized; but it is to be baptized for this reason, in order that it may enter the kingdom of God, that is into the kingdom of heaven.[27]

In Caelestius's vision, babies who are not baptized receive eternal life if they die. But, they must be baptized for the sake of the kingdom of heaven. If they are not baptized and die, there is another place that they will go. In the same sermon, Augustine refutes his opponents and says that "there is no middle place (*medius locus*) left, where you [Pelagians] can put babies. Judgment will be passed on the living and the dead; some will be on the right, others on the left; I do not know any other destiny. You there, bringing in a middle place, get out of the middle, don't make the person seeking the right hand trip over you. And I am advising you for your sake; get out of the middle, but don't go to the left."[28] The theological opinion of limbo would not be developed until the end of the twelfth and beginning of the thirteenth centuries,[29] so we must be cautious about reading back into the fifth century a concept that had not developed yet.[30] It is clear,

---

24. Augustine, *Grat. Chr.* 2.6.6.

25. Augustine, *Grat. Chr.* 2.5.5. See also for Rufinus, *Lib. fid.* 40.

26. The standard dating is that this sermon is from 413, but Dunphy has argued that it was preached in 411. Dunphy, "A Lost Year," 459.

27. Augustine, *Serm.* 294.2. A similar idea can be found in an anonymous quotation in Augustine, *Pecc. merit.* 1.30.58. See also: 1.18.23. Augustine elaborates on his rejection of this idea in 1.23.33–28.26.

28. Augustine, *Serm.* 294.3.

29. International Theological Commission, *Hope of Salvation*, 24.

30. Augustine in this sermon says that "unbaptized babies go to damnation" (294.7). But earlier in his *De libero arbitrio*, Augustine said that "if there can be a life that is intermediate between sin

however, that, in Caelestius's mind, a distinction was being made between salvation from damnation (which unbaptized babies who die can obtain) and the fullness of God's kingdom (which unbaptized babies who die cannot obtain).

When Pelagius discussed baptism, he almost exclusively talked about adult baptism. In the last chapter, we saw that he recognized that babies were often baptized and, although he did not oppose it, he did not actively encourage it. Further, we saw that Pelagius's theology of baptism breaks down when it comes to infants because it is impossible for them to either accept or reject it, which he said was necessary for the efficacy of baptism, and for the autonomy of the individual. When Augustine discusses Caelestius, on the other hand, his focus is entirely on how Caelestius conceived specifically of infant baptism, and does not seem to be very interested in the details of adult baptism. Caelestius, unlike Pelagius, actively encouraged infants to be baptized, saying that "I have always said that infants need baptism and ought to be baptized."[31] In declaring this to Pope Zosimus, Caelestius hoped that his encouragement of this common church practice would be enough to vindicate him. For only a brief moment during the pontificate of Zosimus, it was.

The Theology of the *Liber de Fide*

The *Liber de fide* holds many of the same positions as other Pelagians. It mentions several times that Adam and Eve did not sin again after their first transgression,[32] the sin of Adam and Eve will not condemn the rest of humanity,[33] and that anyone who believes that all people are guilty of sin because of Adam and Eve "are desirous of wickedness."[34] It also lists four Old Testament figures whom it considers to have been sinless: Abel, Enoch, Elijah, and Noah.[35] This list adds Noah to the list from Pelagius's list, but is missing many others from it.[36] It also addresses the issue of infant baptism, stating that babies are not baptized for the remission of sins, but are created

---

and right action, have no fear that our Judge can pronounce a sentence that is intermediate between punishment and reward" (3.22.).

31. Augustine, *Grat. Chr.* 2.23.26; see also: 2.3.4, 2.5.5.
32. Rufinus the Presbyter, *Lib. fid.* 35, 39.
33. Rufinus the Presbyter, *Lib. fid.* 37–38.
34. Rufinus the Presbyter, *Lib. fid.* 39.
35. Rufinus the Presbyter, *Lib. fid.* 39.
36. We saw in an earlier chapter that Pelagius offered an extensive list of sinless biblical figures: "Abel, Henoch, Melchizedek, Abraham, Isaac, Jacob, Joseph, Joshua the son of Nun, Phinehas, Samuel, Nathan, Elijah, Elisha, Micah, Daniel, Hananiah, Azariah, Mishael, Ezekiel, Mordecai, Simeon, Joseph, to whom the Virgin Mary was betrothed, and John . . . Deborah, Anna the mother of Samuel, Judith, Esther, another Anna the daughter of Phanuel, Elizabeth, and also the mother of our Lord and Savior." Augustine, *Nat. grat.* 36.42, 37.44.

in Christ, and receive the heavenly kingdom.[37] Babies who die without baptism, the author insists, do not go to hell.[38]

It is this text's unique contribution to Pelagianism, however, that is more intriguing than the similarities. In contrast with Caelestius, the author of the *Liber* believes that Adam and Eve would not have died had they not committed their one and only sin: "although I have said that the first human beings, Adam and Eve, were created immortal according to the soul, but mortal according to the body; nevertheless they would never have tasted death, as Blessed Enoch merited, if only they had been willing to obey God's command. For although Enoch was mortal, nevertheless, 'he was taken up that he might not see death at all'" (Heb 11:5).[39] At the Synod of Diospolis, as we saw earlier, a number of propositions for which Caelestius was anathematized in Carthage were also leveled against Pelagius. The first of these propositions was that "Adam was created mortal so that he would die whether he sinned or did not sin."[40] Caelestius clearly did not adopt his understanding about the mortality of Adam from the *Liber de fide*.

It must be mentioned that at no point does the *Liber* put forward any definition of grace—Pelagian, Augustinian, or other. This absence is curious. Although the subject of grace did not take center stage in this controversy until Augustine began to fixate on it around 415 with his *De natura et gratia*, both Pelagius[41] and Caelestius[42] had discussed it prior to this, if only in a rudimentary way.[43] The absence of any discussion of grace in the *Liber* indicates that the root of the Pelagian vision of grace cannot be found here.

37. Rufinus the Presbyter, *Lib. fid.* 40.
38. Rufinus the Presbyter, *Lib. fid.* 41.
39. Rufinus the Presbyter, *Lib. fid.* 29.

40. Augustine, *Gest. Pelag.* 11.23. This same quotation also may be found at the very beginning of Augustine's *De peccatorum meritis et remissione et de baptismo parvulorum* when he quotes a nameless author who held that Adam would not have died if he would not have sinned. Augustine, *Pecc. merit.* 1.2.2.

41. Even before Pelagius wrote his *De natura*, he had discussed his basic understanding of grace in his Pauline commentaries. Pelagius, *Expos. (ad Rom.)*, 5:16, 6:14–15, 7:12, 8:2.

42. The extant quotations we have of Caelestius discussing grace comes from Augustine's *De gestis Pelagii*, which Augustine wrote after he wrote *De natura et gratia*. However, the Synod of Diospolis itself took place the same year Augustine wrote *De natura et gratia*. If Augustine quoted the synod faithfully, we can conclude that the issue of grace was discussed. Augustine, *Gest. Pelag.* 14.30, 17.40–18.42.

43. Pelagius does not seem to begin to develop his thought on grace until he wrote his *De natura*. We saw in a footnote in an earlier chapter that scholars disagree when Pelagius wrote *De natura*. Some scholars believe it was written when he was in Sicily in 410–411. Others believe that it was written from Palestine in 413–414. Duval, Teske, and Lancel have argued that it was more likely written 406–410 while in Rome. Teske, vol. 1 "Introduction," 198–99; Lancel, *Saint Augustine*, 326; Duval, "La Date," 274; Rees, "Pelagius," 140.

Chapter 13

The Theology of Augustine (411–418)

Adam and Original Sin

AUGUSTINE'S ANTHROPOLOGY WAS INTIMATELY tied to his exegesis of the story of Adam and Eve in Genesis 3, as it had been with the Pelagians.[1] For Augustine, humanity falls into two distinct categories: prelapsarian humanity (humanity before Adam's disobedience of God's command not to eat of the fruit of the tree of the knowledge of good and evil), and postlapsarian humanity (humanity afterwards).[2] As Adam was the first human and did not come from the generation of parents, he was created in an uncorrupted state of being.[3] Adam's animal body (*corpus animale*) originally had been obedient to the rational soul, because the body was the servant of the soul. His body felt no stirring of disobedience against the soul, just as the soul was obedient to God. It was this obedience of the flesh to the soul that allowed Adam to be naked without any shame.[4]

This unspoiled state, if it had continued without blemish, would have looked quite differently than the reality of the fate that Adam suffered, Augustine speculates. Adam would have lived for "many years" without physical decline (although Augustine does not say exactly how many years).[5] His body would have been sustained from the fruits of the trees in the garden, and he would have been immune from the damages of age.[6] His mortal body would have avoided the punishment of death, and, at some point, passed over into incorruption and immortality through the transformation into the spiritual body that is promised to the saints.[7]

---

1. Bonner argued that the turning point between Augustine and the Pelagians was their different understanding of the fall and original sin. Bonner, *Freedom and Necessity*, 87, 107.

2. Augustine blames Eve for her disobedience as well, but he focuses much more of his attention on Adam than he does on Eve. This is most likely because the biblical passage that was most important for interpreting Genesis 3 was Romans 5:12, which attributes the blame of sin and death on one man (*per unum hominem*), rather than one man and his wife. Augustine, *Pecc. merit.* 1.16.21, 2.21.35.

3. Augustine, *Pecc. merit.* 1.37.68; Rist, "Augustine on Free Will," 434.

4. Augustine, *Pecc. merit.* 2.22.36–23.37.

5. Augustine, *Pecc. merit.* 1.3.3.

6. Augustine, *Pecc. merit.* 1.3.3.

7. Augustine, *Pecc. merit.* 1.2.2–3.3.

But, none of this happened. Adam, instead, chose not to obey God's command,[8] causing the animal body to lose the grace that allowed it to obey the rational soul.[9] When this happened, the "law of disobedience,"[10] that is, the concupiscence of the flesh, reigned in the body, which caused Adam and Eve to become ashamed of their nakedness, and they sewed fig leaves to cover themselves (Gen 3:7).[11] God punished this disobedience by driving Adam out of the garden to toil in labor and sweat as a punishment (Gen 3:23).[12] Their disobedience also caused them to lose their immortality, and, although they lived for many more years, they immediately began to grow old and "to die on that day on which they received the law of death."[13]

Adam's sin did not injure him alone, but his actions caused a domino effect in his progeny that cascaded down through the generations to the present.[14] Augustine called this *peccatum originale*, which is usually translated as "original sin." This translation can be misleading, because it is often viewed only as that transgression that Adam and Eve did in the garden. Augustine did not see it as a one-time sin that occurred in distant history by two people. Rather, it is the root of almost[15] every sin that every person throughout history has done in their life.[16] It might be more helpful, therefore, to translate it as "the origin of sin," rather than "original sin," but, because of convention, we will continue to use the phrase "original sin" here. For Augustine, original sin is the sin of pride (*superbia*).[17] Most often in our common discourse, pride is positive. Students, for example, always want their parents to proud of them when they do well on an exam. *Superbia* for Augustine does not denote this affirming sense of warmth and affection. Rather, it is "a vice which arises when we rely on ourselves and make ourselves our own source of life. Through that stirring of pride one withdraws from the fountain of life from which alone one can draw and drink righteousness, namely, the good life. One also withdraws from that unchangeable light by participation in which the rational soul is in a sense set alight so that it is itself a light that has been made and created."[18] In other words, *superbia* is the turn inwards toward the self.[19] When humans sin, they articulate

---

8. Augustine, *Pecc. merit.* 2.21.35. Augustine offered abundant details about the consequences of Adam's sin, but he never offered a reason why Adam chose to sin in the first place. Bonner, *St. Augustine*, 368.

9. Augustine, *Pecc. merit.* 1.16.21.

10. Augustine, *Pecc. merit.* 2.22.36.

11. Augustine, *Pecc. merit.* 1.16.21.

12. Augustine, *Pecc. merit.* 2.34.55.

13. Augustine, *Pecc. merit.* 1.16.21.

14. Augustine, *Pecc. merit.* 1.9.10; *Perf.* 18.39; *Grat. Chr.* 2.24.28.

15. Augustine does recognize that some sins occur "by the ignorant, by the weak, and often by persons weeping and groaning." *Nat. grat.* 29.33; Mann, "Augustine," 47.

16. Rist, "Augustine on Free Will," 430–32.

17. Augustine, *Pecc. merit.* 2.17.27.

18. Augustine, *Spir. et litt.* 7.11.

19. Bavel, "Anthropology of Augustine," 36.

through word or deed, in effect, I want, what I want, when I want it, and how I want it. I do not care what God says. I do not care about God's commandments. I do not care about God's vision of a flourishing life. I prefer my own vision. This reality of *superbia* is biblically demonstrated first in Adam's consumption of the forbidden fruit, but also is seen daily in the sins swirling all around us.

Postlapsarian humanity suffers from original sin in profound ways. Humanity, he says, "now needs a physician, because it is not in good health. All the goods which it has in its constitution: life, the senses, and the mind, it has from the sovereign God, its creator and maker. But the defect (*vitium*) which darkens and weakens those natural goods so that there is need for enlightenment and healing did not come from its blameless maker. It came from the original sin which was committed by free choice. And thus a nature subject to punishment is part of a punishment that is completely just."[20] The defect of original sin is not something that God has added to our nature as a punishment, nor did God alter humanity such that it is no longer created good in the image and likeness of God. Rather, because sin is not a thing (*res*), but it is an action (*actum*), Augustine described this deficiency in our nature as a lack, similar to a limp.[21] A limp is not something visible when a person is sitting or standing still, nor can it be detected with medical examinations. It is only seen when the person with the limp begins to walk, and an onlooker can observe the deficiency in the person's gait. Similarly, original sin can only be observed in the selfish actions committed by the sinner.

For Augustine, original sin is passed down from generation to generation through propagation (*propagatio*), rather than by imitation (*imitatio*). He referenced many biblical texts to support this claim (such as Rom 7 and 9, and 1 Cor 15),[22] but the "fundamental"[23] biblical proof of the biological cause can be found in Rom 5:12: "through one man sin entered the world, and through sin death, and thus was passed on to all human beings in whom all have sinned."[24] If Paul intended to convey that humanity sins from imitation as Pelagius claimed, then he would have said that sin entered the world "through the devil." Paul, however, stated that sin and death entered "through one man (*homo*)," which, for Augustine, made Paul's meaning plain that sin must come from somewhere more deeply ingrained in our being than mere

20. Augustine, *Nat. grat.* 3.3; Harmless, "Christ as Pediatrician," 7–34.

21. Augustine, *Nat. grat.* 26.29; *Perf.* 2.4.

22. Rigby, "Original Sin," 607.

23. Rondet, *Original Sin*, 128. Azkoul also has said that there is no "more crucial" biblical passage for Augustine other than Romans 5:12. But, Rigby, Lyonnet and Lamberigts offer a minority report. Azkoul, "Peccatum Originale," 42; Rigby, "Original Sin," 607; Lyonnet, "Rom. V,12," 327–29.

24. For example: *Pecc. merit.* 3.7.14. For a description of the mistranslation of Romans 5:12 into Latin that Augustine used, see: Lyonnet, "Rom. V,12," 328; Azkoul, "Peccatum Originale," 42–43; Rondet, *Original Sin*, 128–29; Lamberigts, "Augustine, Julian," 393–94. Although Augustine may have been using a faulty translation, I do not believe that Augustine would have seen this as a problem, for he elsewhere recognized the fruitfulness of different Latin translations from the original Hebrew and Greek. Augustine, *Doctr. chr.* 2.12.17.

parody.²⁵ It is true that Adam may be considered an example (*exemplum*) for sinners in that everyone who sins does so through disobedience of God's commandments, but *exemplum* does not adequately describe Adam's responsibility. More precisely, it must be claimed that Adam is the origin (*origo*) of sin.²⁶ It is also clear to Augustine that original sin rests in our essence, because if the sin of humanity is merely found in imitation of the sin of Adam, then the solution to the problem simply would be imitation of Christ's righteousness: "for, if imitation alone produces sinners through Adam," he asks, "why does imitation alone not produce righteous persons through Christ?"²⁷ Imitation of Christ certainly is admirable and even demanded by Paul (1 Cor 11:1), but imitation of him cannot bring about righteousness. Only God's active agency working within humanity can do that.

Baptism

Augustine had a robust, nuanced, and rich understanding of baptism,²⁸ which he had already honed through the course of his fight with the Donatists.²⁹ During the Pelagian controversy, he was forced to focus his attention on the narrow topic of the baptism of infants, which became the primary battlefield on which the fight over original sin, as well as the meaning of baptism, were fought.³⁰ For Augustine, all humans—including infants, which he most often called "little ones" (*parvuli*)—are crippled by original sin, and therefore need the remedy of baptism.³¹ He readily admits that infants have not accrued any personal sins, because they are not of the age of reason.³² For infants, baptism only washes away the guilt (*reatus*) of their original sin,³³ while the baptism of adults washes away both the guilt of original sin and personal sins.³⁴ The necessity of baptism for the cleansing of the guilt of original sin may be understood in two ways. First, the ancient practice of infant baptism signifies that infants are as implicated in sin as adults. Parents bring their infants to receive the bath of regeneration out of a "holy fear."³⁵ Why, he asks, would parents have anything to fear if their children did not suffer from the punishment for Adam's disobedience? Even though the theology

---

25. Augustine, *Pecc. merit.* 1.9.9.
26. Augustine, *Pecc. merit.* 1.9.10.
27. Augustine, *Pecc. merit.* 1.15.19.
28. For an excellent introduction to Augustine's thought on baptism, see Ferguson, *Baptism*, 776–816.
29. Willis, *Saint Augustine*, 145–68.
30. Augustine, *Pecc. merit.* 1.16.21.
31. Augustine, *Pecc. merit.* 1.12.15, 1.16.24.
32. Augustine, *Pecc. merit.* 1.35.65.
33. Augustine, *Pecc. merit.* 1.9.9, 1.19.25, 1.24.34, 2.4.4, 2.28.45; *Grat. Chr.* 2.3.4.
34. Augustine, *Pecc. merit.* 1.15.20.
35. Augustine, *Pecc. merit.* 1.18.23.

articulating why infants need to be baptized had yet to be developed fully, parents intuitively understood the urgency of baptism for the salvation of the souls of their children. Second, if infants do not suffer from original sin, then Jesus did not die for them. But, Jesus died for everyone, and the salvation won by Jesus on the cross is only shared with those who have received baptism.[36] Baptism both speaks to the reality of the postlapsarian condition, and makes salvation possible.[37]

Although the laver of regeneration releases the baptized from the guilt of original sin, it does not magically return humanity to its prelapsarian purity. The disordered desire of concupiscence—also described as the "law of sin" (*lex peccati*),[38] the "old weakness" (*vetus infirmitas*),[39] and the "old corruption" (*vetus corruptione*)[40]—does not lose its thrall over humanity.[41] It remains in the members of the body wreaking havoc for the duration of one's earthly existence.[42] At the same time, baptism also initiates a transformation that begins to reorient the individual's whole being toward God. "In those who are making good progress," Augustine said, "as their [the baptized] renewal grows from day to day, the fruits of the Spirit transform into themselves what pertains to the old flesh, until the whole is so renewed that even the weakness of the animal body attains spiritual strength and incorruption."[43] This transformation is not instantaneous nor complete, but with God's continual aid throughout life, the individual is able to journey on the path toward God.

If infants die without receiving baptism they will not be saved, because it is necessary for salvation.[44] Augustine does concede that, even though they will not enter the kingdom of heaven, infants "will be under the mildest condemnation of all."[45] Frustratingly, he never explains exactly what this means, but we have already seen him reject the "middle place" (*medius locus*) between heaven and hell.[46] It is safe to say that this is the one of the most difficult parts—if not the most difficult part—of Augustine's anthropology for both Christians and non-Christians today to stomach, because it seems to run counter to God's mercy and compassion.[47]

36. Augustine, *Pecc. merit.* 1.19.24.

37. Augustine, *Pecc. merit.* 1.23.33. See also 1.18.23.

38. Augustine, *Pecc. merit.* 2.4.4.

39. Augustine, *Pecc. merit.* 2.7.9.

40. Augustine, *Pecc. merit.* 2.7.9.

41. Augustine does concede that it is possible for God to choose to grant a miracle to someone and eradicate original sin from that person. He does not mention anyone specifically, but he may have the Virgin Mary in mind. Augustine, *Pecc. merit.* 1.39.70. See also 2.24.38; *Nat. grat.* 36.42; *C. Jul.* 5.15.52.

42. Augustine, *Pecc. merit.* 2.4.4.

43. Augustine, *Pecc. merit.* 2.27.44. See also: 2.7.9.

44. Augustine, *Pecc. merit.* 1.20.28, 1.23.33–25.35, 1.27.42, 3.4.7; *Nat. grat.* 4.4, 8.9.

45. Augustine, *Pecc. merit.* 1.16.21.

46. Augustine, *Serm.* 294.3.

47. Indeed, many people turn away from Christianity because of it. How is it just, they ask, to condemn infants who die without receiving the sacrament of baptism if they are not old enough to ask for

PART II: THEOLOGY

Free Will and Predestination

Of all the layers of Augustine's anthropology, his teaching on free will—and its concomitant moral responsibility—has drawn the most scholarly attention with the least amount of consensus about what, exactly, he meant.[48] This confusion probably can be traced back to the Pelagian controversy itself. How baffled must Pelagius have been after he had quoted Augustine's earlier *De libero arbitrio* in support of his own teaching on free will, only to have Augustine respond that Pelagius misrepresented him?[49] This lack of consensus and confusion on the part of both Pelagius and modern scholars is understandable considering the changing trajectory Augustine took on this subject over the course of his life. Late in his career, Augustine himself recognized that he had shifted his thoughts about free will, saying "I worked hard in defense of the free choice of the human will, but the grace of God conquered."[50] As it would be beyond the scope of this study to trace the long journey of Augustine's thought on free will, only his writings during the Pelagian controversy will be explored here.

God endowed the gift of the free will (*liberum arbitrium*) to humanity from the beginning, setting us apart from the rest of creation. "The free choice," Augustine said, "which the creator has given to the rational soul as part of its nature is a neutral power that can either turn to faith or fall into unbelief. Therefore, human beings cannot be said to have this will by which they believe God unless they have received it, when at God's call it arises from the free choice which they received as part of their nature when they were created."[51] But, as Adam had cursed his offspring, the will of humanity also became compromised (although it was not annihilated),[52] such that we no longer have freedom (*libertas*).[53]

Freedom, for Augustine, means something very different than the way it usually is discussed in our twenty-first-century public discourse. Mattison has succinctly described the contemporary definition: "as long as your actions are truly taken on as your own, then you are fully free. In this view, it does not matter what you choose to

---

it? It should be noted that, despite Augustine's certitude, the church retains hope that infants who have died without baptism might still be saved. As the *Catechism of the Catholic Church* says, "the Church can only entrust them [infants who have died without baptism] to the mercy of God, as she does in her funeral rites for them. Indeed, the great mystery of God who desires that all men should be saved, and Jesus's tenderness toward children . . . allow us to hope that there is a way of salvation for children who have died without Baptism. All the more urgent is the Church's call not to prevent little children coming to Christ through the gift of holy Baptism." Interdicasterial Commission, *Catechism*, 1261.

48. Rist, "Augustine on Free Will," 420; Stump, "Augustine," 124.
49. Augustine, *Nat. grat.* 67.80–81.
50. Augustine, *Praed.* 4.8.
51. Augustine, *Spir. et litt.* 33.58.
52. Rist, "Augustine on Free Will," 424; Stump, "Augustine," 133.
53. Gilson, *Christian Philosophy*, 143–64; Rist, "Augustine on Free Will," 421–23.

do; as long as the action is truly your own, you are free."[54] Freedom, then, is defined as the ability to do whatever you desire without any external pressures, be they governmental, societal, or economic. But, for Augustine, this is untenable in a postlapsarian reality. True freedom, according to him, is not the ability to do whatever the passions desire, but, as Mary Clark has summarized, it is "a power for obtaining what the will naturally desires—the unlimited Good or God—[it] is reconcilable with a grace that enables the human will to choose precisely that for which it was created. The enhancement of free will Augustine calls *libertas* in contrast to *liberum arbitrium*, the natural capacity for free choice."[55] In other words, freedom is liberation from the radical slavery of sin so that we may be able to choose the good, and to become what Christians were intended to be: faithful sons and daughters of God.

This freedom, however, has been lost, because Adam's transgression against God's command "has produced a necessity"[56] (*necessitas*) in humanity. This necessity is a will that is "capable only of sinning."[57] It may sound as if Augustine were scandalously saying that sin is irresistible, and, therefore, that we are not held responsible when we sin because we are compelled to do so by our broken nature (Julian of Eclanum, as we shall see, will level this exact charge against him). On the contrary, Augustine insists that we are responsible for our actions so that when we fall to temptation it is entirely our fault.[58] God is not to blame, nor can we pass the buck of responsibility for our sins to Adam.[59] This is, as John Rist has said, the "Augustinian paradox":[60] we are both unable to choose the good, and, at the same time, responsible for the sins we commit.[61]

Although we may not be able to do the good, we are able to will the good. One way of comprehending what this means is to imagine that a giant boulder fell from the sky and pinned Adam to the ground the day he disobeyed God. Adam undoubtedly would desire to climb out from underneath the boulder, but lacking the requisite upper-body strength would be unable to do so. The only way for Adam to climb out from underneath the boulder would be to receive assistance from a friend with a lever and fulcrum to remove the stone. In an analogous way, when Augustine says that "we can will the good, but cannot carry it out,"[62] he means we may choose to orient our will towards God, but the prideful turn inward towards the self prohibits us from carrying

---

54. Mattison, *Moral Theology*, 51.
55. Clark, *Augustine*, 50.
56. Augustine, *Perf.* 4.9. See also: Alflatt, "Development of Idea," 113–34; Alflatt, "Responsibility," 171–86.
57. Augustine, *Spir. et litt.* 3.5.
58. Augustine, *Pecc. merit.* 2.5.5.
59. Augustine, *Spir. et litt.* 34.60.
60. Rist, "Augustine on Free Will," 424.
61. Djuth, "Stoicism," 393.
62. Augustine, *Spir. et litt.* 33.59.

out those desires. It is Christ's action on the cross that is the friend, lever, and fulcrum that alone can relieve humanity of its burden.

Even more paradoxically, Augustine said that the will to choose the good is itself a gift from God, because, as Paul asked, "what do you have, after all, that you have not received?" (1 Cor 4:7).[63] If everything comes from God, then the will to choose the good must come from God as well; it cannot come from the individual.[64] If one were to say that the will to choose the good comes from one's own efforts, humanity, in effect, is not entirely dependent on the Creator of the universe, which is anathema to the Christian mind. This may sound as if grace renders the will ultimately impotent because any interference by God in human affairs would make the will no longer truly free. If God orients the will towards the good, then, by definition, the individual has no agency. Augustine, however, insisted that it is only through the activity of God's assistance that the will really can be free.[65] Without it, we are slaves to our desires:

> through faith, we obtain grace to struggle against sin; through grace the soul is healed from the wound of sin; through the good health of the soul we have freedom of choice; through free choice we have the love of righteousness; through the love of righteousness we fulfill the law. The law is not done away with but strengthened by faith, because faith obtains the grace by which we fulfill the law. In the same way, free choice is not done away with by grace, but strengthened, because grace heals the will by which we freely love righteousness.[66]

Of course, God's assistance may be accepted or declined by the individual. God does not compel the will to be rightly ordered.[67] When it is accepted by the individual, "these ills of our old condition are healed, as our new condition increases from day to day";[68] when it is declined, we remain in a life of sin.

Our postmodern society, like the Pelagians before, bristles against the twin Augustinian claims of original sin and compromised freedom, although for different reasons. The Darwinian theory of evolution, for one, has relegated to the dustbin the idea of Adam and Eve as the parents of all humanity. The cry of freedom—which has moved beyond the political sphere and saturated every other sphere of existence—and radical individualism, furthermore, have rendered unpalatable the claim that our actions, and our very being, are in some way contingent on influences out of our control. But, Augustine's claim that human freedom is limited because of existential brokenness and, at the same time, that we are responsible for our own actions is not altogether foreign.

---

63. Augustine, *Spir. et litt.* 33.57.

64. Augustine, *Pecc. merit.* 2.5.5, 2.18.29–32; *Spir. et litt.* 3.5, 33.57–34.60; *Nat. grat.* 23.25; *Grat. Chr.* 1.19.20; Rist, "Augustine on Free Will," 425–26; Stump, "Augustine," 134; Bonner, *Freedom and Necessity*, 68.

65. Hanby, *Augustine and Modernity*, 82.

66. Augustine, *Spir. et litt.* 30.52.

67. Augustine, *Spir. et litt.* 34.60.

68. Augustine, *Spir. et litt.* 33.57.

If, for example, a man were to become inebriated and then get into a car accident killing three people, the judicial system rightly would imprison the man for his actions. At the same time, however, geneticists describe how certain genetic traits, such as a disposition for alcoholism, can be passed down from one generation to the next. Although this man may receive compassion because of his genetic code that he did not choose, our society would insist that he is ultimately responsible for his actions. Obviously, Augustine used theological language, not genetic language, to describe the human condition. Both languages, however, describe in different ways how to hold together in our minds both personal responsibility and inherited brokenness.

During the Pelagian controversy,[69] Augustine said surprisingly little about predestination.[70] He probably did not feel compelled to discuss it because the Pelagians did not dwell on it as a grave concern. Most of his serious investigation on the topic would occur during his battle with the so-called Semi-Pelagians.[71] His sparse discussions of it in his anti-Pelagian writings usually centered around Paul's passing line to the Romans: "those whom he foreknew, he predestined to be conformed to the image of his Son so that he might be the firstborn among many brothers and sisters. But those whom he predestined he also called, and those whom he called he also justified, and those whom he justified he also glorified" (8:29–30).[72] Augustine did not expound on Paul's intended meaning, or offer a discussion of the relationship between foreknowledge and predestination with any specificity.[73] Did God predestine someone based on his foreknowledge of that person's behavior? Or, did God predestine that person regardless of what he foreknew? Augustine did not seem to be interested in these types of questions (at least, not during this particular fight).[74] Before the creation of the world,[75] God predestined some to eternal life. Others he predestined to damnation[76] (which later was anathematized by the Second Synod of

---

69. Augustine, *Pecc. merit.* 2.17.26, 2.27.43, 2.29.47; *Spir. et litt.* 5.7; *Perf.* 13.31; *Gest. Pelag.* 3.7, 17.41; *C. du. ep. Pelag.* 2.10.22; *C. Jul.* 5.4.14–18.

70. Lamberigts, "Augustine on Predestination," 282.

71. See Augustine, *Praed.* Lamberigts has shown that most of Augustine's writings on predestination were written upon request by colleagues, or to clarify for his monastic brothers: *Ad Simplicianum, De gratia et libero arbitrio, De correptione et gratia, De praedestinatione sanctorum,* and *De dono perseverantiae.* Lamberigts, "Augustine on Predestination," 288.

72. For example: *Perf.* 20.43.

73. There are many secondary sources that investigate Augustine's teaching on predestination. Some of them are: Bonner, *Freedom and Necessity*; Craig, "Augustine on Foreknowledge," 41–62; Lamberigts, "Augustine on Predestination," 279–305; Rist, "Augustine on Free Will," 420–47; TeSelle, *Augustine the Theologian,* 176–82; Wetzel, "Predestination, Pelagianism," 49–58.

74. Augustine, *Pecc. merit.* 2.29.47.

75. Augustine, *C. Jul.* 5.4.14.

76. Augustine, *Pecc. merit.* 2.17.26, 2.27.43; *Perf.* 13.31.

Orange in 529).[77] But, God's reasons why he chooses some for salvation and others for damnation are entirely mysterious.[78]

Grace

The English word "grace" is derived from the Latin word "*gratia*," which Augustine used throughout his writings in one form or another at least 6,005 times.[79] His thought on the topic developed slowly over time,[80] but by 416 he came to see it as the "heart of the matter [of the entire Pelagian controversy] which is the sole or almost the sole point of contention we have with these people [the Pelagians]."[81] Grace, for Augustine, has a multi-layered and textured definition. It is a freely-given (gratuitous) gift from God to someone who is not worthy of it; it is not given as a reward for good works, or because the law was fulfilled, but that good works may be done by the grace given.[82] God's grace transforms the gifted from within, and is necessary for every action[83]—especially for salvation.[84] In contrast to Pelagius who primarily viewed grace as external assistance from God in the modes of the law, teaching, and Christ's example, Augustine defined grace as "an ineffable sweetness in the depths and interior of the soul, not merely through those who externally plant and water, but also through himself who gives the increase secretly."[85] This ineffable sweetness acts upon the individual in a variety of ways, by forgiving sins, assisting in the pursuit of a virtuous life, healing wounds to help keep God's commands, offering power to do what is right, restoring *libertas*, renewing the will, and giving the will strength to desire and accomplish the good.[86]

Augustine was forced by the Pelagians to clarify his vision of the law and grace, because they viewed the law as part of God's gift to humanity. For him, the law is not part of God's aid to live a flourishing life. It is something that was revealed by God, but it does not have the ability to transform our lives.[87] Alone, the law is not enough. It does not engender righteousness, because righteousness only comes from God's inner illumination of the soul.[88] Only once God has bestowed his divine endowment on

---

77. Pelikan, *Emergence*, 329.
78. Augustine, *C. Jul.* 5.4.14.
79. Rydstrøm-Poulsen, *Gracious God*, 31.
80. Burns, *Development*, 53; Clark, *Augustine*, 45.
81. Augustine, *Nat. grat.* 44.51–52; *Gest. Pelag.* 30.55; Rackett, "What's Wrong?," 231–35.
82. Augustine, *Spir. et litt.* 10.16; *Gest. Pelag.* 14.33.
83. Augustine, *Gest. Pelag.* 14.31.
84. Augustine, *Nat. grat.* 4.4.
85. Augustine, *Grat. Chr.* 1.13.14.
86. Gilson, *Christian Philosophy*, 160; Clark, *Augustine*, 49–50; Creswell, *St. Augustine's Dilemma*, 95.
87. Augustine, *Gest. Pelag.* 9.21.
88. Augustine, *Grat. Chr.* 1.8.9–9.10, 1.13.14.

whom he chooses is the law able to be fulfilled.[89] By itself without grace, the law only brings transgression of God's commandments, because it does not help accomplish what it demands. In fact, without God's assistance, the law is harmful because it causes us to desire that which is forbidden—like a child who wants nothing other than the cookies his parents tell him he cannot have.[90] It "commands, after all, rather than helps; it teaches us that there is a disease without healing it. In fact, it increases what it does not heal."[91] The law without grace is dangerous because it sets before us how we should live our lives—what to do, and what not to do—but it does not bring about what it instructs. It is, in essence, a theologically unfunded mandate.

Augustine also rejected the Pelagian definition of grace that Christ is an example (*exemplum*) to follow in pursuit of perfection. Christ certainly is an example of love, mercy, generosity, and forgiveness that all Christians should follow. But, imitating Christ's example in these does not foster righteousness.[92] Here, we see the second bookend that pairs with the flawed Pelagian understanding of Adam. The Pelagians did not take Adam seriously enough, insisting that he was merely an example whose sin is repeated in imitation. Augustine argued that this vision of the relationship between the first parents and their descendants does not plumb the depths of human brokenness. The Pelagian Adam, then, leads to the Pelagian Christ.[93] For, if Adam is nothing more than a model of human sinfulness, then Christ need not be anything more than an example of righteousness to counterbalance Adam's example. This insufficient Christology, for Augustine, ruptures the soteriological foundation of the gospel.[94] If Christ did not die for the sins of humanity because he is nothing more than a moral model, then Christ died in vain, because his sacrifice was merely symbolic.[95]

Pelagius, as we saw, believed that God's graciousness provided the *posse* to live a life without sin, but that the *velle* and *esse* to attempt such a life come entirely from the individual. God does not interject in the human affairs after providing the *posse*, for to do so would be to sway the will in one direction or another. Augustine found this terribly myopic. Because of original sin, the *velle* and the *esse* require God's continual intervention to enable the baptized Christian to turn towards righteousness.[96]

89. Augustine, *Spir. et litt.* 19.34; *Grat. Chr.* 1.9.10.

90. Augustine, *Gest. Pelag.* 6.20.

91. Augustine, *Grat. Chr.* 8.9.

92. Augustine, *Grat. Chr.* 1.38.42–39.43.

93. Later, in his fight with Julian, Augustine returned to this point: *C. Jul.* 2.146. For a discussion of Christ as example, see: Gore, "Our Lord's Human," 282–313.

94. Although he never wrote one text, or even one section within a text, that offers a condensed soteriological analysis of Pelagian anthropology, Augustine repeatedly claimed that their locus of salvation was too centered on human effort, and not enough on Christ's work on the cross.

95. Throughout the Pelagian controversy, Augustine quoted Gal 2:21 in a variety of contexts to show that flaw in Pelagian soteriology: *Spir. et litt.* 29.50; *Nat. grat.* 1.1, 2.2, 9.10; *Perf.* 7.16; *Gest. Pelag.* 6.20; *C. du. ep. Pelag.* 3.7.22, 4.5.10; *C. Jul.* 4.3.17; *C. Jul. op. imp.* 2.70, 2.188, 2.198–99.

96. Augustine, *Grat. Chr.* 1.13.14–25.26.

He refuted Pelagius's examples of the eyes and the ability to speak that Pelagius used to illustrate his point simply. God must provide not only the *posse* to see, Augustine said, but he must also provide the *velle* and the *esse* to see well.[97] That is, God must provide the active assistance to see an object well—such as viewing a poor person with mercy—and not to misuse the eyes, as one does when viewing a woman with lust.[98] Likewise, God must help in the *velle* and *esse* of speaking well; without God's grace, we would utter any number of lies, blasphemies, and vulgarities.[99] Everything we do must be done with God's infused help. "Let Pelagius, therefore, stop deceiving both himself and others," Augustine summarized, "with his arguments against the grace of God. God's grace toward us should be proclaimed, not merely on account of one of those three elements, namely, on account of the ability to have a good will and good action, but also on account of having a good will and good action."[100]

Sinlessness

Augustine, unfortunately, never wrote a single text that presents his thoughts about sinlessness. These thoughts were spread over a number of texts.[101] One's initial response may be to force these thoughts together to construct a mosaic to give a clear picture of how he conceived of sinlessness.[102] As is often the case with him, however, one cannot capture his thoughts in one picture.[103] Rather, one must approach them as one approaches Claude Monet's *Haystacks*, which must be viewed in succession to see how they changed over time and, only then, to come to a full appreciation of this series. In a similar fashion, we will analyze Augustine's beliefs on the possibility of sinlessness and see that they did not remain static; he changed his position several times over a few short years. We will look at four of his treatises (*De peccatorum meritis et remissione et De baptismo parvulorum, De natura et gratia, De perfectione iustitiae hominis,* and *De gestis Pelagii*) and the canons of the Council of Carthage of 418 (Augustine had been the key figure in constructing them) to track these changes.

Augustine began his reply to the notion of the possibility of living a life free of sin in his text *De peccatorum meritis et remissione et De baptismo parvulorum*. In Book

97. Dupont and Malavasi. "Question of Impact," 556–65.
98. Augustine, *Grat. Chr.* 1.15.16.
99. Augustine, *Grat. Chr.* 1.16.17–17.18.
100. Augustine, *Grat. Chr.* 1.25.26.
101. This section is based largely on one of my earlier publications in *Augustinianum*: "Augustine's Changing Thought on Sinlessness," 447–66.
102. Mary Clark argues that one may think of Augustine's thought as a mosaic, but I am convinced that this way of thinking warps our understanding of him. Clark, *Augustine*, 84.
103. Recent scholarship has attempted to make Augustine's thought homogenous from 386 until his death in 430: Harrison, *Rethinking*. This has caused a stir among Augustinian scholars: Boone, "Rethinking," 154–57; Gerber, "Rethinking," 120–22; Lössl, "Rethinking," 300–302; Meconi, "Rethinking," 180–82; Rist, "Rethinking," 542–44; Rorem, "Rethinking," 519–21; Vinel, "Rethinking," 573–74.

II, Augustine responded to Marcellinus by asking and answering four questions: (1) whether or not one can live life without sin, (2) whether or not there has ever been a person—other than Jesus—who has been sinless, (3) why it is that no human being is sinless, and (4) whether or not someday there will be a person who achieves a state of sinlessness.[104] The first question is only briefly discussed. Augustine claims that it is possible for one to remain sinless. This sinlessness may only be achieved through the grace of God and the movement of the free will. The free will is necessary because God will not force an individual to be sinless. The sinless life must be desired by the individual and only then will God offer His aid.[105] Initially, this may seem to be a surprising claim and that Augustine has agreed with his opponent's arguments. However, he is making what I call a hypothetical claim to sinlessness because, as we will soon see, he does not believe that there have ever been any individuals without sin. If Augustine categorically were to deny the possibility of the sinless life, then he would be placing a limitation on God's power. He would never do so, so he allows for this hypothetical possibility of God's intervention in the life of an individual. Historically, as he makes clear in his second point, there has never been a single individual who has achieved such a state.[106] He refutes his opponents by quoting a variety of biblical passages (Pss 32:5–6; 143:2; 1 John 1:8) and alludes to several others (Rev 14:3–5; Prov 18:17) that prove this impossibility. In his third point, Augustine states that there has never been a sinless individual because there has never been anyone who truly wanted to be without sin. When one is assured that something is good, then one will desire it. This knowledge of goodness, however, is due to the grace of God. At other times, one does not understand the goodness of a deed or take delight in it; it is at these moments that pride leads the individual to sin.[107] Augustine then poses his fourth question: will there ever be anyone in the future who will be free of sin?[108] Despite his earlier claim that it is hypothetically possible for one to be without sin, he claims this will never happen.[109] Returning to an argument from Book I, he links the impossibility of a sinless life to his discussion about the necessity of baptism in infants because of original sin.[110] For, even if one is able to live a life in adulthood free of sin, through grace and the pure desire of the free will, one is still born corrupted.

Augustine's *De natura et gratia* signaled an important shift in his understanding of the arguments of his opponents, and it displayed a more urgent tone in his rhetoric. It is of particular interest because we see a shift in Augustine's thinking about the Virgin Mary. Gerald Bonner offers the standard scholarly view:

104. Augustine, *Pecc. merit.* 2.6.7, 2.7.8–16, 2.16.25, 2.17.26–2.19.33, 2.20.34–36.
105. Augustine, *Pecc. merit.* 2.6.7.
106. Augustine, *Pecc. merit.* 2.7.8.
107. Augustine, *Pecc. merit.* 2.17.26, 2.17.27.
108. Augustine, *Pecc. merit.* 2.20.34.
109. Augustine, *Pecc. merit.* 2.20.34.
110. Augustine, *Pecc. merit.* 1.9.9.

> Augustine, it will be noticed, is careful in his affirmation of universal human sinlessness to give Mary a place apart. It is not so much that he declares her personal sinlessness, as that he absolutely refuses to discuss the matter *propter honorem Domini*, for the honour of the Lord. This specific reference to the Mother of God—and the total number of such references is not very large in the great bulk of Augustine's writings—is evidence of the particular place which Mary enjoyed in the eyes of Christians by the beginning of the fifth century, not only in the Greek east but in the traditionally conservative Latin west.[111]

Augustine, in the passage to which Bonner alludes, says that one should "leave aside the holy Virgin Mary; on account of the honor due to the Lord, I do not want to raise here any question about her when we are dealing with sins. After all, how do we know what wealth of grace was given to her in order to conquer sin completely, since she merited to conceive and bear the one who certainly had no sin?"[112] Bonner, Pelikan, Ferguson, and Doyle agree that Augustine said that Mary was sinless.[113] These scholars, however, ignore a previous discussion, from Book II of *De peccatorum meritis et remissione et De baptismo parvulorum*, where a different understanding of Mary's status is given: "therefore," Augustine says, "he [Jesus] alone, having become man, while remaining God, never had any sin and did not assume sinful flesh, though he assumed flesh from the sinful flesh of his mother (*de materna carne peccati*). Whatever of the flesh he took from her, he either cleansed it to assume it or cleansed it by assuming."[114] Mary, he says, had sinful flesh, but when Jesus took his flesh from his mother, he did not contract her sinfulness. We can see here that there is a shift, over just a few years, from certainty to doubt about Mary's sinfulness.[115]

Two features deserve our attention from his *De perfectione iustittiae hominis*: first, we saw that Augustine believed that, although it is hypothetically possible to achieve a state of sinlessness, in reality this historically has never been achieved. At the end of *De perfectione iustitiae hominis*, however, Augustine changes his mind: "finally, one might claim that, apart from our head, the savior of his body, there have been or are some righteous human beings (*aliqui homines iusti*) without any sin (*sine aliquo peccato*), whether because they never consented to its desires or because we should not consider as a sin something so slight that God does not count it against their holiness. In any case, I do not believe that one should resist this idea too much."[116] Note the shift of focus to allow the possibility of a sinless individual,

---

111. Bonner, *St. Augustine*, 328.

112. Augustine, *Nat. grat.* 36.42.

113. Bonner, *St. Augustine*, 328, n.1; Pelikan, *Mary through Centuries*, 33, 191, 195; Ferguson, *Pelagius*, 166; Doyle, "Mary," 544.

114. Augustine, *Pecc. merit.* 2.24.38.

115. Augustine is not clear when exactly the flesh of Mary was cleansed. This issue would later haunt the medieval theologians. For example, see John Duns Scotus, *Four Questions*, 2:1–2.

116. Augustine, *Perf.* 21.44.

which calls for a few comments. He probably was thinking about some of the figures from the Old and New Testaments (Noah, Daniel, Job, Zechariah, Elizabeth), but Augustine did not want to mention them by name.[117] It is also not a coincidence that Augustine made this claim at the very end of the text while summarizing his argument because this allowed him to avoid expanding this argument. Although he hesitated to defend this new argument with any force, it should not be seen as simply an aberration but as a genuine change of heart.[118]

The second important point comes from the lines shortly after this quotation: "for I know," Augustine says "that such is the view of some whose position on this matter I dare not reprehend, though I cannot defend it either."[119] Teske has argued that Augustine was thinking of Ambrose,[120] but I want to suggest that he is referring to Jerome, who claimed that one may be sinless for a short time.[121] Shortly before Augustine wrote this text, Orosius returned to Hippo from Palestine, as we saw earlier. He had brought with him, among other things, a letter (172) from Jerome and a copy of the *Dialogi contra Pelagianos*.[122] At first glance, this letter seems to praise Augustine, something that is a dramatic turn from their previous correspondence that displayed Jerome's suspicion of Augustine.[123] Jerome said that Augustine had written several books that "were full of learning and resplendent with every sparkle of eloquence."[124] Jerome, however, is actually criticizing Augustine in this letter because he also says that "[in Augustine's texts can be found] the words of the blessed apostle, 'each person abounds in his own ideas (Rom 14:5), one in this way, another in that (1 Cor 7:7).' Certainly whatever could be said and drawn from the sources of holy scriptures by your lofty mind (*ingenium*) you have stated and discussed."[125] This should be read as a subtle criticism because Jerome believed that Augustine was generating his own ideas about sinlessness and has turned away from the writings of the tradition in favor of his own opinions. This criticism is noteworthy for two reasons. First, Jerome earlier had charged Ambrose with plagiarism because Ambrose relied too heavily on the writings of others when he wrote on virginity.[126] Second, Cassian later would criticize Jerome for abandoning tradition in favor of his own views when he wrote

---

117. These people previously had been discussed as possible examples of sinlessness. Augustine, *Pecc. merit.* 2.10.12–16, 2.10.24.

118. Augustine, *Perf.* 21.44. It is unclear exactly what caused this change of heart. It could have occurred because of the change in circumstances in the debate or the context of the situation.

119. Augustine, *Perf.* 21.44.

120. Augustine, *Letters: 156–210*, 18 n. 3.

121. Jerome, *Dial.* 3.12.

122. Frend, "Orosius, Paulus," 616.

123. Squires, "Jerome's Animosity," 181–99. For good introductions to this correspondence: Cavallera, *Saint Jérôme*, 297–306; White, *Correspondence*.

124. Jerome, *Epist.* 172.1.

125. Jerome, *Epist.* 172.1.

126. Adkin, "Ambrose and Jerome," 364–76.

about ascetic practices, a criticism that would have made Jerome furious if he were still alive at the time. Goodrich states that "Jerome, in particular, is made the target of doubt [by Cassian]. He was a particularly eloquent writer, but his ascetic works were drawn from his own ingenuity (*ingenium*). His teachings were the product of his fertile mind, rather than the fruit of *experientia*."[127] Augustine clearly detected Jerome's backhanded compliment because, shortly after receiving this letter, he began to quote authors such as Cyprian, Ambrose, Irenaeus, Hilary, Gregory, and Basil and would rely on tradition throughout his debate with Julian.[128] This letter is also instructive because Jerome recognizes that he and Augustine think differently about sinlessness. He says that "if enemies, and especially heretics, see differences of opinion between us, they will slander us by saying that they stem from rancor of the heart."[129] While Augustine and Jerome see themselves as having the same general agenda against Pelagius, both men recognize that they disagree on the question of sinlessness.

The last text from Augustine that is relevant for our purposes is his *De gestis Pelagii*. Late in this text, Augustine once again returned to the question of sinlessness because he was upset by the fact that the texts of Pelagius neglect any mention of the assistance of God. At Diospolis, Pelagius's verbal testimony diverged from what he had written in his texts by adding the phrase "by the grace of God."[130] Although Augustine's anger at this discrepancy should come as no surprise, his next claim is intriguing. The synod discussed the statement from Caelestius, which was condemned at the Council of Carthage of 411, that before Christ there were human beings without sin.[131] Pelagius distanced himself from this statement. He had stated previously that there were individuals who had been without sin, but now he only said that there were people who were holy and righteous.[132] Augustine says that Pelagius "realized, after all, how dangerous (*periculosus*) and difficult (*molestus*) a point it was [to agree with Caelestius]"[133] since Pelagius knew that Caelestius had been condemned for it. Augustine's mild language—in contrast to his earlier harsh criticisms—is noteworthy; he does not want to use stronger language because he himself allowed for the possibility of just such a claim and he did not want to sound like a hypocrite.[134]

But, he is no longer certain of the possibility of a sinless life. In this text, there is yet another shift in his thinking and he now leaves open for debate the question of sinlessness, saying that "it was not . . . decided [at Diospolis] whether in this flesh

127. Goodrich, *Contextualizing Cassian*, 71.

128. Augustine, *Nupt.* 2.29.52; *C. du. ep. Pelag.* 4.8.20–21, 4.8.31; *C. Jul.* 1.3.5–9. Earlier, Augustine had mentioned some of these authors, but he was responding to Pelagius's claim that his arguments are consistent with tradition. Augustine, *Nat. et. gr.* 61.71–67.81.

129. Jerome, *Epist.* 172.1.

130. Augustine, *Gest. Pelag.* 11.26.

131. Augustine, *Gest. Pelag.* 11.23.

132. Augustine, *Nat. grat.* 36.42.

133. Augustine, *Gest. Pelag.* 11.26.

134. Augustine, *Perf.* 21.44.

lusting against the spirit there has been, is, or will be someone with the use of reason and the choice of the will, whether in human society or monastic solitude, who will not have to say ... 'forgive us our debts' (Matt 6:12) ... that is perhaps a question to be peacefully investigated, not among Catholics and heretics, but among Catholics."[135] We can see that he now abandons his previous position from *De perfectione iustitiae hominis*,[136] but does not yet want to commit himself to the opposite. The shift in Augustine's thought from *De perfectione iustitiae hominis* to *De gestis Pelagii*, I would suggest, was caused by the indecision at Diospolis. Augustine recognized that his acknowledgement of possibility of the sinless life cannot ultimately be sustained, and the hesitancy of Diospolis persuaded him of this.

The final piece of our discussion comes from the Council of Carthage of 418. We know very little about this Council, but we do have nine canons from it—four are important for our purposes here. Although these canons cannot be attributed solely to Augustine, he surely played an important role in the council that was held on the first of May[137] with over two hundred African bishops in attendance.[138] Canons six through nine are important for us because, while Augustine had recently claimed that sinlessness is "perhaps a question to be peacefully investigated,"[139] the Council of Carthage closed the investigation by claiming that it is impossible for anyone to be sinless, including those who are considered "holy persons":

- *Canon six*: They [the bishops at the council] likewise decreed that, if any say that we are given the grace of justification so that we can more easily (*facilis*) do by grace what we are commanded to do by free choice, as though if grace were not given, we could still fulfill the divine commandments without it, though not easily (*facilis*), let them be anathema.

- *Canon seven*: They likewise decreed that, if any think that the statement of Saint John, the apostle, "if we say that we have no sin, we deceive ourselves, and the truth is not in us (1 John 1:8)," is to be interpreted in the sense that one should say that we have no sin on account of humility, not because it is the truth, let them be anathema.

- *Canon eight*: They likewise decreed that, if any say that in the Lord's Prayer holy persons say, "forgive us our debts" (Matt 6:12), so that they do not say this for themselves, because this petition is no longer necessary for them, but for others who are sinners in their people, and that in this way every holy person does not say, "forgive me my debts," but "forgive us our debts," so that the righteous

---

135. Augustine, *Gest. Pelag.* 30.55. I have changed the punctuation of the English translation to make Augustine's words clearer.
136. Augustine, *Perf.* 21.44.
137. Merdinger, "Councils," 249.
138. Ferguson, *Pelagius*, 111.
139. Augustine, *Gest. Pelag.* 30.55.

are understood to say this for others rather than for themselves, let them be anathema.

- *Canon nine*: They likewise decreed that, if any claim that the words of the Lord's Prayer where we say, "forgive us our debts" (Matt 6:12), are said by holy persons in the sense that they say them humbly and not truthfully, let them be anathema.[140]

The discrepancy between Augustine's hesitancy to make any claims for the possibility of sinlessness at the end of *De gestis Pelagii* and these four canons raises several points. Augustine's frustration at the way that the Synod of Diospolis had failed to censure the writings of Pelagius was too much for him to swallow. His leading role in this Council may seem obvious, but we should keep in mind that Augustine had no hand in the Council of Carthage of 411 that dealt with Caelestius.[141] His leadership role, then, should not be assumed.

Two examples from these canons point to Augustine's fingerprints on this Council. The first is from the discussion in canon six which addresses how "easily" (*facilis*) one may keep God's commandments. This brings to mind Augustine's response found in *De gestis Pelagii*. After having received a letter from Pelagius about Diospolis, and having received the minutes of it from Cyril of Alexandria,[142] Augustine noticed an important difference between the two: in the first, Pelagius used the word "easily" (*facilis*), while in the second he did not.[143] This discrepancy was a sign to Augustine of Pelagius's heresy as well as his willful subversion of the synod.[144] Second, the quotation of 1 John 1:8 in canon seven is a quotation that was constantly referenced throughout Augustine's anti-Pelagian writings.[145] The presence of these two examples cannot be coincidental and must be seen as stemming directly from Augustine. It is at also clear that Augustine was behind the council because, of the two hundred bishops in attendance, only he and fourteen other bishops remained in Carthage after the council waiting for a response from the Pope.[146]

Did the other bishops need to convince him of the impossibility of a sinless life, or did Augustine come to this conclusion on his own? We saw earlier that Augustine had reconsidered his understanding of Mary based on the writings of Pelagius and his indecision on the sinlessness because of Diospolis. Here, however, Augustine did not return to his original point through any outside influence. Canons eight and nine give us a glimpse into Augustine's thinking. In the paragraph from *De gestis Pelagii* where

---

140. Dionysius, *Codex Canorum Ecclesiasticorum*, PL, vol. 67 (217B–219C).

141. For an excellent discussion of Caelestius and the Council of Carthage 411, see Wermelinger, *Rom und Pelagius*, 4–28.

142. Augustine, *Epist.* 4*.2.

143. Augustine, *Gest. Pelag.* 30.54.

144. Evans, "Pelagius' Veracity," 21–30.

145. Augustine, *Pecc. merit.* 2.7.8, 2.8.10, 2.10.12, 2.13.18; *Spir. et litt.* 36.65; *Nat. grat.* 14.15, 34.38, 36.42, 62.73; *Perf.* 18.39, 21.44; *Gest. Pelag.* 11.26, 12.27.

146. Lancel, *Saint Augustine*, 339.

he claims that the question of historical sinlessness is open to investigation, Augustine quoted Matt 6:12 saying that "it was not, nonetheless, decided . . . whether in human society or in monastic solitude, who will not have to say, not because of others, but because of himself, 'Forgive us our debts.'"[147] Both canons eight and nine, however, use Matt 6:12 to claim definitively that there never has been, is, or will be anyone without sin. At some point between 416–418, therefore, Augustine's appreciation of this passage from the Lord's Prayer grew and it must have been one of the key factors that convinced him of the impossibility of the sinless life. [148] The importance of this verse can also be seen later in his refutation against Julian's claims of sinlessness.[149]

---

147. Augustine, *Gest. Pelag.* 30.55. This passage from the *Pater Noster* was also crucial to Cassian's understanding of prayer, which is at the heart of his critique of Pelagius. *Coll.* 9.18–24.

148. This argument is similar to one made by scholars, such as Paula Fredriksen, who claim that Augustine had changed his mind about the relationship between grace and free will around 396/97 because of a new assessment of the letters and life of Paul. Prior to this new assessment, in his *De libero arbitio*, Augustine believed that the free will is unencumbered, while after this new assessment, (which changed as he wrote *Ad Simplicianum*), Augustine believed that the will is impeded by the sin of Adam. Fredriksen, "Beyond Body/Soul," 102–5.

149. Augustine, *C. du. ep. Pelag.* 1.14.28, 4.10.27; *C. Jul.* 2.8.23, 4.3.28, 4.3.29.

Chapter 14

The Theology of Jerome

Origen, Sinlessness, and the Pelagians

JEROME HAS BEEN OVERSHADOWED by Augustine in the Pelagian controversy, and his role in the battle needs to be appreciated more by scholars today.[1] Ferguson said that Jerome was in Bethlehem waiting for a fight when Pelagius arrived in Palestine. "Rufinus was dead," he says, "and the old lion was looking for some new adversary on whom to sharpen his claws when Pelagius came on the scene. After a long life of disputation controversy was his meat and drink; to abandon it would mean spiritual starvation."[2] Quite the contrary was true, however. By the time Pelagius fled Rome after 410 and knowledge of his theology began to spread throughout the Mediterranean world, Jerome was nearing the end of his life. He felt pestered by this upstart young man, and did not want to be pulled into yet another contest. At the beginning of his *Dialogi contra Pelagianos*, he reveals that he had not been overly anxious to confront the Pelagians, saying that "I received frequent expostulations from the brethren, who wanted to know why I any longer delayed the promised work in which I undertook to answer all the subtleties of the Preachers of Impassibility."[3] After the Synod at Diospolis, he was content to bite his tongue, writing to Augustine that "a most difficult time has come upon us when it is better for me to be silent than to speak."[4] His writings against Pelagius, furthermore, do not demonstrate the same bite of his earlier works. Jerome was tired, and wanted to be left alone.

His main method of attack on the Pelagians was to link them genealogically to previous heresies to demonstrate their perfidy.[5] Jerome saw intellectual family resemblances in every campaign he ever fought. During his fight with Jovinian, Jerome

---

1. Evans, *Inquiries and Reappraisals*, 4; Zednik, "In Search," 11; Clark, *Origenist Controversy*, 221; Rackett, "What's Wrong?," 228; Jeanjean, "Le *Dialogus*," 60.

2. Ferguson, *Pelagius*, 77.

3. Jerome, *Dial.* 1.pref.

4. Jerome, *Epist.* 134.1. Here, I am using Teske's translation from the Augustinian corpus (*Epist.* 172).

5. Jerome often used this tactic in his writings, but was not the first Christian to do so, as earlier thinkers such as Justin Martyr and Irenaeus of Lyons had already employed this form of attack. Elm, "Polemical Use," 316.

associated him with the Greek philosopher Epicurus, calling him the "Epicurus of Christianity"⁶ in an attempt to demonstrate his moral corruption. In his conflict with Vigilantius over the cult of relics, the practice of all-night vigils, ascetic rigor, and alms sent to Jerusalem,⁷ Jerome linked him back to Jovinian by saying that "in this fellow [Vigilantius] the corrupt mind of Jovinianus has arisen; so that in him, no less than in his predecessor, we are bound to meet the snares of the devil."⁸ In his fight with the Pelagians, Jerome associated them with seemingly everyone whom he could remember: Pythagoras, Xystus, Manichaeans, Priscillian, Evagrius, Jovinian,⁹ Messalians,¹⁰ Basilides,¹¹ and Rufinus.¹² While these genealogies¹³ were the crux of Jerome's attack on the Pelagians, he never put any serious effort into crafting an argument about how they were descendants of these previous heresies.¹⁴ He simply asserted it.

For Jerome, the most important menace to whom the Pelagians could be traced was Origen,¹⁵ whom Jerome described as Pelagius's "special favorite."¹⁶ Specifically, Jerome

6. Jerome, *Jov.* 1.

7. Kelly, *Jerome*, 288.

8. Jerome, *Vigil.* 1.

9. Jerome, *Dial.* 2.24. See also: *In Hier.* 22:24–27.

10. For similarities between the Messalians and the Pelagians, see: Louth, "Messalianism and Pelagianism," 127–35.

11. Pelagius elsewhere associated Priscillian of Avilla with the gnostics, Basilides, and Marcus. Elm, "Polemical Use," 317.

12. For the references for these ancestors, see: Jerome, *Dial.* 1.pref, 2.pref, 2.24, 3.1, 3.15; *Epist.* 130.16; *Epist.* 133.1, 3; *In Hier.* 1.pref, 4.pref, 22:24–27.

13. Scholars have argued about the validity of these genealogical connections. Driver has argued that his entire genealogy is "of little worth." Most scholars, however, have not made such a sweeping claim, and have chosen to be more focused in their assessments. Colish has argued that he incorrectly sensed an influence from the Stoics. McWilliam and Lamberigts agree with Colish and McWilliam adds that Origen, too, was incorrectly seen as an influence. Years before either Colish or McWilliam, Ferguson and Brown claimed that the Stoics had influenced Pelagius. Kelly believes that Origen (through Rufinus) and Xystus did influence Pelagius, but the influence from Jovinian is unfounded. Duval and Hunter have argued that Jovinian, indeed, influenced Pelagius, but Pelagius was attempting to strike a balance between him and Jerome. Driver, "From Palestinian Ignorance," 307; Colish, *Stoic Tradition*, 78; McWilliam, "Letters to Demetrias," 135–36; Lamberigts, "Competing Christologies," 164; Rackett, "What's Wrong?," 228; Ferguson, *Pelagius*, 78; Brown, *Augustine of Hippo*, 369; Kelly, *Jerome*, 315–16; Duval, *L'affaire Jovinien*, 284–365; Hunter, *Marriage, Celibacy*, 259–68.

14. Van Egmond, "Pelagius," 645.

15. We have already seen that Pelagius certainly was influenced by Rufinus's translations of Origen's works, so Jerome is not entirely incorrect in his assessment that Pelagius had been influenced by Origen. However, it should also be noted that Pelagius explicitly condemned theological arguments made by Origen at the Synod of Diospolis, and in his *Libellus fidei* sent to the Pope. Pelagius named Origen explicitly at Diospolis, although he was never mentioned by name in the *Libellus*. Specifically, Pelagius condemned the ideas that (1) we will not be resurrected in this fleshly body, (2) souls are part of the substance of God, (3) souls sinned in a former state and had lived in heaven before being sent into the body, (4) the subordination of the Son to the Father (though this was explicitly linked to Arius), and (5) that on the day of judgment sinners will be spared. Pelagius, *Lib. fid.* 15, 20; Augustine, *Gest. Pel.* 3.9–10. See also: Van Egmond, "Pelagius and the Origenist Controversy in Palestine," 631–47.

16. Jerome, *Dial.* 3.19. For the all times Jerome links Pelagius to Origen, see: *Epist.* 133. 3; *Dial.*

linked the Pelagian claim of the possibility of sinlessness back to Origen (through Rufinus and Evagrius), whom, he claimed, corrupted Christianity with Stoicism.[17] Jerome began to make this connection by asserting that the Latin phrase *sine peccato* (without sin) and the Greek word *anamartetos* (sinless) are synonymous.[18] He said:

> let those blush then for their leaders and companions who say that a man may be "without sin" (*sine peccato*) if he will, or, as the Greeks term it *anamartetos*, "sinless." As such a statement sounds intolerable to the Eastern churches, they profess indeed only to say that a man may be "without sin" (*sine peccato*) and do not presume to allege that he may be "sinless" (*anamartetos*) as well. As if "sinless" and "without sin" had different meanings; whereas the only difference between them is the Latin requires two words to express what Greek gives in one. If you adopt "without sin" (*absque peccato*) and reject "sinless" (*anamartetos*), then condemn the preachers of sinlessness.[19]

He also stated that both *sine peccato* and *anamartetos* are also synonymous with the Greek philosophical word *apatheia*.[20] For the Stoics, *apatheia* was "the complete absence of passions and the resulting tranquility of spirit,"[21] and "a person's utter indifference to any feelings whatsoever, be it joy and love or grief and hate; it is therefore a question of an unconditional equanimity."[22]

Apatheia became a "vexed"[23] term when it was appropriated by Christian theologians in antiquity because it was laden with this Stoic baggage.[24] When Christians began to use this Stoic idea, it initially was used only to describe a characteristic of God, not human beings.[25] In the hands of Clement of Alexandria, however, *apatheia* began to be applied to humans as a goal of attaining likeness with God.[26]

1.pref; *In Hier.* 4.pref. It also should be noted that, although Pelagius never explicitly condemned the following list of Origen's dubious assertions, he also never adopted them personally: (1) the devil could resume his angelic status and be saved, (2) that demons could be transformed into humans, and vice versa, (3) a succession of worlds may have already existed and may exist in the future, (4) hellfire is not eternal, but simply guilty conscience, (5) Christ may return to suffer for the demons, and (6) the superiority of allegorical exegesis.

17. Jerome, *Dial.* 1.pref; *In Hier.* 4.pref.
18. Squires, "Jerome on Sinlessness," 697–709.
19. Jerome, *Epist.* 133.3.
20. Jerome, *In Hier.* 4.pref.
21. Groves, "Mundicia Cordis," 308.
22. Joest, "Part II," 275. See also: Spanneut, "L'*apatheia* Chrétienne," 165–302.
23. Ousley, "Evagrius' Theology," 216.
24. Christians such as Clement of Alexandria, Origen and Evagrius often paired it with the biblical concept of purity of heart (*puritas cordis*). For discussions about *apatheia* concerning Clement and Origen, see: Stewart, *Cassian the Monk*, 42; Groves, "Mundicia Cordis," 312; Driscoll, "Apatheia," 157; Raasch, "Philo," 54.
25. Ignatius of Antioch, Just Martyr, and even Basil of Caesarea used this term in reference to God alone. Joest, "Part II," 276.
26. Joest, "Part II," 276–77.

But, unlike the Stoics who wanted the passions eradicated, Clement wanted them to be controlled and rightly ordered.[27] Origen, who was influenced by both the Stoics and Clement,[28] used this term frequently.[29] *Apatheia*, for him, was the absence of the passions either by preventing them before they arise, or by eliminating them afterwards.[30] While Origen is clear that *apatheia* is a goal of the Christian life that is the necessary precondition that allows the possibility of some form of experience with God,[31] he is less clear if it is an ideal that can be attained in this life. At times, it seems as if he believes *apatheia* is impossible to achieve in this life;[32] at others, he claims that it is possible with God's assistance, although it is extremely difficult and nearly unattainable.[33] Juana Raasch, who has written extensively on *puritas cordis* and *apatheia* in early Christianity, has attempted to make sense of these contradicting statements, and has concluded that it is "likely that Origen thinks of this condition as something that probably will be reached only by a few holy souls, such as the great saints of the Bible, in the present life and is usually reserved for the world to come."[34] In connecting together *sine peccato*, *anamartetos*, and *apatheia*, Jerome cleverly associated Pelagian sinlessness with a pagan origin to show that the Pelagians are corrupting Christianity with Stoic philosophy.[35]

Scholars have disagreed about the viability of Jerome's association of *sine peccato*, *anamartetos*, and *apatheia* with each other. Some have claimed that he was just making baseless accusations in an attempt to discredit the Pelagians in the wake of the Origenist controversy that had just recently settled.[36] Others, however, have not been so dismissive, and have detected an insightful observation on Jerome's part.[37]

In addition to Pelagius's familiarity with many of Origen's texts through Rufinus's translations, and Origen's use of the philosophical term *apatheia*, Pelagius probably first read about the possibility of sinlessness from Origen. The most important example where Pelagius would have found Origen discussing the possibility of sinlessness comes from Origen's *Homiliae in Lucam*, which Jerome had translated into Latin around 389/390.[38] Here, Origen distinguishes between two definitions of sinlessness. The first definition of sinlessness is that a person has never sinned in his entire life.

27. Raasch, "Philo," 21–23.
28. Raasch, "Philo," 35.
29. For example, see: Origen, *Cels.* 8.8; Somos, "Origen," 366–70.
30. Raasch, "Philo," 36, 45.
31. Raasch, "Philo," 35.
32. Joest, "Part II," 276; Raasch, "Philo," 47.
33. Groves, "Mundicia Cordis," 312; Raasch, "Philo," 48.
34. Raasch, "Philo," 49.
35. Jeanjean, *Saint Jérôme*, 395–97; Rackett, "Sexuality and Sinlessness," 283–84.
36. Joest, "Part II," 279–80; Stewart, "Introduction," 8; Sheridan, "Controversy over Apatheia," 287–91; Somos, "Origen," 372; Rackett, "What's Wrong?," 228.
37. Casiday, "Introduction," 16.
38. Kelly, *Jerome*, 143.

Origen rejects this outright. The second definition, which he does accept,[39] is that after one sins, one can return to a virtuous life and refrain from sinning from that point afterwards. What is most striking is Origen's discussion of Zechariah and Elizabeth as examples of sinlessness:

> We say this to teach that someone who has stopped sinning can be called "without sin and spotless." Hence, Scripture says clearly of Zechariah and Elizabeth, "both were just in God's sight and walked without blame in all the Lord's commandments and precepts." Let us consider more attentively the praises of Zechariah and Elizabeth that St. Luke writes in his narrative. We want not only to understand that they deserved praise, but also to make their holy zeal our own and become worthy of praise ourselves. Luke could have written simply, "both were just and walked in all the commandments." But, he had to add, "both were just in God's sight." For, it can happen that someone is just in the sight of men without being just "in God's sight."[40]

It will be recalled that Zechariah and Elizabeth were cited by both Pelagius and Caelestius as examples of biblical figures who lived sinless lives.[41] The use of these two as exemplars of sinlessness by Origen and the Pelagians cannot be coincidental, and points to a direct influence of Origen on the Pelagians.

Augustine focused his attack on Pelagian grace. Jerome was much more panicked by their claim of the sinlessness, and spent much energy refuting this idea.[42] In the beginning of his *Epist.* 133 and the first two books of his *Dialogi contra Pelagianos*, Jerome slammed Pelagian sinlessness as nothing other than placing humans on the same level as God.[43] This hubris, he says, summarizes "into a few words the poisonous doctrines of all the heretics."[44] Only Christ, although fully human, was sinless.[45] Jerome, furthermore, said that anyone who was sinless was, *de facto*, above the apostles. Even the apostles, who were more virtuous than all of the rest of humanity, were not perfect.[46] Pelagius's argument inevitably suggests that one may shine more brightly than the men chosen by Christ to be his followers.

In Book I of Jerome's *Dialogi*, Critobulus (the character who is the voice for the Pelagians) argues that a sinless life does not place oneself equal to God.[47] One may not be perfect as God, he argues, but one may be a perfect human being. Atticus (the character

---

39. Origen, *Hom. Luc.* 2.1.
40. Origen, *Hom. Luc.* 2.2–3, see also 5.
41. For other examples of Origen's take on sinlessness, see: *Cels.* 3.69; *Comm. Rom.* 6:14.
42. Jerome, *In Hier.* 30:1–11. Rackett, "What's Wrong?," 228–31; This section is based largely on an earlier publication of mine with *The Heythrop Journal*: Squires, "Jerome on Sinlessness," 697–709.
43. See my discussion: Squires, "Jerome on Sinlessness," 701–3.
44. Jerome, *Epist.* 133.1.
45. Jerome, *Epist.* 133.8; *Dial.* 1.9.
46. Jerome, *Dial.* 1.14, 2.24.
47. Jerome, *Dial.* 1.16; *In Hier.* 2.pref.

for Jerome) admits that there are degrees of righteousness among people, but he criticizes Critobulus's argument as nonsense. He says that one may have a gift that others do not possess, but no one has all gifts. Hinting at 1 Corinthians (12:29), Atticus asks, "Are all Apostles? Are all prophets? Are all teachers? Are all workers of miracles? Have all gifts of healing? Do all speak with tongues? Do all interpret? But desire earnestly the greater gifts."[48] It is impossible for anyone to be all things to everyone or perfect in all things. "All this goes to prove," he says, "that not only in comparison with Divine majesty are men far from perfection, but also when compared with angels, and other men who have climbed the heights of virtue. You may be superior to someone whom you have shown to be imperfect, and yet be outstripped by another; and consequently may not have true perfection, which, if it be perfect, is absolute."[49] Atticus agrees with Critobulus that one may not be perfect compared to God, but he also argues that one may not even be perfect compared to the rest of humanity.

Although one may be superior to some and inferior to others, Atticus does allow that one may be perfect in one or two virtues—but no one may be perfect in all virtues.[50] Very few individuals, however, may be perfect in even some of the virtues. He does not allow for just any sinner to be so, but the list of examples that he offers suggests that Jerome sees only the elite as having such gifts. Atticus says that "there will not be merely wisdom in Solomon, sweetness in David, zeal in Elias and Phinehas, faith in Abraham, perfect love in Peter, to whom it was said, 'Simon, son of John, do you love me?' zeal for preaching in the chosen vessel, and two or three virtues each in others, but God will be wholly in all, and the company of the saints will rejoice in the whole band of virtues, and God will be all in all."[51] Because the great figures of the Christian past were only blessed with one or two virtues, he argues that it would be impossible for anyone—other than Jesus—to be sinless.

The third book of Jerome's *Dialogi* displays a noticeable difference in outlook, which, I argue, was a result of the arrival of Orosius in Palestine. Upon his arrival, as was mentioned earlier, Orosius gave Jerome two letters from Augustine (166, 167), a copy of Augustine's letter he sent to Hilary (157) and, most likely, provided Augustine's *De peccatorum meritis et remissione et De baptismo parvulorum*, and *De spiritu et littera*.[52] Many scholars have noted the importance of Orosius's gifts to Jerome. Kelly, Clark, and Jeanjean have argued that, through his reading of Augustine, Jerome slavishly adopted Augustine's teachings on original sin and infant baptism, becoming

---

48. Jerome, *Dial.* 1.16.
49. Jerome, *Dial.* 1.17.
50. Jerome, *Dial.* 1.21.
51. Jerome, *Dial.* 1.18.
52. Orosius, *Lib. apol.* 3. Jerome, *Dial.* 3.19. Kelly says that Orosius brought Augustine's *De natura et gratia*, but Orosius tells us that Augustine had not yet completed it. Augustine did not send Jerome *De natura et gratia* until the summer of 416, but by then Jerome's monastery may have been burned. Augustine, *Epist.* 19*.3; Kelly, *Jerome*, 317–18.

nothing more than a crypto-Augustinian.[53] Others, like McWilliam and Lössl, have argued that while he appreciated Augustine's texts, he could not align himself with Augustine completely.[54] Ferguson claimed that Jerome preferred to be a "synergist" between Augustine and Pelagius.[55] No scholar, however, has offered a systematic analysis of the shift in Jerome's thinking because of Augustine's work, which I would suggest he only read between writing Books II and III of his *Dialogi*.[56]

In Book III, he departs from his previous statements that one may not be sinless, and qualifies his remarks by stating that, in fact, one may be sinless due to the effort of the individual. Atticus says that "we, too, say that a man can avoid sinning, if he chooses, according to his local and temporal circumstances and physical weakness, so long as his mind is set upon righteousness and the string is well stretched upon the lyre. But if a man grow a little remiss it is with him as with the boatman pulling against the stream, who finds that, if he slackens but for a moment, the craft glides back and he is carried by the flowing waters whither he would not."[57] Jerome allows for the efficacy of the free will to avoid the traps of sin according to the individual's personal strength and the surrounding temptations. He does not allow this sinlessness to remain a permanent state because no matter how strong the will or how few the temptations, one may not avoid sin for the entirety of one's life. Atticus says that

> this is what I told you at the beginning—that it rests with ourselves either to sin or not to sin, and to put the hand either to good or evil; and thus free will is preserved, but according to the circumstances, time, and state of human frailty; we maintain, however, that perpetual freedom from sin is reserved for God only, and for Him Who being the Word was made flesh without incurring the defects and the sins of the flesh. And, because I am able to avoid sin for a short time, you cannot logically infer that I am able to do so continually. Can I fast, watch, walk, sing, sit, sleep perpetually?[58]

We should not be seduced by his claim that "this is what I told you at the beginning." He now allows for the sinlessness of an individual for a "short time," which Jerome had not done in either Book I or Book II. Why would he, who had gone through great pains to claim that a sinless state is impossible, now claim that it is possible, though only for a short time? This change at the end of Book III, I believe, stems from a rejection of Augustine's position on sinlessness. Jerome read in Augustine's work a theology that he considered to be too pessimistic about the human condition. He felt the need to offer a theological position that attributed more agency to the individual

---

53. Kelly, *Jerome*, 320; Clark, *Origenist Controversy*, 221–26; Jeanjean, "Le *dialogus*," 61–69.
54. McWilliam, "Letters to Demetrias," 136; Lössl, "Who Attacked?," 94.
55. Ferguson, *Pelagius*, 79.
56. Squires, "Reassessing Pelagianism," 93–110.
57. Jerome, *Dial.* 3.4.
58. Jerome, *Dial.* 3.12.

in order to counteract the limitations that Augustine places on the will because of original sin. While it may go too far to ever call him an optimist, Michael Graves has correctly claimed that the *Dialogi* are, by Jerome's standards, "relatively measured."[59] This temperate position was a result of his rejection of Augustine on one extreme and, of course, the Pelagians on the other.

Transmission of Sin

Another issue that Jerome discusses only after he reads the texts from Augustine that Orosius brought him from Africa was the transmission of sin. Towards the end of Book III—just before he explicitly mentions Augustine by name—Jerome draws a connection between the sinfulness of humanity and our first parents. "But all men," he says "are held liable either on account of their ancient forefather Adam, or on their own account. He that is an infant is released in baptism from the chain (*vinculum*) which bound his father. He who is old enough to have discernment is set free from the chain of his own or another's sin by the blood of Christ."[60] Several scholars have found a latent Augustinianism in this quote. Kelly, for example, went so far as to say that this passage shows that Augustine "had converted him to the strict doctrine of original sin."[61] At the beginning of the Pelagian controversy, Augustine himself even suggests that Jerome believes original sin to be true.[62] While it would be foolish to deny Augustine's fingerprints here, I would suggest that scholars have overstated Augustine's influence and, therefore, have made Jerome out to be nothing more than Augustine's theological puppet. It should be noted that Jerome never used the Augustinian phrase original sin.[63] He could have used Augustine's shorthand to describe the state of humanity after the exile of Adam and Eve from the garden, but he used his own vocabulary, *vinculum*.[64] While it may be tempting to read *vinculum* as a theological equivalent to original sin, it is much more likely that he could not stomach Augustine's "strict" doctrine of original sin and consciously resisted it by ignoring Augustine's language.

At the very end of the text, Jerome gives us another clue that he does not embrace fully original sin and places himself on a spectrum between Augustine and Pelagius. He says that "infants also should be baptized for the remission of sins after the likeness of the transgression of Adam (*in similitudinem praevaricationis*

---

59. Graves, "Introduction," xxix. See also Kelly, *Jerome*, 319; Ferguson also says that "the temper of the work is less bitter than many of his controversial writings." Ferguson, *Pelagius*, 79.

60. Jerome, *Dial*. 3.18.

61. Kelly, *Jerome*, 320. See also, Clark, *Origenist Controversy*, 221.

62. Augustine, *Pecc. merit.* 3.6.12–7.14.

63. For original sin, see *Pecc. merit.* 1.9. See also, Bonner, *St. Augustine*, 326–28.

64. This word is used throughout Augustine's *Confessiones*, but there is no evidence that Jerome read that text. Augustine, *Conf.* 3.1.1, 3.8.16, 5.9.16, 6.10.16, 6.12.22, 7.7.11, 8.1.1, 8.6.13, 8.8.19, 8.11.25, 9.1.1, 9.3.5, 9.12.32, 9.13.36.

Adam)."⁶⁵ The term *in similitudinem*, I believe, is used as a third option for the relationship between the sin of Adam and the sin of his descendants. Augustine, as we saw earlier, insisted that sin was passed from Adam to the rest of humanity by way of propagation (*propagatio*), while Pelagius asserted that humanity sins out of imitation (*imitatio*).⁶⁶ Jerome's phrase shows that he rejected Pelagius's *imitatio*, but did not embrace fully Augustine's *propagatio*.

Foreknowledge

Another issue that was brought to Jerome's attention only through reading the Augustinian texts Orosius brought to Palestine was the question of foreknowledge and predestination. He only briefly discussed his understanding of foreknowledge. Atticus said that

> either God knew that man, placed in paradise, would transgress His command, or He did not know. If He knew, man is not to blame, who could not avoid God's foreknowledge (*praescientia*), but He who created him such that he could not escape the knowledge of God. If He did not know, in stripping Him of foreknowledge you also take away His divinity. Upon the same showing God will be deserving of blame for choosing Saul, who was to prove one of the worst of kings. And the Savior must be convicted either of ignorance, or of unrighteousness, inasmuch as He said in the Gospel, "did I not choose you the twelve, and one of you is a devil" (John 6:70)? Ask Him why He chose Judas, a traitor? Why He entrusted to him the bag when He knew that he was a thief? Shall I tell you the reason? God does not make use of His foreknowledge to condemn a man though He knows that he will hereafter displease Him; but such is His goodness and unspeakable mercy that He chooses a man who, He perceives, will meanwhile be good, and who, He knows, will turn out badly, thus giving him the opportunity of being converted and of repenting. This is the Apostle's meaning when he says, "do you not know that the goodness of God leads you to repentance? But after your hardness and impenitent heart you save up for yourself wrath on the day of wrath and revelation of the righteous judgment of God, Who will render to every man according to his works" (Rom 2:4–5). For Adam did not sin because God knew that he would do so; but God, inasmuch as He is God, foreknew what Adam would do of his own free choice.⁶⁷

This paragraph is the only discussion of foreknowledge and predestination in Jerome's writings against the Pelagians, which demonstrates that this question is not pressing in Jerome's mind.

65. Jerome, *Dial.* 3.19.
66. Augustine, *Pecc. merit.* 1.9.9.
67. Jerome, *Dial.* 3.6.

Baptism

Yet another issue that was brought to Jerome's attention only through his reading of Augustine's texts was the row over baptism.[68] In his own contribution to the debate in Book III, Jerome claimed that Pelagius, on this point, was a disciple of Jovinian—going as far as branding him as "Jovinian's heir"[69]—because Jerome saw a connection between the Pelagian claim of the possibility of sinlessness and Jovinian's argument that baptism prevents the baptized from being overthrown by the devil,[70] and even not able to be tempted by the devil.[71] Jerome's refutation of Jovinian, as sometimes was the case with him, was to offer an avalanche of biblical quotations to disprove his opponent.[72] For example, Jerome said that Christians beg God to "forgive us our debts, as we forgive our debtors; and lead us not into temptation, but deliver us from the evil one" (Matt 6:12). "Why do we pray that we may not enter into temptation," Jerome rhetorically asks Jovinian, "and that we may be delivered from the evil one, if the devil cannot tempt those who are baptized?"[73] While Jerome's observation of the connection between Origen and Pelagius concerning sinlessness was astute, Jerome has missed the mark entirely here. There is no suggestion from any of the extant sources from the Pelagians, nor any quotations from them found in the writings of their opponents, to indicate that they believed that baptism preserved the baptized from future transgressions. Every indication we have signals that the Pelagians believed that sinlessness is possible through the movement of the free will, and through the grace of God (as they defined it), not through the effects of baptism.

In Book III of his *Dialogi*, he defended the church's practice of baptizing babies, and had already come to the conclusion of the necessity of baptizing babies over a decade prior to the Pelagian controversy. Laeta, the daughter-in-law of Paula, had written to Jerome asking him for a program of education for her young daughter, also named Paula.[74] In his response to her written around 401/402, we see him insist on the necessity of baptism as it "ensures the salvation of the child."[75] He instructed Laeta to send Paula to Bethlehem for proper formation to become a consecrated virgin, because (clearly still bitter about his exile from Rome) there was no way that Paula would be able to develop into a virtuous young woman amid the corruption of the city. "Let her be brought up in a monastery," Jerome pleads, "let her be one amid companies

---

68. Ferguson, *Pelagius*, 79; Jeanjean, "Le *dialogus*," 61.

69. Jerome, *Dial.* 2.24. See also: *Epist.* 133. 3; *Dial.* 3.15; *In Hier.* 22:24–27.

70. Jerome, *Jov.* 1.3.

71. Jerome, *Jov.* 2.1.

72. This style of argumentation can also be seen, for example in his second book of his *Dialogi contra Pelagianos*, which is almost entirely a list of biblical quotations.

73. Jerome, *Jov.* 2.3.

74. Cavallera, "Saint Jérome," 118.

75. Jerome, *Epist.* 107.6. It is very possible that Jerome's understanding on infant baptism was heavily influenced by Origen. See Origen, *Comm. Rom.* 5.9.

of virgins, let her learn to avoid swearing, let her regard lying as sacrilege, let her be ignorant of the world, let her live the angelic life, while in the flesh let her be without the flesh, and let her suppose that all human beings are like herself."[76]

Against the Pelagians, Jerome said that baptism, of course, washes away personal sins, and if we could spend our lives immersed in the baptismal waters, we might be able to claim to be sinless; but, such an existence is impossible.[77] Even someone who dies immediately after being baptized—or who dies on the same day after being baptized—cannot justly claim to live a sinless life because, although freed from sin by the regenerative waters, the purity of the soul in this case must be attributed to the Holy Spirit, not through the movement of the will of the baptized.[78] Jerome similarly acknowledges the sinlessness of infants who have been baptized: "I will allow it," he admits, "if they have been baptized into Christ; and if you [Critobulus] will not then immediately bind me to agree with your opinion that a man can be without sin if he chooses; for they neither have the power nor the will; but they are free from all sin through the grace of God, which they received in their baptism."[79] Here, again, seems to be another indication that, although Jerome is closer to Augustine than he is to Pelagius on the question of transmission of sin to babies, he cannot bring himself to go as far as Augustine in claiming that babies are always plagued by original sin.

Free Will and Grace

Two Pelagian themes of interest to Jerome—both before and after he read the texts Orosius brought to him—were free will and grace, which he almost always discussed together as he saw them as inseparably intertwined. Jerome rejected the narrow Pelagian definition of grace as the gift of our free will and the commandments of the law given by God to show us how to live our lives.[80] He makes no reference, however, to the part of the Pelagian definition of grace as Christ as an exemplar for how to live sinless lives. It seems he was not aware of this, or he did not find it as troublesome as did Augustine. In his response, Jerome held together free will and grace at the same time, although he never investigated in detail the tension created in holding them together, or exactly how they relate to each other.

Jerome, like all Christians, believed in the existence of the free will.[81] He showed no interest, though, in discussing the effects of sin on the free will, as Augustine obsessively would do throughout this controversy with his insistence on original sin. Does Jerome believe that the free will is inhibited or tarnished in some way by the "ancient

76. Jerome, *Epist.* 107.13.
77. Jerome, *Dial.* 3.1.
78. Jerome, *Dial.* 3.2.
79. Jerome, *Dial.* 3.17.
80. Jerome, *Epist.* 133.5; *Dial.* 1.1–6; *In Hier.* 25:3.
81. Jerome, *Epist.* 133.6, 10. *Dial.* 3.5.

forefather Adam."[82] If so, how? He seems to give the will more agency than Augustine would allow, saying that "to will and to run are mine, but they will cease to be mine unless God brings me His continual aid."[83] At the same time, Jerome could not agree with the Pelagian understanding of the will as it calls into question the necessity of God's assistance, which would lead the Christian faithful to cease turning to God in prayer.[84] His lack of interest in the finer details of the agency of the free will is disappointing, but he was never as theologically probing as many of his contemporaries, such as the Cappadocians or Augustine, as his intellectual gifts leaned more towards translation and biblical commentary.[85]

Like his discussion of free will, Jerome's discussion of grace (*gratia, auxilium, adiutorium*),[86] lacked nuance and precision. Evans even went as far as stating that Jerome "had neither a very clear nor an interesting doctrine of grace with which to oppose Pelagius."[87] Grace, according to Jerome, is necessary for the life of the Christian, but he did not explain exactly how he understood it. He said that it is a help that must continually accompany the will moment by moment in each action.[88] But, he does not offer a more descriptive definition than this. This understanding of grace seems to lean more towards Augustine than it does towards the Pelagians, but an aspect of Jerome's conception of grace would make Augustine nervous. He believed that grace is not simply something that is given freely, but it must be pursued by the individual. God, of course, gives his grace freely, but, at the same time, "if God's grace is limited to this that he formed us with our own wills, and if we are to rest content with free will, not seeking (*petere*) the divine aid lest this should be impaired, we should cease to pray; for we cannot entreat God's mercy to give us daily what is already in our hands having been given to us once for all."[89] It is the responsibility of the individual sinner to pursue God's grace, and not to passively wait for God to bestow it.

---

82. Jerome, *Dial.* 3.18.
83. Jerome, *Epist.* 133.6. See also: *Dial.* 1.5.
84. Jerome, *Epist.* 133.5–10.
85. Ferguson, *Pelagius*, 77; Clark, *Origenist Controversy*, 221.
86. Jerome, *Epist.* 133.5–6, 8; *Dial.* 1. 5.
87. Evans, *Inquiries and Reappraisals*, 7.
88. Jerome, *Epist.* 133.5–6, 10; *Dial.* 1.5; *In Hier.* 25:3.
89. Jerome, *Epist.* 133.5–6.

Chapter 15

The Theology of Orosius

The Theological Vision of Orosius

WE DIVIDED THE THEOLOGICAL analyses in our earlier chapters on Pelagius, Caelestius, Augustine and Jerome into subsections—such as sinlessness, free will, and grace—to approach the thought of each man in an orderly way. This will not be possible with Orosius, because he did not write extensively enough to do so, because writing a comprehensive response to the Pelagians was not his goal.[1] When Orosius responded to the anthropologies of Pelagius and Caelestius, he spent more time critiquing their systems than he did offering one of his own. This is most likely because he was not a theologian of the same caliber as his contemporaries.

Sinlessness was, without question, the most important of all the anthropological issues for Orosius. It was the only one he brought up at the *conventum* in Jerusalem, and he spent more time discussing it in his *Liber apologeticus* than any other. In addition to arguing that the Council of Carthage of 411, Augustine, and Jerome all had condemned sinlessness (and the accompanying claim that the commandments of God easily may be kept),[2] he criticized Pelagius for not writing about the necessity of God's assistance in his *Liber testimoniorum*, despite having verbally affirmed it at the *conventum*.[3] He also refuted the Pelagian claim that Job—who was "a man without blame" and "truthful" (Job 1:8), and that Zechariah who was "without reproach" (Luke 1:6)—were in anyway sinless. He interprets these three descriptions of these men to mean that Job and Zechariah were just and without blame in the eyes of other human beings by the standards of this life, but that does not mean that they were without reproach in the eyes of God.[4] He also accused Pelagius of being "the harbinger of the coming of the Antichrist," for stating that he himself was sinless,[5] which was an odd accusation because there is no indication in any of Pelagius's writings that he ever said such a thing, and Augustine reported

---

1. Orosius, *Lib. apol.* 12.
2. Orosius, *Lib. apol.* 4, 11.
3. Orosius, *Lib. apol.* 11.
4. Orosius, *Lib. apol.* 21. It should be noted that Orosius did not make any reference to other biblical figures discussed in earlier chapters whom the Pelagians claimed were sinless.
5. Orosius, *Lib. apol.* 16.

that Pelagius explicitly said that he was not sinless.[6] Only Christ was sinless, Orosius affirmed.[7] The rest of humanity cannot avoid sin because God alone has the power to forgive sins: "I have had it within my power to sin; I do not have it in my power to be freed from sin. To offer prayer is up to me; to be absolved is not up to me."[8] Even if we were to refrain from sinful actions, our thoughts are forever plagued by sin. Tempering his own argument, however, he did mention in passing that it is possible to be sinless for a short period. But this allowance does not take away from his larger insistence that it is impossible to live an entire life without sin.[9]

Orosius responded to the Pelagian claim that he and his allies believe that human nature is evil by saying that nature is good because it is created by God, but, he does admit, that it is weak (*infirma*). If human nature were evil, then it would not be able to do good at all. But, we all desire (*concupiscere*) and cling (*adhaerere*) to the good, while avoiding (*fugere*) evil, which proves the goodness of our nature.[10] Pelagius's followers, he continued, have "sucked forth vast amounts of poison from your [Pelagius's] breast"[11] when they have imbibed his belief that humanity was originally created mortal,[12] and that no ontological change transformed humanity after the first sin of Adam and Eve. But, Orosius said, the earth has been cursed because of their transgression, and humanity is subject to labor, suffering, and to death until returning to the dust. The descendants of Adam and Eve, furthermore, "still carry with them the original sin (*originale peccatum*) of their unfaithful progenitor."[13] It is because of this first sin that has been passed down that humanity continues to sin, not because of imitation of Adam and Eve. God, he was quick to remind Pelagius, regretted ever having created humanity (Gen 6:6).

Like Jerome and Augustine, Orosius rejected the narrow Pelagian definition of grace as nature and free choice, though he did not discuss the law or the example of Christ as gifts that were also central to the Pelagian conception of grace.[14] Grace

6. Augustine, *Nat. grat.* 13.14.
7. Orosius, *Lib. apol.* 12, 17.
8. Orosius, *Lib. apol.* 13.
9. Orosius, *Lib. apol.* 13.
10. Orosius, *Lib. apol.* 29.
11. Orosius, *Lib. apol.* 26.

12. It is unclear why Orosius would say that Pelagius taught that Adam was created mortal because, as we have already seen, Pelagius condemned this idea as heresy at the Synod of Diospolis when the charge leveled against Caelestius at the Council of Carthage of 411 was leveled against him. Caelestius at that Council did not refute the charge, but neither did he admit teaching it. We also saw that the unknown author of the *Liber* said that Adam and Eve would not have died had they not sinned. Augustine, *Gest Pelag.* 11.24; Rufinus the Presbyter, *Lib. fid.* 29.

13. Orosius, *Lib. apol.* 26. In his *Historiae*, Orosius makes a passing reference to the corruption of humanity: "but I have decided to trace the beginning of men's misery from man's original sin *(ab initio peccantis hominis)*. *C. pag.* 1.1.4. See also: 1.3.1, 2.1.1.

14. Orosius also mentions in passing the grace of baptism, although he does not explore in detail baptism or the grace received through it. He says "truly to be able to be without sin, for someone

(*gratia, adiutorium*), for him, was given by God to the corporate body of Christ, the church, because of the faith of all believers, and given to each person individually.[15] More specifically, he insisted that grace is infused by God throughout the entire life of the believer: "it is the case that God supplies it [grace] specially to all and each individually, in season and out, on every day, at every minute, and in every smallest moment of time."[16] This assistance is even present in our most vulnerable moments when the devil (*seductor*) tempts the faithful.[17]

Orosius said very little about free will, as it obviously was secondary to grace for him. Even when he talked about the free will, it was always in relation to grace. He quoted Paul saying that "by his [God's] grace I am what I am, and his grace has not been lacking in me. On the contrary, I have worked more abundantly than all of them; not I, however, but the grace of God with me" (1 Cor 5:10). Calling him an "imprudent and presumptuous man,"[18] Orosius insisted that Pelagius did not understand that Paul's "not I" and "with me" point away from the will to the grace of God. Even though we have been given a will because we are created in the image and likeness of God, "there operates in the will of a human being the grace of divine virtue which has given him that very will."[19] In other words, even in the action of the will itself, when it chooses the good, can be found the indwelling of grace because God has given to us our wills. But, a truly free will is not found in doing whatever we want, he says. On the contrary, it is only found in giving oneself over to God. "Let each of us," he declares, "offer himself to God as volunteered land (*terra voluntaria*), because this alone results in free will and in this alone free will can go forward."[20] Once again turning to Paul ("for we are God's husbandry; we are God's edifice") (1 Cor 3:9), Orosius shows that the free will is in service to grace by preserving the seed of the Word planted in us by God, and must allow that seed to grow on its own accord. When we take credit for the fruits that develop from the seed, we will be punished by being cut down and cast into the fire (Matt 3:10).[21]

---

who has sinned at one time or another, is impossible without the sole grace of baptism, when, in conformity with the person of the Lord, it is started, 'your sins are forgiven you.' I am urged to believe this because I am allowed to hear, 'I am able, therefore, to be without sin.' I do not embrace this, I do not presume it, nor do I venture to say this, at least in this corrupt state in which we live." Orosius, however, does not discuss the washing away the guilt of original sin by baptism, nor does he discuss infant baptism. Orosius, *Lib. apol.* 13.

15. Orosius, *Lib. apol.* 19–21.
16. Orosius, *Lib. apol.* 19.
17. Orosius, *Lib. apol.* 21.
18. Orosius, *Lib. apol.* 10.
19. Orosius, *Lib. apol.* 10.
20. Orosius, *Lib. apol.* 33.
21. Orosius, *Lib. apol.* 33.

The Influences of Augustine and Jerome on Orosius

Orosius had the rare distinction of personally knowing two giants of the Christian intellectual tradition. This fact invites us to investigate the different ways that Augustine and Jerome had influenced him. Most scholars have detected much more of an influence from Augustine, and largely have ignored Jerome's influence. Otto Bardenhewer, for example, listed Orosius in a subsection titled the "Friends and Disciples of St. Augustine" in a chapter of his *Patrology*.[22] More recently, Van Nuffelen has said that "although he also visited Jerome, it is mainly Augustine with whom Orosius was involved."[23] The scholarly focus on Augustine's influence is most likely due to Orosius's excessive flattery of Augustine in his *Historiae*, which was never duplicated to the same degree for Jerome.[24] I believe, however, that Jerome was equally as influential as Augustine on the ways that Orosius conceived of and attacked the Pelagians.

Several of Orosius's arguments were undoubtedly inspired by Augustine. First, Orosius saw a root of the Pelagian threat originating in the newness of their teachings. In his *Liber apologeticus*, Orosius accused Pelagius of being a "new teacher" (*novus magister*)[25] because he insisted on the possibility of living a sinless life, and later in the same text he repeated this accusation when he called Pelagius a "teacher of new doctrines" (*instructor novorum dogmatum*).[26] Like Augustine, Orosius was suspicious of new theological doctrines because, if they were true, they would have been taught by the church from the beginning. As the Pelagians cannot trace their teachings back to the apostles, they must be deviant. Second, although Jerome was closer to Augustine than Pelagius on the issue of the transmission of sin, we saw in an earlier chapter that he did not fully embrace Augustine's original sin. Orosius did adopt this central Augustinian tenet. Although he only mentioned it a few times, it clearly was a central piece of his understanding of the human person.[27] Third, Orosius seems to have been influenced by Augustine's definition of grace. He insisted that grace must be infused by God in every moment of our lives, as had both Augustine and Jerome.[28] But, as we saw in an earlier chapter, Jerome's discussion of grace lacked nuance and precision compared to the meticulous and clearly crafted definition put forward by Augustine. It is likely that Augustine's thought on grace had more of an effect on Orosius than had Jerome's.[29]

22. Bardenhewer, *Patrology*, 510–11.
23. Van Nuffelen, *Orosius*, 3.
24. Orosius, *C. pag.* 1.pref.1–16, 7.43.19–20.
25. Orosius, *Lib. apol.* 12.
26. Orosius, *Lib. apol.* 24.
27. Orosius, *Lib. apol.* 26; *C. pag.* 1.1.4, 1.3.1, 2.1.1.
28. Orosius, *Lib. apol.* 19; Evans, *Inquiries and Reappraisals*, 7.
29. While Augustine influenced Orosius, Orosius may have influenced Augustine as well. Orosius placed much of the blame for his problems at the *conventum* on a language barrier between the Latin speakers and the Greek speakers, and on an incompetent translator. Augustine, too, had placed much

Several key points are worth reviewing from Jerome's influence on Orosius. First, like Jerome, Orosius saw the Pelagian argument for the possibility of living a sinless life as the most important mistake.[30] Augustine's concern with the Pelagian definition of grace shaped Orosius's thinking, but Orosius never seemed to be as anxious about it as he was about sinlessness.

Second, Orosius used the same two Greek terms *anamartetos* and *apatheia* that Jerome used in his attempt to connect the Pelagian definition of sinlessness with Stoic roots, and thereby show the corruption of Christianity ushered in by the Pelagians. Orosius said of Pelagius that "my 'fellow without sin' claims that the achievement of a pure life can come to him as he is eating, drinking, and sleeping" (*et anamartetos* (ἀναμάρτητος) *meus venire sibi posse perfectionem vitae immaculatae manducanti, bibenti, dormientique, confrimat*)![31] Later in the same section, he said of Pelagius that "our 'untroubled man' has obviously conquered his temptations, so it seems to him, as well as the agent of the temptations, and he believes that he cannot be tempted or disturbed thereafter (*et apathes* (ἀπαθής) *noster, victis sane, ut sibi videtur, cum auctore tentationibus, non posse se ultra tenari perturbarique confidit*)."[32] It is beyond a doubt that Jerome's presence can be felt here because there is no indication that Orosius knew any Greek prior to his arrival in Palestine, and a translator was employed at the *conventum* for the benefit of both the bishops and Orosius. As Orosius only remained in Palestine for about one year, he would not have enough time to learn such sophisticated philosophical vocabulary without the help of Jerome.[33]

Third, we saw that Orosius briefly mentioned that, at times, a sinless life can be realized, although it is impossible to remain sinless forever.[34] Earlier, we saw that Jerome also said that sinlessness is possible for a short time, though it is not possible to sustain indefinitely.[35]

Fourth, although Orosius had repeated Augustine's attack on the Pelagians as teachers of a new theology, he also adopted Jerome's argument that the Pelagians had resurrected errors of the past by claiming that Pelagian roots can be traced to the

---

of the blame of the failure of the bishops at the Synod of Diospolis to condemn Pelagius on a language barrier between Pelagius and the bishops, although he did not disparage the translator. Although it may be possible that both men independently came to the same conclusion that the central problem in both cases was language and translation, it is much more likely that when Orosius returned to Africa from Palestine that he told Augustine about the *conventum* that may have influenced Augustine's assessment of Diospolis.

30. The direct influence can probably be traced to Orosius's reading of Jerome's letter to Ctesiphon (133). Orosius, *Lib. apol.* 11.

31. Orosius, *Lib. apol.* 16.

32. Orosius, *Lib. apol.* 16.

33. The *PL* uses the Greek ἀπαθής and ἀναμάρτητος rather than the Latin transliteration. It is unclear if Orosius used the Greek alphabet in his original text.

34. Orosius, *Lib. apol.* 13.

35. Jerome, *Dial.* 3.12.

errors of Origen, Jovinian, and the Priscillianists.[36] During the *conventum*, for example, John of Jerusalem quoted two passages from Genesis and Luke that he believed hinted at the sinlessness of Abraham, Zechariah, and Elizabeth to get Orosius to make a formal charge against Pelagius.[37] Orosius noted that both examples cited by John had been used earlier by Origen in his argument for the possibility of sinlessness.[38] Orosius undoubtedly knew this from his association with Jerome, because Jerome was Orosius's instructor in all things concerning Origen.

---

36. Orosius, *Lib. apol.* 1, 25.

37. John quoted "walk before me and be without sin" (Gen 17:1) to demonstrate Abraham's sinlessness, and "both righteous before the Lord, walking in all of the just commandments the Lord without blame" (Luke 1:6) to demonstrate the sinlessness of Zechariah and Elizabeth.

38. Orosius, *Lib. apol.* 5.

Chapter 16

The Theology of Julian of Eclanum

Julian's Critique of Augustine as a Manichaean

JULIAN'S THEOLOGY AS A whole is in harmony with his Pelagian contemporaries.[1] Indeed, it is surprising how closely his thought resembles that of Pelagius and Caelestius considering how little direct knowledge he had of their writings. There are no significant differences between these three men about their rejection of original sin,[2] their vision of the free will,[3] their belief that a sinless life is possible,[4] their conviction of the importance of baptism for children and adults,[5] and how they defended grace in the life of the Christian.[6] A deep investigation into Julian's thought on these topics, therefore, would be moot.[7] Julian's contribution to the Pelagian controversy is not in repeating (with slight modifications) the same themes of his Pelagian predecessors that, at that point, had been contested for almost a decade. Rather, his involvement took this fight in altogether new directions.[8]

Augustine's past came back to haunt him, because Julian's general criticism of Augustine—from which all of his more specific criticisms flowed—was that Augustine's anthropology is entirely Manichaean.[9] Having read Augustine's *Confessiones*, Julian knew that Augustine had been an *auditor* for nine years, and, after acquainting himself more thoroughly with Augustine's anti-Pelagian writings, he came to the conclusion that Augustine never entirely left Manichaeism behind.[10] "Between you and Mani," Julian reproached Augustine "there is no disagreement about the character

---

1. Bonner, *Augustine*, 3.
2. Augustine, *C. Jul. op. imp.* 2.29–115.
3. Augustine, *C. Jul. op. imp.* 1.78–94.
4. Augustine, *C. Jul. op. imp.* 1.78, 1.99–100.
5. Augustine, *C. Jul. op. imp.* 1.53–58, 1.95–98.
6. Augustine, *C. Jul. op. imp.* 3.114–119.
7. The important exceptions to this are his views on marriage and sex. Julian has a more positive opinion of them than did Pelagius, as we shall see. His view of marriage and sex was even more starkly contrasted by the views of marriage and sex of the Anonymous Sicilian.
8. Lamberigts, "Recent Research," 193.
9. Beatrice, "Pelagian Critique," 34.
10. Augustine, *C. Jul. op. imp.* 1.25.

of our [human] nature, but only about its author. For you attribute this evil to God whom you admit is the creator of little ones, while Mani attributes it to the prince of darkness who he thought is the creator of human nature."[11]

A few hints from Julian point to the Manichaean and anti-Manichaean sources that were available to him. It is possible that Julian had read some, or even all, of Augustine's anti-Manichaean works, because years earlier Augustine had sent them to their mutual friend Paulinus of Nola. However, Julian only explicitly quotes Augustine's anti-Manichaean *De duabus animabus* that he had written in 392 or 393 while still a presbyter. Of course, Julian would have learned much about the Manichaeans from reading Augustine's *Confessiones*, even though it is not considered to be one of Augustine's anti-Manichean works. In particular, Julian made sure to let Augustine know that he was aware that the Manichaean Faustus had been his teacher, a reminder that undoubtedly would not have made the bishop of Hippo pleased. As we have already seen, Julian had visited Carthage and met Augustine's childhood friend Honoratus, and must have learned more about Manichaeism from that exchange. Furthermore, Julian was acquainted with the *Adversus Manichaeos* from Serapion of Thmuis—an Egyptian monk and later bishop of Thmuis—although Julian had misattributed it to Basil of Caesarea. Finally, Julian was in possession of the Manichaean *Epistula ad Menoch*, which had been sent to him from his friend Florus, and had obtained a copy of Mani's *Epistula ad Patricium*.[12]

All of these sources together gave Julian a basic understanding of Manichaeism, although he never had a sophisticated grasp of the intricacies of Manichaean thought, practice, or history.[13] He was aware of the basics of the Manichaean origin story,[14] the ritual observance of the *electi* eating fruit to release the elements of God imprisoned inside,[15] the Manichaean understanding of the soul,[16] their belief in the transmission of souls,[17] that the devil (through the trap of *concupiscentia*) becomes the author of bodies,[18] and that humanity fell from an original pristine condition.[19] He comprehended the Manichaean cosmology in its fundamental components: the God of Light had fought the Prince of Darkness, but sacrificed his members so as not to lose his

---

11. I have slightly changed the translation from "God who you admit" to "God whom you admit." Augustine, *C. Jul. op. imp.* 3.154.

12. Augustine, *C. Jul.* 1.5.16–17; *C. Jul. op. imp.* 1.25, 1.44, 3.166, 3.172, 3.186, 5.26, 6.6; Paulinus of Nola, *Epp.* 4.5, 6.2; Bruckner, *Julian*, 395; Evans, "Neither a Pelagian," 242 n. 4; Clark, "Vitiated Seeds," 390; Lamberigts, "Was Augustine?," 114–16.

13. Rackett, "Sexuality and Sinlessness," 202; Lamberigts, "Was Augustine?," 119, 135.

14. Augustine, *C. Jul.* 6.68; *C. Jul op. imp.* 1.49.

15. Augustine, *C. Jul op. imp.* 6.20–23.

16. Augustine, *C. Jul op. imp.* 3.166.

17. Augustine, *C. Jul op. imp.* 3.173–4.

18. Augustine, *C. Jul op. imp.* 3.174–5, 6.5–6.

19. Augustine, *C. Jul op. imp.* 3.186.

kingdom.[20] Adam, the "one formed as if from the flower of the first substance," was better than his descendants,[21] but he still was naturally evil.[22] Julian also knew that the Manichaeans excluded the Mosaic law,[23] read only parts of the New Testament,[24] and embraced a muddled Christology that was similar to the Docetists,[25] but also claimed that Jesus had flesh, albeit separated from the flesh of humanity.[26]

This principal accusation of latent Manichaeism led to three connected themes in Julian's assault on Augustine. First, the Manichaean belief in the evil nature of bodies led to the conviction that humans sin out of necessity, giving rise to a rejection of the free will that results in a type of fatalism. Julian sensed a similar fatalism in Augustine's teaching on original sin. How can we truly act freely if we are burdened with the weight of someone else's sin, he asked? Second, Julian perceived no important distinction between Augustine's teaching on original sin and the Manichaean teaching on "evil nature" (*malum naturale*).[27] There is no practical difference between saying humans are created evil, as do the Manichaeans, and saying that humans are born guilty of Adam's transgression, as does Augustine.[28] Third, Julian heard echoes in Augustine of the Manichaean rejection of marriage, sexual desire, and propagation. If bodies are evil, as he believed both the Manichaeans and Augustine taught, then Augustine, like the Manichaeans, must preach the evils of matrimony and the procreative act.[29] As we have already explored the Pelagian emphasis on the unburdened free will, and their rejection of Augustine's original sin, we will focus here on sexual desire, marriage, and procreation.

Concupiscentia

One of the new contributions to the Pelagian controversy from Julian was his attack on Augustine's understanding of *concupiscentia*, and his own championing of it. Julian was convinced that Augustine, like Mani, taught that *concupiscentia* was evil. Julian asked: "What does Mani say? 'through concupiscence the devil is the author of bodies; through it the devil entraps bodies, not souls. Remove . . . the root of the evil tree and you will become spiritual' . . . You see, then, the great agreement that exists between

---

20. Augustine, *C. Jul op. imp.* 1.49.
21. Augustine, *C. Jul op. imp.* 3.186.
22. Augustine, *C. Jul op. imp.* 6.8.
23. Augustine, *C. Jul op. imp.* 3.34.
24. Augustine, *C. Jul op. imp.* 1.25.
25. Augustine, *C. Jul op. imp.* 4.50, 4.58, 4.81.
26. Augustine, *C. Jul op. imp.* 6.33. Clark, "Vitiated Seeds," 390–91; Lamberigts, "Was Augustine?," 117–20.
27. Augustine, *C. Jul. op. imp.* 1.24.
28. Augustine, *C. Jul. op. imp.* 1.98.
29. Rackett, "Sexuality and Sinlessness," 232–35.

you [Augustine] and Mani in your attack on us. You fight with his words; you rely on his arguments, and you call us liars when we say that you not only were, as you yourself write, but are even now his disciple."[30] For Julian, *concupiscentia*, the "fire of life"[31] and the "servant of marital goodness,"[32] is good, first of all and most importantly because it comes from God, who created it as the natural and necessary[33] precondition for procreation.[34] God created the natural sexual drive and placed it in Adam and Eve from the beginning,[35] which is why they did not view their naked bodies as shameful.[36] Even after their sin—which Julian, like the other Pelagians, claimed did not have any substantial effects on either them or their offspring—*concupiscentia* did not change, nor become disordered in any way.[37] The *concupiscentia* that led to the sexual activity by which Cain and Abel were generated was the same as if they had been conceived either prior to the sin of Adam and Eve, or if they had never sinned at all.

This is not to say, however, that because *concupiscentia* is good that it may be indulged in unrestrictedly. God has set limits on it.[38] Specifically, sexual desire only may be considered good when it is employed moderately within marriage; or, if the individual is a virgin,[39] it must be chastely regulated.[40] When *concupiscentia* is made use of within marriage, it also is to be praised and honored because it leads to the offspring that was declared good by God's command to be "fruitful and multiply" (Gen 1:28).[41] This restriction is possible because the soul entirely governs the body[42] so that the mind and the will are able to control *concupiscentia* virtuously, and not become blameworthy.[43] *Concupiscentia* becomes blameworthy, he said, when it becomes evil, which he only vaguely defined as excessive.[44]

Julian argued that the goodness of *concupiscentia* is also witnessed in the rest of God's creation. Plants—and especially animals—experience the same sexual drive as human beings. "At that time [when *concupiscentia* is experienced]," he said, "the wild boar is savage; at that time the tiger is worst. Above all the frenzy of mares is remarkable. In the spring the plants swell; in the spring the abundance of fresh sap flows. And

30. Augustine, *C. Jul. op. imp.* 3.180.
31. Augustine, *C. Jul.* 3.13.26–27.
32. Augustine, *C. Jul.* 4.2.7.
33. Augustine, *Nupt.* 2.7.17; *C. Jul. op. imp.* 5.46; Lamberigts, "Competing Christologies," 167.
34. Augustine, *C. Jul.* 4.13.63; *C. Jul. op. imp.* 3.212, 4.29, 4.40, 5.5; Barclift, "In Controversy," 8–12.
35. Augustine, *C. Jul. op. imp.* 1.71, 4.26.
36. Augustine, *C. Jul.* 5.2.6.
37. Augustine, *C. Jul. op. imp.* 5.8.
38. Augustine, *C. Jul.* 3.14.28, 4.8.52; *C. Jul. op. imp.* 4.41.
39. Augustine, *C. Jul.* 5.16.61.
40. Augustine, *C. Jul.* 3.14.28, 5.7.30; *C. Jul. op. imp.* 4.61.
41. Augustine, *Nupt.* 2.19.34, 2.23.38, 5.4.16; *C. Jul.* 5.4.16, 5.16.60.
42. Augustine, *C. Jul.* 4.4.10, 6.10.30.
43. Augustine, *C. Jul.* 5.9.39, 5.16.61.
44. Augustine, *C. Jul.* 3.13.27–14.28, 4.2.7; *C. Jul. op. imp.* 5.19.

the farm animals seek to mate on certain days."[45] If *concupiscentia* were a disordered desire that is experienced by humans as a result of the sin of the first parents, why, Julian wondered, do plants and animals possess the same drive? Plants and animals, of course, do not sin; the existence of *concupiscentia* in them must point to God as the creator of bodies, and as intentionally having given the desire to all living creation.[46]

This praise of *concupiscentia* led to one of the most bizarre exchanges in the history of Christian theology: a debate over whether Christ experienced it or not. Julian insisted that Christ did experience it, because it is part of human nature, and, as the Logos assumed everything that is human, Jesus did not lack it.[47] Moreover, he accused Augustine of being an Apollinarian because Augustine, Julian claimed, did not believe that Christ experienced it, and that Christ lacked senses of the body.[48] Julian understood Apollinaris to have "first introduced such an incarnation of Christ that he said that he assumed from the human substance only the body, while the deity itself took the place of the soul, and that Christ was thought to have assumed, not a human being, but a cadaver."[49] When Apollinaris was denounced for holding a Christology that reflected a deficient human nature, he, according to Julian, "thought up something else which might give birth to his heresy, which lasts up to the present, and he said that there was indeed a human soul in Christ, but that he did not have the senses of the body, and he declared that he was unable to suffer any sins."[50] Augustine rightly was baffled by this claim, because there is no indication that Apollinaris ever said that Jesus lacked senses of the body.[51]

Although it is difficult to construct a precise picture of his Christology from the extant sources,[52] Apollinaris asserted that the Logos assumed only the human flesh (*sarx*), but not the human mind (*nous*).[53] This meant that the man Jesus was controlled by only one governing divine power, the Logos, not a human power.[54] This conception of Christ led Apollinaris to conclude that Jesus only had one nature (*mia physis*), not two natures (*duo physeis*), because he was concerned that any claim to two natures would divide the unity of Christ. Just as God himself is one, as declared by the Council of Nicaea, so, too, Christ must be.[55] This one nature was neither fully human nor

---

45. Augustine, *C. Jul.* 4.38.
46. Augustine, *C. Jul.* 2.122, 4.38.
47. Augustine, *C. Jul.* 4.45, 4.59, 4.82; Lamberigts, "Competing Christologies," 168.
48. Augustine, *C. Jul. op. imp.* 4.46.
49. Augustine, *C. Jul. op. imp.* 4.47.
50. Augustine, *C. Jul. op. imp.* 4.47. See also 4.48–49.
51. Augustine, *C. Jul. op. imp.* 4.47–49.
52. Young, *From Nicaea*, 246.
53. Grillmeier, *Christ*, 331–39; Davis, *First Seven*, 104–5; Young, *From Nicaea*, 246–49.
54. Meyendorff, *Christ*, 15–20.
55. Grillmeier, *Christ*, 334.

fully divine, but is the meditator, that is the mean, between God and man.[56] "Middle-beings," Apollinaris said, "are formed when different properties are combined in one thing, for example the properties of an ass and a horse in a mule and the properties of white and black . . . in the colour grey; but no middle-being contains the two extremes in full measure—they are there only in part. Now in Christ there is a middle-being of God and man; therefore he is neither fully man nor God (alone), but a mixture of God and man."[57] This "mixed" Christology, though well intentioned to preserve the unity of Christ, led to Apollinaris's condemnation in 377 by Pope Damasus at a synod in Rome, in 379 he was again condemned by a synod at Antioch, and in 381 he was condemned by the Council of Constantinople.[58]

Augustine's Christ, Julian claimed, was a eunuch, because he lacked a fully masculine nature, and therefore lacked something essential to being human, which is why Julian was so eager to equate Augustine with Apollinaris.[59] Julian was not embarrassed to say that Jesus had sex organs;[60] for, although Jesus had genitals, he did not use them, but if he did not have them, again, he would not have been fully human. Although Jesus both experienced *concupiscentia* and had sex organs, he was a model of chastity for everyone to imitate.[61] He "guarded both his mind and his eyes,"[62] Julian said, never relaxing or relenting to those natural desires. It was through the power of his mind that he ruled himself.[63] But, it should never be believed that Jesus's chastity condemned the bodily senses or organs, just as his chastity never condemned marriage.[64]

Sex and Marriage

Julian's thought on sex mirrors his thought on *concupiscentia*. Like *concupiscentia*, sex is good. He viewed Augustine's teaching on sex to be an "invention of the devil,"[65] because the fruit of sex in Augustine's mind is a progeny that is corrupted from the beginning. What else, Julian asked, could be a clearer indication that Augustine persists as a Manichaean? But, for him, because the infant that comes from the sexual act is thoroughly good, the act itself must be good. For, a good fruit—a body—cannot come from an evil

---

56. Young, *From Nicaea*, 251.
57. As translated in Grillmeier, *Christ*, 332.
58. Davis, *First Seven*, 104. Young claims that Apollinaris's condemnation at Constantinople was "in somewhat ambiguous terms." Young, *From Nicaea*, 253.
59. Augustine, *C. Jul. op. imp.* 4.52.
60. Augustine, *C. Jul. op. imp.* 4.54.
61. Augustine, *C. Jul. op. imp.* 4.57.
62. Augustine, *C. Jul. op. imp.* 4.53.
63. Augustine, *C. Jul. op. imp.* 4.53.
64. Augustine, *C. Jul. op. imp.* 4.58.
65. Augustine, *C. du. ep. Pelag.* 1.5.10.

act.[66] More specifically, Julian said that the genitals and the movement of the genitals were instituted by God.[67] God demonstrated the goodness of the genitals by not hiding them when he created Adam and Eve (Gen 2:25),[68] and Adam's ability to be aroused even before his sin further confirms this goodness.[69] Adam's genitals, and the genitals of all men down through the ages afterwards, do not move in rebellion against the soul, but are entirely under the control of the mind and the will, unless illness or "lack of control"[70] (presumably by age) inhibit the governance by the soul.[71]

Julian also rejected the idea that the pain of childbirth is a punishment for the sinfulness of sex. This pain, he insisted, is witnessed not only in human females, but also in female animals, which, he repeats, have never sinned.[72] The pain of childbirth, furthermore, is not felt in all women to the same degree, but varies depending on the physical condition and strength of the woman. Some women, who are accustomed to the physical rigors of life, experience little or no pain at all. "The barbarian and shepherd women," he said, "who have become hardened by exercise surely give birth in the midst of journeys with such great ease that they take care of their babies without interrupting the labor of travel and immediately carry them along, and without being weakened at all by the difficulty of giving birth, they transfer the burden of their belly to their shoulders."[73] These women—and women from lower classes who have lived hardened lives—do not need the assistance of midwives while in labor, but are able to give birth on their own. Other women, who come from privileged families and are "softened by pleasures,"[74] experience tremendously difficult labor pains, and need assistance from midwives. The more midwives there are who surround the woman in labor, the more that woman "learns to get sick and is happy to be sick and thinks she needs as many services as she receives."[75]

This understanding of the goodness of *concupiscentia* and sex takes us to Julian's conception of the goodness of marriage, because he saw all three as intrinsically intertwined.[76] He defined the essence of marriage simply as "nothing but the union of bodies."[77] Because he viewed *concupiscentia* as naturally good, and as he cannot

66. Augustine, *Nupt.* 2.6.16; *C. Jul.* 3.7.14, 3.9.18.
67. Augustine, *C. du. ep. Pelag.* 1.15.21.
68. Augustine, *C. Jul.* 4.12.59.
69. Augustine, *C. Jul.* 4.13.62.
70. Augustine, *C. Jul.* 5.5.20.
71. Augustine, *C. Jul.* 5.5.21–22, 5.7.29; *C. Jul. op. imp.* 4.28.
72. Augustine, *C. Jul. op. imp.* 6.26.
73. Augustine, *C. Jul. op. imp.* 6.26.
74. Augustine, *C. Jul. op. imp.* 6.26.
75. Augustine, *C. Jul. op. imp.* 6.26.
76. Augustine, *C. Jul.* 4.10.56.
77. Augustine, *C. Jul.* 5.16.62; see also: *C. Jul. op. imp.* 1.65.

conceptualize marriage without intercourse (the consequence of *concupiscentia*),[78] marriage, therefore, also must be good.[79] Furthermore, if God, who is goodness, instituted the goodness of *concupiscentia*, and marriage is nothing other than the union of bodies, it follows that God instituted marriage, which therefore must be good.[80] Since Julian understood the relationship between marriage and sex as linked, he concluded that Mary and Joseph were never truly married, because—along with Jerome who furiously wrote against Helvidius[81]—Julian believed that Mary remained a virgin even after Jesus was born.[82]

Augustine, Julian claims, believes that marriage as it is now after Adam and Eve was not instituted by God, which both encourages[83] and supports the Manichaeans.[84] Julian accuses Augustine of believing that marriage is evil because it is through the marital bed that original sin is passed from one generation to the next.[85] If marriage results in the condemnation of children, Julian concludes, then marriage must be evil.[86] Like Pelagius and Caelestius, he holds that the offspring of the marital union is a sinless infant who is free from any fault of their parents, and the fault of the first parents.[87] If marriage is created by a good God and is itself good, then the offspring of that union cannot be evil.[88] But, marriage is evil if it is the cause of the condemnation of the offspring through the infection of original sin.[89] As marriage does not condemn the good offspring to eternal damnation, it must be good.

---

78. Augustine, *C. Jul.* 4.10.56.
79. Augustine, *C. Jul.* 4.10.56, 5.8.31.
80. Augustine, *Nupt.* 2.34.57; *C. du. ep. Pelag.* 1.15.30; *C. Jul. op. imp.* 1.70.
81. Jerome, *Helv.* 2.
82. Augustine, *C. Jul.* 5.12.46.
83. Augustine, *C. du. ep. Pelag.* 1.5.9–10.
84. Augustine, *Nupt.* 2.23.38.
85. Augustine, *C. Jul. op. imp.* 1.61.
86. Augustine, *C. Jul.* 3.24.54.
87. Augustine, *Nupt.* 2.26.41.
88. Augustine, *C. Jul.* 2.9.31.
89. Augustine, *C. Jul.* 2.1.2.

Chapter 17

The Theology of Augustine (419–430)

Introduction

JULIAN, IN MANY WAYS, was a more formidable opponent for Augustine than were Pelagius and Caelestius. Although both Pelagius and Caelestius were educated men, Julian's intellect operated on a deeper level, and his theological insights were more penetrating. His criticisms of Augustine often were more acute than those from the other two, and they probed the tender underbelly of Augustine's anthropology. His rank as a bishop, furthermore, gave him an ecclesiastical gravitas that was absent in Augustine's opponents earlier in the Pelagian controversy, and his aristocratic background added a class dynamic that pulsed underneath all of their exchanges. Even a hint of cultural elitism, as Justo González has shown,[1] pervaded Julian's writing, most noticeably when Julian abused Augustine as "the African,"[2] a "Punic debater,"[3] a "Punic commentator,"[4] a "Punic orator,"[5] a "Punic author,"[6] who demonstrates "Punic dishonesty,"[7] a "Phoenician,"[8] and the "shamelessness of Numidia."[9]

Just as Augustine said a few kind words about Julian, Julian also recognized some positive qualities in Augustine. Julian briefly praised Augustine's "native intelligence" saying that his "learning is evident," that he was "a very pious priest and a very learned speaker,"[10] that he wrote with "rhetorical elegance,"[11] was "very subtle and intelligent"[12]

---

1. González, *Mestizo Augustine*, 24–25, 31, 146–49.
2. Augustine, *C. Jul. op. imp.* 2.19.
3. Augustine, *C. Jul.* 3.17.32.
4. Augustine, *C. Jul. op. imp.* 1.7.
5. Augustine, *C. Jul. op. imp.* 1.48.
6. Augustine, *C. Jul. op. imp.* 1.73.
7. Augustine, *C. Jul. op. imp.* 3.78.
8. Augustine, *C. Jul. op. imp.* 6.18.
9. Augustine, *C. Jul. op. imp.* 1.16, 6.6.
10. Augustine, *C. Jul. op. imp.* 1.48.
11. Augustine, *C. Jul. op. imp.* 4.31.
12. Augustine, *C. Jul. op. imp.* 5.24.

and the "most subtle of debaters."[13] But, Julian also responded to "old"[14] Augustine's *ad hominem* attacks with similar insults that Augustine had showered on him, saying Augustine was part of a "conspiracy of lost souls,"[15] who were "fashioners of deceit,"[16] and "harlots of Manichean teaching."[17] Augustine, he said, was a "new Manichee,"[18] that he and Mani were both "enemies of the truth,"[19] and "disciples"[20] of the devil. He was a "liar,"[21] with a "bad conscience,"[22] a "Jovinian,"[23] a "traducianist,"[24] a "foul criminal,"[25] a "slanderer,"[26] a "blasphemer,"[27] the "Epicurus of our age,"[28] who wallows "in the depth of ignorance,"[29] and "in the swamp of your impiety and fear,"[30] with "dull wits"[31] a "foul mouth,"[32] a "drunken mind,"[33] and who was a "toady"[34] of the prince of darkness. He sarcastically called Augustine a "most noble professor of wisdom,"[35] "O most learned of bipeds,"[36] and an "excellent teacher."[37] "I ought to demand nothing but your excommunication," Julian seethed, because "you have abandoned religion, learning and even the common sensibilities to the point that you regard your God as a criminal—something a barbarian would hardly do."[38] He even took a swipe at Alypius by taunting him as "a slave boy of that man's [Augustine's] errors,"[39] and resurrected

---

13. Augustine, *C. Jul. op. imp.* 5.23.
14. Augustine, *C. Jul. op. imp.* 3.169.
15. Augustine, *C. Jul.* 1.7.29, 1.7.34, 6.22.69.
16. Augustine, *C. Jul. op. imp.* 1.76.
17. Augustine, *C. Jul. op. imp.* 2.9.
18. Augustine, *C. Jul. op. imp.* 1.32.
19. Augustine, *C. Jul. op. imp.* 1.117.
20. Augustine, *C. Jul. op. imp.* 6.20.
21. Augustine, *C. Jul. op. imp.* 1.67, 3.106.
22. Augustine, *C. Jul. op. imp.* 1.11.
23. Augustine, *C. Jul. op. imp.* 1.101, 1.98.
24. Augustine, *C. Jul. op. imp.* 1.6, 2.14, 2.27, 3.7, 3.10, 3.21, 3.35, 3.83, 3.85, 3.91, 3.123, 4.118, 5.6, 5.30, 5.54, 6.3, 6.4, 6.8, 6.14, 6.15, 6.20, 6.31, 6.33.
25. Augustine, *C. Jul. op. imp.* 1.117.
26. Augustine, *C. Jul. op. imp.* 2.19.
27. Augustine, *C. Jul. op. imp.* 3.117.
28. Augustine, *C. Jul. op. imp.* 5.26.
29. Augustine, *C. Jul. op. imp.* 5.24.
30. Augustine, *C. Jul. op. imp.* 3.101.
31. Augustine, *C. Jul. op. imp.* 5.64, 3.181.
32. Augustine, *C. Jul. op. imp.* 6.24.
33. Augustine, *C. Jul. op. imp.* 3.154.
34. Augustine, *C. Jul. op. imp.* 6.20, 6.22.
35. Augustine, *C. Jul. op. imp.* 1.72.
36. Augustine, *C. Jul. op. imp.* 4.90.
37. Augustine, *C. Jul. op. imp.* 6.33.
38. Augustine, *C. Jul. op. imp.* 1.48.
39. Augustine, *C. Jul. op. imp.* 1.7.

Monica's childhood indiscretions by repeating Augustine's description of her from his *Confessiones* as a "tippler."[40]

In the previous chapter, we restricted our investigation to Julian's unique contributions to the Pelagian controversy: his accusation that Augustine persisted as a Manichaean, his belief in the goodness of *concupiscentia*, and his positive views on sex and marriage. In this chapter, likewise, we will refrain from exploring Augustine's responses to Julian's teaching against original sin, his beliefs in the unrestricted free will, his confidence in the possibility of a sinless life, his baptismal theology, and his definition of grace, because doing so would be unnecessarily repetitious. Augustine's arguments against Julian on these issues were fundamentally the same as the ones he had made against Pelagius and Caelestius in the first phase of this controversy. Instead, we will focus our attention on Augustine's reply to Julian's distinctive theological additions.

Augustine's initial response to Julian was with the same patience he showed every new interlocutor whom he believed was misguided, hoping that Julian would see his errors and change his mind. But, by the end of his life when he was still hammering away at Julian's stubborn persistence, Augustine's patience had evaporated, and he came to see their exchange as boring, repetitive, and exhausting. "You repeat the same points in the same words to the point of dreadful boredom,"[41] Augustine exclaimed. "Stop repeating what we have already refuted," he demanded. "Why do you force us to say the same things over and over?"[42]

Augustine's Response to Julian's Claim that He Persists as a Manichaean

Of all of the accusations leveled against Augustine during the Pelagian controversy, Julian's charge that he persisted as a Manichaean stung him the most. It hurt him personally,[43] but he also knew that his entire anthropological project was in jeopardy if he did not successfully show that he had left Mani behind decades earlier.[44] Augustine's response to Julian's charge can be grouped into two general categories: first, he defended himself by discussing the important differences between Christian original sin (*peccatum originale*) and Manichaean natural evil (*malum naturale*). Second, Augustine aggressively attacked Julian by claiming that it was Julian who was the one giving assistance to the Manichaeans.

Augustine repeatedly stressed that *peccatum originale* and Manichaean *malum naturale* are not the same. The Manichaeans believed that the flesh (and everything

---

40. Augustine, *C. Jul. op. imp.*, 1.68. See *Conf.* 9.8.18.
41. Augustine, *C. Jul. op. imp.* 2.44.
42. Augustine, *C. Jul. op. imp.* 2.83. See also: 2.114, 3.27, 3.36, 6.11.
43. Augustine, *C. Jul. op. imp.* 2.164, 4.56.
44. Lancel, *Saint Augustine*, 419.

that is material) is evil because it comes from the evil God. Humans, according to the Manichaeans, are evil in their materiality. Augustine contrasted this with Christian anthropology, saying that all created reality comes from the Creator of all things visible and invisible. The material body, then, is good, although it is vitiated because of our first parents. These two different anthropologies are not the same. "We do not agree," he said, "with the Manichees that this evil has been mixed into us from an evil nature foreign to us. Hence, it remains for you [Julian] to admit that there is something in our nature, like a wound, that needs to be healed, though we hold that its guilt has already been healed by [baptismal] rebirth."[45]

Human nature was corrupted by the devil; but, this claim is not the same thing as stating that the devil is the creator of an evil material nature.[46] The devil is not a co-equal force who is in eternal conflict with God. Rather, the devil is part of God's creation—an angel that fell by his own will.[47] Like the rest of the created order, the devil is ultimately subject to God's will. Augustine endlessly reiterated that this wound (*vulnus*) from the devil was not a substance (*substantia*) in the Manichean sense, but is a defect (*vitium*) of God's original good creation. God permitted the devil's corruption of humanity, which was never an event outside of God's control. We do not know why humanity was allowed to be corrupted, but Augustine assured Julian it was done "by the just and omnipotent God under his judicial ordering of things."[48] Augustine could not understand why it was so hard for Julian to recognize the differences between *peccatum originale* and *malum naturale*, because they seemed so obvious to him.[49]

One of the most important ways that he made this first point, in addition to endlessly quoting biblical passages such as Genesis 3 and Romans 5:12, was to quote repeatedly previous Christian authorities—such as Cyprian,[50] Irenaeus,[51] Reticius of Autun,[52] Olympius,[53] Hilary of Poitiers,[54] Innocent,[55] Gregory of Nazianzus,[56] Basil of Caesarea,[57] the bishops at the Synod of Diospolis,[58] John Chrysostom,[59] and Jerome[60]—who share

45. Augustine, *C. Jul.* 5.16.65. See also: *C. Jul. op. imp.* 4.128.
46. Augustine, *C. Jul.* 6.19.59.
47. Augustine, *C. Jul. op. imp.* 6.10.
48. Augustine, *C. Jul. op. imp.* 1.66.
49. Augustine, *C. Jul. op. imp.* 3.95.
50. Augustine, *C. ep. Pel.* 4.8.21.
51. Augustine, *C. Jul.* 1.3.5.
52. Augustine, *C. Jul.* 1.3.7.
53. Augustine, *C. Jul.* 1.3.8.
54. Augustine, *C. Jul.* 1.3.9.
55. Augustine, *C. Jul.* 1.4.13.
56. Augustine, *C. Jul.* 1.5.15.
57. Augustine, *C. Jul.* 1.5.16.
58. Augustine, *C. Jul.* 1.5.19.
59. Augustine, *C. Jul.* 1.6.21.
60. Augustine, *C. Jul.* 1.7.34.

Augustine's anthropological assumptions about the brokenness of humanity, even if they did not use his exact Latin phrase *peccatum originale*. Unquestionably, the authority whom Augustine quoted against Julian more often than any other was Ambrose.[61] Augustine never grew tired of citing the bishop of Milan, undoubtedly because he knew that it would infuriate Julian to read that Ambrose, Julian's fellow Italian, was on the side of the "Aristotle of the Phoenicians."[62]

The second way that Augustine refuted Julian's claim that he was a secret Manichaean was to turn the tables on him, and accuse him of aiding the Manichaeans. As he grew more frustrated with Julian, Augustine repeated this accusation more often than he had earlier in their exchange. In fact, he made this charge with the last line that he ever wrote before dying a few weeks later: "with your detestable blindness you lend support to the Manichees, and you accuse them foolishly since you wretchedly offer them help."[63] Julian believed that when human beings are born, they do not contract original sin. How, then, Augustine asked, does sin come from something that is not broken by original sin? If sin does not come from the broken goods of God's creation, it must come from something outside of human nature that is not created by God. This is precisely what the Manichaeans claim: anything that is evil comes from outside of the good God. So, although Julian certainly did not intend to support them, Augustine contended that both the Manichaeans and Julian agree that evil comes from something outside of God's purview.[64]

Concupiscentia Carnis

Augustine's response to Julian's championing of *concupiscentia*,[65] as John Cavadini has said, was a "flat, radical, wholesale, scorched earth rejection"[66] of it. The differences between the two men began with how they defined it, and their arguments increasingly diverged from there. For the bishop of Hippo, *concupiscentia carnis* does not trace its origin from God, as Julian had said, but from the devil, the prince of the world.[67] It is not part of our original nature, but is a defect,[68] or disease[69] that has

---

61. Augustine, *C. du. ep. Pelag.* 4.11.29.
62. Augustine, *C. Jul. op. imp.* 3.199.
63. Augustine, *C. Jul. op. imp.* 6.41.
64. Augustine, *C. Jul.* 1.8.36, 5.16.59–66, 6.21.66; *C. Jul. op. imp.* 1.97, 2.110, 2.206, 3.102, 3.170, 3.173, 3.207, 3.212, 4.42.
65. While Augustine preferred the term *concupiscentia* (especially from 410–430), he interchangeably employed the synonyms *cupiditas* and *libido*. Nisula, *Augustine*, 12, 35.
66. Cavadini, "Reconsidering Augustine," 187.
67. Augustine, *Nupt.* 1.22.26, 2.5.14; *C. Jul.* 4.7.37.
68. Augustine, *Nupt.* 2.9.22; *C. Jul.* 4.9.54, 6.11.34, 6.18.53; *C. Jul. op. imp.* 4.29.
69. Augustine, *Nupt.* 1.25.28; *C. Jul.* 3.15.29.

infected humanity as a result of the fall, the first evil;[70] it is "the law of sin"[71] (Rom 7:23) "dwelling in our members"[72] (Rom 6:12–13) that is directed inward towards ourselves, and away from God.[73] In his thought generally, Augustine does not narrowly define *concupiscentia carnis* as disordered sexual desire alone, but may be any disordered desire, such as anger, avarice, obstinacy, ostentation, or the lust for power.[74] Usually in his duel with Julian, however, he specifically meant sexual lust.[75] This lust is "indecency for sinners, a necessity for those who have children, passion for the dissolute, and the source of shame for marriage."[76]

Augustine's claim that *concupiscentia carnis* dwells "in our members" has caused a dispute among modern scholars. Indeed, his understanding of *concupiscentia carnis* is one of the most disputed areas of Augustine's thought by contemporary scholars.[77] All scholars recognize that Augustine asserts that the soul desires,[78] but a disagreement persists over whether Augustine believed that the body desires independently of the will. Some scholars, such as William Babcock, Jesse Couenhoven, William Schumacher, Margaret Miles, Stephen Duffy, (initially) Peter Burnell, and Paul Rigby claim that, for Augustine, the body does not have its own desires.[79] Other scholars, such as Brown, John Rist, Paula Fredriksen, and Cavadini claim that Augustine sometimes says that the body has its own desires, but that this is peripheral to Augustine's anthropology.[80] A third group, including Hunter, (later) Burnell, and William Mann insist that the body does desire independently of the soul, and that this is central to Augustine's anthropological thought.[81] Joshua Evans, who sides with the third group, offers the most thorough and convincing study, I would argue.[82]

This understanding of bodily desires is found from Book I of *De nuptiis et concupiscentia* and consistently can been seen throughout his work until his *Contra Iulianum opus imperfectum*.[83] In his *De nuptiis et concupiscentia*, for example, Augustine claimed that "it was when human beings [Adam and Eve] transgressed the law that

70. Augustine, *Nupt.* 4.2.13.
71. Augustine, *Nupt.* 1.23.25, 1.30.34.
72. Augustine, *Nupt.* 1.23.25, 2.9.22.
73. TeSelle, *Augustine*, 317; Lamberigts, "Augustine, Julian," 409.
74. Lamberigts, "Augustine, Julian," 409–10; Barclift, "In Controversy," 8; Lancel, *Saint Augustine*, 424.
75. Brown, "Sexuality and Society," 64; Brown, *Body and Society*, 418; Hunter, "Introduction," 24–25.
76. Augustine, *Nupt.* 1.12.
77. Evans, "Augustine's Unfinished Work," 208.
78. Augustine, *C. Jul.* 6.14.41.
79. Evans, "Augustine's Unfinished Work," 131 n. 6.
80. Evans, "Augustine's Unfinished Work," 133 n. 10.
81. Evans, "Augustine's Unfinished Work," 134 n. 13.
82. Evans, "Augustine's Unfinished Work," 126–210.
83. Evans, "Augustine's Unfinished Work," 129.

they first began to have another law in their members resisting their mind, and they experienced the evil of their disobedience when they discovered the disobedience of their own flesh as their rightful retribution."[84] Later, in his *Contra Iulianum opus imperfectum*, Augustine, for example, referenced Gregory of Nazianzus as someone with whom he was in harmony: Gregory "clearly and plainly attributed the law of sin which is in our members and resists the law of the mind to this mortal and earthly body of ours. He said that the law of sin which is in our members resists the law of the Spirit."[85] These shameful[86] bodily desires are ordered only towards pleasure.[87] Even when a man, such as a eunuch, is unable to sexually function, these disordered desires still remain in the body, and must be yoked by chastity.[88] This bodily rebellion is a fitting punishment: just as humans disobeyed God's commandments, so, now, the body disobeys the commandments of the human will.[89]

This understanding of postlapsarian bodily desires shaped the way Augustine conceived of bodily desires in Eden before the fall.[90] He concluded that there were four possibilities prior to the first sin: (1) Adam and Eve would have remained the only two people in Eden, thereby negating the necessity of sexual desire or sex; (2) procreation in Eden would have been non-sexual, again negating the necessity of sexual desire or sex; (3) sexual procreation would have occurred without sexual desire; (4) sexual procreation occurred accompanied by a good sexual desire.[91]

Over the course of his life, Augustine's mind changed on this issue. During his fight with Julian,[92] beginning with Book I of *De nuptiis et concupiscentia*, Augustine concluded that *concupiscentia carnis* did not exist prior to the fall, and Adam and Eve had the ability to control their bodies through the movement of their wills just as humans are able to move other parts of their bodies (such as their hands, feet, or mouth) even after the fall.[93] In Book II of the same work, he repeats this claim,[94] but, at the very end, he mentions in passing the possibility in Eden of a good sexual desire that still would obey the will, although he does not favor this possibility.[95] In his *Contra duas epistulas Pelagianorum*, Augustine reaffirms his preference for an Eden void of any type of sexual

---

84. Augustine, *Nupt.* 1.6.7. See also: 1.31.35, 1.27.30.

85. Augustine, *C. Jul. op. imp.* 1.69.

86. Augustine, *Nupt.* 1.6.7, 2.9.22.

87. Augustine, *Nupt.* 1.4.5; *C. Jul.* 6.16.50; Evans, "Augustine's Unfinished Work," 163–65.

88. Augustine, *C. Jul.* 6.14.41. See also: *C. Jul. op. imp.* 4.28.

89. Augustine, *Nupt.* 1.6.7; *C. du. ep. Pelag.* 1.15.31; Brown, *Body and Society*, 416; Nisula, *Augustine*, 58.

90. Evans, "Augustine's Unfinished Work," 210.

91. Evans, "Augustine's Unfinished Work," 231.

92. For a discussion of Augustine's thought on this issue prior to his contest with Julian, see: Evans, "Augustine's Unfinished Work," 232–61.

93. Augustine, *Nupt.* 1.5.6–1.6.7, 1.16.16, 1.21.23; Evans, "Augustine's Unfinished Work," 262.

94. Augustine, *Nupt.* 2.7.17.

95. Augustine, *Nupt.* 2.35.59; Evans, "Augustine's Unfinished Work," 262–64.

desire, good or disordered, but nods to the possibility that there was a good sexual desire under the control of the will.[96] Writing his *Contra Iulianum*, Augustine is not as certain as he had been that there was no sexual desire in Eden. When he discusses good sexual desire, he permits it as a legitimate possibility, but, at the same time, mocks it by telling Julian that he only allows it because he does "not want to make you [Julian] too sad"[97] by insisting that it was not possible. It was in his *Epist. 6**, probably written sometime between 420 and 421,[98] where we see a significant shift in Augustine's thought.[99] He had written it to Atticus, the bishop of Constantinople (406–426), who had succeeded John Chrysostom. After reassuring Atticus that the report that he had heard of Augustine's death was false,[100] he reviewed the possible options of *concupiscentia* in Eden. Here, Augustine allows the possibility that there was good sexual desire in Eden without his earlier sarcastic vituperation.[101] In his last work, the *Contra Iulianum opus imperfectum*, Augustine claims at least twenty times that both options were reasonable possibilities, because at the end of his life he was uncertain which of these two possibilities accurately described the Edenic reality.[102]

If there had been Edenic sexual desire, it would have been very different from the *concupiscentia carnis* humans experience after the fall. In Eden, the flesh only would have desired what, when, and as much as the will commanded it to desire.[103] Regardless of whether there had been no sexual desire or a good sexual desire in Eden before the fall, Augustine's main concern is with the human condition that is now vitiated by this disordered desire, and would not exist if it weren't for the original disobedience.[104]

All babies are born from *concupiscentia carnis* that was passed to them from their parents.[105] Although *concupiscentia carnis* is the result of—and punishment for—sin,

---

96. Augustine, *C. du. ep. Pelag.* 1.17.34–35; Evans, "Augustine's Unfinished Work," 264–66.

97. Augustine, *C. Jul.* 4.11.57; Evans, "Augustine's Unfinished Work," 266–67.

98. Brown suggests 420–421, while Hunter offers around 421, but Teske suggests 416–421. Brown, "Sexuality and Society," 50; Hunter, "Introduction," 24; Teske, "Introduction," in *Augustine*, 250.

99. In this letter, Augustine explained his differences with the Pelagians concerning marriage and *concupiscentia*. He first distinguished between two types of *concupiscentia*: concupiscence of marriage (*concupiscentia nuptiarum*) and concupiscence of the flesh (*concupiscentia carnis*), which is a distinction rarely explicitly detailed in Augustine's writings. *Concupiscentia nuptiarum*, is *concupiscentia* that focuses on making good use of *concupiscentia carnis* by reigning in illicit sexual acts, focuses on the legitimate moral responsibility of the procreation of offspring, and focuses on the bond that unifies married couples. It is this *concupiscentia* that was instituted by God for realizing the command to "increase and multiply" (Gen 1:28). As Peter Brown has summarized, *concupiscentia nuptiarum* is "blessed to this day by God, condensed a sense of the continued urge of men, as social beings, to cohere to an organized society, based, in the first instance, on the joining of husband and wife, for the begetting of children: it was a *concupiscentia vinculi socialis*." Brown, "Sexuality and Society," 53.

100. Augustine, *Epist.* 6*.1.

101. Augustine, *Epist.* 6*.7–8; Evans, "Augustine's Unfinished Work," 267–68.

102. Evans, "Augustine's Unfinished Work," 270 n. 105.

103. Augustine, *C. Jul. op. imp.* 5.14; Evans, "Augustine's Unfinished Work," 272.

104. Augustine, *Nupt.* 1.1.1, 1.6.7, 1.22.24; *C. Jul. op. imp.* 4.79, 5.5, 5.10.

105. Augustine, *Nupt.* 1.19.21, 1.23.25, 1.24.27; Bonner, *St. Augustine*, 377–78.

now, after the fall, procreation cannot happen without it in the "body of this death,"[106] because it is the necessary precondition in men for the sexual act. God, not *concupiscentia carnis*, creates the semen for procreation; but, *concupiscentia carnis* is necessary for insemination: "that pleasure of carnal concupiscence," Augustine said, "does not form the seeds [*semina*]. Rather, those seeds were already created in bodies by the true God who also created the bodies. They are not produced by pleasure, but are aroused and spilled forth with pleasure."[107] *Concupiscentia carnis* is not necessary for the sexual act for women,[108] because procreation may occur without it. It is present, however, in the female body, albeit in a more "hidden"[109] way.

Concupiscentia carnis is not eliminated by the waters of baptism in an infant, nor, as in the case of Augustine's own life, as a young man after a full acceptance of the Christian tradition.[110] Rather, it is the guilt (*reatus*) of it that has been forgiven and wiped away.[111] The *concupiscentia carnis* itself remains hidden (*latere*) in the body, even after the sacrament of rebirth.[112] But, it is no longer counted against the baptized as sin, just as long as they do not consent to it by committing any disordered acts.[113] Even if one does not consent to it, it still is active in some way because the desires remain.[114] Often times, when one does consent to it and does something sinful, one consents to it and hates it at the same time.[115]

We are not slaves to our urges, however. The apostles, for example, were able to harness their desires.[116] *Concupiscentia carnis*, Augustine acknowledges, is amplified in some people because they submit to their urges, but it is diminished in others because of spiritual progress. This progress often is made easier by the aging process when lusts begin to fade with maturity, but this is not always the case.[117] He recounted a story to Julian that he had heard about a man in his eighties "who had lived faithfully with his faithful wife a life of continence for twenty-five years," but who then "had bought a playmate for his sexual desire."[118] Even old age does not necessarily cure this somatic disease. Only at the resurrection will the body be permanently transformed.[119]

106. Augustine, *Nupt.* 1.1.1; see also: 1.8.9.
107. Augustine, *Nupt.* 2.13.26.
108. Augustine, *Nupt.* 2.15.30.
109. Augustine, *C. Jul.* 4.13.62.
110. Augustine, *Nupt.* 1.25.28; *C. Jul.* 6.16.50–52.
111. Augustine, *Nupt.* 1.25.28; *C. Jul.* 6.17.51.
112. Augustine, *Nupt.* 1.25.28, 1.32.37; *C. Jul.* 6.16.50.
113. Augustine, *Nupt.* 1.23.25, 1.25.28, 1.31.36.
114. Augustine, *Nupt.* 1.27.30, 1.39.32.
115. Augustine, *Nupt.* 1.28.31.
116. Augustine, *C. du. ep. Pelag.* 1.11.24.
117. Augustine, *Nupt.* 1.25.28–27.30.
118. Augustine, *C. Jul.* 3.11.22.
119. Augustine, *C. Jul.* 3.20.39, 6.16.50; *C. Jul. op. imp.* 3.167.

Augustine does not assert that *concupiscentia carnis* can ever be eradicated, but he does say that after baptism it can be "controlled"[120] (*domare*), "defeated"[121] (*vincere*), "reined in"[122] (*frenare*), and "diminished"[123] (*minuere*) by good habits in all people—chaste and married couples alike—so that it does not cause any harm by instigating forbidden actions. Unfortunately, it never can be controlled entirely, because dreams produce "those motions in the bodies"[124] in even the most chaste. When it is uncontrolled, either when one is awake or asleep, *concupiscentia carnis* unleashes "everything that horrifies us in the shamefulness of any sins committed by the sexual organs."[125]

Augustine rejected Julian's claim that the presence of *concupiscentia* in animals is proof that it is a good gift given by God, and that it is not a punishment because animals do not sin. He dismissed in principle Julian's comparison of animal bodies and human bodies as equivalent simply because they are constituted by the same physical material and come from the same Creator. The human body, Augustine said, had a fundamentally different beginning than the animal body because humans are created in the image and likeness of God (Gen 1:27); if Adam and Eve would not have sinned, the flesh would have "remained in eternity and incorruptibility," and that the body is "destined to see eternity with a very different end"[126] than animals. He admitted that animals do experience sexual desire, but it is not the same desire that haunts humanity after the fall. For animals, sexual desire is not the same "misery"[127] as human desire, because animal desire is not characterized by the flesh lusting against the spirit as it is in the human body.[128] Sexual desire, which is appropriate in animals, is punishment for human sin after the fall.[129]

Augustine also defended himself against the charge that he was an Apollinarian. He did not deny that he had taught that Jesus did not experience *concupiscentia carnis* during his life, but he rejected the claim that this made him an Apollinarian. Christ, Augustine insisted, was free of all desires for sin, because *concupiscentia carnis* had not been passed to him as he had not been conceived by it. His sinless flesh meant that his body did not rebel against his soul. If he had chosen to do so through an act of his will, he could have experienced such desires, but his virtue prevented him from

---

120. Augustine, *Nupt.* 2.35.59.
121. Augustine, *C. Jul.* 3.20.39.
122. Augustine, *C. Jul.* 4.2.7.
123. Augustine, *C. Jul. op. imp.* 3.167.
124. Augustine, *C. Jul.* 3.20.38.
125. Augustine, *C. Jul.* 3.20.38.
126. Augustine, *C. Jul. op. imp.* 4.39.
127. Augustine, *C. Jul. op. imp.* 4.38.
128. Augustine, *C. Jul. op. imp.* 4.38–41.
129. Augustine, *C. Jul. op. imp.* 4.43.

it.[130] Christ did have bodily senses like every other human, such as vision that allowed him to see beauty and ugly sights, smell that allowed him to experience fragrant and noxious scents, hearing that allowed him to listen to consonant and dissonant sounds, taste that allowed him to enjoy the range of flavors, and touch that allowed him to feel various textures.[131] But, *concupiscentia carnis* is not a bodily sense in the same way, and, therefore, it is not necessary for Christ to have it in order to be fully human.

Even though Jesus did not experience *concupiscentia carnis* because he was without sin, he did have reproductive organs. His organs were never aroused by sexual desire either by his will—because as he was celibate he never would will this—or against his will either while he was asleep[132] or awake.[133] Julian insisted that Augustine's thinking necessitated that Jesus was a eunuch. If he did not have *concupiscentia carnis*, it would have been impossible for him to have father a child. Augustine retorted that Jesus could have fathered a child if he so willed it because he was not a eunuch, but he never chose to do so.[134] Jesus's refusal to enjoy sexual pleasures, or to father a child, was not a result of a struggle to resist any urges deeply ingrained within, but was a chaste decision that should not be understood to condemn sex, marriage, or offspring.[135]

Sex and Marriage

Augustine mocked Julian's praise of the goodness of the sexual act, scoffing that a couple need not display even the slightest bit of bodily control: "I suppose that married couples lie down together whenever they like, and enter each other, whenever the desire moves them. This desire for intercourse is not postponed even for an hour; rather, the union of their bodies is seen as permissible at the very moment when this natural good of yours is spontaneously aroused."[136] He also called into question Julian's own sexual behavior with his wife, speculating whether or not they comported themselves in a sexually indulgent manner. "If you have lived such a married life," he said, "stop presenting yourself with your experiences in this discussion, and learn rather from others how to live and how to teach others to live a married life. I wonder, nonetheless, whether you did not at least rein in desires for adultery and did not think that they should be reined

---

130. Augustine, *C. Jul. op. imp.* 4.48, 4.58.
131. Augustine, *C. Jul. op. imp.* 4.49.
132. Augustine, *C. Jul. op. imp.* 4.58.
133. Augustine, *C. Jul. op. imp.* 4.53–54.
134. Augustine, *C. Jul. op. imp.* 4.49, 4.52.
135. Augustine, *C. Jul. op. imp.* 4.57–58.
136. Augustine, *C. Jul.* 3.14.28.

in."[137] Furthermore, if sex were to be lauded, why, Augustine mused, do parents engage in sex privately away from their children?[138]

In paradise, prior to the first sin, the sexual act would have been different from the way it is now after the fall. Augustine presents four possibilities of how it would have happened prior to the first sin: (1) Adam and Eve would have had intercourse whenever they wanted it; (2) they would curb their desires when sex was not necessary; (3) desire would have arisen only at the command of the will when it saw the necessity for sex; (4) intercourse would have occurred (without sexual desire) when the members were moved by the will, just as any other part of the body is moved by the will.[139] Augustine dismissed the first two options, claiming that Adam and Eve's "moral excellence" excludes option one, and their "great happiness" excludes the second.[140] As we saw earlier, Augustine, at the end of his life, was unsure whether or not there was good *concupiscentia* in paradise, or if the members would have moved entirely at the instigation of the will without *concupiscentia*, so he does not insist on either of the last two options. By the end of his life, however, he is confident that the sexual act of procreation would have been bodily, and it would have been a shameless act.[141]

For Augustine, postlapsarian sex was not an unrestricted good to be enjoyed the moment desire begins to stir. Within the bonds of the marital union, the sexual act must be ordered properly. Marital intercourse is not free from the evil of *concupiscentia carnis*, but it makes appropriate use of this evil. Married couples make good use of the evil desire, just as adulterers evilly use the good body.[142] Sex for the purposes of procreation is the rightly ordered exercise of the sexual organs, and it is sanctioned by God.[143] It is not sinful in this situation because the good will directs the bodily desire toward the end of procreation; the bodily desire does not drive the will.[144] Sex, therefore, is neither inherently good as Julian claimed, nor inherently evil, as the Manichaeans claimed. The intention of the will determines the morality or immorality of the act. If the intention is to fulfill God's commandment to "be fruitful and multiply" (Gen 1:28), then sex is morally praiseworthy. If, however, the intention is to satisfy sexual urges alone, then it is morally blameworthy.

Although sexual acts that are intended only for sexual gratification within marriage are intrinsically disordered in that they do not tend toward procreation,

---

137. Julian ignored Augustine's speculations, and never publicly discussed his own behavior as a model to emulate or to avoid. Augustine, *C. Jul.* 3.14.28.

138. Augustine, *C. Jul.* 2.5.14.

139. Augustine, *C. du. ep. Pelag.* 1.17.34.

140. Augustine, *C. du. ep. Pelag.* 1.17.34.

141. Augustine, *Nupt.* 2.22.37; *C. Jul.* 4.11.57; *C. Jul. op. imp.* 5.16.

142. Augustine, *C. Jul. op. imp.* 6.26.5.18.

143. Augustine, *Nupt.* 1.14.16–15.17.

144. Augustine, *Nupt.* 1.12.

Augustine says that they must be "tolerated" (*tolerare*), and "permitted" (*concedere*)[145] lest one spouse or the other fall into the greater sins of fornication or adultery. They are "pardonable" (*venia*) sins, because even though the intention of the act is for pleasure, procreation is still a possible result.[146] Not every sexual act is permissible, however, even within marriage. "If one has relations even with one's wife," he said, "in a part of the body which was not made for begetting children, such relations are against nature and indecent," are "unclean," and "wicked."[147]

Augustine rejected Julian's claim that the pain women experience in childbirth is not a punishment for sin. He insisted that, prior to the first sin, Eve would not have experienced any pain in labor, but after her transgression pain became part of God's punishment.[148] Again turning to the story in Genesis that was so important for his theological anthropology, he showed that God would "multiply your [Eve's] sorrows" (Gen 3:16) in labor because of her disobedience. To "multiply" her sorrows does not mean that Eve already had experienced such sorrows in labor prior to the fall, and that God now is increasing those pains. Rather, those sorrows came into being only after the first sin.[149] This curse is passed down to every woman after Eve. It is true, he concedes to Julian, that this pain is more intense for some women (those who are not accustomed to a life of physical difficulties) than it is for others (those who live physically demanding lives). However, all women—regardless of their tolerance for pain—experience at least some suffering during labor.[150]

Marriage and sex, for Augustine, are not the same thing. Sex often is a component of marriage, but it is not a necessary aspect of marriage.[151] If the two were necessarily linked, he insisted, there would not be a qualitative difference between marriage and adultery. Adultery, like marriage, sometimes results in the good of procreation, even if offspring was not intended in the moment of the act.[152] But, marriage should not be likened to adultery because marriage is good while adultery is evil. This distinction between marriage and sex set Augustine apart from his contemporaries (such as Jerome), because they (as well as Julian)[153] necessarily linked the two together. Without the sexual act, his contemproaries concluded, there is no marital bond.[154]

Unlike *concupiscentia carnis* (which is perverted after the fall), and the sexual act (which is no longer essentially attached to the procreative act after the fall), marriage

---

145. Augustine, *Nupt.* 1.14.16.
146. Augustine, *Nupt.* 1.15.17, 1.24.27.
147. Augustine, *Nupt.* 2.20.35.
148. Augustine, *C. Jul. op. imp.* 6.26.
149. Augustine, *C. Jul. op. imp.* 6.26.
150. Augustine, *C. Jul. op. imp.* 6.29.
151. Augustine, *Nupt.* 1.11.12.
152. Augustine, *C. Jul. op. imp.* 1.66.
153. Augustine, *C. Jul.* 5.16.62.
154. Clark, "'Adam's Only Companion,'" 161.

was instituted by God from the beginning ("increase and multiply", Gen 1:28),[155] and was not distorted because of the first sin.[156] An element was added to marriage after the fall, however, that was not originally planned by God—the struggle against the desires of the flesh. Because of our first parents' transgression, "there was added to marriage, not as a matter of happiness, but of necessity, a struggle so that by its goodness it too fights against the evil of concupiscence."[157] But, this additional struggle does not corrupt the goodness of marriage itself.[158] For, when virtue prevails in the struggle against *concupiscentia carnis*, marriage makes good use of it,[159] at which marriage "still blushes."[160] The good use of *concupiscentia carnis* is only what is permitted by God, not whatever the desire itself craves.[161] Nor does original sin, which is passed down by marriage through the sexual act to the next generation, destroy or condemn the goodness of marriage either.[162]

Marriage, for Augustine, has two more goods in addition to the good of offspring.[163] The second is the good of fidelity. Fidelity entails two aspects: it preserves the sexual faithfulness of the marriage bed of the couple,[164] and, for couples who engage in sexual activity and for those who do not, it also entails "willing affections"[165] of the heart. Fidelity would have existed effortlessly between two spouses in paradise, but since the fall it always is in danger from one's own sinful desires, or the temptations from someone else.[166] This fidelity is something that even non-Christians have and demand of their spouses.[167] The third good is marriage as a sacrament. Sacramentally, marriage is an inseparable union[168] that "stands in horror at the impiety of divorce."[169] It ensures that a husband will not divorce his wife if she cannot conceive, and that a husband who does not want many children will not give his wife to someone else to impregnate her.[170] It is not lost to a couple if they separate, nor even when either spouse

---

155. Augustine, *Nupt.* 1.21.23.
156. Augustine, *Nupt.* 1.1.1, 2.32.54; *C. du. ep. Pelag.* 1.5.9.
157. Augustine, *C. Jul.* 3.16.30.
158. Augustine, *Nupt.* 1.7.8, 1.14.16.
159. Augustine, *Nupt.* 1.4.5; *C. Jul. op. imp.* 1.65, 1.68, 5.18.
160. Augustine, *Nupt.* 1.24.27.
161. Augustine, *Epist.* 6*.4.
162. Augustine, *C. Jul. op. imp.* 1.61.
163. Augustine, *Nupt.* 1.4.5; *C. du. ep. Pelag.* 1.5.10; *C. Jul.* 3.16.30; *Epist.* 6*.5; *C. Jul. op. imp.* 1.65.
164. Augustine, *C. Jul.* 3.16.30, 5.12.46; *C. Jul. op. imp.* 1.65.
165. Augustine, *Nupt.* 1.11.12; Clark, "Adam's Only Companion," 154.
166. Augustine, *Nupt.* 1.21.23; *C. Jul.* 3.16.30.
167. Augustine, *Nupt.* 1.17.19.
168. Augustine, *Nupt.* 1.21.23.
169. Augustine, *C. Jul.* 3.16.30.
170. Augustine, *C. Jul.* 5.12.46.

(or both) commits adultery.[171] This sacramental bond is as unbreakable a union as the union between Christ and the church.[172]

All three of these goods were present in the marriage of Mary and Joseph, according to Augustine. Jesus was the offspring of their marriage (even though he was not generated by the sexual act between them). The marriage was faithful because there was no adultery, and it was sacramental because they did not divorce.[173] Although they never engaged in intercourse, Augustine claimed that they experienced an affection of the mind,[174] which, for him, made their marriage stronger, not weaker, than any physical joining. Marital abstinence allowed them to "have entered more deeply into those agreements with each other, which have to be observed in greater love and harmony, not by pleasureful embraces of their bodies, but by willing affections of their hearts."[175] Just as Augustine was unique among the Fathers for not having equated marriage and sex, he also was unique for claiming—as early as 397—that Mary and Joseph had a full marriage, even though they never physically consummated it.[176]

Augustine's vision of marriage, as Elizabeth Clark has shown, primarily[177] developed in the crucible of controversy—first against the Manichaeans, then against Jovinian and Jerome, and later against the Pelagians. That vision, she says, became skewed toward the reproductive good of marriage (especially during the Pelagian controversy) such that procreation came to overshadow the "companionate" aspects of marriage.[178] Although Augustine had claimed earlier in his career against the Manichaeans that mental intimacy is more profound than physical intimacy in marriage,[179] his fear of Julian's incessant accusations that he was a Manichaean forced Augustine to stress the procreative good of marriage.[180] Clark critiques Augustine for failing to develop fully the companionate aspects of marriage,[181] and wonders if he would have elaborated on the non-procreative goods of marriage had he not been pressured by his various opponents to focus his attention on procreation.[182] She does credit Augustine's theology of marriage for establishing the foundation

---

171. Augustine, *Nupt.* 1.17.19.

172. Augustine, *Nupt.* 1.21.23.

173. Augustine, *Nupt.* 1.11.13, 1.11.12; *C. Jul.* 5.12.46.

174. Clark, "Adam's Only Companion," 152.

175. Augustine, *Nupt.* 1.11.12.

176. Clark, "Adam's Only Companion," 151.

177. Clark points to two other instigators to Augustine's thought, but these do not apply directly to his arguments against Julian: his assessment of women as secondary, and Late Antique law. Clark, "Adam's Only Companion," 157–62.

178. Clark, "Adam's Only Companion," 139.

179. Clark, "Adam's Only Companion," 151.

180. Clark, "Adam's Only Companion," 157.

181. Clark, "Adam's Only Companion," 140.

182. Clark, "Adam's Only Companion," 162.

that would allow later theological developments of the social aspects of marriage.[183] Although Clark does not specifically name any later developments on the theology of marriage, one recent emphasis on the social aspect of marriage that she may have in mind is from Vatican II's *Gaudium et Spes* (47–52) that emphasizes the unitive aspect of marriage as well as the procreative.

---

183. Clark, "Adam's Only Companion," 149–50, 162.

Chapter 18

The Theology of Cassian

Adam, Adam's *Praeuaricatio*, and the Fall

LIKE ALL CHRISTIANS, CASSIAN believed that the good God made creation good. Probably with the Manichaeans in mind, he rejected those who said that God created a world that was less than perfect that needed to be improved over time, and he insisted that God's creation was perfect from the beginning.[1] His understanding of the human person, like the other authors we have discussed, was rooted in the biblical narrative of Adam. Prior to his indiscretion, Adam was originally created upright (*rectum*),[2] and naturally possessed knowledge of the law.[3] Adam was immortal[4] with an unrestricted will, which inevitably chose the good, because the good was the only choice Adam knew to make.[5] He also was entirely in control of his bodily desires because concupiscence of the flesh was a reality only after Adam's sin.[6]

Cassian recognized that something happened to Adam and to his descendants as a result of his transgression,[7] although his understanding of the human person after the first sin ultimately was more optimistic than Augustine's.[8] The fall itself was caused by his pride,[9] "a most savage beast,"[10] and Adam's envious acquiescence to Eve.[11] Cassian used the phrase *peccatum originale* coined by Augustine to de-

---

1. Cassian, *Coll.* 8.24. See also: 8.6, 23.3.
2. Cassian, *Coll.* 13.12. See also 7.4.
3. Cassian, *Coll.* 8.23–24.
4. Cassian, *Coll.* 8.25.4. See also: 18.16.
5. Cassian, *Coll.* 13.12.1–3.
6. Cassian, *Coll.* 5.6.1–7, 4.7; Stewart, *Cassian the Monk*, 64–67; Rea, "Grace and Free Will," 70–72.
7. Several studies are important for an understanding of Cassian's overall theological anthropology: Rea, "Grace and Free Will," 65–106; Pristas, "Theological Anthropology," 134–369; Ogliari, *Gratia et Certamen*, 265–305.
8. Chadwick, *Primitive Monasticism*, 129; Ogliari, *Gratia et Certamen*, 148–49, 273–74, 406; Pristas, "Theological Anthropology," 217.
9. Cassian, *Inst.* 12.4–5.
10. Cassian, *Inst.* 12.1.
11. Cassian, *Coll.* 8.11, 8.16.

scribe the fall, but he only used it once,[12] and preferd to use the term "transgression" (*praeuaricatio*) to describe Adam's mistake so as to avoid any Augustinian baggage.[13] His conception of Adam's sin, furthermore, is not understood or employed in exactly the same way that Augustine did.

Cassian believed that, through the first sin, the image and likeness of God was violated (*violare*) in humanity.[14] Knowledge of evil was ushered in,[15] and we have become inclined towards vice either through ignorance of what is good, or through passionate attachments.[16] He claimed that Adam's failure was a "damnable dealing and deceitful transaction,"[17] in which Adam was seduced by the serpent. Like a man selling himself into slavery, Adam forfeited his natural freedom (*naturalis libertas*), and, in so doing, condemned not only himself but also his future offspring into perpetual slavery because children of slaves are born into slavery.[18] God, as the true master of Adam, could have prevented Adam from making this tragic mistake, but God respected Adam's freedom to make the decision he made, and would have infringed unjustly upon that freedom if Adam were prevented from selling what had been given to him as a gift to be used as he so desired.[19] By succumbing to the devil's lies, Adam and his descendants have become mortal.[20]

But, humanity has not been completely vitiated by Adam's act; it is not totally depraved. Even after the fall, there remains the "seeds of virtue" in every soul that are not destroyed, but they also must be nurtured by God's aid because the soul cannot make progress in its pursuit of perfection without it.[21] Adam had knowledge of evil after his transgression, but he and his offspring still did not lose the knowledge of good that they naturally possessed. Cassian points to Paul's claim that even the Gentiles, who were not under the law, still had the law written on their hearts (Rom 2: 14–16).[22] This knowledge of natural law also allows the individual to discern what is just (*aequus*).[23] The will, though crippled because of humanity's slavery, is not entirely eliminated or destroyed, but still retains freedom to a partial degree. Two angels, one good and one bad, are attached to each person, but unlike Luther who later would say that the will is ridden

---

12. Cassian, *Coll.* 13.7.3.
13. Ogliari, *Gratia et Certamen*, 275–76.
14. Cassian, *Coll.* 5.6.1.
15. Cassian, *Coll.* 13.12.7.
16. Cassian, *Coll.* 13.12.7.
17. Cassian, *Coll.* 13.12.7.
18. Glancy, *Slavery*, 18.
19. Cassian, *Coll.* 23.12.4–6.
20. Cassian, *Coll.* 8.15.4, 18.16.8, 5.6.2.
21. Cassian, *Coll.* 13.12.7; Hwang, *Intrepid Lover*, 154.
22. Cassian, *Coll.* 13.12.2–3.
23. Cassian, *Coll.* 13.12.5.

either by Satan or God like a beast of burden,[24] Cassian says that the will chooses which angel it follows.[25] "Consequently," Cassian said, "there always remains in the human being a free will that can either neglect or love the grace of God."[26] At the same time, the will cannot choose the good without God's assistance.[27]

Grace and Free Will in Cassian's *Institutio* 12 and *Collatio* 3

Since Prosper of Aquitaine in the fifth century derided him for opposing Augustine (as he put it),[28] and continuing with current scholarly reevaluations that try to decipher what Cassian truly thought,[29] Cassian's writings on grace and free will have drawn more attention than anything else he wrote. In all three of his texts, he stressed the importance of both of grace and free will. But, how did he conceive of the relationship between the two? Did he believe that God's grace comes first and spurs the will towards the good? Did he believe that the will must desire and seek God's assistance before God will provide it? Did he believe that grace and free will somehow move simultaneously together? Cassian focused on grace and free will three times throughout his writings: his *Institutio* 12, *Collatio* 3, and his controversial *Collatio* 13. Although Cassian's *Collatio* 13 is his most important work on grace and free will, serious attention first must be paid to his *Institutio* 12 and *Collatio* 3 that also address them.

In his *Institutio* 12, Cassian's primary agenda was to complete his discussion of eight vices, which he had started in *Institutio* 5, by concluding with the vice of pride.[30] Towards the end, he shifted his attention to grace and free will. His presentation here of the relationship between the two is often ignored by scholars because his depiction of grace and free will is not controversial. Quoting the apostle that the pursuit of perfection "is not of the one who wills or of the one who runs, but of God who is merciful" (Rom 9:16), Cassian insisted that the origin of any sinner's confession of repentance, and the eternal salvation received by the sinner, are not from our own work (*opus*), but from God's gift (*donum*) and grace (*gratia*).[31] He continued to say that the efforts of the monk to be cleansed of fleshly vices are inadequate, and cannot be efficacious without God's compassion and help. No matter how much individual effort through fasting, vigils, reading, isolation—which undoubtedly are important—this

24. Cassian, *Coll.* 5.6.1.
25. Cassian, *Coll.* 5.6.1.
26. Cassian, *Coll.* 5.6.1.
27. Cassian, *Coll.* 5.6.1.
28. Prosper of Aquitaine, *C. coll.* 22.
29. For example: Chadwick, *John Cassian*, 110–36; Rea, "Grace and Free Will," 107–225; Ogliari, *Gratia et Certamen*, 265–304; Casiday, *Tradition and Theology*, 94–118; Macqueen, "John Cassian," 5–28; Morey, "How Unsearchable."
30. His seven previous *institutiones* addressed gluttony, fornication, avarice, anger, sadness, acedia, and vainglory.
31. Cassian, *Inst.* 12.11.2.

work is nothing without God. "For never will a person's own effort and human diligence," he said, "be equal to the divine gift, if it has not been granted by the divine compassion to the one who desires it."[32]

At the same time that he emphasized grace, Cassian stressed the importance of individual effort, because he understood the possibility that his monastic audience could misinterpret his emphasis on grace, and that he might instigate a crisis over the efficacy of ascetic renunciation as the monks of Hadrumetum had experienced when they read Augustine's letter (194) to the priest Sixtus.[33] Repeating once again that his teaching does not come from his own creativity but from the teachings of the monastic elders, he acknowledged that the pursuit of perfection requires diligence (*industria*) and intense toil (*labor*) on the part of the monk. He reiterated that perfection cannot be attained without God's grace. Thus, God's grace and individual effort are both intimately intertwined and necessary for spiritual progress, because God's mercy and grace, he says, are given to those who toil, labor, will, and run.[34]

Without wanting to seem as if he unduly emphasizes monastic renunciation, Cassian repeated that individual effort cannot be executed without the help of God's protection (*protectio*), inspiration (*inspiratio*), correction (*castigatio*) and encouragement (*exhoratio*). This grace, he says, can either come mediated through another's presence, or directly from God.[35] How, Cassian demands, can human beings, who are dust and ashes, work towards salvation without God's assistance when Christ said that he himself could do nothing without the Father (John 5:30, 14:10)? All sinners, even the most advanced renunciants, need God's grace at every moment.[36]

At no point in his *Institutio* 12 does Cassian say whether he thinks that God's grace must come before human effort is possible, or if the will must show a modicum of initiation before God will provide his assistance. He simply asserts that both grace and free will are necessary. It is unclear why Cassian did not explore the question of priority. It could be that, as a monastic thinker rather than a theoretician, it wasn't a question that interested him. It also could be that, at this moment, he hadn't yet come to his own answer to the question. But, he certainly knew that the question itself was contested, because he was aware of the Pelagians and their teachings on the relationship between grace and the will at least as early as the writing of this *Institutio*.

Cassian never explicitly named the Pelagians in this *Institutio*. There are some clues he leaves, however, that indicate that his description of grace and free will was intended to refute them.[37] Towards the end of the *Institutio*, Cassian exhorts

---

32. Cassian, *Inst.* 12.13.
33. Weaver, *Divine Grace*, 4–16.
34. Cassian, *Inst.* 12.14.1.
35. Cassian, *Inst.* 12.12.16.
36. Cassian, *Inst.* 12.17.1.
37. Casiday makes a similar argument. Casiday, "Cassian against Pelagians," 7–23.

his readers to give thanks for the graces that God has bestowed on humanity that is worth quoting at length:

> Let us offer him [God] thanks not only for these things, that he created us rational, gave us the power of free will, bestowed on us the grace of baptism, and granted us the knowledge and help of the law, but also for the things that are conferred on us by the daily exercise of his providence—namely, that he frees us from the snares of our adversaries, that he works with us in order that we may be able to overcome the vices of the flesh, that he protects us from dangers even unbeknownst to us, and he guards us from falling into sin, that he helps and enlightens us so that we may be able to understand and recognize this very help of ours (which some wish to be interpreted as nothing other than the law [*quod non aliud quidam interpretari uolunt quam legem*], that by his inspiration we are secretly struck with compunction for our heedlessness and wrongdoing, that we are most salutarily chastened when he deigns to visit us, that we are often even against our will drawn to salvation by him, and lastly, that, when he visits and moves us, he turns even our free will itself, which is readily inclined to vice, to better things and to the path of virtue.[38]

It will be recalled, as discussed in an earlier chapter, that the Pelagians did believe in the necessity of God's grace, but their definition of grace was too narrowly defined for Augustine, and, as we now see here, too narrowly defined for Cassian as well. Cassian's initial description of the graces of reason, free will, baptism, and knowledge and assistance of the law—which he does not deny are important gifts from God—clearly echoes the narrow Pelagian definition of grace that is limited to human nature and external aids in the pursuit of a sinless life. But, Cassian, again like Augustine, asserts that grace also must be understood as God's active agency in "the daily exercise"[39] of life. Daily, God internally transforms the individual to avoid sin and vice; God does not simply offer signposts for the individual to decipher and follow. The most noteworthy part of the long quotation above is his vague statement that "some" (*quidam*) want to interpret God's grace as nothing other than the law. Although Cassian does not specify the identity of these mysterious people, it seems evident from his description of the definition of grace that he rejects that he had the Pelagians in mind.

In Cassian's *Collatio* 3, *De tribus abrenuntiationibus*, we see a slightly different presentation of grace and free will. This *Collatio* was a conversation between Cassian, Germanus, and Paphnutius, who was the elderly priest of the Scetis community, and "resplendent with brilliant knowledge as if he were a large celestial body."[40] As a young man, Paphnutius began his training in a cenobium, and attempted to eradicate his vices, and perfect his virtues. Desiring to advance more deeply in the spiritual life, he moved into the most remote corners of the desert where he was rarely seen by anyone.

38. Cassian, *Inst.* 12.18.
39. Cassian, *Inst.* 12.18.
40. Cassian, *Coll.* 3.1.1.

When Cassian and Germanus knew him, he was over ninety years old. He had lived five miles from their church for many years, but moved closer to it so he would not have to travel far on Saturdays and Sundays. When he returned to his cell, he would bring back enough water for an entire week on his shoulders, and refused any assistance from younger men, thus gaining him the nickname "The Buffalo."[41]

The first half of the *Collatio*, which is not relevant for our purposes, addresses three different monastic callings (from God, from human agency, and from need),[42] and three different monastic renunciations (rejection of wealth and the resources of the world, rejection of vices and affections of the soul and body, and a rejection of everything present and visible).[43] In the second half, Paphnutius discussed grace and free will, because Germanus grew uncomfortable with how Paphnutius seemingly diminished the importance of the will.[44] Paphnutius did insist that the free will is important. It is the responsibility of the individual "to be either more or less attentive to the opportunities"[45] that God's grace offers. In other words, it is the obligation of the individual to respond to God's assistance. God never forces anyone against their will. Just as Abraham had to respond to God's call to leave his homeland (Gen 12:1–4), so, too, every Christian must respond to God's call as well.[46] God, furthermore, gratuitously offers salvation; at the same time, however, God does not unilaterally determine how one will spend eternity after this life. The salvation of each soul also depends on "the extent that we have either neglected or been zealous to conform with devout obedience"[47] to God's providence. Neither God's graciousness nor the individual's will are sufficient to be saved. God must offer salvation, but it must be accepted.[48]

Germanus correctly intuited Paphnutius's stress on grace, however. While Cassian emphasized the necessity of both grace and free will in his *Institutio* 12, here, in his *Collatio* 3, he noticeably championed grace over the will. More forcefully than in his *Institutio* 12, Cassian insisted that good habits and untiring effort are important, but God must cooperate (*cooperor*) with human effort.[49] God's assistance sustains and strengthens the will when it falters, as it inevitably will do as it is wounded by sin.[50] The movement of the will and its work are completed (*implere*) by grace,[51] which liberates the enchained (Ps 146:7), lifts up the fallen (Ps 146:8b), and makes the blind see

---

41. Cassian, *Coll.* 3.1.1–3.
42. Cassian, *Coll.* 3.4.1.
43. Cassian, *Coll.* 3.6.1.
44. Cassian, *Coll.* 3.11.
45. Cassian, *Coll.* 3.12.1.
46. Cassian, *Coll.* 3.12.1.
47. Cassian, *Coll.* 3.19.1.
48. Cassian, *Coll.* 3.19.3.
49. Cassian, *Coll.* 3.12.2, 3.15.3.
50. Cassian, *Coll.* 3.12.3–5.
51. Cassian, *Coll.* 3.15.2.

(Ps 146:8a).⁵² Everything that relates to salvation comes from God. Even faith is a gift, which, like the will, is flawed and needs God's assistance to strengthen it.⁵³ The will, furthermore, is insufficient to persevere through the travails of life; only God's charity can provide the endurance needed to navigate the difficult waters of existence.⁵⁴ "Nothing," Paphnutius summarizes, "at all can be done in this world without God."⁵⁵

The most important difference between *Institutio* 12 and *Collatio* 3 is not this emphasis on grace, but that Cassian specifies that grace comes before the movement of the will.⁵⁶ Four times throughout this short section, Paphnutius says that the beginning (*initium, principium*) of salvation comes from God's side, not the side of the will. For example, he says that "the beginning [*initium*] of our conversion and faith and the endurance of sufferings are all granted us by the Lord."⁵⁷ Also, in reference to the Psalmist who said "Confirm, O God, what you have worked in us" (Ps 68:28), Cassian says that "the beginnings [*principia*] of salvation and the grace conferred by God's gift are not enough for him [David] unless they have been perfected by his mercy and daily assistance."⁵⁸ Three times in this same section, Paphnutius claims that spiritual fruit, the beginning of a good will, and salvation all are preceded by God's inspiration (*inspiratio, inspirare*). He says, for example, that "we hasten to the way of salvation as result of the Lord's inspiration [*inspiratio*],"⁵⁹ and later he says that "no one can bring forth spiritual fruit without his [God's] inspiration (*inspiratio*) and cooperation."⁶⁰ This precedence of grace before the will that is not found in *Institutio* 12 probably arose out of a growing concern over the persistence of Pelagianism in Gaul, which Cassian felt compelled to correct here in his *Collatio* 3.⁶¹

Grace and Free Will in Cassian's Collatio 13

Cassian's discourse on the relationship between grace and free will in his *Collatio* 13, which may have been written between 426 and 428,⁶² is the centerpiece of his con-

52. Cassian, *Coll.* 3.15.3.
53. Cassian, *Coll.* 3.3.16.1–2.
54. Cassian, *Coll.* 3.17.
55. Cassian, *Coll.* 3.20.1.
56. Ramsey, "General Introduction," In *The Institutes*, 115.
57. Cassian, *Coll.* 3.15.1.
58. Cassian, *Coll.* 3.15.2. See also: "the beginning [*initium*] of our salvation is by the Lord's call," (3.10.6.), and "by these words [Ezek 11:18–20] we are very clearly taught that the beginning [*initium*] of a good will is bestowed upon us at the Lord's inspiration" (3.19.1.).
59. Cassian, *Coll.* 3.10.6.
60. Cassian, *Coll.* 3.16.4. See also: "by these words [Ezek 11:18–20] we are very clearly taught that the beginning of a good will is bestowed upon us at the Lord's inspiration [*inspirare*]" (3.19.1.).
61. Casiday, "Cassian against Pelagians," 14–15.
62. Weaver and Casiday claim that it was written in 426, while Chadwick claims that it was written in 428. Weaver, *Divine Grace*, 97; Casiday, *Tradition and Theology*, 114; Chadwick, *Primitive Monasticism*, 116.

tribution to the Pelagian controversy. For this reason, too often it has received an excessive amount of scholarly attention at the expense of his other contributions that are also discussed in this chapter.

Cassian's and Germanus's interlocutor was Abba Chaeremon, whom they had met shortly after they had disembarked in Egypt when Bishop Archebius took them just outside of Panephysis to sit at his feet.[63] Chaeremon was over one hundred years old when they met him. His body was broken by age and constant prayer causing his back to curve to the point that his hands touched the ground.[64] His bodily extremities were "already weak and dying,"[65] but he did not abandon his strict ascetic observance. When Cassian and Germanus asked him to share "a word"[66] of wisdom with them, he initially hesitated, because he felt that his tired body did not allow him to perform as rigorously as he had in his younger days, so his advice would be deficient as he did not practice the same advice he would give them.[67] Despite his lack of confidence, Cassian and Germanus prevailed on him, and what he taught them constituted Cassian's *Collationes* 11, 12, and 13.

The first eight sections of *Collatio* 13 are virtually identical to *Collatio* 3. Here, like in *Collatio* 3, Cassian asserts that grace must move prior to a good act of the will because "human frailty can accomplish nothing which pertains to salvation" without God's assistance.[68] Human striving, he says, should never be placed on the same plane as grace, nor should it be believed that individual "efforts have brought upon it the divine generosity, boasting that its own deserving toil has been responded to with an abundant harvest."[69] The good movement of the will as well as good thoughts, rather, find their origin (*principium*) in God's grace, and that God inspires (*inspirare*), begins (*incipere*), carries out (*exsequor*), and fulfills (*consummare*) the good that the will does.[70] At the same time, Cassian reaffirms that grace is not tyrannical, and that the individual must conform (*subsequor*) to God's daily aid.[71] A farmer's toil of tilling the field is nothing without God's gift of rain, while, at the same time, the farmer cannot be lazy and neglect plowing it on a regular basis.[72]

Beginning in section nine, Cassian complicated his previous claims of the prerequisite of grace, and indicated that sometimes the good movement of the will antecedes

63. Cassian, *Coll.* 11.2.1–4.2.
64. Cassian, *Coll.* 11.4.1–2.
65. Cassian, *Coll.* 11.4.2.
66. Cassian, *Coll.* 11.4.2. In monastic literature, especially the literature of the Egyptian monks, the ascetics are often asked to "speak a word" of advice.
67. Cassian, *Coll.* 11.11.4.2–3.
68. Cassian, *Coll.* 13.6.1.
69. Cassian, *Coll.* 13.3.2.
70. Cassian, *Coll.* 13.3.5.
71. Cassian, *Coll.* 13.3.6.
72. Cassian, *Coll.* 13.3.1–3.

grace that then prompts God to respond to the will, which scandalized Prosper in Cassian's own time. "Even by his own activity," Cassian said, "a person can occasionally be brought to a desire for virtue."[73] Cassian offered Zacchaeus (who—without receiving any instruction from Jesus—gave half of his possessions to the poor, and repaid fourfold to whomever he had cheated (Luke 19:1–10), and the thief on the cross (who—unprompted by any show of mercy—asked Jesus to remember him when he went into his kingdom (Luke 23:40–43) as examples of men who, "by their own desire,"[74] stirred Jesus to reward them with salvation.

This new claim of the agency of the will did not supplant his earlier claims about grace and free will, for he continued to insist that God often instigates the good actions of the will. By the end of this *Collatio*, Cassian failed to definitively articulate if he believed that God's grace must initiate the good will to act, or if the good movement of will is able to stir prior to God's assistance. The issue itself, he said, is "a great question,"[75] and he purposefully refused to answer it. The spiritual physics of grace and free will seem to be logically irreconcilable, and they seem impossible to harmonize with each other; but, the paradox of the reality still does not invalidate that both statements must be accepted as true.[76] Sometimes God's grace inspires those who desire a deeper devotion, while sometimes God compels (*conpellere*) others against their will. Sometimes God assists those good actions that the will already desires, while at other times God inspires the beginning of the desire, the beginning of the good action, and the perseverance in the action. When God inspires and leads us towards salvation (even sometimes against our will), God rightly can be called the protector and savior. At the same time, when God assists, supports, and defends us after we have sought God's salvation, he rightly can be called the supporter and refuge.[77] Cassian's apparent inability to resolve this dilemma, was, in fact, an attempt to strike a balance between the necessity of both grace and free will.[78] As Ogliari has succinctly put it: "what he [Cassian] wishes to retain, at the expense of metaphysical clarity, is the inner (and inclusive) coherence of the dialectical co-operation between grace and free will."[79] Cassian did not see his *Collatio* as logically incoherent, but that he was bowing to yet another Christian mystery that is not fundamentally different than the trinitarian, christological, and ecclesial mysteries that Christians hold together in tension in their minds every day.

A simple image Cassian employed to drive home the confluence of grace and the will is the care that a nurse has for an infant. In the beginning, the nurse carries

---

73. Cassian, *Coll.* 13.9.4.
74. Cassian, *Coll.* 13.11.4.
75. Cassian, *Coll.* 13.11.1.
76. Cassian, *Coll.* 13.11.4.
77. Cassian, *Coll.* 13.17.1. See also: 13.18.2.
78. Ramsey, "John Cassian," 124.
79. Ogliari, *Gratia et Certamen*, 148.

the child in her arms. When the child has reached a certain age, she allows the child to crawl. Later, she takes the child by the hands and supports him as he takes his first steps. If the child is able to make progress on his own, the nurse will allow him to walk without any assistance, but she remains hovering over the child so that, when the child begins to lose his balance, she will either prevent the child from falling, or she will pick him up after she has allowed the child to fall softly. As the child matures, the nurse will place obstacles in his way in the hopes that his muscles will be strengthened through the physical exertion. In the same way, God knows who is a spiritual infant, toddler, or adolescent, and God will shed his grace as appropriate.[80]

The most contentiously debated aspect of *Collatio* 13 among scholars, without a doubt, addresses the object (or objects) of Cassian's critique. Although he did not name anyone explicitly, it is clear that Cassian did not simply repeat what he had learned in the Egyptian desert. Rather, he envisioned *Collatio* 13 as a correction to what he saw as unsatisfactory answers previously given about grace and the free will. Answers given by whom? Prosper of Aquitaine was convinced that Cassian wrote against Augustine for not giving enough agency to the will.[81] For this reason, Christians down the centuries often have approached Cassian with suspicion (including not canonizing him as a saint in the West).[82] While some scholars have agreed with Prosper that Cassian wrote against Augustine,[83] others have argued that Cassian was writing against Pelagius.[84] Others have argued that he was writing against both Pelagius and Augustine simultaneously,[85] and Prosper himself has been offered as Cassian's object of attack.[86] I agree with those scholars who suggest that Cassian took issue with both Pelagius and Augustine, as it seems evident to me that Cassian was well-versed in the thought of both men, and he found fault with both.[87]

---

80. Cassian, *Coll.* 13.14.9. Over one thousand years later in his fight with Luther, Erasmus will repeat almost the exact same illustration. In Erasmus's image, it is a father who lifts up his child to help it walk across a room to obtain an apple at the other side. The father holds the child's hand, and steadies his footsteps. Although the child cannot stand if the father does not lift him, the child does participate in the endeavor with his own efforts, no matter how feeble his efforts may be. Erasmus on Rotterdam, "On Freedom," 91.

81. Prosper of Aquitaine, *C. coll.* 2.1, 22.

82. Stewart, *Cassian the Monk*, 21 n. 196.

83. Chadwick, *Primitive Monasticism*, 29–30; Stewart, *Cassian the Monk*, 20; Weaver, *Divine Grace*, 110–14; Ogliari, *Gratia et Certamen*, 133–35; Driver, *John Cassian*, 16; Chadwick, *Early Church*, 182; Hwang, *Intrepid Lover*, 146.

84. Markus, *End of Ancient Christianity*, 178.

85. Ramsey, "Student of Augustine," 5–6; Rousseau, *Ascetics, Authority*, 231; Rea, "Grace and Free Will," 155.

86. Casiday, *Tradition and Theology*, 117. Elsewhere, Casiday puts forward another possibility that Cassian was writing against unwritten ideas among his local peers. Casiday, "Cassian against Pelagians," 20–22.

87. Ramsey, I believe, has convincingly shown that in several places of this *Collatio* where Cassian leveled pointed criticisms at both Augustine and Pelagius, although, admittedly, Cassian did not mention either man by name. Section seven rejects Augustine's pessimism regarding the salvation;

PART II: THEOLOGY

Sinlessness

Like Augustine, Jerome, and Orosius before him, Cassian denounced the Pelagians for their claim that people can choose to be sinless if they want it badly enough, but his analysis of sinlessness is significantly different from these other authors.[88] Cassian's arguments against sinlessness begin in *Collationes* 22 and 23,[89] which were dialogues between Cassian, Germanus, and with Abba Theonas.[90] Abba Theonas most likely lived in Scetis.[91] The beginning of *Collatio* 21 tells us that his parents made him marry at a young age, because they were concerned about his chastity, believing that marriage would prevent him from falling into sin. He had been living with his spouse for five years when he went to Abba John—who was in charge of alms for the poor—to offer him a tithe.[92] After listening to John's teaching, Theonas decided that he must leave his wife and devote himself to the ascetic life.[93]

In his *Collatio* 22, Cassian offers his first of two critiques of the idea that one may live a sinless life. He rests this first critique on a christological foundation. It is Christ, and Christ alone, whose life was lived without falling to temptation. "But," Cassian says, "what would be the meaning of what the apostle says—namely, that he came in the likeness of sinful flesh—if we too could have a flesh unpolluted by any stain of sin? For he says this of him who alone is without sin as if it were something unique: 'God sent his Son in the likeness of sinful flesh'" (Rom 8:3).[94] For Cassian, one can never claim that one may be sinless because sinlessness is reserved only for Christ, and anyone who claims such a place with Christ is anathema. "Whoever [*quisquis*] dares to say that he is without sin, therefore, claims for himself, by a criminal and blasphemous pride, an equality in the thing that is unique and proper to him alone."[95] To whom does this *quisquis* refer?

---

section eleven takes issue with Augustine for his primacy on grace at the exclusion of the will, while, at the same time, takes issue with Pelagius for his emphasis on the will; section sixteen addresses the Pelagian definition of grace. Ramsey, "General Introduction," in *The Institutes*, 461–62.

88. This section is based largely on an earlier publication in *Cistercian Studies Quarterly*: Squires, "Cassian on Sinlessness," 411–32.

89. Rebillard claims that *Collatio* 11 was written against Pelagius. Cassian's only brief mention of sinlessness (11.9.5.), I argue, leads to the conclusion that Cassian had probably only heard of Pelagius's argument through Augustine or Jerome at that point; it was not until later that he had actually read Pelagius's own writings. Rebillard, "*Quasi Funambuli*," 209.

90. We cannot know exactly when they were written, but Weaver says that we can be certain that the third group "would have been completed between Honoratus's accession in late 426 and his death, probably early in 429. Because of the close relation among the three groups, it seems reasonable that the third group was composed soon after the first two, thus probably 427." Weaver, *Divine Grace*, 94.

91. Stewart suggests that "the evidence seems to converge on Scetis, rather than either Panephysis or Diolcos, as Theonas' monastic home." See Stewart's analysis of the available data on Theonas's geographic location. Stewart, *Cassian the Monk*, 137.

92. Cassian, *Coll.* 21.1.1.

93. Cassian, *Coll.* 21.9.7.

94. Cassian, *Coll.* 21.11.1.

95. Cassian, *Coll.* 22.12.3.

It cannot be Germanus, because he never made any claim that sinlessness is possible. Cassian must be arguing against someone outside of the dialogue between Theonas and Germanus. It is clear that he was referring to the Pelagians.

The main focus of this *Collatio* was on the problem of nocturnal emissions. A discussion about sinlessness was a tangent leading away from this stated goal. Theonas, therefore, did not wish to pursue the topic of sinlessness and stopped the dialogue before going any further.[96] He resumed his discussion—and introduced a second critique of Pelagius—in *Collatio* 23,[97] the "companion"[98] to *Collatio* 22, which often is ignored in favor of others, and does not receive the proper scholarly attention it deserves.[99] Scholars often believe that it is tedious and offers little for a greater understanding of Cassian's thought. Ramsey, for example, dismissed it when he stated that it "is little else than a lengthy and somewhat repetitive commentary."[100] We will see that it is much more than that.

Collatio 23 begins as a close analysis of Paul's statement that "the good that I want to do I do not do, but the evil that I hate, this I do. But if I do what I do not want, it is no longer I who do it but sin dwelling in me . . . I delight in the law of God according to the inner man, but I see another law in my members at war with the law in my mind and making me captive to the law of sin that is in my members" (Rom 7:19), which was introduced at the end of *Collatio* 22. Few of Cassian's *Collationes* confined themselves to a close analysis of only one particular passage,[101] but he used this passage from Paul as a springboard to criticize Pelagius's understanding of sinlessness. Germanus believed that Paul was speaking about common sinners,[102] and could not believe that the apostle would ever refer to himself in such a disparaging way. Theonas countered Germanus saying that Paul, in fact, was talking about himself (and those who also were spiritually mature),[103] and only appears to be speaking about sinners.[104] For Theonas, sinners would never claim that they do not want to do evil.[105]

---

96. Cassian, *Coll.* 22.16.

97. Julien Leroy and Ansgar Kristensen argue that this *Collatio* was intended for a cenobitic audience. Leroy, "Les préfaces," 171–74; Kristensen, "Cassian's Use," 271. Stewart, however, argues that "there is no geographical reference in them that fixes Theonas' location, though the milieu seems to be anchoritic." Stewart, *Cassian the Monk*, 137.

98. Stewart, *Cassian the Monk*, 86.

99. Kardong. "John Cassian's Teaching," 249–63; Macqueen. "John Cassian," 5–28; Fiske, "Cassian and Monastic Friendship," 190–205.

100. Ramsey, "General Introduction," in *The Conferences*, 785. Rebillard is an exception who has argued that it is "*au cœur de la controverse pélagienne.*" Rebillard, "*Quasi Funambuli*," 198.

101. Haag, "Precarious Balance," 180.

102. Boniface Ramsey claims that Germanus was following Origen's exegesis here and that Theonas's contradiction to this claim goes against Origen. Ramsey, "General Introduction," 783.

103. Cassian, *Coll.* 23.16.2, 23.1.1.

104. Cassian, *Coll.* 23.2.1.

105. Cassian, *Coll.* 23.1.3.

It is impossible to know exactly what were Paul's failures until one is on his spiritual level. Although he certainly had "splendid and precious jewels"[106] that few other men could obtain, he would give them all up to reach the perfection that had eluded him. What is this perfection? Theonas used the biblical example of Mary and Martha (Luke 10: 38–42)[107] to indicate that even though Paul (and the other apostles) was virtuous in chastity, abstinence, prudence, hospitality, sobriety, temperance, mercy, and justice,[108] the perfection that he sought, and could not permanently obtain, was *theoria*, or the contemplation of God (*contemplatio Dei*).[109] While it is good to possess all virtues, permanent contemplation of God is superior to everything else.[110] He insists that it only will be in the future when the corruption of this life has been replaced by grace that one will be able to bask ceaselessly in the beatific vision.[111] This definition of sinlessness is noteworthy as it differs from the definitions of sinlessness from Augustine and Jerome. Cassian allows for an individual (someone as holy as Paul) to be perfectly virtuous. No one is entirely sinless, however, because one cannot remain vigilant in prayer.[112] One may be *sanctus*, but not *immaculatus*.[113]

No matter how virtuous one is in this life, or how much one wants to devote oneself to contemplation, one inevitably must act. Even when one is able to have a quiet mind for a time, the needs of the flesh inevitably force the mind to lose focus. Not even Paul, blessed with many gifts, was able to sustain his gaze upon God, because of Paul's earthly distractions.[114] To common sinners, the inability to maintain unceasing prayer seems like an insignificant problem. To men like Paul who strive to keep their gaze on God's splendor and ignore the trials of daily life, however, this mental endeavor is no trivial matter.[115] These holy men understand that the briefest lapse in contemplation is a great offense against God because to turn away from Eternal Beatitude to the finitude of the sensorial world is a sin of impiety. Theonas tells Germanus why

---

106. Cassian, *Coll.* 23.2.4.

107. This story of Mary and Martha would become the standard story recited by monks throughout the medieval period to indicate the superiority of the contemplative life over the active life. Pelikan, *Growth*, 119–20.

108. Cassian, *Coll.* 23.2.2.

109. It is the definition of sinlessness as *theoria* where we can best see the Evagrian foundation for Cassian's rejection of Pelagius. Evagrius claimed that the monk's goal was to achieve a state of pure prayer after having gone through a rigorous ascetic process that harnessed the mind. This pure prayer leads to the contemplation of the Trinity. While Cassian did not use the exact same vocabulary as Evagrius (Cassian often avoided Evagrius's vocabulary), the Evagrian ideal is present in *Collatio* 23. Cassian's rejection of Pelagius's belief in the possibility of sinlessness, then, is clearly rooted in Evagrian soil.

110. Cassian, *Coll.* 23.4.4.

111. Cassian, *Coll.* 23.3.4.

112. Cassian, *Coll.* 23.5.9.

113. Cassian, *Coll.* 20.12.

114. Cassian, *Coll.* 23.5.1, 23.5.30, 23.5.5–6.

115. Cassian, *Coll.* 23.6.2.

Paul took this seemingly insignificant problem so seriously, saying that "rightly will a person be guilty not only of no insignificant sin but in fact of the very serious crime of impiousness if, while pouring forth his prayer to God, he suddenly goes after a vain and immoral thought and abandons his presence, as if he neither saw nor heard."[116] Contrary to Paul and those like Paul, those who "cover the eyes of their heart with a thick veil of vice"[117] are constantly running from pleasure to pleasure in hopes of finding fleeting moments of happiness.

The problem with sinners, Theonas says, is that they are unaware that they should even strive for the perfection of sinlessness. Sinners are only capable of realizing the severity of the "capital crimes"[118] that they commit and feel that it is only the worst sins which need to be avoided. When such sins are successfully averted, the sinner feels that he has done his duty and has achieved a state of sinlessness. This false sense of spotlessness precludes the sinner from seeking forgiveness from God.[119]

In chapter 11, Cassian shifts his discussion from articulating the problem of the impossibility of permanent contemplation of God to the cause of this problem: a broken humanity where the flesh is constantly at "war with the law of [the] mind."[120] One is forced to abandon *contemplatio* because the human condition, after the fall of Adam and Eve, no longer has the capacity to remain forever turned towards God. The necessity of sin is "inserted in the nature of the human condition . . . which leads captive their understanding by the violent law of sin, forcing it to abandon the chief good and to submit to earthly thoughts."[121] Cassian rejects the Pelagian idea of the unadulterated free will in *Collatio* 23, because every descendent of Adam suffers from this "violent law of sin."

Just as earlier we saw in his *Institutio* 12 that Cassian anonymously pointed to "some" (*quidam*) who narrowly defined grace as reason, will, baptism, and the law, which clearly was a reference to the Pelagians, and in *Collatio* 22 where Cassian criticized "whoever" (*quisquis*) claimed that they are without sin was also a reference to the Pelagians, here, in *Collatio* 23, Cassian once again (anonymously) criticizes the Pelagians for their insistence on the possibility of a sinless life. Towards the end of the *Collatio*, Theonas says that

> whoever [*quisquis*], then, ascribes sinlessness [*anamarteton*]—that is, impeccability [*impeccantia*]—to human nature must go against not empty words but the witness and proof of his own conscience, which is on our side, and he may declare that he is without sin only when he feels that he has not been violently torn away [*avellere*] from the highest good. For, indeed, whoever looks into his

116. Cassian, *Coll.* 23.6.4.
117. Cassian, *Coll.* 23.6.5.
118. Cassian, *Coll.* 23.7.1.
119. Cassian, *Coll.* 23.7.2.
120. Cassian, *Coll.* 23.11.1.
121. Cassian, *Coll.* 23.11.1.

own conscience, to give but one example, and sees that he has attended even one synaxis without having been interrupted [*interpellatio*] by any word or deed or thought may declare that he is sinless.[122]

The remark that "whoever" (*quisquis*) claims that a sinless life is possible, I am convinced, is yet another reference to the Pelagians, because neither Cassian, nor Germanus, nor Theonas made such a claim.

Christology

In an earlier chapter, we reviewed the scholarly debate over the christological worth of Cassian's *De incarnatione*. We saw that most scholars have deemed it to be theologically deficient, while Casiday and Fairbairn want to rehabilitate its reputation. Everyone agrees, however, that the text did not make an important contribution to Nestorius's downfall. While Cassian's *De incarnatione* is often examined by scholars for its Nestorian content, it is rarely mentioned in scholarship on the Pelagian controversy, or even the so-called "Semi-Pelagian Controversy."[123] Weaver, for example, never references it in her *Divine Grace and Human Agency: A Study of the Semi-Pelagian Controversy*, and does not even feel that it is worth including in her bibliography.[124] Although a discussion of Cassian's own Christology and his understanding of Nestorius's Christology would be outside the focus of this study, I believe that the *De incarnatione* offers a christological critique of the Pelagians that has been overlooked by modern scholars.

Cassian claimed that Pelagius's Christ was simply an example for humanity to emulate in the quest for sinlessness: "if Christ who was born of Mary," he said, "is not the same Person as He who is of God, you [Nestorius] certainly make two Christs; after the manner of that abominable error of Pelagius ... [who] said that he [Christ] was the teacher rather than the redeemer of mankind; for he did not bring to men redemption of life but only an example [*exemplum*] of how to live."[125] Pelagius, as was discussed earlier, stated several times the importance of the example of Christ. In his *Expositiones ad Romanos*, he says of Romans 5:12 ("just as through one person sin came into the world, and through sin death") that sin and death happen "by example or by pattern. Just as through Adam sin came at a time when it did not yet exist, so in the same way through Christ righteousness was recovered at a time when it survived in almost no one. And just as through the former's sin death came in, so also through the latter's righteousness life was regained."[126] Later, in the same text, he said that Jesus

---

122. Cassian, *Coll.* 23.19.1. I have changed Ramsey's translation here from "snatched away" to "violently torn away" to indicate the severity of the force at hand.

123. A notable exception to this is Rousseau, *Ascetics, Authority*, 174 n. 31.

124. Weaver, *Divine Grace*, 241.

125. Cassian, *De inc.* 6.14. See also 1.2–3.

126. Pelagius, *Expos. (ad Romanos)* 5:12, and 8:3; *Ad Dem.* 8.4.

"offered, by way of grace to overcome sin, teaching [and] example."[127] For Pelagius, Christ is the exemplar on which we can model our lives if we want to live lives free of sin because Christ was without sin.

Pelagius, according to Cassian, asserted that Christ was no more than an *exemplum* for our own spiritual journeys because Pelagius's Christology did not adequately account for Christ's divinity. Throughout the *De incarnatione*, Cassian repeatedly returned to the accusation that Pelagius believed that Christ was a "mere man" (*solitarius homo*). At the beginning of the text, for example, Cassian says that "in saying that Jesus Christ lived as a mere man without any stain of sin, they [Pelagians] actually went so far as to declare that men could be without sin if they liked."[128] Later in the same text, he said, that "you [Nestorius] say then that Christ was born a mere man. But certainly this was asserted by the wicked heresy of Pelagius, as we clearly showed in the first book [of the *De incarnatione*]; viz., that Christ was born a mere man."[129] He repeatedly accused Nestorius of reviving Pelagian errors, saying that Nestorius was "trying to fan the flame of the ashes of Pelagianism," and "belching out the poison of Pelagianism, and hissing with the very spirit of Pelagianism."[130]

Cassian[131] understood the christological implications of Pelagius's belief of Christ as *exemplum* and a "mere man."[132] For Cassian, as for Augustine and Jerome, Christ is more than an example to imitate and more than a mere human being. Christ is the savior of humanity. "For all the prophets and all the saints," he said, "received from God some portion of the Divine Spirit as they were able to bear it. But in Christ 'all the fullness of the Godhead' dwelt and 'dwells bodily' (Col 2:9). And therefore they all fall short of His fullness, from whose fullness they received something; for the fact that they are filled is the gift of Christ: because they would all certainly be empty were He not the fullness of all."[133] To say that Christ is simply a human exemplar to emulate is to call into question Christ's role as mediator between God and humanity.

127. Pelagius, *Expos. (ad Romanos)* 6:14.

128. Cassian, *De inc.* 1.3.

129. Cassian, *De inc.* 5.2. See also 1.3, 5.1.

130. Cassian, *De inc.* 5.1.

131. Hanby more recently has also explored Pelagian Christology. Hanby, *Augustine and Modernity*, 73–81. Although Hanby attributes to Augustine a correct assessment of Pelagius's Christology, he does not recognize that Cassian understood this problem as well. Hanby sees Cassian as almost as dangerous as Pelagius.

132. Casiday, I argue, does not adequately grasp the soteriological problems of Pelagius's Christology. He claims that "in their defense, it should be acknowledged that they espoused a broadly sacramental view of salvation that belies Cassian's insinuation about the Pelagian Christ being merely a teacher." While Casiday is right to point towards the Pelagian belief in the necessity of baptism, he overestimates the sacramental value of Pelagius's understanding of baptism. Baptism for Pelagius was an entrance into the Christian community for both babies and adults and a washing away of sins in adults. Casiday, *Tradition and Theology*, 111.

133. Cassian, *De inc.* 5.14.

Conclusion

THE COUNCIL OF EPHESUS of 431 that condemned the Pelagians, but whose main focus was the condemnation of Nestorius for his insistence on using the title *Christotokos* to describe Mary, was not so much of a triumphant blow against the Pelagians as it was an eastern pro forma affirmation of earlier western conciliar, papal, and imperial condemnations against them. The Pelagian controversy, which by then had raged for two decades, sputtered to its conclusion simply because it had run out of steam. Jerome had died over a decade earlier. Pelagius and Orosius most likely had died not long after him.[1] Augustine, who had been invited to attend the council, had died essentially with his pen in his hand the year before it.[2] Caelestius, Julian, and Cassian had ceased writing, and did not live much longer after it. Death, in the end, got the final word.

Despite the definitive outcome against the Pelagians, fights repeatedly sprang up over the next sixteen hundred years that wrestled with similar anthropological issues—or often the exact same fights were repeated all over again. Before the Pelagian controversy even came to an end, the so-called "Semi-Pelagian Controversy"—which is a moniker that is universally disliked by scholars today,[3] but a better one has yet to catch on—was already underway. The first phase of this controversy comprised of a group of monks at a monastery in Hadrumetum in North Africa who were upset with Augustine's emphasis on grace to the detriment, in their minds, of monastic effort. Around 426, a certain Florus from that community was visiting Uzalis where he read a copy of a letter (194) Augustine wrote to the future Pope Sixtus III around 418 in which he described his understanding of grace.[4] Florus copied the letter and sent it back to Hadrumetum with his colleague, Felix, and then went to Carthage. Before Florus returned to Hadrumetum, Felix shared the letter with some of the other monks who became greatly disturbed by it, because they

---

1. Gennadius says that Orosius "flourished almost at the end of the reign of the emperor Honorius." This could be a reference to the fact that Orosius completed his *Historiae* in 418. It also could be a hint that Orosius died before Honorius did in 423. Gennadius, *De vir. Inlustr.* 40.
2. Davis, *First Seven*, 154.
3. Hwang, *Intrepid Lover*, 1–10.
4. Augustine, *Epist.* 214.3.

took it to mean that meritorious actions in this life are ultimately inconsequential.[5] After his arrival, Florus informed Valentinus, the superior of the monastery, of the scandal the letter had caused, leading Valentinus to write to Evodius, the bishop of Uzalis, for clarification.[6] Evodius's response was less than edifying, so Valentinus appealed to a priest named Januarius, who also did not satisfactorily resolve the drama. Valentinus then sent two monks, Cresconius and a different Felix than the Felix who brought the letter from Uzalis, to visit Augustine.[7]

Augustine explained to them the meaning of his letter to Sixtus, and asked that they stay in Hippo for further conversations, but they wanted to return home to celebrate Easter. He wrote a letter (214) to Valentinus elaborating on his teaching on the relationship between grace and the will, but Cresconius and Felix, despite their expressed desire to go back to Hadrumetum, remained in Hippo through Easter.[8] The Felix who originally had brought the letter written to Sixtus back from Uzalis then arrived in Hippo. The bishop of Hippo continued teaching all three men, and, when they eventually returned to Hadrumetum, he sent his initial letter to Valentinus, a second letter to him (215), and some of the most important sources of the Pelagian controversy, including the two letters (175, 176) to Pope Innocent from the Council of Carthage and the Council of Milevis in 416, the letter (177) to Pope Innocent from five North African bishops, Innocent's three letters (181, 182, 183) in response, a letter (no longer extant) to Pope Zosimus from an African council that was held in the winter of 417–418, Zosimus's *Tractoria*, and the canons of the Council of Carthage of 418. He also hinted to Valentinus that he should review Cyprian's *De dominica oratione*, which Augustine somehow knew that Valentinus already owned.[9] Most importantly, Augustine wrote and sent his *De gratia et libero arbitrio*, which discussed the will, and, more importantly, the need for grace.[10]

These texts did not quell the debate at Hadrumetum. Valentinus wrote a letter (216) to Augustine recounting the history of the events in his monastery, and sent it to Augustine with Florus, whose presence Augustine had requested.[11] Augustine then learned that an unnamed monk there had concluded that if grace is of primary importance, then the correction of any monk for failing to live up to the monastic ideal would be moot. Prayer on behalf of the monk should be the only appropriate measure of rebuke. This prompted Augustine to write a third letter to Valentinus,[12] and to write

5. Augustine, *Epist.* 216.2–3.

6. This letter is not found in Augustine's corpus of letters translated by WSA, but may be found on pages 42–44 of vol. 4 of *Answer to the Pelagians* by WSA.

7. Augustine, *Epist.* 214.1.

8. Augustine, *Epist.* 215.1.

9. Augustine, *Epist.* 215.2–3.

10. Augustine, *Grat.* 1.1.

11. Augustine, *Epist.* 214.6, 215.8.

12. This letter is not found in Augustine's corpus of letters translated by WSA, but may be found on page 53 of vol. 4 of *Answer to the Pelagians* by WSA.

his second treatise to the monks at Hadrumetum, his *De correptione et gratia*,[13] in which he argued for the necessity and efficacy of brotherly rebuke.[14]

This treatise may have appeased the African monks, because we do not hear from them again. But, it caused a new outbreak of drama in southern Gaul. At some point between 427 and 429, Prosper of Aquitaine and a certain Hilary wrote separate letters (225, 226) informing Augustine of the turmoil there. Little is known about Hilary, a layman, but Prosper's modest literary output made him an important figure in Late Antiquity, although, these days, he is often overlooked and underappreciated. Almost nothing is known about the life of Prosper (c. 388–c. 456–466), who continued to clash with the Gallic monks after Augustine died. He was a layman, like Hilary, and probably was born into an aristocratic family in Aquitaine. Undoubtedly, he received a first-class education, which came to an end around 406 when he was taken into captivity for a time by the Goths. At some point, he was released from bondage for unknown reasons, and around 416 he moved to Marseilles, also for unknown reasons.[15]

Prosper's literary career unfolded in a fascinating arc that consisted of three distinct periods.[16] Initially, from the time he wrote his *Epistula ad Rufinum* around 427 until he wrote his *Pro Augustino responsiones ad excerpta Genuensium* in 432, Prosper, as Weaver has stated, "became the recognized interpreter of the African bishop and the chief spokesman for the Augustinians in Gaul,"[17] especially when it came to predestination. In the second period, from 432 to 435, Prosper still defended Augustine, but, at the same time, he softened his statements by giving more efficacy to the will. It was during this time that Prosper wrote the text for which he is best known, his *Pro Augustino liber contra collatorem* against Cassian's *Collatio* 13, *De protectione Dei*. In it, Prosper insisted that Cassian's description of the relationship between grace and the will significantly differed from Augustine, leading him to sharply demand why Cassian would "leave the impregnable fortress of truth and step by step run down the precipice of the Pelagian heresy."[18] The third period began after he moved to Rome and joined the administration of Pope Leo I (440–461),[19] and was characterized by a new understanding of the authority of the bishop of Rome, which led him to place even more emphasis on the free will. As Hwang has remarked about the last phase of his life, Prosper "began to move away

---

13. Augustine, *Corrept.* 3.5.

14. Weaver, *Divine Grace*, 4–35; Ogliari, *Gratia et Certamen*, 28–89.

15. Hwang, *Intrepid Lover*, 37–51, 233.

16. Weaver, *Divine Grace*, 152–53; Hwang similarly argues that there were distinct periods in Prosper's life, but he demarcates them differently than Weaver. He argues that the four periods are (1) 417–425; (2) 426–430; (3) 430–440; (4) 440–455. Hwang, *Intrepid Lover*, 1–2.

17. Weaver, *Divine Grace*, 118.

18. Prosper, *C. coll.* 14.2.

19. Weaver says that Prosper went to Rome in 435, while Hwang has said that he didn't move until 440. Weaver, *Divine Grace*, 139; Hwang, *Intrepid Lover*, 187.

from strict adherence to Augustine's doctrine of predestination as [his] appreciation of the Roman Church began to emerge."[20]

The monks in southern Gaul had been acquainted with at least some of Augustine's anti-Pelagian writings, but they were uncomfortable with certain aspects of them.[21] When they obtained a copy of his *De correptione et gratia*, some of them were appeased by it, but others were even more disturbed than they had been before they read it. They asserted that the human will has more agency than Augustine allowed, and they believed that God foreknew from the beginning of time who would believe in Jesus, but that God did not predestine them. If God had already decided who would be saved and who would not be saved based on his sovereign decision, then there would be no incentive for anyone, monk or lay person, to strive for sanctity.[22] They also had beliefs, Prosper said, that were close to the Pelagians in that they define grace as "the creation of every human being."[23] In other words, when God created human beings, he gave them free will and reason that alone are sufficient for choosing good and avoiding evil. They also disagreed with Augustine on the death of infants who die without baptism, insisting that infants would be saved or not saved based on God's knowledge of how they would have acted in this life had they lived.[24]

Hilary's letter to Augustine similarly claimed that the monks were uncomfortable with Augustine's vision that God chooses to give to some people the grace to believe, but not others. One must inevitably conclude, if Augustine were right, that preaching is fruitless for those who have not been given that grace. The belief of the sinner, they said, comes from us after God has given us our nature that has the ability to choose to believe. When a sinner believes, he will receive assistance from God, but the initial movement comes from the individual to either turn towards or away from God.[25] Furthermore, they said that the gospel is preached to people when God foreknows that they will believe.[26] God foreknows who will believe the gospel and who will not believe it, but he does not predestine them either way. Human nature, though damaged, still has the ability to choose to believe and to persevere, but, because of that damage, belief and perseverance also can be lost.[27] Similar to the monks of Hadrumetum, they also complained that Augustine's vision of grace renders exhortation and rebuke useless, insisting that God rejects or accepts those who choose to receive

---

20. Hwang, *Intrepid Lover*, 9.

21. As was mentioned in an earlier chapter, scholars usually relegate Cassian to the Semi-Pelagian controversy, and ignore his contributions to the Pelagian controversy.

22. Augustine, *Epist.* 225.3.

23. Augustine, *Epist.* 225.4.

24. Augustine, *Epist.* 225.5.

25. Augustine, *Epist.* 226.2.

26. Augustine, *Epist.* 226.3.

27. Augustine, *Epist.* 226.4.

the exhortation and rebuke.[28] Finally, they insisted that the list of those who have been saved, and those who have not been saved, is not fixed, but that God wills that all humans be saved.[29] In response to these letters from Prosper and Hilary, Augustine wrote his *De praedestinatione sanctorum*,[30] in which he reasserted that the *initium fidei* is entirely gratuitous, that the grace given by God does not simply allow one to believe, but that it makes one believe, that the grace to believe is not given to everyone, and that predestination, not foreknowledge, is how salvation is brought about.[31] Augustine also composed his *De dono perseverantiae*,[32] in which he says that the gift of perseverance in belief, like the gift of belief itself, is unearned.[33]

This controversy did not end after the deaths of Prosper and Hilary,[34] but took on a new form with Faustus of Riez (c. 405–c. 490) and Fulgentius of Ruspe (c. 467–c. 532). Faustus, like Pelagius, probably was born in Britain, but moved to Gaul with his family when he was still very young. Sometime around 424, he joined the monastery at Lérins, and became its third superior around 433. Later, around 457, he became the bishop of Riez.

During a council in Arles in 473, a certain priest named Lucidus came under scrutiny because he apparently had taught a form of predestination that had made the bishops there nervous. Eventually, he would disavow his own teaching, but the synod asked Faustus to write a treatise that summarized their views on grace, the will, and predestination, and to present it the following year at the next council. Before that next council, the Council of Lyons met in 474. Faustus's treatise, his *De gratia* written in 474, distilled the thinking on these anthropological issues from both synods. His position, like the Gallic monks before him, took nothing away from God's grace, but he also wanted to emphasize the importance of the will, and individual effort. Most importantly, he tried to walk a middle path between an extreme predestinarian view on the one hand, and an extreme emphasis on the will on the

---

28. Augustine, *Epist.* 226.5–6.

29. Augustine, *Epist.* 226.7–8.

30. Augustine, *Praed.* 1.1–2, 9.17–19.38.

31. Creswell, "St. Augustine's Dilemma," 186–91; Lamberigts, "Augustine on Predestination," 279–305; Rist, "Augustine on Free Will," 420–47; Wetzel, "Predestination, Pelagianism," 49–58.

32. Augustine, *Persev.* 2.2.

33. Weaver, *Divine Grace*, 37–69; Ogliari, *Gratia et Certamen*, 93–183; Hwang, *Intrepid Lover*, 137–86.

34. Often times Vincent of Lérins is included in conversations about this controversy, but not every scholar believes that his famous *Commonitorium* was intentionally written against Augustine, and, therefore, should not be included as part of this fight. Thomas Guarino, for example, has argued that "because of Vincent's sophisticated reflection on these questions, it makes little sense—and is textually unjustified—to reduce his small but incisive *Commonitorium* to a semi-Pelagian manifesto dedicated to attacking Augustine's theory of grace and predestination." Guarino, *Vincent of Lérins*, xxviii.

other hand.[35] The result of his effort, however, was to place more emphasis on human effort than even Cassian had done decades earlier.[36]

During his lifetime, Faustus was highly esteemed by his contemporaries. But, because of his emphasis on the will, his reputation began to suffer after his death, primarily because of Fulgentius, whom Robert Eno has called "the greatest North African theologian after the time of Augustine."[37] Like Faustus, Fulgentius seems to have come from a prominent family and received a quality education. As a young man in North Africa, he had been his family's estate manager for a time, and a procurator. He then lived on his family's property as a monk, but later moved to a monastery to live in community where he would become its superior. For a time, he had wanted to flee to the Egyptian desert—because of his admiration for Cassian—but only made it as far as Syracuse before he was convinced to turn around. He became the bishop of Ruspe around 507, and would serve in that capacity for approximately twenty-five years. Immediately after his ordination, he and sixty other bishops were sent into exile to Sardinia by the Arian Vandal Thrasamund, because he had forbidden any Nicene bishops to be ordained. Fulgentius was recalled to North Africa by Thrasamund in 516 in order to debate him, but, when Thrasamund could not demonstrate the superiority of Arianism, he sent Fulgentius back to Sardinia in 519 where Fulgentius would stay until King Hilderic allowed him to return in 523 after Thrasamund died.[38]

At approximately the same time that Fulgentius was sent to Sardinia for the second time, a certain African bishop named Possessor, who was in exile in Constantinople, wrote to Pope Hormisdas (514–523) asking about the trustworthiness of Faustus. Hormisdas replied that Augustine's teaching on grace was authoritative, but Faustus's teaching should be considered his own personal opinion, and not an articulation of Christian teaching. A group of Scythian monks, who were also in Constantinople at the time, caught wind of this, and concluded that if Augustine's teaching on the centrality of grace is correct, then Faustus's emphasis on the will must be incorrect. These monks wrote to the African bishops in Sardinia for confirmation, and Fulgentius responded with a letter, and his *De veritate praedestinationis et gratiae Dei*.

In this treatise, composed in 523 after his return to North Africa, Fulgentius countered Faustus's emphasis on the will with an emphasis on grace and predestination. Predestination, he insisted, was the only reasonable conclusion to the Christian doctrine of salvation by grace. Foreknowledge alone does not adequately safeguard God's sovereignty. For, if God simply knows how an individual will behave in life, then God's decisions concerning salvation become dependent on the individual's actions. Such a claim is anathema, as it calls into question God's immutability. God does not change, and therefore God does not change his will about who will receive eternal life, or who

---

35. Smith, *De Gratia*, 1–20, 55–59; Weaver, *Divine Grace*, 157–80.
36. Weaver, *Divine Grace*, 174.
37. Eno, "Introduction," xv.
38. Eno, "Introduction," xv–xvii; Fairbairn, "Introduction," 3–22; Weaver, *Divine Grace*, 180–98.

will not, because of human action. Those who will be saved and those who will not have been chosen by God long before the creation of the world. That cannot change. Fulgentius did envision predestination a bit differently than Augustine did, however. First, he said that if God's grace is infused in an individual, that person will inevitably choose the good. Second, he passed over any consideration of Christians who had been faithful but, for whatever reason, lapsed in their religious commitment. Third, Fulgentius claimed that individuals can know in this lifetime whether or not they will be saved. Fourth, he insisted that knowledge of one's election to heaven does not eliminate the necessity of submission to ecclesiastical teaching and commands.[39]

This controversy seemed to have no end in sight when Caesarius of Arles (469/70–542) stepped onto the scene. Caesarius became a lector at the age of seventeen. At the age of nineteen, he joined the monastery at Lérins. Five to seven years after that, he went to Arles to recuperate from health problems. During his time there, he began to study Roman literature, but concluded that such literature was more harmful than helpful for the spiritual life, so he ceased reading it, just as Jerome had done for a time. The bishop of Arles at that time, Aeonius, was related to Caesarius, and ordained him first to the diaconate, then to the priesthood, and later made him the superior of the monastery in Arles. In 502, Caesarius succeeded him, and would be the bishop there for the next forty years until his death. He gained a reputation as a powerful preacher, even though he shunned sophisticated rhetoric in favor of a style that was understandable to the masses. Primarily, he was concerned with the moral striving of those in his charge, so his sermons were less focused on grace, and more concerned with exhorting his flock to live more rigorous Christians lives. He also wrote a short theological treatise, his *Opusculum de gratia*, for a more educated audience that emphasized grace over individual effort.[40]

This controversy finally concluded almost one hundred years after it began when Caesarius convened the Second Council of Orange in July of 529 at which "essential Augustinism was vindicated."[41] It gathered at the same time that a new basilica that had been funded by a certain Liberius, the praetorian prefect of Gaul, was dedicated. Fourteen bishops (including Caesarius) and eight influential laymen in attendance promulgated twenty-five canons that were followed by a *Definitio fidei*. This Council was confirmed by Pope Boniface II (530–532) in 531. It took a clear Augustinian position in its teaching on original sin, claiming that both the body and the soul were spoiled by Adam's first sin. Like all the other authors in this controversy, it asserted the importance of God's grace. Against Cassian, it stated that the *initium fidei* always comes from the prompting of God, and never comes from the individual. At the same time, it also asserted the importance of human effort.

---

39. Klingshirn, "General Introduction," xi–xvii; Weaver, *Divine Grace*, 199–225.
40. Klingshirn, "General Introduction," xi–xvii; Weaver, *Divine Grace*, 199–225.
41. Pelikan, *Emergence*, 327.

CONCLUSION

The Council made two crucial contributions. The first was that baptism was the avenue by which the will gains its freedom. "The choice of the will," canon thirteen proclaimed, "which was weakened in the first human being can be restored only through the grace of baptism. Once something is lost, it can be returned only by someone who could give it in the first place. Thus Truth himself says 'if the Son sets you free, then you will be free indeed'" (John 8:36).[42] In other words, prior to baptism, the will can choose nothing good. But, after baptism, the will now has the ability to turn towards good or evil. The decision where to turn is now entirely up to the will. At the same time, the council reaffirmed the necessity of God's assistance for accomplishing the good. The second contribution was to definitively declare that no one is predestined to hell. The *Definitio fidei* stated that "not only do we not believe ourselves that the divine power predestines anyone to evil, but we also completely detest and condemn any who choose to believe such a terrible thing."[43] While predestination to damnation was officially condemned here for the first time, it should be noted that the fight over God's foreknowledge of one's future faithfulness or predestination to heaven based on God's sovereignty was not settled.[44]

In the ninth century, a conflict over grace, the will, foreknowledge, and predestination once again exploded. This time, the fight was between Gottschalk of Orbais, Ratramnus, Servatus Lupus (the abbot of Ferrières), and Florus of Lyons (all of whom Pelikan dubbed the "latter-day Augustinians"[45]) on one side of the split, and Hincmar of Reims, and Rabanus Maurus on the other side. Hincmar charged Gottschalk with upholding grace while ignoring the will. Unsurprisingly, Gottschalk shot back with the opposite charge that Hincmar upheld the will at the expense of grace. This time, angels were dragged into the fray when Hincmar claimed that God gave free will to both angels and humanity, but Gottschalk responded that both humanity and angels always need God's assistance. In 853, Hincmar convened the Council of Quiercy that asserted both the importance of the will, and election to heaven based on foreknowledge. Florus protested that both of Quiercy's conclusions were devoid of God's grace. Two years later, a synod in Valence denounced the Council of Quiercy, and a synod in Langres in 859 affirmed the Council of Valence.[46]

It was, of course, the Protestant Reformation in the sixteenth century—and the early modern Catholic[47] response to it—when anthropological fights volcanically erupted yet again, this time irreparably tearing apart Christianity, devastating Europe

---

42. Second Council of Orange, "Synod of Orange," 116.

43. Second Council of Orange, "Synod of Orange," 119.

44. Second Council of Orange, "Synod of Orange," 112–28; Mathisen, "Councils of Orange," 250–51; Pelikan, *Emergence*, 327–31; Weaver, *Divine Grace*, 225–34.

45. Pelikan, *Growth*, 90.

46. Pelikan, *Growth*, 80–95.

47. O'Malley, *Trent*, 1–15.

through decades of war, and setting the stage for our postmodern milieu.[48] Anyone who attempts to appreciate adequately this revolution first must grasp the fifth century, for, as Diarmaid MacCulloch has said, "it is impossible to understand why the Reformation happened or the profound nature of the issues at stake"[49] unless one comprehends Augustine's thought in general, and his anti-Pelagian thought in particular. Virtually all of the old ghosts were back from the grave for reconsideration: original sin, grace, the will, baptism, predestination, and the role of the monastic life, to name just some of the most important. In their anthropological assertions, both Protestants and Catholics "claimed to be defending the Augustinian heritage and to be recovering the true Augustine"[50] (as Prosper of Aquitaine had considered himself to have done after Augustine died), and of carrying forward his legacy. Neither side, however, could fully lay claim to the bishop of Hippo, because, in their interpretations of him, "both sides were right, and both were wrong."[51]

Martin Luther (1483–1546), as legend has it,[52] ignited the Reformation by nailing his *Ninety-Five Theses* to the doors of the *Schlosskirche* in Wittenberg on October 31, 1517. Although Luther was an Augustinian Friar prior to abandoning his vows, his early intellectual formation did not include Augustine, because, at that time, Augustine was not required reading for the Friars. It was only during the 1509–1510 academic year that Luther encountered Augustine in a serious way when he read his *De Trinitate*, and *De civitate Dei*.[53] Through reading Augustine and Paul's Epistle to the Romans, Luther began to develop his mature theological anthropology.[54] He also gradually began to conclude that Thomism, Nominalism, and his contemporary rival the humanist Erasmus of Rotterdam (who was more partial to Jerome than to Augustine)—in fact all of Catholicism—was thoroughly Pelagian, and in desperate need of theological rehabilitation.[55]

A detailed study of Protestant anthropology—which would include not only Luther's anthropology, but also anthropologies from other important Protestants such as John Calvin, Ulrich Zwingli, Martin Bucer, Menno Simons, Thomas Müntzer, and others—necessarily would be massive, and is outside the scope of our project here. For the sake of brevity, it is enough to focus our attention on the Lutheran *Confessio Augustana* that was drafted by Philipp Melanchthon, because it was not only a foundational document for the Lutheran tradition, but it also became part of the DNA

---

48. Gregory, *Unintended Reformation*, 1–24.
49. MacCulloch, *Reformation*, 107.
50. Pelikan, *Emergence*, 331.
51. Pelikan, *Emergence*, 331.
52. MacCulloch, *Reformation*, 119.
53. Pereira, *Augustine of Hippo*, 265–342; Oberman, *Luther*, 158–61.
54. Janz, *Luther*, 6–33.
55. Oberman, *Dawn of Reformation*, 108–14; Janz, *Luther*, 4, 25; O'Malley, *Trent*, 104; Pelikan, *Reformation*, 16–18, 139–40, 258–59, 262; Pereira, *Augustine of Hippo*, 307–20.

of the statements of faith of other Protestant traditions.⁵⁶ It was presented to the Emperor Charles V (1500–1558) in 1530⁵⁷ when Charles gathered a number of Protestant groups together at a diet, and invited them to present their differing views to him.⁵⁸ In addition to the Lutheran statement, Zwingli sent his own, as did four German cities (Strasbourg, Constance, Memmingen, and Lindau) that sent their *Confessio Tetrapolitana*, which was written by Bucer and Wolfgang Capito.⁵⁹ Luther was not present, as he could not leave Saxony for fear of capture.⁶⁰

The *Confessio Augustana* summarized Lutheran teaching in twenty-eight sections, including descriptions on original sin, justification, free will, and faith and good works, among others. The second article, concerning original sin, stated that, after Adam's fall, "all men begotten according to nature, are born with sin, that is, without the fear of God, and with concupiscence; and that this disease or vice of origin is truly sin, even now condemning and bringing eternal death upon those not born again through baptism and the Holy Ghost."⁶¹ The claim that humanity has suffered dire consequences because of Adam's sin has been a contested theme throughout this book. We see in this Lutheran claim, however, that *concupiscentia* is not simply the first evil⁶² or defect⁶³ as Augustine described it, or even a "spark"⁶⁴ (*fomes*) as the medieval scholastics described it, but that *concupiscentia* itself "is truly sin" (*vere sit peccatum*). The article continues to condemn "the Pelagians and others, who deny that the vice of origin is sin, and who, to obscure the glory of Christ's merit and benefits, argue that man can be justified before God by his own strength and reason."⁶⁵ The fourth article, on justification, asserted that "men cannot be justified before God by their own strength, merits or works, but are freely justified for Christ's sake through faith, when they believe that they are received into favor and that their sins are forgiven for Christ's sake, who, by his death, has made satisfaction for our sins. This faith God imputes [*imputare*] for righteousness in his sight."⁶⁶ The eighteenth article, on the free will, insisted that the will does have limited freedom concerning "the attainment of civil righteousness, and for the choice of things subject to reason," but that "it has no power, without the Holy Ghost, to work the righteousness of God, that is,

---

56. MacCulloch, *Reformation*, 169.
57. Kittelson, *Luther*, 233.
58. Oberman, *Luther*, 29.
59. Oberman, *Luther*, 237.
60. Kittelson, *Luther*, 230–39.
61. Melanchthon, *Augsburg Confession*, 66.
62. Augustine, *C. Jul.* 4.2.13.
63. Augustine, *Nupt.* 2.9.22; *C. Jul.* 4.9.54, 6.11.34, 6.18.53; *C. Jul. op. imp.* 4.29.
64. Pelikan, *Reformation*, 278–79.
65. Melanchthon, *Augsburg Confession*, 66.
66. Melanchthon, *Augsburg Confession*, 79.

spiritual righteousness."[67] Furthermore, it condemned "the Pelagians and others who teach that, without the Holy Ghost, by the power of nature alone, we are able to love God above all things," because the will "cannot work the inward motions, such as the fear of God, trust in God, chastity, patience, etc."[68] The twentieth article, concerning good works, claimed that "our works cannot reconcile God or merit forgiveness of sins, grace and justification, but that we obtain this only [*tantum*] by faith, when we believe that we are received into favor for Christ's sake, who alone has been set forth as the Mediator and Propitiation, in order that the Father may be reconciled through him."[69] Good works are necessary, but sinners do not "merit grace by them."[70] They should be done simply "because it is the will of God. It is only [*tantum*] by faith that forgiveness of sins and grace are apprehended."[71]

The Council of Trent (1545–1563) was one of the Catholic responses to the challenges posed by the Protestants. As early as 1536, some Catholics expressed a desire for a conciliar gathering to address these Protestant arguments. But, it wasn't until Pope Paul III (1534–1549) convened the first of three periods (1545–1547, 1551–1552, 1562–1563) of the council in the small town of Trent that it finally got under way.[72] Throughout the three periods, the council primarily focused its attention on the challenges brought by Luther, who died the year after the first period began. Doctrinal decisions were promulgated, but pastoral problems, such as the problem of prelates not residing in their diocese for extended periods of time,[73] also were confronted. At the beginning, Trent was in danger of failure, as only a small group of thirty-one bishops and fifty theologians made the arduous trip to the Italian Alps. By the end, it became one of the most important councils in the history of Christianity.[74]

The Council participants decided that they wanted to take up those issues that were the most controversial—the issues of original sin and justification—right from the beginning, rather than waiting for the council to gather momentum by commencing with peripheral issues. In June 1546, at the fifth session, the council issued six anathemas concerning original sin. The first anathematized anyone who claimed that Adam had not lost his holiness and justice with which he had been made, that Adam had not suffered death because of his sin, and that Adam was not changed in body and soul. The second anathematized anyone who claimed that Adam's sin only changed him, and not his progeny. The third anathematized anyone who claimed that original sin may

---

67. Melanchthon, *Augsburg Confession*, 125.
68. Melanchthon, *Augsburg Confession*, 125.
69. Melanchthon, *Augsburg Confession*, 137.
70. Melanchthon, *Augsburg Confession*, 138.
71. Melanchthon, *Augsburg Confession*, 138.
72. The number of inhabitants of Trent were approximately seven to eight thousand people. O'Malley, *Trent*, 2.
73. The sixth session of 1547 addressed this problem.
74. O'Malley, *Trent*, 1–22.

be taken away by natural means, or any means other than Jesus. It also anathematized anyone who denied that Christ's merit is applied to both adults and infants in the baptismal waters. The fourth anathematized anyone who denied that newly born infants need baptism. The fifth, and most important for our purposes, anathematized "anyone [who] denies that by the grace of our Lord Jesus Christ which is conferred in baptism, the guilt [*reatus*] of original sin is remitted, or says that the whole of that which belongs to the essence of sin is not taken away but says that it is only canceled or not imputed [*imputare*]."[75] It continued to claim that an inclination to sin and *concupiscentia* remain in those who are baptized. This *concupiscentia* must be understood as "of sin," and that it "inclines to sin"; it is not, as the *Confessio Augustana* claimed, "truly" sin.[76] The sixth simply stated that this session would not discuss the Virgin Mary.[77]

The bishops, in January 1547, at the sixth session promulgated a decree (which was passed unanimously) and thirty-three canons concerning justification. The decree declared that the free will was not extinguished (*exstinguere*) by the sin of Adam, although it was weakened (*attenuare*). Sinners are translated from being children of Adam to being children of Christ through baptism, or the desire for it. The beginning of justification in adults comes from the grace of Christ so that those in sin may "convert themselves to their own justification by freely assenting to and cooperating with that grace," and that "man himself neither does absolutely nothing while receiving that inspiration, since he can also reject it, nor yet is he able by his own free will and without the grace of God to move himself to justice in his [God's] sight."[78] When sinners cooperate with this grace, they "are disposed to that justice when, aroused and aided by divine grace . . . they are moved freely toward God."[79] After this preparation for justification, justification itself is not limited to the forgiveness of sins, but it is the "sanctification and renewal of the inward man through the voluntary reception" of Christ's grace.[80] This decree, like the Council of Orange in 529, did not address the question of predestination to heaven, but it did declare that sinners do not know in this life whether or not they have been predestined to heaven (with the exception of a special revelation), or even if they have been given the gift of perseverance.[81] Justification can be lost through sin, but it also can be regained through the sacrament of reconciliation. The last chapter of the decree took up the ever-contentious issue of good works. It asserted that "since Christ Jesus . . . continually infuses strength into those justified, which strength always precedes [*antecedere*], accompanies [*comitare*], and follows [*subsequi*] their good works, and without which they could not in any manner

75. Council of Trent, *Canons and Decrees*, 23.
76. Council of Trent, *Canons and Decrees*, 21–23.
77. O'Malley, *Trent*, 102–8.
78. Council of Trent, *Canons and Decrees*, 31–32.
79. Council of Trent, *Canons and Decrees*, 32.
80. Council of Trent, *Canons and Decrees*, 33.
81. Council of Trent, *Canons and Decrees*, 38.

be pleasing and meritorious before God, we must believe that nothing further is wanting to those justified."[82] The canons of this session reinforced the decree by offering anathemas on a variety of Protestant claims concerning justification.[83]

More infighting came to a head during the seventeenth century between the Jesuits and the so-called Jansenists, a term that was coined by the Jesuits in the 1640s even though Jansen's admirers simply called themselves "Friends of the Truth." Cornelius Jansen (1585–1638) had been a student in Paris starting in 1604. In 1617, he became a professor at Louvain, and the bishop of Ypres in 1636. He claims to have read everything that Augustine had ever written ten times, and to have read his anti-Pelagian writings thirty times.[84]

His love of Augustine, and his suspicion of the Jesuits, led him to begin writing his *Augustinus* in 1628, and finally completed it just before his death in 1638. He directed his executors to publish the text after he died; it was printed two years later in 1640. In this three-volume tome, he criticized the Jesuits (and others) for worldliness, moral laxity, a disordered emphasis on the will and human reason, and excessive reception of communion. Jansen asserted a theology that stressed the brokenness of humanity, the need for grace, the irresistibility of grace, a limited will, and predestination to heaven and to hell.[85]

Because Jansen already had died, it was left to his admirers to carry his cause forward. One of the most important of these admirers was Antoine Arnauld (1612–1694). Arnauld had studied at the Sorbonne and was ordained a priest in 1641. He wrote a series of books attacking his opponents on a number of fronts. In 1643, he wrote his *De la fréquente communion* that criticized the growing practice of frequent reception of communion, claiming that it devalued the Eucharist by making it common. It was widely read and supported by bishops, theologians, and the masses, as it had been written in French, rather than Latin. That same year, he wrote his *Théologie morale des Jésuites*, in which he reprimanded the Jesuits for their systems of morality that they had developed after the Council of Trent that seemed loose. The following year, he anonymously wrote his *Première Apologie pour Jansénius* (although the author was known to all) that articulated Jansen's ideas in French. The next year, 1645, he penned his *Seconde Apologie*.[86]

The anti-Jansenist furor manifested itself in several ways. Almost immediately after *Augustinus* was published, the Jesuits at Louvain strongly condemned it. The Inquisition in Rome examined it, and the first of several papal condemnations was published in 1643 by Urban II (1623–1644) with his bull *In eminenti*. Six years later,

---

82. Council of Trent, *Canons and Decrees*, 41.

83. O'Malley, *Trent*, 109–16.

84. Doyle, *Jansenism*, 1; Bireley, *Refashioning of Catholicism*, 188; MacCulloch, *Christianity*, 797.

85. Cragg, *Church and Age*, 25–26; Bireley, *Refashioning*, 188; MacCulloch, *Christianity*, 797; Doyle, *Jansenism*, 1, 17–22.

86. Bireley, *Refashioning*, 188–89; Doyle, *Jansenism*, 22–24.

the Sorbonne considered a series of Jansenist propositions for condemnation. Five of these propositions were condemned in the 1653 bull *Cum occasione* by Pope Innocent X (1644–1655). The five condemned propositions were:

> (1) Some of God's commandments are impossible for the Just to obey, because they lack the grace to make it possible; (2) in the state of fallen nature, there can be no resistance to interior grace; (3) for merit and demerit after the fall, it is not necessary to have freedom from necessity, it is enough to have freedom from constraint; (4) the Semi-Pelagians admitted the necessity of an interior and prevenient grace, even for the beginning of faith, but they were heretical in holding that it might be either resisted or obeyed; (5) it is a Semi-Pelagian error to say that Christ died for all men.[87]

None of these five propositions may be found word-for-word in *Augustinus*, so Innocent was forced to write a letter the following year clarifying that the five condemned propositions came from Jansen. Pope Alexander VII (1655–1622) promulgated yet another bull, *Ad sacram*, in 1656 that reaffirmed Innocent's claim that the five propositions came from Jansen. In February 1665, Alexander issued another bull, *Regiminis apostolici*, that required bishops, priests, deacons, female religious, and teachers to sign a formulary condemning the five propositions. Pope Clement XI (1700–1721) published yet another encyclical, *Unigenitus*, in 1713 that condemned not only the five propositions, but the entire Jansenist movement.[88]

In our own time, Christianity continues to struggle over the issue of the efficacy of the will in light of God's sovereign activity. Pope Francis,[89] in particular, has repeatedly denounced what he believes to be a dangerous and persistent threat that he has labeled as "neopelagianism." His concerns do not come from a specific theological controversy between two individuals or two parties, but come from what he sees as an intellectual malady infecting Christianity today.[90] Just eight months after he was elected pope on March 23, 2013 after Pope Benedict XVI shocked the world by stepping down, Francis published *Evangelii gaudium*, his first apostolic exhortation, on November 24, 2013, in which he described "the self-absorbed promethean neopelagianism" of people who trust "only in their own powers and feel superior to others because they observe certain rules or remain intransigently faithful to a particular

---

87. Doyle, *Jansenism*, 91.

88. Bireley, *Refashioning*, 188–89; MacCulloch, *Christianity*, 797–98; Doyle, *Jansenism*, 22–31.

89. Pope Pius XI is another recent pope who described what he saw as a new manifestation of Pelagianism. In 1928 he said that "the wise men of this age of ours, who follow the ancient error of Pelagius, ascribe to human nature a certain native virtue by which of its own force it can go onward to higher things." Two years later, he said that "it is abundantly clear that readers of Augustine will not be caught in the toils of that pernicious [Pelagian] error, which was widespread during the eighteenth century, namely, that the inborn impulses of the will should neither be feared nor curbed, since all of them are right and sound." Pope Pius XI, *Miserentissimus Redemptor*, 8; *Ad salutem*, 32.

90. As of the publication of this book, Francis is still the Pope. It is possible that Francis may return to this theme again in the future.

Catholic style from the past. A supposed soundness of doctrine or discipline leads instead to a narcissistic and authoritarian elitism, whereby instead of evangelizing, one analyzes and classifies others, and instead of opening the door to grace, one exhausts his or her energies in inspecting and verifying."[91]

Almost five years later,[92] in his third apostolic exhortation, *Gaudete et exsultate*,[93] Francis elaborated on this concern, saying that

> the same power that the gnostics attributed to the intellect, others now began to attribute to the human will, to personal effort. This was the case with the pelagians and semi-pelagians. Now it was not intelligence that took the place of mystery and grace, but our human will. It was forgotten that everything "depends not on human will or exertion, but on God who shows mercy" (Rom 9:16) and that "he first loved us" (1 John 4:19). Those who yield to this

---

91. Pope Francis, *Evangelii Gaudium*, 94.

92. On November 10, 2015, Francis addressed the Fifth Convention of the Italian Church, and discussed the dangers of a new form of Pelagianism: "Pelagianism leads us to trust in structures, in organizations, in planning that is perfect because it is abstract. Often it also leads us to assume a controlling, harsh and normative manner. Norms give Pelagianism the security of feeling superior, of having a precise bearing. This is where it finds its strength, not in the lightness of the Spirit's breath. Before the evils or problems of the Church it is useless to seek solutions in conservatism and fundamentalism, in the restoration of obsolete practices and forms that even culturally lack the capacity to be meaningful. Christian doctrine is not a closed system, incapable of raising questions, doubts, inquiries, but is living, is able to unsettle, is able to enliven. It has a face that is supple, a body that moves and develops, flesh that is tender: Christian doctrine is called Jesus Christ. The reform of the Church then—and the Church is *semper reformanda*—is foreign to Pelagianism. She is not exhausted in the countless plans to change her structures. It instead means being implanted and rooted in Christ, allowing herself to be led by the Spirit. Thus everything will be possible with genius and creativity." Pope Francis, "Pastoral Visit."

93. The Congregation for the Doctrine of Faith (CDF), on February 22, 2018 (less than a month before Francis published his *Gaudete et exsultate*), also described a "new form of Pelagianism [that] is spreading in our days, one in which the individual, understood to be radically autonomous, presumes to save oneself, without recognizing that, at the deepest level of being, he or she derives from God and from others. According to this way of thinking, salvation depends on the strength of the individual or on purely human structures, which are incapable of welcoming the newness of the Spirit of God . . . Clearly, the comparison with the Pelagian and gnostic heresies intends only to recall general common features, without entering into judgments on the exact nature of the ancient errors. In fact, there is a great difference between modern, secularized society and the social context of early Christianity, in which these two heresies were born. However, insofar as Gnosticism and Pelagianism represent perennial dangers for misunderstanding the biblical faith, it is possible to find similarities between the ancient heresies and the modern tendencies just described . . . Both neo-Pelagian individualism and the neo-Gnostic disregard of the body deface the confession of faith in Christ, the one, universal Savior. How would Christ be able to mediate the Covenant of the entire human family, if human persons were isolated individuals, who fulfil themselves by their own efforts, as proposed by neo-Pelagianism? Also, how could it be possible for the salvation mediated by the Incarnation of Jesus, his life, death and Resurrection in his true body, to come to us, if the only thing that mattered were liberating the inner reality of the human person from the limits of the body and the material, as described by the neo-Gnostic vision?" Interestingly, there seems to be a difference in the way that the CDF and Francis conceive of this new form of Pelagianism, because the CDF here does not include in its definition a description of what Francis calls an obsession with rules. Congregation for the Doctrine of Faith, *Placuit Deo*, 3–4.

pelagian or semi-pelagian mindset, even though they speak warmly of God's grace, "ultimately trust only in their own powers and feel superior to others because they observe certain rules or remain intransigently faithful to a particular Catholic style." When some of them tell the weak that all things can be accomplished with God's grace, deep down they tend to give the idea that all things are possible by the human will, as if it were something pure, perfect, all-powerful, to which grace is then added. They fail to realize that "not everyone can do everything," and that in this life human weaknesses are not healed completely and once for all by grace. In every case, as Saint Augustine taught, God commands you to do what you can and to ask for what you cannot, and indeed to pray to him humbly: "Grant what you command, and command what you will" [*Confessiones*, 10.29.40].[94]

Later, in the same text, he continued:

> Not infrequently, contrary to the promptings of the Spirit, the life of the Church can become a museum piece or the possession of a select few. This can occur when some groups of Christians give excessive importance to certain rules, customs or ways of acting. The Gospel then tends to be reduced and constricted, deprived of its simplicity, allure and savour. This may well be a subtle form of pelagianism, for it appears to subject the life of grace to certain human structures. It can affect groups, movements and communities, and it explains why so often they begin with an intense life in the Spirit, only to end up fossilized . . . or corrupt.[95]

On the one hand, Francis's description of this new Pelagianism that is characterized by a confidence in human powers certainly is in harmony with the original Pelagian view. On the other hand, Francis sees in these new Pelagians an element not in the original. This new element is born from attachments to certain rules, customs, disciplines, an obsession with taxonomy, ways of behaving that harken back to an earlier age of Catholicism, and a supreme confidence in a specific vision of doctrinal orthodoxy. His meaning is not entirely clear, because he does not enumerate the specific rules, customs, disciplines, behaviors, and assumptions about orthodoxy that he is critiquing. It is odd that Francis characterizes this new Pelagianism as elitist, because, as we saw earlier, the Pelagians rejected a church stratified between an ascetic minority and a majority who have not abandoned society. They wanted an egalitarian one where every Christian strives for a life without sin, not just a select few. Perhaps Francis is using the slander Neo-Pelagian as a weapon against those who have criticized his *Amoris Laetitia* (which was published two years before *Gaudete et exsultate*) for what they perceived to be a change in the definition of

---

94. Pope Francis, *Gaudete et exsultate*, 48–49.
95. Pope Francis, *Gaudete et exsultate*, 58.

marriage.[96] It might be more accurate for Francis to use the phrase Neo-Pharisee to describe those he has in mind, rather than Neo-Pelagian.

Future anthropological controversies eventually will emerge, because Christians will continue to wrestle with the foundational questions about what it means to be human, and how humans relate to God. New scientific discoveries, technological advancements, metaphysical horizons, and exegetical methods will shape the way that these questions will be answered. At the same time, the answers will be rooted in the Bible, and the decrees that have come from previous disputes.

---

96. Douthat, *To Change*, 126–208.

Bibliography

Primary Literature (Original Languages)

Ambrose of Milan. *De officiis ministrorum*, PL xvi. 25–187.
———. *Epistolae*, PL xvi. 875–1289.
Anonymous Pelagian. *De homine paenitente et adhuc in saeculo commorante*, PL xxx. 242–45.
———. *De induratione cordis Pharaonis et de uasis honoris et contumeliae*, PLS i. 1506–39.
———. *De viduitate servanda*, PL cxvii. 1094–98.
———. *Epistula ad Pammachium et Oceanum de renuntiatione saeculi*, PL xxx. 239–42.
———. *Epistula ad virginem devotam*, PL xvii. 579–84.
———. *Epistula sancti Severi presbyteri ad Claudiam sororem suam de ultimo iudicio*, PL xx. 223–27.
———. *Epistula sancto Fatali de vita christiana*, PLS i. 1699–704.
———. *Humelia de penetentibus*, PLS i. 1694–98.
Anonymous Sicilian. *Ad adolescentem*, PLS i. 1375–80.
———. *De castitate*, PLS i. 1464–505.
———. *De divitiis*, PLS i. 1380–418.
———. *De malis doctoribus et operibus fidei et de iudicio futuro*, PLS i. 1418–57.
———. *De possibilitate non peccandi*, PLS i. 1457–62.
———. *Honorificentiae tuae*, PLS i. 1687–94.
Augustine. *Ad Simplicianum de diversis quaestionibus*, CC, ser. lat. xliv.
———. *Beata vita*, PL xxxii. 959–76.
———. *Confessiones*, 2 vols. The Loeb Classical Library. Cambridge: Harvard University Press, 1999.
———. *Contra academicos*, PL xxxii. 905–58.
———. *Contra duas epistulas Pelagianorum*, CSEL lx. 423–570.
———. *Contra Iulianum*, PL xliv. 641–875.
———. *Contra Iulianum opus imperfectum: Libri I–III*, CSEL lxxxv/i. 3–506.
———. *Contra Iulianum opus imperfectum: Libri IV–VI*, PL xlv. 1337–1608.
———. *Contra Priscillianistas et Origenistas*, PL xlii. 669–76.
———. *De civitate Dei*, PL xli. 13–804.
———. *De correptione et gratia*, PL xliv. 915–46.
———. *De doctrina christiana*, PL xxxiv. 16–121.
———. *De dono perseverantiae*, PL xlv. 993–1034.
———. *De gestis Pelagii*, CSEL xlii. 51–122.
———. *De gratia Christi et de peccato originali*, CSEL xlii. 125–206.

———. *De gratia et libero arbitrio*, PL xliv. 881–912.
———. *De haeresibus*, PL xlii. 21–51.
———. *De libero arbitrio*, PL xxxii. 1221–300.
———. *De natura et gratia*, CSEL lx. 233–99.
———. *De nuptiis et conscupiscentia*, CSEL xlii. 211–319.
———. *De ordine*, PL xxxii. 977–1020.
———. *De peccatorum meritis et remissione et de baptismo parvulorum*, CSEL lx. 3–151.
———. *De perfectione iustitiae hominis*, CSEL xlii. 3–48.
———. *De praedestinatione sanctorum*, PL xliv. 959–92.
———. *De spiritu et littera*, CSEL lx. 155–229.
———. *Epistulae*, CSEL xxxiv.i–ii, xliv, lvii, lviii.
———. *Retractationes*, CC, ser. lat. lvii.
———. *Sermones ad populum*, PL xxxviii. 23–1484.
———. *Sermones ad populum*, PL xxxix. 1493–735.
———. *Soliloquia*, PL xxxii. 869–904.
Bede. *Historia ecclesiastica*, PL xcv. 23–289.
Benedict of Nursia. "Regula Sancti Benedicti." In *The Rule of St. Benedict in Latin and English with Notes*, edited by Timothy Fry, 156–297. Collegeville, MN: Liturgical, 1980.
Caelestius. *Libellus fidei*, PL xlviii. 497–505.
Cassiodorus. *De divinis electionibus*, PL lxx. 1105–49.
Council of Ephesus. *Ad Coelestinum papam*, PL l. 511–22.
Council of Trent. *Canons and Decrees of the Council of Trent: Original Text with English Translation*. St. Louis: B. Herder, 1941.
Dionysius. *Codex canorum ecclesiasticorum*, PL lxvii. 217B–219C.
Epiphanius of Salamis. *Ancoratus*, PG xliii. 11–237.
———. *Panarion*, PG xli. 173–1199, xlii. 9–832.
Eusebius of Caesarea. *De vita Constantini*, PG xx. 910–1234.
———. *Historia ecclesiastica*, PG xx. 9–909.
Gennadius. *Liber de scriptoribus ecclesiasticis (De viris illustribus)*, PL lviii. 1058–120.
Gregory the Great. *Epistulae*, PL lxxvii. 441–1368.
Gregory Thaumaturgus. *Oratio prosphonetica ac panegyrica in Origenem*, PG x. 1052–104.
Isaac of Nineveh. *The Second Part, Chapters IV–XLI*. Leuven: Peeters, 1995.
Jerome. *Chronicon*, PL xxvii. 509–652.
———. *Commentaria in Amos*, PL xxv. 989–1096.
———. *Commentaria in epistolam ad Ephesios*, PL xxvi. 439–554.
———. *Contra Vigilantium*, PL xxiii. 339–71.
———. *De perpetua virginitatae Mariae adversus Helvidium*, PL xxiii. 194–221.
———. *Dialogi contra Pelagianos*, CC, ser. lat. lxxx.
———. *Ad Demetriadem*, CC, ser. lat. lvi.
———. *Ad Ctesiphontem*, CC, ser. lat. lvi.
———. *Interpretatio libri Didymi de Spiritu Sancto*, PL xxiii. 101–54.
———. *Praefatio Hieronymi in quatuor evangelia*, PL xxix. 525–30.
———. *Sancti Eusebii Hieronymi in Hieremiam prophetam libri sex*, CSEL lix.
———. *Vita Hilarionis*, PL xxiii. 29–55.
———. *Vita Malchi Monachi*, PL xxiii. 55–65.
———. *Vita Pauli primi eremitae*, PL xxiii. 17–29.
John Cassian. *Collationes*, CSEL xiii. 3–673.

———. *De incarnatione Domini contra Nestorium*, CSEL xvii. 235–391.

———. *De institutis coenobiorum et de octo principalium uitiorum remediis*, CSEL xvii. 3–231.

Lactantius. *Divinarum institutionum*, PL vi. 111–1016.

———. *Liber de mortibus persecutorum*, PL vii. 190–275.

Marius Mercator. *Commonitorium de Coelestio*, PL xcviii. 63–108.

———. *Liber subnotationum in verba Iuliani*, PL xcviii. 109–72.

———. *Libri Marii Mercatoris. In Acta conciliorum oecumenicorum: concilium universale Ephesenum*, v. 5–70.

Origen of Alexandria. *Commentaria in epistolam Pauli ad Romanos*, PG xiv. 839–1291.

———. *Homiliae in Lucam*, PG xiii. 1801–901.

———. *Origenes Werke / herausgegeben im Auftrage der Kirchenväter—Commission der Königl. Preussischen Akademie der Wissenschaften*. 13 vols. Griechischen Christlichen Schriftsteller Der Ersten Drei Jahrhunderte. Leipzig: JC Hinrichs, 1899–1955.

Orosius. *De errore Priscillianistarum et Origenistarum*, PL xlii. 669–77.

———. *Liber apologeticus, contra Pelagianum*, PL xxxi. 1173D–1213.

Palladius. *Dialogus de vita sancti Ioannis Chrysostomi*, PG xlvii. 5–83.

———. *Historia Lausiaca*, PL lxxiii. 1065–218.

Pamphilus. *Apologia Pamphili pro Origene*, PG xvii. 541–615.

Paulinus of Milan. *Libellus Paulini diaconi aduersum Caelestium Zosimo episcopo datus*, CSEL xxxv.i. 108–11.

———. *Vita sancti Ambrosii*, PL xiv. 27–46.

Paulinus of Nola. *Epistolae*, PL cxi. 153–437.

———. *Poemata*, PL cxi. 437–743.

Pelagius. *Epistula ad sacram Christi uirginem Demetriadem*, PL, xxx. 15–45.

———. *Libellus fidei Pelagii, ad Innocentium ab ipso missus, Zosimo redditus*, PL xlv. 1716–18.

———. *Expositiones XIII epistularum Pauli: ad Romanos (Etc.)*, vol. 2. Alexander Souter: Cambridge, 1926.

———. *Testimoniorum liber unus*, PL xlviii. 593–96.

Photius. *Bibliotheca*, PG ciii. 41–1588.

Pope Anastasius. *Ad Ioannem episcopum Hierosolymitanum*, PL xx. 68–73.

Pope Celestine. *Epistolae*, PL l. 417–567.

Pope Innocent I. *Epistolae*, CSEL xxxv.i. 92–99.

Pope Zosimus. *Epistolae*, CSEL xxxv.i. 99–117.

Possidius. *Vita Augustini*, PL xxxii. 33–66.

Priscillian of Avila. *The Complete Works*. Oxford: Oxford University Press, 2010.

Prosper of Aquitaine. *Chronicum integrum*, PL li. 535–608.

———. *De gratia Dei et libero arbitrio liber contra collatorem*, PL li. 213–76.

Rufinus of Aquileia. *Apologia ad Anastasium*, PL xxi. 623–28.

———. *De adulteratione librorum Origenis*, PG xvii. 615–33.

———. *Prologus in libros de principiis Origenis presbyteri*, PG xi. 112–15.

———. *Prologus in omelias Origenis super numeros*, CCL xx. 285.

Rufinus the Presbyter. *Rufini presbyteri liber de fide: A Critical Text and Translation with Introduction and Commentary*. xcvi. Washington, DC: The Catholic University of America Press, 1964.

Severus of Minorca. *De virtutibus ad Iudaeorum conversionem in minoricensi insula factis in praesentia reliquiarum sancti Stephani*, PL xli. 821-32.
Sextus. *The Sentences of Sextus: A Contribution to the History of Early Christian Ethics.* Cambridge: The Cambridge University Press, 1959.
Socrates. *Historia ecclesiastica*, PG lxvii. 30-842.
Sozomen. *Historia ecclesiastica*, PL cxix. 879-1213.
Sulpicius Severus. *Chronicorum libri duo*, PL xx. 95-158.
———. *De vita beati Martini*, PL xx. 159-75.
———. *Dialogi*, PL xx. 183-223.
Theodore of Mopsuestia. *Ex libro contra defensores peccati originalis*, PG lxvi. 1005-12.
Vincent of Lérins. *Commonitoria*, PL c. 637-38.

Primary Literature (Translation)

Augustine. "Acts or Disputation against Fortunatus the Manichaean." In *Augustin: The Writings against the Manichaeans and against the Donatists*, 113-24. NPNF IV. Peabody, MA: Hendrickson, 2004.
———. "Against the Academicians." In *Against the Academicians and the Teacher*, 1-93. Indianapolis: Hackett, 1995.
———. "Answer to Letters of Petilian, Bishop of Cirta." In *Augustin: The Writings against the Manichaeans and against the Donatists*, 519-628. NPNF IV. Peabody, MA: Hendrickson, 2004.
———. "Answer to Julian." In *The Works of Saint Augustine: A Translation for the 21st Century: Answer to the Pelagians: III*, edited by John E. Rotelle, 222-536. Hyde Park, NY: New City, 1998.
———. "Answer to the Two Letters of the Pelagians." In *The Works of Saint Augustine: A Translation for the 21st Century: Answer to the Pelagians: II*, edited by John E. Rotelle, 98-221. Hyde Park, NY: New City, 1998.
———. *Confessions*. Translated by Henry Chadwick. Oxford: Oxford World Classics, 1998.
———. "The Deeds of Pelagius." In *The Works of Saint Augustine: A Translation for the 21st Century: Answer to the Pelagians: I*, edited by John E. Rotelle, 309-72. Hyde Park, NY: New City, 1997.
———. "The Gift of Perseverance." In *The Works of Saint Augustine: A Translation for the 21st Century: Answer to the Pelagians: IV*, edited by John E. Rotelle, 191-240. Hyde Park, NY: New City, 1999.
———. "The Grace of Christ and Original Sin." In *The Works of Saint Augustine: A Translation for the 21st Century: Answer to the Pelagians: I*, edited by John E. Rotelle, 273-450. Hyde Park, NY: New City, 1997.
———. "Grace and Free Choice." In *The Works of Saint Augustine: A Translation for the 21st Century: Answer to the Pelagians: IV*, edited by John E. Rotelle, 70-107. Hyde Park, NY: New City, 1999.
———. "The Heresies." In *Arianism and Other Heresies*, edited by John Rotelle, I/18. Hyde Park, NY: New City, 1995.
———. *Letters: 1-99*. In *The Works of Saint Augustine: A Translation for the 21st Century*, edited by John E. Rotelle. Translated by Roland Teske. Hyde Park, NY: New City, 2001.
———. *Letters:100-155*. In *The Works of Saint Augustine: A Translation for the 21st Century*, edited by Boniface Ramsey. Translated by Roland Teske. Hyde Park, NY: New City, 2003.

———. *Letters: 156–210*. In *The Works of Saint Augustine: A Translation for the 21st Century*, edited by Boniface Ramsey. Translated by Roland Teske. Hyde Park, NY: New City, 2004.

———. *Letters: 211–270, 1*–29**. In *The Works of Saint Augustine: A Translation for the 21st Century*, edited by Boniface Ramsey. Translated by Roland Teske. Hyde Park, NY: New City, 2005.

———. "Marriage and Desire." In *The Works of Saint Augustine: A Translation for the 21st Century: Answer to the Pelagians: II*, edited by John E. Rotelle, 12–97. Hyde Park, NY: New City, 1998.

———. "Nature and Grace." In *The Works of Saint Augustine: A Translation for the 21st Century: Answer to the Pelagians: I*, edited by John E. Rotelle, 197–268. Hyde Park, NY: New City, 1997.

———. "The Nature and Origin of the Soul." In *The Works of Saint Augustine: A Translation for the 21st Century: Answer to the Pelagians: I*, edited by John E. Rotelle, 451–542. Hyde Park, NY: New City, 1997.

———. *On Christian Doctrine*. Translated by D. W. Robertson. Upper Saddle River, NJ: Prentice Hall, 1997.

———. *On Free Choice of the Will*. Translated by Thomas Williams. Indianapolis: Hackett, 1993.

———. "The Perfection of Human Righteousness." In *The Works of Saint Augustine: A Translation for the 21st Century: Answer to the Pelagians: I*, edited by John E. Rotelle, 269–308. Hyde Park, NY: New City, 1997.

———. "The Predestination of the Saints." In *The Works of Saint Augustine: A Translation for the 21st Century: Answer to the Pelagians: IV*, edited by John E. Rotelle, 149–90. Hyde Park, NY: New City, 1999.

———. "The Punishment and Forgiveness of Sins and the Baptism of Little Ones." *The Works of Saint Augustine: A Translation for the 21st Century: Answer to the Pelagians: I*, edited by John E. Rotelle, 1–134. Hyde Park, NY: New City, 1997.

———. "Rebuke and Grace." In *The Works of Saint Augustine: A Translation for the 21st Century: Answer to the Pelagians: IV*, edited by John E. Rotelle, 108–48. Hyde Park, NY: New City, 1999.

———. *The Retractions*. Fathers of the Church, vol. 60. Translated by Sister Mary Inez Bogan. Washington, DC: The Catholic University of America Press, 1968.

———. "The Spirit and the Letter." In *The Works of Saint Augustine: A Translation for the 21st Century: Answer to the Pelagians: I*, edited by John E. Rotelle, 135–96. Hyde Park, NY: New City, 1997.

———. "To Orosius in Refutation of the Priscillianists and Origenists." In *Arianism and Other Heresies*, 115–27. Hyde Park, NY: New City, 1995.

———. "Unfinished Work in Answer to Julian." In *The Works of Saint Augustine: A Translation for the 21st Century: Answer to the Pelagians: III*, edited by John E. Rotelle, 55–721. Hyde Park, NY: New City, 1999.

Bede. *Ecclesiastical History of the English People*. Translated by Leo Sherley-Price. New York: Penguin, 1990.

Benedict of Nursia. "The Rule of St. Benedict." In *The Rule of St. Benedict in Latin and English with Notes*, edited by Timothy Fry, 156–297. Collegeville, MN: Liturgical, 1980.

Cassiodorus. *Institutions of Divine and Secular Learning and on the Soul*. Translated by James Halporn. Liverpool: Liverpool University Press, 2004.

Congregation for the Doctrine of Faith. *Placuit Deo*, 2018, http://www./roman_curia/congregations/cfaith/documents/rc_con_cfaith_doc_20180222_placuit-deo_en.html.

Council of Ephesus. "The Letter of the Synod to Pope Celestine." In *The Seven Ecumenical Councils*, NPNF XIV, 237–39. Peabody, MN: Hendrickson, 2004.

Council of Trent. *The Canons and Decrees of the Council of Trent*. Translated by H. J. Schroeder. Rockford, IL: Tan, 1978.

Epiphanius of Salamis. *Ancoratus*. Translated by Young Richard Kim. Washington, DC: The Catholic University of America, 2014.

———. *The Panarion of Epiphanius of Salamis: Book I (Sects 1–46)*. 2nd ed. Translated by Frank Williams. Boston: Brill, 2009.

———. *The Panarion of Epiphanius of Salamis, Books II and III. De Fide*. 2nd ed. Translated by Frank Williams. Boston: Brill, 2013.

Erasmus of Rotterdam. "On the Freedom of the Will." In *Luther and Erasmus: Free Will and Salvation*, 35–97. Philadelphia: Westminster, 1969.

Eusebius of Caesarea. *The History of the Church*. Translated by G. A. Williamson. New York: Penguin, 1989.

———. "The Life of Constantine." In *Eusebius: Church History, Life of Constantine the Great, and Oration in Praise of Constantine*, NPNF I, 481–561. Peabody, MA: Hendrickson, 2004.

Fulgentius of Ruspe. *Fulgentius of Ruspe and the Scythian Monks: Correspondence on Christology and Grace*. Translated by Rob McGregor and Donald Fairbairn. Washington, DC: The Catholic University of America Press, 2013.

———. *Fulgentius: Selected Works*. Translated by Robert Eno. Washington, DC: The Catholic University of America Press, 1997.

Gennadius. "Lives of Illustrious Men." In *Theodoret, Jerome, Gennadius, Rufinus: Historical Writings, etc.*, NPNF III, 385–402. Peabody, MA: Hendrickson, 2004.

Gerontius. *The Life of Melania the Younger*. Translated by Elizabeth Clark. New York: Edwin Mellen, 1985.

Gregory the Great. "Epistles." In *Leo the Great, Gregory the Great*, NPNF XII, 1–243. Peabody, MA: Hendrickson, 2004.

Gregory Thaumaturgus. "The Oration and Panegyric Addressed to Origen." In *Gregory Thaumaturgus, Dionysius the Great, Julius Africanus, Anatolius and Minor Writers, Methodius, Arnobius*, ANF VI, 21–39. Peabody, MA: Hendrickson, 2004.

Isaac of Nineveh. *The Second Part, Chapters IV–XLI*. Translated by Sebastian Brock. Leuven: Peeters, 1995.

Interdicasterial Commission for the Catechism of the Catholic Church. *Catechism of the Catholic Church*. Vatican: Liberia Editrice Vaticana, 1994.

International Theological Commission. *The Hope of Salvation for Infants Who Die without Being Baptized*, 2007, http://www.vatican.va/roman_curia/congregations/cfaith/cti_documents/rc_con_cfaith_doc_20070419_un-baptised-infants_en.html.

Jerome. "Against Jovinianus." In *Jerome: Letters and Select Works*, NPNF VI, 346–416. Peabody, MA: Hendrickson, 2004.

———. "Against Vigilantius." In *Jerome: Letters and Select Works*, NPNF VI, 417–24. Peabody, MA: Hendrickson, 2004.

———. *The Commentaries of Origen and Jerome on St. Paul's Epistle to the Ephesians*. Translated by Ronald Heine. Oxford: Oxford University Press, 2002.

———. *Commentary on Jeremiah*. Edited by Thomas C. Oden and Gerald L. Bray. Translated by Michael Graves. Ancient Christian Texts. Downers Grove, IL: IVP Academic, 2011.

———. "Dialogue against the Pelagians." In *Jerome: Letters and Select Works*, NPNF VI, 447–82. Peabody, MA: Hendrickson, 2004.

———. "Letters." In *Jerome: Letters and Select Works*, NPNF VI, 1–298. Peabody, MA: Hendrickson, 2004.

———. "The Life of Malchus, the Captive Monk." In *Jerome: Letters and Select Works*, NPNF VI, 315–18. Peabody, MA: Hendrickson, 2004.

———. "The Life of Saint Hilarion." In *Jerome: Letters and Select Works*, NPNF VI, 303–15. Peabody, MA: Hendrickson, 2004.

———. "Life of Saint Paul the First Hermit." In *Jerome: Letters and Select Works*, NPNF VI, 299–303. Peabody, MA: Hendrickson, 2004.

———. "The Perpetual Virginity of Blessed Mary: Against Helvidius." In *Jerome: Letters and Select Works*, NPNF VI, 334–46. Peabody, MA: Hendrickson, 2004.

———. "Prefaces to the Four Gospels: Addressed to Pope Damasus." In *Jerome: Letters and Select Works*, NPNF VI, 487–88. Peabody, MA: Hendrickson, 2004.

———. "Prologue to Jerome's Commentary on Ezekiel in Jerome's Prologues to His Commentaries on the Prophets." Translated by Brigid Pauline Nugent. Austin: The University of Texas at Austin, 1992.

———. "Prologue to Jerome's Commentary on Jeremiah in Jerome's Prologues to His Commentaries on the Prophets." Translated by Brigid Pauline Nugent. Austin: The University of Texas at Austin, 1992.

———. *A Translation of Jerome's Chronicon with Historical Commentary*. Translated by Malcom Drew Donalson. Lewiston, NY: Mellen, 1996.

John Cassian. "Apophthegmata Patrum." In *The Sayings of the Desert Fathers: The Alphabetical Collection*, edited by Benedicta Ward, 112–15. Kalamazoo: Cistercian Publications, 1975.

———. *The Conferences*. Edited by John Dillon, Dennis D. McManus, and Walter J. Burghardt. Ancient Christian Writers, vol. 57. Translated by Boniface Ramsey. New York: Newman, 1997.

———. *The Institutes*. Edited by Dennis D. McManus. Ancient Christian Writers, vol. 58. Translated by Boniface Ramsey. New York: Newman, 2000.

———. "The Seven Books on the Incarnation of the Lord, against Nestorius." In *Sulpitius Severus, Vincent of Lerins, John Cassian*, NPNF XI, 547–621. Peabody, MA: Hendrickson, 2004.

John Duns Scotus. *Four Questions on Mary*. Translated by Allan B. Wolter. St. Bonaventure: The Franciscan Institute, 2000.

John of Nikiu. *The Chronicle of John, Coptic Bishop of Nikiu*. Translated by Robert Charles. Amsterdam: Philo, 1916.

Lactantius. "The Divine Institutes." In *Lactantius, Venantius, Asterius, Victorinus, Dionysius, Apostolic Teaching and Constitutions, 2 Clement, Early Liturgies*, ANF VII, 9–223. Peabody, MA: Hendrickson, 1994.

———. "On the Manner in Which the Persecutors Died." In *Lactantius, Venantius, Asterius, Victorinus, Dionysius, Apostolic Teaching and Constitutions, 2 Clement, Early Liturgies*, ANF VII, 301–22. Peabody, MA: Hendrickson, 2004.

Luther, Martin. "On the Bondage of the Will." In *Luther and Erasmus: Free Will and Salvation*, 101–334. Philadelphia: Westminster, 1969.

Melanchthon, Philipp. *The Augsburg Confession*. Translated by J. L. Neve. Philadelphia: The United Lutheran Publication House, 1914.

Origen of Alexandria. *Commentary on the Epistle to the Romans, Books 1–5*. Translated by Thomas Scheck. Washington, DC: The Catholic University of America Press, 2009.

———. *Commentary on the Epistle to the Romans, Books 6–10*. Translated by Thomas Scheck. Washington DC: The Catholic University of America, 2012.

———. *Homilies on Luke*. Translated by Joseph Lienhard. Washington, DC: The Catholic University of America Press, 1996.

———. "On First Principles." In *Minucius Felix; Commodian; Origen*, ANF IV, 239–384. Peabody, MA: Hendrickson, 2004.

Orosius. "Book in Defense against the Pelagians." In *Iberian Fathers: Pacian of Barcelona; Orosius of Braga*, 3, 115–67. Washington, DC: The Catholic University of America Press, 1999.

———. "Orosius's Inquiry or Memorandum to Augustine on the Error of the Priscillianists and Origenists." In *Iberian Fathers: Pacian of Barcelona; Orosius of Braga*, 3, 168–74. Washington, DC: The Catholic University of America Press, 1999.

———. *Seven Books of History against the Pagans*. Translated by A. T. Fear. Liverpool: Liverpool, 2010.

Palladius. *Dialogue on the Life of St. John Chrysostom*. Translated by Robert Meyer. Mahwah, NJ: Newman, 1985.

———. *The Lausiac History*. Ancient Christian Writers, vol. 34. Translated by Robert T. Meyer. Westminster: Newman, 1965.

Pamphilus. *Apology for Origen*. Fathers of the Church, vol. 120. Translated by Thomas Scheck. Washington, DC: The Catholic University of America Press, 2010.

Paulinus of Milan. "The Life of Saint Ambrose." In *Ambrose*, edited by Boniface Ramsey, 195–232. New York: Routledge, 1997.

Paulinus of Nola. *Letters of St. Paulinus of Nola: Letters 1–22*, vol. 1. Translated by P. G. Walsh. Westminster: Newman, 1966.

———. *Letters of St. Paulinus of Nola: Letters 23–51*, vol. 2. Translated by P. G. Walsh. Westminster: Newman, 1968.

———. *The Poems of Paulinus of Nola*. Translated by P. G. Walsh. New York: Newman, 1975.

Pelagius. *Pelagius's Commentary on St. Paul's Epistle to the Romans*. Translated by Theodore De Bruyn. Oxford: Clarendon, 2002.

———. "On the Christian Life." In *Pelagius: Life and Letters*, II, 105–26. Woodbridge: Boydell, 1998.

———. "On the Divine Law." In *Pelagius: Life and Letters*, II, 88–104. Woodbridge: Boydell, 1998.

———. "On Virginity." In *Pelagius: Life and Letters*, II, 71–87. Woodbridge: Boydell, 1998.

———. "To Celantia." In *Pelagius: Life and Letters*, II, 127–44. Woodbridge: Boydell, 1998.

———. "To Demetrias." In *Pelagius: Life and Letters*, II, 29–70. Woodbridge: Boydell, 1998.

Photius. *The Bibliotheca*. Translated by N. G. Wilson. London: Duckworth, 1994.

Plato. "Phaedo." In *The Last Days of Socrates*, 109–91. New York: Penguin, 1993.

Pope Anastasius. "The Letter of Anastasius, Bishop of the Church of Rome to John Bishop of Jerusalem Concerning the Character of Rufinus." In *Theodoret, Jerome, Gennadius, Rufinus: Historical Writings, Etc.*, NPNF III, 432–33. Peabody, MA: Hendrickson, 2004.

Pope Francis. *Evangelii Gaudium*, 2013, http://w2.vatican.va/content/francesco/en/apost_exhortations/documents/papa-francesco_esortazione-ap_20131124_evangelii-gaudium.html.

———. *Gaudete et Exsultate*, 2018, http://w2.vatican.va/content/francesco/en/apost_exhortations/documents/papa-francesco_esortazione-ap_20180319_gaudete-et-exsultate.html

———. "Pastoral Visit of His Holiness Pope Francis to Prato and Florence: Meeting with the Participants in the Fifth Convention of the Italian Church," 2015, http://m.vatican.va/content/francesco/en/speeches/2015/november/documents/papa-francesco_20151110_firenze-convegno-chiesa-italiana.html.

Pope Innocent I. "Letters." In *The Principal Works of St. Jerome*, NPNF VI, 280–81. Peabody, MA: Hendrickson, 2004.

Pope Leo XIII. *Libertas praestantissimum*, 1888.

Pope Pius XI. *Ad salutem*, 1930.

———. *Lux veritatis*, 1931.

———. *Miserentissimus redemptor*, 1928.

Pope Pius XII. *Doctor mellifluus*, 1953.

Possidius. "The Life of Saint Augustine." In *Soldiers of Christ: Saints and Saints' Lives from Late Antiquity and the Early Middle Ages*, edited by Thomas Noble and Thomas Head, 31–73. University Park: The Pennsylvania State University Press, 1995.

Priscillian of Avila. *The Complete Works*. Translated by Marco Conti. Oxford: Oxford University Press, 2010.

Prosper of Aquitaine. "Chronicle." In *From Roman to Merovingian Gaul*, 62–76. Tonawanda: University of Toronto Press, 2008.

———. "On Grace and Free Will, against Cassian the Lecturer." In *Prosper of Aquitaine: Defense of St. Augustine*, 70–138. New York: Newman, 1963.

Rufinus of Aquileia. "Apology of Rufinus Addressed to Anastasius, Bishop of Rome." In *Theodoret, Jerome, Gennadius, Rufinus: Historical Writings, Etc.*, NPNF III, 430–32. Peabody, MA: Hendrickson, 2004.

———. *The Church History of Rufinus of Aquileia: Books 10 and 11*. Translated by Philip Amidon. Oxford: Oxford University Press, 1997.

———. *A Commentary on the Apostles' Creed*. Translated by J. N. D. Kelly. New York: Newman, 1978.

———. *On the Falsification of the Books of Origen*. Fathers of the Church, vol. 120. Translated by Thomas Scheck. Washington, DC: The Catholic University of America Press, 2010.

———. "Preface to Origen's Homilies on Numbers." In *Theodoret, Jerome, Gennadius, Rufinus: Historical Writings, Etc.*, NPNF III, 568. Peabody, MA: Hendrickson, 2004.

———. "Prologue of Rufinus to Origen's *De Principiis*." In *Tertullian, Minicius Felix; Commodian; Origen*, NPNF IV, 237–38. Peabody, MA: Hendrickson, 2004.

Rufinus the Presbyter. *Rufini Presbyteri Liber De Fide: A Critical Text and Translation with Introduction and Commentary*, vol. XCVI. Translated by Sister Mary William Miller. Washington, DC: The Catholic University of America Press, 1964.

Second Council of Orange. "The Synod of Orange, A.D. 529." In *Theological Anthropology*, 112–28. Philadelphia: Fortress, 1981.

Severus of Minorca. *Letter on the Conversion of the Jews*. Translated by Scott Bradbury. Oxford: Clarendon, 1996.

Sextus. *The Sentences of Sextus: A Contribution to the History of Early Christian Ethics.* Translated by Henry Chadwick. Cambridge: The Cambridge University Press, 1959.

Socrates. "Church History." In *Socrates, Sozomenus: Church Histories*, NPNF II, 1–178. Peabody, MA: Hendrickson, 2004.

Solomon of Borsa. *The Book of the Bee.* Translated by Earnest A. Wallis Budge. Oxford: Clarendon, 1886.

Sozomen. "Ecclesiastical History." In *Socrates, Sozomenus: Church Histories*, NPNF II, 179–427. Peabody, MA: Hendrickson, 2004.

Sulpicius Severus. *The Complete Works*, Ancient Christian Writers, vol. 79. Mahwah, NJ: The Newman, 2015.

Theodore of Mopsuestia. "The Creation of Adam and Eve." In *Theodore of Mopsuestia*, 86–94. New York: Routledge, 2009.

Theophilus of Alexandria. "First Synodal Letter." In *Theophilus of Alexandria*, 91–93. New York: Routledge, 2007.

———. "Letter Written at Constantinople (403)." In *Theophilus of Alexandria*, 139–43. New York: Routledge, 2007.

———. "Letters to the Origenist Monks." In *Theophilus of Alexandria*, 100–1. New York: Routledge, 2007.

———. "Nineteenth Festal Letter (404)." In *Theophilus of Alexandria*, 143–59. New York: Routledge, 2007.

———. "Second Synodal Letter to the Bishops of Palestine and Cyprus." In *Theophilus of Alexandria*, 93–100. New York: Routledge, 2007.

———. "Seventeenth Festal Letter (402)." In *Theophilus of Alexandria*, 118–39. New York: Routledge, 2007.

———. "Sixteenth Festal Letter (401)." In *Theophilus of Alexandria*, 101–18. New York: Routledge, 2007.

———. "Tractate on Isaiah 6:1–7." In *Theophilus of Alexandria*, 159–73. New York: Routledge, 2007.

Vincent of Lérins. "A Commonitory." In *Sulpitius Severus, Vincent of Lérins, and John Cassian*, NPNF XI, 131–56. Peabody, MA: Hendrickson, 2004.

Secondary Literature

Adkin, Neil. "Ambrose and Jerome: The Opening Shot." *Mnemosyne* 46 (1993) 364–76.

———. "Gregory of Nazianzus and Jerome: Some Remarks." In *Georgica: Greek Studies in Honour of George Cawkwell*, 13–24. London: University of London Institute of Classical Studies, 1991.

Ahl, Frederick. "The Art of Safe Criticism in Greece and Rome." *The American Journal of Philology* 105 (Summer 1984) 174–208.

Alexander, Archibald. "The Early History of Pelagianism." *The Biblical Repertory and Theological Review* 2 (1830) 77–113.

Alexanderson, Bengt. "Le commentaire sur les Psaumes de Julien d'Éclane et le texte du Psautier." *Studia Patristica* 49 (2010) 319–24.

Alflatt, Malcom E. "The Development of the Idea of Involuntary Sin in St. Augustine." *Revue des Études Augustiniennes* 20 (1974) 113–34.

———. "The Responsibility for Involuntary Sin in Saint Augustine." *Recherches Augustiniennes* 10 (1975) 171–86.

Alföldi, Andrew. *The Conversion of Constantine and Pagan Rome.* Translated by Harold Mattingly. Oxford: Clarendon, 1948.

Allan, Mowbray. "Augustine the Semi-Pelagian." *Augustiniana* 62 (2012) 189–249.

Altaner, Berthold. "Der *Liber de fide*: ein Werk des Pelagianers Rufinus des 'Syrers.'" *Theologische Quartalschrift* 130 (1950) 432–49.

Amidon, Philip. "Introduction." In *The Church History of Rufinus of Aquileia*, vii–xvii. Oxford: Oxford University Press, 1997.

Antin, Paul. "Rufin et Pélage dans Jérôme, Prologue 1 *In Hieremiam.*" *Latomus* 22 (1963) 792–94.

Armstrong, C.B. "St. Augustine and Pelagius as Religious Types." *Church Quarterly Review* 162 (1961) 150–64.

Augusto, Diego. "... At Tum Instantius, Salvianus et Priscillianus Romam Profecti: El Viaje de los Priscilianistsas Hacia la Ciudad Eterna." *Antiquité Tardive* 22 (2014) 156–76.

———. "... *Exim in Gallaeciam Priscillianistarum Haeresis invasit.* The Success of Priscillianism in Gallaecia Following the Trials at Trier." *Kilo* 98 (2016) 634–52.

Ayres, Lewis. *Nicaea and Its Legacy: An Approach to Fourth-Century Trinitarian Theology.* Oxford: Oxford University Press, 2004.

Azkoul, Michael. "Peccatum Originale: The Pelagian Controversy." *Patristic and Byzantine Review* 3 (1984) 39–53.

Babcock, William. "Augustine on Sin and Moral Agency." *Journal of Religious Ethics* 16 (1988) 28–55.

Babut, Ernest. *Priscillien et le Priscillianisme.* Paris: Champion 1909.

Backus, Irena and Aza Goudriaan. "'Semipelagianism': The Origins of the Term and Its Passage into the History of Heresy." *Journal of Ecclesiastical History* 65 (2014) 25–46.

Baker-Brian, Nicholas. *Manichaeism: An Ancient Faith Rediscovered.* New York: T. & T. Clark, 2011.

Bamberger, John. "Desert Calm. Evagrius Ponticus: The Theologian as Spiritual Guide." *Cistercian Studies Quarterly* 7 (1992) 185–98.

Bammel, C.P. "Rufinus' Translation of Origen's Commentary on Romans and the Pelagian Controversy." In *Storia ed esegesi in Rufino di Concordia*, edited by A. Scotta, 39, 131–42. Udine: Antichità Altoadriatiche, 1992.

Banev, Krastu *Theophilus of Alexandria and the First Origenist Controversy: Rhetoric and Power.* Oxford: Oxford University Press, 2015.

Barclift, Philip. "In Controversy with Saint Augustin: Julian of Eclanum on the Nature of Sin." *Recherches de Théologie Ancienne et Médiévale* 58 (1991) 5–20.

Bardenhewer, Otto. *Patrology: The Lives and Works of the Fathers of the Church.* Translated by Thomas Shahan. St. Louis: B. Herder, 1908.

Bardy, Gustave. "Grecs et Latins dans les Premières Controverses Pélagiennes." *Bulletin de Littérature Ecclésiastique* 49 (1948) 3–20.

Bark, William. "The Doctrinal Interests of Marius Mercator." *Church History* 12 (September 1943) 210–16.

Barnard, L.W. "Pelagius and Early Syriac Christianity." *Recherches de Théologie Ancienne et Médiévale* 35 (1968) 193–96.

Barnes, Timothy. *Athanasius and Constantius: Theology and Politics in the Constantinian Empire.* Cambridge: Harvard University Press, 1993.

———. *Constantine and Eusebius.* Cambridge: Harvard University Press, 1981.

———. "Constantine's Prohibition of Pagan Sacrifice." *American Journal of Philology* 105 (1984) 69–72.

———. "Religion and Society in the Age of Theodosius." In *Grace, Politics and Desire: Essays on Augustine*, edited by H.A. Meynell, 157–78. Calgary: University of Calgary Press, 1990.

Barnhart, Bruno and Joseph Wong, ed. *Purity of Heart and Contemplation: A Monastic Dialogue between Christian and Asian Traditions*. New York: Continuum, 2001.

Barr, James. "The Pelagian Controversy." *Evangelical Quarterly* 21 (1949) 253–64.

Barron, Robert. *Catholicism: A Journey to the Heart of the Faith*. New York: Image, 2011.

Batka, L'ubomír. "Luther's Teaching on Sin and Evil." In *The Oxford Handbook of Martin Luther's Theology*, 233–53. Oxford: Oxford University Press, 2014.

Bavel, Johannes van. "The Anthropology of Augustine." *Louvain Studies* 5 (1974) 34–47.

Beatrice, Pier Franco. "Chromatius and Jovinus at the Synod of Diospolis: A Prosopographical Inquiry." *Journal of Early Christian Studies* 22 (2014) 437–64.

———. *The Transmission of Sin: Augustine and the Pre-Augustinian Sources*. Translated by Adam Kamesar. Oxford: Oxford University Press, 2013.

Beck, John. "The Pelagian Controversy: An Economic Analysis." *American Journal of Economics and Sociology* 66 (2007) 681–96.

BeDuhn, Jason. *Augustine's Manichaean Dilemma, I: Conversion and Apostasy, 373–388 C.E.* Philadelphia: University of Pennsylvania Press, 2010.

———. "The Battle for the Body in Manichaean Asceticism." In *Asceticism*, edited by Vincent L. Wimbush and Richard Valantasis, 513–19. Oxford: Oxford University Press, 1998.

———. *The Manichaean Body: In Discipline and Ritual*. Baltimore: The Johns Hopkins University Press, 2000.

Beeley, Christopher. *Gregory of Nazianzus on the Trinity and the Knowledge of God: In Your Light We Shall See Light*. Oxford: Oxford University Press, 2013.

Bell, David. "Apatheia: The Convergence of Byzantine and Cistercian Spirituality." *Cîteaux* 38 (1987) 141–63.

Bireley, Robert. *The Refashioning of Catholicism, 1450–1700: A Reassessment of the Counter Reformation*. Washington, DC: The Catholic University of America Press, 1999.

Birley, A.R. "Magnus Maximus and the Persecution of Heresy." *Bulletin of the John Rylands Library* 66 (1983) 13–43.

Bogan, Sister Mary Inez. "Introduction." In *St. Augustine: The Retractions*, xiii–xxvi. Washington, DC: The Catholic University of America Press, 1968.

Bohlin, Torgny. *Die Theologie des Pelagius und Ihre Genesis*. Uppsala: Almquist, 1957.

Bonaiuti, Ernesto. "The Genesis of St. Augustine's Idea of Original Sin." *The Harvard Theological Review* 10 (1917) 159–75.

Bonner, Ali. "The Manuscript Transmission of Pelagius' *Ad Demetriadem*: The Evidence of Some Manuscript Witnesses." *Studia Patristica* LXX (2013) 619–30.

———. "The Manuscript Transmission of Pelagius' Works and Its Implications, with Special Reference to His *Letter to Demetrias*." *Studia Patristica* LXXIV (2016) 341–52.

Bonner, Gerald. "Anti-Pelagian Works." In *Augustine through the Ages: An Encyclopedia*, edited by Allan D. Fitzgerald, 41–47. Grand Rapids: Eerdmans, 1999.

———. *Augustine and Modern Research on Pelagianism*. Edited by Robert P. Russell. The Saint Augustine Lecture Series. Villanova, PA: Augustinian Institute, Villanova University Press, 1972.

———. "Augustine and Pelagianism." *Augustinian Studies* 24 (1993) 27–47.

———. "The Desire for God and the Need for Grace in Augustine's Theology." In *Congresso Internazionale Su S. Agostino Nel XVI Centenario Della Conversione*, edited by V. Grossi, I, 203–15. Rome: Institutum Patristicum Augustinianum, 1987.

———. "Dono preseverantiae, De." In *Augustine through the Ages: An Encyclopedia*, edited by Allan D. Fitzgerald, 287. Grand Rapids: Eerdmans, 1999.

———. *Freedom and Necessity: St. Augustine's Teaching on Divine Power and Human Freedom*. Washington, DC: The Catholic University of America Press, 2007.

———. "Gestis Pelagii, De." In *Augustine through the Ages: An Encyclopedia*, edited by Allan D. Fitzgerald, 382–83. Grand Rapids: Eerdmans, 1999.

———. "Gratia et libero arbitrio, De." In *Augustine through the Ages: An Encyclopedia*, edited by Allan D. Fitzgerald, 400–1. Grand Rapids: Eerdmans, 1999.

———. "Gratia et de peccato originali, De." In *Augustine through the Ages: An Encyclopedia*, edited by Allan D. Fitzgerald, 399–400. Grand Rapids: Eerdmans, 1999.

———. "How Pelagian Was Pelagius? An Examination of the Contentions of Torgny Bohlin." In *Studia Patristica: Classica, Philosophica et Ethica, Theologica, Augustiniana, Post-Patristica. Texte und Untersuchungen zur Geschichte der altchristlichen Literatur*, edited by F.L. Cross, 9, 350–58. Berlin: Akademie-Verlag, 1966.

———. "A Last Apology for Pelagianism?" In *Studia Patristica*, 49, 325–28. Walpole: Peeters, 2010.

———. "Natura et gratia, De." In *Augustine through the Ages: An Encyclopedia*, edited by Allan D. Fitzgerald, 582. Grand Rapids: Eerdmans, 1999.

———. "Peccatorum meritis et remissione et de baptismo parvulorum, De." In *Augustine through the Ages: An Encyclopedia*, edited by Allan D. Fitzgerald, 632–33. Grand Rapids: Eerdmans, 1999.

———. "Pelagianism and Augustine." *Augustinian Studies* 23 (1992) 33–51.

———. "Pelagianism Reconsidered." In *Studia Patristica: Cappadocian Fathers, Greek Authors after Nicaea, Augustine, Donatism, and Pelagianism*, edited by Elizabeth A. Livingstone, 237–41. Leuven: Peeters, 1993.

———. "Perfectione iustitiae hominis, De." In *Augustine through the Ages: An Encyclopedia*, edited by Allan D. Fitzgerald, 646. Grand Rapids: Eerdmans, 1999.

———. "Praedestinatione sanctorum, De." In *Augustine through the Ages: An Encyclopedia*, edited by Allan D. Fitzgerald, 669. Grand Rapids: Eerdmans, 1999.

———. "Rufinus of Syria and African Pelagianism." *Augustinian Studies* 1 (1970) 31–47.

———. "Spiritu et littera, De." In *Augustine through the Ages: An Encyclopedia*, edited by Allan D. Fitzgerald, 815–16. Grand Rapids: Eerdmans, 1999.

———. *St. Augustine of Hippo: Life and Controversies*. Third ed. Norwich: Canterbury, 2002.

Boone, Mark. "Rethinking Augustine's Early Theology: An Argument for Continuity, by Carol Harrison." *Augustinian Studies* 40 (2009) 154–57.

Bostock, Gerald. "The Influence of Origen on Pelagius and Western Monasticism." In *Origeniana Septima: Origenes in den Auseinandersetzungen des 4. Jahrhunderts*, edited by W.A. Bienert and Kühbeweg, 381–96. Leuven: Leuven University Press, 1999.

Bowersock, G.W. *Julian the Apostate*. Cambridge: Harvard University Press, 1978.

Bradbury, Scott. "Constantine and the Problem of Anti-Pagan Legislation in the Fourth Century." *Classical Philology* 89 (1994) 120–39.

Brakke, David. "Introduction." In *Talking Back: A Monastic Handbook for Combating Demons*, 1–48. Collegeville, MN: Liturgical, 2009.

Breyfogle, Todd. "Magic, Women, and Heresy in the Late Empire: The Case of the Priscillianists." In *Ancient Magic and Ritual Power*, edited by Marvin Meyer and Paul Mirecki, 435–54. Boston: Brill, 2001.

Brochet, J. *Saint Jérôme et ses Ennemis: Etude sur la Querelle de Saint Jérôme avec Rufin d'Aquilée et sur l'Ensemble de son Oeuvre Polémique*. Edited by Albert Fontemoing. Paris: Libraire des Écoles Françaises d'Athènes et de Rome du Collège de France et de l'École Normale Supérieure, 1905.

Brown, Peter. "Aspects of the Christianization of the Roman Aristocracy." In *Religion and Society in the Age of Saint Augustine*, 161–82. New York: Harper & Row, 1972.

———. *Augustine of Hippo: A Biography*. Berkeley: University of California Press, 2000.

———. *The Body and Society: Men, Women and Sexual Renunciation in Early Christianity*. New York: Columbia University Press, 1988.

———. "The Patrons of Pelagius: The Roman Aristocracy between East and West." In *Religion and Society in the Age of Saint Augustine*, 208–26. New York: Harper & Row, 1972.

———. "Pelagius and His Supporters: Aims and Environment." In *Religion and Society in the Age of Saint Augustine*, 183–207. New York: Harper & Row, 1972.

———. *The Ransom of the Soul: Afterlife and Wealth in Early Western Christianity*. Cambridge: Harvard University Press, 2015.

———. "The Rise and Function of the Holy Man in Late Antiquity." *The Journal of Roman Studies* 61 (1971) 80–101.

———. "Sexuality and Society in the Fifth Century A.D.: Augustine and Julian of Eclanum." In *Tria Corda: Scritti in onore di Arnaldo Momigliano*, edited by E. Gabba, 49–70. Como: New Press, 1983.

———. *Through the Eye of a Needle: Wealth, the Fall of Rome, and the Making of Christianity in the West, 350–550 AD*. Princeton: Princeton University Press, 2014.

———. *The World of Late Antiquity*. London: Hartcourt Brace Jovanovich, 1971.

Bruckner, Albert. *Julian von Eclanum: Sein Leben und seine Lehre*. Leipzig: J.C. Hinrichs, 1897.

Burnaby, John. *Amor Dei: A Study of the Religion of St. Augustine: The Hulsean Lectures for 1938*. London: Hodder & Stoughton, 1947.

Burnett, Carole. "Dysfunction at Diospolis: A Comparative Study of Augustine's *De gestis Pelagii* and Jerome's *Dialogus adversus Pelagianos*." *Augustinian Studies* 34 (2003) 153–73.

Burns, J. Patout. "Augustine's Role in the Imperial Action against Pelagius." *Journal of Theological Studies* 30 (1979) 67–83.

———. *The Development of Augustine's Doctrine of Operative Grace*. Paris: Études Augustiniennes, 1980.

———. "The Economy of Salvation: Two Patristic Traditions." *Theological Studies* 37 (1976) 598–619.

———. "Grace." In *Augustine through the Ages: An Encyclopedia*, edited by Allan D. Fitzgerald, 391–98. Grand Rapids: Eerdmans, 1999.

———. "The Interpretation of Romans in the Pelagian Controversy." *Augustinian Studies* 10 (1979) 43–53.

———. "Introduction." In *Theological Anthropology*. Philadelphia: Fortress, 1981.

Burrus, Virginia. "Ascesis, Authority, and Text: The Acts of the Council of Saragossa." *Semei* 58 (1992) 95–108.

———. "Canonical References to Extra-Canonical 'Texts': Priscillian's Defense of the Apocrypha." In *Society of Biblical Literature Seminar Papers*, edited by David J. Lull, 29, 60–67, 1990.

———. *The Making of a Heretic: Gender, Authority, and the Priscillianist Controversy*. Berkeley: University of California Press, 1995.

Byrne, Richard. "Cassian and the Goals of Monastic Life." *Cistercian Studies Quarterly* 22 (1987) 3–16.

Cain, Andrew. *Jerome's Epitaph on Paula: A Commentary on the Epitaphium Sanctae Paulae with an Introduction, Text, and Translation*. Oxford: Oxford University Press, 2013.

———. *The Letters of Jerome: Asceticism, Biblical Exegesis, and the Construction of Christian Authority in Late Antiquity*. Oxford: Oxford University Press, 2009.

Callam, Daniel. "Clerical Continence in the Fourth Century: Three Papal Decretals." *Theological Studies* 41 (1980) 3–50.

Cameron, Averil. *The Later Roman Empire: AD 284–430*. Cambridge: Harvard University Press, 1993.

Cannon, Stephen. "The Jerome-Augustine Correspondence." In *Word and Spirit: A Monastic Review*, 9, 35–45. Ann Arbor: St. Bede's Publications, 1987.

Cary, Phillip. *Inner Grace: Augustine in the Traditions of Plato and Paul*. Oxford: Oxford University Press, 2008.

Casiday, Augustine. "Apatheia and Sexuality in the Thought of Augustine and Cassian." *St. Vladimir's Theological Quarterly* 45 (2001) 359–94.

———. "Cassian against the Pelagians." *Studia Monastica* 46 (2004) 7–23.

———. "Cassian, Augustine, and *De incarnatione*." In *Studia Patristica: St. Augustine and His Opponents; Other Latin Writers*, edited by M.F. Wiles and E.J. Yarnold with the assistance of P.M. Parvis, XXXVIII, 41–47. Leuven: Peeters, 2001.

———. "Introduction." In *Evagrius Ponticus*. New York: Routledge, 2006.

———. "Rehabilitating John Cassian: An Evaluation of Prosper of Aquitaine's Polemic against the 'Semipelagians.'" *Scottish Journal of Theology* 58 (2005) 270–84.

———. *Tradition and Theology in St John Cassian*. Oxford: Oxford University Press, 2007.

Caspari, C.P. *Briefe, Abhandlungen, und Predigten aus den zwei letzen Jahrhunderten des kirchlichen Altertums und dem Anfang des Mittelalters*. Brussels: Christiana, 1964.

Cavadini, John. "Eucharistic Exegesis in Augustine's *Confessions*." *Augustinian Studies* 41 (2010) 87–108.

———. "Reconsidering Augustine on Marriage and Concupiscence." *Augustinian Studies* 48 (2017) 183–99.

Cavallera, Ferdinand. "Saint Jérôme et la Vie Parfaite." *Revue d'Ascétique et de Mystique* 2 (1921) 101–27.

———. *Saint Jérôme: sa Vie et son Oeuvre*. 2 vols. Louvain: Spicilegium Sacrum Lovaniense, 1922.

Chadwick, Henry. *Augustine*. Edited by Keith Thomas. Past Masters. Oxford: Oxford University Press, 1996.

———. *Augustine of Hippo: A Life*. Oxford: Oxford University Press, 2009.

———. *The Early Church: The Story of Emergent Christianity from the Apostolic Age to the Foundation of the Church of Rome*. New York: Penguin, 1990.

———. "Pelagius, Caelestius, and the Roman See in Gaul and North Africa." In *The Church in Ancient Society: From Galilee to Gregory the Great*, 446–63. Oxford: Oxford University Press, 2003.

———. *Priscillian of Avila: The Occult and the Charismatic in the Early Church*. Oxford: Oxford University Press, 1976.

———. *The Sentences of Sextus: A Contribution to the History of Early Christian Ethics*. Cambridge: The Cambridge University Press, 1959.

Chadwick, Owen. *John Cassian*. Second ed. Cambridge: Cambridge University Press, 1968.

———. *John Cassian: A Study in Primitive Monasticism*. Cambridge: The Syndics of the Cambridge University Press, 1950.

Chéné, Jean. "Saint Augustin Enseigne-t-il dans le *De Spiritu et Littera* l'Universalité de la Volonté Salvifique de Dieu?" *Recherches de Science Religieuse* 47 (1959) 215–24.

Chepey, Stuart. *Nazirites in Late Second Temple Judaism: A Survey of Ancient Jewish Writings, the New Testament, Archaeological Evidence, and Other Writings from Late Antiquity*. Boston: Brill, 2005.

Chin, Catherine M. "Prayer and *Otium* in Cassian's *Institutes*." In *Studia Patristica: Ascetica, Gnostica, Liturgica, Orientalia*, edited by M.F. Wiles and E.J. Yarnold with the Assistance of P.M. Parvis, XXXV, 24–29. Leuven: Peeters, 2001.

Chitty, Derwas. *The Desert a City: An Introduction to the Study of Egyptian and Palestinian Monasticism under the Christian Empire*. Crestwood: St. Vladimir's, 1999.

Christensen, Torben. "The So-Called Edict of Milan." *Classica et Mediaevalia* 35 (1984) 129–75.

Chronister, Andrew. "Augustine and Patristic Argumentation in His Anti-Pelagian Works: Change or Continuity?" *Augustiniana* 64 (2014) 187–226.

Clark, Elizabeth. "'Adam's Only Companion': Augustine and the Early Christian Debate on Marriage." *Recherches Augustiniennes* 21 (1986) 139–62.

———. "Friendship between the Sexes: Classical Theory and Christian Practice." In *Jerome, Chrysostom, and Friends: Essays and Translations*, 35–106. New York: Mellen, 1979.

———. "From Origenism to Pelagianism: Elusive Issues in an Ancient Debate." *Princeton Seminary Bulletin* 12 (1991) 283–303.

———. *The Origenist Controversy: The Cultural Construction of an Early Christian Debate*. Princeton: Princeton University Press, 1992.

———. "Theory and Practice in Late Ancient Asceticism: Jerome, Chrysostom, and Augustine." *Journal of Feminist Studies in Religion* 5 (Fall 1989) 25–46.

———. "Vitiated Seeds and Holy Vessels: Augustine's Manichean Past." In *Images of the Feminine in Gnosticism*, edited by Karen King, 367–401. Harrisburg: Trinity, 1988.

Clark, Gillian. *Monica: An Ordinary Saint*. Oxford: Oxford University Press, 2015.

———. "Women and Asceticism in Late Antiquity: The Refusal of Status and Gender." In *Asceticism* edited by Vincent L. Wimbush and Richard Valantasis, 33–48. Oxford: Oxford University Press, 1998.

Clark, Mary T. *Augustine*. Washington, DC: Georgetown University Press, 1994.

———. *Augustine: Philosopher of Freedom*. New York: Desclée, 1958.

Clebsch, William. "Preface." In *Athanasius: The Life of Antony and the Letter to Marcellinus*, xiii–xxi. Mahwah, NJ: Paulist, 1980.

Colish, Marcia. *The Stoic Tradition from Antiquity to the Early Middle Ages: Stoicism in Christian Latin Thought through the Sixth Century*, vol. II. New York: Brill, 1990.

Conio, Caterina. "Theory and Practice in Evagrius Ponticus." In *Philosophy, Theory and Practice: Proceedings of the International Seminar on World Philosophy*, 49–62. Madras: University of Madras, 1974.

Conti, Marco. "Introduction." In *Priscillian of Avila: The Complete Works*, 1–30. Oxford: Oxford University Press, 2010.

Conybeare, Catherine. *The Irrational Augustine*. Oxford: Oxford University Press, 2006.

Cragg, Gerald. *The Church and the Age of Reason: 1648–1789*. New York: Penguin, 1990.

Craig, William Lane. "Augustine on Foreknowledge and the Free Will." *Augustinian Studies* 15 (1984) 41–62.

Creswell, Dennis R. "St. Augustine's Dilemma: The Conflict between Eternal Law and Grace, Its Resolution in Double Predestination, and Its Effect on Freedom in the Late Pelagian Controversy." PhD diss., Luther Northwestern Theological Seminary, 1991.

———. *St. Augustine's Dilemma: Grace and Eternal Law in the Major Works of Augustine of Hippo*. New York: Lang, 1997.

Cristiani, Léon. *Jean Cassien: La Spiritualité du Désert*. 2 vols. Abbaye S. Wandrille: Éditions de Fontenelle, 1946.

Curran, John. *Pagan City and Christian Capital: Rome in the Fourth Century*. Oxford: Oxford University Press, 2000.

Dalmon, Laurence. "La correspondance antipélagienne de l'Afrique avec Rome: Présentation d'un dossier de l'Épistolaire augustinien (416-8)." In *Studia Patristica XLIX*, 313–18. Leuven: Peeters, 2010.

Damian, Theodor. "Some Critical Considerations and New Arguments Reviewing the Problem of St. John Cassian's Birthplace." *Orientalia Christiana Periodica* 57 (1991) 257–80.

Daniélou, Jean. *Origen*. Translated by Walter Mitchell. Eugene, OR: Wipf and Stock, 1955.

Davis, Leo Donald. *The First Seven Ecumenical Councils (325–787) Their History and Theology*. Collegeville, MN: Liturgical, 1990.

De Bruyn, Theodore. "General Introduction." In *Pelagius's Commentary on St. Paul's Epistle to the Romans*, edited by Henry Chadwick and Rowan Williams, 1–53. Oxford: Clarendon, 2002.

———. "Pelagius's Interpretation of Rom. 5:12–21: Exegesis within the Limits of Polemic." *Toronto Journal of Theology* 4 (1989) 30–43.

De Clerq, V.C. "Ossius of Cordova and the Origins of Priscillianism." In *Studia Patristica*, 601–6. Berlin: Akademie Verlag 1957.

De Plinval, Georges. *Essai sur le Style et la Langue de Pélage*. Fribourg en Suisse: L'Université de Fribourg en Suisse, 1947.

———. "L'Heure est-elle Venue de Redécouvrir Pélage?" *Revue des Études Augustiniennes* 19 (1973) 158–62.

———. *Pélage: Ses Écrits, Sa Vie et Sa Réforme*. Lausanne: Librairie Payot, 1943.

———. "Points de Vues Récents sur la Théologie de Pélage." *Recherches de Science Religieuse* 46 (1958) 227–36.

———. "Le Problème de Pélage sous son Dernier État." *Revue d'Histoire Ecclésiastique* 35 (1939) 5–21.

———. "Recherches sur l'Oeuvre Littéraire de Pélage." *Revue de Philologie, de Littérature et d'Histoire Anciennes* 8 (1934) 9–42.

———. "Vue d'Ensemble sur la Littérature Pélagienne." *Revue des Études Latines* 29 (1951) 284–94.

De Plinval, Georges et J. De La Tullaye. "Introduction: La Grande Crise du Pélagianisme. Première Phase: 413–417." In *La Crise Pélagienne I*, 21, 9–23. Paris: L'Institut d'Etudes Augustiniennes, 1966.

Dechow, Jon. *Dogma and Mysticism in Early Christianity: Epiphanius of Cyprus and the Legacy of Origen*. Macon, GA: Mercer University Press, 1988.

Decret, François. "Du bon usage du mensonge et du parjure. Manichéens et Priscillianistes face à la persécution dans l'Empire chrétien (IVe–Ve siècles)." *Annales littéraires de l'Université de Besançon* 413 (1990) 141–49.

Den Boeft, Jan. "Augustine's Letter to Pelagius." In *Augustiniana Traiectina: Communications Présentées au Colloque International d'Utrecht 13-14 Novembre 1986*, 73–84. Paris: Études Augustiniennes, 1987.

Devos, Paul. "Saint Jean Cassien et Saint Moïse l'Éthiopien." *Analecta Bollandiana* (1985) 61–73.

Dewart, Joanne. "The Christology of the Pelagian Controversy." In *Studia Patristica: In Three Parts*, XVII, Pt. 2, edited by Elizabeth A. Livingstone, 1221–41. Oxford: Pergamon, 1982.

Djuth, Marianne. "Cassian's Use of the Figure *Uia Regia* in *Collatio* II 'On Discretion.'" In *Studia Patristica: Biblica et Apocrypha, Ascetica, Liturgica*, XXX, edited by Elizabeth A. Livingstone, 167–74. Leuven: Peeters, 1997.

———. "Stoicism and Augustine's Doctrine of Human Freedom after 396." In *Collectanea Augustiniana: Augustine: 'Second Founder of Faith,'* edited by Joseph C. Schnaubelt and Frederick Van Fleteren, 387–401. New York: Lang, 1990.

Dodaro, Robert. "Note on the Carthaginian Debate over Sinlessness, A.D. 411–412 (Augustine, *Pecc. Mer.* 2.7.8–16.25)." *Augustinianum* 40 (2000) 187–202.

———. "*Sacramentum Christi*: Augustine on the Christology of Pelagius." In *Studia Patristica: Papers Presented at the Eleventh International Conference on Patristic Studies Held in Oxford 1991: Cappadocian Fathers, Greek Authors after Nicaea, Augustine, Donatism, and Pelagianism*, XXVII, edited by Elizabeth A. Livingstone, 274–80. Leuven: Peeters, 1993.

Douthat, Ross. *To Change the Church: Pope Francis and the Future of Catholicism*. New York: Simon & Schuster, 2018.

Doyle, Daniel. "Mary, Mother of God." In *Augustine through the Ages: An Encyclopedia*, edited by Allan D. Fitzgerald, 542–45. Grand Rapids: Eerdmans, 1999.

Doyle, William. *Jansenism: Catholic Resistance to Authority from the Reformation to the French Revolution*. New York: St. Martin's, 2000.

Drake, H.A. *Constantine and the Bishops: The Politics of Intolerance*. Baltimore: John Hopkins University Press, 2000.

Drecoll, Volker Henning. "Rethinking Augustine's Early Theology: An Argument for Continuity, by Carol Harrison." *Vigiliae Christianae* 63 (2009) 202–10.

Driscoll, Jeremy. "Apatheia and Purity of Heart in Evagrius Ponticus." In *Purity of Heart in Early Ascetic and Monastic Literature: Essays in Honor of Juana Raasch, O.S.B.*, edited by Harriet Luckman and Linda Kulzer, 141–59. Collegeville, MN: Liturgical, 1999.

———. *Steps to Spiritual Perfection: Studies on Spiritual Progress in Evagrius Ponticus*. New York: Newman, 2005.

Driver, Steven. "The Development of Jerome's Views on the Ascetic Life." *Recherches de Théologie Ancienne et Médiévale* 62 (1995) 44–70.

———. "From Palestinian Ignorance to Egyptian Wisdom: Jerome and Cassian on the Monastic Life." *American Benedictine Review* 48 (1997) 293–315.

———. *John Cassian and the Reading of Egyptian Monastic Culture* Studies in Medieval History and Culture. Edited by Francis G. Gentry. New York: Routledge, 2002.

———. "A Reconsideration of Cassian's Views on the Communal and Solitary Lives." In *Religion, Text, and Society in Medieval Spain and Northern Europe: Essays in Honor of J.N. Hillgarth*, 277–301. Toronto: Pontifical Institute of Mediaeval Studies, 2002.

Duffy, Stephen J. "Anthropology." In *Augustine through the Ages: An Encyclopedia*, edited by Allan D. Fitzgerald, 24–31. Grand Rapids: Eerdmans, 1999.

Dulles, Avery. "Changing Concepts of Church Membership." In *The Resilient Church: The Necessity and Limits of Adaptation*, 133–52. Garden City, NY: Doubleday, 1977.

Dunn, Geoffrey. "Augustine, Cyril of Alexandria, and the Pelagian Controversy." *Augustinian Studies* 37 (2006) 63–88.

———. "Cassian in Syria?: The Evidence of Innocent I." *Vigiliae Christianae* 59 (2015) 3–17.

———. "The Christian Networks of the Aniciae: The Example of the Letter of Innocent I to Anicia Juliana." *Revue d'études Augustiniennes et Patristiques* (2009) 53–72.

———. "Did Zosimus Pardon Caelestius?" *Lex et Religio* 135 (2013) 647–56.

———. "Zosimus' Synod of Rome in September 417 and His Letter to Western Bishops (*Cum Aduersus*)." *Antiquité Tardive* 23 (2015) 395–405.

Dunphy, Walter. "Caelestius: A Preliminary Investigation." *Journal of the Nanzan Academic Society* 9 (1994) 33–59.

———. "Caelestius's *De possibilitate non peccandi*?" *Academia* 66 (1997) 65–81.

———. "Concerning the Synod of Diospolis and Its Acts." *Journal of the Nanzan Academic Society* (1996) 101–17.

———. "Eucherius of Lyons in Unexpected (Pelagian?) Company." *Augustinianum* 33 (1997) 483–94.

———. "Glosses on Glosses: On the Budapest Anonymous and Pseudo-Rufinus: A Study on Anonymous Writings in Pelagian Circles (Part 1)." *Augustinian Studies* 44 (2013) 227–47.

———. "Glosses on Glosses: On the Budapest Anonymous and Pseudo-Rufinus: A Study on Anonymous Writings in Pelagian Circles (Part 2)." *Augustinian Studies* 45 (2013) 49–68.

———. "Glosses on Glosses: On the Budapest Anonymous and Pseudo-Rufinus: A Study on Anonymous Writings in Pelagian Circles (Part 3)." *Augustinian Studies* 46 (2015) 43–70.

———. "Jerome against Jovinian, and Other(s): A Note on *Epp.* 50 and 133." *Academia* 64 (1996) 25–53.

———. "The Lost Manuscript of Pseudo-Rufinus: *De Fide*." *Augustinianum* 40 (2000) 89–103.

———. "A Lost Year: Pelagianism in Carthage, 411 A.D." *Augustinianum* 45 (2005) 389–466.

———. "A Manuscript Note on Pelagius' *De Vita Christiana* (Paris, Bn Lat. 10463)." *Augustinianum* 21 (1981) 589–91.

———. "Marius Mercator on Rufinus the Syrian: Was Schwartz Mistaken?" *Augustinianum* 32 (1992) 279–88.

———. "Pauline *Fragmenta*: An Unlisted Commentary on the Pauline Letters from the Hiberno-Latin Tradition (St Gal 877)." *Peritia* 26 (2015) 65–80.

———. "A Pelagian Commentary on Genesis? Pseudo-Rufinus: *De Fide*." *Academia* 71 (2000) 67–97.

———. "The Pelagians and Their Eastern (Antiochene) Sources: Theodore of Mopsuestia on Lk 2.52 in the *Liber De Fide* by Pseudo-Rufinus?" *Revue d'études Augustiniennes et Patristiques* 58 (2012) 97–111.

———. "Pelagius or Caelestius? An Unidentified Text." *Academia* 6 (1997) 147–65.

———. "A Prelude to the Synod of Diospolis: *The Liber Apologeticus* of Orosius." *Academia* 62 (1995) 123–53.

———. "Ps-Rufinus (the "Syrian") and the Vulgate: Evidence Wanting!" *Augustinianum* 52 (2012) 219–56.

———. "Rufinus of Aquileia in the Middle Ages: The Evidence of Manuscripts." *Nanzan Journal of Theological Studies* 34 (2011) 93–141.

———. "Rufinus the Syrian: Myth and Reality." *Augustiniana* 59 (2009) 79–157.

———. "Rufinus the Syrian's 'Books.'" *Augustinianum* 23 (1983) 523–29.

———. "Saint Jerome and the Gens Anicia (Ep. 130 to Demetrias)." In *Studia Patristica: Augustine, Post-Nicene Fathers, Oriental Texts, Nachleben of the Fathers*, XVIII, 4, edited by Elizabeth A. Livingstone, 139–45. Leuven: Peeters, 1990.

———. "Unexplored Paths: Relating to the Outbreak of the Pelagian Debate." *Nanzan Journal of Theological Studies* 30 (2007) 27–54.

———. "Who Was Flavius Marcellinus?" *Academia* 75 (2002) 233–49.

———. "The Writings of Caelestius." *Academia* 61 (1995) 25–47.

Dupont, Anthony. "The Christology of the Pre-Controversial Pelagius: A Study of *De natura* and *De fide trinitatis*, Complemented by a Comparison with *Libellus fidei*." *Augustiniana* 58 (2008) 235–57.

———. *Gratia in Augustine's Sermones ad Populum during the Pelagian Controversy*. Boston: Brill, 2012.

———. "*Gratia Fidei* in the Anti-Pelagian *Sermones ad Populum Sermones* 143 and 144: the Rare Appearance of Ioh. 16, 7–11." In *Ministerium Sermonis: Philological, Historical, and Theological Studies on Augustine's Sermones Ad Populum*, edited by Gert Partoens, Antony Dupont, and Mathijs Lamberigts. Turnhout: Brepolis, 2009.

Dupont, Anthony, and Giulio Malavasi. "The Question of the Impact of Divine Grace in the Pelagian Controversy. Human *posse, uelle et esse* According to Pelagius, Jerome, and Augustine." *Revue d'Histoire Ecclésiastique* 112 (2017) 539–68.

Duval, Y.M. *L'affaire Jovinien: d'une crise de la société romaine à une crise de la pensée chrétienne à la fin du IVe et au début du Ve siècle*. Rome: Institutum patristicum Augustinianum, 2003.

———. "La correspondance entre Augustin et Pélage." *Revue des Études Augustiniennes* 45 (1999) 363–84.

———. "La Date du *De natura* de Pélage: Les Premières Étapes de la Controverse sur la Nature de la Grâce." *Revue des Études Augustiniennes* 36 (1990) 257–83.

———. *La décrétale Ad Gallos Episcopos: son texte et son auteur*. Leiden: Brill, 2005.

———. *L'extirpation de l'Arianism en Italie du Nord et en Occident*. Brookfield: Ashgate, 1998.

———. *Jérôme entre l'Occident et l'Orient*. Paris: Études Augustiniennes, 1988.

———. "Julien d'Éclane et Rufin d'Aquilée: Du Concile de Rimini à la Répression Pélagienne L'Intervention Impériale en Matière Religieuse." *Revue des Études Augustiniennes* 24 (1978) 243–71.

———. "Pélage en son temps: Données chronologiques nouvelles pour une présentation nouvelle." In *Studia Patristica*, edited by M.F. Wiles and E.J. Yarnold, 38, 95–118. Leuven: Peeters, 2001.

———. "Pélage est-il le Censeur Inconnu de l'*Adversus Iovinianum* A Rome en 393? Ou: Du 'Portrait-Robot' de l'Hérétique chez S. Jérôme." *Revue d'Histoire Ecclésiastique* 75 (1980) 525–57.

Dysinger, Luke. *Psalmody and Prayer in the Writings of Evagrius Ponticus*. Oxford: Oxford University Press, 2005.

Elm, Susanna "The Polemical Use of Genealogies: Jerome's Classification of Pelagius and Evagrius Ponticus." In *Studia Patristica: Augustine and His Opponents, Jerome, Other Latin Fathers after Nicaea, Orientalia. Papers Presented at the Twelfth International Conference on Patristic Studies Held in Oxford 1995*, XXXIII, edited by Elizabeth A. Livingstone, 311–18. Leuven: Peeters, 1997.

Eno, Robert. "Introduction." In *Fulgentius: Selected Works*, xv–xviii. Washington, DC: The Catholic University of America, 1997.

Escribano, Victoria. "Heresy and Orthodoxy in Fourth-Century Hispania: Arianism and Priscillianism." In *Hispania in Late Antiquity: Current Perspectives*, edited by Kim Bowes and Michael Kulikowski, 121–49. Boston: Brill, 2005.

Evans, Gillian R. "Neither a Pelagian nor a Manichee." *Vigiliae Christianae* 35 (1981) 232–44.

Evans, Joshua. "Augustine's Unfinished Work against Julian: The Ancient and Contemporary Dispute over Concupiscence." PhD diss., The Catholic University of America, 2016.

Evans, Robert F. *Four Letters of Pelagius*. New York: Seabury, 1968.

———. "Pelagius, Fastidius, and the Pseudo-Augustinian *De vita christiana*." *Journal of Theological Studies* XIII (1962) 72–98.

———. *Pelagius: Inquiries and Reappraisals*. New York: Seabury, 1968.

———. "Pelagius' Veracity at the Synod of Diospolis." In *Studies in Medieval Culture*, edited by John R. Sommerfeldt, 21–30. Kalamazoo: Western Michigan University, 1964.

Fairbairn, Donald. *Grace and Christology in the Early Church*. Oxford: Oxford University Press, 2003.

———. "Introduction." In *Fulgentius of Ruspe and the Scythian Monks: Correspondence on Christology and Grace*, 3–22. Washington, DC: The Catholic University of America Press, 2013.

Fear, A.T. "Introduction." In *Orosius: Seven Books of History against the Pagans*, 54, 1–30. Liverpool: Liverpool University, 2010.

Ferguson, Everett. *Baptism in the Early Church: History, Theology, and Liturgy in the First Five Centuries*. Grand Rapids: Eerdmans, 2009.

Ferguson, John. "In Defence of Pelagius." *Theology* 83 (1980) 114–19.

———. *Pelagius: A Historical and Theological Study*. Cambridge: W. Heffer & Sons, 1956.

Fiske, Adele. "Cassian and Monastic Friendship." *American Benedictine Review* 12 (1961) 190–205.

Fitzgerald, Allan. "Retractationes." In *Augustine through the Ages: An Encyclopedia*, edited by Allan D. Fitzgerald, 723–24. Grand Rapids: Eerdmans, 1999.

Fox, F. Earle. "Biblical Theology and Pelagianism." *The Journal of Religion* 41 (1961) 169–81.

Fox, Robin Lane. *Augustine: Conversions to Confessions*. Grand Rapids: Baker, 2015.

Frank, Karl "John Cassian on John Cassian." In *Studia Patristica: Augustine and His Opponents, Jerome, Other Latin Fathers after Nicaea, Orientalia*, 33, edited by Elizabeth A. Livingstone, 418–33. Leuven: Peeters, 1997.

Fredriksen, Paula. "Beyond the Body/Soul Dichotomy: Augustine on Paul against the Manichees and the Pelagians." *Recherches Augustiniennes* 23 (1988) 87–114.

———. "Response to 'Vitiated Seeds and Holy Vessels: Augustine's Manichean Past' by Elizabeth A. Clark." In *Images of the Feminine in Gnosticism*, edited by Karen King, 402–9. Harrisburg: Trinity, 1988.

Freeman, Charles. *A.D. 381: Heretics, Pagans, and the Dawn of the Monotheistic State*. New York: Overlook, 2008.

Frend, W.H.C. "Augustine and Orosius: On the End of the Ancient World." *Augustinian Studies* 20 (1989) 1–38.

———. "The Divjak Letters: New Light on St. Augustine's Problems, 416–428." *Journal of Ecclesiastical History* 34 (1983) 497–512.

———. "Orosius, Paulus." In *Augustine through the Ages: An Encyclopedia*, edited by Allan D. Fitzgerald, 615–17. Grand Rapids: Eerdmans, 1999.

———. *The Rise of Christianity*. Philadelphia: Fortress, 1984.

Garcia-Allen, C.A. "Was Pelagius Influenced by Chromatius of Aquileia?" In *Studia Patristica*, edited by Elizabeth A. Livingston, 17.3, 1251–57. Oxford: Pergamon, 1982.

García-Sánchez, Carlos. "Pelagius and Christian Initiation: A Study in Historical Theology." PhD diss., The Catholic University of America, 1978.

Gaustad, Edwin. *Sworn on the Altar of God: A Religious Biography of Thomas Jefferson*. Grand Rapids: Eerdmans, 1996.

Georgieva, Silvia. "The Letters of Jerome, Augustine, and Pelagius to the Virgin Demetrias. The Epistolary Education of Early Christianity." *Studia Patristica* LXXIV (2016) 329–40.

Gerber, Chad Tyler. "Rethinking Augustine's Early Theology: An Argument for Continuity, by Carol Harrison." *Journal of Early Christian Studies* 15 (2007) 120–22.

———. *The Spirit of Augustine's Early Theology: Contextualizing Augustine's Pneumatology*. Burlington, VT: Ashgate, 2012.

Gibson, Edgar. "Prolegomena." In *Sulpitius Severus, Vincent of Lerins, John Cassian*, XI, edited by Philip Schaff and Henry Wace, 183–97. Peabody, MA: Hendrickson, 2004.

Gillette, Gertrude. "Purity of Heart in St. Augustine." In *Purity of Heart in Early Ascetic and Monastic Literature: Essays in Honor of Juana Raasch, O.S.B.*, edited by Harriet Luckman and Linda Kulzer, 175–95. Collegeville, MN: Liturgical, 1999.

Gilson, Etienne. *The Christian Philosophy of Saint Augustine*. Translated by L. E. M. Lynch. New York: Octagon, 1988.

Glancy, Jennifer. *Slavery in Early Christianity*. Minneapolis: Fortress, 2006.

González, Justo. *The Mestizo Augustine: A Theologian between Two Cultures*. Downers Grove, IL: IVP Academic, 2016.

Goodrich, Richard J. *Contextualizing Cassian: Aristocrats, Asceticism, and Reformation in Fifth-Century Gaul*. Oxford: Oxford University Press, 2007.

———. "Introduction." In *Sulpicius Severus: The Complete Works*, 70, 1–21. Mahwah, NJ: Newman, 2015.

Gore, Bishop. "Our Lord's Human Example." *Church Quarterly Review* XVI (1883) 282–313.

Graves, Michael. "Introduction." In *Commentary on Jeremiah*, xxiii–li. Downers Grove, IL: IVP Academic, 2011.

Greer, Rowan. "Introduction." In *Origen: An Exhortation to Martyrdom, Prayer and Selected Works*. Mahwah, NJ: Paulist, 1979.

Gregg, Robert. "Introduction." In *Athanasius: The Life of Antony and the Letter to Marcellinus*, 1–26. Mahwah, NJ: Paulist, 1980.

Gregg, Robert, and Dennis Groh. *Early Arianism: A View of Salvation*. Minneapolis: Fortress, 1981.

Gregory, Brad. *The Unintended Reformation: How a Religious Revolution Secularized Society*. Cambridge: Belknap, 2012.

Griffe, E. "Cassien a-t-il été Prêtre d'Antioche?" *Bulletin de Littérature Ecclésiastique* 55 (1954) 240–44.

Grillmeier, Aloys. *Christ in Christian Tradition: From the Apostolic Age to Chalcedon (451),* vol. 1. Second revised ed. Translated by John Bowden. Atlanta: John Knox, 1975.

Groves, Nicholas. "Mundicia Cordis: A Study of the Theme of Purity of Heart in Hugh of Pontigny and the Fathers of the Undivided Church." In *One Yet Two: Monastic Tradition East and West. Orthodox-Cistercian Symposium. Oxford University: 26 August–1 September 1973,* edited by M. Basil Pennington, 304–31. Kalamazoo: Cistercian Publications, 1976.

Guarino, Thomas. *Vincent of Lérins and the Development of Christian Doctrine.* Grand Rapids: Baker Academic, 2013.

Guevin, Benedict. "The Beginning and End of Purity of Heart: From Cassian to the Master and Benedict." In *Purity of Heart in Early Ascetic and Monastic Literature: Essays in Honor of Juana Raasch, O.S.B.,* edited by Harriet Luckman and Linda Kulzer, 197–214. Collegeville, MN: Liturgical, 1999.

Haag, Modestus. "A Precarious Balance: Flesh and Spirit in Cassian's Works." *American Benedictine Review* 19 (1968) 180–92.

Habermas, Jürgen. *The Philosophical Discourse of Modernity: Twelve Lectures (Studies in Contemporary German Thought).* Translated by Frederick Lawrence. Cambridge: The MIT Press, 1990.

Hadot, Pierre. *Philosophy as a Way of Life.* Translated by Michael Chase. Malden, MA: Blackwell, 1995.

Haight, Roger. "Notes on the Pelagian Controversy." *Philippine Studies* 22 (1974) 26–48.

Hamman, Adalbert. "Orosius de Braga et le Pélagianisme." *Bracara Augusta* 21 (1968) 346–55.

Hanby, Michael. *Augustine and Modernity.* New York: Routledge, 2003.

Hanson, Craig L. "Introduction." In *Iberian Fathers: Pacian of Barcelona; Orosius of Braga,* edited by Thomas P. Halton, 3, 97–114. Washington, DC: The Catholic University of America Press, 1999.

Hanson, Richard. *The Search for the Christian Doctrine of God: The Arian Controversy, 318–381.* Edinburgh: T. & T. Clark, 1988.

Harbert, Bruce. "Romans 5:12: Old Latin and Vulgate in the Pelagian Controversy." In *Studia Patristica,* 22, edited by Elizabeth Livingstone, 261–64. Leuven: Peeters, 1989.

Harmless, William. "Christ as Pediatrician: Infant Baptism and Christological Imagery in the Pelagian Controversy." *Augustinian Studies* 28 (1997) 7–34.

Harnack, Adolph. *History of Dogma,* vol. V. Third ed. Translated by Neil Buchanan. Boston: Little, Brown, 1899.

Harrill, Albert J. *Paul the Apostle: His Life and Legacy in Their Roman Context.* Cambridge: Cambridge University Press, 2012.

Harrington, Daniel. *The Church According to the New Testament: What the Wisdom and Witness of Early Christianity Teach Us Today.* Lanham: Rowman & Littlefield, 2001.

Harrison, Carol. *Rethinking Augustine's Early Theology: An Argument for Continuity.* Oxford: Oxford University Press, 2006.

———. "Truth in Heresy? 1. Pelagianism." *The Expository Times* 112 (2000) 78–82.

Harrison, Simon. *Augustine's Way into the Will: The Theological and Philosophical Significance of De libero arbitrio.* Oxford: Oxford University Press, 2006.

Heine, Ronald. "Introduction." In *The Commentaries of Origen and Jerome on St. Paul's Epistle to the Ephesians*. Oxford: Oxford University Press, 2002.

Hellenga, Virginia. "The Exchange of Letters between Saint Augustine and Saint Jerome." In *Daidalikon: Studies in Memory of Raymond V. Schroder, S.J.*, edited by Robert F. Sutton Jr., 177–82. Wauconda: Bolchazy-Carducci, 1988.

Henry, Patrick. "Why Is Contemporary Scholarship So Enamored of Ancient Heretics?" In *Studia Patristica*, edited by Elizabeth A. Livingston, 17.1, 123–26. Oxford: Pergamon, 1982.

Henry, Paul. "The Place of Plotinus in the History of Thought." In *Plotinus: The Enneads*, xlii–lxxxiii. New York: Penguin Classics, 1991.

Hickey, Anne. *Women of the Roman Aristocracy as Christian Monastics*. Ann Arbor: UMI Research Press, 1987.

Hoare, F.R. "Introduction." In *Soldiers of Christ: Saints and Saints' Lives from Late Antiquity and the Early Middle Ages*, edited by Thomas F.X. Noble and Thomas Head, 1–3. University Park: The Pennsylvania State University Press, 2000.

Hollingworth, Miles. *Saint Augustine of Hippo: An Intellectual Biography*. Oxford: Oxford University Press, 2013.

Holloway, Ross. *Constantine and Rome*. New Haven: Yale University Press, 2004.

Hombert, Pierre-Marie. *Nouvelles Recherches de Chronologie Augustinienne*. Paris: Institut d'Études Augustiniennes, 2000.

Honnay, Guido. "Caelestius, Discipulus Pelagii." *Augustiniana* 44 (1994) 271–302.

Hopkins, M.K. "The Age of Roman Girls at Marriage." *Population Studies* 18 (1965) 309–27.

Huber, Karen Cash. "The Pelagian Heresy: Observations on Its Social Context." PhD diss., Oklahoma State University, 1979.

Hunter, David. "Ambrosiaster, Astral Fatalism and the Prehistory of the Pelagian Controversy." North American Patristic Society: Loyola University, Chicago, 1990.

———. "Augustinian Pessimism? A New Look at Augustine's Teaching on Sex, Marriage, and Celibacy." *Augustinian Studies* 25 (1994) 153–77.

———. "Introduction." In *Marriage in the Early Church*, 1–28. Minneapolis: Fortress, 1992.

———. *Marriage, Celibacy and Heresy in Ancient Christianity: The Jovinianist Controversy*. Oxford: Oxford University Press, 2007.

Hušek, Vít. "Perfection Appropriate to the Fragile Human Condition: Jerome and Pelagius on the Perfection of Christian Life." In *Studia Patristica*, edited by Markus Vinzent, 67, 385–92. Walpole: Peeters, 2013.

Hwang, Alexander. *Intrepid Lover of Perfect Grace: The Life and Thought of Prosper of Aquitaine*. Washington, DC: The Catholic University of America Press, 2009.

Ingham, Mary Beth and Mechtild Dreyer. *The Philosophical Vision of John Duns Scotus: An Introduction*. Washington, DC: The Catholic University Press, 2004.

Jacobs, Andrew. "The Disorder of Books: Priscillian's Canonical Defense of Apocrypha." *Harvard Theological Review* 93 (2000) 135–59.

———. *Epiphanius of Cyprus: A Cultural Biography of Late Antiquity*. Oakland: University of California Press, 2016.

Jacobs, Andrew S. "Writing Demetrias: Ascetic Logic in Ancient Christianity." *Church History* 69 (2000) 719–48.

Janz, Denis. *Luther and Late Medieval Thomism: A Study in Theological Anthropology*. Waterloo, ON: Wilfrid Laurier University Press, 1983.

Jeanjean, Benoît. "Le *Dialogus Attici et Critobuli* de Jérôme et la Prédication Pélagienne en Palestine entre 411 et 415." In *Jerome of Stridon: His Life, Writings, and Legacy*, edited by Andrew Cain and Josef Lössl, 73–83. Farnham & Burlington, VT: Ashgate, 2009.

———. *Saint Jérôme et l'Hérésie*. Paris: Institut d'Études Augustiniennes, 1999.

Joest, Christoph. "The Significance of *Acedia* and *Apatheia* in Evagrius Ponticus: Part I." *American Benedictine Review* 55 (2004) 121–50.

———. "The Significance of *Acedia* and *Apatheia* in Evagrius Ponticus: Part II." *American Benedictine Review* 55 (2004) 273–307.

Johnson, David. "The Myth of the Augustinian Synthesis." *Lutheran Quarterly* 5 (1991) 157–69.

———. "Purging the Poison: The Revision of Pelagius' Pauline Commentaries by Cassiodorus and His Students." PhD diss., Princeton Theological Seminary, 1989.

Kalvesmaki, Joel and Robin Darling Young, ed. *Evagrius and His Legacy*. Notre Dame: University of Notre Dame Press, 2016.

Kannengiesser, Charles. "Athanasius of Alexandria and the Ascetic Movement of His Time." In *Asceticism*, edited by Vincent L. Wimbush and Richard Valantasis, 479–92. Oxford: Oxford University Press, 1998.

Kardong, Terrence. "Aiming for the Mark: Cassian's Metaphor for the Monastic Quest." *Cistercian Studies Quarterly* 22 (1987) 213–20.

———. "John Cassian's Evaluation of Monastic Practices." *American Benedictine Review* 43 (1992) 82–105.

———. "John Cassian's Teaching on Perfect Chastity." *American Benedictine Review* 30 (1979) 249–63.

Karfíková, Lenka. *Grace and Will According to Augustine*. Translated by Markéta Janebová. Boston: Brill, 2012.

Katos, Demetrios. *Palladius of Helenopolis: The Origenist Advocate*. Oxford: Oxford University Press, 2011.

Kavvadas, Nestor. "An Eastern View: Theodore of Mopsuestia's *Against the Defenders of Original Sin*." In *Grace for Grace: The Debates after Augustine and Pelagius*, edited by Alexander Hwang, Brian Matz, and Augustine Casiday, 271–93. Washington, DC: The Catholic University of America Press, 2014.

Keech, Dominic. *The Anti-Pelagian Christology of Augustine of Hippo, 396–430*. Oxford: Oxford University Press, 2012.

Kelly, J.N.D. *Early Christian Doctrines*. London: Adam and Charles Black, 1958.

———. *Golden Mouth: The Story of John Chrysostom: Ascetic, Preacher, Bishop*. Grand Rapids: Baker, 1995.

———. "Introduction." In *A Commentary on the Apostles' Creed*, 3–27. New York: Newman, 1978.

———. *Jerome: His Life, Writings, and Controversies*. Peabody, MA: Hendrickson, 2000.

———. *The Oxford Dictionary of Popes*. Oxford: Oxford University Press, 1986.

Kessler, Andreas. *Reichtumskritik und Pelagianismus. Die pelagianische Diatribe de divitiis: Situierung, Lesetext, Übersetzung, Kommentar*. Paradosis 43. Freiburg, Schweiz: Universitäts-Verlag, 1999.

Kim, Young Richard. *Epiphanius of Cyprus: Imagining an Orthodox World*. Ann Arbor: University of Michigan Press, 2015.

King, N.Q. *The Emperor Theodosius and the Establishment of Christianity*. Philadelphia: Westminster, 1960.

King, Peter. *Western Monasticism: A History of the Monastic Movement in the Latin Church.* Kalamazoo: Cistercian Publications, 1999.

Kittelson, James. *Luther the Reformer: The Story of the Man and His Career.* Minneapolis: Fortress, 1986.

Klingshirn, William E. "General Introduction." In *Caesarius of Arles: Life, Testament, Letters,* xi–xvii. Liverpool: Liverpool University Press, 1994.

Konstantinovsky, Julia. *Evagrius Ponticus: The Making of a Gnostic.* Burlington, VT: Ashgate, 2009.

Koopsmans, J.H. "Augustine's First Contact with Pelagius and the Dating of the Condemnation of Caelestius at Carthage." *Vigiliae Christianae* 8 (1954) 149–53.

Krabbe, Sr. M. Kathryn Clare, ed. *Epistula ad Demetriadem: De Vera Humilitate: A Critical Text and Translation with Introduction and Commentary.* Washington, DC: The Catholic University of America Press, 1965.

Krannich, Torsten. *Von Leporius bis zu Leo dem Großen: Studien zur lateinischsprachigen Christologie im fünften Jahrhundert nach Christus.* Tübingen: Mohr Siebeck, 2005.

Kristensen, Ansgar. "Cassian's Use of Scripture." *American Benedictine Review* 28 (1977) 276–88.

La Bonnardière, A.M. "Quelques Remarques sur les Citations Scripturaires du *De Gratia et Libero Arbitrio*." *Revue des Études Augustiniennes* 9 (1963) 77–83.

Lacroix, Benoît. *Orose et ses idées.* Montréal: Institut d'Études Médiévales, 1965.

Lamberigts, Mathijs. "Augustine, Julian of Aeclanum, and E. Pagels' *Adam, Eve, and the Serpent*." *Augustiniana* 39 (1989) 393–435.

———. "Augustine and Julian of Aeclanum on Zosimus." *Augustiniana* 42 (1992) 311–30.

———. "Augustine on Predestination: Some *Quaestiones Disputatae* Revisited." *Augustiniana* 54 (2004) 279–305.

———. "Augustine's Use of Tradition in His Reaction to Julian of Aeclanum's *Ad Turbantium*: *Contra Iluianum I-II*." *Augustinian Studies* 41 (2010) 183–200.

———. "Augustine's View on Love as Grace in the Controversy with Julian of Aeclanum." *Augustiniana* 64 (2014) 75–91.

———. "Caelestius." In *Augustine through the Ages: An Encyclopedia*, edited by Allan D. Fitzgerald, 114–15. Grand Rapids: Eerdmans, 1999.

———. "Competing Christologies: Julian and Augustine on Jesus Christ." *Augustinian Studies* 36 (2005) 159–94.

———. "Co-operation of Church and State in the Condemnation of the Pelagians: The Case of Zosimus." In *Religious Polemics in Context: Papers Presented to the Second International Conference of the Leiden Institute for the Study of Religions (Lisor) Held at Leiden, 27-28 April 2000*, edited by T.L. Hettema and A. Van Der Ikooij, 363–75. Assen: Royal Van Gorcum, 2004.

———. "Les évêques pélagiens déposés, Nestoriuus et Ephèse." *Augustiniana* 35 (1985) 264–80.

———. "Julian of Aeclanum and Augustine of Hippo on 1 Cor. 15." In *Studia Patristica: Papers Presented at the Fourteenth International Conference on Patristic Studies Held in Oxford 2003: Augustine; Other Latin Writers*, XLIII, edited by M. Edwards, P. Parvis, and F. Young, 155–72. Leuven: Peeters, 2006.

———. "Julian of Aeclanum on Grace: Some Considerations." In *Studia Patristica: Papers Presented at the Eleventh International Conference on Patristic Studies Held in Oxford*

1991: Cappadocian Fathers, Greek Authors after Nicaea, Augustine, Donatism, and Pelagianism, XXVII, edited by Elizabeth A. Livingstone, 342–49. Leuven: Peeters, 1993.

———. "Julian of Aeclanum: A Plea for a Good Creator." *Augustiniana* 38 (1988) 5–24.

———. "Julian and Augustine on the Origin of the Soul." *Augustiniana* 46 (1996) 243–60.

———. "Julian of Eclanum." In *Augustine through the Ages: An Encyclopedia*, edited by Allan D. Fitzgerald, 478–79. Grand Rapids: Eerdmans, 1999.

———. "Julien d'Éclane et Augustin d'Hippone: Deux Conceptions d'Adam." *Augustiniana* 40 (1990) 373–410.

———. "Le Mal et le Péché. Pélage: la Réhabilitation d'un Hérétique." *Revue d'Histoire Ecclésiastique* 95 (2000) 97–111.

———. "The Philosophical and Theological Background of Julian of Aeclanum's Concept of Concupiscence." In *Die christlich-philosophischen Diskurse der Spätantike: Texte, Personen, Institutionen: Akten der Tagung vom 22.–25. Februar 2006 am Zentrum für Antike und Moderne der Albert-Ludwigs-Universität Freiburg*, edited by Therese Fuhrer, 245–60. Stuttgart: Franz Steiner Verlag, 2008.

———. "The Presence of 1 Cor. 4,7 in the Anti-Pelagian Works of Augustine." *Augustiniana* 56 (2006) 374–99.

———. "Recent Research into Pelagianism with Particular Emphasis on the Role of Julian of Aeclanum." *Augustiniana* 52 (2002) 175–98.

———. "Was Augustine a Manichaean? The Assessment of Julian of Aeclanum." In *Augustine and Manichaeism in the Latin West: Proceedings of the Fribourg-Utrecht Symposium of the International Association of Manichaean Studies (Iams)*, edited by Johannes Van Oort, Otto Wermelinger, and Gregor Wurst, 113–36. Boston: Brill, 2001.

Lancel, Serge. *Saint Augustine*. Translated by Antonia Nevill. London: SCM, 2002.

Lavender, Earl Dale. "The Development of Pelagius' Thought within a Late Fourth Century Ascetic Movement in Rome." PhD diss., Saint Louis University, 1991.

Lawrence, C.H. *Medieval Monasticism: Forms of Religious Life in Western Europe in the Middle Ages*. New York: Longman, 2001.

Le Nain de Tillemont, Louis Sébastien. *The Life of Augustine of Hippo: Part Three: The Pelagian Crisis: (411–430)*. Translated by Frederick Van Fleteren. New York: Lang, 2015.

Leclercq, Jean. *The Love of Learning and the Desire for God: A Study of Monastic Culture*. Translated by Catharine Misrahi. New York: Fordham University Press, 2003.

Lee, Kam-Iun E. "Augustine, Manichaeism and the Good." PhD diss., Saint Paul University, 1996.

Leithart, Peter. *Defending Constantine: The Twilight of an Empire and the Dawn of Christendom*. Downer's Grove, IL: IVP Academic, 2010.

Leroy, Julien. "Le Cénobitisme Chez Cassien." *Revue d'Ascétique et de Mystique* 43 (1967) 121–58.

———. "Les Préfaces des Écrits Monastiques de Jean Cassien." *Revue d'Ascétique et de Mystique* 42 (1966) 157–80.

Levering, Matthew. *The Theology of Augustine: An Introductory Guide to His Most Important Works*. Grand Rapids: Baker, 2013.

Leyser, Conrad. "*Lectio Divina, Oratio Pura*: Rhetoric and the Techniques of Asceticism in the *Conferences* of John Cassian." In *Modelli di Santità e Modelli di Comportamento*, 79–105. Torino: Rosenberg & Sellier, 1994.

———. "Semi-Pelagianism." In *Augustine through the Ages: An Encyclopedia*, edited by Allan D. Fitzgerald, 761–66. Grand Rapids: Eerdmans, 1999.

Liebeschuetz, W. "Did the Pelagian Movement Have Social Aims?" *Historia: Zeitschrift für Alte Geschichte* 12 (April 1963) 227–41.

Lieu, Iain and Samuel Gardner, ed. *Manichaean Texts from the Roman Empire*. Cambridge: Cambridge University Press, 2004.

Lof, L.J. Van der. "The Man in the Shadow Behind Pelagius." In *Studia Patristica*, XV, edited by Elizabeth A. Livingstone, 247–54. Berlin: Akademie-Verlag, 1984.

Löhr, Winrich. "Pelagius' Schrift *De natura*: Rekonstruktion und Analyse." *Recherches Augustiniennes* (1999) 235–94.

Lössl, Josef. "Augustine, 'Pelagianism,' Julian of Aeclanum and Modern Scholarship." *Journal of Ancient Christianity* 11 (2007) 129–50.

———. "Julian of Aeclanum's 'Prophetic Exegesis.'" In *Studia Patristica: Papers Presented at the Fourteenth International Conference on Patristic Studies Held in Oxford 2003*, edited by M. Edwards and P. Parvis F. Young, XLIII, 409–21. Leuven: Peeters, 2006.

———. "Julian of Aeclanum's 'Rationalist' Exegesis: Albert Bruckner Revisited." *Augustiniana* 53 (2003) 77–106.

———. *Julian von Aeclanum: Studien zu seinem Leben, seinem Werk, seiner Lehre und ihrer Überlieferung*. Supplements to Vigiliae Christianae, 60. Leiden: Brill, 2001.

———. "Rethinking Augustine's Early Theology: An Argument for Continuity, by Carol Harrison." *The Journal of Theological Studies* 58 (2007) 300–2.

———. "A Shift in Patristic Exegesis: Hebrew Clarity and Historical Verity in Augustine, Jerome, Julian of Aeclanum and Theodore of Mopsuestia." *Augustinian Studies* 32 (2001) 157–75.

———. "'Te Apulia Genuit' (*C. Iul. Imp.* 6.18): Some Notes on the Birthplace of Julian of Eclanum." *Revue des Études Augustiniennes* 44 (1998) 223–37.

———. "Who Attacked the Monasteries of Jerome and Paula in 416 A.D.?" *Augustinianum* 44 (2004) 91–112.

Louth, Andrew. "Messalianism and Pelagianism." In *Studia Patristica: In Three Parts*, Part One, XVII, edited by Elizabeth A. Livingstone, 127–35. Oxford: Pergamon, 1978.

Lucas, J.R. "Pelagius and St. Augustine." *Journal of Theological Studies* XXII (1971) 73–85.

Lyonnet, Stanislaus. "A Propos de Romains 5:12 dans l'Oeuvre de S. Augustin." *Biblica* 45 (1964) 541–42.

———. "Rom. V,12 Chez Saint Augustin: Note sur l'Élaboration de la Doctrine Augustinienne du Péché Originel." In *L'Homme Devant Dieu: Mélanges Offerts au Pére Henri de Lubac*, 327–39. Paris: Aubier, 1963.

MacCulloch, Diarmaid. *Christianity: The First Three Thousand Years*. New York: Penguin, 2009.

———. *The Reformation: A History*. New York: Viking, 2003.

Macqueen, D.J. "John Cassian on Grace and Free Will with Particular Reference to *Institutio* XII and *Collatio* XIII." *Recherches de Théologie Ancienne et Médiévale* 44 (1977) 5–28.

Malavasi, Giulio. "The Involvement of Theodore of Mopsuestia in the Pelagian Controversy: A Study of Theodore's Treatise *Against Those Who Say That Men Sin by Nature and Not by Will*." *Augustiniana* 64 (2014) 227–60.

Mann, William. "Augustine on Evil and Original Sin." In *The Cambridge Companion to Augustine*, edited by Eleonore Stump and Norman Kretzmann, 40–48. Cambridge: Cambridge University Press, 2001.

Markus, R.A. "Augustine's *Confessions* and the Controversy with Julian of Eclanum: Manicheism Revisited." In *Collectanea Augustiniana: Mélanges T.J. Van Bavel* 2, 913–25. Leuven: University Press, 1994.

———. *The End of Ancient Christianity*. Cambridge: Cambridge University Press, 1990.

———. "The Legacy of Pelagius: Orthodoxy, Heresy and Conciliation." In *The Making of Orthodoxy: Essays in Honour of Henry Chadwick*, edited by Rowan Williams, 214–34. Cambridge: Cambridge University Press, 1989.

———. "Life, Culture, and Controversies of Augustine." In *Augustine through the Ages: An Encyclopedia*, edited by Allan Fitzgerald, 498–504. Grand Rapids: Eerdmans, 1999.

———. "Pelagianism: Britain and the Continent." *Journal of Ecclesiastical History* 37 (April 1986) 191–204.

Marrou, Henri Irénée. "La Canonisation de Julien d'Eclane." *Historisches Jarbuch* 77 (1958) 434–37.

———. "Jean Cassien à Marseille." *Revue du Moyen Age Latin* 1 (1945) 5–26.

———. "La Patrie de Jean Cassien." *Orientalia Christiana Periodica* (1947) 588–96.

Marsili, D. Salvatore. *Giovanni Cassiano ed Evagrio Pontico*. Rome: Herder, 1936.

Mathewes, Charles. "The Career of the Pelagian Controversy: Introductory Essay." *Augustinian Studies* 3 (2002) 201–12.

Mathisen, Ralph W. "Councils of Orange." In *Augustine through the Ages: An Encyclopedia*, edited by Allan D. Fitzgerald, 250–51. Grand Rapids: Eerdmans, 1999.

Mattison, William. *Introducing Moral Theology: True Happiness and the Virtues*. Grand Rapids: Brazos, 2008.

McGrath, Alister. "Divine Justice and Divine Equity in the Controversy between Augustine and Julian of Eclanum." *The Downside Review* 101 (1983) 312–19.

McGuckin, John. *Gregory of Nazianzus: An Intellectual Biography*. Crestwood: St. Vladimir's, 2001.

McLeod, Frederick. "Introduction." In *Theodore of Mopsuestia*, 3–68. New York: Routledge, 2009.

McWilliam, Joanne. "Letters to Demetrias: A Sidebar in the Pelagian Controversy *Helenae, Amicae Meae*." *Toronto Journal of Theology* 16 (2000) 131–39.

Meconi, David. "Rethinking Augustine's Early Theology: An Argument for Continuity, by Carol Harrison." *Theological Studies* 68 (2007) 180–82.

Merdinger, Jane. "Councils of North African Bishops." In *Augustine through the Ages: An Encyclopedia*, edited by Allan D. Fitzgerald, 248–50. Grand Rapids: Eerdmans, 1999.

———. *Rome and the African Church in the Time of Augustine*. New Haven: Yale University Press, 1997.

Merenciano, Alicia, and Ramon Rosat. "New Perspectives on St. Augustine and Priscillianism." In *Studia Patristica* 49, edited by J. Baun, A. Cameron, M. Edwards et al., 307–12. Walpole: Peeters, 2010.

Meyendorff, John. *Christ in Eastern Christian Thought*. Crestwood: St. Vladimir's, 1975.

———. *Imperial Unity and Christian Divisions: The Church 450–680 A.D.* Crestwood: St. Vladimir's, 1989.

Meyer, Paul W. "Augustine's *the Spirit and the Letter* as a Reading of Paul's Romans." In *The Social World of the First Christians: Essays in Honor of Wayne A. Meeks*, edited by L. Michael White and O. Larry Yarbrough, 366–81. Minneapolis: Fortress, 1995.

Miller, Sister Mary William. "Introduction." In *Rufini Presbyteri Liber De Fide: A Critical Text and Translation with Introduction and Commentary*, 1–49. Washington, DC: The Catholic University of America Press, 1964.

Mommsen, Theodor. "Aponius and Orosius on the Significance of the Epiphany." In *Medieval and Renaissance Studies*, 299–324. Ithaca, NY: Cornell University Press, 1959.

———. "Orosius and Augustine." In *Medieval and Renaissance Studies*, 325–48. Ithaca, NY: Cornell University Press, 1959.

Morey, Lawrence Charles. "How Unsearchable God's Ways: Grace and Free Will in the Thought of Cassian and Augustine." PhD diss., Toronto School of Theology, 2005.

Morris, John. "Pelagian Literature." *Journal of Theological Studies* XVI (April 1965) 26–60.

Munz, Peter. "John Cassian." *Journal of Ecclesiastical History* 11 (1960) 1–22.

Murphy, Francis. *Rufinus of Aquileia (345–411): His Life and Works*. Washington, DC: The Catholic University of America Press, 1945.

———. "St. Jerome as an Historian." In *A Monument to Saint Jerome: Essays on Some Aspects of His Life, Works and Influence*, edited by Francis Murphy, 115–41. New York: Sheed & Ward, 1952.

———. "St. Jerome: The Irascible Hermit." In *A Monument to Saint Jerome: Essays on Some Aspects of His Life, Works and Influence*, edited by Francis Murphy, 3–12. New York: Sheed & Ward, 1952.

Myres, J.N.L. "Pelagius and the End of Roman Rule in Britain." *The Journal of Roman Studies* 50 (1960) 21–36.

Nautin, Pierre. "Études de chronologie hiéronymienne (393–397)." *Revue des Études Augustiniennes* 19 (1973) 69–86.

Newlands, G.M. *Hilary of Poitiers: A Study in Theological Method*, vol. 108. European University Studies. Bern: Lang, 1978.

Newman, John Henry. "Demetrias." *Historical Sketches* 2 (1906) 163–84.

Nisula, Timo. *Augustine and the Functions of Concupiscence*. Boston: Brill, 2012.

Nolan, John Gavin. *Jerome and Jovinian*, vol. 97. The Catholic University of America Studies in Sacred Theology (Second Series). Washington, DC: The Catholic University of America, 1956.

Oberman, Heiko. *The Dawn of the Reformation*. Grand Rapids: Eerdmans, 1992.

———. *Luther: Man between God and the Devil*. Translated by Eileen Walliser-Schwarzbart. New York: Image, 1989.

O'Collins, Gerald. *Christology: A Biblical, Historical, and Systematic Study of Jesus*. Oxford: Oxford University Press, 1995.

O'Connell, Robert. "St. Augustine's Criticism of Origen in the *Ad Orosium*." *Revue des Études Augustiniennes* 30 (1984) 84–99.

———. "When Saintly Fathers Feuded: The Correspondence between Augustine and Jerome." *Thought* 57 (1979) 344–64.

O'Connell, Robert J. "Augustine's Rejection of the Fall of the Soul." *Augustinian Studies* 4 (1973) 1–32.

O'Donnell, James. *Augustine: A New Biography*. New York: HarperCollins, 2005.

———. "The Authority of Augustine." *Augustinian Studies* 22 (1991) 7–35.

———. *Pagans: The End of Traditional Religions and the Rise of Christianity*. New York: HarperCollins, 2015.

———. *The Ruin of the Roman Empire*. New York: HarperCollins, 2008.

Ogliari, Donato. *Gratia et Certamen: The Relationship between Grace and Free Will in the Discussion of Augustine with the So-Called Semipelagians*. Leuven: Leuven University Press, 2003.

Olphe-Galliard, Michel. "La Pureté de Coeur d'Après Cassien." *Revue d'Ascétique et de Mystique* 17 (1936) 28–60.

O'Malley, John. *Trent and All That: Renaming Catholicism in the Early Modern Era*. Cambridge: Harvard University Press, 2000.

———. *Trent: What Happened at the Council*. Cambridge: Belknap, 2013.

———. *Vatican I: The Council and the Making of the Ultramontane Church*. Cambridge: Belknap, 2018.

———. *What Happened at Vatican II*. Cambridge: Belknap, 2008.

Opalinski, Brett. "Pelagius and Galatians: An Ascetic Approach to Grace and Human Effort." PhD diss., University of Denver, 2008.

Ousley, David Alan. "Evagrius' Theology of Prayer and the Spiritual Life." PhD diss., University of Chicago, 1979.

Outrata, Filip. "Differing Defenders of Free Will: Possible Origenian Influences in Julian of Aeclanum." In *Origeniana Undecima: Origen and Origenism in the History of Western Thought*, edited by Anders-Christian Jacobsen, 489–500. Bristol: Peeters, 2016.

Paredi, Angelo. "Paulinus of Milan." *Sacris Erudiri* 14 (1963) 206–30.

———. *Saint Ambrose: His Life and Times*. Translated by M. Joseph Costelloe. Notre Dame: University of Notre Dame Press, 1964.

Pelikan, Jaroslav. *The Emergence of the Catholic Tradition (100–600)*, vol. 1. Chicago: The University of Chicago Press, 1971.

———. *The Growth of Medieval Theology (600–1300)*, vol. 3. Chicago: University of Chicago Press, 1978.

———. *Mary through the Centuries: Her Place in the History of Culture*. New Haven: Yale University Press, 1996.

———. *Reformation of Church and Dogma (1300–1700)*, vol. 4. Chicago: University of Chicago Press, 1984.

———. "Some Anti-Pelagian Echoes in Augustine's *City of God*." *Concordia* 23 (1952) 448–52.

———. *Whose Bible Is It? A History of the Scriptures through the Ages*. New York: Viking, 2005.

Pellegrino, Michele Cardinal. "Introduction." In *Sermons I (1–19): On the Old Testament*, edited by John Rotelle, 1, 13–137. New York: New City, 1990.

Penaskovic, Richard. "The Fall of the Soul in Saint Augustine: A Quaestio Disputata." *Augustinian Studies* 17 (1986) 135–45.

Pereira, Jairzinho. *Augustine of Hippo and Martin Luther on Original Sin and Justification of the Sinner*. Bristol: Vandenhoeck and Ruprecht, 2013.

Phipps, William E. "The Heresiarch: Pelagius or Augustine?" *Anglican Theological Review* LXII (1980) 124–33.

Picard-Mawji, Zohra. "Le passage de Célestius à Carthage: un moment clé du pélagianisme." *Mondes Anciens* 4 (2013) 1–18.

Plagnieux, Jean. "Le grief de complicité entre erreurs Nestorienne et Pélagienne d'Augustin à Cassien par Prosper d'Aquitaine?" *Revue des Études Augustiniennes* 2 (1956) 391–402.

Pourkier, Aline. *L'hérésiologie chez Épiphane de Salamine*. Paris: Beauchesne, 1992.

Pristas, Lauren. "The Theological Anthropology of John Cassian." PhD diss., Boston College, 1993.

Quasten, Johannes. *Patrology: The Golden Age of Greek Patristic Literature*, vol. 3. Allen: Christian Classics, 1983.

Raasch, Juana. "The Monastic Concept of Purity of Heart and Its Sources." *Studia Monastica* 8 (1966) 7–33.

———. "The Monastic Concept of Purity of Heart and Its Sources: Among the Second Century Apologists and Anti-Heretical Writers and in the Literature of the Third Century, Not Including the Alexandrians." *Studia Monastica* 8 (1966) 183–213.

———. "The Monastic Concept of Purity of Heart and Its Sources: Early Monasticism." *Studia Monastica* 11 (1969) 269–314.

———. "The Monastic Concept of Purity of Heart and Its Sources: Philo, Clement of Alexandria, and Origen." *Studia Monastica* 10 (1968) 7–55.

———. "The Monastic Concept of Purity of Heart and Its Sources: Symeon-Macarius, the School of Evagrius Ponticus, and the Apophthegmata Patrum." *Studia Monastica* 12 (1970) 7–41.

Rackett, Michael. "Anti-Pelagian Polemic in Augustine's *De continentia*." *Augustinian Studies* 26 (1995) 25–50.

———. "Sexuality and Sinlessness: The Diversity among Pelagian Theologies of Marriage and Virginity." PhD diss., Duke University, 2002.

———. "What's Wrong with Pelagianism? Augustine and Jerome on the Dangers of Pelagius and His Followers." *Augustinian Studies* 33 (2002) 223–38.

Rahner, Hugo. *Church and State in Early Christianity*. San Francisco: Ignatius, 2005.

Ramsey, Boniface. "General Introduction." In *John Cassian: The Conferences*, 57, 5–24. New York: Newman, 1997.

———. "General Introduction." In *John Cassian: The Institutes*, 3–17. New York: The Newman, 2000.

———. "John Cassian and Augustine." In *Grace for Grace: The Debates after Augustine and Pelagius*, edited by Alexander Hwang, Brian Matz, and Augustine Casiday, 114–30. Washington, DC: The Catholic University of America Press, 2014.

———. "John Cassian: Student of Augustine." *Cistercian Studies Quarterly* 28 (1993) 5–15.

Rapp, Claudia. *Holy Bishops in Late Antiquity: The Nature of Christian Leadership in an Age of Transition*. Oakland: University of California Press, 2013.

Rea, Robert Floyd. "Grace and Free Will in John Cassian." PhD diss., Saint Louis University, 1990.

Rebenich, Stefan. *Hieronymus und sein Kreis: Prosopographische und Sozialgeschichtliche Untersuchungen*. Stuttgart: Franz Steiner Verlag, 1992.

———. *Jerome*. New York: Routledge, 2002.

Rebillard, Éric. "Deviance Theory and Orthodoxy: The Case of the Pelagian Controversy." In *Transformations of Religious Practices in Late Antiquity*, 159–77. Burlington, VT: Ashgate, 2013.

———. "*Dogma Populare*: Popular Belief in the Controversy between Augustine and Julian of Eclanum." *Augustinian Studies* 38 (2007) 175–87.

———. "A New Style of Argument in Christian Polemic: Augustine and the Use of Patristic Citations." In *Transformations of Religious Practices in Late Antiquity*, 179–98. Burlington, VT: Ashgate, 2013.

———. "*Quasi Funambuli*: Cassian and the Pelagian Controversy on Perfection." In *Transformations of Religious Practices in Late Antiquity*, 213–26. Burlington, VT: Ashgate, 2013.

———. "*Quasi Funambuli*: Cassien et la Controverse Pélagienne sur la Perfection." *Revue des Études Augustiniennes* 40 (1994) 197–210.

———. "Sociologie de la Déviance et Orthodoxie: Le Cas de la Controverse Pélagienne sur la Grâce." In *Orthodoxie, Christianisme, Histoire*, edited by Susanna Elm, 221–40. Rome: École Française de Rome, 2000.

Rees, B.R. "Introduction." In *Pelagius: Life and Letters*, II, 1–25. Woodbridge: Boydell, 1998.

———. "Pelagius: A Reluctant Heretic." In *Pelagius: Life and Letters*, I, ix–132. Woodbridge: Boydell, 1998.

Refoulé, François. "Datation du Premier Concile de Carthage Contre les Pélagiens et du *Libellus Fidei* de Rufin." *Revue des Études Augustiniennes* 9 (1963) 41–49.

———. "La Distinction 'Royaume de Dieu-Vie Éternelle' Est-Elle Pélagienne?" *Recherches de Science Religieuse* 51 (1963) 247–54.

———. "Julien d'Éclane, Théologien et Philosophe." *Recherches de Science Religieuse* 52 (1964) 42–84, 233–47.

Rigby, Paul. "Original Sin." In *Augustine through the Ages: An Encyclopedia*, edited by Allan D. Fitzgerald, 607–14. Grand Rapids: Eerdmans, 1999.

Riggi, Calogero. "Catechesi escatologica dell' 'Ancoratus' di Epifanio." *Augustinianum* 18 (1978) 163–71.

Rist, John. *Augustine: Ancient Thought Baptized*. Cambridge: Cambridge University Press, 1994.

———. "Augustine on Free Will and Predestination." *The Journal of Theological Studies* 20 (1969) 420–47.

———. "Rethinking Augustine's Early Theology: An Argument for Continuity, by Carol Harrison." *New Blackfriars* 87 (2006) 542–44.

Rivière, Jean. "Hétérodoxie des Pélagiens en fait de Rédemption?" *Revue d'Histoire Ecclésiastique* 41 (1946) 5–43.

Roberts, James W. "An Assessment of the Changes in the Early Church as Seen in the Condemnations of the Heretics Arius and Pelagius." PhD diss., New Orleans Baptist Theological Seminary, 2009.

Robertson, A. "Introduction." In *Athanasius: Select Works and Letters*, 4. Peabody, MA: Hendrickson, 2004.

Robinson, Samuel. "Christian Asceticism and the Emergence of the Monastic Tradition." In *Asceticism*, edited by Vincent L. Wimbush and Richard Valantasis, 49–57. Oxford: Oxford University Press, 1998.

Rogers, Katherin. "Fall." In *Augustine through the Ages: An Encyclopedia*, edited by Allan D. Fitzgerald, 351–52. Grand Rapids: Eerdmans, 1999.

Rondet, Henri. *Original Sin: The Patristic and Theological Background*. Translated by Cajetan Finegan. Shannon: Ecclesia, 1972.

———. "Rufin le Syrien et le *Liber de Fide*." *Augustiniana* 22 (1972) 531–39.

Rorem, Paul. "Rethinking Augustine's Early Theology: An Argument for Continuity, by Carol Harrison." *Scottish Journal of Theology* 62 (2009) 519–21.

Rousseau, Philip. "Ancient Ascetics and Modern Virtue: The Case of Anger." In *Prayer and Spirituality in the Early Church*, edited by Pauline Allen, Lawrence Cross, and Wendy Mayer, 4, 213–31. Strathfield, NSW: St Paul's Publications, 2006.

———. *Ascetics, Authority, and the Church in the Age of Jerome and Cassian*. Oxford: Oxford University Press, 1978.

———. "Cassian, Contemplation and the Coenobitic Life." *Journal of Ecclesiastical History* XXVI (1975) 113–26.

———. "Cassian: Monastery and World." In *The Certainty of Doubt: Tributes to Peter Munz*, edited by Miles Fairburn and W.H. Oliver, 68–89. Wellington: University of Victoria Press, 1996.

———. "Cassian and Perverted Virtue," 1–15. Tenth Annual Lecture as Andrew W. Mellon Distinguished Professor of Early Christian Studies. Washington, DC, September 17, 2009.

———. "Christian Culture and the Swine's Husks: Jerome, Augustine, and Paulinus." In *The Limits of Ancient Christianity: Essays on Late Antique Thought and Culture in Honor of R.A. Markus*, edited by William E. Klingshirn, 172–87. Ann Arbor: University of Michigan Press, 1999.

———. *The Early Christian Centuries*. New York: Longman, 2002.

———. "Jerome on Jeremiah: Exegesis and Recovery." In *Jerome of Stridon: His Life, Writings, and Legacy*, edited by Andrew Cain and Josef Lössl, 73–83. Burlington, VT: Ashgate, 2009.

———. "Jerome's Search for Self-Identity." In *Prayer and Spirituality in the Early Church*, edited by Pauline Allen, 125–42. Everton Park, Queensland: Australian Catholic University, 1998.

———. *Pachomius: The Making of a Community in Fourth-Century Egypt*. Berkeley: University of California Press, 1999.

Russell, Kenneth. "John Cassian on a Delicate Subject." *Cistercian Studies Quarterly* 27 (1992) 1–12.

Russell, Norman. "Introduction." In *Theophilus of Alexandria*, 3–41. New York: Routledge, 2007.

Ryan, Christopher J. "Pelagius' View of the Nature of Revelation." In *Studia Patristica: Augustine, Post-Nicene Latin Fathers, Oriental Texts, Nachleben of the Fathers*, XVIII, 4, edited by Elizabeth A. Livingstone, 184–89. Leuven: Peeters, 1990.

Rydstrøm-Poulsen, Aage. *The Gracious God: Gratia in Augustine and the Twelfth Century*. Copenhagen: Akademisk, 2002.

Saldarini, Anthony. "Asceticism and the Gospel of Matthew." In *Asceticism and the New Testament*, edited by Leif Vaage and Vincent Wimbush, 11–29. New York: Routledge, 1999.

Scheck, Thomas. "Introduction." In *St. Pamphilus: Apology for Origen*, edited by Thomas Scheck. Washington, DC: The Catholic University of America Press, 2010.

———. *Origen and the History of Justification: The Legacy of Origen's Commentary on Romans*. Notre Dame: University of Notre Dame Press, 2008.

Scholl, Lindsey Anne. "The Pelagian Controversy: A Heresy in Its Intellectual Context." PhD diss., University of California Santa Barbara, 2011.

Scott, Mark. *Journey Back to God: Origen on the Problem of Evil*. Oxford: Oxford University Press, 2012.

Sell, Alan P.F. "Augustine Versus Pelagius: A Cautionary Tale of Perennial Importance." *Calvin Theological Journal* 12 (1977) 117–43.

Sessa, Kristina. *Daily Life in Late Antiquity*. Cambridge: Cambridge University Press, 2018.

Sheridan, Mark. "The Controversy over Apatheia: Cassian's Sources and His Use of Them." *Studia Monastica* 39 (1997) 287–310.

———. "Models and Images of Spiritual Progress in the Works of John Cassian." In *Spiritual Progress: Studies in the Spirituality of Antiquity and Early Monasticism. Papers of the Symposium of the Monastic Institute of Rome, Pontificio Ateneo S. Anselmo 14–15 May 1992*, edited by Jeremy Driscoll and Mark Sheridan, 101–25. Rome: Pontificio Ateneo S. Anselmo, 1994.

———. "Monastic Terminology: Monk, Cenobite, Nun." In *The Rule of St. Benedict*, edited by Timothy Fry, 301–21. Collegeville, MN: Liturgical, 1981.

Sillem, Aelred. "A New Study of John Cassian." *The Downside Review* 69 (1951) 333–47.

Simon, Ed. "Why Sin is Good." *Essays* (blog), *Marginalia*, March 2, 2017, http://marginalia.lareviewofbooks.org/sin-good-ed-simon/.

Sinkewicz, Robert. "Introduction." In *Evagrius of Pontus: The Greek Ascetic Corpus*, xvii–xl. Oxford: Oxford University Press, 2003.

Slenczka, Notger. "Luther's Anthropology." In *The Oxford Handbook of Martin Luther's Theology*, 212–32. Oxford: Oxford University Press, 2014.

Smith, A.J. "Pelagius and Augustine." *Journal of Theological Studies* 31 (1930) 21–35.

Smith, Thomas. *De Gratia: Faustus of Riez's Treatise on Grace and Its Place in the History of Theology*. Notre Dame: University of Notre Dame Press, 1990.

Somos, Róbert. "Origen, Evagrius Ponticus and the Ideal of Impassibility." In *Origeniana Septima: Origenes in den Auseinandersetzungen des 4. Jahrhunderts*, edited by W.A. Bienert and U. Kühneweg, 365–73. Leuven: Leuven University Press, 1999.

Souter, Alexander. "Introduction." In *Pelagius's Expositions of Thirteen Epistles of St. Paul*, I, edited by J. Armitage Robinson, vii–344. Cambridge: At the University Press, 1922.

———. "Prolegomena to the Commentary of Pelagius on the Epistles of St. Paul." *The Journal of Theological Studies* 7 (1905, 1906) 568–75.

Spanneut, Michel. "L'apatheia Chrétienne aux quatre premiers siècles." *Proche-Orient Chrétien* 52 (2002) 165–302.

Squires, Stuart. "Augustine's Changing Thought on Sinlessness." *Augustinianum* 54 (2014) 447–66.

———. "Cassian on Sinlessness." *Cistercian Studies Quarterly* 48 (2013) 411–32.

———. "*Contra Academicos* as Autobiography: A Critique of the Historiography on Augustine's First Extant Dialogue." *Scottish Journal of Theology* 64 (2011) 251–64.

———. "Jerome on Sinlessness: A *Via Media* between Augustine and Pelagius." *The Heythrop Journal* 57 (2016) 697–709.

———. "Jerome's Animosity against Augustine." *Augustiniana* 58 (2008) 181–99.

———. "Reassessing Pelagianism: Augustine, Cassian, and Jerome on the Possibility of a Sinless Life." PhD diss., The Catholic University of America, 2013.

Staniforth, Maxwell. "Introduction." In *Marcus Aurelius: Meditations*, 7–27. London: Penguin, 1964.

Stelzer, Wilbert. *A New Reconstruction of the Text of 2 Corinthians in Pelagius' Commentary on the Pauline Epistles*. Piscataway: Gorgias, 2018.

Stewart, Columba. *Cassian the Monk*. Oxford: Oxford University Press, 1998.

———. "Introduction." In *Purity of Heart in Early Ascetic and Monastic Literature: Essays in Honor of Juana Raasch, O.S.B.*, edited by Harriet Luckman and Linda Kulzer, 1–15. Collegeville, MN: Liturgical, 1999.

———. "John Cassian on Unceasing Prayer." *Monastic Studies* 15 (1984) 159–77.

Stortz, Martha Ellen. "Exegesis, Orthodoxy, and Ethics: Interpretations of Romans in the Pelagian Controversy." PhD diss., The University of Chicago, 1984.

Studer, Basil. *Trinity and Incarnation: The Faith of the Early Church*. Edinburgh: T. & T. Clark, 1993.

Stump, Eleonore. "Augustine on Free Will." In *The Cambridge Companion to Augustine*, edited by Eleonore Stump and Norman Kretzmann, 124–47. Cambridge: Cambridge University Press, 2001.

Tardieu, Michel. *Manichaeism*. Translated by M. B. DeBevoise. Urbana: University of Illinois Press, 2008.

TeSelle, Eugene. *Augustine the Theologian*. New York: Herder and Herder, 1970.

———. "The Background: Augustine and the Pelagian Controversy." In *Grace for Grace: The Debate after Augustine and Pelagius*, edited by Alexander Hwang, Brian Matz, and Augustine Casiday, 1–13. Washington, DC: The Catholic University of America Press, 2014.

———. "Rufinus the Syrian, Caelestius, Pelagius: Explorations in the Prehistory of the Pelagian Controversy." *Augustinian Studies* 3 (1972) 62–96.

Teske, Roland. "1 Timothy 2:4 and the Beginnings of the Massalian Controversy." In *Grace for Grace: The Debates after Augustine and Pelagius*, edited by Alexander Hwang, Brian Matz, and Augustine Casiday, 14–34. Washington, DC: The Catholic University of America Press, 2014.

———. "Introduction." In *Arianism and Other Heresies*, 91–106. Hyde Park, NY: New City, 1995.

———. "Introduction." In *Augustine. Letters: 211–270, 1*–29**, 11–17. Hyde Park, NY: New City, 2005.

———. "Introduction." In *The Works of Saint Augustine: A Translation for the 21st Century: Answer to the Pelagians: I*, edited by John E. Rotelle, 23. Hyde Park, NY: New City, 1997.

———. "De Libero Arbitrio." In *Augustine through the Ages: An Encyclopedia*, edited by Allan D. Fitzgerald, 494–95. Grand Rapids: Eerdmans, 1999.

Thompson, E.A. *Saint Germanus of Auxerre and the End of Roman Britain*. Suffolk: Boydell, 1984.

Ticciati, Susannah. "Augustine and Grace *Ex Nihilo*: The Logic of Augustine's Response to the Monks of Hadrumetum and Marseilles." *Augustinian Studies* 41 (2010) 401–22.

Toczko, Rafal. "Heretic as Bad Rhetorician: How Augustine Discredited Pelagius." *Augustinian Studies* 42 (2011) 211–31.

———. "The Image of *Templum Dei* in Pelagius and Augustine." *Augustiniana* 63 (2013) 231–55.

———. "Rome as the Basis of Argument in the So-Called Pelagian Controversy (415–418)" In *Studia Patristica LXX*, 649–59. Leuven: Peeters, 2013.

Tougher, Shaun. *Julian the Apostate*. Edinburgh: Edinburgh University Press, 2007.

Trout, Dennis. "Damasus and the Invention of Early Christian Rome." *Journal of Medieval and Early Modern Studies* 33 (2003) 519–36.

———. *Damasus of Rome: The Epigraphic Poetry*. Oxford: Oxford University Press, 2015.

———. *Paulinus of Nola: Life, Letters, and Poems*. Berkeley: University of California Press, 1999.

Turner, C.H. "Pelagius' Commentary on the Pauline Epistles and Its History." *The Journal of Theological Studies* 4 (1902, 1903) 132–41.

Van Dam, Raymond. *Leadership and Community in Late Antique Gaul.* Berkeley: University of California Press, 1992.

———. "Sheep in Wolves Clothing": The Letters of Consentius to Augustine." *Journal of Ecclesiastical History* 37 (1986) 515–35.

Van Egmond, Peter. "The Confession of Faith Ascribed to Caelestius." *Sacris Erudiri* 50 (2011) 317–39.

———. "*Haec Fides Est*: Observations on the Textual Tradition of Pelagius's '*Libellus Fidei.*'" *Augustiniana* 57 (2007) 345–85.

———. "Pelagius and the Origenist Controversy in Palestine." In *Studia Patristica*, edited by Markus Vinzent, 18, 631–47. Walpole: Peeters, 2013.

Van Nuffelen, Peter. *Orosius and the Rhetoric of History.* Oxford: Oxford University Press, 2012.

Van Oort, Johannes. "Augustine and Mani on *Concupiscentia Sexualis*." In *Augustiniana Traiectina: Communications Présentées au Colloque International d'Utrecht 13–14 Novembre 1986*, 137–52. Paris: Études Augustiniennes, 1987.

———. "Was Julian Right? A Re-Evaluation of Augustine's and Mani's Doctrines of Sexual Concupiscence and the Transmission of Sin: Part I." *Journal of Early Christian History* 6 (2016) 111–25.

Van Reyn, Geert and Anthony Dupont. "Why Donatists and Pelagians Really Deny That Christ Has Come in the Flesh: An Argumentative Reading of Augustine's *Sermo* 183" *Augustiniana* 65 (2015) 115–40.

Vessey, Mark. "Jerome." In *Augustine through the Ages: An Encyclopedia*, edited by Allan D. Fitzgerald, 460–62. Grand Rapids: Eerdmans, 1999.

———. "Jerome's Origen: The Making of a Christian Literary Persona." In *Studia Patristica: Latin Authors (Other Than Augustine and His Opponents), Nachleben of the Fathers*, XXVIII, edited by Elizabeth A. Livingstone, 135–45. Leuven: Peeters, 1993.

Vind, Anna. "The Human Being According to Luther." In *Anthropological Reformations: Anthropology in the Era of Reformation*, 69–85. Bristol: Vandenhoeck and Ruprecht, 2015.

Vinel, Françoise. "Rethinking Augustine's Early Theology: An Argument for Continuity, by Carol Harrison." *Revue des Sciences Religieuses* 82 (2008) 573–74.

Wallis, R.T. *Neoplatonism.* 2nd ed. Indianapolis: Hackett, 1995.

Ward, Graeme. "All Roads Lead to Rome? Frechulf of Lisieux, Augustine and Orosius." *Early Medieval Europe* 22 (2014) 492–505.

Weaver, Rebecca Harden. *Divine Grace and Human Agency: A Study of the Semi-Pelagian Controversy.* Macon, GA: Mercer University Press, 1996.

Weidman, Clemens. "The Corpus of Augustinian Sermons Recently Discovered at Erfurt: With a New Edition of *Sermo* 207." In *Ministerium Sermonis: Philological, Historical, and Theological Studies on Augustine's Sermones Ad Populum*, edited by Gert Partoens, Antony Dupont, Mathijs Lamberigts, 11–37. Turnhout: Brepolis, 2009.

Weinandy, Thomas. *Athanasius: A Theological Introduction.* Burlington, VT: Ashgate, 2007.

Wermelinger, Otto. *Rom und Pelagius.* Stuttgart: Anton Hiersemann, 1975.

Wetzel, James. "Pelagius Anticipated: Grace and Election in Augustine's *Ad Simplicianum*." In *Augustine: From Rhetor to Theologian*, edited by Joanne McWilliam, 121–32. Waterloo, ON: Wilfrid Laurier University Press, 1992.

———. "Predestination, Pelagianism, and Foreknowledge." In *The Cambridge Companion to Augustine*, edited by Eleonore Stump and Norman Kretzmann, 49–58. Cambridge: Cambridge University Press, 2001.

———. "The Recovery of Free Agency in the Theology of St. Augustine." *The Harvard Theological Review* 80 (1987) 101–25.

———. "Simplicianum, Ad." In *Augustine through the Ages: An Encyclopedia*, edited by Allan D. Fitzgerald, 798–99. Grand Rapids: Eerdmans, 1999.

White, Carolinne. *The Correspondence (394-419) between Jerome and Augustine of Hippo*. Lewiston, NY: Mellen, 1990.

Wickham, Lionel. "Pelagianism in the East." In *The Making of Orthodoxy: Essays in Honor of Henry Chadwick*, edited by Rowan Williams, 200–13. Cambridge: Cambridge University Press, 1989.

Wiesen, David. *St. Jerome as a Satirist*. Ithaca, NY: Cornell University Press, 1964.

Wiles, Maurice. "In Defence of Arius." *Journal of Theological Studies* 13 (1962) 339–47.

Wilkinson, Kate. "Spectacular Modesty: The Self-Representation of Ascetic Noblewomen in the Context of the Pelagian Controversy." PhD diss., Emory University, 2009.

Williams, Michael Allen. *Rethinking "Gnosticism": An Argument for Dismantling a Dubious Category*. Princeton: Princeton University Press, 1996.

Williams, Rowan. *Arius: Heresy and Tradition*. Grand Rapids: Eerdmans, 2002.

Williams, Stephen. *Diocletian and the Roman Recovery*. New York: Routledge, 1997.

Williams, Stephen, and Gerard Friell. *Theodosius: The Empire at Bay*. New Haven: Yale University Press, 1994.

Williams, Thomas. "Introduction." In *On Free Choice of the Will*. Indianapolis: Hackett, 1993.

Willis, Geoffrey Grimshaw. *Saint Augustine and the Donatist Controversy*. Eugene, OR: Wipf and Stock, 2005.

Wilson, N.G. "Introduction." In *Photius: The Bibliotheca*, 1–21. London: Duckworth, 1994.

Winslow, Donald. *The Dynamics of Salvation: A Study in Gregory of Nazianzus*. Macon, GA: Mercer University Press, 1979.

Winterbottom, Michael. "Pelagiana." *The Journal of Theological Studies* 38 (1987) 106–29.

Wolfson, Harry Austryn. "St. Augustine and the Pelagian Controversy." In *Religious Philosophy: A Group of Essays*, 158–76. Cambridge: Belknap, 1961.

Yamada, Nozomu. "The Influence of Chromatius and Rufinus of Aquileia on Pelagius—as seen in his Key Ascetic Concepts: *exemplum Christi, sapientia* and *imperturbabilitas*." In *Studia Patristica*, edited by Markus Vinzent, 18, 661–70. Walpole: Peeters, 2013.

Yarbrough, Anne. "Christianization in the Fourth Century: The Example of Roman Women." *Church History* 45 (1976) 149–65.

Yates, Jonathan. "Anti-Pelagian or Anti-Semipelagian? A Close Reading of Augustine's *Sermones* 168 and 333." In *Ministerium Sermonis: Philological, Historical, and Theological Studies on Augustine's Sermones Ad Populum*, edited by Gert Partoens, Antony Dupont, Mathijs Lamberigts, 97–119. Turnhout: Brepolis, 2009.

Young, Frances. *From Nicaea to Chalcedon: A Guide to the Literature and Its Background*. Second ed. Grand Rapids: Baker Academic, 2010.

Zednik, Margaret Jean. "In Search of Pelagius: A Reappraisal of His Controversy with Augustine." PhD diss., The University of Texas at Austin, 1975.

Text Index

Ambrose of Milan

De officiis, 57

Anastasius I

Ad Ioannem episcopum Hierosolymitanum, 37–38

Athanasius

Vita Antonii, 18–19, 83, 94

Augustine

Ad Orosium contra Priscillianistas et Origenistas, 98, 101–2
Confessiones, 9, 15, 17, 51, 58, 68–84, 101, 192, 227, 248
Contra Academicos, 79–80, 83
Contra duas epistulas Pelagianorum, 48, 61, 141, 144, 152–53, 188, 209, 211, 216, 219, 243–45, 250, 252–54, 257, 259
Contra Julianum, 145–46, 148, 150, 188, 205, 209, 210–11, 216, 219, 239, 241–42, 244–47, 249, 250–60, 287
Contra Julianum opus imperfectum, 144–45, 147–48, 151–54, 157–58, 185, 188, 211, 238–50, 252–59, 287
De bono viduitatis, 166
De civitate, 85
De correptione et gratia, 280
De doctrina Christiana, 203
De dono perseverantiae, 250, 161, 282
De gestis Pelagii, 43, 52, 59, 95, 97, 102, 104–5, 109, 117, 121, 124, 128, 130–36, 139, 188, 194–95, 200, 209–11, 216–19
De gratia Christi, et de peccato originali, 41, 46, 49, 54, 59–60, 67, 114, 132, 140, 142–43, 184–86, 188–91, 193, 195, 198–99, 202, 204, 208, 210–12
De gratia et libero arbitrio, 279
De haeresibus, 158
De natura et gratia, 49, 121–22, 133, 142, 184, 186–88, 192–93, 196, 199, 202–3, 205–6, 208, 210, 211, 214, 216, 218, 233
De nuptiis et concupiscentia, 61, 119, 152–53, 216, 241, 244–45, 250–55, 257–60, 287
De peccatorum meritis et remissione et de baptismo parvulorum, 42, 49, 60, 64, 102, 104–6, 157, 195, 198, 200–5, 207–9, 213–15, 218, 227–28
De perfectione justitiae hominis, 123, 125, 195–97, 202–3, 207, 209, 211, 214–18
De praedestinatione sanctorum, 206, 209, 282
De spiritu et littera, 106-7, 188, 194, 202, 206–21, 218
Retractationes, 54, 59, 97, 102, 104–5, 153, 157

Bede

Historia ecclesiastica gentis Anglorum, 41, 148

Benedict of Nursia

Regula Sancti Benedicti, 162

Cassian

Collationes, 164–69, 174–75, 180, 219, 262–64, 266–76
De incarnatione Domini contra Nestorium, 165, 169–70, 177–80, 276–77
De institutis coenobiorum, 56, 164–66, 169, 173–74, 180, 262, 264–66

Cassiodorus

De divinis lectionibus, 164

Council of Ephesus (431)

Ad Coelestinum Papam, 158

Eusebius of Caesarea

Historia ecclesiastica, 3, 7, 10, 26–27
Vita Constantini, 6–10

Gennadius

De viris inlustribus, 19–20, 28, 30, 41, 53, 55, 97, 99, 131, 145, 148, 151, 160, 164–65, 169–71, 177, 278

Jerome

Apologia adversus libros Rufini, 28, 31, 35–36, 39, 62, 66, 87, 90, 118
Commentaria in Amos, 94
Commentarii in Ezechielem, 30, 51, 88, 108
Contra Joannem Hierosolymitanum, 31–35, 57, 90–91
Contra Jovinianum, 48, 55, 90, 93, 119
De viris illustribus, 28, 87–88, 90, 93
Dialogi contra Pelagianos, 103, 124, 157, 215, 220–22, 224–31, 236
In Hieremiam prophetam Libri Sex, 40, 42, 47, 93, 108, 117–19, 125, 221–22, 224, 229–31
Interpretatio libri Didymi de Spiritu Sancto, 94
Praefatio Hieronymi in quatuor evangelia, 91
Vita Hilarionis, 89
Vita Malchi monachi captivi, 89
Vita Pauli, 89

John of Nikiu

Chronicon, 33

Lactantius

Liber de mortibus persecutorum, 3–6

Marius Mercator

Commonitorium de Coelestio, 151
Subnotationes in verba Iuliani, 41, 43, 53, 62, 140, 142, 148

Origen

Commentaria in epistolam Pauli ad Romanos, 224, 229
Contra Celsum, 223–24
Homiliae in Lucam, 224
De Principiis (Peri archon), 27–28

Orosius

Commonitorium de errore Priscillianistarum et Origenistarum, 98–101, 122
Historiarum adversum paganos, 50, 97–98, 100, 102–4, 125, 127, 233, 235
Liber apologeticus contra Pelagianum, 41–42, 56, 123–24, 127–31, 225, 232–37

Palladius

Dialogus de vita sancti Joannis Chrysostomi, 30, 33, 169
Historia Lausiaca, 19–21, 28–29

Pamphilus of Caesarea

Apologia pro Origene, 27

Paulinus of Milan

Vita sancti Ambrosii, 56–57

Paulinus of Nola

Poemata, 145, 148–50

Pelagius

Epistula [ad amicum] de divina lege, 44, 186–87, 189, 192–93

Epistula ad Celantiam [matronan], 48–49, 187, 189
Epistula ad Claudiam de virginitate, 43, 186–87, 189, 193
Epistula ad sacram Christi virginem Demetriadem, 43, 44, 110–11, 113, 183–87, 189–90, 276
Expositiones XIII epistularum, 48, 50, 120, 184–90, 192–93, 200, 276–77
Libellus fidei, 119, 186, 190, 221
Liber de vita Christiana (Christianorum), 110, 184, 187, 189, 192–193

Possidius

Vita Sancti Aurelii Augustini, 68–70, 84–86

Prosper of Aquitaine

Chronicum integrum, 41, 160, 164
Pro Augustino liber contra collatorem, 142, 145, 162, 264, 271, 280

Rufinus (*presbyter*)

Liber de Fide, 63–65, 196, 198–200, 233

Rufinus of Aquileia

De adulteratione librorum Origenis, 35
Apologia ad Anastasium, 37, 65
Apologia contra Hieronymum, 29–30, 35–36, 38–39, 108, 117
Prologus in libros peri archon Origenis Presbyteri, 30, 35
Prologus in omelias Origenis super Numeros, 30

Socrates

Historia ecclesiastica, 6, 8–15, 31, 34, 37, 168, 192

Sozomen

Historia ecclesiastica, 6–15, 30–31, 37, 169–70

Theodore of Mopsuestia

Ex libro contra defensores peccati originalis, 155–56

Vincent of Lérins

Commonitorium, 33, 54

Subject Index

Acholius, 14
Adeodatus, 75, 84
Aemilius, 148
Aeneas, 71
Aeonius, 284
Alaric, 30, 50, 55–56, 109, 151, 170
Albina, 24, 142, 188, 191
Alexander VII, 291
Alexander of Antioch, 170
Alypius, 17, 44, 82–84, 115–17, 120, 136–37, 153–54, 158, 247
Alypius (Governor of Britain), 13
Amachius, 12
Ambrose, 15, 37, 56–59, 77–78, 81–84, 93, 122, 178, 192, 215–16, 250
Ambrosiaster, 49
Anastasius, 37, 62, 64–65, 114
Anonymous Commentator on Paul, 49
Anthropomorphites, 32, 168–69
Antony, 17–20, 22–24, 27, 43, 94
Apollinarianism, 63, 242
Apollinaris of Laodicea, 12, 26, 118, 242–43
Archebius, 166, 269
Arianism, 63, 189
Aristotle, 185, 196, 250
Arius, 10, 26
Arnauld, Antoine, 290
Arpingius, 103–4
asceticism, 16–25
astral determinists, 39
Atarbius, 28, 30
Athanasius of Alexandria, 12, 17–19, 22–24, 33, 94, 159, 179
Atticus, 120, 140, 224–26, 228, 253
Augustine, xxi–xxii, 8–9, 17, 26, 29, 31, 39, 41–49, 51–54, 56, 58–59, 61, 63–64, 67, 93–95, 97–101, 103–7, 111, 114–17, 119–28, 131–32, 134–39, 142–48, 150–58, 161–62, 178–79, 187–88, 191–92, 195, 197–200, 220, 224–33, 235–36, 238–43, 245–60, 262–64, 266, 271, 274, 277–82, 284, 286, 290, 293
baptism, 204–6
biography, 68–86
concupiscentia, 250–56
free will, 206–10
grace, 210–12
Manichaean, 248–50
original sin, 201–04
predestination, 206–10
sex and marriage, 256–61
sinlessness, 212–19
Augustine of Aquileia, 152
Augustine's companion, 75, 80
Augustine's fiancé, 80
Augustine's sister, 69–70, 110
Aurelius, 45, 55, 59–60, 109, 121, 131, 136–37
Auxentius, 56–57
Avitus, 98, 101
Avitus of Braga, 98, 101, 129, 131

Basil of Caesarea, 23, 216, 239, 249
Basilica Constantiniana, 10
Basilica Portiana, 15
Basilides, 221
Bede, 41
Benedict, 162–163
Benedict XVI, 291
Bernard of Clairvaux, 163
Blesilla, 23, 92
Boniface, 142, 152–154
Boniface II, 284
Bonosus, 66, 88
Bucer, Martin, 286

Caecilian, 103

SUBJECT INDEX

Caelestius, xxi, 16, 23, 61, 63, 65, 67, 104, 121, 123-25, 127, 134-36, 138, 140-44, 152, 159-60, 163, 170, 178, 200, 216, 218, 224, 232, 238, 245-46, 248, 278
    Adam, 194-95
    baptism, 197-99
    biography, 53-59
    Council of Carthage (411), 56, 59-60, 128, 134, 194-95, 216, 232
    original sin, 194-95
    sinlessness, 195-97
Caesar Baronius, 7
Caesarius of Arles, 284
Calvin, John, 286
capital punishment, 12
Capito, Wolfgang, 287
Cappadocians, 231
Cassian, xxi, 39, 56, 92, 144, 159, 215-16, 278, 280, 283-84
    biography, 161-80
    christology, 276-77
    fall, 262-64
    free will, 264-71
    grace, 264-71
    sinlessness, 272-76
Cassiodorus, 164
Castor, 173-74
Castorina, 87
Celestine, 142, 159-60
Cerealis, 23
Chaeremon, 269
Charles V, 287
Chromatius, 30, 39, 49
Cicero, 38, 72, 89
Claudius, 61, 65
Claudius (bishop), 157
Clement XI, 291
Clement of Alexandria, 222-23
Confessio Augustana, 286-87, 289
Constans, 11
Constantine, 5-11, 14, 17, 26, 44, 192
Constantine II, 11
Constantine III, 131
Constantius, 3
Constantius II, 11, 69, 90
Conventum of Jerusalem, 126-31, 137, 232, 237
Cornelius, 22
Council of Carthage (411), 56, 59-60, 128, 134, 140, 194-95, 216, 232
Council of Carthage (416), 136-38, 140
Council of Carthage (418), 45, 141, 144, 217-19
Council of Chalcedon, 190
Council of Constantinople, 15, 81, 117, 190, 243
Council of Ephesus, 64, 142, 144, 158, 160, 278

Council of Lyons, 282
Council of Nicaea, 10, 14-15, 17, 26, 81, 86, 90, 117, 190
Council of Trent, 93, 288-90
Cresconius, 279
Crispus, 8
Critobulus, 120, 224-25, 230
Ctesiphon, 108, 111, 120, 128, 180
Cunctos populous, 14
Cyprian, 49, 77, 216, 249, 279
Cyril of Alexandria, 33, 132, 159, 218
Cyril of Jerusalem, 159

Damasus, 14, 23, 90-92, 94, 243
Decian persecution, 17, 27
Demetrias, 44, 109-17, 143, 178, 183
Demetrius, 27
Demophilus, 14
Dido, 71
Didymus the Blind, 29, 118
Diocletian, 3-5
Diodore, 154
Docetists, 240
Domnio, 47-48
Domnus, 129
Donatists, 9, 12, 25, 69, 86, 102, 128, 133, 204

Edict of Milan, 7
Eleusius of Cyzicus, 13
Epicurus, 221, 247
Epiphanius, 30-40, 57, 90
Erasmus of Rotterdam, 66, 286
Eucherius, 175
Euethius, 4
Eulogius, 131
Eunomianism, 63
Eunomians, 14
Eusebius of Caesarea, 6, 27, 30, 66, 125-26, 155, 159
Eusebius of Cremona, 33, 35-37, 117
Eusebius (Jerome's father), 87
Eusebius of Nicomedia, 8, 192
Eustochium, 23, 91-92, 95, 112-13, 115, 120, 180
Eutropius, 122
Evagrius of Antioch, 22, 88
Evagrius Pontius, 167, 221-22
Evodius of Uzalis, 98, 137, 279

Fausta, 8
Faustus, 76-78, 239
Faustus of Riez, 282-83
Feast of the Epiphany, 11
Felix, 90
Felix (monk), 278-79

SUBJECT INDEX

Felix (second monk), 279
Firmus, 153
Florentius, 66, 88
Florus, 278–79
Florus (bishop), 158, 160, 239
Florus of Lyons, 285
Francis, 291–94
Fulgentius of Ruspe, 282–84

Galerius, 3–6
Gennadius, 19–20, 28, 41, 55, 97, 99, 145, 164–65
George (Arian bishop of Alexandria), 13
Germanus, 165–69, 174, 266–67, 269, 272–74, 276
Gnostics, 25, 39, 108
Gottschalk, 285
Gratian, 45, 109
Great Persecution, 3–7, 15, 25
Gregory the Great, 162
Gregory of Nazianzus, 14, 90, 159, 179, 216, 249, 252
Gregory of Nyssa, 90
Gregory Thaumaturgus, 27

Helena, 10
Helladius, 174
Helvidius, 91
Heraclian, 103, 109
Heraclius, 86
Heros, 120, 131–32, 135–36, 140
Hesiod, 11
Hexapla, 27
Hilarion, 8
Hilary, 124–25, 127, 134, 225
Hilary (Gaul), 280–82
Hilary of Poitiers, 12, 88, 122, 178, 216, 249
Hilderic, 283
Hincmar, 285
Historia Monachorum in Aegypto, 23
Homer, 11
Honoratus, 151, 239
Honoratus (bishop), 175
Honorius, 16, 102, 104, 141, 144
Hormisdas, 283
Hortentius, 72

Ignatius of Loyola, 163
Innocent I, 94–95, 114, 129, 137–39, 141, 143, 151–52, 169–70, 249, 279
Innocent X, 291
Irenaeus, 216, 249
Isidore, 34

James, 120–121

Jansen, Cornelius, 290–91
Januarius, 279
Jerome, xxi–xxii, 22–25, 28–42, 47–51, 54–57, 61–63, 65–66, 97–98, 103, 107–8, 111–20, 122–27, 132–33, 137, 152–57, 161, 165, 171–72, 179–80, 215–16, 232–33, 235–36, 249, 258, 260, 272, 274, 277–78, 284, 286
    baptism, 229–30
    biography, 87–96
    foreknowledge, 228–29
    free will, 230–31
    grace, 230–31
    sinlessness, 220–27
    transmission of sin, 227–28
Jesuits, 290
John (abba), 272
John (Brother of Pachomius), 20
John Chrysostom, 31, 39, 122, 154, 169–70, 249, 253
John of Jerusalem, 29, 32–40, 57, 95, 121, 127–32, 237
John of Nikiu, 33
Joseph, 168
Jovian, 14
Jovinian, 47, 48, 55, 63, 93–94, 118, 221, 229, 237, 247, 260
Jovinianus, 175
Juliana, 44–45, 109–11, 113, 115–16
Julian the Apostate, 11–14
Julian of Eclanum, xxi, 16, 45, 142–43, 216, 219, 246–50, 278
    biography, 144–60
    concupiscentia, 240–43
    Julian's critique of Augustine as a Manichaean, 238–40
    sex and marriage, 243–45
Juliana (Julian of Eclanum's mother), 148
Justina, 15

Labarum, 6–7,
Lactantius, 3, 5–6, 49, 122
Laeta, 229
Lampius, 58
Lazarus, 120, 131–32, 135–36, 140
Leo, 113, 170, 176–77, 280
Leonides, 26
Leontius, 175
Leontius (bishop), 174
Liber de fide, 63–67, 104, 199–200
Liberius, 90
Liberius (prefect), 284
Libri Platonicorum, 80–81
Licinius, 7, 20

limbo, 198
Lucian, 6
Lucianus, 131
Lucidus, 282
Luther, Martin, 286, 288

Macarius, 29–30, 35, 38
Macarius (legate), 69
Macedonius, 12
Magnus Maximus, 84
Malchus, 89
Mani, 73, 151, 239–41, 247
Manichaeans, 14, 49–50, 72–78, 81, 83, 86, 100–101, 119, 184, 186, 196, 221, 238–40, 243, 245, 247–50, 257, 260, 262
Marcella, 23–25, 35, 44, 91, 110
Marcellian, 160
Marcellinus, 102–6, 109, 213
Marcion of Sinope, 25
Mardonius, 11
Marinus, 103–4
Marius Mercator, 41, 43, 53, 62–63, 65–66, 105, 142, 152, 155, 160
Martin of Tours, 131
Maxentius, 6, 8, 10
Maximian, 3, 5
Maximin Daia, 5, 6, 19, 20
Maximus, 11
Melanchthon, Philipp, 286
Melania the Elder, 29–30, 110
Melania the Younger, 30, 50, 142, 188, 191
Melitian schism, 170
Memorius, 148, 150, 151
Merton, Thomas, 163
Messalians, 221
Minervus, 175
Monica, 8–9, 15, 69–70, 74–77, 80, 83–84, 248
Müntzer, Thomas, 286

Navigius, 69, 70, 84
Nazarites, 16
Nemo se hostiis polluat, 15
Neoplatonism, 101
Neoplatonists, 81
Nero, 3
Nestorius, 33, 65, 142, 159–60, 170, 176–77, 276–78
Niceas, 89
Novatian, 22
Novatianism, 63

Oceanus, 35, 36, 38
Olybrius, 109
Olympius, 249

Origen, 17, 26–27, 49, 63–64, 90, 94, 114, 117–18, 154, 163, 167–68, 220–27, 229, 237
Origenism, 63, 101, 114, 126
Origenist controversy, xxii, 25–40, 94, 117, 223
Orontius, 160
Orosius, 39, 41, 43, 50, 102–4, 122–23, 125–30, 132, 136–37, 161, 163, 215, 225, 227–28, 230, 272, 278
   biography, 97–101
   influences, 235–37
   theology, 232–34
otium, 22, 44–45, 56, 85, 151, 172

Pachomius, 19–24, 27, 43, 180
Pachonius, 98
Palamon, 20
Palchonius, 131
Palladius, 19, 20, 28–29, 33
Palladius (Roman prefect), 141
Pammachius, 35–36, 38, 47, 60–62
Pamphilus, 27, 29, 35, 39
Paphnutius, 266–68
Passerius, 129
Patricius, 68–69
Patricius (Augustine's nephew), 70
Patroclus of Arles, 16, 175, 178
Paul, 122
Paul (the hermit), 89
Paul III, 288
Paula, 23, 87, 91–92, 95, 110, 229
Paula (daughter of Laeta), 229
Paulinian, 32–33, 57–58, 87
Paulinus of Antioch, 57, 90
Paulinus of Milan, 56–57, 59–60, 140
Paulinus of Nola, 45–47, 56, 58–59, 94, 121, 143, 145, 148–50, 171, 239
Pelagius, xxi–xxii, 16, 23, 25, 40, 45–48, 53–56, 61–62, 65, 95, 102, 104, 106, 109–15, 117–24, 128–29, 131–36, 138–44, 152, 160, 163, 170, 177–78, 194–95, 197–200, 206, 210–12, 216, 218, 220, 223–24, 226, 228–30, 232–33, 238, 245–46, 248, 271, 273, 276–78, 282
   Africa, 50–52
   baptism, 192–93
   biography, 41–48
   christology, 189–91
   commentaries, 48–50
   free will, 185–86
   grace, 188–91
   original sin, 48, 183–85, 193
   predestination, 185–86
   sinlessness, 186–88
Peter of Alexandria, 6, 14, 22, 24

SUBJECT INDEX

Petronius Probus, 44
Photius, 155–56
Plato, 25
Platonists, 81
Plotinus, 22, 80
Photinians, 14
Pinianus, 30, 142, 188, 191
Pinufius, 166
Ponticianus, 82, 84
Possessor, 283
Possidius, 68, 85, 137, 150–51
Praesidius, 160
Praylius, 140–41
Priscillian, 221
Priscillianism, 100, 101, 237
Proba, 109–11, 113, 115–16
Prosper of Aquitaine, 41, 142, 145, 151, 162, 164, 264, 270–71, 280, 282, 286
Pythagoras, 221

Quodvultdeus, 158

Rabanus Maurus, 285
Ratramnus, 285
Respecta, 162
Reticius of Autun, 249
Riparius, 96
Rogatianus, 22
Romanianus, 69
Romanus, 4
Rufinus of Aquileia, xxii, 23, 28–40, 49, 62–67, 93, 108–9, 112, 117–18, 179, 220–23
Rufinus ("Holy Priest"), 59–67, 194
Rufus of Thessalonica, 152–53

Saint Peter's Basilica, 10
Salutius, 14
Saracens, 19
Semi-Pelagian controversy, 161, 186, 209, 276, 278
Septimius Severus, 26
Septuagint, 27, 93, 95, 155
Serapaeum, 15
Serapion of Thmuis, 239
Serapis, 15
Servatus Lupus, 285
Severus, 5
Sextus, 122
Sextus Petronius Probus, 109
Shah of Persia, 73
Simons, Menno, 286
Simplicianus, 37, 81
Siricius, 91
Sixtus, 45, 265

Sixtus III, 160, 278–79
Skepticism, 79–80
Socrates, 12–13, 31, 33
Sozomen, 13, 31
Stoicism, 222, 223
Sulpicius Severus, 58, 171
Symmachus, 77
Synod of Diospolis, 43, 46, 109, 120, 124, 130–37, 139, 143, 188, 194–95, 200, 216–18, 220, 249
Synod of Orange, 209–10, 284–85, 289

Tall brothers, 33, 37, 39
Tatian, 12
Temple, 13
Terminalia, 4
Terminus, 4
Tertullian, 49
Tetrarchy, 3
Theodore, 175
Theodore of Mopsuestia, 65, 154–57, 159–60
Theodosian Code, 50
Theodosius I, 14–16
Theodosius II, 16, 142, 160, 178
Theodotus of Antioch, 141
Theodulus, 12
Theonas, 272–76
Theophilus of Alexandria, 15, 31, 33–40, 94, 168
Theresa of Avila, 163
Thomas à Kempis, 163
Thomas Aquinas, 163
Thrasamund, 283
Timasius, 120–21
Titia, 148–150
Tractoria, 16, 45, 141, 144, 153, 160, 279
Turbantius, 153

Ulysses, 107
Unconquered Sun, 8
Urban II, 290
Ursacius, 30
Ursinus, 90–91

Valentinian II, 15, 77, 109
Valentinian III, 16, 178
Valentinus, 279
Valerius, 152–53, 157–58
Valerius (bishop), 16, 58, 85–86
Vatican I, 138
Vatican II, 261
Verecundus, 83
Vettius Agorius Praetextatus, 91
Victorinus, 80, 101
Victricius of Rouen, 55

Vigilantius, 94, 221
Vincent of Lérins, 33, 54
Vincentius, 34, 57
Vindemialis, 153
Virgil, 71
Vita Antonii, 17–19, 22, 82
Vulgate, xxi, 93

Xystus, 221

Zosimus, 16, 43, 45, 139–44, 152–54, 197, 199, 279
Zwingli, Ulrich, 286

Scripture Index

Acts

2:45	18
8:37	192
9:1–31	8
9:32	131 n. 269

Colossians

2:9	277

1 Corinthians

3:5–7	116
3:9	234
4:7	208
5:10	234
7:7	215
7:9	135
7:25	135
7:39–40	119
11:1	190, 204
12:29	225

2 Corinthians

3:6	107

Deuteronomy

31:3	106

Ephesians

5:22–33	149
5:27	43, 193

Ezekiel

11:18–20	268 n. 60

Galatians

1:13–24	8
1:28	241
2:11–14	95
2:21	211 n. 95

Genesis

1:26–27	9, 183
1:27	255
1:28	253 n. 99, 258, 259
2:25	244
3	201 n. 2, 249
3:7	202
3:16	258
3:21	26 n. 177
3:23	202
6:6	233
12:1–4	267
17:1	128, 237 n. 37

Hebrews

11:5	200

SCRIPTURE INDEX

James

2:10	126, 137

Job

1:8	232

John

1:1–2	81
5:30	265
6:70	228
8:36	285
14:10	265

1 John

1:8	213, 217, 218
4:19	292

Lamentations

5:17	76

Luke

1:6	128, 232, 237 n. 37
10:38–42	274
19:1–10	270
23:40–43	270

Matthew

3:1–12	16
3:10	234
6:12–13	51 n. 87
6:12	217–19, 229
6:25–34	18
14:24	107
19:12	27
19:21	18, 83
19:24–26	106
24:2	13
26:53	106

Numbers

6:1–8	16

Proverbs

18:17	213

Psalms

5:8	69
32:5–6	213
54:21	107
68:28	268
72:27	77
138:22	77
143:2	213
146:7	267
146:8a	268
146:8b	267

Revelation

14:3–5	213

Romans

1:21	150
2:4–5	228
2:14–16	263
5:12	201 n. 2, 203, 203 n. 23 and n. 24, 249, 276
6:12–13	251
7:7–12	189
7:19	273
7:23	251
8:3	272
8:29–30	186, 209
9:6	264
9:16	29
13:13–14	83
14:5	215

1 Timothy

1:15	142
5:9	119

www.ingramcontent.com/pod-product-compliance
Lightning Source LLC
Chambersburg PA
CBHW080407300426
44113CB00015B/2429